U.S.

A NARRATIVE HISTORY
VOLUME 2: SINCE 1865

U.S.

A NARRATIVE HISTORY
VOLUME 2: SINCE 1865
Ninth Edition

James West Davidson

Brian DeLay
University of California, Berkeley

Christine Leigh Heyrman
University of Delaware

Mark H. Lytle
Bard College

Michael B. Stoff
University of Texas, Austin

Mc
Graw
Hill

U.S.: A NARRATIVE HISTORY, VOLUME 2: SINCE 1865, NINTH EDITION

Published by McGraw Hill LLC, 1325 Avenue of the Americas, New York, NY 10121. Copyright ©2022 by McGraw Hill LLC. All rights reserved. Printed in the United States of America. Previous editions ©2018, 2015, and 2012. No part of this publication may be reproduced or distributed in any form or by any means, or stored in a database or retrieval system, without the prior written consent of McGraw Hill LLC, including, but not limited to, in any network or other electronic storage or transmission, or broadcast for distance learning.

Some ancillaries, including electronic and print components, may not be available to customers outside the United States.

This book is printed on acid-free paper.

1 2 3 4 5 6 7 8 9 LWI 26 25 24 23 22 21

ISBN 978-1-260-70578-2 (bound edition)
MHID 1-260-70578-1 (bound edition)
ISBN 978-1-260-70573-7 (loose-leaf edition)
MHID 1-260-70573-0 (loose-leaf edition)

Senior Portfolio Manager: *Jason Seitz*
Product Development Manager: *Dawn Groundwater*
Marketing Manager: *Michael Gedatus*
Lead Content Project Manager (Core): *Susan Trentacosti*
Lead Content Project Manager (Assessment): *Jodi Banowetz*
Senior Buyer: *Laura Fuller*
Designer: *Beth Blech*
Lead Content Licensing Specialist: *Brianna Kirschbaum*
Cover Image: *McGraw Hill LLC*
Compositor: *Aptara®, Inc.*

All credits appearing on page or at the end of the book are considered to be an extension of the copyright page.

Library of Congress Cataloging-in-Publication Data

Names: Davidson, James West, author.
Title: U.S.: a narrative history / James West Davidson [and four others].
Other titles: United States: a narrative hsitory
Description: Ninth edition. | New York, NY : McGraw-Hill Education, [2022]
   | Includes bibliographical references and index. | Contents: v. 1. To
   1877 —
Identifiers: LCCN 2020047141 (print) | LCCN 2020047142 (ebook) | ISBN
   9781260243048 (v. 1 ; hardcover) | ISBN 9781260705720 (v. 1 ; spiral
   bound) | ISBN 9781260705782 (v. 2 ; hardcover) | ISBN 9781260705737
   (v. 2 ; spiral bound) | ISBN 9781264251155 (hardcover) | ISBN 9781260705669
   (v. 1 ; ebook) | ISBN 9781260705683 (v. 2 ; ebook)
Subjects: LCSH: United States—History—Textbooks.
Classification: LCC E178.1 .D23 2022 (print) | LCC E178.1 (ebook) | DDC
   973—dc23
LC record available at https://lccn.loc.gov/2020047141
LC ebook record available at https://lccn.loc.gov/2020047142

mheducation.com/highered

U.S. BRIEF CONTENTS

Contents

19 THE NEW INDUSTRIAL ORDER 1870–1900

20 THE RISE OF AN URBAN ORDER 1870–1900

25 THE GREAT DEPRESSION AND THE NEW DEAL 1929–1939

26 THE UNITED STATES'S RISE TO GLOBALISM 1927–1945

27 THE UNITED STATES AND THE COLD WAR 1945–1954

28 THE SUBURBAN ERA 1945–1963

31 THE CONSERVATIVE CHALLENGE 1976–1992

Out of many stories, one *U.S.*

In an approachable and compelling way, *U.S.: A Narrative History* tells the stories of the American people as the colonies grew from scattered settlements into fifty united states. The engaging narrative, crafted by a team of scholars representing different eras, regions, topics, and approaches, showcases the diversity and complexity of the American past and guides students to develop a more nuanced understanding of our present and future.

This extremely readable program provides opportunities to engage with and uncover the history of the United States using the tools and practices that historians employ to illuminate the past. The approachable narrative is supported by a comprehensive set of learning activities found in Connect U.S. History. By harnessing the power of Connect, your students will get the help they need, when and how they need it, so that your class time can be more rewarding for your students and you.

In this text, we hope to show you that history has multiple voices, like our diverse nation. The Many Histories feature presents two primary source documents that offer contrasting perspectives on key events for analysis and discussion. With our Historian's Toolbox feature, we explore how historians cross-examine all sorts of evidence, from newspapers and paintings to furniture, photographs, and comic books. In short, this program is designed to let students experience history the way historians do.

Primary Sources Help Students Think Critically about History

Primary sources help students think critically about history and expose them to contrasting perspectives on key events. The Ninth Edition of *U.S.: A Narrative History* provides several different ways to use primary source documents in your course.

POWER OF PROCESS FOR PRIMARY SOURCES

Power of Process for Primary Sources is a critical thinking tool for reading and writing about primary sources. As part of Connect U.S. History, McGraw Hill Education's learning platform Power of Process contains a database of over 400 searchable primary sources in addition to the capability for instructors to upload their own sources. Instructors can then select a series of strategies for students to use to analyze and comment on a source. The Power of Process framework helps students develop essential academic skills such as understanding, analyzing, and synthesizing readings and visuals such as maps, leading students toward higher order thinking and writing.

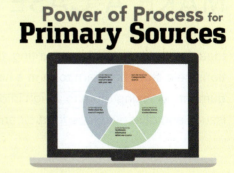

The Power of Process landing page makes it easy for instructors to find prepopulated documents or to add their own.

MANY HISTORIES

Within the print or eBook, Many Histories features pair two primary source documents that offer contrasting perspectives on the same key event. Introductions and Thinking Critically questions provide a framework to guide analysis and discussion. For example, how did Spaniards and the Aztec differ in their account of first contact? Or, what were the arguments used to justify the internment of Japanese Americans during World War II and how did they compare to the experiences of those imprisoned?

HISTORIAN'S TOOLBOX

Also available within the print or eBook, Historian's Toolbox features showcase historical images and artifacts. Introductions and Thinking Critically questions frame the images and guide students in "reading" visual evidence and examining material culture.

MAKE A CASE

Ideal for class discussion or writing, these questions help students learn to form a historical argument by asking them to weigh in on debated issues and give evidence for their answer.

Make a Case

Dose the Electoral College ensure fair outcomes in presidential contests.

You select the primary source documents that meet the unique needs of your course. No two history courses are the same. McGraw Hill Education's Create allows you to quickly and easily create custom course materials with cross-disciplinary content and other third-party sources.

>> **CHOOSE YOUR OWN CONTENT:** Create a book that contains only the chapters you want, in the order you want. Create will even renumber the pages for you!

>> **ADD READINGS:** Use our American History Collections to include primary sources, or Taking Sides: Annual Editions. Add your own original content, such as syllabus or History major requirements!

>> **CHOOSE YOUR FORMAT:** Print or eBook? Softcover, spiral-bound, or loose-leaf? Black-and-white or color? Perforated, three-hole punched, or regular paper?

>> **CUSTOMIZE YOUR COVER:** Pick your own cover image and include your name and course information right on the cover. Students will know they're purchasing the right book—and using everything they purchase!

Map Tools to Promote Student Learning
MAPPING THE PAST

The Mapping the Past feature, appearing in most chapters, guides students in reading and understanding the historical content depicted in maps. Each features includes a full-sized map, along with questions designed to develop map-reading skills and launch an interpretive analysis of the map.

INTERACTIVE MAPS

Interactive maps give students a hands-on understanding of geography. *U.S.: A Narrative History* offers over 30 interactive maps that support geographical as well as historical thinking. These maps appear in both the eBook and Connect U.S. History exercises. For some interactive maps, students click on the boxes in the map legend to see changing boundaries, visualize migration routes, or analyze war battles and election results. With others, students manipulate a slider to help them better understand change over time. New interactive maps offer advanced navigation features, including zoom, as well as audio and textual animation.

A complete list of maps can be found in a separate section of the frontmatter.

SmartBook 2.0 Tailors Content to the Individual Student

SMARTBOOK®

Available within Connect U.S. History, SmartBook has been updated with improved learning objectives to ensure that students gain foundational knowledge while also learning to make connections to help them formulate a broader understanding of historical events. SmartBook 2.0 personalizes learning to individual student needs, continually adapting to pinpoint knowledge gaps and focus learning on topics that need the most attention. Study time is more productive and, as a result, students are better prepared for class and coursework. For instructors, SmartBook 2.0 tracks student progress and provides insights that can help guide teaching strategies.

Writing Assignment Plus

McGraw Hill's new Writing Assignment Plus tool delivers a learning experience that improves students' written communication skills and conceptual understanding with every assignment. Assign, monitor, and provide feedback on writing more efficiently and grade assignments within McGraw Hill Connect®. Writing Assignment Plus gives you time-saving tools with a just-in-time basic writing and originality checker.

Features include:

- Grammar/writing checking with McGraw Hill learning resources
- Originality checker with McGraw Hill learning resources
- Writing stats
- Rubric building and scoring
- Ability to assign draft and final deadline milestones
- Tablet ready and tools for all learners

Contexualize History

Help students experience history in a whole new way with our new Podcast Assignments. We've gathered some of the most interesting and popular history podcasts currently available and built assignable questions around them. These assignments allow instructors to bring greater context and nuance to their courses while engaging students through the storytelling power of podcasts.

New Content in *U.S.: A Narrative History*, 9e

>> NEW THEN AND NOW features in every chapter make timely connections between historical events, trends, or social conditions and current events and challenges. These provide historical context for some of the United States' most pressing concerns—such as economic inequality in the nineteenth and early twenty-first centuries, and the development and use of nuclear weapons during World War II and current nuclear threats.

>> NEW MAP EXERCISES, "Mapping the Past," in most chapters provide students with a map's historical context and then take them through a series of questions designed to develop map-reading skills as well as to launch an interpretive analysis of the map.

>> CHAPTER BIBLIOGRAPHIES have been updated to reflect new scholarship.

>> CHAPTERS have been revised to reflect new trends in scholarship. For example, CHAPTER 21, REALIGNMENT AT HOME AND EMPIRE ABROAD, expands discussion of the major political parties and the importance of the currency issue, African American responses to Jim Crow, and the power of yellow journalism.

>> CHAPTER 24, THE NEW ERA, features refined discussions of nativism and immigration restrictions, the growth of the KKK, Prohibition, and the causes of the Great Crash and the Great Depression.

>> CHAPTER 25, THE GREAT DEPRESSION AND THE NEW DEAL, presents a fresh appraisal of Hoover's strengths and weaknesses as a leader, the political use of mass media, and those excluded from the benefits of relief programs.

>> CHAPTER 26, THE UNITED STATES'S RISE TO GLOBALISM, incorporates a revised discussion of the features of fascism, new material on the Greater East Asia Co-Prosperity Sphere, and a revised assessment of the importance of the war in the Pacific to the larger war effort.

>> CHAPTER 30, THE VIETNAM ERA, adds material on political motivations for U.S. involvement in Vietnam and updates the discussions of the end of Vietnam and the significance of the Pentagon Papers.

>> CHAPTER 32, THE UNITED STATES IN A GLOBAL COMMUNITY, includes updates on Donald Trump's presidency, including U.S. withdrawal from the Paris Agreement on global warming; the attack on Obamacare; the passage of a new tax cut; the controversy over Russian meddling in the election; and the failed impeachment attempt.

Instructor Resources

U.S.: A Narrative History, 9e offers an array of instructor resources:

Instructor's manual. The instructor's manual provides a wide variety of tools and resources for presenting the course, including learning objectives and ideas for lectures and discussions.

Test bank. By increasing the rigor of the test bank development process, McGraw Hill has raised the bar for student assessment. Each question has been tagged for level of difficulty, Bloom's taxonomy, and topic coverage. Organized by chapter, the questions are designed to test factual, conceptual, and higher order thinking.

Test Builder. New to this edition and available within Connect, Test Builder is a cloud-based tool that enables instructors to format tests that can be printed and administered within a Learning Management System. Test Builder offers a modern, streamlined interface for easy content configuration that matches course needs, without requiring a download. Test Builder enables instructors to:

- Access all test bank content from a particular title.
- Easily pinpoint the most relevant content through robust filtering options.
- Manipulate the order of questions or scramble questions and/or answers.
- Pin questions to a specific location within a test.
- Determine your preferred treatment of algorithmic questions.
- Choose the layout and spacing.
- Add instructions and configure default settings.

PowerPoint. The PowerPoint presentations highlight the key points of the chapter and include supporting visuals. New to this edition, all slides are WCAG compliant.

Remote Proctoring. New remote proctoring and browser-locking capabilities are seamlessly integrated within Connect to offer more control over the integrity of online assessments. Instructors can enable security options that restrict browser activity, monitor student behavior, and verify the identity of each student. Instant and detailed reporting gives instructors an at-a-glance view of potential concerns, thereby avoiding personal bias and supporting evidence-based claims.

List of MAPS

List of AUTHOR-SELECTED PRIMARY SOURCE DOCUMENTS IN POWER OF PROCESS

Power of Process for Primary Sources is a critical thinking tool for reading and writing about primary sources. As part of Connect U.S. History, McGraw Hill Education's learning platform, Power of Process, contains a database of over 400 searchable primary sources in addition to the capability for instructors to upload their own sources. Instructors can then select a series of strategies for students to use to analyze and comment on a source. The Power of Process framework helps students develop essential academic skills such as understanding, analyzing, and synthesizing readings and visuals such as maps, leading students toward higher order thinking and writing.

The following primary source documents, carefully selected by the authors to coordinate with this chapter, are available in the Power of Process assignment type within Connect U.S. History.

Acknowledgments

We would like to express our deep appreciation to the following individuals who contributed to the development of our U.S. history programs:

Melissa Anyiwo,
Curry College

Shelly D. Bailess,
Liberty University

Jeremiah Bauer,
Metropolitan Community College

Mark Ehlers,
United States Military Academy

Robert Galler,
St. Cloud University

Ronald E. Goodwin,
Prairie View A&M University

J. Toby Graves,
Copiah-Lincoln Community College

Joshua Hammack,
Santiago Canyon College

Lisa Johnson,
Paris Junior College

Richard D. Kitchen,
New Mexico Military Institute

Jennifer S. Lawrence,
Tarrant County College

Carmen Lopez,
Miami Dade College

Mary Lyons-Carmona,
Metro Community College

Thomas Massey,
Cape Fear Community College

George Reklaitis,
Brookdale Community College

Walton P. Sellers III,
Louisiana State University, Eunice

Daniel Spegel,
Metropolitan Community College

Joanne Sundell,
Erie Community College

Melissa Weinbrenner,
Northeast Texas Community College

Scott M. Williams,
Weatherford College

Nancy Beck Young,
University of Houston

Special thanks and gratitude to the McGraw Hill Academic Integrity Board of Advisors who were instrumental *in providing guidance on chapter content, illustration program, and language and conventions. Our advisors include:*

Susan Bragg,
Georgia Southwestern State University

Jennifer Epley Sanders,
Texas A&M

Eileen Ford,
California State University, Los Angeles

Nicholas Fox,
Houston College

Rudy Jean-Bart,
Broward Community College

Darnell Morehand-Olufade,
University of Bridgeport

Sharon Navarro,
University of Texas at San Antonio

Jeffrey Ogbar,
University of Connecticut

Andrea Oliver,
Tallahassee Community College

Birte Pfleger,
California State University, Los Angeles

Linda Reed,
University of Houston

About the Authors

James West Davidson received his Ph.D. from Yale University. A historian who has pursued a full-time writing career, his works include *After the Fact: The Art of Historical Detection* (with Mark H. Lytle), *The Logic of Millennial Thought: Eighteenth-Century New England*, and *Great Heart: The History of a Labrador Adventure* (with John Rugge). He is co-editor with Michael Stoff of the *Oxford New Narratives in American History*, which includes his study *'They Say': Ida B. Wells and the Reconstruction of Race*. Most recently he wrote *A Little History of the United States*.

Brian DeLay received his Ph.D. from Harvard and is an Associate Professor of History at the University of California, Berkeley. He is a frequent guest speaker at teacher workshops across the country and has won several prizes for his book *War of a Thousand Deserts: Indian Raids and the U.S.-Mexican War*. His current book project, *Shoot the State*, explores the connection between guns, freedom, and domination around the Western Hemisphere, from the American Revolution through World War II.

Christine Leigh Heyrman is the Robert W. and Shirley P. Grimble Professor of American History at the University of Delaware. She received her Ph.D. in American Studies from Yale University. The author of *Commerce and Culture: The Maritime Communities of Colonial Massachusetts, 1690–1750*, she received the Bancroft Prize for her second book, *Southern Cross: The Beginnings of the Bible Belt,* and the Parkman Prize for her third, *American Apostles: When Evangelicals Entered the World of Islam*. Her latest book, forthcoming, is *Doomed Romance: A Story of Broken Hearts, Lost Souls and Sexual Politics in Nineteenth-Century America.*

Mark H. Lytle, a Ph.D. from Yale University, is the Lyford Paterson and Mary Gray Edwards Professor of History Emeritus at Bard College. He served two years as Mary Ball Washington Professor of American History at University College Dublin, in Ireland. His publications include *The Origins of the Iranian-American Alliance, 1941–1953, After the Fact: The Art of Historical Detection* (with James West Davidson), *America's Uncivil Wars: The Sixties Era from Elvis to the Fall of Richard Nixon*, and most recently, *The Gentle Subversive: Rachel Carson, Silent Spring, and the Rise of the Environmental Movement*. His forthcoming book, *The All-Consuming Nation*, considers the tension between the post–World War II consumer democracy and its environmental costs.

Michael B. Stoff is Associate Professor of History and University Distinguished Teaching Associate Professor at the University of Texas at Austin. The recipient of a Ph.D. from Yale University, he has been honored many times for his teaching, most recently with the University of Texas systemwide Regents Outstanding Teaching Award. In 2008, he was named an Organization of American Historians Distinguished Lecturer. He is the author of *Oil, War, and American Security: The Search for a National Policy on Foreign Oil, 1941–1947*, co-editor (with Jonathan Fanton and R. Hal Williams) of *The Manhattan Project: A Documentary Introduction to the Atomic Age*, and series co-editor (with James West Davidson) of the *Oxford New Narratives in American History*. He is currently working on a narrative of the bombing of Nagasaki.

U.S.

A NARRATIVE HISTORY
VOLUME 2: SINCE 1865

17 Reconstructing the Union

1865–1877

"There were swaying chimneys, tottering walls, streets impassable from piles of brick, stones, and rubbish," reported one journalist in Richmond, Virginia, at war's end. "Men stood speechless, haggard . . . gazing at the desolation." Many white southerners must have felt that way in defeat. But despite the widespread ruins, newly freed African Americans were understandably happy about their changed status.

Library of Congress, Prints and Photographs Division

>> An American Story

A SECRET SALE AT DAVIS BEND

Joseph Davis had had enough. Well on in years and financially ruined by the war, he decided to sell his Mississippi plantations Hurricane and Brierfield to Benjamin Montgomery and his sons in 1866. Selling a plantation was common enough after the war, but this transaction was unusual, since Joseph Davis was the elder brother of Jefferson Davis. Indeed, before the war the ex-Confederate president had operated Brierfield as his own plantation. But the sale was

unusual for another reason—so unusual that the parties involved agreed to keep it secret. The plantation's new owners were Black, and Mississippi law prohibited African Americans from owning land.

Even before the war, when he was still enslaved, Benjamin Montgomery had acted as business manager of the two Davis plantations. He had also operated a plantation store with his own line of credit in New Orleans. In 1863 Montgomery fled to the North, but when the war was over, he returned to Davis Bend, where the federal government had confiscated the Davis plantations and was leasing plots of the land to Black farmers. Montgomery quickly emerged as the leader of the African American community at the Bend.

Then, in 1866, President Andrew Johnson pardoned Joseph Davis and restored his lands. Davis was over 80 years old and lacked the stamina to rebuild; yet, unlike many former slaveholders, he felt bound by obligations to those he had enslaved. Convinced that with encouragement African Americans could

succeed in freedom, he sold his land secretly to Benjamin Montgomery. Only when the law prohibiting African Americans from owning land was overturned in 1867 did Davis publicly confirm the sale.

Montgomery undertook to create a model society at Davis Bend based on mutual cooperation. He rented land to Black farmers, hired others to work his own fields, sold supplies on credit, and marketed the crops. The work was hard indeed: Davis Bend's farmers faced the destruction caused by several disastrous floods, insects, droughts, and declining cotton prices. Yet before long, cotton production exceeded that of the prewar years. The Montgomerys eventually became the third-largest planters in the state, and won national and international awards for the quality of their cotton. Their success demonstrated what African Americans, given a fair chance, might accomplish.

The experiences of Benjamin Montgomery were not those of most Black southerners, who did not own land or have a white benefactor. Yet

all African Americans shared Montgomery's dream of economic independence. As one Black veteran noted: "Every colored man will be a slave, and feel himself a slave until he can raise [his] own bale of cotton and put [his] own mark upon it and say this is mine!" Blacks could not gain effective freedom simply through a proclamation of emancipation. They needed economic power, including land that no one could unfairly take away. And political power too, if the legacy of slavery was to be overturned.

How would the republic be reunited, now that slavery had been abolished? War, in its blunt way, had roughed out the contours of a solution, but only in broad terms. The North, with its industrial might, would be the driving force in the nation's economy and retain the dominant political voice. But would African Americans receive effective power? How would North and South readjust their economic and political relations? These questions lay at the heart of the problem of Reconstruction. <<

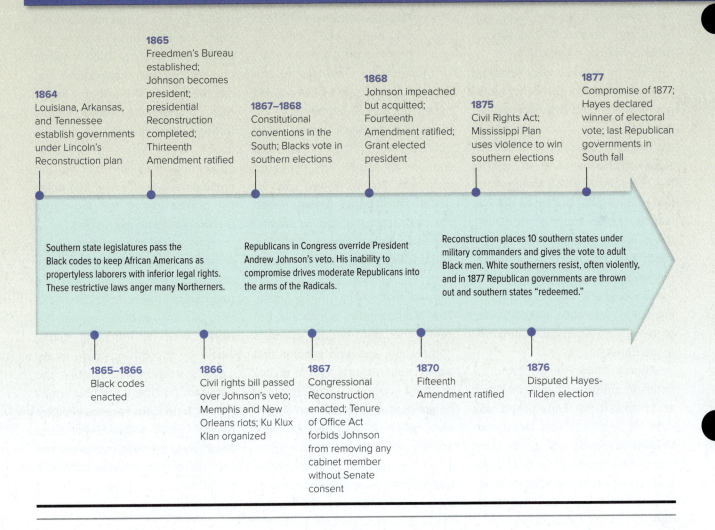

1864
Louisiana, Arkansas, and Tennessee establish governments under Lincoln's Reconstruction plan

1865
Freedmen's Bureau established; Johnson becomes president; presidential Reconstruction completed; Thirteenth Amendment ratified

1867–1868
Constitutional conventions in the South; Blacks vote in southern elections

1868
Johnson impeached but acquitted; Fourteenth Amendment ratified; Grant elected president

1875
Civil Rights Act; Mississippi Plan uses violence to win southern elections

1877
Compromise of 1877; Hayes declared winner of electoral vote; last Republican governments in South fall

Southern state legislatures pass the Black codes to keep African Americans as propertyless laborers with inferior legal rights. These restrictive laws anger many Northerners.

Republicans in Congress override President Andrew Johnson's veto. His inability to compromise drives moderate Republicans into the arms of the Radicals.

Reconstruction places 10 southern states under military commanders and gives the vote to adult Black men. White southerners resist, often violently, and in 1877 Republican governments are thrown out and southern states "redeemed."

1865–1866
Black codes enacted

1866
Civil rights bill passed over Johnson's veto; Memphis and New Orleans riots; Ku Klux Klan organized

1867
Congressional Reconstruction enacted; Tenure of Office Act forbids Johnson from removing any cabinet member without Senate consent

1870
Fifteenth Amendment ratified

1876
Disputed Hayes-Tilden election

PRESIDENTIAL RECONSTRUCTION

Throughout the war Abraham Lincoln had considered Reconstruction his responsibility. Elected with less than 40 percent of the popular vote in 1860, he understood that once the states of the Confederacy were restored to the Union, the Republicans would be weakened unless they ceased to be a sectional party. By a generous peace, Lincoln hoped to attract former Whigs in the South, who supported many of the Republicans' economic policies, and build up a southern wing of the party.

Lincoln's 10 Percent Plan >> Lincoln outlined his program in a Proclamation of **Amnesty** and Reconstruction, issued in December 1863. When a minimum of 10 percent of the qualified voters from 1860 took a **loyalty oath** to the Union, they could organize a state government. The new state constitution had to abolish slavery and provide for Black education, but Lincoln did not insist that high-ranking Confederate leaders be barred from public life.

Lincoln meant to be generous in granting pardons to Confederate leaders and did not rule out compensation for slave property. And while he privately advocated limited Black suffrage in the disloyal southern states, he did not demand social or political equality for Black Americans. In Louisiana, Arkansas, and Tennessee he recognized pro-Union governments that allowed only white men to vote.

Many members of Congress, known as the Radical Republicans, found Lincoln's approach much too lenient. Strongly antislavery, they had led the struggle to make

amnesty general pardon granted by a government, usually for political crimes.

loyalty oath oath of fidelity to the state or to an organization.

<< The mood of white southerners at the end of the war was mixed. Many, like the veteran caricatured here by northern cartoonist Thomas Nast, remained hostile. Others, like Texas captain Samuel Foster, came to believe that the institution of slavery "had been abused, and perhaps for that abuse this terrible war . . . was brought upon us as a punishment."
Library of Congress, Prints and Photographs Division [LC-USZ62-131562]

emancipation a war aim. Now they led the fight to guarantee the rights of freedpeople. The Radicals believed that it was the duty of Congress, not the president, to determine how states would regain their rights in the Union. Though the Radicals often disagreed among themselves about other matters, they all agreed that southern states should be readmitted only after slavery had been ended, Black rights protected, and the power of the planter class destroyed.

Led by Senator Benjamin Wade of Ohio and Representative Henry Winter Davis of Maryland, Congress proposed a much stricter plan of Reconstruction. The Wade-Davis bill required fully half the white adult males to take an oath of allegiance before drafting a new state constitution, and it restricted political power to the hardcore Unionists. Lincoln vetoed this approach, but as the war drew to a close, he appeared ready to make concessions to the Radicals, such as placing the defeated South temporarily under military rule. Then Booth's bullet found its mark, and Lincoln's final approach to Reconstruction would never be known.

Reconstruction under Andrew Johnson >>

In the wake of defeat, many white southerners felt shock, despair, and hopelessness. Some former Confederates were openly antagonistic. A North Carolina innkeeper remarked bitterly that Yankees had stolen those he had enslaved, burned his house, and killed all his sons, leaving him only one privilege: "To hate 'em. I git up at half-past four in the morning, and sit up till twelve at night, to hate 'em." Most Confederate soldiers were less defiant, having had their fill of war. Even among hostile civilians the feeling was widespread that the South must accept northern demands. A South Carolina paper admitted that "the conqueror has the right to make the terms, and we must submit."

This psychological moment was critical. To prevent a resurgence of resistance, the president needed to lay out in unmistakable terms what white southerners had to do to regain their old status in the Union. Perhaps even a clear and firm policy would not have been enough. But with Lincoln's death, the executive power had come to rest in far less capable hands.

Andrew Johnson, the new president, had been born in North Carolina and moved to Tennessee, where he worked as a tailor. Barely able to read and write when he married, he gained political power by campaigning as the champion of the people against the wealthy planter class. "Some day I will show the stuck-up aristocrats who is running the country," he vowed. Although he accepted emancipation as one result of the war, Johnson cared little about the welfare of African Americans. "Damn the negroes," he said during the war, "I am fighting these traitorous aristocrats, their masters." After he had served in Congress and as military governor of Tennessee once Union forces occupied it, Lincoln tapped Johnson, a Democrat, as his running mate in 1864 on the rechristened "Union" ticket.

The Radicals expected Johnson to uphold their views on Reconstruction, and on assuming the presidency he spoke of prosecuting Confederate leaders and breaking up planters' estates.

⌃ Andrew Johnson was a staunch Unionist, but his contentious personality and inflexibility masked a deep-seated insecurity, which was rooted in his humble background. As a young man, he worked and lived in this rude tailor shop in Greeneville, Tennessee.
(left) Library of Congress, Prints and Photographs Division [LC-BH-832-2417] (right) Library of Congress, Prints and Photographs Division [LC-USZ62-130976]

Unlike most Republicans, however, Johnson strongly supported states' rights, and his political shortcomings sparked conflicts almost immediately. Scarred by his humble origins, he became tactless and inflexible when challenged or criticized, alienating even those who sought to work with him.

Johnson wanted the southern states to return to the Union quickly. He prescribed a loyalty oath that most white southerners would have to take to regain their civil and political rights and to have their property restored, except for enslaved African Americans. High Confederate officials and those with property worth over $20,000 had to apply for individual pardons. Once a state drafted a new constitution and elected state officers and members of Congress, Johnson promised to end martial law and recognize the new state government. Suffrage was limited to white citizens who had taken the loyalty oath. This plan was similar to Lincoln's, though more lenient. Only informally did Johnson require southern states to renounce their ordinances of secession, repudiate the Confederate debt, and ratify the Thirteenth Amendment abolishing slavery. That amendment had been passed by Congress in January 1865 and was in the process of being ratified by the states.

The Failure of Johnson's Program >> The

southern delegates who met to construct new governments were in no mood to follow even Johnson's more lenient recommendations. Several states merely repealed instead of repudiating their ordinances of secession, rejected the Thirteenth Amendment, or refused to repudiate the Confederate debt.

Black codes laws passed by southern states in 1865 and 1866, modeled on the slave codes in effect before the Civil War. The codes did grant African Americans some rights not enjoyed by the enslaved, but their primary purpose was to keep African Americans as propertyless agricultural laborers.

Nor did the new governments give African Americans any political rights or provide for Black education. In addition, each state passed laws, often modeled on its old slave code, that applied only to African Americans. These "**Black codes**" did grant some new rights. They legalized marriages that had been made under slavery and allowed Black southerners to hold and sell property and to sue and be sued in state courts. Yet their primary intent was to keep African Americans as propertyless agricultural laborers with inferior legal rights. The new freedpeople could not serve on juries, testify against whites, or work as they pleased. Mississippi prohibited them from buying or renting farmland, and most states ominously provided that Black people who were vagrants could be arrested and hired out to landowners. Many northerners were incensed by the restrictive Black codes, which violated their conception of freedom.

Southern voters under Johnson's plan also defiantly elected prominent Confederate military and political leaders to office. At this point, Johnson could have called for new elections or admitted that a different program of Reconstruction was needed. Instead, he caved in. For all his harsh rhetoric, he shrank from the prospect of social upheaval, and as the lines of ex-Confederates waiting to see him lengthened, he

began issuing special pardons almost as fast as they could be printed. Publicly Johnson put on a bold face, announcing that Reconstruction had been successfully completed. But many members of Congress were deeply alarmed, and the stage was set for a serious confrontation.

Johnson's Break with Congress >> The new Con-

gress was by no means of one mind. A few Democrats and conservative Republicans backed the president's program of immediate restoration. At the other end of the spectrum, a larger group of Radical Republicans, led by Thaddeus Stevens, Charles Sumner, and Benjamin Wade, was bent on remaking southern society in the image of the North. Reconstruction must "revolutionize Southern institutions, habits, and manners," insisted Representative Stevens, "or all our blood and treasure have been spent in vain."

As a minority the Radicals needed the aid of the moderate Republicans, the largest bloc in Congress. Led by William Pitt Fessenden and Lyman Trumbull, the moderates had no desire to foster social revolution or promote racial equality in the South. But they wanted to keep Confederate leaders from reassuming power, and they were convinced that freedpeople needed federal protection. Otherwise, Trumbull declared, they would "be tyrannized over, abused, and virtually reenslaved."

The central issue dividing Johnson and the Radicals was the place of African Americans in American society. Johnson accused his opponents of seeking "to Africanize the southern half of our country," while the Radicals championed civil and political rights for African Americans. The only way to maintain loyal governments and develop a Republican party in the South, Radicals argued, was to give Black men the ballot. Moderates agreed that the new southern governments were too harsh toward African Americans,

∧ Thaddeus Stevens, Radical Republican leader in the House.
Library of Congress, Prints and Photographs Division [LC-USZ62-63460]

but they feared that too great an emphasis on Black civil rights would alienate northern voters.

In December 1865, when southern representatives to Congress appeared in Washington to take their seats, a majority in Congress voted to exclude them. Congress also appointed a joint committee, chaired by Senator Fessenden, to look into Reconstruction.

The growing split with the president became clearer after Congress passed a bill extending the life of the Freedmen's Bureau. Created in March 1865, the bureau provided emergency food, clothing, and medical care to war refugees (including white southerners) and took charge of settling freedpeople on abandoned lands. The new bill gave the bureau the added responsibilities of supervising special courts to resolve disputes involving freedpeople and establishing schools for Black southerners. Although this bill passed with virtually unanimous Republican support, Johnson vetoed it.

Johnson also vetoed a civil rights bill designed to overturn the harshest provisions of the Black codes. The law made African Americans citizens of the United States and granted them the right to own property, make contracts, and have access to courts as parties and witnesses. (The law did not go so far as to grant freedpeople the right to vote.) For most Republicans, Johnson's veto was the last straw, and in April 1866 Congress overrode it. Congress then approved and promptly overrode the president's veto of a slightly revised Freedmen's Bureau bill in July. Johnson's refusal to compromise drove the moderates into the arms of the Radicals.

The Fourteenth Amendment >> To prevent hardcore Confederates from taking over the reconstructed state governments and denying African Americans basic freedoms, Congress's Joint Committee on Reconstruction proposed an amendment to the Constitution, which passed both houses with the necessary two-thirds vote in June 1866.

The amendment guaranteed repayment of the national war debt and prohibited repayment of the Confederate debt. To counteract the president's wholesale pardons, it disqualified prominent Confederates from holding office. Because moderates balked at giving the vote to African Americans, the amendment merely gave Congress the right to reduce the representation of any state that did not have impartial male suffrage. The practical effect of this provision, which Radicals labeled a "swindle," was to allow northern states to retain white suffrage, since unlike southern states they had few African Americans in their populations and thus would not be penalized.

The amendment's most important provision, Section 1, defined an American citizen as anyone born in the United States or naturalized, thereby automatically making African Americans citizens. Section 1 also prohibited states from abridging "the privileges or immunities" of citizens, depriving "any person of life, liberty, or property, without due process of law," or denying "any person . . . equal protection of the laws." The framers of the amendment probably intended to prohibit laws that applied to one race only, such as the Black codes, or that made certain acts felonies when committed by Black but not white people, or that decreed different penalties for the same crime when committed by white and Black lawbreakers. The framers probably did not intend to prevent segregation (the legal separation of the races) in schools and public places.

Johnson denounced the amendment and urged southern states not to ratify it. Only Tennessee, the president's home state, did ratify, and Congress readmitted it with no further restrictions. The telegram sent to Congress by a longtime foe of Johnson officially announcing Tennessee's approval ended with this sardonic salutation: "Give my respects to the dead dog in the White House."

The Election of 1866 >> When Congress blocked his policies, Johnson undertook a speaking tour of the East and Midwest in the fall of 1866 to drum up support for the upcoming elections. But northern audiences were skeptical that white southerners had fully repented. Only months earlier white mobs in Memphis and New Orleans had attacked Black residents and killed nearly 100 in two major race riots. "The negroes now know, to their sorrow, that it is best not to arouse the fury of the white man," boasted one Memphis newspaper. When the president encountered hostile audiences during his northern tour, he made matters only worse by trading insults and charging that the Radicals were traitors.

Not to be outdone, the Radicals vilified Johnson as a traitor aiming to turn the country over to former rebels. Resorting to the tactic of "waving the **bloody shirt**," they appealed to voters by reviving bitter memories of the war. Republican Governor Oliver Morton of Indiana proclaimed that "every bounty jumper, every deserter, every sneak who ran away from the draft calls himself a Democrat. Every 'Son of Liberty' who conspired to murder, burn, rob arsenals

> **bloody shirt** campaign tactic of "waving the bloody shirt" invoked the deaths and casualties from the Civil War as a reason to vote for Republicans as the party of the Union rather than Democrats, who had often opposed the war.

SCENES IN MEMPHIS, TENNESSEE, DURING THE RIOT—BURNING A FREEDMEN'S SCHOOL-HOUSE.

⌃ In 1866 white mobs in Memphis and New Orleans attacked African Americans in two major riots. Here rioters set fire to a schoolhouse used by freedpeople.
Library of Congress, Prints and Photographs Division [LC-USZ62-111152]

and release rebel prisoners calls himself a Democrat. In short, the Democratic party may be described as a common sewer."

Voters soundly repudiated Johnson, as the Republicans won more than a two-thirds majority in both houses of Congress. The Radicals had reached the height of their power, propelled by genuine alarm among northerners that Johnson's policies would lose the fruits of the Union's victory. Johnson was a president virtually without a party.

 REVIEW

What were Lincoln's and Andrew Johnson's approaches to Reconstruction, and why did Congress reject Johnson's approach?

CONGRESSIONAL RECONSTRUCTION

With a clear electoral victory, congressional Republicans passed their own program of Reconstruction, beginning with the first Reconstruction Act in March 1867. Like all later pieces of Reconstruction legislation, it was repassed over Johnson's veto.

Placing the 10 unreconstructed states under military commanders, the act provided that in enrolling voters, officials were to include Black adult males but not former Confederates, who were barred from holding office under the Fourteenth Amendment. Delegates to the state conventions were to frame constitutions that made these provisions part of state law as well as ratify the Fourteenth Amendment. Once Congress approved the new state constitution, a state could send representatives to Congress.

White southerners found these requirements so insulting that officials took no steps to register voters. Congress then enacted a second Reconstruction Act, also in March,

ordering the local military commanders to put the machinery of Reconstruction into motion. Johnson's efforts to limit the power of military commanders produced a third act, passed in July, that upheld their superiority in all matters. When the first election was held in Alabama to ratify the new state constitution, whites boycotted it in sufficient numbers to prevent a majority of voters from participating. Undaunted, Congress passed the fourth Reconstruction Act (March 1868), which required ratification of the constitution by only a majority of those voting rather than those who were registered.

By June 1868 Congress had readmitted the representatives of seven states. Texas, Virginia, and Mississippi did not complete the process until 1869. Georgia finally followed in 1870.

Post-Emancipation Societies in the Americas >>

With the exception of Haiti's revolution (1791–1804), the United States was the only society in the Americas in which the destruction of slavery was accomplished by violence. But the United States, uniquely among these societies, gave the vote to formerly enslaved people almost immediately after the emancipation. Thus, in the United States, freedpeople and their former slaveholders battled for control in ways that did not occur in other post-emancipation societies.

In most of the Caribbean, property requirements for voting left the planters in political control. Jamaica, for example, with a population of 500,000 in the 1860s, had only 3,000 voters. Moreover, a movement to mobilize disenfranchised Black peasants led Jamaican planters to dissolve the assembly and revert to being a British Crown colony governed from London. Of the sugar islands, all but Barbados adopted the same policy, thereby blocking the potential for any future Black peasant democracy. Nor did any of these societies have the counterparts of the Radical Republicans, a group of outsiders with political power that promoted the fundamental transformation of the post-emancipation South. These comparisons highlight the radicalism of Reconstruction in the United States, which alone saw an effort to forge an interracial democracy.

MAP 17.1: THE SOUTHERN STATES DURING RECONSTRUCTION

The Land Issue >> While the political process of Reconstruction proceeded, Congress debated whether land should be given to freedpeople to foster economic independence. "The way we can best take care of ourselves," African American leaders declared, "is to have land, and till it by our own labor." The Second Confiscation Act of 1862 had authorized the government to seize and sell the property of supporters of the rebellion. In June 1866, however, President Johnson ruled that confiscation laws applied only to wartime.

After more than a year of debate, Congress rejected all proposals to distribute land to freedpeople. Given Americans' strong belief in self-reliance, little sympathy existed for the idea that government should support any group. In addition, land redistribution represented an attack on property rights, another cherished American value. "A division of rich men's lands amongst the landless," argued the *Nation*, a Radical journal, "would give a shock to our whole social and political system from which it would hardly recover without the loss of liberty." By 1867 land reform was dead.

Impeachment >> Throughout 1867 Congress routinely overrode Johnson's vetoes, but the president undercut congressional Reconstruction in other ways. He interpreted the new laws narrowly and removed military commanders who vigorously enforced them. Congress responded by restricting his power to issue orders to military commanders in the South. It also passed the Tenure of Office Act, which forbade Johnson to remove any member of the cabinet without the Senate's consent. The principal reason for this law was to prevent him from firing Secretary of War Edwin Stanton, the only remaining Radical in the cabinet.

When Johnson tried to dismiss Stanton in February 1868, the House of Representatives angrily approved articles of impeachment. The articles focused on the violation of the Tenure of Office Act, but the charge with the most substance was that Johnson had acted to systematically obstruct Reconstruction legislation. In the trial before the Senate, the president's lawyers argued that impeachment could be charged only for an indictable crime, which Johnson clearly had not committed. Seven moderate Republicans agreed with this sentiment and in May 1868 the Senate voted 35 to 19 to convict. The tally had come up one vote short of the two-thirds majority needed. Johnson was allowed to serve out his term.

THEN&NOW

Impeachment is the most drastic remedy the Constitution offers for curbing the misbehavior of federal officials. Before Andrew Johnson, it had never been used against a president. It was not threatened again until 1974, when President Richard Nixon resigned before he could be impeached. Again in 1998, President Bill Clinton was impeached but then acquitted. A little over 20 years later, President Donald J. Trump was impeached twice.

The fight during Reconstruction laid out the lines of battle over the proper scope of impeachment—and similar arguments have echoed during the Trump presidency and his first impeachment trial. Trump's defenders insisted it would be unconstitutional to impeach unless there was "substantial evidence that, while in office, [Trump] committed treason, bribery, or other high crimes and misdemeanors." In contrast, the Radical Republicans of Reconstruction insisted that a president could be impeached for the "grave misuse of his powers . . . for any conduct which harms the public or perils its welfare." That is, the process could properly be as much political as criminal in its orientation.

The same argument was made by members of the House who voted to impeach Trump in 2019. But a political case is harder to win when a two-thirds majority in the Senate is needed to convict and fierce partisan lines are drawn. As evidence mounted that Trump had withheld U.S. aid to Ukraine in order to pressure its government to investigate a potential political rival, Republicans argued that such actions did not constitute an impeachable offense. Voters should decide such political matters, they insisted, in the election of 2020.

 REVIEW

What was Congress's approach to Reconstruction, and why did it not include a provision for giving land to freedpeople?

RECONSTRUCTION IN THE SOUTH

As the power of the Radicals in Congress waned, the fate of Reconstruction increasingly hinged on events in the southern states themselves. Power in these states rested with the new Republican parties, representing a coalition of Black and white southerners and transplanted northerners.

Black and White Republicans >> Once African Americans received the right to vote, Black men constituted as much as 80 percent of Republican voters in the South. They steadfastly opposed the Democratic Party with its appeal to white supremacy. But during Reconstruction, African Americans never held office in proportion to their voting strength. No African American was ever elected governor. And only in South Carolina, where more than 60 percent of the population was Black, did they control even one house of the state legislature. Between 15 and 20 percent of the state officers and 6 percent of members of Congress (2 senators and 15 representatives) were Black. Only in South Carolina did Black officeholders approach their proportion of the population.

Those who held office came from the top levels of African American society. Among state and federal officeholders,

^ Hiram Revels, a minister and educator, became the first African American to serve in the U.S. Senate, representing Mississippi. Later he served as president of Alcorn University.
Library of Congress, Prints and Photographs Division [LC-DIG-cwpbh-03275]

Originally from the North, they allegedly had arrived with all their worldly possessions stuffed in a carpetbag, ready to loot and plunder the defeated South. Some did, certainly, but northerners moved south for a variety of reasons. Though carpetbaggers made up only a small percentage of Republican voters, they controlled almost a third of the offices in the South. More than half of all southern Republican governors and nearly half of Republican members of Congress were originally northerners.

The Republican Party in the South had difficulty maintaining unity. Scalawags were especially susceptible to the race issue and social pressure. "Even my own kinspeople have turned the cold shoulder to me because I hold office under a Republican administration," testified a Mississippi white Republican. As Black southerners pressed for greater recognition, white southerners increasingly defected to the Democrats. Carpetbaggers, in contrast, were less sensitive to race, although most felt that their Black allies should be content with minor offices. The animosity between scalawags and carpetbaggers, which grew out of their rivalry for party honors, was particularly intense.

Reforms under the New State Governments

>> The new southern state constitutions enacted several significant reforms. They devised fairer systems of legislative representation and made many previously appointive offices elective. The Radical state governments also assumed some responsibility for social welfare and established the first statewide systems of public schools in the South.

Although all the new constitutions proclaimed the principle of equality and granted Black adult males the right to vote, on social relations they were much more cautious. No state outlawed segregation, and South Carolina and Louisiana were the only ones that required integration in public schools (a mandate that was almost universally ignored). Sensitive to status, biracial citizens pushed for prohibition of social discrimination, but white Republicans refused to adopt such a radical policy.

Economic Issues and Corruption

>> With the southern economy in ruins at the end of the war, problems of economic reconstruction were severe. The new Republican governments encouraged industrial development by providing subsidies, loans, and even temporary exemptions from taxes. These governments also largely rebuilt the southern railroad system, offering lavish aid to railroad corporations. In the two decades after 1860, the region doubled its manufacturing establishments, yet the South steadily slipped further behind the booming industrial economy of the North.

The expansion of government services offered temptations for corruption. Southern officials regularly received bribes and kickbacks for awarding railroad charters, franchises, and other contracts. The railroad grants and new social services such as schools also left state governments in debt, even though taxes rose in the 1870s to four times the rate in 1860.

Corruption, however, was not only a southern problem but a national one. During these years, the Democratic Tweed

perhaps 80 percent were literate, and over a quarter had been free before the war, both marks of distinction in the Black community. Their occupations also set them apart: many were professionals (mostly clergy), and of the third who were farmers, nearly all owned land. In their political and social values, African American leaders were more conservative than the rural Black population, and they showed little interest in land reform.

Black citizens were a majority of the voters only in South Carolina, Mississippi, and Louisiana. Thus in most of the South the Republican Party had to secure white votes to stay in power. Opponents scornfully labeled white southerners who allied with the Republican Party **scalawags**, yet an estimated quarter of white southerners at one time voted Republican. They were primarily Unionists from the upland counties and hill areas and largely yeoman farmers. Such voters approved Republican promises to rebuild the South, restore prosperity, create public schools, and open isolated areas to the market with railroads.

The other group of white Republicans in the South were known as **carpetbaggers**.

scalawags white southerners who supported the Republican Party.

carpetbaggers northern white Republicans who came to live in the South after the Civil War. Most were veterans of the Union army; many were teachers, Freedmen's Bureau agents, or investors in cotton plantations.

Ring in New York City alone stole more money than all the southern Radical governments combined. Moreover, corruption was hardly limited to southern Republicans: many Democrats and white business leaders participated. Louisiana governor Henry Warmoth, a carpetbagger, told a congressional committee: "Everybody is demoralizing down here. Corruption is the fashion."

Corruption in Radical governments existed, but southern Democrats exaggerated its extent for partisan purposes. They opposed honest Radical regimes just as bitterly as notoriously corrupt ones. In the eyes of most white southerners, the real crime of the Radical governments was that they allowed Black citizens to hold some offices and tried to protect the civil rights of Black Americans. Race was white conservatives' greatest weapon. And it would prove the most effective means to undermine Republican power in the South.

 REVIEW

What roles did African Americans, southern whites, and northern whites play in the Reconstruction governments of the South?

BLACK ASPIRATIONS

Emancipation came to enslaved African Americans in different ways and at different times. Betty Jones's grandmother was told about the Emancipation Proclamation by another worker while hoeing corn. Mary Anderson received the news from her slaveholder near the end of the war when Sherman's army invaded North Carolina. Whatever the timing, freedom meant a host of precious blessings to people who had been in bondage all their lives.

Experiencing Freedom >> The first impulse was to think of freedom as a contrast to slavery. Emancipation immediately released enslaved African Americans from the most oppressive aspects of bondage—the whippings, the breakup of families, the sexual exploitation. Freedom also meant movement, the right to travel without white permission. Above all, freedom meant that African Americans' labor would be for their own benefit. One Arkansas freedman, who earned his first dollar working on a railroad, recalled that on payday, "I felt like the richest man in the world."

Freedom included finding a new place to work. Changing jobs was one concrete way to break the psychological ties of slavery. Even slaveholders with reputations for kindness sometimes saw most of their former hands depart. The cook who left a South Carolina family, despite the offer of higher wages than her new job's, explained: "I must go. If I stays here I'll never know I'm free."

Symbolically, freedom meant having a full name. African Americans now adopted last names, most commonly the name of the first slaveholder in the family's oral history as far back as it could be recalled. Most, however, retained their first name, especially if the name had been given to them by their parents (as was most often the case). Whatever the name, Black Americans insisted on making the decision themselves.

The Black Family >> African Americans also sought to strengthen the family in freedom. Since the marriages of those held in bondage had not been recognized as legal, thousands of freedpeople insisted on being married again by proper authorities, even though this was not required by law. Those who had been forcibly separated in slavery and later remarried confronted the dilemma of which spouse to take. Laura Spicer, whose husband had been sold away from her plantation, wrote him after the war seeking to resume their marriage. In a series of wrenching letters, he explained that he had thought her dead, had remarried, and had a new family. "You know it never was our wishes to be separated from each other, and it never was our fault. I had rather anything to had happened to me most than ever have been parted from you and the children," he wrote. "As I am, I do not know which I love best, you or Anna." Declining to return, he closed, "Laura, truly, I have got another wife, and I am very sorry."

As in white families, Black husbands deemed themselves the head of the family and acted legally for their wives. They often insisted that their wives would not work in the fields as they had in slavery. "The [Black] women say they never mean to do any more outdoor work," one planter reported, "that white men support their wives and they mean that their husbands shall support them." In negotiating contracts, a father also demanded the right to control his children and their labor. All these changes were designed to insulate the Black family from white control.

The Schoolhouse and the Church >> In freedom, the schoolhouse and the Black church became essential institutions in the Black community. "My Lord, Ma'am, what a great thing learning is!" a South Carolina freedman told a northern teacher. "White folks can do what they likes, for they know so much more than we." At first, northern churches and missionaries, working with the Freedmen's Bureau, set up Black schools in the South. Tuition at these schools represented 10 percent or more of a laborer's monthly wages, yet these schools were full. Eventually, states established public school systems, which by 1867 enrolled 40 percent of African American children.

Black adults, who often attended night classes, had good reasons for seeking literacy. They wanted to be able to read the Bible, to defend their newly gained civil and political rights, and to protect themselves from being cheated. Both races saw that education would undermine the servility that slavery had fostered.

The teachers in the Freedmen's Bureau schools were primarily northern middle-class white women sent south by

<< When Beale Street Baptist Church was founded by African Americans after the Civil War, the congregation was so poor, it met in a brush arbor—a canopy of leaves and branches held up by log poles. But the Memphis church soon grew by leaps and bounds. Contributions to the weekly collection plate financed the building of this stately church. By the early 1880s, Memphis boasted more Black than white Protestant churches.
Library of Congress, Prints and Photographs Division [HABS TENN,79-MEMPH,7—1]

northern missionary societies. "I feel that it is a precious privilege," Esther Douglass wrote, "to be allowed to do something for these poor people." Many saw themselves as peacetime soldiers, struggling to make emancipation a reality. Indeed, hostile white southerners sometimes destroyed Black schools and threatened and even murdered white teachers. Then there were the everyday challenges: low pay, run-down buildings, few books, classes of 100 or more children. By 1869 most teachers in these Freedmen's Bureau schools were Black, trained by the bureau.

Most enslaved people had attended white churches or services supervised by whites. Once free, African Americans quickly established their own congregations led by Black preachers. Mostly Methodist and Baptist, Black churches were the only major organizations in the African American community controlled by Blacks themselves. A white missionary reported that "the Ebony preacher who promises perfect independence from White control and direction carried the colored heart at once." Just as in slavery, religion offered African Americans a place of refuge in a hostile white world and provided them with hope, comfort, and a means of self-identification.

New Working Conditions >> As a largely property-less class, Blacks in the postwar South had no choice but to work for white landowners. Except for paying wages, whites wanted to retain the old system of labor, including close supervision, gang labor, and physical punishment. Determined to remove all emblems of servitude, African Americans refused to work under these conditions, and they demanded time off to devote to their own interests. Because of shorter hours and the withdrawal of children and women from the fields, Blacks' output declined by an estimated 35 percent in freedom. They also refused to live in the old slave quarters

located near the slaveholder's house and instead erected cabins on distant parts of the plantation. Wages initially were $5 or $6 a month plus provisions and a cabin; by 1867, they had risen to an average of $10 a month.

These changes eventually led to the rise of sharecropping. Under this arrangement African American families farmed discrete plots of land and divided the crop with the white landowner, normally on an equal basis, at the end of the year. Sharecropping had higher status and offered greater personal freedom than being a wage laborer. "I am not working for wages," one Black farmer declared, "but am part owner of the crop and as [such,] I have all the rights that you or any other man has." Although Black agricultural workers earned about 40 percent more once they were free, sharecropping was a harshly exploitative system in which Black families often sank into perpetual debt.

The task of supervising the transition from slavery to freedom on southern plantations fell to the Freedmen's Bureau, a unique experiment in social policy supported by the federal government. Assigned the task of protecting freedpeople's economic rights, approximately 550 local agents regulated working conditions in southern agriculture after the war. The racial attitudes of Bureau agents varied widely, as did their commitment and competence.

Most agents required written contracts between white planters and Black laborers, specifying wages and the conditions of employment. Although agents sometimes intervened to protect freedpeople from unfair treatment, they also provided important help to planters. They insisted that Black laborers not leave at harvest time, they arrested those who violated their contracts or refused to sign new ones at the beginning of the year, and they preached the need to be orderly and respectful. Because of such attitudes, freedpeople increasingly complained that Bureau agents were mere tools of the planter class.

>> MAPPING THE PAST <<

GEORGIA PLANTATION AFTER THE WAR

After emancipation, sharecropping became the dominant form of agricultural labor in the South. Black families no longer lived in the old enslaved worker quarters but dispersed to separate plots of land that they farmed for themselves. At the end of the year, each sharecropper turned over part of the crop to the white landowner.

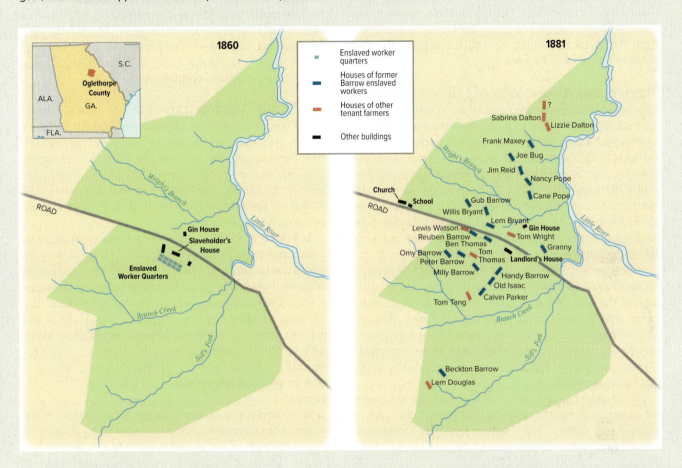

MAP READING

1. Compare the location of the slaveholder's house in relationship to the enslaved worker quarters with the location of the landlord's house and the houses of former slaves and other tenant farmers.
2. What buildings appear on the 1881 map but not on the 1860s map?
3. Describe the location of the houses of other tenant farmers in relationship to the houses of former enslaved workers.

MAP INTERPRETATION

1. What might explain the positioning of the slaveholder's house between the enslaved worker quarters and the gin house on the 1860 map?
2. What does the location of houses on the 1881 map suggest about relations between former enslaved workers and other tenant farmers? Between all tenant farmers and the landlord?
3. What do the names and colors of the tenant farmer homes suggest about the mobility of families during Reconstruction?

To avoid the discrimination African Americans received in southern state courts, Congress created the Freedmen's Courts in 1866. These new courts functioned as military tribunals, and often the agent was the entire court. The sympathy Black laborers received varied from state to state. But since Congress was opposed to creating any permanent welfare agency, it shut down the Freedmen's Bureau, and by 1872 it had gone out of business. Despite its mixed record, it was the most effective agency in protecting Blacks' civil and political rights. Its disbanding signaled the beginning of the northern retreat from Reconstruction.

Planters and a New Way of Life >> Planters and other white southerners faced emancipation with dread. "All the traditions and habits of both races had been suddenly overthrown," a Tennessee planter recalled, "and neither knew just what to do, or how to accommodate themselves to the new situation." Slavery had been a complex institution that welded Black and white southerners together in intimate relationships. The old ideal of a paternalistic planter, which required Blacks to act subservient and grateful, gave way to an emphasis on strictly economic relationships. Only with time did planters develop new norms to judge Black behavior.

After the war, however, planters increasingly embraced the ideology of segregation. Since emancipation significantly reduced the social distance between the races, white southerners sought psychological separation and kept dealings with African Americans to a minimum. Increasingly, white planters developed a new way of life based on the institutions of sharecropping and segregation, and undergirded by a militant white supremacy.

While most planters kept their land, they did not regain the economic prosperity of the prewar years. Cotton prices began a long decline, and southern per-capita income suffered as a result. By 1880 the value of southern farms had slid 33 percent below the level of 1860.

 REVIEW

In what ways were the church and the school central to African American hopes after the Civil War?

THE ABANDONMENT OF RECONSTRUCTION

On Christmas Day 1875 a white acquaintance approached Charles Caldwell in Clinton, Mississippi, and invited him to have a drink. A freedman, Caldwell was a state senator and the leader of the Republican Party in Hinds County. But the Black leader's fearlessness made him a marked man. Only two months earlier, Caldwell had fled the county to escape an armed white mob. Despite further threats, he had returned home to vote in the November election. Now, as Caldwell and

his "friend" raised their glasses in a toast, a gunshot exploded through the window and Caldwell collapsed, mortally wounded. He was taken outside, where his assassins riddled his body with bullets. He died alone in the street.

A number of Black Republican leaders in the South shared Charles Caldwell's fate. Resorting to violence and terror, white southerners challenged the commitment of the federal government to sustaining Reconstruction. After Andrew Johnson was acquitted at his impeachment trial in May 1868, the crusading idealism of the Republican Party began to wane. Ulysses S. Grant was hardly the cause of this change, but he certainly came to symbolize it.

The Grant Administration >> In 1868 Grant was elected president—and Republicans were shocked. Their candidate, a great war hero, had won by a margin of only 300,000 votes. Furthermore, with an estimated 450,000 Black Republican votes cast in the South, a majority of whites had voted Democratic. The election helped convince Republican leaders that an amendment securing Black suffrage throughout the nation was necessary.

In February 1869 Congress sent the Fifteenth Amendment to the states for ratification. It forbade any state to deny the right to vote on grounds of race, color, or previous condition of servitude. It did not forbid literacy and property requirements, as some Radicals wanted, because the moderates feared that only a conservative version of the amendment could be ratified. As a result, when the amendment was ratified in March 1870, loopholes remained that eventually allowed southern states to **disenfranchise** African Americans.

> **disenfranchise** deny a citizen's right to vote.

Advocates of women's suffrage were bitterly disappointed when Congress refused to outlaw voting discrimination on the basis of sex as well as race. The Women's Loyal League, led by Elizabeth Cady Stanton and Susan B. Anthony, had pressed for first the Fourteenth and then the Fifteenth Amendment to recognize that women had a civic right to vote. But even most Radicals were unwilling to back women's suffrage, contending that Black rights had to be ensured first. As a result, the Fifteenth Amendment divided the feminist movement. Although disappointed that women were not included in its provisions, Lucy Stone and the American Woman Suffrage Association urged ratification. Stanton and Anthony, however, denounced the amendment and organized the National Woman Suffrage Association to work for passage of a new amendment giving women the ballot. The division hampered the women's rights movement for decades to come.

When Ulysses S. Grant was a general, his quiet manner and well-known resolution served him well in maneuvering troops. As president he proved much less certain of his goals and therefore less effective at corralling politicians.

A series of scandals wracked his administration, so much so that *Grantism* soon became a code word in American politics for corruption and cronyism. Although Grant did not

THE FIFTEENTH AMENDMENT.

CELEBRATED MAY 19ᵀ 1870.

∧ The Fifteenth Amendment, ratified in 1870, secured the right of African American males to vote as free citizens. In New York, Black citizens paraded in support of Ulysses S. Grant for president (*center*). But citizenship was only one component of what African Americans insisted were central aspects of their freedom. What other features of a free life does the poster champion?
Library of Congress, Prints and Photographs Division [LC-DIG-ppmsca-34808]

profit personally, he remained loyal to his friends and displayed little zeal to root out wrongdoing. Nor was Congress immune from the lowered tone of public life. In such a climate ruthless state political machines, led by politicians who favored the status quo, came to dominate the party.

As corruption in both the North and the South worsened, reformers became more interested in cleaning up government than in protecting Black rights. In 1872 Congress passed an amnesty act, allowing many more ex-Confederates to serve in southern governments. That same year, liberal Republicans broke with the Republican Party and nominated for president Horace Greeley, the editor of the *New York Tribune*. A one-time Radical, Greeley had become disillusioned with Reconstruction and urged a restoration of home rule in the South as well as adoption of civil service reform. Democrats decided to back the Liberal Republican ticket. The Republicans renominated Grant, who, despite the defection of a number of prominent Radicals, won an easy victory.

<< As president, Ulysses Grant's gratitude toward friends led him to appoint a number of officials who betrayed his trust. But the president acted firmly to prosecute terrorism pursued by the Ku Klux Klan, and he appointed a record number of African Americans to government positions. Frederick Douglass approvingly noted that one federal department he visited included 249 Black officials and there were "many positions . . . in different parts of the country."
Library of Congress, Prints and Photographs Division

Make a Case

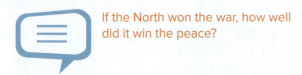

If the North won the war, how well did it win the peace?

Growing Northern Disillusionment >> During Grant's second term Congress passed the Civil Rights Act of 1875, the last major piece of Reconstruction legislation. This law prohibited racial discrimination in public accommodations, transportation, places of amusement, and juries. But Congress refused to ban segregation in public schools, which was almost universal in the North as well as the South. And the federal government made little attempt to enforce the Civil Rights Act. Finally in 1883 the Supreme Court struck down its provisions, except the one relating to juries.

Despite passage of the Civil Rights Act, many northerners were growing disillusioned with Reconstruction. They were repelled by the corruption of the southern governments, they were tired of the violence and disorder that accompanied elections in the South, and they had little faith in Black Americans. William Dodge, a wealthy New York capitalist and an influential Republican, wrote in 1875 that the South could never develop its resources "till confidence in her state governments can be restored, and this will never be done by federal bayonets." It had been a mistake, he went on, to make Black southerners feel "that the United States government was their special friend, rather than those . . . among whom they must live and for whom they must work. We have tried this long enough," he concluded. "Now let the South alone."

The wounds of the war faded even more as the Panic of 1873 sparked a severe four-year depression. Battered by the panic and the corruption issue, the Republicans lost a shocking 77 seats in Congress in the 1874 elections, and along with them control of the House of Representatives for the first time since 1861.

"The truth is our people are tired out with the worn out cry of 'Southern outrages'!!" one Republican concluded. More and more, he and others in his party spoke about cutting loose the unpopular southern governments.

The Triumph of White Supremacy >> Meanwhile, southern Democrats set out to overthrow the remaining Radical governments. Already, white Republicans in the South felt heavy pressure to desert their party. To poor white southerners who lacked social standing, the Democratic appeal to racial solidarity offered special comfort. The large landowners and other wealthy groups that led southern Democrats objected less to Black southerners voting, since they were confident that if outside influences were removed, they could control the Black vote.

Democrats also used economic pressure to undermine Republican power. In heavily Black counties, newspapers published the names of Black residents who cast Republican ballots and urged planters to discharge them. But terror and violence provided the most effective weapon against radical governments. A number of paramilitary organizations broke up Republican meetings, terrorized white and Black Republicans, assassinated Republican leaders, and prevented Black citizens from voting. The most notorious of these organizations was the Ku Klux Klan, which along with similar groups functioned as an unofficial arm of the Democratic Party.

In the war for supremacy, contesting control of the night was paramount to both southern whites and Blacks. Before emancipation slaveholders regulated nighttime hours, with a system of passes and patrols that chased African Americans who went hunting or tried to sneak a visit to a family member at a neighboring plantation. For those in bondage the night provided precious free time: to read, to meet for worship, school, or dancing. During Reconstruction African Americans actively took back the night for a host of activities, including torchlight political parades and meetings of such organizations as the Union League. Part of the Klan's mission was to recoup this contested ground and to limit the ability of African Americans to use the night as they pleased. When indirect threats of violence were not enough (galloping through Black neighborhoods rattling fences with lances), beatings and executions were undertaken—again, facilitated by the dark of night.

What became known as the Mississippi Plan was inaugurated in 1875, when Democrats decided to use as much violence as necessary to carry the state election. Local papers trumpeted, "Carry the election peaceably if we can, forcibly if we must." Recognizing that northern public opinion had grown sick of federal intervention in southern elections, the Grant administration rejected the request of Republican governor Adelbert Ames for troops to stop the violence. Bolstered by terrorism, the Democrats swept the election in Mississippi. Violence and intimidation prevented as many as 60,000 Black and white Republicans from voting, converting the normal Republican majority into a Democratic majority of 30,000. Mississippi had been "redeemed."

The Disputed Election of 1876 >> The 1876 presidential election was crucial to the final overthrow of Reconstruction. The Republicans nominated Ohio governor Rutherford B. Hayes to oppose Samuel J. Tilden, governor of New York. Again violence prevented an estimated quarter of a million Republican votes from being cast in the South. Tilden had a clear majority of 250,000 in the popular vote, but the outcome in the Electoral College was in doubt because both parties claimed South Carolina, Florida, and Louisiana, the only reconstructed states still in Republican hands.

To arbitrate the disputed returns, Congress established a 15-member electoral commission. By a straight party vote of

Historian's TOOLBOX

Dressed to Kill

Klan members drawn for *Harper's Weekly* magazine.

These three Klansmen were arrested in Tishomingo County, Mississippi, for attempted murder.

Why wear a hooded mask? Might there be more than one reason?

The costumes of Ku Klux Klan night riders—pointed hoods and white sheets—have become a staple of history books. But why use such outlandish disguises? To hide the identity of members, according to some accounts, or to terrorize freedpeople into thinking they were being menaced by Confederate ghosts. Historian Elaine F. Parsons has suggested that KKK performances took their cues from American popular culture; they imitated the costumes of Mardi Gras and similar carnivals, as well as minstrel shows. In behaving like carnival revelers, KKK members may have hoped to fool northern authorities into viewing the night rides as humorous pranks, not a threat to Radical rule. For southern white Democrats the theatrical night rides helped overturn the social order of Reconstruction, just as carousers at carnivals disrupted the night. The ritual garb provided seemingly innocent cover for what was truly a campaign of terror and intimidation that often turned deadly.

THINKING CRITICALLY

In what ways do these disguises affect the people who wear them? Assess how the combination of horror and jest might have worked in terms of the different groups perceiving the Klan's activities: white northerners, white southerners, and African American southerners. In terms of popular culture, do modern horror films sometimes combine both terror and humor?

(left, right) Library of Congress, Prints and Photographs Division [LC-USZ62-119565]; (middle) Library of Congress, Prints and Photographs Division [LC-USZ62-49988]

---

8 to 7, the commission awarded the disputed electoral votes—and the presidency—to Hayes.

When angry Democrats threatened a filibuster to prevent the electoral votes from being counted, key Republicans met with southern Democrats and reached an informal understanding, later known as the Compromise of 1877. Hayes's supporters agreed to withdraw federal troops from the South and not oppose the new Democratic state governments. For their part, southern Democrats dropped their opposition to Hayes's election and pledged to respect African Americans' rights.

Without federal support, the last Republican southern governments collapsed, and Democrats took control of the remaining states of the Confederacy. By 1877 the entire South was in the hands of the **Redeemers**, as they called themselves. Reconstruction and Republican rule had come to an end.

Redeemers southerners who came to power in southern state governments between 1875 and 1877, claiming to have "redeemed" the South from Reconstruction. The Redeemers looked to undo many of the changes wrought by the Civil War.

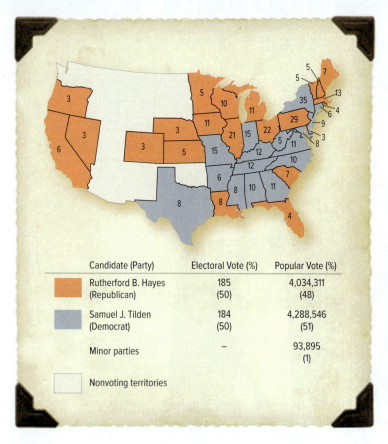

Candidate (Party)	Electoral Vote (%)	Popular Vote (%)
Rutherford B. Hayes (Republican)	185 (50)	4,034,311 (48)
Samuel J. Tilden (Democrat)	184 (50)	4,288,546 (51)
Minor parties	–	93,895 (1)
Nonvoting territories		

MAP 17.2: ELECTION OF 1876

Racism and the Failure of Reconstruction >>

Reconstruction failed for a multitude of reasons. The reforming impulse behind the Republican Party of the 1850s had been battered and worn down by the war. The new materialism of industrial America inspired a jaded cynicism in many Americans. In the South, African American voters and leaders inevitably lacked a certain amount of education and experience; elsewhere, Republicans were divided over Reconstruction policies and options.

Yet beyond these obstacles, the sad fact remains that the ideals of Reconstruction were most clearly defeated by a deep-seated racism throughout American life. Racism stimulated white southern resistance, undercut northern support for Black rights, and eventually made northerners willing to write off Reconstruction, and with it the welfare of African Americans. Although Congress could pass a constitutional amendment abolishing slavery, it could not overturn at a stroke the social habits of two centuries.

REVIEW

What factors in the North and the South led the federal government to abandon Reconstruction in the South?

With the overthrow of Reconstruction, the white South had won back some of the power it had lost in 1865—but not all. In the longer term, the political equations of power had been changed. Even under the new Redeemer governments, African Americans did not return to the social position they had occupied before the war. They were no longer enslaved, and Black southerners who walked dusty roads in search of family members, sent their children to school, or worshiped in their own Black churches knew what a momentous change this was. Even under the exploitative sharecropping system, Black income rose significantly in freedom. Then, too, the guarantees of "equal protection" and "due process of law" had been written into the Constitution and would be available for later generations to use in fighting once again for the Radicals' goal of racial equality.

But this was a struggle left to future reformers. For the time being, the clear trend was away from change or hope—especially for freedpeople like Benjamin Montgomery and his sons, the owners of the old Davis plantations in Mississippi. In the 1870s bad crops, lower cotton prices, and falling land values undermined the Montgomerys' financial position, and in 1875 Jefferson Davis sued to have the sale of Brierfield invalidated. Following the overthrow of Mississippi's Radical government, a white conservative majority of the court awarded Brierfield to Davis in 1878. The Montgomerys lost Hurricane as well.

The waning days of Reconstruction were times filled with such ironies. State governments were being "redeemed" by violence; Fourteenth Amendment rights were being used by conservative courts to protect not Black people but giant corporations; disillusioned reformers took up other causes. Increasingly, the industrial North focused on an economic task: integrating both the South and the West into the Union. In the case of both regions, northern factories sought to use southern and western raw materials to produce goods and to find national markets for those products. Indeed, during the coming decades European nations also scrambled to acquire natural resources and markets. In the onrushing age of imperialism, Western nations would seek to dominate newly acquired colonies in Africa and Asia, with the same disregard for their "subject peoples" that was seen with African Americans, Latinos, and Native Americans in the United States.

Disowned by its northern supporters and unmourned by public opinion, Reconstruction was over.

CHAPTER SUMMARY

Presidents Abraham Lincoln and Andrew Johnson and the Republican-dominated Congress each developed a program of Reconstruction to quickly restore the Confederate States to the Union.

- Lincoln's 10 percent plan required that 10 percent of qualified voters from 1860 swear an oath of loyalty to begin organizing a state government.
- Following Lincoln's assassination, Andrew Johnson eased up on Lincoln's terms over how Confederate States returned to the Union.
- The more radical Congress rejected Johnson's state governments and eventually enacted its own program of Reconstruction, which included the principle of Black suffrage.
  - Congress passed the Fourteenth and Fifteenth Amendments and also extended the life of the Freedmen's Bureau, a unique experiment in social welfare.
  - Congress rejected land reform, however, which would have provided the freedpeople with a greater economic stake.
  - The effort to remove Johnson from office through impeachment failed.
- The Radical governments in the South, led by Black and white southerners and transplanted northerners, compiled a mixed record on matters such as racial equality, education, economic issues, and corruption.
- Reconstruction was a time of both joy and frustration for freedpeople.
  - Those who had been enslaved took steps to reunite their families and establish Black-controlled churches.
  - They eagerly sought their own land and a good education.
  - Black resistance to the plantation system of labor led to the adoption of sharecropping.
  - The Freedmen's Bureau fostered these new working arrangements and also the beginnings of Black education in the South.
- Northern public opinion became disillusioned with Reconstruction during the presidency of Ulysses S. Grant.
- Southern whites used violence, economic coercion, and racism to overthrow the Republican state governments.
- In 1877 Republican leaders agreed to end Reconstruction in exchange for Rutherford B. Hayes's election as president.
- Racism played a key role in the eventual failure of Reconstruction.

Digging Deeper

Historians' views of Reconstruction have dramatically changed over the past half century. Modern studies view Reconstruction and the experience of African Americans with more sympathy. Prime among them is Eric Foner, *Reconstruction* (1988), and his briefer treatment *Forever Free* (2005); see also Michael W. Fitzgerald, *Splendid Failure* (2007). Brenda Wineapple covers the impeachment and trial of Andrew Johnson in *The Impeachers: The Trial of Andrew Johnson* (2019). Political affairs in the South during Reconstruction are examined in Dan T. Carter, *When the War Was Over* (1985); and Thomas Holt, *Black over White* (1977), an imaginative study of Black political leadership in South Carolina. Ron Chernow's majestic *Grant* (2017) argues that the general-turned-president worked actively to crush the Ku Klux Klan and defend African American rights. Hans Trefousse, *Thaddeus Stevens: Nineteenth-Century Egalitarian* (1997), provides a sympathetic reassessment of the influential Radical Republican. Mark W. Summers, *A Dangerous Stir* (2009), examines the ways in which fear and paranoia shaped Reconstruction.

Leon Litwack, *Been in the Storm So Long* (1979), vividly portrays the transition of enslaved African Americans to freedom. Heather Andrea Williams, *Self-Taught* (2005), illustrates the Black drive for literacy and education. James L. Roark, *Masters without Slaves* (1977), shows how former slaveholders adjusted to the end of slavery. Steven Hahn lays out the continuing tug of Black-white relations from the antebellum years through Reconstruction and beyond in *A Nation under Our Feet* (2003). Two excellent studies of changing labor relations in southern agriculture are Julie Saville, *The Work of Reconstruction* (1995); and John C. Rodrigue, *Reconstruction in the Cane Fields* (2001). For the Freedmen's Bureau, consult Donald Nieman, *To Set the Law in Motion* (1979). William Gillette, *Retreat from Reconstruction, 1869–1879* (1980), focuses on national politics and the end of Reconstruction; while Michael Perman, *The Road to Redemption* (1984), looks at developments in the South. Heather Cox Richardson explores the postwar context in the North in *The Death of Reconstruction* (2004), and considers Reconstruction in the West in *West from Appomattox* (2008). Faye E. Dudden, *Fighting Chance* (2011) traces the growing conflict between the woman suffrage and Black suffrage movements.

18 The New South and the Trans-Mississippi West

1870–1890

African American migrants, known as Exodusters, are depicted in these four scenes from the April 19, 1879 issue of *Leslie's Illustrated Newspaper.* The illustrations show them arriving in St. Louis, one of the jumping-off places for their trip to Kansas, by way of Mississippi River steamboats. The Exodusters often traveled with few resources, and as the drawings show, they were greeted, fed and supported by local Black citizens as they made their way west from Louisiana, Mississippi and other southern states.

Bettmann/Getty Images

>> An American Story

"COME WEST"

The news spread across the South during the late 1870s. Perhaps a man came with a handbill, telling of cheap land; or a letter arrived and was read aloud at church. The news spread in different ways, but in the end, it always spelled KANSAS.

Few Black farmers had been to Kansas themselves. More than a few knew that the abolitionist John Brown had made his home there before coming east to raid Harpers Ferry and help ignite the Civil War. Black folks, it seemed, might be able to live more freely in Kansas: "They do not kill Negroes here for voting," wrote one Black settler.

St. Louis learned of these rumblings in the first raw days of March 1879, as steamers from downriver began unloading freedpeople in large numbers. By the end of the year, crowds overwhelmed the wharves and temporary shelters. The city's Black churches banded together to house the "refugees," feed them, and help them continue toward Kansas. The "Exodusters," as they became known, pressed westward, many of the Black emigrants settling in growing towns such as Topeka, St. Louis and Kansas City.

The thousands of Exodusters who poured into Kansas were part of a human flood westward. It had many sources: played-out farms of New England and the South, crowded cities, much of Europe. Special trains brought the settlers to the plains, all eager to start anew. But the optimism of migrants Black and white could not mask the strains in the rapidly expanding nation, especially in the South and the lands beyond the Mississippi River—the Trans-Mississippi West. As largely agricultural regions, they struggled to find their place in the new industrial age emerging after Reconstruction.

In the South, despite a strong push to industrialize, white supremacy undercut economic growth. Sharecropping and farm tenancy mushroomed, and a system of violence and caste replaced slavery to sustain the old racial hierarchy. For its part, the booming West began to realize some of the dreams of antebellum reformers: free land, a transcontinental railroad, and colleges to educate its people. Yet the West, too, built a society based on violence and hierarchy, racial and economic, that challenged their hopes for a more democratic future.

By the end of the nineteenth century both the South and the West had assumed their place as suppliers of raw materials, providers of foodstuffs, and consumers of finished goods. A nation of "regional nations" hardly equal in stature was thus drawn together in the last third of the nineteenth century, despite the growing frustrations of inhabitants Black and white, old and new. <<

THEMATIC TIME LINE

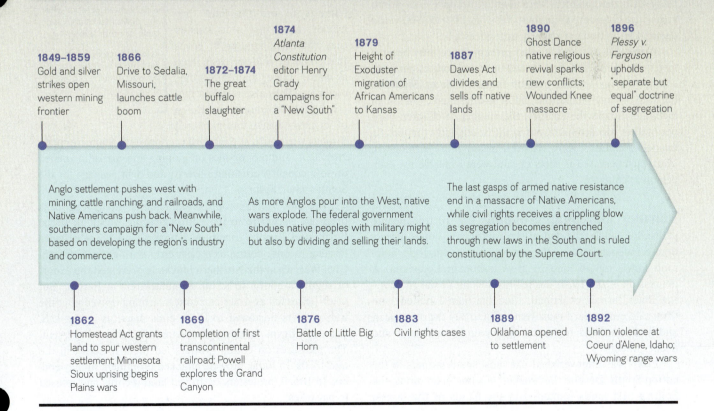

1849–1859 Gold and silver strikes open western mining frontier

1866 Drive to Sedalia, Missouri, launches cattle boom

1872–1874 The great buffalo slaughter

1874 *Atlanta Constitution* editor Henry Grady campaigns for a "New South"

1879 Height of Exoduster migration of African Americans to Kansas

1887 Dawes Act divides and sells off native lands

1890 Ghost Dance native religious revival sparks new conflicts; Wounded Knee massacre

1896 *Plessy v. Ferguson* upholds "separate but equal" doctrine of segregation

Anglo settlement pushes west with mining, cattle ranching, and railroads, and Native Americans push back. Meanwhile, southerners campaign for a "New South" based on developing the region's industry and commerce.

As more Anglos pour into the West, native wars explode. The federal government subdues native peoples with military might but also by dividing and selling their lands.

The last gasps of armed native resistance end in a massacre of Native Americans, while civil rights receives a crippling blow as segregation becomes entrenched through new laws in the South and is ruled constitutional by the Supreme Court.

1862 Homestead Act grants land to spur western settlement; Minnesota Sioux uprising begins Plains wars

1869 Completion of first transcontinental railroad; Powell explores the Grand Canyon

1876 Battle of Little Big Horn

1883 Civil rights cases

1889 Oklahoma opened to settlement

1892 Union violence at Coeur d'Alene, Idaho; Wyoming range wars

THE SOUTHERN BURDEN

It was just such regional inequities that infuriated Henry Grady, the editor of the *Atlanta Constitution.* He liked to tell the story of the poor cotton farmer buried in a pine coffin in the pine woods of Georgia. However, the coffin had been made in Cincinnati, not in Georgia. Despite its rich resources, the "South didn't furnish a thing on earth for that funeral but the corpse and the hole in the ground!" Grady fumed. The irony of the story was the tragedy of the South: the region had human and natural resources aplenty but, alas, few factories to manufacture the goods it needed.

In the 1880s Grady campaigned to bring about a "New South" based on bustling industry, cities, and commerce. The business class and its values would displace the old planter class as southerners raced "to out-Yankee the Yankee." Like modern alchemists, they would transform resources into riches. The region encompassed a third of the nation's farmlands, vast tracts of lumber, and rich deposits of coal, iron, oil, and fertilizers. To overcome the devastation of the Civil War and the loss of wealth from slavery, apostles of the New South campaigned to catch up with the North by creating an economy based more on industry and less on agriculture.

For all the hopeful talk of industrialization, the economy of the postwar South remained agricultural, tied to cash crops such as tobacco, rice, sugar, and especially cotton. By using fertilizers, planters were able to introduce cotton into areas once considered marginal. Yet from 1880 to 1900 world demand for cotton grew slowly, and prices fell.

Worse still, as farms in other parts of the country became larger, more efficient, and tended by fewer workers per acre, southern farms actually became smaller. This reflected the breakup of large plantations, but it also resulted from a high birthrate. Across the country, the number of children born per mother was dropping, but in the South, large families remained common. More children meant more farmhands. Thus each year, fewer acres of land were available for each person to cultivate.

Tenancy and Sharecropping >> To freedpeople

across the South, the end of slavery brought hopes of economic independence. After the war a hopeful John Solomon Lewis rented land to grow cotton in Louisiana. A depression in the 1870s dashed his dreams. "I was in debt," the Black farmer explained, "and the man I rented land from said every year I must rent again to pay the other year, and so I rents and rents and each year I gets deeper and deeper in debt."

Lewis was impoverished like most small farmers in the cotton South. Despite the breakup of some plantations, the South's best lands remained in the hands of the largest owners. Few freedpeople or poor whites had money to acquire property. Like Lewis, most rented perhaps a plot of 15 to 20 acres as tenants in hopes of buying someday. Since cotton was king and money scarce, rents were generally set in pounds of cotton rather than dollars. Rents usually amounted to between one-quarter and one-half the value of the crop.

Among the most common and exploitative forms of farm tenancy was sharecropping. Unlike renters, who leased land and controlled what they raised, sharecroppers worked a parcel of land in exchange for a share of whatever crop the owner wanted to plant. The croppers' portion typically amounted to about a third after deducting what they owed. It was rarely enough to make ends meet. Like other forms of tenancy, sharecropping left farmers in perpetual debt.

This system might not have proved so ruinous if the South had possessed a fairer system of credit. Before selling crops in the fall, farmers without cash had to borrow money in the spring to buy seeds, tools, and other necessities. Most often the only source of supplies was the local store, run by the landlord, where prices for goods bought on credit could be as much as 60 percent higher. To secure a loan, the only asset most renters and sharecroppers could offer was a mortgage, or **lien**, on their crops. The lien gave the shopkeeper first claim on the crop until the debt was paid off.

Year after year tenants and croppers borrowed against their harvests to use the land they farmed. Most landlords insisted that sharecroppers grow crops that could be sold for cash, such as cotton, rather than things they could eat. They also required that raw cotton be ginned or cleaned of its seeds, baled, and marketed through their mills at a price they controlled. Sharecropping, crop liens, and monopolies on ginning and marketing added up to inequality, crushing poverty, and **debt peonage** for the South's small farmers.

The slide of sharecroppers and tenants into debt peonage occurred elsewhere in the cotton-growing world. In India, Egypt, and Brazil agricultural laborers gave up **subsistence farming** to raise cotton as a cash crop during the American Civil War, when the Northern blockade prevented the export of southern cotton to textile manufacturers in Europe. But when prices fell as American cotton farming revived after the war, growers borrowed to make ends meet, as in the U.S. South. In Egypt, interest rates soared as high as 60 percent. The pressures on cotton growers led them to revolt in the mid-1870s. In India, growers attacked prominent moneylenders. In Brazil, protesters destroyed land records and refused to pay taxes.

> **lien** legal claim against property used to obtain a loan, which must be paid when the property is sold.
>
> **debt peonage** paying off a debt through labor when the debtor lacks sufficient cash or other assets.
>
> **subsistence farming** farming in which individuals and families produce most of what they need to live on.

TENANT FARMING, 1900

Tenant farming dominated southern agriculture after the Civil War. It spread rapidly across the states of the former Confederacy and replaced slavery as the principal source of farm labor. By 1900, it had moved west of the Mississippi River, where low crop prices, high costs, and a harsh environment forced many independent farmers into tenancy.

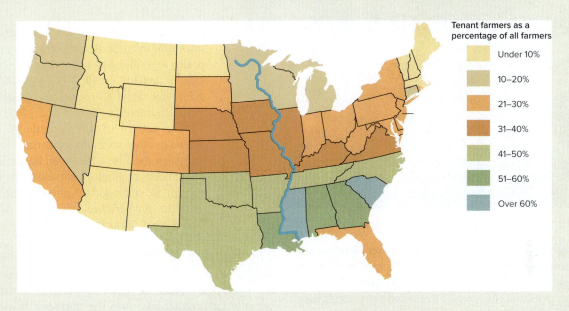

Tenant farmers as a percentage of all farmers

- Under 10%
- 10–20%
- 21–30%
- 31–40%
- 41–50%
- 51–60%
- Over 60%

MAP READING

1. In what region is farm tenancy most heavily concentrated?
2. Which states have the lowest concentrations of tenant farmers?
3. Where is the Mississippi River? In what states west of the Mississippi do we find tenant farmers? Where do they form more than 30 percent of all farmers?

MAP INTERPRETATION

1. What geographic factors help account for the low percentage of tenant farmers in the band of states extending south from Montana and Idaho? In the Northeast?
2. The information above suggests that a harsh environment helped push independent farmers into tenancy. Yet in the Black Belt areas of the South and in South Carolina, conditions are good for raising crops. What other factors lead these states to have such high rates of tenancy?

Southern Industry >> The crusade for a New South did bring change. From 1869 to 1909, industrial production grew faster in the South than it did nationally. A boom in railroad building after 1879 furnished the region with good transportation. In two areas, cotton textiles and tobacco, southern advances were striking. With cotton fiber and cheap labor close at hand, 400 cotton mills were humming by 1900. They employed almost 100,000 workers.

Most new textile workers were white southerners escaping competition from Black farm laborers or fleeing the hardscrabble life of the mountains. Entire families worked in the cramped mills. But only over time, as farm folk slowly adapted to the tedious rhythm of factories, did southerners become competitive with workers from other regions of the United States and western Europe.

The tobacco industry also thrived in the New South. Before the Civil War, American tastes had run to cigars, snuff (powdered tobacco that is inhaled), and chewing tobacco. In 1876 James Bonsack invented a machine to roll cigarettes. That was just the device Washington Duke and his son James needed to boost the fortunes of their growing tobacco and cigarette businesses. Cigarettes suited the new urban market in the North. Unlike snuff and chewing tobacco, they were, in the words of one observer, "clean, quick, and potent." Between 1860 and 1900, Americans spent more money on tobacco than on clothing or shoes.

turning out iron pipe for gas, water, and sewer lines vital to cities. But Birmingham's iron deposits were ill-suited to produce the kinds of steel in demand. In 1907 TCI was sold to the giant U.S. Steel Corporation, controlled by northern interests.

The pattern of lost opportunity was repeated in other southern industries. Under the campaign for a New South, all industries grew dramatically in employment and value, but not enough to end regional poverty. For all the drive to industrialize, the South remained largely rural, agricultural, and poor.

In the postwar era the South possessed over 60 percent of the nation's timber resources. With soaring demand from towns and cities, lumber and turpentine became the South's chief industries and employers. The environmental costs were high. In the South, as elsewhere, destructive logging practices stripped hillsides bare. As spring rains eroded soil and unleashed floods, forests lost their capacity for self-renewal. With them went the golden eagles, peregrine falcons, and other native species.

The iron and steel industry most disappointed promoters of the New South. The availability of coke as a fuel made Chattanooga, Tennessee, and Birmingham, Alabama, major centers for foundries. By the 1890s the Tennessee Coal, Iron, and Railway Company (TCI) of Birmingham was

The Sources of Southern Poverty >> Why did poverty persist in the New South? Three factors peculiar to the South best explain the region's poverty. First, the South began to industrialize later than the Northeast. Northerners had a head start on learning new manufacturing techniques. And it was difficult to catch up. The South contained only a small technological community to guide its industrial development. Northern engineers and mechanics seldom followed northern capital into the region. Few experts were available to adapt modern technology to southern conditions or to teach southerners how to do it themselves.

Education might have overcome the problem by upgrading the region's workforce, were it not for a second factor: school budgets. No region spent less on schooling than the South. Southern leaders, drawn from the ranks of the upper class, cared little about educating poor whites and openly resisted educating Black southerners. Education, they contended, "spoiled" otherwise contented

<< The booming timber industry often left the South poorer due to the harsh methods of extracting lumber. Here logs that have been floated down Lost Creek, Tennessee, are loaded onto a train. Getting the logs out was a messy affair: skidding them down rude paths to a creek and leaving behind open fields piled with rotting branches and leaves or needles, where once a forest stood. Rains eroded the newly bare hillsides, polluting streams. Downriver, tanneries, pulp mills, and sawmills emptied waste and sewage into the water, making many streams into little more than open sewers.
Historical \Corbis\Getty Images

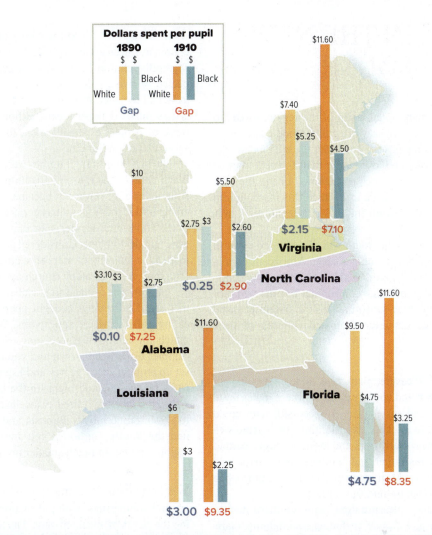

MAP 18.1: SPENDING ON EDUCATION IN THE SOUTH BEFORE AND AFTER DISENFRANCHISEMENT

With disenfranchisement and segregation, education was separate, but hardly equal, for Blacks and whites. In these states, after Blacks were disenfranchised, spending on white students rose while spending on Black students decreased.
Why were differences between expenditures on Black and white students smaller in 1890 than in 1910?

Source: Robert A. Margo, *Disenfranchisement, School Finance, and the Economics of Segregated Schools in the U.S. South, 1890–1910*. New York, NY: Garland Press, 1985, table I-1.

workers by leading them to demand higher wages and better conditions.

Lack of education aggravated the third and most important source of southern poverty: the isolation of its labor force. In 1900 agriculture still dominated the southern economy. It required unskilled, low-paid sharecroppers and wage laborers. Southerners feared that outsiders, whether capitalists, industrialists, or experts in technology, would spread discontent among workers. So southern states discouraged social services and opportunities that might have attracted human and financial resources. As a result, their workforce remained secluded and uneducated and capital scarce. Despite what some southerners believed, the South remained poor because it received too little, not too much, outside investment.

 REVIEW

What factors explain the failure of the campaign for a "New South"?

LIFE IN THE NEW SOUTH

Many a southern man, noted a son of the region, loved "to toss down a pint of raw whiskey in a gulp, to fiddle and dance all night, to bite off the nose or gouge out the eye of a favorite enemy, to fight harder and love harder than the next man, to be known far and wide as a hell of a fellow." Life in the New South was a constant struggle to balance this masculinized love of sport and leisure with the pull of a feminized Christian piety.

Divided in its soul, the South was also divided by race. After the Civil War, 90 percent of African Americans continued to live in the rural South. Without slavery, white southerners lost the system of social control that had defined race relations. Over time they substituted a new system of racial separation that eased but never eliminated white fear of Black Americans.

Rural Life >> Pleasure, piety, race, and gender—all split southern life in town and country alike. Southern males loved hunting for sport and sustenance. A successful hunt could add meat and fish to a scanty diet. Hunting also offered welcome relief from heavy farmwork and for many boys a path to manhood. Seeing his father and brothers return with wild turkeys, young Edward McIlhenny longed "for the time when I would be old enough to hunt this bird."

The thrill of illicit pleasure drew many southern men to events of violence and chance, including cockfighting. Gambling between bird owners and among spectators heightened the thrills. Such sport and the hard-drinking, sometimes brutal culture that accompanied it offended churchgoing southerners. They condemned as sinful "the beer garden, the baseball, the low theater, the dog fight and cock fight and the ring for the pugilist and brute."

Many southern customs involved no such disorderly behavior. Work-sharing festivals such as house raisings, log rollings, and quilting bees gave isolated farm folk the chance to break their daily routine, to socialize, and to work for a common good. These events, too, were generally segregated along gender lines. Men did the heavy chores and competed in contests of physical prowess. Women shared more domestic tasks such as quilting. These community gatherings also offered young southerners an opportunity for courtship. In one courting game, the young man who found a rare red ear of corn "could kiss the lady of his choice."

For rural folk a trip to town brought special excitement and a bit of danger. Saturdays, court days, and holidays provided an occasion to mingle. For men, the saloon, the blacksmith shop, or the storefront were places to do business and to let off steam. Few men went to town without participating in social drinking. The threat of brawling and violence kept most women away.

The Church >> At the center of southern life stood the church as the custodian of social order. "When one joined the Methodist church," a southern woman recalled, "he was expected to give up all such things as cards, dancing, theatres, in fact all so called worldly amusements." Many devout southerners pursued these ideals, although such restraint asked more of people, especially men, than many were willing to show, except on Sunday.

By 1870 southern churches were segregated by race. The Black church was the only institution controlled by African Americans after slavery. It became a principal source of leadership and identity as well as comfort. Within churches, both Black and white, gender split congregations too. Churches were female domains. Considered guardians of virtue, women made up a majority of members, attended church more often than men, and ran many church activities.

Church was a place to socialize as well as worship. Picnics and all-day sings brought people together for hours of eating, talk, services, and hymns. Weekly rituals could not match the fervor of a weeklong camp meeting. In the late summer or early fall, town and countryside emptied as folks set up tents in shady groves and listened to two or three ministers preach day and night, in the largest event of the year. The camp meeting refired evangelical faith among the majority Protestants, mostly Baptists and Methodist, who inhabited the South. Catholics and Jews worshiped across the region, too, but in much smaller numbers.

Segregation >> After Reconstruction, white northerners and southerners achieved sectional harmony by sacrificing the rights of Black citizens. During the 1880s, Redeemer governments (Chapter 17) moved to formalize a new system of **segregation**, or racial separation. Redeemers were white Democrats who came to power in southern states vowing to end the Republican rule that had been established during Reconstruction.

> **segregation** separation of people by race, imposed through law and custom.

The pressure to reach a new racial accommodation in the South increased as more African Americans moved into southern towns and cities. They competed for jobs and living space with poor whites and for public space on railroads and trolley cars. One way to preserve the social and economic hierarchy imposed by whites was to separate Blacks as an inferior caste. Within 20 years, every southern state had enacted segregation laws. The earliest laws legalized racial separation in trains and other public conveyances. Soon a web of "Jim Crow" statutes segregated the races in almost all public places except streets and stores. (The term denoted a policy of segregation and originated in a song of the same name sung in minstrel shows of the day.)

In the 1896 case of *Plessy* v. *Ferguson,* the Supreme Court validated a Louisiana law requiring segregated railroad facilities. Racial separation did not constitute discrimination, the Court argued, so long as accommodations for both races

⌃ For Baptists in the South, the ceremony of adult baptism included immersion, often in a nearby river. The ritual symbolized the waters of newfound faith washing away sins. Virginia's James River was the site of this occasion.
Bayard Wooten/Library of Congress/Corbis/Getty Images

were equal. In reality, of course, this "separate-but-equal" doctrine rarely produced equal facilities for African Americans and always stigmatized them.

THEN&NOW

The new legal doctrine, already legislated across the South, separated the races and shaped the lives of Americans, Black and white, for almost seven decades. White proponents saw segregation as a scientific means of managing race relations and a mark of white superiority. Black Americans saw it as a badge of discrimination and social servitude. As intended, separate was never equal and always favored whites. African Americans ended up with higher rates of poverty and mortality and lower levels of employment, income, and education. More than 100 years later, racial divides, often physical, still persist in housing, education, employment, and business. They come about not from law but from persistent inequalities with the same roots and similar consequences as the legal separation of races. And precisely because they are no longer part of our legal fabric, these inequalities are, ironically, more difficult to eliminate.

By the turn of the century, segregation was firmly in place, stifling economic competition between the races and reducing African Americans to second-class citizenship. Many kinds of employment, such as work in the textile mills, went largely to whites. Skilled and professional Black workers generally served Black clients. African Americans could enter some white residences only as servants and hired help, and then only through the back door. They were barred from juries and usually received far stiffer penalties than whites for the same crimes. Any African American who crossed this "color line" risked violence. Some were tarred and feathered, others whipped and beaten, and many lynched. Of the 187 lynchings averaged each year of the 1890s, some 80 percent occurred in the South, mostly among Blacks.

Segregation, lynching, and disfranchisement (see Chapter 17) were not the only means by which southern states sought to control African Americans and replace the labor lost with the abolition of slavery. Among the harsher and more corrupt practices was the convict leasing system. Southern states leased convicts, predominantly African Americans often imprisoned for minor offenses, to plantations and private industry. Employers received cheap labor, and state governments large revenues. The convicts were worked mercilessly, poorly fed, housed in dilapidated buildings, and beaten, sometimes to death. It was, wrote one historian, "slavery by another name."

The cost of Jim Crow and other discriminatory practices to southerners Black and white was incalculable. The race question trumped all other issues and produced a one-party region, where fear of Black Republicans hamstrung any opposition to all-white Redeemer Democrats. Supporting a two-tiered system of public services drained money from southern treasuries that might have been used for other public purposes. All suffered under the rule of racial separation, whether they realized it or not.

 REVIEW

How did segregation work as an instrument of social control?

WESTERN FRONTIERS

The Black Exodusters flooding into the treeless plains of Kansas in the 1870s and 1880s were only part of the vast migration west. Looking beyond the Mississippi in the 1840s and 1850s, "overlanders" had moved over land (as opposed to sailing around the southern tip of South America), setting their sights on California and Oregon in search of opportunity and "free" land.

Those without money or power found opportunity elusive. They also found native peoples and "Hispanos" (settlers of Spanish descent), who hardly considered the land free for use by Anglos. And they discovered the West was not one frontier but many, all moving in different directions. Before the Civil War the frontier for easterners had moved westward beyond the Mississippi to the timberlands of Missouri, but skipped over the Great Plains, as the overlanders settled in California and Oregon. A mining frontier pushed east from the Pacific coast, following diggers into the Sierra Nevada. For Texans the frontier moved from south to north as cattle ranchers sought new grazing land. For native people the frontier was constantly shifting and disrupting their ways of life.

Western Landscapes >> The varied landscapes of the West begin with the region between the 98th meridian and the West Coast. Called the "Great Plains," it receives less than 20 inches of rain a year. The first Anglo settlers called the treeless expanse of prairie grass and dunes the "Great American Desert."

⌃ The cultures of western native people were remarkably varied, ranging from the nomadic plains tribes to the settled peoples of the northwest coast who lived off the sea. This Sioux woman carries firewood she has gathered; the photograph was taken by Edward Curtis, who spent many years recording the faces and lives of the native peoples of the West.
Library of Congress, Prints and Photographs Division [LC-USZ62-46975]

The Great Plains are only part of the Trans-Mississippi West. Beyond the plains the jagged peaks of the Rocky Mountains stretch from Alaska to New Mexico. On the far side of the mountains lies the Great Basin of Utah, Nevada, and eastern California, where temperatures climb above 100 degrees. Farther west the towering Sierra Nevada and the Cascades rise near the coast and then slope into the temperate shores of the Pacific.

Already in the 1840s, the Great Plains and mountain frontier constituted a complex web of cultures and environments. The horse, for example, had been introduced into North America by Spanish colonizers. By the eighteenth century, horses were grazing on prairie grass across the Great Plains. By the nineteenth century, the Comanche, Cheyenne, Apache, and other indigenous peoples had become master riders and hunters who could shoot their arrows with deadly accuracy at a full gallop. Their new mobility far extended the area in which they could hunt buffalo. Their lives shifted from settled, village-centered agriculture to a nomadic existence.

Native Peoples and the Western Environment >> Some whites embraced the myth of the "noble savage" who lived in perfect harmony with the natural world. To be sure, plains people were inventive in using scarce resources. Cottonwood bark fed horses in winter, while the

FOREST
- Woodland
- Deciduous
- Coniferous
- Mixed
- Margin of semiarid zone (20" of rainfall)

GRASSLAND
- Tall grass
- Short grass
- Mesquite grass

DESERT
- Sage brush
- Creosote brush

MAP 18.2: NATURAL ENVIRONMENT OF THE WEST

With the exception of the Pacific Northwest, few areas west of the 20-inch rainfall line receive enough annual precipitation to support agriculture without irrigation. Consequently, water has been the key to development west of the 98th meridian, an area that encompasses more than half the country.

Which two western states have the largest proportion of land that receives enough annual rainfall to support agriculture without irrigation? How might heavily forested areas on the map help us answer the question?

buffalo supplied not only meat but also bones for tools, fat for cosmetics, and sinews for thread.

For all their ties to the natural world, Native Americans did shape the ecosystems around them, not always for the better. Plains people hunted buffalo by stampeding herds over cliffs, hardly a natural end for the animals and sometimes an inefficient use of this valuable resource. They irrigated crops and set fires to improve vegetation. By the mid-nineteenth century, some tribes had become so enmeshed in the white fur trade that they overtrapped their own hunting grounds. Waste and scarcity could easily be the result.

Ecological diversity produced a stunning variety of smaller bands, larger tribes, and people who nonetheless

<< John Wesley Powell's second expedition into the Grand Canyon launched on the Green River in 1871. Despite near drownings as well as the loss of boats and supplies, Powell successfully explored the wild Colorado River at a time when local legends suggested the river might disappear underground in some spots. Library of Congress, Prints and Photographs Division [LC-USZC4-8292]

shared experiences and values. Most bands, components of tribes, were small kinship groups of 300 to 500 people in which the well-being of all outweighed the needs of each member. Although some bands were materially better off than others, the gap between rich and poor within them was seldom large. Among plains peoples wealth often revolved around the possession of horses and mules. Such small material differences frequently promoted communal decision making. The Cheyenne, for example, employed a council of 44 to advise the chief.

Indigenous people also shared a reverence for nature, whatever their actual impact on the natural world. They believed human beings were part of an interconnected world of animals, plants, and other natural elements. All had souls of their own but were bound together, as if by contract, to live in balance through the ceremonial life of the tribe and the customs related to specific plants and animals. The Tao of New Mexico believed that each spring the pregnant earth issued new life. To avoid disturbing "mother" earth, they walked in bare feet or soft moccasins and removed the hard shoes from their horses.

Whites and the Western Environment: Competing Visions >> As discoveries of gold and silver lured white settlers into Native American territory, many adopted the decidedly un-native outlook of Missouri politician William Gilpin. Only a lack of vision prevented the opening of the West for exploitation, Gilpin told a Missouri audience in 1849. What westerners needed most was cheap land for farms and a railroad linking the two coasts, he said, "like ears on a human head." In his expansive view, land was nothing sacred, only property to be owned and exploited. Native peoples were merely obstacles.

By 1868 a generous Congress had granted western settlers their two greatest wishes: free land, under the Homestead Act of 1862, and a transcontinental railroad. As the

new governor of Colorado, Gilpin crowed about the West's near limitless possibilities for growth. Scarce water and rainfall did not daunt him. He believed in the widely accepted theory that "rain follows the plow."

Early climatologist Cyrus Thomas and amateur scientist Charles Dana Wilbur popularized the notion that plowing dry land released moisture into the air, thereby increasing cloud cover and rainfall. Settlers and speculators in the United States justified their actions as transforming "desert into a farm or garden," as did wheat growers cultivating marginal land in southern Australia. An unusually wet cycle from 1878 to 1886 helped sustain the myth in the states. When the normally dry conditions returned, some 2 million farmers who had settled the plains discovered that the skeptics who argued plowing produced no change in climate were right.

Unlike the visionary Gilpin, John Wesley Powell knew something about water and farming. In 1869 and 1871 Powell led scientific expeditions down the Green and Colorado Rivers through the Grand Canyon. He returned to warn Congress that developing the West required more scientific planning. Much of the region had not yet been mapped nor its resources identified.

In 1880 Powell became director of the recently formed U.S. Geological Survey. He, too, had a vision of the West, but one based on the limits of its environment. The key was water, not land. Unlike the rainy East, water in the parched West should be treated as community rather than private property. The practice would benefit many rather than a privileged few owners at the headwaters. Powell suggested that the federal government establish political boundaries defined by large watersheds and regulate the distribution of the scarce resource. But his scientific realism could not overcome the popular vision of the West as the American Eden. Powerful interests ensured that development occurred with the same laissez-faire credo that ruled the East.

✔ REVIEW

How did native conceptions of the environment compare and contrast with white conceptions?

THE WAR FOR THE WEST

Beginning in 1848, a series of gold and silver discoveries signaled the first serious interest by white settlers in the arid and semiarid lands beyond the Mississippi. The government had forced native peoples there, but whites had avoided the harsh environment and the unwelcoming tribes. In 1851, federal officials introduced a policy of "concentration" among the tribes. They were pressured into signing treaties limiting the boundaries of their hunting grounds to "reservations"—the Sioux to the Dakotas, the Crow to Montana, the Cheyenne to the foothills of Colorado. There they would be taught to abandon their wandering ways and instead to farm. Some, like the Navajo, were ripped from their homelands and forced on the "Long Walk" some 450 miles to eastern New Mexico and an infamous 40-square-mile stretch of scorching desert called the *Bosque Redondo*. Over the next four years, nearly one in three Navajo died there.

Such treaties often claimed that their provisions would last "as long as waters run," but time after time land-hungry pioneers broke the promises of their government by squatting on native lands and demanding federal protection. The government, in turn, forced more-restrictive agreements on the western tribes. This cycle of agreements made and broken was repeated, until a full-scale war for the West raged between whites and natives.

Contact and Conflict >> The policy of concentration
began in the Pacific Northwest and produced some of the earliest clashes. In an oft-repeated pattern, white encroachment led to native resistance and war and finally to native defeat.

By 1862 the lands of the Santee Sioux had been whittled down to a strip 10 miles wide and 150 miles long along the Minnesota River in present-day South Dakota. Lashing out in frustration, the tribe attacked several undefended white settlements along the Minnesota frontier. In response, General John Pope arrived in St. Paul declaring his intention to wipe them out. When Pope's forces captured 1,800 Sioux, white Minnesotans were outraged that President Lincoln ordered only 38 hanged. Still, it was the largest mass execution in U.S. history.

The campaign under General Pope was the opening of a guerrilla war that continued off and on for 30 years. The conflict gained momentum in November 1864. A force of Colorado volunteers under Colonel John Chivington fell upon a band of friendly Cheyenne gathered at Sand Creek under army protection. Chief Black Kettle raised an American flag to signal friendship, but Chivington would have none of it. "Kill and scalp all, big and little," he told his men. The troops massacred well over 100, including women and

Make a Case

Could whites and native peoples have lived together peaceably in the Trans-Mississippi American West? What would have had to happen for this to occur?

children. In 1865 virtually all plains peoples joined in the First Sioux War to drive whites from their lands.

Among the soldiers who fought the plains natives were African American veterans of the Civil War. In 1866 two regiments of Black soldiers formed the Ninth and Tenth Cavalry under the command of white officers. Native people called them "Buffalo Soldiers," reflecting both the similarity they saw between African American and buffalo hair and the hard-won respect the Black soldiers earned in battle. The Buffalo Soldiers fought native peoples across the West for more than 20 years. They also served as protectors of white settlement, subduing bandits, cattle thieves, and gunmen. They located water, wood, and grasslands for eager homesteaders and laid the foundations for army posts such as Fort Sill in Oklahoma.

War was only one way in which contact with whites undermined tribal cultures. Liquor and disease killed more indigenous peoples than combat. On the Great Plains the railroad disrupted the migratory patterns of the buffalo and thus the patterns of the hunt. As hides became popular in the East, commercial companies hired hunters who could kill more than 100 bison an hour. Military commanders promoted the bison butchery as a way of weakening native resistance. In three short years, from 1872 to 1874, approximately 9 million head were slaughtered. Nature played its part. Reduced rainfall, competitive domesticated animals, and deadly new diseases introduced by settlers helped nearly wipe the plains clean of bison by 1883. In other areas, mines, crops, grazing herds, and fences competed with the herds for space.

Custer's Last Stand—and the Natives' >> The
Sioux War ended in 1868 with the signing of the Treaty of Fort Laramie. It established two large reservations, one in Oklahoma and the other in the Dakota Badlands. Only six years later, however, Colonel George Armstrong Custer led an expedition into Paha Sapa, the sacred Black Hills of the Sioux in the Dakotas. He marched in search of the Sioux and in violation of the treaty of 1868. Custer, a Civil War veteran, already had a reputation as a "squaw killer" for his cruel warfare against Native Americans in western Kansas. To draw whites into the Black Hills, his expedition spread rumors of gold "from the grass roots down." Prospectors poured into what was called "Indian country." Federal authorities tried to force yet another treaty to gain control of the Black Hills. When negotiations failed, President

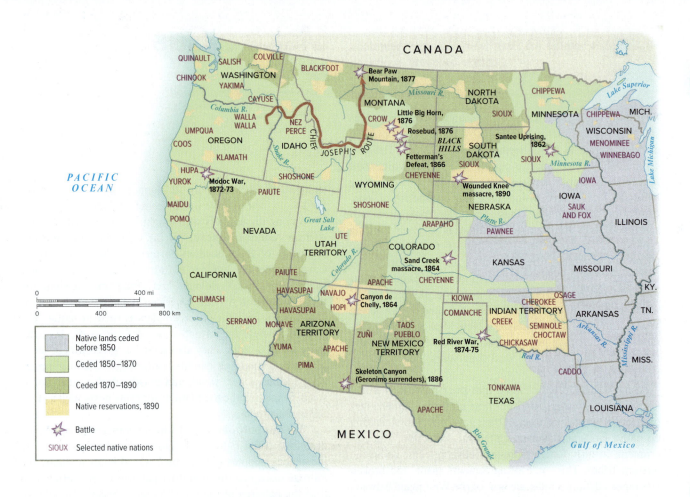

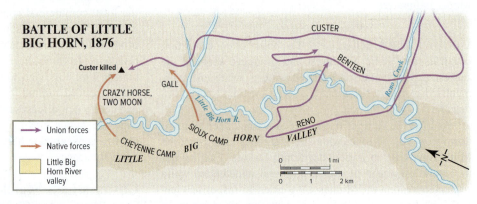

MAP 18.3: THE NATIVE AMERICAN FRONTIER

As conflict erupted between indigenous and white cultures in the West, the government sought increasingly to concentrate tribes on reservations. Resistance to the reservation concept helped unite the Sioux and the Cheyenne, traditionally enemies, in the Dakotas during the 1870s. Along the Little Big Horn River, the impetuous Custer underestimated the strength of his opponents and attacked before the supporting troops of Reno and Benteen were in a position to aid him.
Based on the dates of land cessions, which native groups held out against white expansion the longest?

Grant ordered all "hostiles" in the area driven onto the reservations.

In the summer of 1876 several army columns, including Custer's Seventh Cavalry of about 600 troops, marched into the territory. Custer, eager for glory, arrived at the Little Big Horn River a day earlier than the other columns. Hearing of a native village nearby, he attacked, only to discover that he had stumbled onto an encampment of more than 7,000 Sioux and Cheyenne. From a deep ravine Sioux leader Crazy Horse and his braves charged Custer, killing him and 267 soldiers.

Historian's TOOLBOX

Why would natives want the scalps of the dead?

What weapons do the Sioux warriors use?
What does this suggest about the nature of warfare in the late nineteenth century?

What indicates that some soldiers have been scalped?
Why would natives want the scalps of the dead?

American flags seem to be drawn upside down
Art Collection 2/Alamy Stock Photo

Firsthand historical accounts come in a variety of forms. Some are spoken and recorded, others written, and still others drawn. In 1881, five years after the Battle of Little Big Horn, a Minneconjou Lakota Sioux warrior named Red Horse composed 42 drawings of the battle at the behest of Army physician Charles E. McChesney at the Cheyenne River Agency, a reservation in South Dakota where Red Horse lived. He had fought at Little Big Horn and surrendered a year later. The result was a series of stunning colored-pencil-and-ink drawings that depict the horror of war from a Native American point of view. Members of the cavalry flee charging natives, while the bloody and beheaded bodies of soldiers litter the bottom of the drawing, some of them with their hair scalped. Among the dead at the lower right side is a man wearing what appears to be a plaid shirt and pants without the typical stripe of an army uniform. Red Horse mentioned the presence of civilians among the American force when using sign language to tell his story. The body may be either George Armstrong Custer's youngest brother, Boston Custer, or his nephew, Henry Armstrong Reed. This is hardly the image most white Americans have of Custer's heroic "last stand."

THINKING CRITICALLY

At the center and foot of the illustration, American flags have been drawn upside down, surely not the way soldiers carried them. Why would Red Horse have depicted them this way? Recall that he was, in effect, a prisoner of war with only the power of his pens and pencils to express himself.

National Anthropological Archives/Smithsonian Institution

Even in the midst of victory, defeat loomed for Crazy Horse and his people. Although Custer had been beaten, railroads stood ready to extend their lines, prospectors to make fortunes, settlers to lay down roots, and soldiers to protect them. By late summer the Sioux were forced to split into small bands to evade the army. While the legendary Lakota chief Sitting Bull barely escaped to Canada, Crazy Horse and 800 with him surrendered in 1876 after a winter of suffering and starvation. Custer's "last stand" began the end of native military successes.

Even the peaceful Nez Percé of Idaho found no security once whites began to hunger for their land. In 1877, rather than see his people herded into a small reservation, Chief Joseph led almost 600 Nez Percé toward Canada, pursued by the U.S. Army. In 75 days they traveled more than 1,300 miles. Every time the soldiers closed to attack, Chief Joseph's warriors drove them off. But before they could reach the border, the Nez Percé were trapped and forced to surrender. The government shipped the defeated tribe to the bleak "Indian Country" of Oklahoma. Disease and starvation finished the job the army had begun.

Killing with Kindness >> Some whites and Native Americans began speaking out against the tragedy taking place on the Great Plains. In the 1870s, Susan La Flesche, daughter of an Omaha chief and the first indigenous woman in the United States to become a physician, lectured eastern audiences about the mistreatment of native peoples and inspired reformers to action. Moved by such reports, the poet Helen Hunt Jackson lobbied for native rights. In 1881 she published *A Century of Dishonor*, a best-selling exposé that detailed government fraud and corruption in native affairs.

Reformers began pressing for assimilation of indigenous peoples into white society, ironically as the only means of preserving them in a world that seemed bent on their destruction. In 1881, the newly formed Women's National Indian Association and the later Indian Rights Association sought to end traditional culture. They suppressed communal activities, "reeducated" native children in boarding schools, and established homesteads owned by individuals, not by tribes.

By the late 1880s reformers also recognized that the policy of concentrating native peoples on reservations had failed to manage their relations with whites well. With a mix of good intentions and unbridled greed, Congress adopted the Dawes Severalty Act in 1887. It sought to eliminate reservations, which were collectively owned by tribal members, and replace them with plots of land owned by individuals—160 acres to the head of a family and 80 acres to single adults or orphans. Tribes stood in the way of "civilizing" their people, according to the law's backers. Doing away with collective property would eventually destroy tribes.

In practice, the Dawes Act was more destructive than any blow struck by the army. It undermined the communal structure at the core of tribal life. And as John Wesley Powell had warned, small homestead farms in the West could not support a family—white or Native American—unless they were irrigated. Most native peoples, moreover, had no experience with farming, managing money, or other white ways. Perhaps worst of all, reservation lands not allocated to Native Americans were opened to nonnative homesteaders. By 1900 native landholding had dropped by almost half from 20 years earlier.

Against such a dismal future, some native peoples sought protection in the spirits of the past. In 1890 a religious revival spread when word came from the Nevada desert that a humble Paiute named Wovoka had received revelations from the Great Spirit. If his followers adopted his mystical rituals and lived together in love and harmony, the native dead would rise, whites would be driven from the land, and game would be thick again. As the rituals spread, alarmed settlers called the shuffling and chanting practiced by Wovoka's followers the "Ghost Dance." The army moved to stamp out Ghost Dancing for fear of another uprising. At Wounded Knee in South Dakota the cavalry fell upon one band and with devastating artillery fire killed some 300 Sioux men, women, and children. Twenty-five soldiers lay dead as well.

Wounded Knee was yet another violent blow against native life. But after 1890 the battle was over assimilation, not extinction. The system of markets, rail networks, and extractive industries was linking the West with the rest of the nation. Free-roaming bison were replaced by herded cattle and sheep, nomadic tribes by prairie sodbusters, and sacred hunting grounds by gold fields. Reformers relied on education, citizenship, and allotments to move indigenous peoples into white society. Most of

<< The all-male Carlisle Indian School Band was formed in 1881, two years after this boarding school was founded in Pennsylvania. School authorities saw music as one way to "civilize" their charges. Writing a wealthy donor, the school's superintendent suggested, "If you will give me a set of brass band instruments, I will give them to the 'tom tom' boys and they can toot on them and this will stop the 'tom tom.'" Pianos were also donated for the girls.
Library of Congress, Prints and Photographs Division [LC-USZ62-26786]

them were equally determined to preserve their tribal ways and separateness as a people.

Borderlands >>

The coming of the railroad in the 1880s and 1890s brought wrenching changes to the Southwest, but with an ethnic twist characteristic of the region. As new markets and industries sprang up, new settlers poured in from the east but also from the south, across the Mexican border. Nations such as the Navajo and the Apache faced the hostility of Anglos *and* Hispanos, those settlers of Spanish descent already in the region.

Like native peoples, Hispanos discovered that they had either to embrace or resist the flood of new Anglos. The elite, or *Ricos,* often aligned themselves with Anglos to protect their status and property. Others pushed back. When Anglo cattle ranchers began forcing Hispanos off their lands near Las Vegas, Juan José Herrera assembled a band of masked night riders known as *Las Gorras Blancas* (the White Caps). In 1889 and 1890, as many as 700 White Caps burned Anglo fences, haystacks, and occasionally barns and houses. They targeted symbols of corporate wrongdoing as well, attacking railroads that refused to raise the low wages of Hispano workers.

The railroads withstood the attacks, and with them came Mexican laborers to build them. Just as the southern economy depended on African American labor, the Southwest grew on the backs of Mexicans. Mexican immigrants worked mostly as contract and seasonal laborers for railroads and large farms. Many of them settled in the growing cities along the rail lines: El Paso, Albuquerque, Tucson, Phoenix, and Los Angeles. They lived in segregated *barrios*, Spanish neighborhoods, where their cultural traditions persisted.

To focus on cities alone would distort the experience of most southwesterners of Spanish descent, who lived in small villages like those in northern New Mexico and southern Colorado. There, a pattern of adaptation and resistance to Anglo penetration developed. As the market economy advanced, Hispanic villagers turned to migratory labor to adapt. While women continued to work in the old villages, men traveled from job to job. The resulting "regional communities" of villages and migrant workers allowed Hispanic residents to preserve their distinctive culture, while incorporating those aspects of Anglo life—like the sewing machine—that suited their needs. At the same time, the regional community sustained migrant workers with a base of operations and a haven from harsh working conditions.

Ethno-Racial Identity in the New West >>

The New West met the Old South in the diamond-shaped Blackland Prairie of central Texas. Before the Civil War, King Cotton had thrived in its rich soil. Afterward, Texas became the leading cotton-producing state in the country. Having embraced the slave system of the Old South, Texas also adopted the New South's system of crop liens and segregation, with its racial separation, restrictions on Black voting, and biracial labor force of African Americans and poor whites.

Yet Texas was also part of the borderlands of the American West, where the Anglo culture of European Americans met the Latin culture of Mexicans and Mexican Americans. "Mexicanos" had lived in Texas since before the 1840s, when it had been part of Mexico. In the late nineteenth and early twentieth centuries, as political violence undercut economic growth south of the border, more Mexicans crossed the Rio Grande in search of work and safety. Between 1890 and 1910, the Spanish-speaking population of the Southwest nearly doubled.

In central Texas the presence of this large and growing force of Mexicano laborers complicated racial matters. The Black-and-white poles of Europeans and African Americans that defined identity in the New South as they had in the Old were replaced by a new racial triad of Black, white, and brown. Unlike African Americans, Texans of Mexican descent sometimes found themselves swinging between the white world of privilege and the Black world of disadvantage. And whites could lose status, as had the many Texans who had sunk into landlessness and poverty in the decades after the Civil War. White landowners disdained them as "white trash" and a "white scourge."

By the 1920s a multiracial labor force of agricultural wage earners worked on giant ranches and large farms across the Southwest. In Texas

<< Western cities attracted ethnically diverse populations. This market in San Antonio, Texas, known as Military Plaza, served the city's large Latino population in 1887.
Library of Congress, Prints and Photographs Division [LC-USZ62-24772]

the labor force was triracial, but in California it also included Asian Americans and, elsewhere, Native Americans. Racial identity in the New West would be more complicated and, for Mexicans and Mexican Americans, more fluid than in other parts of the country.

✔ REVIEW

Through what means did native peoples lose their independence and land?

BOOM AND BUST IN THE WEST

Opportunity in the West lay in land and resources, but wealth also accumulated in the towns. Each time a speculative fever hit a region, new communities sprouted to serve those who rushed in. The western boom began in mining with the California gold rush of 1849 and the rise of San Francisco. In the decades that followed, new hordes threw up towns in Park City, Utah, and other promising sites. All too often, busts followed booms, transforming boom towns into ghost towns.

Mining Sets a Pattern >> The gold and silver strikes of the 1840s and 1850s set a pattern of rapid growth. Stories of easy riches attracted prospectors from all over the world, with their shovels and wash pans. Almost all were male and nearly half foreign-born. Muddy mining camps sprang up, where a prospector could register a claim, get provisions, bathe, and buy a drink or a companion. The opportunity of outfitting these small boom towns siphoned riches into the pockets of storeowners and other suppliers and became the most important source of growth in the West. Once the quick profits were gone, a period of consolidation and settlement often brought more order to these communities and larger scale to regional businesses.

In the mine fields, order and scale meant corporations. They alone had the capital for hydraulic water jets to blast ore loose and other heavy equipment to extract silver and gold in greater quantities and from deeper veins. In their quest for quick profits, such large-scale operations often led to environmental disaster, even as they spawned riches for owners, managers, and townsfolk. Machinery clawed into mountainside, stripping them bare of protective vegetation. The resulting floods, mud slides, and dirty streams threatened the livelihood of farmers in the valleys below.

In corporate mining operations, paid laborers replaced the independent prospectors of earlier days. Like other industrial workers, miners sought shorter hours, higher wages, and better working conditions; like others in charge, management fought back. In Coeur d'Alene, Idaho, troops crushed a strike in 1892, killing seven miners. To consolidate their strength, the miners created the Western Federation of Miners. In the decade after 1893 the union attracted some 50,000 members and gained a reputation for militancy. Across the West, the once-rowdy mining frontier of small-scale prospectors and independent operators would become integrated into the orderly industrial system of wage labor, large-scale resource extraction, and high-finance capital.

The Transcontinental Railroad >> As William Gilpin predicted in 1849, the development of the West required railroads. Before the Central and

<< Blasting away with pressurized water jets, miners loosen gold-bearing gravel from this hillside. Such techniques damaged the environment, spurring erosion, flooding and mudslides as well as destroying habitats of native species. These miners are working in Nevada County, California, in 1866.
Library of Congress, Prints and Photographs Division

Union Pacific Railroads were joined in 1869, travel was slow and dusty. Vast distances and scarce population gave entrepreneurs little opportunity to follow the eastern practice of building local railroad lines from city to city.

The federal government helped overcome the challenges of distance and scarcity, often at the expense of other interests. Generous loans and gifts of federal and state lands allowed the lines to cut a path westward and reap immense profits for owners. For every mile of track completed, the rail companies received between 200 and 400 square miles of land—eventually totaling some 45 million acres. Fraudulent stock practices, corrupt accounting, and wholesale bribery (involving even a vice president of the United States and at least two members of Congress) swelled profits even more.

General Grenville Dodge, an army engineer on leave to the Union Pacific Railroad, was placed in charge of completing the section of the line west of Omaha, Nebraska, which was to meet the Central Pacific Railroad working its way east from California. Dodge recruited his immense labor force from Irish and other European immigrants, more populous in the East, while Charles Crocker of the Central Pacific relied on some 10,000 Chinese laborers from the West Coast. With wheelbarrows, picks, shovels, and baskets they inched eastward, building giant trestles and chipping away at the Sierras' looming granite walls with axes and dangerous dynamite. On May 10, 1869, a golden spike joined the two lines at Promontory Summit, Utah,

As the railroads pushed west in the 1860s, they helped spawn cities such as Denver and later awakened sleepy communities such as Los Angeles. Railroads opened the Great Plains to cattle drives that in the 1870s brought great herds to "cow towns" such as Sedalia, Missouri, and Cheyenne, Wyoming. From there, cattle could be shipped East to market. The rail companies recognized the strategic position they held. Just by threatening to bypass a town, a railroad could extract concessions on rights of way, taxes, and loans. If a key to profiting from the gold rush was supplying miners, one way to prosper from the West was to control transportation.

Cattle Kingdom >> Westerners recognized that railroads were keys to the cattle kingdom. By 1860 some 5 million longhorns were wandering the grassy plains of Texas. Ranchers allowed their herds to roam the unbroken or "open" range freely. A distinct brand from each ranch identified them. In 1866, Texas ranchers began driving their herds north to railheads for shipment to market. These "long drives" lasted two to three months and might cover more than 1,000 miles. When early routes to Sedalia, Missouri, proved unfriendly, ranchers scouted alternatives. The Chisholm Trail led from San Antonio to Abilene and Ellsworth in Kansas. More westerly routes ran to Dodge City and even Denver and Cheyenne.

Since cattle grazed on the open range, early ranches were primitive. They consisted of little more than a house for the rancher and his family, a bunkhouse for the hired hands, and about 30 to 40 acres per animal. Women were scarce in the cattle kingdom. Most were ranchers' wives, but some ranched themselves. When Helen Wiser Stewart learned that her husband had been murdered, she took over their Nevada spread—buying and selling cattle, managing the hands, and tending to family and crops.

Ranchers came to expect profits of 25 to 40 percent a

<< A line of Chinese men stands outside a refreshment stand. The Chinese worked on rail lines and also prospected for gold and silver in the West. Their long queues, or braided ponytails, dangle from their heads. This distinctive hairstyle was introduced by the Manchus in China in the early seventeenth century as a symbol of their dominance.
Library of Congress, Prints and Photographs Division [LC-W7-938]

MAP 18.4: THE MINING AND CATTLE FRONTIERS

In the vast spaces of the West, railroads, cattle trails, and gold mining usually preceded the arrival of enough settlers to establish towns and cities. The railroads forged a crucial link between the region's natural resources and urban markets in the East and in Europe, but by transecting the plains they also disrupted the migratory patterns of the buffalo herds, undermining cultures of native peoples while opening the land to cattle grazing and farming.
Which state was at the southern end of every major cattle route?

year. As in all booms, forces were at work to bring the inevitable bust. High profits soon swelled the size of the herds and led to overproduction and lower prices. Increased competition from cattle producers in Canada and Argentina caused beef prices to fall still further. And in the end, nature imposed its own limits—blizzards, droughts, and floods sometimes pushed losses as high as 90 percent.

By the 1890s cattle ranching was changing. Sodbusters were fencing the open range, and the long drives had largely ceased. Cattle corporations such as the King Ranch of Texas, which grew bigger than the state of Rhode Island, dominated the industry. Only corporate giants had enough capital to acquire and enclose massive grazing lands, hire

ranchers to manage herds, and pay for feed during winter months. As for the cowboys, most became wage laborers employed by the ranching corporations. Like the mining industry, the cattle business was succumbing to the eastern pattern of economic concentration, corporate control, and labor specialization.

 REVIEW

How did the pattern of labor and management introduced in mining function in other businesses such as cattle ranching?

THE FINAL FRONTIER

In the 1860s they came in a trickle; by the 1870s they had become a torrent. Farmers from the East and Midwest, Black freedpeople from the rural South, and peasant-born immigrants from Europe flooded the West. What bound them together was a craving for land. They read railroad and steamship advertisements and heard stories from friends about millions of free acres in the plains west of the 98th meridian. Hardier strains of wheat such as Turkey Red (imported from Russia), improved machinery, and new farming methods made it possible to raise crops in the "Great American Desert." The number of farms in the United States jumped from around 2 million on the eve of the Civil War to almost 6 million in 1900.

Farming on the Plains >> Farmers looking to plow the plains faced a daunting task. Under the Homestead Act, government land could be bought for $1.25 an acre or claimed free if homesteaders worked their parcel for five years. But the best tracts—near a railroad line, with access to eastern markets—were owned by the railroads or speculators and sold for around $25 an acre. Raising costs still further, successful farming on the plains demanded expensive machinery.

Steel-tipped plows and harrows (which left a blanket of dust to keep moisture from evaporating too quickly) permitted **dry farming** in arid climates.

> **dry farming** farming system to conserve water in semiarid regions receiving less than 15 to 20 inches of rain a year.

Threshers, combines, and harvesters brought in the crop, while steam tractors pulled the heavy equipment.

That was just the beginning. With little rain, many farmers had to install windmills and pumping equipment to draw water from deep underground. The threat of cattle trampling the fields forced farmers to erect costly fences. Lacking wood, they found the answer in barbed wire, first marketed in 1874. When all was said and done, the average farmer spent what was for the poor a small fortune. Bigger operators invested 10 or 20 times as much.

Land and weather favored those big farmers. Tracts of 160 acres granted under the Homestead Act might be enough for eastern farms, but in the drier West more land was needed to produce the same harvest. Farms of more than 1,000 acres, known as "bonanza farms," were most common in the wheatlands of the northern plains. A steam tractor working a bonanza farm could plow, harrow, and seed up to 50 acres a day—20 times more than a single person could do without machinery. Against such competition, small-scale farmers could scarcely survive. As in the South, many became tenants on land owned by others.

⌃ Farm equipment was often the most important and proudest possession of farm families. In the 1890s, this Nebraska farmer was so taken with his horse-drawn reaper that he had his whole family photographed on top of it. He occupies the highest point on the giant machine, used for harvesting crops. This one was so large and heavy that it required an entire team of horses to pull it.
Fotosearch/Archive Photos/Getty Images

A Plains Existence >> For poor farm families, home on the range meant sod houses or dugouts carved into hillsides for protection against the wind. Tough, root-bound sod was cut into bricks a foot wide and three feet long and laid edgewise to create walls. Sod bricks also covered rafters for a roof. The average house was seldom more than 18 by 24 feet and in severe weather had to accommodate animals as well as people. The thick walls kept the house warm in winter and cool in summer, but a heavy, soaking rain or snow could bring the roof down or drip mud and water (and sometimes snakes) into the living area.

The heaviest burdens fell to women. They cooked and kept house under trying conditions. And with stores and supplies scarce, they also spent days at a time over hot tubs preparing tallow wax for candles or soaking ashes to make lye to mix with rendered pork rinds to make soap. Buttons had to be fashioned from old wooden spoons. Without doctors, women learned how to care for the hurt and sick, treating anything from frostbite to snakebite to burns and rheumatism.

Nature imposed its own hardships. Blizzards piled snow to the rooftops and halted travel. Weeks could pass before farm families saw an outsider. In the summers, searing winds blasted the plains for weeks. Nothing spelled disaster like locusts. They descended without warning in swarms 100 miles long. Beating against houses like hailstones, they devoured all vegetation, including the bark of trees. An entire year's labor might be destroyed in a day.

In the face of such hardships many westerners found comfort in religion. Native peoples turned to traditional spiritualism and Hispanics to the Catholic Church to cope with nature and hardship. Though some white Catholics and Jews came west, evangelical Protestants dominated the Anglo frontier. Worship offered an emotional outlet, intellectual stimulation, a means of preserving old values and sustaining hope. In the West as in the rural South, circuit riders compensated for the shortage of preachers, while huge camp meetings offered the chance to socialize. Both brought the world beyond the prairie a little closer. In many communities, it was the churches that first instilled order into public life, addressing local problems such as the need for schools and charity for the poor.

The Urban Frontier >> Not all westerners lived in isolation. By 1890 the percentage of those found in cities of 10,000 or more was greater than in any other section of the country except the Northeast.

Some western cities—San Antonio, El Paso, Los Angeles—were old Spanish towns whose growth had been reignited by the westward march of Anglo migrants, the northward push of Mexican immigrants, and the spread of railroads. Other cities, such as Portland near the Columbia River in Oregon, blossomed because they stood astride commercial routes. Still others, such as Wichita, Kansas, arose to serve the cattle and mining booms. As technology freed people from the need to produce their own food and clothing, westerners turned to the business of supplying goods and services. These enterprises required the labor of densely populated cities.

Denver was typical. Founded in 1859, the city profited from the discovery of gold in nearby Cherry Creek. The completion of the Denver Pacific and Kansas Pacific Railroads sparked a second growth spurt in the 1870s. By the 1890s, with with more than 100,000 residents, it ranked in population behind only Los Angeles and Omaha among western cities. Like much of the urban West, Denver grew outward rather than upward, breaking the pattern set by the cramped cities of the East. In the West, such urban sprawl produced living environments with sharply divided districts for business, government, and industry. Workers lived in one section of town; managers, owners, and wealthier citizens in another.

The West and the World Economy >> In its cities or its open range, deep in its mine shafts or on the sun-soaked fields of its huge bonanza farms, the West was being linked to the world economy more tightly each year. Longhorn cattle that grazed on Texas prairies fed city dwellers in the eastern United States and in Europe as well. Wood from the forests of the Pacific Northwest found its way into the hulls of British schooners and the furniture that adorned Paris parlors. Wheat grown on the Great Plains competed with grain from South America and Australia. Gold and silver mined in the Rockies were minted into coins around the world.

The ceaseless search for western resources depended ultimately on money. As raw materials flowed out of the region, capital flowed in. Most of it came from the East but some also from Europe. Foreign investment varied from industry to industry, but generally came in two forms: direct stock purchases and loans to western corporations and individuals. The great open-range cattle boom of the 1870s and 1880s, for example, brought an estimated $45 million into the western livestock industry from Great Britain alone. By 1887 Congress had become so alarmed at foreign ownership of western land that it enacted the Alien Land Law. Under it, no land in western territories could be bought by foreign corporations or by individuals who did not intend to become citizens.

Westerners were becoming part of a vast network of production and trade that spanned the globe. Between 1865 and 1915, world population increased by more than 50 percent, and demand mushroomed. Better and cheaper transportation, fed by a new industrial order, allowed westerners to supply raw materials and agricultural goods to places they knew only as exotic names on a map. Global reach came at a price. Decisions made elsewhere—in London and Paris, Tokyo and Buenos Aires—now determined the prices that westerners charged and the profits they made.

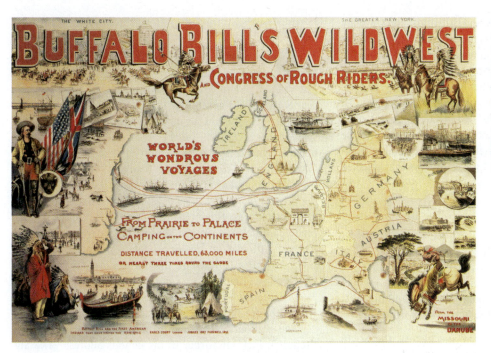

<< Buffalo Bill Cody's Wild West show provided Americans with mythical stereotypes of the "vanishing frontier," making the West seem a savage land in need of taming but also an Eden of boundless opportunity and adventure. The reach of such fantasies was truly global, and Buffalo Bill's show traveled widely in Europe, as this poster shows. DeAgostini/SuperStock

Packaging and Exporting the "Wild West" >>

No popular figure linked the West to the wider world and shaped perceptions of the region more than William F. ("Buffalo Bill") Cody. In 1883, trading on his fame as an army scout and buffalo hunter, Cody packaged the West in his "Wild West, Rocky Mountain, and Prairie Exhibition." Rope-twirling cowboys, war-painted Native Americans, and Annie Oakley, celebrated as much for her beauty as for her aim with a gun, entertained audiences across the globe. For many Americans, Buffalo Bill's "Wild West" was the West, where six-shooters administered justice and native peoples lived in tepees and made war on whites. Cody's depictions of romance and adventure obscured the realities of conquest, exploitation, and corporate control. Instead, cowboys and native peoples were glamorized, commercialized, and packaged for domestic as well as international consumption. Cody took his troupe not only across the United States but also to London, Paris, and even Outer Mongolia.

 REVIEW

What problems did the environment of the West present for farmers and ranchers?

History in Global Context >> Examining the returns from 1890, the superintendent of the census noted that landed settlements in the continental United States now stretched so far that "there can hardly be said to be a frontier line." Between 1867 and 1889, eight western states entered the Union. A new West was emerging as a frontierless mosaic of ethnicities, races, cultures, and climate with the shared identity of a single region, much as the wider world was seeing its frontiers disappear.

The sense of a regional identity was heightened for both westerners and southerners because so many of them felt isolated from the mainstream of the industrial United States. Ironically, it was not their isolation from northern industry but their links to it that marginalized them. The campaign for a New South to out-Yankee the industrial Yankee could not overcome the low wages and high fertility rates of an older South. The promoters of the West had greater success in adapting large-scale industry and investment to mining, cattle ranching, and farming. But they, too, confronted the limits of their region, whose resources were not endless and whose climate, especially rainfall, was fickle. Large projects like the transcontinental railroads were possible only with government support.

What beggared the South and conquered the West was a vast new industrial order that was reshaping the world, knitting it together in an interdependent network. Southerners and westerners were being linked to the world economy and faced the same confounding problems as their foreign counterparts. The small cotton growers in India, Egypt, and Brazil who faced plummeting prices were just as baffled by market economics as cotton farmers in the American South who found themselves deep in debt to merchants. And racialism, the widely accepted practice of categorizing people according to race, was being used to justify the exploitation of foreign workers just as it was used to thwart southern Black sharecroppers or to drive native peoples from their land.

Near the end of the century, one British official traveling into a remote cotton-growing region of India reported that growers found "some difficulty in realizing . . . that, by means of the Electric Telegraph, the throbbings of the pulse of the Home markets communicate themselves instantly to Hingunghat and other trade centres throughout the country." It was the "pulse of Home markets" worldwide that controlled the prospects of those in the cotton fields of India and the United States. A global industrial system increasingly determined interest rates, prices, and wages in ways that affected ordinary folk everywhere.

CHAPTER SUMMARY

In the years after the Civil War, both the South and the West became more closely linked to the industrial Northeast.

- Despite differences in geography and history, the South and the West shared many features.
  - ► Both became sources of agricultural goods and raw materials that fed urban and industrial growth in the northeastern and north central states.
  - ► Both were racially divided societies in which whites often used violence to assert their dominance.
  - ► Both looked beyond their regions for the human and financial resources needed to boost their economies.
- Southerners embraced the philosophy of the "New South," which hoped that industrialization would bring prosperity.
- The South nonetheless remained wedded to agriculture, especially cotton, and to a system of labor that exploited poor whites and Blacks.
  - ► In the South the crop-lien system shackled poor southerners to the land through debt, and Jim Crow segregation kept Blacks and whites apart.
- White westerners, too, exploited people of other races and ethnicities through settlement, conquest, and capture.
- By 1890 the emergence of the Ghost Dance and the closing of the frontier signaled that native peoples must adapt to life within the boundaries set by white culture, despite their efforts at resistance.
- Hispanos were increasingly subjected to similar exploitation but resisted and adapted more effectively to the intrusions of white culture and market economy.
- In a pattern that became typical for western mining, ranching, and agriculture, small operators first grabbed quick profits and then were followed by large corporations that increased both the scale and the wealth of these industries.
- As world economies became increasingly interdependent, a global industrial system more and more determined interest rates, prices, and wages across the world.

Digging Deeper

The themes of change and continuity have characterized interpretations of southern history after Reconstruction. For years C. Vann Woodward's classic *The Origins of the New South* (1951) dominated thinking about the region with its powerful argument for a changing South. Edward Ayers, *The Promise of the New South* (1992), offers a fresh, comprehensive synthesis that sees both change and continuity. Gavin Wright, *Old South, New South* (1986), destroys the myth of the southern colonial economy. Ted Ownby, *Subduing Satan* (1990), provides a valuable discussion of southern social life, especially the role of religion. On the issue of race relations, see Steven Hahn, *Under Our Feet: Black Political Struggles in the Rural South from Slavery to the Great Migration* (2003); on the convict leasing system, see Douglas A. Blackmon, *Slavery by Another Name: The Re-Enslavement of Black Americans from Reconstruction to World War II* (2008).

The contours of western history were first mapped by Frederick Jackson Turner in his famous address "The Significance of the Frontier in American History" (1893) but have been substantially reshaped by Richard White, *"It's Your Own Misfortune and None of My Own": A New History of the American West* (1992); and Patricia Limerick, *A Legacy of Conquest: The Unbroken Past of the American West* (1987). Each describes the history of the West less as a traditional saga of frontier triumphs than of the exploitation of the region and its resources. Richard White adds to his critique of western development in *The Transcontinental Railroad and the Making of Modern America* (2011). Donald Worster's *A River Running West: The Life of John Wesley Powell* (2002) chronicles that naturalist's feats. David Treuer provides an excellent survey of Native Americans in *The Heartbreak of Wounded Knee: Native America from 1890 to the Present* (2019). For a study of the Great Plains as a contested zone among environment, animals, and people, see Elliott West's *The Contested Plains: Indians, Goldseekers, and the Rush to Colorado* (1998). See also his *The Last Indian War: The Nez Perce Story* (2009), which places the episode in a national political context. Ari Kelman's award-winning *A Misplaced Massacre: Struggling over the Memory of Sand Creek* (2013) looks at the contested terrain of memory; while Jeffery Ostler's *The Lakotas and the Black Hills: The Struggle for Sacred Ground* (2010) carefully examines the Native American point of view of "sacred ground." S. C. Gwyne's *Empire of the Summer Moon: Quanah Parker and the Rise and Fall of the Comanches, the Most Powerful Indian Tribe in American History* (2011) tells the story of a mixed-race Comanche chief and the native nation that dominated the southern plains. Margaret D. Jacobs brings a comparative dimension to native boarding schools in *White Mother to a Dark Race: Settler Colonialism, Materialism, and the Removal of Indigenous Children in the American West and*

Australia, 1880-1940 (2009). Louis S. Warren's *God's Red Son: The Ghost Dance Religion and the Making of Modern America* (2017) offers a striking reinterpretation of the Ghost Dance as forward rather than backward-looking. Studies of the of the impact of native peoples on the environment include Shepherd Krech III, *The Ecological Indian: Myth and History* (1999); Karl Jacoby, *Crimes against Nature: Squatters, Poachers, Thieves, and the Hidden History of American Conservation* (2001); and Dan Flores, *The Natural West: Environmental History in the Great Plains and Rocky Mountains* (2001).

Sarah Deutsch, *No Separate Refuge: Culture, Class, and Gender on an Anglo-Hispanic Frontier in the American Southwest, 1880-1940* (1987), develops the concept of regional community. On the growing literature of ethno-racial identity in the West, see Neil Foley, *White Scourge: Mexicans, Blacks, and Poor Whites in Texas Cotton Culture* (1997); and David Gutiérrez, *Walls and Mirrors: Mexican Americans, Mexican Immigrants, and the Politics of Ethnicity* (1995). John Weber's *From South Texas to the Nation: The Exploitation of Mexican Labor in the Twentieth Century* (2015) builds on their work to examine mobility and immobility as devices for exploiting Mexican workers. For an excellent account of the African American experience in shaping the West, see Quintard Taylor, *In Search of the Racial Frontier: African Americans in the American West, 1528-1990* (1998). Gordon Chang brings the Chinese experience in the American West into sharp relief, *Ghosts of Gold Mountain: The Epic Story of the Chinese Who Built the Transcontinental Railroad* (2019).

19 The New Industrial Order

1870–1900

The magnificent steel arches of the Eads Bridge awed T. S. Hudson in his train travel across the continent. When it opened in 1874, it was the longest bridge in the world and the first to cross the Mississippi and to carry railroad tracks. It could not have been built without the newly achieved industrial systems of transportation, mining, finance, and, above all, the manufacture of steel.

Library of Congress, Prints and Photographs Division

>> **An American Story**

SCAMPERING THROUGH THE UNITED STATES

It was so dark that Robert Ferguson could not see his own feet. Inching along the railroad tracks, he suddenly pitched forward and found himself wedged between two railroad ties. His legs were dangling in the air.

Ferguson, a Scot visiting the United States in 1866, had been in Memphis only two days earlier, ready to take the "Great Southern Mail Route" east some 850 miles to Washington. Things had gone badly from the start. A broken bridge not 50 miles outside Memphis had forced him to take a ferry across the river. There followed a bumpy 10-mile ride on a mule-drawn truck to where the track was supposed to resume—but didn't. Disheartened, he and his fellow travelers rode back to Memphis aboard a train, only to have it derail just outside the city.

When a few passengers decided to hike the remaining distance, Ferguson tagged along. At dawn he discovered that the tracks led onto a flimsy, high river bridge. That was when he fell between the ties. Slowly, cautiously, he crawled to safety on the other side.

Less than 20 years later a second industrial revolution had transformed the transportation system. T. S. Hudson, another British tourist, undertook a self-proclaimed "Scamper through America" in 1882. In just 60 days he traveled from England to San Francisco and back. He crossed the continental United States on a ticket booked by a single agent in Boston. Such speed and centralization would have been unthinkable in 1866, when Ferguson made his ill-fated trip. Hudson's cross-country scamper would have been impossible as well. The transcontinental railroad was still three years from completion.

By the 1880s, Hudson's trains had Pullman Palace cars with posh sleeping quarters, full meals, and air brakes that smoothed stops. Bridges appeared where none had been before. A graceful, steel-and-stone structure supported by three giant arches now spanned the Mississippi at St. Louis. Hudson judged it "magnificent." He also found himself in the midst of a communications revolution. Traveling across the plains, he was struck by the number of telephone poles along the route.

What made the United States in the 1880s so different from the 1860s was a new industrial order. The process of industrialization had begun at least three decades before the Civil War, with small factories producing light consumer goods such as clothing, shoes, and furniture. Manufacturers catered to local markets made up mostly of farmers and merchants. After the 1860s, a second industrial revolution took hold as the industrial economy matured, producing larger factories, more machines, greater efficiency, and national, even international markets.

The transformation brought pain along with progress. Virgin forests vanished from the Pacific Northwest, the hillsides of Pennsylvania and West Virginia were pockmarked with open-pit mines, and the rivers of the Northeast grew toxic with industrial wastes. In 1882, the year Hudson crossed the United States by rail, an average of 675 people were killed on the job every week. Like most Americans, workers scrambled—sometimes literally—to adjust. Change came nonetheless. Industrialization swept from Great Britain to the European continent to the United States. Within a span of three decades, the republic of merchants and small farmers turned into an industrial powerhouse. «

THEMATIC TIME LINE

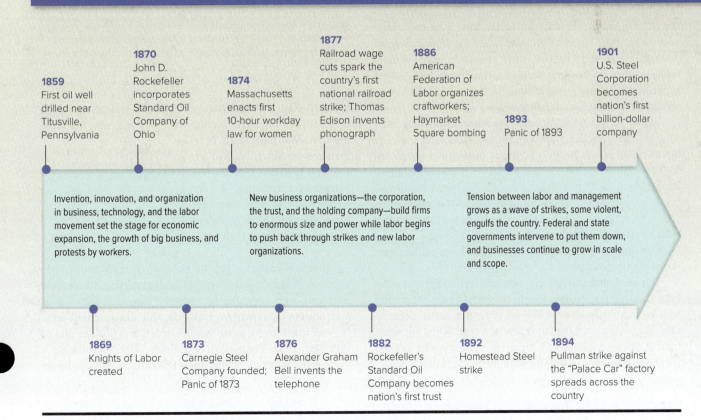

1859 First oil well drilled near Titusville, Pennsylvania

1870 John D. Rockefeller incorporates Standard Oil Company of Ohio

1874 Massachusetts enacts first 10-hour workday law for women

1877 Railroad wage cuts spark the country's first national railroad strike; Thomas Edison invents phonograph

1886 American Federation of Labor organizes craftworkers; Haymarket Square bombing

1893 Panic of 1893

1901 U.S. Steel Corporation becomes nation's first billion-dollar company

Invention, innovation, and organization in business, technology, and the labor movement set the stage for economic expansion, the growth of big business, and protests by workers.

New business organizations—the corporation, the trust, and the holding company—build firms to enormous size and power while labor begins to push back through strikes and new labor organizations.

Tension between labor and management grows as a wave of strikes, some violent, engulfs the country. Federal and state governments intervene to put them down, and businesses continue to grow in scale and scope.

1869 Knights of Labor created

1873 Carnegie Steel Company founded; Panic of 1873

1876 Alexander Graham Bell invents the telephone

1882 Rockefeller's Standard Oil Company becomes nation's first trust

1892 Homestead Steel strike

1894 Pullman strike against the "Palace Car" factory spreads across the country

THE DEVELOPMENT OF INDUSTRIAL SYSTEMS

The new industrial order can best be understood as a web of complex industrial systems. Look, for example, at the bridge across the Mississippi that Hudson admired. When James B. Eads constructed its soaring arches in 1874, he needed steel, most likely made from iron ore mined in northern Michigan. Giant steam shovels scooped up the ore and loaded whole freight cars in a few strokes. A transportation system—railroads, boats, and other carriers—moved the ore to Pittsburgh, where giant mills furnished the labor and machinery to finish the steel. The capital to create such factories came from a system of finance, linking investment banks and stock markets to entrepreneurs in need of money. Only with a national network of industrial systems could the Eads bridge be built and a new age of industry arise.

Natural Resources and Industrial Technology >>

The earliest European settlers had marveled at the "merchantable commodities" of America, from the glittering silver mines of the Spanish Empire to the continent's hardwood forests. What set the new industrial economy apart from that older America was the scale and efficiency of using those resources. New technologies made it possible to employ natural riches in ways undreamed of only decades earlier.

Iron, for example, had been forged into steel as far back as the Middle Ages, when it was used for fine swords. In the 1850s, inventors in Great Britain and the United States discovered a cheaper way—called the Bessemer process for its British designer, Sir Henry Bessemer—to convert large quantities of iron into steel. Steel was lighter than iron, could support 20 times as much weight, and lasted 20 years instead of 3. Steel tracks soon carried most rail traffic; steel girders replaced the old cast-iron frames in buildings; steel cables supported new suspension bridges. It became the indispensable metal of the new industrial order.

Industrial technology made some natural resources more valuable. New distilling methods transformed a thick, smelly liquid called *petroleum* into kerosene for lighting lamps, oil for lubricating machinery, and paraffin for making candles. Beginning in 1859, new drilling techniques began to tap vast pools of petroleum below ground. About the same time, Étienne Lenoir, a Belgian engineer, constructed the first practical internal combustion engine. After 1900 new vehicles such as gasoline-powered carriages turned the oil business into a major industry.

The environmental price of industrial technology was often high. Coal mining, logging, and the industrial wastes of factories were only the most obvious sources of environmental degradation. Sometimes even the cure came at a cost. When engineers tried to cleanse the polluted Chicago River by reversing its flow, they succeeded only in shifting pollution to rivers downstate.

STEEL PRODUCTION, 1880 AND 1914

While steel production jumped in many Western industrial nations from 1880 to 1914, it skyrocketed in the United States because of rich resources, cheap labor, and aggressive management.
Everett Collection/SuperStock

Systematic Invention >>

Industrial technology rested on invention. For sheer inventiveness, the 40 years following the Civil War have rarely been matched in American history. Between 1790 and 1860, 36,000 **patents** were registered with the government. Over the next three decades the U.S. Patent Office granted more than half a million.

> **patent** legal document issued by the government giving the holder exclusive rights to use, make, and sell a process, product, or device for a specified period of time.

One fact accounts for the number of innovations. The process of invention became systematized. Small-scale inventors were replaced by orderly "invention factories"—forerunners of expensive research and development labs. No one did more to bring system, order, and profitability to invention than Thomas Alva Edison. After developing a more efficient stock printer for a telegraph company, he set

^ In 1901 Spindletop Hill, just south of Beaumont, Texas, yielded a gusher that began the modern oil industry. Known as "black gold," oil became one of the most profitable businesses in the world, but drilling for it was dangerous, especially for workers on-site. Wells could ignite, producing a deadly blast and then a fire that might last for days.
Beaumont Texas oil black gold gusher/Texas Energy Museum, Beaumont, Texas

himself up as an independent inventor. For the next five years, Edison patented a new invention almost every five months.

Edison was determined to organize the process of invention. Only then could breakthroughs come in a steady and profitable stream. He moved 15 of his workers to Menlo Park, New Jersey, where in 1876 he created an "invention factory." Like a manufacturer, Edison subdivided the work among gifted inventors, engineers, toolmakers, and others. This orderly bureaucracy quickly evolved into the Edison Electric Light Company. It was soon delivering not only lightbulbs but a unified electrical power system of central stations to generate electric current, wired to users, all powering millions of small bulbs in homes and businesses.

George Eastman revolutionized photography by making the consumer a part of his system. In 1888 Eastman marketed the "Kodak" camera at the affordable price of $25. The small black box weighed two pounds and contained a strip of celluloid film that replaced hundreds of pounds of photography equipment. After 100 snaps of the shutter, the owner simply sent the camera back to the factory and waited for the developed photos, along with a reloaded camera, to return by mail, all for $10.

What united these innovations was the notion of rationalizing inventions by making a systematic business out of them. By 1913 Westinghouse Electric, General Electric, Armour meatpackers, and other firms had set up research laboratories. By the middle of the twentieth century, research labs had spread beyond business to the federal government, universities, trade associations, and labor unions.

Transportation and Communication >> Abundant resources and new inventions remained worthless to industry until they could be moved to processing plants, factories, and offices. With more than 3.5 million square miles of land in the United States, distances were daunting. Where 100 miles of railroad track would do for shipping goods in Germany and Britain, 1,000 miles was necessary in the United States.

An efficient internal transportation network tied the country into an emerging international system. By the 1870s railroads crisscrossed the country and steam-powered ships (introduced before the Civil War) were pushing barges down rivers and carrying passengers and freight across the oceans. Between 1870 and 1900 the value of American exports tripled. Eventually the rail and water transportation systems merged. By 1900 railroad companies owned nearly all of the country's domestic steamship lines.

In an innovative industrial nation, information was a precious commodity, as essential as natural resources or technology to industry. Effective communication helped move that information where it was needed. In 1844 Samuel Morse succeeded in testing his new telegraph. Communication using Morse's code of dots and dashes became virtually instantaneous. So useful to railroads was the telegraph that they allowed poles and wires to be set along their rights-of-way in exchange for free service. By the turn of the century, a million miles of telegraph wire handled some 63 million messages a year, not to mention those flashing across underwater cables to Europe, Asia, Africa, and South America.

The telephone vastly improved on the telegraph as an instrument of communication across great distances. Alexander Graham Bell, a Scottish immigrant, was teaching the deaf when he began experimenting with ways to transmit speech electrically. In 1876 he transmitted his famous first words to his young assistant: "Mr. Watson, come here! I want you." No longer did messages require a telegraph office, unwieldy dots and dashes, and couriers to deliver the translated messages. Communication could be instantaneous *and* direct. Before the turn of the century, the Bell-organized American Telephone and Telegraph Company combined more than 100 local companies to furnish business and government with long-distance service. The telephone patent proved to be the most valuable ever granted.

Finance Capital >> As industry grew, so did the demand for investment capital—the money spent on land, buildings, and machinery. The need for capital was great because so many new industrial systems were being put into place at

⌃ In 1915, years after its invention, a man demonstrates one of Alexander Graham Bell's first "speaking telegraphs." Early phones were cumbersome, and no one knew quite how to use them with one device for listening and another for speaking. Nor did people know what to say when a call came in. Bell himself suggested "ahoy" (as on a ship), but eventually users settled on Thomas Edison's "hello."
Underwood Archives /Archive Photos/Getty Images

once. Each carried enormous start-up costs. Industrial processes involving so many expensive systems could not take shape until someone raised the money to finance them.

For the first three-quarters of the nineteenth century, investment capital had come mostly from the savings of firms. In the last half of the century, "capital deepening," a process essential for industrialization, took place. Simply put, as national wealth increased, more people had more money to save and invest. This meant that more funds could be lent to companies seeking to start up or expand. Capital deepening was the key to financing the new industrial order.

Savings and investment grew more attractive with the development of a complex web of financial institutions. Commercial and savings banks, investment houses, and insurance companies moved money from savers to businesses. The New York **Stock Exchange,** in existence since 1792, linked eager investors with money-hungry firms.

> **stock exchange** market in which shares of ownership in corporations are bought and sold.

The Corporation >> For those business leaders with the skill to knit the pieces together, large profits awaited. This was the era of the notorious "robber baron." And to be sure, sheer ruthlessness went a long way in the fortune-building game. "Law? Who cares about law!" railroad magnate Cornelius Vanderbilt once boasted. "Hain't I got the power?"

To survive over the long term, business leaders could not depend on ruthlessness alone. They needed ingenuity, an eye for detail, and the gift of foresight. The growing scale of enterprise and need for capital, for example, led them to adapt an old device, the corporation, to new needs.

The corporation had several advantages over the traditional forms of ownership: single proprietors and partnerships. A corporation could raise large sums quickly by selling "stock certificates," or shares in its business, while single owners could not. It could also outlive its owners (or stockholders), because it required no legal reorganization if one died. It limited liability, since owners were no longer personally responsible for corporate debts. And it separated owners from day-to-day management of the company. Professional managers could now operate complex businesses. So clear were these benefits that before the turn of the century, corporations were making two-thirds of all manufactured products in the United States.

An International Pool of Labor >> No new industrial order could arise without an abundant pool of labor. In 1860 it took about 4.3 million workers to run all the factories, mills, and shops in the United States. By 1900 there were approximately 20 million industrial workers in the United States.

In part, the United States relied on a vast global network to fill its need for workers. In Europe as well as Latin America, Asia, Africa, and the Middle East, seasonal migrations provided a rich source of workers. Mechanization, poverty, oppression, and ambition pushed many of these laborers

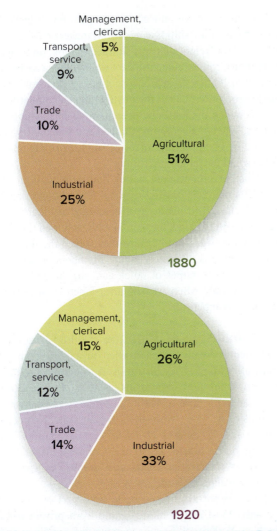

OCCUPATIONAL DISTRIBUTION, 1880 AND 1920

Between 1880 and 1920, management and industrial work—employing white- and blue-collar workers—grew at the expense of farmwork.

from farms into industrial cities and to other continents. By the 1880s, steamships cut travel time across the Atlantic to about a week.

Between 1870 and 1890 more than 8 million immigrants arrived in the United States, another 14 million by 1914. Some came from Asia and Latin America, but most came from Europe and settled in industrial cities. Like migratory laborers elsewhere, they hoped to find work, fill their purses, and go home. According to one estimate, perhaps as many as 60 percent of all immigrants returned to their homelands from the United States during these years.

Immigrants relied on well-defined migration chains of friends and family. A young man from Poland might find work with other Slavs in the mines of Pennsylvania; or the daughter of Greek parents, in a New England textile mill filled with relatives. Labor contractors also served as a funnel

to industry. Tough and savvy immigrants themselves, they met newcomers at the docks and train stations with contracts. Among Italians they were known as *padrones;* among Mexicans, as *enganchistas.* By 1900 they controlled two-thirds of the labor in New York.

Some 11 million rural Americans provided a homegrown source of labor between 1865 and 1920. Driven from the farm by machines or bad times, or just following dreams of a new life, they moved first to small, then to larger cities. Most lacked the skills for high-paying work. But they spoke English, and many could read and write. In iron and steel cities as well as in coal-mining towns, the better industrial jobs and supervisory positions went to them. Others found work in retail stores or offices and slowly entered the new urban middle class of white-collar workers.

While most African Americans continued to work fields in the South, about 300,000 moved to northern cities between 1870 and 1910. Like the new immigrants, they were trying to escape discrimination and follow opportunity. One by one, they brought their families, forming domestic migration chains. Discrimination dogged them, but they found employment. Often they worked in low-paying jobs as day laborers or laundresses and domestic servants. Black entrepreneurship also thrived as Black-owned businesses served growing Black communities.

Mexicans, too, came in search of jobs, mainly in agriculture but also in industry. With Chinese immigrants, they helped build the transcontinental railroad. After the turn of the century, a small number turned farther north for jobs in the tanneries, meatpacking plants, foundries, and rail yards of Chicago and other midwestern industrial cities.

✓ REVIEW

What factors led to the development of industrial systems?

RAILROADS: THE UNITED STATES'S FIRST BIG BUSINESS

In 1882, the year of T. S. Hudson's "scamper through America," clocks in New York and Boston were 11 minutes 45 seconds apart. Stations often had several clocks showing the time on different rail lines. In 1883, without consulting anyone, the railroad companies divided the country into four zones an hour apart to standardize time. Congress did not get around to making the zones official until 1916.

At the center of the new industrial systems lay the railroads, moving people and freight, spreading communications, reinventing time, tying the nation together. Railroads also stimulated economic growth, simply because they required so many resources to build: coal, wood, glass, rubber, brass, and, by the 1880s, 75 percent of all U.S. steel. Lowering transportation costs, railroads allowed manufacturers to reduce prices, attract more buyers, and increase business. Equally important, railroads operated year-round, even when canals and rivers froze or mud made roads impassable. As the country's first big business they created techniques of modern management, soon adopted by other companies.

A Managerial Revolution >> To those who ran them, railroads presented challenges in organization and finance. In the 1850s one of the largest industrial enterprises in the United States, the Pepperell textile mills of Maine, employed about 800 workers. By the early 1880s the Pennsylvania Railroad had nearly 50,000 employees. From paying workers to setting schedules and rates to determining costs and profits, the sheer scale of operations required a level of coordination unknown in earlier businesses.

The so-called trunk lines devised new systems of management. Scores of early companies serviced local cities and communities, often with fewer than 50 miles of track. During the 1850s longer trunk lines emerged east of the Mississippi to connect major cities and the shorter branches, or "feeder" lines. By the outbreak of the Civil War, with four great trunk lines under single management, railroads linked the Eastern Seaboard with the Great Lakes and western rivers.

The operations of large lines spawned a new managerial elite. They stood beneath owners but had wide authority over daily operations. Daniel McCallum, superintendent of the New York and Erie Railroad in the 1850s, laid the foundation for this system by creating the first table of organization for an American company. A tree trunk with roots represented the president and board of directors; five branches constituted the main operating divisions; leaves stood for the local agents, train crews, and others. Information moved up and down the trunk so that managers could get reports to and from the separate parts.

These managerial techniques soon spread to other industries. Local superintendents were responsible for daily activities. Central offices served as corporate nerve centers and housed divisions for purchases, production, transportation, sales, and accounting. A new class of middle managers ran them and imposed new order on business operations. Executives, managers, and workers were being taught to operate in precise and coordinated ways. It was a revolution in management and the most important contribution of the railroads to the rise of big business.

Competition and Consolidation >> While managers made operations more systematic, the fierce struggle among railroad companies to dominate the industry was anything but orderly. In the 1870s and 1880s, rate wars and bankruptcies spread as rapidly as tracks and trestles.

The most savage and costly competition came over the prices charged for shipping goods. Managers lowered prices, or "rates," for freight that was shipped in bulk, on long hauls, or on return routes, since the cars would otherwise be empty. They used "rebates"—secret discounts to preferred customers—to drop prices below the posted rates of competitors and then recouped the losses by overcharging small shippers like farmers. When the economy plunged or a weak line sought to improve its position, rate or price wars broke out. By 1880, 65 lines had declared bankruptcy.

Consolidation worked better than competition. During the 1870s railroads created regional federations to pool traffic, set prices, and divide profits among members. Initially these loosely affiliated lines, or "pools," achieved their goal of reducing rate wars, but because they lacked the force of law, their agreements ultimately failed. Members broke ranks by cutting prices in hopes of quick gain. In the end, rate wars died down only when weaker lines failed or stronger ones bought up competitors.

The Challenge of Finance >> Earlier in the nineteenth century many railroads relied on state governments for financial backing. They also looked to counties, cities, and towns for bonds and other forms of capital. People took stock in exchange for land or labor, particularly those living near the ends of rail lines, who stood to gain most from construction. In the 1850s and 1860s western promoters went to Washington for federal assistance. Congress loaned $65 million to six western railroads and granted railroads some 131 million acres of land.

Government aid helped build only part of the nation's railroads. Most of the money came from private investors. The New York Stock Exchange expanded rapidly as railroad corporations began to trade stocks there. Large investment banks tracked down money at home but also abroad. By 1898 a third of the assets of American life insurance companies had gone into railroads, while Europeans owned nearly a third of all American railroad securities.

Because investment bankers played such large roles in funding railroads, they found themselves advising companies about business affairs. If a company fell into bankruptcy, bankers sometimes served as the "receivers" who oversaw the property until financial health returned. By absorbing smaller lines into larger ones, eliminating rebates, and stabilizing rates, the bankers helped reduce competition and impose order and centralization on railroads and other corporations. In the process, they often gained control of the companies they advised.

By 1900 the new industrial systems had transformed American railroads. Some 200,000 miles of track were in operation, 80 percent of it owned by only six groups of railroads. Time zones allowed for coordinated schedules; standardized track permitted easy cross-country freighting. Soon passengers were traveling 16 billion miles a year, along with large quantities of farm goods, raw materials, and factory-finished products. Everything moved with new regularity that allowed businesses to plan and prosper.

RAILROADS, 1870–1890

In just a few decades, railroad companies built a web of lines that tied the nation together as never before. As this map reveals, by 1890 the railroad network stretched from one end of the country to the other, with more miles of track than in all of Europe. New York City and Chicago, linked by the New York Central "trunk" line, became the new commercial axis. Beyond the Mississippi River a less dense network of trunk lines snaked their way to the West Coast. Note the cities they serviced along their lines.

MAP READING

1. Which regions of the country had their railroad lines built earliest?
2. Which regions had the most major lines added between 1870 and 1890?
3. What cities are the terminal points of the Transcontinental Railroad?
4. Which cities are the terminal points of the New York Central Railroad?

MAP INTERPRETATION

1. Why are the earliest rail lines built in the East? What geographic factors caused the railroad network in other regions to be less dense than in the East?
2. Why is the New York Central trunk line so important? Which cities did it most benefit?
3. What role did railroads play in the settlement of the West?
4. What role did cities play in mapping the national railroad network?

 REVIEW

How did the railroads contribute to the rise of big business?

THE GROWTH OF BIG BUSINESS

In 1865, near the end of the Civil War, 26-year-old John D. Rockefeller sat blank-faced in the office of his Cleveland oil refinery. He was about to conclude the biggest deal of his life. Rockefeller's business was thriving, but he had fallen out with his partner over pace of expansion. Rockefeller was eager to grow fast; his partner was not. They dissolved their partnership and agreed to bid for the company. Bidding opened at $500, rocketed to $72,500, and abruptly stopped. "The business is yours," said the partner. The men shook hands, and a thin smile crept across Rockefeller's angular face.

Twenty years later, Rockefeller's Standard Oil Company controlled 90 percent of the nation's refining capacity and an empire that stretched well beyond Cleveland. Trains swept Standard executives to New York, Philadelphia, and other eastern cities. It was a fitting form of transportation for Rockefeller's company. Railroads were the key to his oil empire. They pioneered the big business systems on which he was building it. And they carried his oil products for discounted rates, giving him the edge to squeeze out rivals and dominate the industry.

Strategies of Growth >> Before Rockefeller could achieve such dominance, a bedeviling business riddle had to be solved: how to grow and still control the ravages of competition? In Michigan in the 1860s, salt producers found themselves fighting for their existence. The presence of too many salt makers had begun an endless round of price-cutting that was driving everyone out of business. Seeing salvation in combination, they drew together in the nation's first pool, a strategy which the railroads later copied to minimize rivalries and end costly rate wars. In 1869 the salt producers formed the Michigan Salt Association, through which they voluntarily allocated production, divided markets, and set prices—at double the previous rate.

Since salt processing and other industries that specialized in **consumer goods** had low start-up costs, they were often plagued by competition. **Horizontal combination**—joining together loosely with rivals that offered the same goods or services—saved Michigan salt producers. Others created similar agreements. By the 1880s there was a whiskey pool, a cordage pool, and countless rail and other pools. In the end, pools proved to be unenforceable and therefore unsatisfactory. (After 1890 they were

consumer goods products such as food and clothing that fill the needs and wants of individuals.

horizontal combination strategy of business growth (sometimes referred to as "horizontal integration") that attempts to stifle competition by combining more than one firm involved in the same level of production, transportation, or distribution into a single firm.

also considered illegal restraints on trade under new federal law.) But other forms of horizontal growth, such as formal mergers or the consolidation of companies, spread in the wake of an economic panic in the 1890s.

Some makers of consumer products worried less about direct competition and concentrated on boosting efficiency and sales. They adopted a vertical-growth strategy in which one company gained control of two or more stages of a business. Take Gustavus Swift, a New England butcher, for example. Aware of the demand for fresh beef in the East, Swift moved to Chicago in the mid-1870s to be closer to its stockyards. He acquired refrigerated railcars to ship meat from western slaughterhouses and a network of ice-cooled warehouses in eastern cities to store it. By 1885 he had created the first national meatpacking enterprise, Swift and Company.

Swift moved upward, closer to consumers, by putting together a fleet of wagons to distribute his beef to retailers. He moved down toward raw materials, extending and coordinating the purchase of cattle at the Chicago stockyards. By the 1890s Swift and Company was a fully integrated, vertically organized corporation operating on a nationwide scale. His research lab created new products such as glue from the products his slaughterhouses discarded.

Vertical growth generally moved producers of consumer goods closer to the marketplace in search of high-volume sales. The Singer Sewing Machine Company and the McCormick Harvesting Machine Company created their own retail sales arms. Manufacturers began furnishing ordinary consumers with technical information, credit, and repair services. Advertising expenditures grew, to some $90 million by 1900, in an effort to identify markets, shape buying habits, and increase sales.

Carnegie Integrates Steel >> Industrialization encouraged vertical integration in heavy industry, but more often down toward reliable sources of raw materials. Heavy industry firms made products for big users such as railroads and construction companies. Their markets were easily identified and changed little. For them, success lay in securing limited raw materials and in holding down costs.

Andrew Carnegie led the way in steel. A Scottish immigrant, he began as a lowly bobbin boy in a textile mill, became an expert telegrapher, and then the superintendent of the Pennsylvania Railroad's western division at the age of 24. A string of wise investments paid off handsomely. Among other things, he owned a locomotive factory and an iron factory that became the nucleus of his steel empire.

In 1872, on a trip to Great Britain, Carnegie chanced to see the Bessemer process in action. Awestruck and dreaming of the profits to be made from cheap steel, he rushed home to build the biggest steel mill in the world. It opened in 1875, in the midst of a severe depression. Over the next 25 years, Carnegie added mills at Homestead and elsewhere in Pennsylvania and moved from railroad-building to city-building.

Carnegie succeeded, in part, by taking advantage of the boom-and-bust business cycle. He jumped in during hard times, building and buying when equipment and businesses were cheap. But he also found skilled managers who employed the administrative techniques of the railroads. And Carnegie knew how to compete: he scrapped machinery, workers, even a new mill to keep down costs and undersell competitors.

The final key to Carnegie's success was expansion. He spread his empire horizontally by purchasing rival steel mills and constructing new ones. He also spread it vertically, buying up sources of supply, transportation, and eventually sales. Controlling such an integrated system, Carnegie could ensure a steady flow of materials from mine to mill and market, as well as reap profits at every stage. In 1900 his company turned out more steel than Great Britain and netted $40 million.

Rockefeller and the Great Standard Oil

Trust >> John D. Rockefeller accomplished in oil what Carnegie achieved in steel. And he went further, developing an innovative business structure—the trust—that promised greater control than even Carnegie's integrated system. At first, Rockefeller, who specialized in refining petroleum, grew horizontally by buying out or joining with other refiners. To cut costs, he expanded vertically, with oil pipelines, warehouses, and barrel factories. By 1870, when he and five partners formed the Standard Oil Company of Ohio, his

high-quality, low-cost products achieved the promise of the company's name. It set the standard for the whole industry.

Because the oil-refining business was a jungle of competitive firms, Rockefeller proceeded to twist arms. He bribed rivals, spied on them, created phony companies, and slashed prices. His decisive advantage came from the railroads. Desperate for business, they granted Standard Oil not only rebates on shipping rates but also "drawbacks." These involved an additional fee from the railroad to Rockefeller for any product shipped by a rival oil company. Within a decade, Standard Oil topped the American refining industry with a vertically integrated empire from drilling to selling.

Throughout the 1870s Rockefeller kept his empire stitched together through informal pools and other business combinations. But they were weak and afforded too little control. He could try to expand further, except that corporations were restricted by state law. In Rockefeller's home state of Ohio, for example, corporations could not own plants in other states or own stock in out-of-state companies.

In 1879 Samuel C. T. Dodd, chief counsel of Standard Oil, came up with a new device, the **trust**. The stockholders of a corporation surrendered their shares "in trust" to a central board of directors with the power to control all property. In exchange, stockholders received certificates of trust that paid hefty dividends. Since

trust business arrangement in which owners of shares in a business turn over their shares "in trust" to a board with power to control those businesses for the benefit of the trust.

it did not literally own other companies, the trust violated no state laws.

In 1882 the Standard Oil Company of Ohio formed the country's first great trust. It brought Rockefeller what he sought so fiercely: centralized management of the oil industry. Other businesses soon created trusts of their own—in meatpacking, wire-making, and farm machinery, for example. Just as quickly, trusts became notorious for crushing rivals and fixing prices.

The Mergers of J. Pierpont Morgan >> The
trust was only a stepping-stone to an even more effective means of avoiding competition, managing people, and controlling business: the corporate merger. The merging of two corporations—one buying out another—remained impossible until 1889, when New Jersey began to permit corporations to own other companies through what became known as the "holding company" (a company that held stock in other companies). Many industries converted their trusts into holding companies, including Standard Oil, which moved to New Jersey in 1899.

Two years later came the biggest corporate merger of the era. It was the creation of a financial wizard named J. Pierpont Morgan. His orderly mind detested the chaotic competition that threatened his profits. "I like a little competition," Morgan used to say, "but I like combination more." He had taken over his father's powerful investment bank after the Civil War. For the next 50 years the House of Morgan played a part in consolidating almost every major industry in the country.

Morgan's greatest triumph came in steel. In 1901 a colossal war loomed between Andrew Carnegie and other steelmakers. Morgan convinced Carnegie to put a price tag on his company. When a messenger brought back a scrawled reply of over $400 million, Morgan nodded agreement. He then added Carnegie's eight largest competitors to the new company and announced the formation of the United States Steel Corporation. The mammoth holding company produced nearly two-thirds of all American steel. With a value of $1.4 billion, a sum almost three times larger than the federal budget in 1901, U.S. Steel became the country's first billion-dollar corporation.

What Morgan helped create in steel was rapidly coming to pass in other industries. A wave of mergers swept through American business after the depression of 1893. As the economy plunged, cutthroat competition bled businesses until they were eager to sell out. Giants sprouted almost overnight. By 1904, one firm came to account for 60 percent or more of the total output in some 50 industries.

Corporate Defenders >> As Andrew Carnegie's empire grew, so did his social conscience. Preaching a "gospel of wealth," he told the rich their money obligated them to act as agents for the poor, "doing for them better than they would or could do for themselves." He devoted more and more of his time to philanthropy, creating foundations and endowing libraries and universities with some $350 million.

^ Andrew Carnegie around 1868. A decade later, after a world tour, he tempered his social Darwinist view that evolution had produced the superiority of Western technology and ideas. "Go and see for yourself how greatly we are bound by prejudices, how checkered and uncertain are many of our own advances," he told friends. "No nation has all that is best."
Hulton Archive/Getty Images

Defenders of the new corporate order were less troubled than Carnegie about the rough-and-tumble world of business. They justified the system by stressing the opportunities created for individuals by economic growth. Through frugality, acquisitiveness, and discipline—the sources of cherished American individualism—they believed anyone could rise like Andrew Carnegie.

Since most ordinary workers were unable to follow in Carnegie's footsteps, defenders blamed them as individuals. People who failed were lazy, ignorant, or morally depraved, they said. British philosopher Herbert Spencer explained failure—and success—by applying Charles Darwin's theories of evolution to human relations. Spencer maintained that in society, as in biology, only the "fittest" survived. The competitive social jungle doomed the unfit to poverty and rewarded the fit with property and privilege.

Spencer's American apostle, William Graham Sumner, argued that competition was natural and had to proceed without any interference, including government regulation. Millionaires were simply the "product of natural selection." Such "social Darwinism" found strong support among turn-of-the-century business leaders. The philosophy certified their success even as they worked to destroy the very competitiveness it celebrated.

Corporate Critics >>

At the other end of the political spectrum, radical critics mounted a powerful attack on corporate capitalism. Seeing the income inequality of his day, Henry George, a journalist and self-taught economist, attacked large landowners as the source of the problem. They bought land while it was cheap and held it until the forces of society—labor, technology, and speculation on nearby sites—increased its value. These "unearned" profits should be distributed among all, George argued, for he believed that land was common property and forces larger than any owner increased its value. In *Progress and Poverty* (1879), he proposed a single tax on the profits from land ownership. In effect, owners would become renters. Monopoly landholding would end and income would be redistributed. Millions supported the idea, and "single-tax" clubs sprang up across the country. In 1886, George nearly won the race for mayor of New York City.

The journalist Edward Bellamy tapped the same popular resentment against the inequalities of corporate capitalism in his utopian novel, *Looking Backward* (1888). A fictional Bostonian falls asleep in 1887 and awakens Rip-Van-Winkle–like in the year 2000. The competitive, caste-ridden society of the nineteenth century is gone. In its place is an orderly utopia, managed by a benevolent government trust. "Fraternal cooperation" and shared abundance reign. Like George's ideas, Bellamy's philosophy inspired a host of clubs. His followers demanded redistribution of wealth, civil service reform that awarded merit rather than connections, and nationalization of railroads and utilities, all for the common good.

Less popular but equally hostile to capitalism was the Socialist Labor Party, formed in 1877. Under Daniel De Leon, a West Indian immigrant, it stressed class conflict and called for a revolution to give workers control over production. De Leon refused to compromise his radical beliefs, and the **socialists** ended up attracting more intellectuals than workers. Some immigrants found its class consciousness appealing, but most rejected its rigidity. A few party members revolted and in 1901 founded the more successful and pragmatic Socialist Party of America. Workers were beginning to organize political responses to industrialism.

socialists philosophy of social and economic organization in which the means of producing and distributing goods are owned collectively or by government.

In 1890 the public clamor against trusts and other business combinations finally forced Congress to act. State laws limiting the size of corporations had proved all too easy to evade. The Sherman Antitrust Act relied on the only constitutional authority Congress had over business: its right to regulate interstate commerce. The act outlawed "every contract, combination in the form of trust or otherwise, or conspiracy, in restraint of trade or commerce" where business crossed state lines. "Restraint of commerce or trade" referred to attempts to limit competition. Outlawing such practices effectively made monopoly businesses illegal, because they were the only entities large enough to restrict competition. The United States stood practically alone among developed countries in regulating the size of business combinations.

Its language was purposefully vague, but the Sherman Antitrust Act did give the government the power to break up trusts and other big businesses. So high was the regard for the rights of private property, however, that few in Congress expected Washington to exercise that power or the courts to uphold it.

They were right. In 1895 the Supreme Court dealt the law a major blow by severely limiting its scope in *United States* v. *E. C. Knight Co.* The court held that businesses involved in manufacturing (as opposed to "trade or commerce") lay outside the authority of the Sherman Antitrust Act. Not until after the turn of the century, when more aggressive presidents and a more responsive court were in place, would the law finally bust a trust. Until then, its vague wording and the court rulings that weakened it left the law toothless and rarely employed. When it was used, it was against workers, whose strikes courts deemed a "restraint of trade."

The Costs of Doing Business >>

The heated debates between the critics and defenders of industrial capitalism made it clear that the changes in U.S. society were two-edged. Big businesses helped rationalize the economy, increase national wealth, and connect the country. Yet they also concentrated power, corrupted politics, and made the gap between rich and poor wider than ever.

The double edge was most obvious in the enormous disruptions to which big business subjected the economy. The banking system could not always keep pace with the demand for capital, and businesses failed to distribute enough of their profits to sustain the purchasing power of consumers. The supply of goods periodically outstripped demand, and a wrenching cycle of boom and bust set in. Three severe depressions—1873–1879, 1882–1885, and 1893–1897—rocked the economy in the last third of the nineteenth century. With hard times came fierce competition, ruthless cost cutting, high unemployment, and intense human suffering.

THEN&NOW

In trying to understand the role of innovation in the boom-and-bust business cycle, the Austrian economist Joseph Schumpeter came up with an intriguing theory. The "gale of creative destruction," he wrote in 1942, "incessantly revolutionizes the economy from within, incessantly destroying the old one, incessantly creating a new one." Schumpeter argued that entrepreneurship and innovation combine at regular intervals to produce tectonic shifts in the economy. Pioneering technologies and fresh forms of business replace existing ones. Creativity seeds economic growth, with "boom industries"

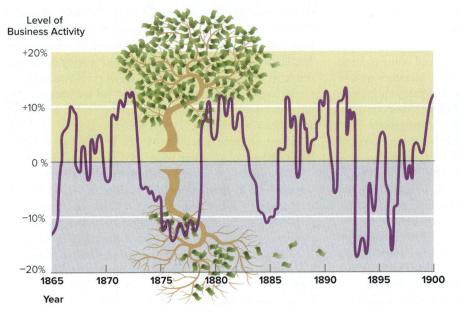

Level of Business Activity

+20%

+10%

0 %

−10%

−20%

1865   1870   1875   1880   1885   1890   1895   1900

Year

BOOM-AND-BUST BUSINESS CYCLE, 1865–1900

Between 1865 and 1900, industrialization produced great economic growth but also wild swings of prosperity and depression. During booms, productivity soared and near-full employment existed. But the rising number of industrial workers meant high unemployment during deep busts.

and new sources of energy leading the way. But it also destroys outmoded ways of doing business, thus producing busts. Today, in a new era of creative destruction, we have seen a digital revolution, powered by electricity and spawning boom industries in computers and communications. It has ignited the economy but also destabilized it.

The environmental costs of industrialization were often steep and plain to see as well. In Pittsburgh, some 14,000 smokestacks spewed so much coal dust into the air that the city was permanently covered in haze. Sulfur, cyanide, ammonia, acid fumes, and other toxic gases filled the air. Lead paint was the norm on many buildings, even though authorities knew it could damage muscles, nerves, and the brain. Equally normal was dumping industrial wastes into nearby rivers and streams. Hardly anyone worried, assuming as they did that it promoted public health by killing infectious bacteria in the water.

Not all costs were clear at the time. In the nineteenth century most people, scientists included, believed that nature would maintain its own balance, largely unaffected by human action. And for the handful of observers interested in climate change, only the most basic calculations were possible.

It took a Brit and a Swede consumed with discovering the cause of the prehistoric Ice Age to work out the climatic ramifications of new smokestack industries. In 1859 British scientist John Tyndall took up the question of precisely what in the atmosphere *prevented* the Earth from freezing. By testing the "coal gas" (gas emitted by burning coal) from a jet in his laboratory, he found that methane and carbon dioxide captured heat. Historically such gases had come from volcanic eruptions and other natural occurrences, but growing amounts were now being thrown aloft by industry.

In Sweden, Svante Arrhenius carried the idea a step further in 1896. If heat-trapping gases raised global temperatures

even slightly, warmer air would absorb more of the most potent heat trapper—water vapor. Temperatures would rise still higher, setting off a new, planetary cycle of climate. With the age of industry in its infancy, few paid attention to the implications of human contributions to what would later be called "climate change."

 REVIEW

What strategies and structures did businesses use to grow and at what costs?

THE WORKERS' WORLD

At seven in the morning, Sadie Frowne sat at her sewing machine in a Brooklyn garment factory. Her boss, a man she barely knew, dropped a pile of unfinished skirts next to her. She pushed one under her needle and began to rock her foot on the pedal that powered her machine. Sometimes Sadie pushed the skirts too quickly, and the needle pierced her finger. "The machines go like mad all day because the faster you work the more money you get," she explained of industrial work in 1902.

The cramped sweatshops, the vast steel mills, the dank tunnels of the coal fields—all demanded workers and required them to work in new ways. Farmers or peasants who had once timed themselves by the movement of the sun now lived by the clock and labored in the twilight of gaslit factories. Instead of being self-employed, they were under the thumb of a supervisor and paid by the piece or hour. Not the seasons but the relentless cycle of machines set their pace. They bore the brunt of depressions, faced periodic unemployment, and toiled under dangerous conditions as they struggled to make ends meet. And, like their managers, some workers sought to bring the new industrial processes under control.

Industrial Work >>

In 1881 the Pittsburgh Bessemer Steel Company opened its new mill in Homestead, Pennsylvania. Nearly 400 men and boys went to work in its 60 acres of sheds. They kept the mill going around the clock in two 12-hour shifts. In the furnace room, some men fainted from the heat, while the vibration and screeching machinery deafened others. There were no breaks, not even for lunch.

Few industrial laborers worked under such extreme conditions, but the Homestead mill reflected common characteristics of industrial work: the use of machines for mass production; the division of labor into intricately organized, often repetitive tasks; and the dictatorship of the clock. At the turn of the century, two-thirds of all industrial work took place in large-scale mills.

Under such conditions labor paid dearly for industrial progress. By 1900 most of those earning wages in industry worked 6 days a week, 10 hours a day. They held jobs that increasingly required more machines and fewer skills. Repetition of small chores replaced fine craftwork. In the 1880s, for example, almost all of the 40 steps that previously went into making a pair of shoes could be performed by a novice or "green hand" with a few days of instruction at a simple machine.

With machines came danger. Tending furnaces in a steel mill or plucking tobacco from cigarette-rollers was tedious. If a worker became bored or tired, disaster could strike. Each year from 1880 to 1900, industrial mishaps killed an average of 35,000 wage earners and injured more than 500,000. Workers could expect no payment from employers or government for death or injury. The law presumed such accidents were the victim's fault.

Higher productivity and profits were the ends, and for Frederick W. Taylor, efficiency was the means. During the 1870s and 1880s Taylor undertook careful time-and-motion studies of workers' movements in the steel industry. He set up standard procedures and offered pay incentives for beating his production quotas. One hundred forty men were soon doing the work of 600. By the early twentieth century "Taylorism" was a full-blown philosophy, complete

≈ Chicago laborer.
Library of Congress, Prints and Photographs Division
[LC-USZ62-5422]

with its own professional society. "Management engineers" prescribed routines from which workers could not vary.

For all the high ideals of Taylorism, ordinary laborers refused to perform as cogs in a vast industrial machine. In a variety of ways they worked to exert control. Many European immigrants continued to observe the numerous saints' days and other religious holidays of their homelands, regardless of factory rules. When the pressure of six-day weeks became too stifling, workers took an unauthorized "blue Monday" off. Or they slowed down production to reduce the grueling pace. Or they walked off the job. Come spring and warm weather, factories reported turnover rates of 100 percent or more as workers looked for jobs elsewhere.

For some, seizing control of work was more than a matter of survival or self-respect. Many workers regarded themselves as citizens of a democratic republic. They expected to earn a "competence"—enough money to support and educate their families and enough time to stay abreast of current affairs. Only a relatively few high-skilled workers could realize such democratic dreams. More and more, labor was being managed as another part of an integrated system of industry.

Children, Women, and African Americans at Work >>

The demand for industrial workers was so great that groups traditionally left out of industry—children, women, African Americans—found themselves drawn into it. In the mines of Pennsylvania, nimble-fingered eight-year-olds snatched bits of slate from the chunks of coal. In Illinois glass factories, "dog boys" dashed with trays of red-hot bottles to the cooling ovens. By 1900 the industrial labor force included some 1.7 million children, more than double the number 30 years earlier. Parents often had no choice. As one union leader observed, "Absolute necessity compels the father . . . to take the child into the mine." On average, children worked 60 hours a week and carried home paychecks a third the size of adult males.

Women had always labored on family farms, but by 1870 one out of every four nonagricultural workers was female. Industrialization inevitably pushed women into new jobs. Mainly they worked in industries considered extensions of housework: food processing, textiles and clothing, cigar making, and domestic service. In general they earned one-half of what men did.

Nearly all women working in industry were single and young, anywhere from their mid-teens to their mid-20s. Most lived in boardinghouses or at home with their parents. Usually they contributed their wages to the family kitty. Once married, they often took on a life of full-time housework and child rearing. Only 5 percent of married women held jobs outside the home in 1900. However, married Black women were four times more likely than married white women to hold jobs. They needed the income because their husbands had fewer opportunities and brought home smaller paychecks than their white counterparts.

Pay scales for women never matched those for men, but new methods of management and marketing opened

^ Clerks' jobs, traditionally held by men, came to be filled by women as growing industrial networks created more managerial jobs for men. Here a factory floor full of neatly dressed female clerks work at their "Type-Writers," patented first in 1868.
Bettmann/Getty Images

positions for white-collar women as "typewriters" and "telephone girls" that did not exist earlier. On rare occasions women entered the professions, though law and medical schools were reluctant to admit them. Such discrimination drove ambitious, educated women into teaching and hospital nursing, among other fields considered forms of female nurturance. The growing numbers of women soon "feminized" these professions, pushing men upward into managerial slots or out entirely.

Even more than white women, African Americans faced discrimination in the workplace. They were usually given menial jobs and always for lower pay. Their greatest opportunities in industry came when they worked as "scabs," replacing white workers on strike. Once a strike ended, Black workers lost their jobs but gained the hatred of white strikers.

African Americans fought discrimination in a variety of ways. Many found jobs outside of industry, especially in service trades, such as railroad porters. Others learned crafts,

and still others became professionals. After the turn of the century, Black-owned businesses thrived in the growing Black neighborhoods of the North and the South by catering to African American patrons.

The American Dream of Success >> Whatever their separate experiences, working-class Americans did improve their overall lot. Though the gap between the very rich and the very poor widened, most wage earners made gains. Between 1860 and 1890 real daily wages—pay in terms of buying power—climbed some 50 percent as prices gradually fell. After 1890, partly as a result of labor agitation for an 8-hour day, the number of hours on the job began a slow decline.

For all the progress, most factory workers continued to receive low pay. In 1890 an unskilled laborer could expect about $1.50 for a 10-hour day; a skilled one, perhaps twice that amount. It took about $600 a year just to scrape by, but

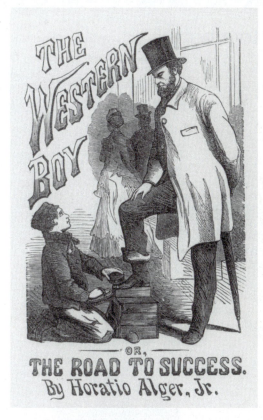
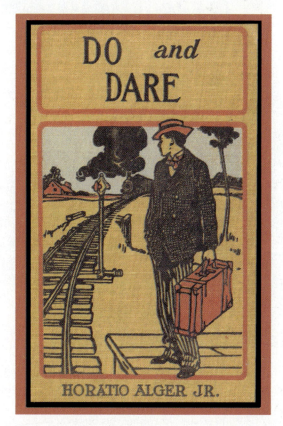

∧ Horatio Alger, the author of these widely popular "dime novels" (named for their price), was a minister and school teacher turned children's book author. He achieved great success with his tales of down-and-out youngsters who worked hard and through "luck" (good fortune) and "pluck" (industriousness) got ahead in life. Generations of young Americans who believed in the American dream of success found confirmation of it on every page. Early novels, such as *The Western Boy* (1878), were printed with black-and-white covers, but the presses kept turning out the books even after Alger died in 1899. His novel *Do and Dare*, originally published in 1884, appeared in this early-twentieth-century edition with a color cover and characters whose style of dress was updated to reflect more current fashions.
(left) Library of Congress, Prints and Photographs Division [LC-USZ62-61588]; (right) Buyenlarge/Getty Images

most manufacturing workers made under $500 a year. Native-born white Americans tended to earn more than immigrants, those who spoke English earned more than those who did not, men earned more than women, and all others earned more than African Americans, Latinos, and Asians.

Few workers repeated the rags-to-riches rise of Andrew Carnegie. But some did rise, despite periodic unemployment and ruthless wage cuts. About one-quarter of the manual laborers in one study entered the lower middle class in their lifetime. More often such unskilled workers climbed within their own class. Most workers, seeing some improvement, believed in the American dream of success, even if they did not fully share in it.

Make a Case

Who deserves more credit for making the United States an industrial powerhouse, industrialists or workers? What evidence might you use to make your case?

REVIEW

How did industrialization change the working day for people employed in factories?

THE SYSTEMS OF LABOR

To negotiate industrialization, many ordinary workers sought to combine, just as businesses did. They sought to join together horizontally—organizing workers doing the same thing not just locally but on a national scale. They were less inclined to integrate vertically by coordinating action across a wide range of jobs and skills. Unions were the workers' systematic response to industrialization.

Early Unions >> In the United States, unions began forming before the Civil War. Skilled craft workers—carpenters, iron molders, cigar makers—united to counter the

Historian's TOOLBOX

Digital Detecting

Eastport, Maine: what adjectives would you use to describe the scene?

At first the view looks somewhat rural, but at least three elements in the photograph suggest otherwise. What are they?

What strikes you about this digitally enlarged portion of the photo?

Photographs can be both revealing and deceptive, but technology can help historians detect what the camera lens actually captured. This print (*lower right*) of a photo by Lewis Hine, a turn-of-the-century photographer, shows eight-year-old Phoebe Thomas returning to her house in Eastport, Maine. The scene seems to be nothing more than a little girl making her way home up a set of stairs. Hine tells us that the young Syrian worked all day in a cannery, shearing the heads off sardines with a butcher's knife. When the Library of Congress scanned the image nearly a century later, a portion of the photo could be digitally enlarged to reveal much more than meets the unaided eye. What appears to be an ordinary homecoming is, in fact, something much worse, as Hine's notes reveal. Phoebe was "running home from the factory all alone, her hand and arm bathed with blood, crying at the top of her voice. She had cut the end of her thumb nearly off, cutting sardines in the factory, and was sent home alone, her mother being busy."

THINKING CRITICALLY

How does the close-up of Phoebe Thomas change the nature of the photograph? What would we make of the photograph without Hine's explanatory notes? Google "Lewis Hine" to learn what he photographed and why.

(photo and detail) (left): Library of Congress, Prints and Photographs Division; (right): Library of Congress, Prints and Photographs Division

growing power of management. Railroad "brotherhoods" furnished insurance for those hurt or killed on the accident-plagued lines. Largely local and exclusively male, these early unions remained weak and unconnected to each other as well as to the growing mass of less skilled workers.

After the war a group of craft unions, brotherhoods, and reformers united skilled and unskilled workers in a nationwide organization. The National Labor Union (NLU) hailed the virtues of a simpler United States, when workers controlled their workday, earned a decent living, and had time to be good informed citizens. NLU leaders attacked the wage system as unfair and enslaving and urged workers to manage their own factories. By the early 1870s NLU ranks swelled to more than 600,000.

Among the gains it sought, the NLU pressed for the eight-hour workday, the most popular labor demand of the era. Workers saw it as a way not merely of limiting their time on the job but of limiting the power of employers over their lives. "Eight hours for work; eight hours for rest; eight hours for what we will!" proclaimed a banner at one labor rally. Despite the popularity of the issue, the NLU languished during the depression of 1873.

The Knights of Labor

The Knights of Labor >> More successful was a national union born in secrecy. In 1869 Uriah Stephens and nine Philadelphia garment cutters founded the Noble and Holy Order of the Knights of Labor. They draped themselves in ritual and regalia to deepen their sense of solidarity and met in secret to evade hostile owners. The Knights remained small and fraternal for a decade. Their strongly Protestant tone repelled Catholics, who made up almost half the workforce in many industries.

In 1879 the Knights elected Terence V. Powderly as their Grand Master Workman. Handsome, dynamic, Irish, and Catholic, Powderly threw off the Knights' secrecy, dropped their rituals, and opened their ranks. He called for "one big union" of skilled and unskilled, men and women, natives and immigrants, all religions, all races. By 1886 membership had leapt to more than 700,000, including nearly 30,000 African Americans and 3,000 women.

Like the NLU, the Knights of Labor looked to abolish the wage system and in its place create a cooperative economy of worker-owned businesses. The Knights set up more than 140 cooperative workshops. Workers shared decisions and profits, and sponsored some 200 political candidates. To tame the new industrial order, they supported the eight-hour workday and the regulation of trusts. Underlying this program was a moral vision of society. If only people renounced greed, laziness, and dishonesty, Powderly argued, corruption and class division would disappear. Democracy would flourish. To reform citizens inside and outside of the workplace, the Knights promoted the prohibition of child labor, convict labor, and liquor.

It was one thing to proclaim a moral vision for his union, but quite another to coordinate the activities of so many members. Locals resorted to strikes and violence, actions Powderly condemned. In the mid-1880s such stoppages wrung concessions from the western railroads, but the organization soon became associated with unsuccessful strikes and violent extremists. By 1890 the Knights of Labor faced extinction.

The American Federation of Labor

The American Federation of Labor >> The Knights' position as the premier union in the nation was taken by the rival American Federation of Labor (AFL). The AFL reflected the practicality of its leader, Samuel Gompers. Born in a London tenement, the son of a Jewish cigar maker, in 1863 he had emigrated with his family to New York's Lower East Side. Unlike the visionary Powderly, Gompers accepted capitalism and the wage system. He rejected resistance and visionary goals and instead sought accommodation with owners. What he wanted was "pure and simple unionism"—higher wages, fewer hours, improved safety, more benefits.

⌃ This 1883 political cartoon depicts a mismatched jousting contest between "Monopoly" and "Labor." Such cartoons were filled with symbols. Why, for instance, does the larger knight have wheels? Why use the color scheme for the two contestants? Some of the labels may be hard to read, but it's possible to guess where they belong. Where would you place the label "Subsidized press" and why? "Poverty"? "Strike"? "Corruption of the Legislature"?
Library of Congress, Prints and Photographs Division

Gompers chose to organize highly skilled craft workers because they were difficult to replace. He then bargained with employers, using strikes and boycotts only as last resorts. With the Cigar Makers' Union as his base, Gompers helped create the first national federation of craft unions in 1881. In 1886 it was reorganized as the American Federation of Labor. Twenty-five labor groups joined, representing some 150,000 workers. Stressing gradual, concrete gains, he made the AFL the most powerful union in the country. By 1901 it had more than a million members, almost a third of all skilled workers in the United States.

Gompers was less interested in vertical integration: combining skilled and unskilled workers. For most of his career he preserved the privileges of male craft workers and accepted their prejudices against women, Blacks, and immigrants. Only two locals–the Cigar Makers' Union and the Typographers' Union–enrolled women. Most affiliates restricted Black membership through high entrance fees and other discriminatory practices.

Despite the success of the AFL the laboring classes did not organize themselves as systematically as the barons of industry. At the turn of the century, union membership included less than 10 percent of industrial workers. Separated by different languages and nationalities, divided by issues of race and gender, most workers resisted unionization during the nineteenth century. In fact, a strong strain of individualism often made them regard all collective action as un-American.

The Limits of Industrial Systems >> As managers
sought to increase their control over the workplace, workers often found themselves at the mercy of the new industrial order. Even in boom times, one in three workers was out of a job at least three or four months a year.

When a worker's pay dropped and frustration mounted, when a mother worked all night and fell asleep during the day while caring for her children, when food prices suddenly jumped, violence might erupt. "A mob of 1,000 people, with women in the lead, marched through the Jewish quarter of Williamsburg last evening and wrecked half a dozen butcher shops," reported the *New York Times* in 1902.

In the late nineteenth century a wave of labor activism swept the nation. More often than mob violence, strikes and boycotts challenged the authority of employers. Generally peaceful, they expressed working-class identity and discontent. Most strikes broke out spontaneously, organized by informal leaders in a factory. Thousands of rallies and work stoppages were staged as well, often on behalf of the eight-hour workday, in good times and bad, by union and nonunion workers alike.

In 1877 the country's first nationwide strike opened an era of confrontation between labor and management. When the Baltimore and Ohio Railroad cut wages by 20 percent, a crew in Martinsburg, West Virginia, seized the local depot and blocked the line. Two-thirds of the nation's track shut down in sympathy. When companies hired strikebreakers, workers torched rail yards, smashed engines and cars, and tore up track. Local police, state militia, and federal troops finally crushed the strike after 12 bloody days. The Great Railroad Strike of 1877 left 100 people dead and $10 million worth of railroad property in rubble. "This may be the beginning of a great civil war . . . between labor and capital," warned one newspaper.

The Civil War was still fresh in the minds of residents of Atlanta when 3,000 laundresses struck for higher wages in

⌃ In this painting by Robert Koehler, *The Strike* (1886), labor confronts management in a strike that may soon turn bloody. One worker reaches for a stone as an anxious mother and her daughter look on.
Library of Congress, Prints and Photographs Division

1881. Over 98 percent of the city's domestic workers were African American women. Laundresses were among the most privileged domestics because they did not live in the homes where they worked. They washed clothes in common spaces in their own neighborhoods, where they built first social, then political networks. In 1881, they formed the Washer Society and threatened to refuse to wash the city's clothes unless their demands for higher wages were met. Little came of the strike, but it showed the appeal of organized dissent against economic exploitation and laid the groundwork for later civil rights protests.

In 1886 tension between labor and capital exploded in the "Great Upheaval"—a series of strikes, boycotts, and rallies that strengthened bonds among workers. These disruptions also turned national sympathies against labor. One of the most violent episodes occurred at Haymarket Square in Chicago. A group of anarchists were protesting the recent killing of workers by police at the McCormick Harvesting Company. As rain drenched the small crowd, police moved in and ordered everyone out of the square. Suddenly a bomb exploded. One officer was killed, and 6 others were mortally wounded. When police opened fire, the crowd fired back. Nearly 70 more police officers were injured, and at least 4 civilians died.

Conservatives charged that radicals were responsible for the "Haymarket Massacre." Ordinary citizens who had supported labor grew fearful of its power to spark violence and disorder. Though the bomb thrower was never identified, eight anarchists were found guilty of conspiracy to murder. Seven were sentenced to death. Cities enlarged their police forces, and states built more National Guard armories in middle-class neighborhoods to protect them from labor upheavals.

Management Strikes Back >> Beginning in 1892, a second surge of labor activism erupted. In the silver mines of Coeur d'Alene, Idaho, and the coal mines near Tracy City, Tennessee, strikes flared and failed. In July, at Andrew Carnegie's steel mill in Homestead, Pennsylvania, manager Henry Clay Frick announced that no union members could work there any longer, despite having negotiated a contract with the Amalgamated Association of Iron and Steel Workers. When the workers struck, Frick enlisted paramilitary support from the Pinkerton Detective Agency. Three hundred armed Pinkertons waged a fierce battle with the strikers and lost, but not before three Pinkertons and seven workers had been killed. After an appeal from Frick, the governor of Pennsylvania sent 8,000 state militia to restore order. The strike was broken, the mill reopened, and the union was smashed.

The broadest confrontation between labor and management took place two years later in 1894. A terrible depression had shaken the economy for almost a year when George Pullman, owner of the Palace Car factory and inventor of the plush railroad car, laid off workers and cut wages. At the same time, he kept rents high on company-owned housing in Pullman, Illinois, the site of his factory. It was there that the cars carrying T. S. Hudson, our British tourist scampering across the United States, were made.

In 1894, Pullman's workers struck. They convinced the new American Railway Union (ARU) to support them by boycotting all trains with Pullman cars. The strike spread to 27 states and territories. Anxious railroad owners appealed to President Grover Cleveland for federal help. On the slim pretext that the strike obstructed mail delivery (strikers had actually been willing to handle mail trains without Pullman cars), Cleveland secured a court order halting the strike and called several thousand special deputies into Chicago to enforce it. In the rioting that followed, 12 people died and scores were arrested. But the strike was quashed.

In all the labor disputes in this era the central issue was the power to shape the new industrial systems. Employers always enjoyed the advantage. They hired and fired workers, set the terms of employment, and ruled the workplace. They forced workers to sign "yellow dog" contracts, forbidding them from joining unions. Blacklists circulated the names of labor organizers. Lockouts kept protesting workers from plants, and labor spies infiltrated their associations. With a growing pool of labor and support from the government, employers could replace strikers and break strikes.

In addition, businesses used a powerful new legal weapon, the **injunction**, to attack labor. These court orders prohibited certain actions, including strikes, by barring workers from interfering with their employer's business. Just such an order had brought federal deputies into the Pullman strike and put Eugene Debs, head of the railway union, behind bars.

> **injunction** court order requiring individuals or groups to participate in or refrain from a certain action.

✔ REVIEW

Through what means, organized and unorganized, did workers respond to industrialization?

History in Global Context >> In a matter of only 30 or 40 years, the new industrial order transformed the landscape of the United States and much of the world. Railroads led the way. In Great Britain, some 20,000 miles of track covered the country by the 1870s, while Germany and France built even larger systems. Japan began constructing its network in the 1870s. In India, the British built the world's fourth-longest railway system. None outstripped the United States. By 1915 its rail network was longer than the next seven-largest systems combined.

With remarkable speed, networks of communication and transportation spread across the globe. Underwater telegraph cables were laid from the United States to Europe in 1866, to Australia in 1871 and 1872, to Latin America in 1872 and 1873, and to West Africa by 1886. The completion of the Suez Canal in 1869 sliced thousands of miles from the journey between Europe and Asia and hastened the switch from sail-powered to steam-driven ships.

As these networks tied together national economies, swings in the business cycle produced global consequences. When an Austrian bank failed in 1873, depression soon reached the United States. In the mid-1880s and again in the mid-1890s, recessions drove prices down and unemployment up across the world.

Industrial workers bore the brunt of the burden. In Europe more than the United States, they had greater success in unionizing, especially after anti-combination laws forbidding strikes were abolished after 1850. By 1900 British unions had signed up 2 million workers. As strikes multiplied and labor unions became more powerful, industrializing nations passed legislation that included the first social security systems and health insurance plans. Neither came to the United States until the Great Depression of the 1930s.

CHAPTER SUMMARY

In the last third of the nineteenth century, a new industrial order reshaped the United States.

- New systems—of resource development, technology, invention, transportation, communications, finance, corporate management, and labor—boosted industrial growth and productivity in the late nineteenth century.
- Businesses, pioneered by the railroads, grew big, expanding vertically and horizontally to curb costs and competition and to increase control and efficiency.
- Industrialization came at a price.
  - ► Workers found their power, job satisfaction, and free time reduced as their numbers in factories mushroomed.
  - ► The environment was degraded.
  - ► A vicious cycle of boom and bust afflicted the economy.
- Workers both resisted and accommodated the new industrial order.
  - ► Some resisted through informal mechanisms such as slowdowns, absenteeism, and quitting and through spontaneous and formal ones, including radical unions like the Knights of Labor.
  - ► Other workers were more accommodating, creating "pure-and-simple" unions, such as the American Federation of Labor, that accepted the prevailing system of private ownership and wage labor while bargaining for better wages and working conditions.
- The benefits of industrialization were equally undeniable.
  - ► Life improved materially for many Americans.
  - ► The real wages of even industrial workers climbed.

Digging Deeper

Robert Gordon, *The Rise and Fall of American Growth: The U.S. Standard of Living Since the Civil War* (2016), argues that the United States will never have another era as fruitful as the late nineteenth century. For a useful introduction, see Edward C. Kirkland, *Industry Comes of Age: Business, Labor, and Public Policy, 1860–1897* (1967). Thomas Piketty's sweeping *Capital in the Twenty-First Century* (2013) examines wealth and income inequality across three centuries in Europe and the United States. Steven Stoll, *Ramp Hollow: The Ordeal of Appalachia* (2017), shows how industrialism systematically displaced the region's subsistence farmers.

The best overview of American labor is American Social History Project, *Who Built America? Working People and the Nation's Economy, Politics, Culture, & Society,* Volume Two: *From the Gilded Age to the Present* (1992). Herbert Gutman, *Work, Culture, and Society in Industrializing America: Essays in American Working-Class History* (1976), explores the development of working-class communities in the nineteenth century; while David Montgomery assesses the impact of industrialization on American labor in *The Fall of the House of Labor: The Workplace, the State, and American Labor Activism, 1865–1925* (1987). Leon Fink, *Workingmen's Democracy: The Knights of Labor and American Politics* (1983), examines early efforts of the Knights of Labor to challenge corporate capitalism. Alice Kessler-Harris, *Out to Work: A History of Wage-Earning Women in the United States* (1982), surveys female wage earners and their effect on American culture, family life, and values. Thomas G. Andrews's *Killing for Coal: America's Deadliest Labor War* (2008), uses the Ludlow Massacre and the Colorado Coalfield War of 1913–1914 to examine the changes in the industrial United States in the late nineteenth and early twentieth centuries.

Ron Chernow's *Titan: The Life of John D. Rockefeller Sr.* (1998); and Jean Strouse's definitive *Morgan: American Financier* (1999) help debunk the image of business leaders as "robber barons" without minimizing their ruthlessness. David Nasaw's *Andrew Carnegie* (2006) gives us the most human portrait of the legendary steel baron; for the rise of big railroads, consult T. J. Stiles, *The First Tycoon: The Epic Life of Cornelius Vanderbilt* (2009). Charlotte Gray, *Reluctant Genius: The Passionate and Inventive Mind of Alexander Graham Bell* (2006), explores the invention of the telephone and the struggle to control its future. Edmund Morris's *Edison* (2019) offers a rich, illuminating biography of the inventor. Richard White's *Railroaded: The Transcontinentals and the Making of Modern America* (2012) makes a powerful case for the profligacy of the transcontinental railroad lines in a revisionist retelling of the epic story.

20 The Rise of an Urban Order

1870–1900

A stiff wind out of the southwest sent swirling bands of flame into the air, spreading the blaze that became the Great Chicago Fire of 1871. But the city would be rebuilt with remarkable speed, for it was located at the center of a new urban-industrial complex.

Chicago History Museum/Contributor/Getty Images

>> An American Story
"THE DOGS OF HELL"

"The dogs of hell were upon the housetops . . . bounding from one to another," gasped Horace White, a Chicago reporter, as he described the fire consuming his city on a hot October day in 1871. Whipped by dry prairie winds, tornadoes of flame whirled through Chicago, at times faster than fleeing residents. The flaming twisters, called "fire devils" by the locals, leapt from building to building, block to block, spinning and spewing fiery debris that fed the inferno. The heat was so intense that stone walls collapsed with a force that

shook the earth. A burning ember set the roof of the Waterworks ablaze, leaving the city without enough water to fight the fire. Even the Chicago River burst into flame as industrial grease and oil floating on its surface ignited.

The Great Chicago Fire was the worst disaster in the city's history. When the flames finally burned themselves out more than a day later, a smoldering scar of cinders and rubble four miles long and three-quarters of a mile wide cut through the city. The fire destroyed the business district and left a third of the city's 300,000 residents homeless. As many as 300 people died. Could the city—any city— recover from such a calamity?

Unitarian minister Robert Collyer had the answer. "We have not lost, first, our geography," he told his congregation, displaying little doubt that geography was destiny. "Nature called the lakes, the forests, the prairies together in convention long before we were born, and they decided that on this spot a great city would be built." Linking eastern railroads and the Great Lakes with the West, Chicago's prime location at the crossroads of continental commerce had not moved one inch.

More than geography favored recovery. An astounding assortment of assets survived the fire. The city's stockyards and packinghouses, the center of a meat industry that made Chicago "Hog Butcher of the World," lay untouched. Along the wharves on the river, lumberyards and mills miraculously survived. To the west, two-thirds of the city's grain elevators still stood, their giant silos holding corn, wheat, and other grains for processing and shipment. And the rails that connected Chicago to the rest of the country remained largely intact.

With opportunity beckoning, people poured into the city. Chicago grew vertically, attracting a school of young architects whose soaring structures created a new cityscape. It grew horizontally, with new rail and telephone lines spreading onto empty prairie. By 1900 Chicago was the fastest-growing city in the world, with a population that topped a million and a half people.

Other American cities flourished as well. In 1898 New York's five boroughs merged into one giant metropolis. As in Chicago, a series of bridges and rail lines allowed New York and other industrial cities to function with new precision and efficiency on an unprecedented scale. The industrial city reshaped the environment, created a new urban landscape, and gave opportunity to politicians drawn from the ranks of ordinary people, many of them immigrants or their children. They came from the streets and saloons, the slums and tenements, the firehouses and funeral homes. Their families had only recently arrived in the United States. While the Irish of Tammany Hall ran New York City, Germans governed St. Louis, Scandinavians Minneapolis, and Jews San Francisco.

In an earlier age, the United States had been an agrarian republic where personal relationships were grounded in small communities. Political leaders came from the ranks of the wealthy and native-born. By the late nineteenth century, the country was in the midst of an urban explosion. Industrial cities of unparalleled size and diversity remade American life. They lured people from all over the globe, created tensions between natives and newcomers, and refashioned the social order in a fluid urban world. A new urban age was dawning. The golden door of opportunity opened onto the city. <<

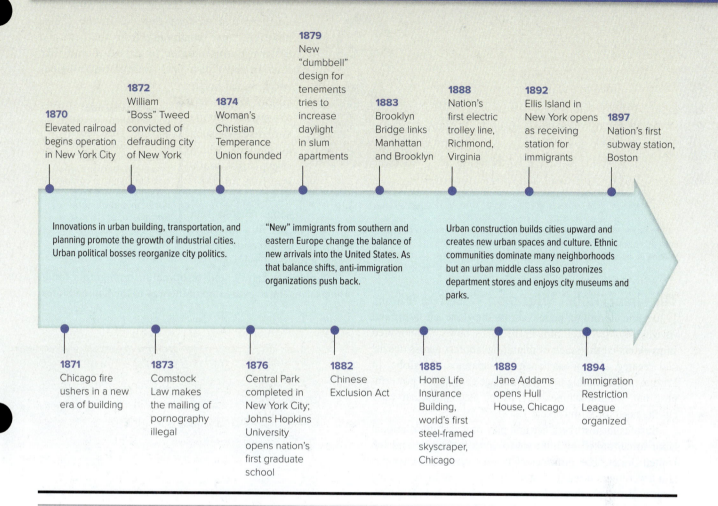

1870 Elevated railroad begins operation in New York City

1872 William "Boss" Tweed convicted of defrauding city of New York

1874 Woman's Christian Temperance Union founded

1879 New "dumbbell" design for tenements tries to increase daylight in slum apartments

1883 Brooklyn Bridge links Manhattan and Brooklyn

1888 Nation's first electric trolley line, Richmond, Virginia

1892 Ellis Island in New York opens as receiving station for immigrants

1897 Nation's first subway station, Boston

Innovations in urban building, transportation, and planning promote the growth of industrial cities. Urban political bosses reorganize city politics.

"New" immigrants from southern and eastern Europe change the balance of new arrivals into the United States. As that balance shifts, anti-immigration organizations push back.

Urban construction builds cities upward and creates new urban spaces and culture. Ethnic communities dominate many neighborhoods but an urban middle class also patronizes department stores and enjoys city museums and parks.

1871 Chicago fire ushers in a new era of building

1873 Comstock Law makes the mailing of pornography illegal

1876 Central Park completed in New York City; Johns Hopkins University opens nation's first graduate school

1882 Chinese Exclusion Act

1885 Home Life Insurance Building, world's first steel-framed skyscraper, Chicago

1889 Jane Addams opens Hull House, Chicago

1894 Immigration Restriction League organized

A NEW URBAN AGE

Industrialization created the modern city with its great investment banks, smoky mills and dingy sweatshops, railroad yards, tenements, mansions, and new department stores. Opportunity drew people from as near as the countryside and as far away as Italy, Russia, Armenia, and China. By the end of the nineteenth century the United States had entered a new urban age, with tens of millions of "urbanites," an urban landscape, and a growing urban culture.

The Urban Explosion >> During the 50 years after the Civil War the population of the United States tripled—from 31 million to 92 million. Yet the number of Americans living in cities increased nearly sevenfold. By 1910 nearly half the nation lived in cities large and small.

Cities grew in every region of the country. In the Northeast and upper Midwest, early industrialization created more cities than in the West and the South, although big cities sprouted there as well. Atlanta, Nashville, and later Dallas and Houston boomed under the influence of railroads. By 1900 Los Angeles, with its 100,000 residents, boasted a population second only to San Francisco on the West Coast.

Large urban centers dominated whole regions, tying the country together in a vast urban network. New York, the nation's banker, printer, and chief marketplace, ruled the East; Chicago with its stockyards, silos, and prime location, the Midwest. Smaller cities operated within narrower spheres of influence and often specialized. Milwaukee was famous for beer, Tulsa for oil, and Hershey, Pennsylvania, for chocolate.

Cities shaped the natural environment hundreds of miles beyond their limits. Chicago became a powerful agent of ecological change. As its lines of commerce and industry radiated outward, the city transformed the rich ecosystems of the West. Wheat to feed Chicago's millions replaced sheltering prairie grasses. Great stands of white pine in Wisconsin vanished, only to reappear in the furniture and frames of Chicago houses, or as fence rails shipped to prairie farms.

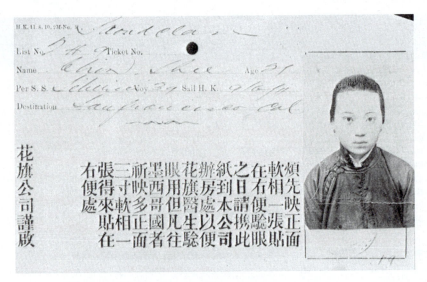

Chin Shee was 21 years old and bound for San Francisco at the time this boarding pass was issued in Hong Kong in 1911.
National Archives & Records Administration

右張三新墨眼花瓣紙之在軟煩
便得寸映西用旗房到日 右相先
處來軟多哥但醫處木請便一映
貼相正國凡生以公攜驗張正
在一面者往驗便司此眼貼面

花旗公司謹啟

Immigration from Europe dwarfed all others as new regions of the continent contributed growing numbers of people. Earlier in the century, most European immigrants had come from northern and western Europe. In the 1880s, however, **"new" immigrants** from southern and eastern Europe began to arrive. Some, like Russian and Polish Jews, were fleeing religious and political persecution. Others left to evade famine and diseases such as cholera, which swept across southern Italy in 1887. Most came for the same reasons that moved migrants from the countryside: a job, more money, a fresh start.

"new" immigrants newcomers from eastern and southern Europe who were largely non-Protestant (Catholics, Jews, and Russian Orthodox Christians) in contrast to earlier arrivals from northern and western Europe.

Ambitious, hardy, and resourceful, immigrants found themselves tested every step of the way to the United States.

The Great Global Migration >> Between 1820 and 1920 some 60 million people across the globe left farms and villages for cities. Beginning in the 1870s, new steam-powered ships extended the reach of migrating laborers across oceans and created a labor exchange that spanned the globe. In Europe mushrooming populations gave emigrants a powerful push out, while machines such as the mechanical harvester cut the need for farmworkers.

Surplus farmworkers became part of a vast international labor force, pulled by industry to cities in Europe and the United States. The prospect of factory work for better pay and fewer hours lured the young. In the United States, young farm women spearheaded the urban migration. Mechanization and the rise of commercial agriculture made them less valuable in the fields; mass-produced goods from mail-order houses made them less useful at home. City factories and offices furnished the employment they needed.

Asia sent comparatively fewer newcomers to the United States, Canada, and other industrializing nations. Those that came followed migration patterns similar to those of workers leaving Europe and relocated for many of the same reasons. Between 1850 and 1882 rising taxes and rents on land and declining markets drove some 370,000 Chinese across the Pacific to the United States. Nearly 400,000 Japanese arrived between 1885 and 1924.

IMMIGRATION, 1870–1914

Between 1860 and 1920 immigration increased dramatically and the sources of immigrants shifted increasingly from northern Europe toward southeastern Europe.
In which year was the proportion of southeastern Europeans highest? About what percentage of the total did they comprise in that year?
Photo: Library of Congress, Prints and Photographs Division

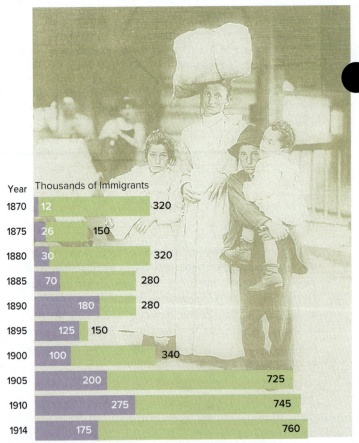

Year	Thousands of Immigrants (Southeastern Europeans)	(Northern Europeans)
1870	12	320
1875	26	150
1880	30	320
1885	70	280
1890	180	280
1895	125	150
1900	100	340
1905	200	725
1910	275	745
1914	175	760

Southeastern Europeans: Includes immigrants from Poland, Russia, Italy, and other Baltic and eastern European countries.

Northern Europeans: Includes immigrants from Great Britain, Ireland, Germany, and the Scandinavian countries.

Make a Case

Did massive immigration from eastern and southern Europe help or hinder the United States in the late nineteenth century? Might it have done both? How would we know?

Getting to a port city took time to make the overland trek and money to pay off border guards. It took another week or two to cross the Atlantic. Immigrants spent most of the voyage below decks in cramped, filthy compartments called "steerage." Most landed at New York's Castle Garden or the newer facility on nearby Ellis Island, opened in 1892. If arriving from Asia, they landed at Angel Island in San Francisco Bay. They had to pass a medical examination, have their names recorded by customs officials, and pay an entry tax. At any point, they could be detained or shipped home.

Most newcomers were young, between the ages of 15 and 40. Few spoke English or had skills or much education. Unlike earlier arrivals, who were mostly Protestant, these new immigrants worshiped in Catholic, Greek, or Russian Orthodox churches or Jewish synagogues. Almost two-thirds were men. A large number came for money to buy land or start businesses back home. Some stayed and sent for relatives. Those returning home were common enough to be labeled "birds of passage." Still, by 1900 some 30 million immigrants had arrived. They made up nearly 15 percent of the population.

Holding the City Together >> Cities of the late nineteenth century exhibited a ringed pattern of settlement as sprawling industrial cities spilled across their colonial limits. The wealthy lived at the outskirts of the city, the middle class closer in, and the poor and working poor at the industrial center.

For all their differences, the circles of settlement held together as part of an interdependent whole. One reason was an evolving system of urban transportation. By the mid-nineteenth century, horse-drawn railways were conveying some 35 million people a year in New York. Their problems were legendary: so slow, a person could walk faster; so crowded (according to Mark Twain), you "had to hang on by your eyelashes and your toenails"; so dirty, people had to pick their way through tons of horse manure left daily in the streets.

Civic leaders came to understand that the modern city could not survive, much less grow, without improved transportation. San Francisco installed trolley cars pulled by steam-driven cables in 1873. The innovation worked so well in the hilly city that Chicago, Seattle, and others installed cable systems in the 1880s. Some cities experimented with elevated trestles to carry steam locomotives or cable lines high above crowded streets. None of the breakthroughs quite did the trick. Cables remained slow and unreliable; the elevated railways, or "els," were dirty, ugly, and noisy.

Electricity rescued city travelers. In 1888 Frank Julian Sprague, a naval engineer who had once worked for Thomas Edison, installed the first electric trolley line in Richmond, Virginia. Electrified streetcars were soon speeding along at 12 miles an hour, twice as fast as horses. By 1902, electricity drove nearly all city railways. Sprague's breakthroughs also meant that "subways" could be built beneath ground without tunnels filling with smoke and soot from steam engines. Boston built the first underground electric line between 1895 and 1897. New York followed in 1904, with a subway from the southern tip of Manhattan north to Harlem.

The rich had long been able to keep homes outside city limits, traveling to and fro in private carriages. New systems of mass transit freed the middle class and even the poor to live miles from work. For a nickel or two, anyone could ride a streetcar from central shopping and business districts to the suburban fringes. A network of moving vehicles held the segmented and sprawling city together and widened its reach out to "streetcar suburbs."

Bridges and Skyscrapers >> Since cities often grew along rivers and harbors, their separate parts sometimes had to be joined over water. The principles of building large river bridges had already been worked out by the railroads. It remained for a German immigrant, John Roebling, and his son, Washington, to make the bridge a symbol of urban growth.

Their creation—the legendary Brooklyn Bridge linking Manhattan with Brooklyn—took 13 years to complete, cost $15 million and 20 lives, and killed designer John Roebling. When it opened in 1883, it stretched more than a mile across the East River, with passage broad enough for a footpath, two double carriage lanes, and two railroad lines. Its arches were cut like giant cathedral windows, and its supporting cables hung, said an awestruck observer, "like divine messages from above." Soon other suspension bridges were spanning the railroad yards in St. Louis and the bay at Galveston, Texas.

Even as late as 1880, church steeples towered over squat factories and office buildings. Growing congestion and increasing land values challenged architects to search for ways to make buildings taller. Thin air became valuable real estate. In place of thick, heavy walls of brick that restricted factory floor space, builders used cast-iron columns. The new "cloudscrapers" were strong, durable, and fire-resistant, ideal for warehouses and also for office buildings and department stores.

Steel, with greater flexibility and strength than iron, turned cloudscrapers into skyscrapers. William LeBaron Jenney first used steel in his 10-story Home Life Insurance

RIDING THE CHICAGO LOOP

Railroads shaped travel across the nation but also within cities, first on city streets, then elevated above them, and finally in subterranean tunnels below them. This map shows one of Chicago's earliest elevated railway systems. "Els" first appeared in Chicago in 1892 as a way of providing mass transit across the city without disrupting street traffic. The earliest lines did not extend downtown, but by 1897 elevated railways were whisking passengers from the outskirts to the center of the city. The circular elevated line downtown was known as "the Loop."

Library of Congress, Geography and Map Division [g4104c pm001523]

MAP READING

1. Chicago is located along the shore of Lake Michigan. Where is the lake on the map? Where is the Chicago River?
2. Locate "the Loop" on the map.
3. Where is the Chicago Rock Island and Pacific Railway Station? Chicago is nowhere near the Pacific Ocean. Why does the railroad have "Pacific" as a part of its name?

MAP INTERPRETATION

1. This map shows the location of the El's tracks and its stations, but also those for the Rock Island and Pacific Railway (marked in red as A, B, and C). Is the map promoting the El or the Rock Island Railway? How can you tell?
2. The drawing at lower-left is labeled "Elevated Station of the 'Rock Island' Van Buren St. Station" and shows a large flag proclaiming "Rock Island Route." Where is the station on the map? Why draw the station larger-than-life?
3. In this new industrial age, why is it significant that the local and national rail systems are shown on this city map?

Designed by Chicago architect Daniel Burham and completed in 1902, the Fuller Building quickly became known as the "Flatiron Building" for its uniquely triangular shape. With a steel frame, it soared to a height of 22 stories, making it one of the tallest structures in New York City. "I found myself agape," wrote science fiction novelist H. G. Wells when he saw the building, "admiring a sky-scraper, the prow of the Flat-iron Building, to be particular, ploughing up through the traffic of Broadway and Fifth Avenue in the afternoon light."
Library of Congress, Prints and Photographs Division

Building (1885) in Chicago. By the end of the century, steel frames and girders raised buildings to 30 stories or more. New York City's triangular Flatiron Building used the new technology to project an angular, yet remarkably delicate elegance. In Chicago, Daniel Burnham's Reliance Building (1890) made such heavy use of new plate glass windows that contemporaries called it "a glass tower fifteen stories high."

Slum and Tenement >> Far below the skyscrapers lay the slums and **tenements** of the inner city. In cramped rooms and sunless hallways, along narrow alleys and in flooded basements, lived the city poor. They often worked there in "sweaters' shops," where as many as 18 people labored and slept in foul two-room flats.

> **tenement** building often in disrepair and usually five or six stories in height, in which cheap apartments were rented to tenants.

Slum dwellers usually lived on poor diets that left them vulnerable to epidemics, especially in the densely packed quarters of inner cities. Cholera, typhoid, and an outbreak of yellow fever in Memphis in the 1870s killed tens of thousands. Tuberculosis was deadlier still. Slum children—all city children—were most susceptible to such diseases. Almost a quarter of American children born in cities in 1890 never saw their first birthday.

All too often cities dumped waste into old private vaults or rivers used for drinking water. Sanitation became as vital to city growth as transportation. The installation of sewage and water purification systems reduced the incidents of disease. The modern flush toilet came into use only after the turn of the century. Until then people relied on water closets and communal privies, some of which catered to as many as 800.

Slum housing was often more dangerous than polluted water. The tubercle bacillus flourished in musty, windowless tenements. In 1879 New York enacted a new housing law requiring a window in all bedrooms of new apartment buildings. Architect James E. Ware won a competition with a creative design that contained an indentation on both sides of the building. When two tenements abutted, the indentations formed a narrow shaft for air and light that led to the nickname "dumbbell" tenement. From above, the buildings resembled giant dumbbells and packed up to 16 families on a floor.

Originally hailed as an innovation, Ware's dumbbell tenement spread through such cities as Cleveland, Cincinnati, and Boston "like a scab," said an unhappy reformer. The airshafts became giant silos for trash, which blocked what little light had entered and, worse still, served as breeding grounds for disease and carried fires from one story to the next. When the New York housing commission met in 1900, it concluded that conditions were worse than when reformers had started 33 years earlier.

 REVIEW

How did industrial cities grow and at what costs?

⌃ "Dumbbell" tenements were designed to use every inch of available space in the standard 25-by-200-foot city lot while providing ventilation and reducing the spread of disease.
Irma and Paul Milstein Division of United States History, Local History and Genealogy/The New York Public Library

RUNNING AND REFORMING THE CITY

Every new arrival to the city brought dreams and altogether too many needs. Schools and houses had to be built, streets paved, garbage collected, sewers dug, fires fought, utility lines laid. As running the city became a full-time job, a new breed of politician rose to the task. So, too, did a new breed of reformer, determined clean up corruption and to help the disadvantaged cope with urban life.

The need for change was clear. Many city charters dated from the eighteenth century and included a paralyzing system of checks and balances. Mayors vetoed city councils; councils ignored mayors. Jealous state legislatures allowed cities only the most limited and unpopular taxes, such as those on property. At the same time, city governments were often decentralized—fragmented, scattered branches often at odds with one another. Each branch was a tiny kingdom with its own regulations and taxing authority. As immigrants and rural newcomers flocked to factories and tenements, the structures of urban government strained to adapt.

Boss Rule >> "Why must there be a boss," news reporter Lincoln Steffens asked Boss Richard Croker of New York,

"when we've got a mayor—and a city council?" "That's why," Croker said. "It's because we've got a mayor and a council and judges—and—a hundred other men to deal with." Cities were so disorganized that they could not provide the leadership required to run them. Boss rule supplied the centralization, authority, and services needed.

Bosses ruled through the **political machine.** Often, as with New York City's Tammany Hall, machines dated back to the late eighteenth and early nineteenth centuries. Like Tammany, they began as fraternal and charitable organizations. Over the years, they became centers of political power. In New York the machine was Democratic; in Philadelphia, Republican. Machines could even be found in rural areas. In Duval County, Texas, the Spanish-speaking Anglo boss Archie Parr molded a powerful alliance with Mexican American landowners.

> **political machine**
> hierarchical political organization developed in the nineteenth century that controlled the activities of a political party and was usually headed by a political boss.

In an age of enterprise, the boss operated his political machine like a corporation. His office might be a saloon, a funeral home, or, like New York's George Washington Plunkitt's, a shoeshine stand. His managers were party activists, connected in a corporate-like hierarchy. Local committee members reported to district captains, captains to district leaders, district leaders to the boss or bosses who directed the machine.

With no mincing of words, William M. Tweed of New York was featured as "Our Boss" on a tobacco label (*left*). Tweed made millions in graft but eventually wound up in jail wearing a different sort of "pinstripe" suit, as in this cartoon by Thomas Nast (*right*).
(left): Library of Congress, Prints and Photographs Division; *(right):* Library of Congress, Prints and Photographs Division

The goods and services of the machine were basics: a Christmas turkey, a load of coal for the winter, jobs for the unemployed, English-language classes for recent immigrants. Bosses sponsored fun, too: sports teams, glee clubs, balls, and barbecues. In return, citizens expressed their gratitude at the ballot box by voting to keep bosses and their machines in power.

When grateful voters were not enough, bosses marshaled the "graveyard vote" by drawing names from tombstones to pad lists of registered voters. They hired "repeaters," who voted more than once under phony names. When reformers introduced the Australian (secret) ballot in the 1880s to prevent fraud, bosses pulled the "Tasmanian dodge" by premarking ballots for voters. Failing that, they dumped whole ballot boxes into rivers or used hired thugs to scare independent-minded voters from the polls.

Rewards, Accomplishments, and Costs >> Why
did bosses go to such lengths? Some simply loved the game of politics. More often, bosses loved the money and power they acquired from running the city. Their success was limited only by their ingenuity or the occasional victory of an outraged reformer. The record for brassiness must go to Boss William Tweed. During his reign in the 1860s and 1870s, Tweed swindled New York City out of a fortune. His masterpiece was a chunky three-story courthouse in Lower Manhattan originally budgeted at $250,000. When Tweed was through, the city had spent more than $13 million on it. Over 60 percent of it lined the pockets of Tweed and his cronies. Tweed died in prison, but with such profits to be made, it was small wonder that bosses nearly matched the emperors of Rome as builders.

In their fashion, bosses played a vital role in the industrial city. Rising from the bottom ranks, they guided immigrants into American life and helped some of the underprivileged up from poverty. They changed the urban landscape with a massive construction program and modernized city government by uniting it and making it work. Choosing the council members, municipal judges, mayors, and administrative officials, bosses exerted new control to provide the contracts and franchises to run cities. Such accomplishments fostered the notion that government could be called on to help the needy. The "welfare state," as yet unnamed and still decades away, had roots here.

The toll was often outrageous. Inflated taxes, extorted revenue, unpunished vice and crime were only the most obvious costs. Unsafe working and unhealthy living conditions often took lives. A woman whose family enjoyed a boss's Christmas turkey might be widowed by an accident to her husband in a sweatshop kept open by timely bribes to the local political club. Filthy buildings might claim her children's lives as corrupt inspectors ignored serious violations. Buying votes and selling favors, bosses turned democracy into a petty business—as much a "business," said George Washington Plunkitt, "as the grocery or dry-goods or the drug business."

Nativism, Revivals, and the Social Gospel >>
Urban blight and the condition of the poor inspired social as well as political activism, often within churches. Not all of it was constructive. The popular Congregationalist minister Josiah Strong concluded that the city was "a menace to society." Along with anxious economists and social workers, he blamed everything from corruption to

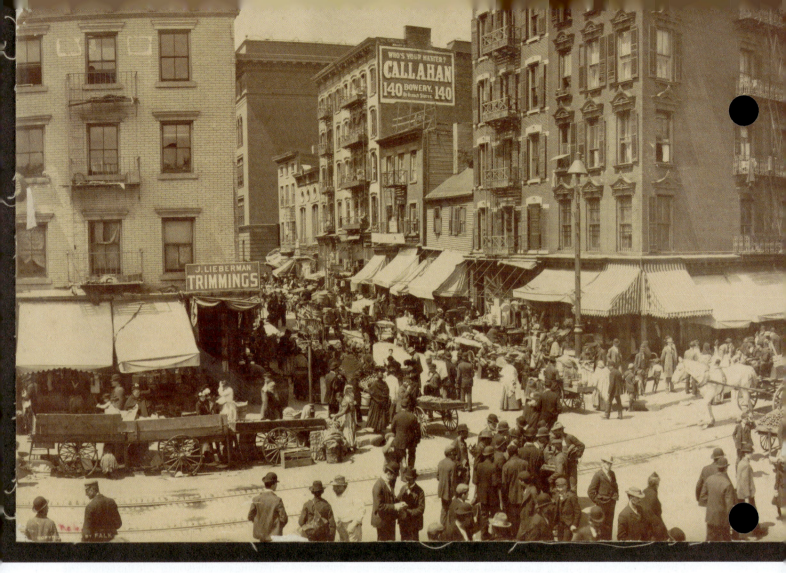

^^ Hester Street, Lower East Side, New York City.
Library of Congress, Prints and Photographs Division

unemployment on immigrant city dwellers and urged restricting their entry.

The depressions of the 1880s and 1890s sharpened anxieties. Nativism, a defensive and fearful nationalism, peaked as want and unemployment ignited prejudice. Organizations such as the new Immigration Restriction League attacked Catholics and foreigners. Already the victims of racial prejudice, the Chinese were easy targets. In 1882 Congress enacted the Chinese Exclusion Act banning the entry of Chinese laborers. The act was the first instance of race being used to exclude people from entry and represented a fateful step in the drive to restrict immigration.

THE GREAT FEAR OF THE PERIOD
THAT UNCLE SAM MAY BE SWALLOWED BY FOREIGNERS.

<< By the 1800s a flood of southern and eastern European immigrants were streaming into the new receiving center of Ellis Island in New York Harbor, while the relatively few Asian immigrants who arrived (most were barred from entry by the Chinese Exclusion Act of 1882) came through Angel Island in San Francisco Bay. The rapid rise in immigration ignited nativist fears that immigrants were taking over the country. In the 1870s cartoon pictured here, Irish and Chinese immigrants literally gobble up Uncle Sam.
Library of Congress, Prints and Photographs Division

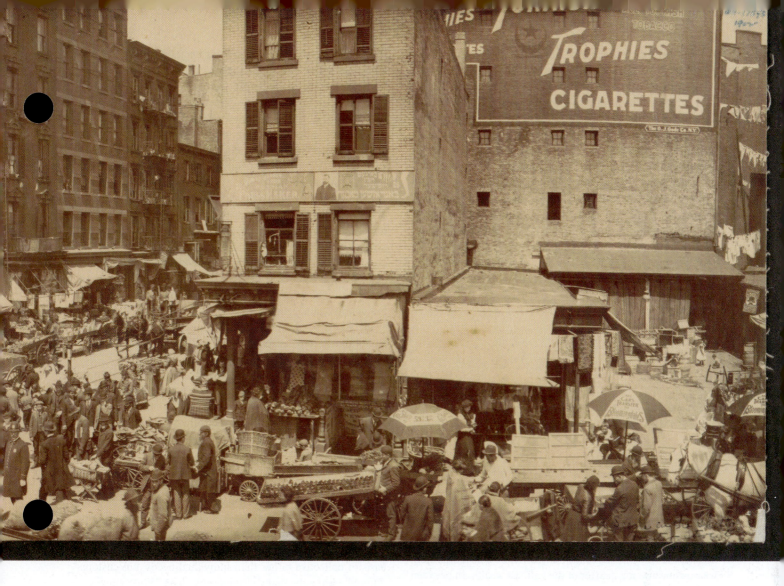

To bridge the gap between the middle class and the poor, some clergy took their missions to the slums. Beginning in 1870, Dwight Lyman Moody, a former shoe salesman, won armies of converts with revivals in Boston, Chicago, and other cities. The baseball player William Ashley "Billy" Sunday turned into an evangelist whose religious revivals attracted thousands. "Going to church doesn't make you a Christian," he told critics of his unorthodox preaching and revivals, "any more than going to a garage makes you a car." Evangelists helped found American branches of the British-born Young Men's Christian Association (YMCA) and Salvation Army.

A small group of ministers rejected the traditional notion that weak character explained sin and that society would be perfected only as individual sinners were converted. They spread a new "Social Gospel" that focused on improving the conditions of society to save individuals. In *Applied Christianity* (1886), the influential pastor Washington Gladden preached that the church must be responsible for correcting social injustices, including dangerous working conditions and unfair labor practices. Houses of worship, such as William Rainford's St. George's Episcopal Church in New York City, became centers of social activity, with boys' clubs, gymnasiums, libraries, glee clubs, and industrial training programs.

The Social Settlement Movement >> Church-sponsored programs sometimes repelled the immigrant poor, especially when they were seen as thinly disguised missionary efforts. Immigrants and other slum dwellers were more receptive to a bold experiment called the **settlement house**. Situated in the worst slums, often in renovated old houses, these early community centers were run by middle-class women and men to help the poor and foreign-born. At the turn of the century, there were more than 100 of them, the most famous being Jane Addams's Hull House in Chicago. In 1898 the Catholic Church sponsored

settlement house neighborhood center in which social reformers lived and worked among the poor, often in slum neighborhoods.

its first settlement house in New York City, and in 1900 Bronson House opened its doors to the Latino community in Los Angeles.

High purposes inspired settlement workers, who actually lived in the settlement houses. They left comfortable middle-class homes and dedicated themselves (like the "early Christians," said one) to service and sacrifice. They taught immigrants American ways and created a community spirit of "right living through social relations." Immigrants were also encouraged to preserve their heritages through festivals, parades, and museums. Settlement reformers furnished practical help, from day nurseries to English-language and cooking classes to playgrounds and libraries. Armed with statistics and their own experiences, they lobbied for social legislation to improve housing, women's working conditions, and public schools.

REVIEW

In what ways did boss rule represent "reform" of city government, and at whose expense did such reform come?

CITY LIFE

City life reflected the stratified nature of American society in the late-nineteenth century. Every city had its slums and tenements but also its fashionable avenues, where mansions housed the tiny one percent of city dwellers considered rich, who owned about a quarter of the nation's wealth. In between tenement and mansion lived the broad middle of urban society, which made up nearly a third of the population and owned about half the nation's wealth. With more money and leisure time than ever, the middle class was increasing its power and influence.

The Immigrant in the City >> When they put into port, the first thing immigrants were likely to see was a city. Perhaps it was Boston or New York City or Galveston, Texas, where an overflow of Jewish immigrants were directed beginning in 1907. Most immigrants, exhausted physically and financially, settled in cities.

Cities developed a well-defined mosaic of ethnic communities, since immigrants usually clustered together on the basis of their villages or provinces. But these neighborhoods were in constant flux. As many as half the residents moved every 10 years, often because of better-paying jobs or more members of their family working.

Ethnic communities served as havens from the strangeness of American society and springboards to a new life. From the moment they stepped off the boat, newcomers felt pressed to learn English, don American clothes, and drop their "greenhorn" ways. Yet in their neighborhoods they also found comrades who spoke their language, theaters that performed their plays and music, restaurants that served their food. Foreign-language newspapers reported events from both the old world and the new in a native tongue that first-generation immigrants could understand. Meanwhile, immigrant aid societies furnished assistance with housing and jobs and sponsored baseball teams, insurance programs, and English-language classes.

Houses of worship were always at the center of immigrant life. They often catered to the practices of individual towns or provinces. Occasionally they changed their ways under the cultural pressures of American life. The Irish dominated the American Catholic Church, and other immigrants formed new churches with priests from their homelands. Eastern European Jews began to break the old law against men sitting next to their wives and daughters in synagogues. The Orthodox churches of Armenians, Syrians, Romanians, and Serbians gradually lost their national identifications.

On the whole, immigrants married later and had more children than did the native-born. Greeks and eastern European Jews prearranged marriages, according to tradition. They imported "picture brides," betrothed by mail with a photograph. After marriage, men ruled the household, but women managed it. Although child-rearing practices varied, immigrants resisted the relative permissiveness of American parents. Youngsters were expected to contribute like little adults to family finances.

In these "family economies" of working-class immigrants, key decisions—over whether and whom to marry, over work and education, over when to leave home—were made on the basis of collective rather than individual needs, but customs differed among the many immigrant groups. While many valued the ideal of women staying home, financial reality often meant that women worked outside as well as inside the home. Italian women were more likely to stay home, taking in boarders or doing sewing, laundry, and other forms of piece work to earn money. Jewish women could often be found working alongside their husbands in a family-owned business. Though immigrant boys were more likely to be employed outside the home than girls, some daughters went to work at an early age so sons could continue their education. For other immigrant families, education for daughters was seen as the only path to well-paying jobs. Among still others, it was customary for one daughter to remain unmarried so she could care for younger siblings or aged parents.

The Chinese were an exception to the pattern. The ban on the immigration of Chinese laborers in the 1880s had frozen the gender ratio of Chinese communities into a curious imbalance. Like other immigrants, most Chinese newcomers had been single men. In the wake of the ban, those in the United States could not bring over their wives and families. Nor by law in 13 states could they marry white Americans. With few women, Chinese communities suffered from high rates of prostitution, large numbers of gangs and secret

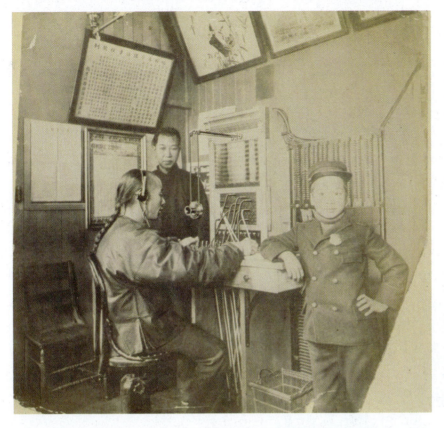

⌃ The first Chinese telephone operator in San Francisco's Chinatown, the largest community of Chinese outside Asia, is pictured here handling calls from local subscribers. The first switchboard was installed in 1894. Chinese operators had to memorize the names of their users because residents often asked to be connected by name, believing it was impolite to ask by number. This was no easy task. Some subscribers had the same name, so operators also had to learn the occupation and the address of each person on their service. And they had to master the five Chinese dialects spoken by residents.
Library of Congress, Prints and Photographs Division

plague, taking jobs, lowering wages, increasing crime, corrupting politics, eroding culture, and contaminating the gene pool. The federal government took control of immigration from the states with the Immigration Act of 1882. It ended once-free entry by shutting out those who could not support themselves. Over the next half century, new barriers denied entry to the sick and illiterate as well as those considered immoral and, in the first case of exclusion based on race, all Chinese laborers. In the 1920s, national origin became another source of denial with caps on totals and quotas on countries. Those bars set the terms for today's debates over who gains entry. As a new wave of arrivals seeks refuge and opportunity, it is worth remembering that the country has absorbed millions of immigrants during its history, despite repeated predictions of doom and efforts to keep them out.

Urban Middle-Class Life >>

Life for the urban middle class revolved around home and family. By the turn of the century, just over a third of middle-class urbanites owned their home. Often two or three stories, made of brick or brownstone, these houses were a measure of social standing. Inside, the plush furniture, heavy drapes, elaborate furniture, and curios all signaled the status and refinement of their owners.

societies, and low birth totals. When the San Francisco earthquake and fire destroyed birth records in 1906, resourceful Chinese immigrants created "paper sons" (and less often "paper daughters") by forging birth certificates and claiming their China-born children as American citizens.

Caught between past and present, pressed to adopt American ways, immigrants nonetheless clung to tradition and assimilated slowly. Their children adjusted more quickly. They soon spoke English like natives, married whomever they pleased, and worked their way out of old neighborhoods. Rapid as it was for many children, this process of assimilation was not always easy. Children often faced heartrending clashes with parents and rejection from peers.

THEN&NOW

In the closing decades of the nineteenth century, as immigrants flooded into the United States, native-born Americans worried that the newcomers were a

Such homes, usually on their own lot, also served as refuge to protect and nourish the family in the chaotic world of the industrial city. Calm and orderly households with nurturing mothers would launch children on the right course and ensure a genial home life for all. "A clean, fresh, and well-ordered house," stipulated a domestic adviser in 1883, "exercises over its inmates a moral, no less than physical influence, and has a direct tendency to make members of the family sober, peaceable, and considerate of the feelings and happiness of each other."

A typical homemaker prepared elaborate meals, cleaned, laundered, and sewed. Each task took time. The process of baking a loaf of bread required nearly 24 hours from start to finish. In 1890 four of five loaves were still made at home. New labor-saving technologies such as indoor plumbing, washing machines, vacuums, and stoves in some ways made women's lives harder and housework more time-consuming, by raising the standards of cleanliness and the expectations for more elaborate meals.

CITY SCENES

In the late-nineteenth and early twentieth centuries, city scenes of daily life were the subject of countless renderings, from pen-and-ink drawings to lithographs and paintings to photographs, beginning in the mid-nineteenth century. Each brought a different perspective to the bustling life of industrial cities, and all reflected the point of view of the artist creating them. Two street scenes appear below, both from turn-of-the-century New York but in very different forms. Both offer panoramic views of busy New York streets. The top photograph was taken in 1900 of an Easter Day parade on Fifth Avenue. The bottom painting shows a crowded New York intersection, titled simply New York *and painted in 1911 by the realist painter George Bellows.*

DOCUMENT 1

National Archives & Records Administration

DOCUMENT 2

Courtesy National Gallery of Art, Washington

THINKING CRITICALLY

How many different types of urban transport can you see in each image? (Note, for example, an early automobile driving toward the camera on the left side of Fifth Avenue in the top photograph.) What can these various forms of transportation tell us about the speed and nature of technological change? Which rendering—the photograph at the top or the painting at the bottom—captures the vibrancy of the city best? Why? What is each artist— photographer and painter—trying to say about city life? How, if at all, does each medium shape the message?

By the 1890s, a host of new consumer products eased some of the burdens of housework. Brand names trumpeted a new age of commercially prepared food—Campbell's soup, Quaker oats, Pillsbury flour, Jell-O, and Cracker Jacks, to name a few. New appliances, such as "self-working" washers, offered mechanical assistance, but shredded shirts and aching arms testified to the imperfections of mechanization.

Toward the end of the century, Saturday became less of a workday and more of a family day. Sunday mornings remained a time for church, still an important center of family life. Afternoons had a secular flavor. There were shopping trips (city stores often stayed open) and visits to lakes, zoos, and amusement parks (usually built at the end of trolley lines to attract more riders). Outside institutions—fraternal organizations, uplift groups, athletic teams, and church groups—were becoming part of middle-class urban family life.

Victorianism and the Pursuit of Virtue >>

Middle-class life reflected a rigid social code called Victorianism, named for Britain's long-reigning Queen Victoria. It emerged in the 1830s and 1840s as part of an effort to tame the turbulent urban-industrial society developing in Europe.

Victorianism dictated that personal conduct be based on orderly behavior and disciplined moralism. It stressed sobriety, industriousness, self-control, and sexual modesty and taught that demeanor, particularly proper manners, was the backbone of society. According to its sexual precepts, women were "pure vessels," devoid of carnal desire. Their job was to control the "lower natures" of their husbands by withholding sex except for procreation.

Victorian values migrated across the Atlantic. In the United States, even women's fashions mirrored them. Strenuously laced corsets ("an instrument of torture," according to one woman) pushed breasts up, stomachs in, and rear ends out. The resulting wasplike figure accentuated the busts and hips, promoting the image of women as child bearers. Ankle-length skirts were draped over bustles, hoops, and petticoats to make the pelvis look even larger and suggest fertility. Such elegant dress set off middle- and upper-class women from those below. Their plain clothes signaled lives of drudgery and want.

When working-class Americans failed to follow Victorian cues, reformers urged them to pursue virtue. In 1879 Frances Willard, fearing the ill effects of alcohol on the family, became the second president of the newly formed Woman's Christian Temperance Union (WCTU), founded in 1874. Under her leadership the WCTU worked relentlessly to stamp out alcohol and promote sexual purity and other middle-class virtues. By the turn of the century it was the largest women's organization in the country, with 500,000 members.

temperance movement
reform movement, begun in the 1820s, to temper or restrain the sale and use of alcohol.

Initially the WCTU focused on **temperance**—the movement, begun in the 1820s, to stamp out the sale of alcoholic beverages and to end drunkenness. For many women, the campaign seemed a way not merely to reform society but to protect their homes and families from abuse at the hands of drunken husbands and fathers. And in attacking the saloon, the WCTU also sought to spread democracy, by storming these all-male bastions where political bosses often conducted political business and women were barred from entry. Soon, under the slogan "Do Everything," the WCTU was promoting women's suffrage, prison reform, better working conditions, and an end to prostitution. Just as important, the organization offered talented, committed women an opportunity to move out of their homes and churches and into the public arena of lobbying and politics.

Anthony Comstock crusaded with equal vigor against what he saw as moral pollution, ranging from pornography and gambling to the use of nude art models. In 1873 President Ulysses S. Grant signed the so-called Comstock Law, a statute banning from the mails all materials "designed to incite lust." Two days later, Comstock went to work as a special agent for the post office. In his 41-year career he claimed to have made more than 3,000 arrests and destroyed 160 tons of books and photographs.

Victorian crusaders like Comstock were not simply missionaries of a stuffy morality. They were apostles of a middle-class creed of social control, responding to increasing incidences of alcoholism, venereal disease, gambling debts, prostitution, and unwanted pregnancies. No doubt they overreacted in warning that the road to ruin lay behind the door of every saloon, gambling parlor, or bedroom. Yet the new urban environment did reflect the disorder and dangers of a rapidly industrializing society.

The insistence with which moralists warned against "impropriety" suggests that many people did not heed their advice. Three-quarters of the women surveyed toward the turn of the century reported that they enjoyed sex. The growing variety of contraceptives—including spermicidal douches, sheaths made of animal intestines, rubber condoms, and forerunners of the diaphragm—testified to the desire for pregnancy-free intercourse. Abortion, too, was available. According to one estimate, a third of all pregnancies were aborted, usually with the aid of a midwife. (By the 1880s abortion had been made illegal in most states following the first antiabortion statute in England in 1803.) Despite Victorian marriage manuals, middle-class Americans became more conscious of sexuality as an emotional dimension of a satisfying union.

Challenges to Convention >>

A few bold women and men challenged conventions of gender and propriety. Victoria Woodhull, publisher of *Woodhull & Claflin's Weekly,* divorced her husband, became the first woman to run for president in 1872 on the Equal Rights Party ticket, and pressed the case for sexual freedom. "I am a free lover!" she shouted to a riotous audience in New York. "I have the inalienable, constitutional, and natural right to love whom I may, to love as long or as short a period as I can, to change that love every day if I please!" Despite making a strong public case for sexual freedom, Woodhull adhered to strict monogamy and romantic love in private.

The same cosmopolitan conditions that provided protection for Woodhull's unorthodox beliefs made possible the growth of communities of homosexual men and women. Earlier in the century, Americans had idealized romantic friendships among members of the same sex, without necessarily attributing sexual overtones to them. For friendships with an explicitly sexual dimension, the anonymity of large cities provided new meeting grounds. Single factory workers and clerks, living on their own rather than with their families in small towns and on farms, were freer to seek others who shared their sexual orientation. Homosexual men and women began forming social networks. They met on the streets and at specific restaurants and clubs, which, to avoid controversy, sometimes passed themselves off as athletic associations or chess societies.

^ Strongman and bodybuilder Eugen Sandow
Rischgitz/Hulton Archive/Getty Images

Only toward the end of the century did physicians begin to take note of homosexual behavior, usually to condemn it as a disease or an inherited infirmity. Not until the turn of the century did the term *homosexual* even come into existence. Certainly homosexual love was not new. But for the first time in the United States, the conditions of urban life allowed gays and lesbians to define themselves in terms of a larger, self-aware community, even if they were stoutly condemned by prevailing standards of morality.

The Decline of "Manliness" >> The corrupting
influence of city life on manhood troubled some onlookers as much as political or moral corruption distressed reformers. The components of traditional "manliness"—physical vigor, honor and integrity, courage and independence—seemed under assault by life in the industrial city. White middle- and upper-class men who found themselves working at desks and living in cushy comfort appeared particularly at risk. As early as the 1850s Oliver Wendell Holmes Sr. (father of a famous Supreme Court justice) lamented that "such a set of stiff-jointed, soft-muscled, paste-complexioned youth as we can

boast in our Atlantic cities never before sprang from the loins of Anglo-Saxon lineage."

Anxious observers worried that the decline in "Anglo-Saxon" manliness courted catastrophe. Soft, listless white men lacked vitality but also the manly discipline and character that came from living what Theodore Roosevelt called the "Strenuous Life" of action and struggle. Debased by the seamy pursuit of business, Roosevelt warned, such "weaklings" left the nation "[trembling] on the brink of doom," its future imperiled by laziness, timidity, and dishonesty. The "virile qualities" essential for achievement and leadership would vanish. Roosevelt saw himself as a model. Frail and asthmatic as a boy, he turned himself into a strapping man through backbreaking workouts. He commanded deskbound, "civilized" white men to follow his lead, even to reinvigorate their intellects with the "barbarian virtues" of physical strength he saw in darker-hued "primitives." Gender and race were thus being blended into a heady brew of white supremacy.

A frenzy of fitness spread across the nation. Bicycling, rowing, boxing, and what one historian called a college "cult of sports" promised to return middle- and upper-class men to "vigorous and unsullied manhood." Prussian bodybuilder Eugen Sandow ignited a weightlifting craze when he toured the country in the 1890s with feats of strength and poses he dubbed "muscle display performances." In a show of manly courage, a young Roosevelt lit out for the Dakota Badlands, writer Richard Harding Davis for Cuba in the middle of the Spanish-American War, and explorers Robert Peary and Matthew Henson for the North Pole in 1898. Exploration and adventure became exercises in undaunted manliness.

REVIEW

How did class and ethnicity determine life for city dwellers?

CITY CULTURE

"We cannot all live in cities," bemoaned the reformer Horace Greeley just after the Civil War, "yet nearly all seemed determined to do so." Economic opportunity drew people to the teeming industrial city. But so, too, did a vibrant urban culture.

By the 1890s cities had begun to clean things up in downtown business districts, paving streets, widening thoroughfares, erecting fountains and marble buildings. This "city beautiful" movement aimed also to elevate public tastes and, like Victorian culture itself, refine the behavior of urbanites. Civic leaders pressed for public education and built museums, libraries, and parks to uplift unruly city masses.

Public parks followed the model of New York's Central Park. When it opened in 1858 Central Park was meant to serve as a pastoral retreat from the turbulent industrial city. Its rustic paths, leafy glades, and placid lakes, said designer Frederick Law Olmsted, would have "a distinctly harmonizing and refining influence" on even the rudest fellow. Bustling industrial cities looked to be modern, but public parks reflected the age-old human need to connect to the tranquility of the natural world.

Public Education in an Urban Industrial World

>> Those at the bottom and in the middle of city life saw public education as a key to success. Although the campaign for public education began in the Jacksonian era, it did not make much headway until after the Civil War. As late as 1870 half the children in the country received no formal education, and one in five American 14-year-olds could not read.

Between 1870 and 1900 an educational awakening occurred. As more and more businesses required workers who could read, write, and tally numbers, attendance in public schools more than doubled. The length of the school term rose from 132 to 144 days. Illiteracy fell by half. By the turn of the century, nearly all the states outside the South had enacted mandatory education laws. Almost three of every four school-age children were enrolled. Even so, the average American adult still attended school for only about five years, and less than 10 percent of those eligible continued beyond the eighth grade.

The average school day started early, but by noon most girls were released under the assumption that they needed less formal education than boys. Curricula stressed the fundamentals of reading, writing, and arithmetic. Courses in manual training, science, and physical education were added as the demand for technical knowledge grew and opportunities to exercise shrank. Few schools encouraged creative thinking, so, instead, students learned by memorization. In an age of industrialization, massive immigration, and rapid change, schools taught conformity and values as much as facts and figures. Teachers acted as drillmasters, shaping their charges for the sake of an orderly society. "Teachers and books are

^ Educational reformers in the 1870s pushed elementary drawing as a required subject. Their goal was not to turn out gifted artists but to train students in the practical skills needed in an industrial society. Winslow Homer's portrait of a teacher by her blackboard shows the geometric shapes behind practical design.
National Gallery of Art, Washington (1990.60.1./DR)

better security than handcuffs and policemen," wrote a New Jersey college professor in 1879.

As much as anyone, urban middle-class young women profited from education. Liberated from household chores, many attended primary school and some went on to high school. They walked city streets, met their peers beyond the watchful eyes of parents, and extended childhood into the new intermediate stage of "adolescence." Through education, prim and sheltered "young ladies" became "school girls," with newfound freedom to be who and what they wanted.

As Reconstruction faded, so did the impressive gains made in Black education. Most of the first generation of former enslaved people had been illiterate. So eager were they to learn that by the end of the century more than half over the age of 14 could read. Discrimination soon took its toll. For nearly 100 years after the Civil War, the doctrine of "separate but equal," upheld by the Supreme Court in *Plessy v. Ferguson* (1896), kept Black and white students apart but scarcely equal. By 1882 public schools in a half-dozen southern states were racially segregated by law, the rest by practice. Black schools were underfunded and ill-equipped and served dirt-poor families whose every member had to work.

Like African Americans, immigrants saw education as a way of getting ahead. Some educators saw it as a means of Americanizing newcomers. They assumed that immigrant and native-born children would learn the same lessons in the same language and turn out the same way. Only toward the end of the 1800s, as immigration mounted, did eastern cities begin to offer night classes that taught English, along with civics lessons, to foreigners. When public education proved inadequate, immigrants established their own schools. Catholics, for example, started an elaborate expansion of their parochial schools in 1884.

By the 1880s educational reforms were helping schools respond to the needs of an urban society. Opened first in St. Louis in 1873, U.S. versions of innovative German "kindergartens" put four-to six-year-olds in school while parents went off to work. **Normal schools** multiplied to provide teachers with more professional training. And in the new industrial age, science and manual training supplemented more conventional subjects in order to supply industry with skilled workers.

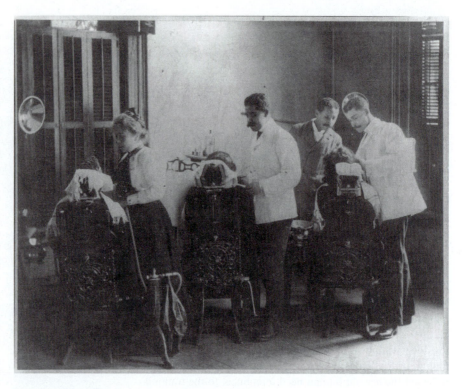

⌃ Black dentistry students at Howard University, 1900.
Library of Congress, Prints and Photographs Division

normal schools schools that trained teachers, usually for two years and mostly for teaching in the elementary grades.

Higher Learning and the Rise of the Professional

>> Colleges served the urban industrial society, too, not by controlling mass habits but by providing leaders and managers. Early in the nineteenth century, most Americans regarded higher learning as unmanly and irrelevant. The few who sought it often preferred the superior universities of Europe to those in the United States.

As American society grew more organized, mechanized, and complex, the need for professional, technical, and literary skills brought greater respect for college education. The Morrill Act of 1862 generated a dozen new state colleges and universities, eight mechanical and agricultural colleges, and six Black colleges. Private charity added more. Railroad barons such as Johns Hopkins and Leland Stanford used parts of their fortunes to found colleges named after them (Hopkins in 1873, Stanford in 1890). The number of colleges and universities nearly doubled between 1870 and 1910, though less than 5 percent of college-age Americans enrolled in them.

A practical impulse inspired the founding of several Black colleges. In the late nineteenth century, few institutions mixed races. Church groups and private foundations, such as the Peabody and Slater funds (supported by white donors from the North), underwrote Black colleges after Reconstruction. By 1900 a total of 700 Black students were enrolled. About 2,000 had graduated. Through hard work and persistence, some even received degrees from institutions reserved for whites.

In keeping with the new emphasis on practical learning, a growing number of professional schools provided training beyond college. American universities adopted the German model, requiring young scholars to perform research as part of their education. The number of law schools more than doubled between 1870 and 1900; medical students almost tripled. Ten percent of medical students were women, though their numbers shrank as the medical profession became more organized and exclusively male.

Professionals of all kinds—in law, medicine, engineering, business, academics—swelled the ranks of the middle class. Slowly they were becoming a new force in the urban United States, replacing the ministers and gentlemen freeholders of an earlier day as community leaders.

Higher Education for Women

>> Before the Civil War, women could attend only three private colleges. After the war they had new ones all their own, including Smith (1871), Wellesley (1875), and Bryn Mawr (1885). Such schools, with their mostly female faculties and administrators,

^ American impressionist Mary Cassatt painted this mural of women picking apples (in entirely unsuitable clothing) for the Women's Building at the Chicago World's Columbian Exposition in 1893. Titled *Young Women Plucking the Fruits of Knowledge or Science*, it stood on its head the story of Eve and her famous apple. According to the Bible, the fruit was the source of forbidden knowledge: when it was eaten by Eve, who shared it with Adam, the result was humankind's original sin. But Cassatt's mural suggested that the place of women in society was changing. No longer bound by cultural conventions against the dangers of educated women, a new generation of well-schooled females was to be celebrated for its achievements in science, the arts, and the professions.
Harper's New Monthly Magazine, May 1893, Courtesy of Cornell University Library

deepened an emerging sense of membership in a special community of women. Many land-grant colleges, chartered to serve all people, also admitted women. By 1910, some 40 percent of college students were women, almost double the 1870 figure.

Potent myths of gender continued to plague even college women. As Dr. Edward Clarke of the Harvard Medical School told thousands of students in *Sex in Education* (1873), the rigors of a college education could lead the "weaker sex" to physical or mental collapse, infertility, and early death. Women's colleges therefore included a program of physical activity to keep their students healthy. Many offered an array of courses in "domestic science"—cooking, sewing, and other such skills—to counter the claim that higher education would be of no value to women.

College students, together with office workers and female athletes, became role models for ambitious young women. These "new women" were impatient with custom and cast off Victorian restrictions. Fewer married, and more, perhaps 25 percent, were self-supporting. They shed their corsets and bustles and donned lighter, more comfortable clothing, such as "shirtwaist" blouses (styled after men's shirts) and lower-heeled shoes. Women were moving beyond the domestic sphere of home and family.

A Culture of Consumption >> The city spawned a
new material culture built on consumption. As standards of living rose, U.S. industries began providing "ready-made" clothing to replace garments that had once been made at home. Similarly, food and furniture were mass-produced in greater quantities. The city became a giant marketplace for these goods, where new patterns of consumption took hold

and radiated outward to rural areas. The leveling effect was demonstrable. City businesses sold the same goods to farmer and clerk, rich and poor, native-born and immigrant.

Well-made, inexpensive merchandise in standard sizes and shapes found outlets in new palaces of consumption known as "department stores." The name came from the fact that they displayed their goods in separate sections or departments. Unlike the small exclusive shops of Europe, department stores were palatial, public, and filled with an array of furniture, housewares, and fashions. The creation of "plate glass" allowed stores to display their goods in windows and cases.

The French writer Émile Zola claimed that department stores "democratized luxury." Anyone could enter, handle the most expensive goods, and buy whatever was affordable. When consumers found goods too pricey, department stores pioneered layaway plans with deferred payments. They educated people by showing them what "proper" families owned. In the process, they socialized consumers into their need for products of all kinds.

Chain stores, a term coined in the United States, spread the culture of consumption without frills. They catered to the working class, who could not afford department stores, and operated on a cash-and-carry basis. Owners kept their costs down by buying in volume to fill stores in growing neighborhood chains. Founded in 1859, the Great Atlantic and Pacific Tea Company (later A&P supermarkets) was the first of the chain stores. By 1876 its 76 branch stores had added groceries to its line of teas.

Far from department and chain stores, rural Americans joined the community of consumers by mail. In 1872 Aaron Montgomery Ward sent his first price sheet to farmers from a livery stable in Chicago. Ward avoided intermediaries and

"LAGGED BEFORE SHOP WINDOWS"

promised savings of 40 percent on fans, needles, trunks, harnesses, and scores of other goods available to city dwellers. By 1884 his catalog boasted 10,000 items, each illustrated by a lavish woodcut. Similarly, Richard W. Sears and Alvah C. Roebuck built a $500 million mail-order business by 1907. Schoolrooms that had no encyclopedia used a Montgomery Ward or Sears catalog instead. When asked the source of the Ten Commandments, one farm boy guessed they came from Sears, Roebuck.

Leisure >> As mechanization gradually reduced the number of hours on the job, factory workers found themselves with more free time. So did the middle class, with free weekends, evenings, and vacations. A stricter division between work and play developed. City dwellers turned this new leisure time into a consumer item that reflected differences in class, gender, and ethnicity.

Sports, for example, had been a traditional form of recreation for the rich. They continued to play polo, golf, and the newly imported English game of tennis. A new craze—bicycling—quickly grabbed their attention. Bicycles evolved

∧ "Wheelman clubs" formed in many cities, to take advantage of the popularity of bicycling as a leisure-time activity. This illustration of cyclists returning from a ride along Manhattan's Riverside Drive in 1897 indicates that women eagerly undertook the sport, though debates raged over its suitability for them. In 1893 the *New York Times* pronounced the use of "bicycles by the weaker sex" a question that had been "decisively settled in the affirmative."
Lebrecht Music and Arts Photo Library/Alamy Stock Photo

from unstable contraptions with large front wheels into "safety" bikes with equal-sized wheels, a dropped middle bar, pneumatic tires, and coaster brakes. On Sunday afternoons, city parks became crowded with cyclists, at least those wealthy enough to pay the $100 price tag. Women rode the new safety bikes, too, although social convention prohibited them from riding alone. Still, cycling broke down norms. It required looser garments, freeing women from corsets. And female cyclists demonstrated that they were hardly too fragile for physical exertion.

Organized spectator sports attracted crowds from every walk of life. Baseball overshadowed all others. For city dwellers with dull work, stuffy quarters, and isolated lives, baseball offered the chance to join thousands of others for an exciting outdoor spectacle. The first professional teams appeared in 1869. Slowly the game evolved. Umpires began to call balls and strikes; the overhand replaced the underhand pitch; fielders put on gloves. Teams from eight cities formed the National League of Professional Baseball Clubs in 1876, followed by the American League in 1901.

At first, teams featured some Black players. When African Americans were barred in the 1880s, Black professionals formed their own team, the Cuban Giants of Long Island, New York. They played anyone they could and took the name "Cuban" (rather than "Negro") in hopes of playing white teams.

Perhaps the most violent sport of all, bare-knuckled prizefighting, was illegal in some states. In others, it gave young men from the streets the chance to stand out from the crowd, win some cash, and prove how manly they were. Football offered the elite a similar opportunity. In 1869, without pads or helmets, Rutgers beat Princeton in the first intercollegiate football match. College football soon attracted crowds of 50,000 or more.

Arts and Entertainment >> Other forms of city entertainment also divided along lines of class. For the wealthy and upper-middle class, there were symphonies, operas, and theater. Highbrow productions of Shakespearean plays catered to the aspirations of upwardly mobile Americans for culture and European refinement. Popular melodramas gave middle-class audiences the chance to ignore the ambiguities of modern life, booing villains and cheering heroes. By 1900 people were bringing their entertainment home, snapping up some 3 million new phonograph recordings a year.

Workingmen discovered a refuge from the drudgery of factory, mill, and mine in the saloon. It was an all-male preserve—a workingman's club—where one could drink and talk free from Victorian finger-wagging. Young working-women found escape alone or with dates at dance halls or the new amusement parks, with their mechanical "thrill rides." In the all-Black gaming houses and honky-tonks of St. Louis and New Orleans, the syncopated rhythms of African American composer Scott Joplin's "Maple Leaf Rag" (1899) and other ragtime tunes heralded the coming of jazz.

With an eye on the potential business of middle-class housewives with children, resourceful theater owners cleaned up the bawdy acts of saloons and music halls, required audiences to be well mannered, and came up with a new form of variety show called "vaudeville," after the French slang *voix de ville* ("songs of the town"). For anywhere from a dime to two dollars, a customer could enjoy up to nine acts of singers, jugglers, acrobats, magicians, trained animals, and comics. During its heyday from 1890 to 1920, vaudeville was popular and profitable. Nearly one in five city dwellers went to a show once a week.

As much as any form of entertainment, the traveling circus embodied the changes of the new urban, industrial world. Moving outward from their city bases, circuses rode the new rail system across the country and, with the advent of steamships, crisscrossed the globe. The mammoth New York–based Barnum & Bailey Circus carried dozens of gilded show wagons, scores of animals, and tons of equipment to the faraway capitals of Europe and Asia.

At home the shows drew patrons from every class, ethnicity, and race, sometimes numbering in the tens of thousands. Circus workers erected huge "big top" tents with the factory-like precision of modern industry. And, like the city itself, circuses both supported and subverted social conventions. Owners reassured customers that their scantily clad dancers came from respectable families and their muscular female acrobats prized the Victorian values of motherhood and domesticity. But they winked slyly because they knew that the very appearance of these women, let alone their talents, defied the Victorian ideal of dainty and demure femininity.

✔ REVIEW

How did city culture shape national culture?

History in Global Context >> Industrialization ignited the growth of cities not just in the United States but all over the world. Great Britain, the birthplace of the Industrial Revolution, became the world's first country to house over half its people in towns and cities, reaching this mark in 1851. Fifty years later, London's population had more than doubled, from 2.7 million to 6.6 million. On the eve of World War I in 1914, 8 of every 10 Britons lived in cities, as did 6 of 10 Germans and nearly half of all French.

Just as European immigrants poured into cities across the United States, newcomers from Europe, Asia, and the Middle East flowed into South America, Australia, and the Caribbean. Before 1900, two of every three emigrating Italians booked passage not for the United States but for Brazil or Argentina. Chinese immigrants harvested sugar cane in Cuba, built railroads and opened restaurants in Peru, and launched businesses in Trinidad. By 1920, São Paulo, the largest city in Brazil, was exploding with Asian immigrants, and Brazil boasted the world's largest Japanese population outside that island nation.

The hubbub, the overcrowding, and the corruption of cities like Boss Plunkitt's New York were reflected elsewhere in the world. Before the arrival of mass transit, British urban workers had to live within walking distance of factories, in dingy row houses beset by the overflow from privies and garbage in the streets. A deadly cholera epidemic in 1848 spurred a campaign to install iron pipes and drains for running water and sewers throughout major cities. About the same time, Paris underwent a radical renovation in which workers tore down the city's medieval fortress walls, widened major streets into boulevards, and set aside land for green parks. Borrowing innovations from the United States, Europeans adopted horse-drawn streetcars and, later, electric trolleys. With an intracity transportation network in place, the old "walking cities" of Europe, like those in the United States, added suburbs, partially easing the crush of earlier crowding.

The world over, industrial cities transformed both the urban landscape and the daily lives of city dwellers. Critics damned the city's crime and corruption; defenders celebrated its vibrancy and diversity. No matter how they felt, Americans had to search for ways to make new industrial cities work.

CHAPTER SUMMARY

The modern city was the product of industrialization, lying at the center of the new integrated systems of transportation, communications, manufacturing, marketing, and finance.

- Fed by a great global migration of laborers, cities began to grow and to assume their modern shape of ringed residential patterns around central business districts and strict divisions among different classes, races, and ethnic groups.
- The challenge for the political system was to find within its democratic traditions a way to bring order out of the seeming chaos of unchecked urban growth.
- The urban boss and the urban political machine met the needs of cities for centralized authority but at a terrible cost in corruption, while social settlement houses, the Salvation Army, and the Social Gospel churches represented only a start at coping with the problems of poverty and urban blight.
- As cities grew, the middle-class code of behavior—called Victorianism by historians—spread, teaching the values of sobriety, hard work, self-control, and modesty. Such traits served the needs of the new industrial society for efficiency and order and the middle-class need for protection against the turbulence of city life.
- Yet for all the emphasis on skills, discipline, and order, the vibrancy of city culture remained attractive. It drew millions in search of education, entertainment, and opportunity, and it radiated outward to almost every corner of the country.

Digging Deeper

The best treatment of the rise of cities is Howard B. Chudacoff, *The Evolution of American Urban Society* (rev. ed., 1981). John Stilgoe, *Borderland: The Origins of the American Suburb, 1820–1929* (1988), chronicles the growth of the suburban United States. William Cronon, *Nature's Metropolis: Chicago and the Great West* (1991), sees Chicago as part of the ecological landscape. In *Boss Cox's Cincinnati: Urban Politics in the Progressive Era* (1968), Zane Miller reassesses the urban political machine. Paul Boyer explores efforts at controlling city life in *Urban Masses and Moral Order in America, 1820–1920* (1978). John F. Kasson, *Rudeness and Civility: Manners in Nineteenth-Century Urban America* (1990); and Lawrence Levine, *Highbrow/Lowbrow: The Emergence of Cultural Hierarchy in America* (1988), investigate the emerging urban culture. To understand traveling circuses as conduits for cultural exchanges, see Janet M. Davis's *The Circus Age: Culture and Society Under the American Big Top* (2002). On the origins of baseball, see David Block's *Baseball before We Knew It: A Search for the Roots of the Game* (2004).

Marcus Lee Hanson's classic *The Atlantic Migration, 1607–1860* (1940) began the shift in immigration history away from the national and toward a global perspective. For richly detailed comparative examinations of the immigrant experience, see Roger Daniels, *Coming to America: A History of Immigration and Ethnicity in American Life* (1990); and Ronald Takaki, *A Different Mirror: A History of Multicultural America* (1993). Daniel Okrent, *The Guarded Gate: Bigotry, Eugenics, and the Law That Kept Two Generations of Jews, Italians, and Other Europeans out of America* (2019), explores the effort to restrict immigration. Susan A. Glenn, *Daughters of the Shtetl: Life and Labor in the Immigrant Generation* (1990), probes the lives and labor of immigrant women, especially the shaping effect of old world Jewish culture. Her *Female Spectacle: The Theatrical Roots of Modern Feminism* (2002) looks at female actresses and comics as a source of modern feminism. Virginia Yans-McLaughlin, ed., *Immigration Reconsidered: History, Sociology, and Politics* (1990), places American immigration in its international context. Madeline Y. Hsu examines Chinese immigrants in her award-winning *The Good Immigrants: How the Yellow Peril Became the Model Minority* (2015). Mae Ngai's *Impossible Subjects: Illegal Aliens and the Making of Modern American* (2004) explores the history of undocumented immigrants. In *New Spirits: Americans in the Gilded Age, 1865–1905* (2006), Rebecca Edwards makes the "Gilded Age" the birth of the modern United States by emphasizing the anxieties and optimism of ordinary people, many of them city dwellers. Helen Lefkowitz Horowitz's *Rereading Sex: Battles over Sexual Knowledge and Suppression in Nineteenth-Century America* (2002) explores the contradictions of Victorian thinking about contraception, abortion, pornography, and free speech. Jane Hunter's *How Young Ladies Became Girls: The Victorian Origins of American Girlhood* (2003) surveys the liberating experiences of female adolescents in the Victorian United States.

21 Realignment at Home and Empire Abroad

1877–1900

The exotic buildings of the Chicago World's Columbian Exposition of 1893, with their domes, minarets, and foreign flags, show how conscious Americans were becoming of the wider world. A woman takes a camel ride (*right*) while many foreigners wander through the plaza.

Stock Montage/Getty Images

>> **An American Story**

"THE WORLD UNITED AT CHICAGO"

On May 1, 1893, nearly half a million people crushed into a dramatic plaza fronted on either side by gleaming white buildings. Named the Court of Honor, the plaza was the center of a strange, ornamental city that was awesome and entirely imaginary.

At one end stood the Administration Building, whose magnificent dome exceeded the height of the Capitol in Washington, D.C. Unlike the marble-built Capitol, however, it was all surface: a stucco shell plastered onto a steel frame and then sprayed with white-oil lead paint to make it glisten. Beyond it stretched thoroughfares encompassing over 200 colonnaded buildings, piers, islands, and watercourses. Located five miles south of Chicago's center, this imagined city proclaimed itself the "World's Columbian Exposition" to honor the 400th anniversary of Columbus's voyage to America. The Exposition declared the United States one of the great developed countries of the globe.

In the short space between 1860 and 1890, American industrial production had rocketed from third to first place in the world. President Grover Cleveland opened the fair in a way that symbolized the transformation. He pressed a telegrapher's key. Instantly, electric current put 7,000 feet of shafting into motion—unfurling flags, setting fountains pumping, lighting 10,000 electric bulbs. The lights played over an array of exhibition buildings soon known as the "White City."

One visitor dismissed the displays within as "the contents of a great dry goods store mixed up with the contents of museums." In a sense he was right. Visitors paraded by typewriters, watches, agricultural machinery, and refrigerators, to say nothing of a map of the United States fashioned out of pickles. This riot of mechanical marvels and bric-a-brac was symbolic, too, of the nation's industrial transformation. The fair resembled nothing so much as a tangible version of the new mail-order catalogs that were now showing the goods of the city to the countryside of the United States and the world at large.

The connections made by the fair were clearly international. This was the *World's* Columbian Exposition, with exhibits from 36 nations. Germany's famous manufacturer of armaments, Krupp, had its own building. It housed a 120-ton rifled gun capable of launching a 1-ton shell 20 miles. At the fair's amusement park, visitors encountered exotic cultures—and not just temples, huts, and totems, but exhibits in the flesh. The Arabian village featured Saharan camels, veiled ladies, and elders in turbans. Nearby, Irish peasants boiled potatoes over turf fires and Samoan men threw axes.

Like all such fairs the Columbian Exposition trafficked in fantasy. Beyond its boundaries the real world was showing signs of strain. Early in 1893 the Philadelphia and Reading Railroad had gone bankrupt, setting off a financial panic. By the end of the year nearly 500 banks and 15,000 businesses had failed. Crowds of worried and unemployed workers gathered in Chicago. On Labor Day, Illinois governor John Altgeld told one such assemblage that the government was powerless to soften the "suffering and distress" caused by the devastating downturn.

In truth the political system was ill-equipped to cope with the economic and social revolutions reshaping the United States. The executive branch remained weak, while Congress and the courts found themselves easily swayed by the financial interests of the industrial class. The crises of the 1890s forced the political order to respond to such inequities.

The political system also had to take into account developments abroad. Industrialization sent American businesses around the world searching for raw materials and new markets. As their quest intensified, many influential Americans argued that, like European nations, the United States needed to acquire territory overseas and a navy powerful enough to defend them.

By the end of the century the nation's political system had taken its first steps toward modernization at home and abroad. They included a major political realignment and a growing overseas empire. Both changes and the tensions that accompanied them launched the United States into the twentieth century and an era of prosperity and global power. «

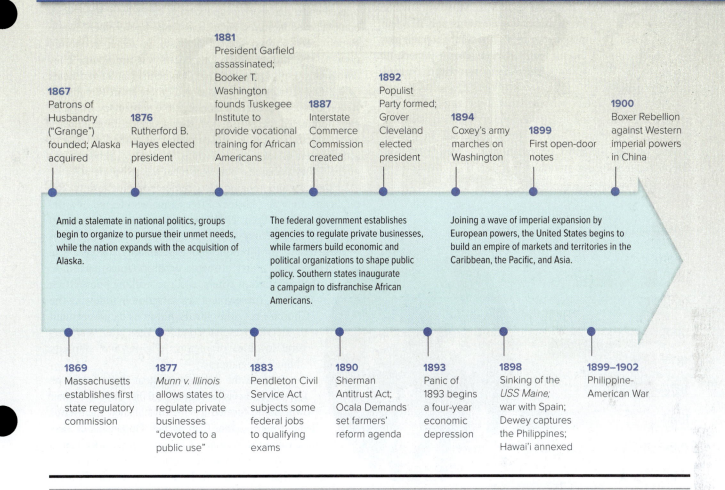

1867
Patrons of Husbandry ("Grange") founded; Alaska acquired

1876
Rutherford B. Hayes elected president

1881
President Garfield assassinated; Booker T. Washington founds Tuskegee Institute to provide vocational training for African Americans

1887
Interstate Commerce Commission created

1892
Populist Party formed; Grover Cleveland elected president

1894
Coxey's army marches on Washington

1899
First open-door notes

1900
Boxer Rebellion against Western imperial powers in China

Amid a stalemate in national politics, groups begin to organize to pursue their unmet needs, while the nation expands with the acquisition of Alaska.

The federal government establishes agencies to regulate private businesses, while farmers build economic and political organizations to shape public policy. Southern states inaugurate a campaign to disfranchise African Americans.

Joining a wave of imperial expansion by European powers, the United States begins to build an empire of markets and territories in the Caribbean, the Pacific, and Asia.

1869
Massachusetts establishes first state regulatory commission

1877
Munn v. Illinois allows states to regulate private businesses "devoted to a public use"

1883
Pendleton Civil Service Act subjects some federal jobs to qualifying exams

1890
Sherman Antitrust Act; Ocala Demands set farmers' reform agenda

1893
Panic of 1893 begins a four-year economic depression

1898
Sinking of the *USS Maine*; war with Spain; Dewey captures the Philippines; Hawai'i annexed

1899–1902
Philippine-American War

THE POLITICS OF PARALYSIS

During the 1880s and 1890s, the balding, bespectacled Moisei Ostrogorski was traveling across the United States. Like other foreign visitors, the Russian political scientist had come to see the new democratic experiment in action. His verdict was as blunt as it was common: "The constituted authorities are unequal to their duty." The experiment, he suggested, had fallen victim to greed, indifference, and political mediocrity.

In fact there were deeper problems: a great gulf between rich and poor; a wrenching cycle of boom and bust; the unmet needs of African Americans, women, native peoples, and other "others." These problems had scarcely been addressed let alone resolved. Politics was the traditional medium of resolution, but it was grinding into a dangerous stalemate.

Political Stalemate >> From 1877 to 1897 American politics rested on a delicate balance of power that left neither Republicans nor Democrats in control of Washington. Republicans inhabited the White House for 12 years; Democrats, for 8. Margins of victory in presidential elections were paper thin. No president could count on having a majority of his party in Congress for his entire term. Usually Republicans controlled the Senate, Democrats the House of Representatives.

With elections so tight both parties worked hard to turn out the vote. Brass bands, parades, cheering crowds of flag-wavers were "the order of the day and night from end to end of the country," reported a British visitor. When Election Day arrived, stores closed and businesses shut down. At political clubs and corner saloons men lined up to get voting orders and free drinks from ward bosses. Fields went untended as farmers took their families to town, cast their ballots, and bet on the outcome.

An average of nearly 80 percent of eligible voters turned out for presidential elections between 1860 and 1900, a figure higher than at any time since. In that era, however, the electorate made up a smaller percentage of the population than it does currently. About one American in five actually voted in presidential elections from 1876 to 1892. Most were white males. Women could vote in national elections only in a few western states. Beginning in the 1880s, the South erected barriers that eventually disenfranchised most African American voters. In the West, Latinos and Asians were largely barred from the ballot box.

Party loyalty rarely wavered. It was the key to electoral success and thus to the stalemate. In every election, 16 states voted for Republicans and 14 for Democrats. In only 6 "swing" states—the most important being New York and Ohio—were results ever in doubt.

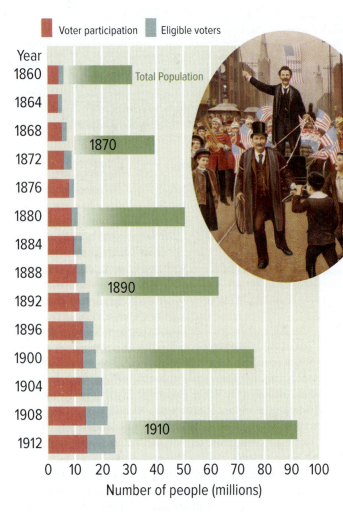

THE VOTING PUBLIC

Between 1860 and 1910 the population of the United States increased nearly threefold while the number of eligible voters increased over fourfold. But, as reforms of the early twentieth century reduced the power of political machines and parties to turn out voters, the percentage of eligible voter participation actually declined in presidential elections through 1912. *Photo*: Library of Congress, Prints and Photographs Division

The Parties >> What inspired such loyalty? Republicans and Democrats had similarities but also differences. Both parties supported business and condemned radicalism; neither offered embattled workers and farmers much help. But Democrats believed in states' rights and limited government, while Republicans favored federal activism to foster economic growth. The stronghold of Democrats was the South. They continually reminded voters that Democrats had led the states of the Old Confederacy, "redeemed" them from Republican Reconstruction, and championed white supremacy. Republicans dominated the North, with strong support from industry and business. They, too, invoked memories of the Civil War to secure voters, Black as well as white. "Not every Democrat was a rebel," they declared, "but every rebel was a Democrat."

Ethnicity and religion also cemented voter loyalty. Republicans drew on old-stock Protestants, who feared new immigrants and put their faith in promoting pious behavior. In the Republican Party they found support for immigration restriction, prohibition, and English-only schools. The Democratic Party attracted urban political machines, their immigrant voters, and the working poor. Often Catholic, these voters saw salvation in following the Church's religious rituals, not in using government to dictate personal conduct. Year after year, cultural loyalties of region, religion, and ethnicity shaped allegiances.

Outside the two-party system impassioned reformers often fashioned political instruments of their own. Some formed groups that aligned themselves behind issues rather than parties. Opponents of alcohol created the Woman's Christian Temperance Union (1874) and the Anti-Saloon League (1893). Champions of women's rights joined the National American Woman Suffrage Association (1890), a reunion of two branches of the women's suffrage movement that had split in 1869.

Third parties might also crystallize around a single concern or a particular group. Those who sought inflation of the currency formed the Greenback Party (1874). Farmers in the West and South, frustrated with high interest rates, deep debts, and powerful industrialists, created the People's, or Populist, Party (1892). All drew supporters from both conventional parties, but as single-interest groups they mobilized minorities, not majorities.

The Issues >> In the halls of Congress, attention focused on the well-worn issues of veterans' benefits, appointments, tariffs, and money. The impeachment of Andrew Johnson, the scandals of Ulysses S. Grant, and the contested victory of Rutherford B. Hayes in 1876 had weakened the presidency. Congress enjoyed the initiative in making policy, just as the founders intended.

Some divisive issues were the bitter legacy of the Civil War. Republicans and Democrats waved symbolic "bloody shirts," tarring each other with responsibility for the war. The Civil War also surfaced in the lobbying efforts of veterans. The Grand Army of the Republic, an organization of more than 400,000 Union soldiers, petitioned Congress for pensions to make up for poor wartime pay and to support the widows and orphans of fallen comrades. By 1900 Union army veterans and their families were receiving $157 million annually. The payments turned out to be one of the largest public assistance programs in American history and laid the foundation for the modern welfare state.

Such welfare programs drew little interest from either party, but both cared keenly about how to staff federal offices. Barely 53,000 federal employees at the end of the Civil War had mushroomed to 166,000 by the early 1890s, with far more jobs requiring special skills. The reigning "spoils system" valued party loyalty above merit. It proved difficult to reform because, without such rewards, politicians feared that they could attract neither voters nor money.

The spoils system remained in place until it led to the assassination of President James Garfield in 1881. A deranged office seeker, who believed Garfield should have rewarded his support with a diplomatic post in Vienna or Paris, shot him. Congress finally acted in 1883 by passing the Civil Service, or Pendleton, Act. It created a bipartisan commission to administer competitive examinations for some federal jobs. Later presidents expanded the positions covered. By 1896, almost half of all federal workers came under civil service jurisdiction.

The protective tariff also split Congress. As promoters of economic growth, Republicans usually championed tariffs on manufactured imports to protect industries at home. Democrats, with their strength in the agrarian South, generally opposed such price protection. They backed tariff reduction to encourage freer trade. The resulting profits, they believed, would reduce prices on manufactured goods and cut the federal surplus. In 1890, when Republicans controlled the House, Congress passed the McKinley Tariff. It raised tariffs to all-time highs but contained a novel twist designed to satisfy both parties. With "reciprocity," the president could lower rates if other countries did the same.

Just as divisive was the issue of currency. Until the mid-1800s money was coined from both gold and silver under a policy known as "bi-metalism." The need for more money during the Civil War had led Congress to issue "greenbacks"—currency printed on paper with a green back—that were not backed by gold or silver. For the next 15 years, Americans argued over whether to print more paper money or take it out of circulation. Farmers and other debtors favored greenbacks and opposed coining gold, with the hope of inflating prices. Inflation—too much money chasing too few goods—would reduce the real cost of their debts by raising prices while their debts remained constant. Conversely, bankers and creditors supported "sound money" backed by gold alone, the so-called gold standard, to keep prices stable and interest rates high. Fearing inflation, Congress first cut the number of greenbacks and then, in 1879, made all remaining paper money convertible into gold.

A more heated battle developed over silver-backed money. By the early 1870s so little silver was being used that

Make a Case

Does government work more effectively when one party controls both the presidency and the Congress or when government is divided between the parties? How would you define "effectively"?

Congress stopped coining it in 1873. The money supply shrank and interest rates rose, leading indebted farmers and other advocates of silver- *and* gold-backed money to call it the "Crime of '73." A mining boom in Nevada soon revived demands for more silver money. In 1878 the Bland-Allison Act began a limited form of silver coinage. But pressure for unlimited coinage of silver—coining all silver presented at U.S. mints—mounted as silver production quadrupled between 1870 and 1890 and its price plummeted. In 1890 pressure for silver resulted in the Sherman Silver Purchase Act, which obligated the government to buy 4.5 million ounces of silver every month. Paper tender called "treasury notes," redeemable in either gold or silver, would pay for it. The compromise satisfied both sides only temporarily.

The White House from Hayes to Harrison >>

From the 1870s through the 1890s a string of near-anonymous presidents presided over the country. Not all were mere caretakers. Some tried to revive the office, but Congress continued to curb the executive and control policy.

Republican Rutherford B. Hayes was the first of the "Ohio dynasty," which included three presidents from 1876 to 1900. Once elected, Hayes moved quickly to end Reconstruction and tried unsuccessfully to woo southern Democrats with promises of economic support. His pursuit of civil service reform ended only in splitting his party between "Stalwarts" (who favored the spoils systems) and "Half-Breeds" (who opposed it). Hayes left office after a single term, relieved to be "out of a scrape."

In 1880 Republican James Garfield, another Ohioan, succeeded Hayes by a handful of votes. He spent his first hundred days in the White House besieged by office hunters and failing to placate the rival sections of his party. After Garfield's assassination, only six months into his term, Chester A. Arthur, the "spoilsman's spoilsman," became president.

To everyone's surprise, the dapper Arthur turned out to be an honest president who broke with machine politicians. He worked to lower the tariff, warmly endorsed the new Civil Service Act, and reduced the federal surplus by beginning construction of a modern navy. Such evenhanded administration left little likelihood that party leaders would renominate him in 1884.

The election of 1884 was one of the dirtiest ever waged. Senator James Blaine, the beloved "Plumed Knight" from Maine and leader of the Half-Breeds, ran against Democrat Grover

Cleveland, the former governor of New York. Despite superb talents as a leader and vote-getter, Blaine was haunted by charges of illegal favoritism for the Little Rock and Fort Smith Railroad. For his part, "Grover the Good" had built a reputation for honesty by fighting corruption and the spoils system in New York. The portly Cleveland worked so hard, sighed a reporter, that he "remains within doors constantly, eats and works, eats and works, and works and eats." Cleveland spent enough time away from his desk to father an illegitimate child. The campaign rang with Republican taunts of "Ma, ma, where's my pa?"

In the last week of the tight race, the Irish vote in New York swung to the Democrats when a local Protestant minister labeled them the party of "Rum, Romanism, and Rebellion" (alcohol, Catholicism, and the Civil War). New York went to Cleveland, and with it, the election. Democrats crowed over where to find the bachelor "pa" now: "Gone to the White House, ha, ha, ha!"

⌃ This splashy poster welcomes the National Democratic Convention to St. Louis in 1888. It was a foregone conclusion that incumbent Grover Cleveland would be the party's nominee. Displayed prominently are the Capitol in Washington and the famous Eads Bridge as well as Cleveland's young wife, Frances Folsom. When the pious Benjamin Harrison won the election, he crowed, "Providence has given us the victory." "Providence hadn't a damn thing to do with it," one irritated senator complained, irked that Harrison seemed to have no idea how many Republicans "were compelled to approach the gates of the penitentiary to make him President." Universal History Archive/Getty Images

Cleveland, the first Democrat elected to the White House since James Buchanan in 1856, was more active than many of his predecessors. He pleased reformers by expanding the civil service. His devotion to gold, economy, and efficiency earned him praise from business and the anger of farmers. He supported the growth of federal power by endorsing the Interstate Commerce Act (1887), new agricultural research, and federal arbitration of labor disputes. Still, his activism remained limited. He vetoed two of every three bills brought to him, more than twice the number vetoed by all his predecessors.

In 1888 Republicans nominated a sturdy defender of tariffs, Benjamin Harrison, the grandson of President William Henry Harrison. Cleveland won a **plurality** of the popular vote but lost in the Electoral College. Called the "human iceberg" for his frostiness in dealing with people, Harrison worked productively with Congress and turned the White House into a well-run office. He helped shape the Sherman Silver Purchase Act (1890), kept abreast of the McKinley Tariff (1890), and accepted the Sherman Antitrust Act (1890) to limit the size of big businesses.

plurality receiving more votes than any other candidate but less than half of all votes cast. Receiving more than half of the votes cast is called a majority.

By the end of Harrison's term in 1892, Congress had completed its most productive session of the era, including passing the first billion-dollar peacetime budget. To Democrat jeers of a "Billion Dollar Congress," Republican House Speaker Thomas Reed shot back, "This is a billion-dollar country!"

Ferment in the States and Cities >> Despite growing expenditures and more legislation, most people expected little from the federal government. Public pressure to curb the excesses of the new industrial order mounted closer to home, in state and city governments. Experimental and often effective, state programs began to grapple with the problems of corporate power, discriminatory railroad rates, political corruption, and urban disorder.

Starting with Massachusetts in 1869, states established commissions to investigate and regulate industry, especially railroads, the United States's first big business. By the turn of the century almost two-thirds of the states had them. The first commissions gathered and publicized information on shipping rates and business practices and furnished advice about public policy, but had little power.

In the Midwest, on the Great Plains, and in the Far West, merchants and farmers pressed state governments to reduce railroad rates and stop the rebates or kickbacks given to large shippers. On the West Coast and in the Midwest, state legislatures empowered commissions to end rebates and monitor railroad rates. In 1870 Illinois became the first of several states to define railroads as public highways. The reclassification subjected them to public regulation, including setting maximum rates.

Mary Shelley's novel of a human-made creature who turns against its creator strikes the theme for this anti-railroad cartoon titled "The American Frankenstein" (1874). "Agriculture, commerce, and manufacture are all in my power," bellows the mechanical monster with the head of a locomotive.
Cornell University Library, Ithaca, NY

 REVIEW

What factors led to the paralysis of politics in the late nineteenth century?

THE REVOLT OF THE FARMERS

In 1890 the politics of stalemate shattered as farmers across the South and the western plains lost patience with business-oriented government. Beginning in the 1880s, a sharp depression drove down agricultural prices, pushed up surpluses, and forced thousands from their land. Farmers also suffered from a great deal more, including heavy mortgages, widespread poverty, and railroad rates that discriminated against them.

populism political outlook that supports the rights and powers of the common people in opposition to the interests of the privileged elite.

In 1890 their resentment boiled over. An agrarian revolt—called **populism**—swept across the political landscape and broke the stalemate of the previous 20 years.

The Harvest of Discontent >> The revolt of the farmers stirred first on the southern frontier, spreading eastward from Texas through the rest of the Old Confederacy, then west across the plains. Farmers blamed their troubles on obvious inequalities: manufacturers protected by the tariff, railroads charging sky-high rates, bankers who held their mounting debts, and expensive intermediaries such as grain elevator operators and millers who stored and processed farm commodities. Monopoly allowed them to pay low prices for crops and overcharge for their services.

The true picture was more complex. The tariff protected industrial goods but also supported some farm commodities. Railroad rates, however high, actually fell from 1865 to 1890. Although mortgages were expensive, most were short, no more than four years. Farmers often refinanced them and used the extra money to buy more land and machinery, thereby increasing their debts. Millers and operators of grain elevators earned handsome profits; yet every year more of them came under state regulation.

In hard times, when debts mounted and families went hungry, complexity mattered little. In the South many poor farmers seemed condemned to hard times forever. A credit crunch lay at the root of the problem, since most southern farmers had to borrow money to plant and harvest their crops. The inequities of sharecropping and the crop-lien system forced them deeper into debt. When crop prices fell, farmers borrowed still more, stretching financial resources beyond their meager limits. Within a few years after the Civil War, Massachusetts's banks had five times as much money as all the banks of the Old Confederacy.

Beginning in the 1870s, nearly 100,000 debt-ridden farmers a year picked up stakes across the Deep South and fled to Texas to escape debt and the crop-lien system, only to find it waiting for them. Others stood and fought, as one pamphlet exhorted in 1889, "not with glittering musket, flaming sword and deadly cannon, but with the silent, potent and all-powerful ballot."

The Origins of the Farmers' Alliance >> Before farmers could vote together, they had to join together. Harsh and isolated life on the farm limited opportunities to unify. Such conditions shocked Oliver Hudson Kelley as he traveled across the South after the Civil War. In 1867 the young government clerk founded the Patrons of Husbandry to brighten the lives of farmers and broaden their horizons. Local chapters, called "granges," brought a dozen or so farmers and their families together to pray, sing, and learn new farming techniques. The Grangers sponsored fairs, picnics, dances, lectures—anything to break the isolation of farm life. After a slow start the Patrons of Husbandry grew quickly. By 1875 there were 800,000 members in 20,000 locales, most in the Midwest, South, and Southwest.

At first the Grangers swore off politics. But in a pattern often repeated, socializing led to a recognition of common problems, and recognition to economic and then political solutions. By pooling their money for supplies and equipment to store and market their crops, for example, Grangers sought to avoid the high charges of middlemen such as millers and operators of giant silos or "elevators" for storing grain. By the early 1870s they were lobbying midwestern legislatures to adopt "Granger laws" regulating rates charged by railroads and intermediaries.

Eight "Granger cases" came before the Supreme Court in the 1870s to test the new regulatory measures. The most important, *Munn v. Illinois* (1877), upheld the right of Illinois to regulate private property "devoted to a public use"(in this case, grain elevators). Later decisions allowed state regulation of railroads but only within state lines. Congress responded in 1887 by creating the Interstate Commerce Commission, a federal agency to regulate commerce across state boundaries. Although it had little power, it was a key step toward establishing the right to police corporations.

Slumping prices in the 1870s and 1880s bred new farm organizations. Slowly they blended into what the press called the "Alliance Movement." The Southern Alliance, formed in Texas in 1875, spread rapidly after Dr. Charles W. Macune took command in 1886. A doctor and lawyer as well as a farmer, Macune planned to expand the state's network of local chapters, or "sub-alliances," into a national network of state Alliance exchanges. The exchanges pooled resources in jointly owned businesses for buying and selling, milling and storing, banking and manufacturing.

Soon the Southern Alliance was publicizing its activities in local newspapers, publishing a journal, and sending lecturers across the country. For a brief period, between 1886 and 1892, the Alliance cooperatives, as the jointly owned businesses were called, multiplied throughout the South. They grew to more than a million members and challenged accepted ways of doing business. Macune claimed that his new Texas Exchange saved members 40 percent on plows and 30 percent on wagons. But most Alliance cooperatives failed, the result of poor management and business hostility.

Although the Southern Alliance admitted no African Americans, it encouraged them to organize. A small group of Black and white Texans founded the Colored Farmers' National Alliance and Cooperative Union in 1886. By 1891 a quarter of a million Black farmers had joined. Their operations were largely secret, since public action often brought swift retaliation from white supremacists. When the Colored Farmers' Alliance organized a strike of Black cotton pickers near Memphis in 1891, white mobs hunted down and lynched 15 strikers. The murders went unpunished, and the Colored Alliance began to founder.

The Alliance Peaks >> The key to success for what soon became known as the National Farmers' Alliance lay not in organization but leadership. Alliance lecturers fanned out across the South and the Great Plains, creating sub-alliances and teaching new members about finance and cooperative businesses. Women were often as active as men, sometimes more active. In the summer of 1890 alone, Alliance organizer Mary Elizabeth Lease, the "Kansas Pythoness" known for her biting attacks on big business, gave 160 speeches.

In 1890 members of the Alliance met in Ocala, Florida, and issued the "Ocala Demands." The manifesto reflected their deep distrust of the "money power"—large corporations and banks whose financial clout gave them the ability to manipulate markets. The Ocala Demands called on government to reduce tariffs, abolish national banks, regulate railroads, and coin silver freely. The platform also demanded a federal income tax to counteract land taxes, which fell most heavily on farmers, and the popular election of senators to make government more responsive to the public.

The most innovative feature came from Charles Macune. His "subtreasury system" would have required the federal government to furnish warehouses for storing crops until prices rose and low-interest loans to tide farmers over. Under such a system, farmers would no longer have to sell in a low-price, glutted market, as they did under the crop-lien system. And they could expand the money supply simply by borrowing at harvest time.

"You ought to be ashamed of yourself!"

⌃ This illustration by artist W. W. Denslow, titled *You Ought to Be Ashamed of Yourself,* is from *The Wonderful Wizard of OZ,* published in 1900 by L. Frank Baum. It was the first of 14 best-selling books on the mythical land. Although Baum claimed only to be telling children's stories, some readers have found a symbolic resemblance to the Populist politics of the day. The "yellow brick road" is the gold standard, they say, leading to a place of false promises (the Emerald City of Oz) under the spell of a bellowing politician (the Wizard), who is exposed by the Scarecrow (farmers), the Tin Man (laborers), and the Lion (the Populists).
Library of Congress, Prints and Photographs Division

In the off-year elections of 1890 the old parties faced hostile farmers across the nation. In the South, the Alliance worked within the Democratic Party and elected 4 governors, won 8 legislatures, and sent 44 members of the House and 3 senators to Washington. In the Midwest, newly created farmer parties elected 5 representatives, 2 senators, and took over both houses of the Nebraska legislature.

In February 1892, as the presidential election year opened, a convention of 900 labor, feminist, farm, and other reform delegates, 100 of them Black, met in St. Louis. They founded the People's, or Populist, Party, which they said was open to all "toilers." They called for another convention to nominate a presidential ticket. Initially southern Populists held back, clinging to their strategy of working within the Democrat Party. But when newly elected Democrats failed to support Alliance programs, southern leaders, led by Tom Watson of Georgia, abandoned the Democrats and began recruiting Black and white farmers for the Populists. Although a wealthy farmer, Watson sympathized with the poor of both races.

The national convention of Populists met in Omaha, Nebraska, on Independence Day, 1892. Their impassioned platform promised to return government "to the hands of 'the plain people.'" Planks advocated the subtreasury plan, unlimited coinage of silver as well as an increase in the money supply, direct election of senators, an income tax, and government ownership of railroads, telegraph, and telephone. To attract wage earners, the party endorsed the eight-hour workday, restriction of immigration, and a ban on the use of Pinkerton detectives in labor disputes. Pinkertons had engaged in a savage gun battle with strikers that year at Andrew Carnegie's Homestead Steel Plant. Delegates rallied behind the old greenbacker and Union general James B. Weaver, carefully balancing their presidential nomination with a one-legged Confederate veteran as his running mate.

The Election of 1892 >>

The Populists enlivened the otherwise dull campaign, as Democrat Grover Cleveland and Republican incumbent Benjamin Harrison refought the election of 1888. This time, however, Cleveland won, and for the first time since the Civil War, Democrats gained control of both houses of Congress. The Populists, too, enjoyed success. Weaver became the first third-party candidate to poll over a million votes in a presidential election. Populists elected 3 governors, 5 senators, 10 representatives, and nearly 1,500 members of state legislatures.

Despite these short-term strengths, the election revealed dangerous longer-term weaknesses in the People's Party. A campaign of intimidation and repression hurt the People's Party in the South, where Tom Watson's courtship of Blacks appalled white Democrats. In the North, Populists failed to win over labor and most city dwellers, who were concerned with family budgets, not the problems of farmers and the downtrodden.

The darker side of populism also put off many Americans. Its rhetoric was often violent and laced with anti-immigrant, nativist slurs; it spoke ominously of conspiracies and stridently in favor of immigration restriction. In fact the Alliance

lost members, an omen of defeats to come. But the People's Party had demonstrated two conflicting truths: how far from the needs of many ordinary Americans the two parties had drifted, and how difficult it would be to break their power.

THEN&NOW

"When we hear populism," observed one journalist in 2019, "we think Donald Trump." Yet the man and his followers bear little resemblance to the nineteenth-century agrarian revolt from which the word comes. Unlike the forty-fifth president, a city boy from a wealthy family, most nineteenth-century Populists were poor farm folk. Frustrated over the rising power of corporations and bankers, they believed that only government regulation and increased voter participation could set things right. Modern-day populists may come from countryside or city, may be poor or rich, and likely believe that the power of corporations ought to be unleashed through deregulation and that voting requirements should be tighter, not looser. As it turns out, what we call populism is less a coherent set of beliefs than a political style. Anger ignites it, and distant enemies animate it: "elites," outsiders, and craven politicians. Grievances, real or imagined, feed the anger; conspiracy theories sustain it. The Populists of old shared all these traits and employed all these techniques, just as populism does today, whatever its current targets.

✔ **REVIEW**

How did the National Farmers' Alliance and the People's Party attempt to resolve the problems faced by farmers?

THE NEW REALIGNMENT

On May 1, 1893, President Cleveland was in Chicago to throw the switch that set ablaze 10,000 electric bulbs and opened the World's Columbian Exposition. Four days later, a wave of bankruptcies destroyed major firms across the country and stock prices sank to all-time lows, setting off the depression of 1893.

At first Chicago staved off the worst, thanks to the business generated by the world's fair. But when its doors closed in October, thousands of workers found themselves without a job. Chicago's mayor estimated the number of unemployed in the city to be near 200,000. He had some firsthand experience on which to base his calculations. Every night desperate men slept on the floors and stairways of City Hall, and every police station in the city put up 60 to 100 additional homeless people.

The sharp contrast between the exposition's White City and the nation's economic misery demonstrated the inability

^ Charles Dana Gibson, the Massachusetts-born illustrator famous for his portraits of well-bred young women in the 1890s, tackles a different subject in this ink drawing: a bread line of mixed classes during the depression of 1893.
Buyenlarge/SuperStock

of the political system to smooth out the economic cycle of boom and bust. The new industrial order had brought prosperity by increasing production, opening markets, and tying Americans closer together. In 1893 the price of interdependence came due. A major downturn in one area affected the other sectors of the economy. Overexpansion led to a massive contraction. With no way to control swings in the business cycle, depression came on a scale as large as that of the booming prosperity. Out of the crisis emerged a political realignment that left the Republican Party in control of national politics.

The Depression of 1893 >> The depression of 1893, the deepest the nation had yet undergone, lasted until 1897. Railroad baron and descendant of two presidents Charles Francis Adams Jr. called it a "convulsion," but the country experienced it as crushing idleness. By the end of 1894, unemployment hit nearly 20 percent.

The federal government turned a deaf ear to cries for help. "While the people should patriotically and cheerfully support their Government," President Cleveland declared, "its functions do not include the support of the people." The states offered little more. Relief, like poverty, was considered a private matter. The burden fell on local charities, benevolent societies, churches, labor unions, and ward bosses.

Many had little sympathy for those in need. The popular preacher Henry Ward Beecher told his congregation what most Americans believed: "No man in this land suffers from poverty unless it be more than his fault—unless it be his sin." But the scale of hardship was so great, its targets so random, that anyone could be thrown out of work—an industrious

neighbor, a factory supervisor with 20 years on the job, a bank president. Older attitudes about sinfulness and personal responsibility for poverty began to give way to new ideas about its social origins and the obligation of public agencies to help.

The Rumblings of Unrest >> Even before the depression, rumblings of unrest had begun to roll across the country. The Great Railroad Strike of 1877 ignited nearly two decades of labor strife. After 1893 discontent mounted as wages were cut, employees laid off, and factories closed. During the first year of the depression, 1,400 strikes sent more than half a million workers from their jobs. It was the closest the country had ever come to class warfare.

Uneasy business executives and politicians saw radicalism and the possibility of revolution in every strike. But the depression of 1893 had unleashed another force: popular discontent. In the spring of 1894, "General" Jacob Coxey, a 39-year-old Populist and factory owner, proved the point. On Easter Sunday he launched the "Tramps' March on Washington" from Massillon, Ohio. His "Commonweal Army of Christ," consisting of some 500 men, women, and children, descended on Washington to offer "a petition with boots on" for a federal program of public works. Security around the White House tightened as other "armies" of unemployed mobilized. On May 1, Coxey's troops, armed with "clubs of peace," massed at the foot of the Capitol. When Coxey entered the grounds, 100 mounted police routed the protestors and arrested him for trespassing. Nothing significant came of the protest, other than to signal a growing demand for government action.

Federal help was not forthcoming. President Cleveland had barely moved into the White House when the depression struck. The country blamed him; he blamed silver. In his view the Sherman Silver Purchase Act of 1890 had shaken business confidence by forcing the government to use its shrinking reserves of gold to purchase (though not coin) silver. Panicked conservatives worried that the national gold reserves were going to run out. Repeal of the Sherman Act, Cleveland believed, was the way to build gold reserves and restore confidence. After bitter debate, Congress complied. The economic tinkering only strengthened the resolve of "silverites" in the Democratic Party to overwhelm Cleveland's conservative "gold" wing.

Worse for the president, repeal of silver purchases brought no economic revival and cost the Democrats in Congress. In the short run, abandoning silver hurt the economy by contracting the money supply just when expansion might have

WHAT SHOULD THE GOVERNMENT DO?

In 1887 President Grover Cleveland vetoed the "Texas Seed Bill," legislation designed to aid drought-stricken Texas farmers (Document 1). Four years later, Nebraska farmer W. M. Taylor made a desperate plea for help in the face of natural and human-made disasters (Document 2).

DOCUMENT 1
President Grover Cleveland: Government Should Not Help Individuals

It is represented that a long-continued and extensive drought has existed in certain portions of the State of Texas, resulting in a failure of crops and consequent distress and destitution. Though there has been some difference in statements concerning the extent of the people's needs in the localities thus affected, there seems to be no doubt that there has existed a condition calling for relief; and I am willing to believe that, notwithstanding the aid already furnished, a donation of seed grain to the farmers located in this region, to enable them to put in new crops, would serve to avert a continuance or return of an unfortunate blight.

And yet I feel obliged to withhold my approval of the plan as proposed by this bill, to indulge a benevolent and charitable sentiment through the appropriation of public funds for that purpose.

I can find no warrant for such an appropriation in the Constitution, and I do not believe that the power and duty of the general government ought to be extended to the relief of individual suffering which is in no manner properly related to the public service or benefit. A prevalent tendency to disregard the limited mission of this power and

duty should, I think be steadfestly resisted, to the end that the lesson should be constantly enforced that, though the people support the government, the government should not support the people.

The friendliness and charity of our countrymen can always be relied upon to relieve their fellow citizens in misfortune. This has been repeatedly and quite lately demonstrated. Federal aid in such cases encourages the expectation of paternal care on the part of the government and weakens the sturdiness of our national character, while it prevents the indulgence among our people of that kindly sentiment and conduct which strengthens the bonds of a common brotherhood.

It is within my personal knowledge that individual aid has, to some extent, already been extended to the sufferers mentioned in this bill. The failure of the proposed appropriation of $10,000 additional to meet their remaining wants, will not necessarily result in continued distress if the emergency is fully made known to the people of the country.

It is here suggested that the Commissioner of Agriculture is annually directed to expend a large sum of money for the purchase, propagation, and distribution of

seeds and other things of this description, two-thirds of which are, upon the request of senators, representatives, and delegates in Congress, supplied to them for distribution among their constituents.

The appropriation of the current year for this purpose is $100,000, and it will probably be no less in the appropriation for the ensuing year. I understand that a large quantity of grain is furnished for such distribution, and it is supposed that this free apportionment among their neighbors is a privilege which may be waived by our senators and representatives.

If sufficient of them should request the Commissioner of Agriculture to send their shares of the grain thus allowed them, to the suffering farmers of Texas, they might be enabled to sow their crops; the constituents, for whom in theory this grain is intended could well bear the temporary deprivation, and the donors would experience the satisfaction attending deeds of charity.

"President Grover Cleveland Vetoes Disaster Relief Legislation, February 16, 1887," reprinted in J. F. Watts and Fred Israel, eds., Presidential Documents: The Speeches, Proclamations, and Policies That Have Shaped the Nation from Washington to Clinton (New York: Routledge, 2000), pp. 164–165.

DOCUMENT 2
W. M. Taylor: Farmers' Problems Are Beyond Their Control

This season is without a parallel in this part of the country. The hot winds burned up the entire crop, leaving thousands of families wholly destitute, many of whom might have been able to run through this crisis had it not been for the galling yoke put on them by the money loaners and sharks—not by charging 7 per cent per annum, which is the lawful rate of interest or even 10 per cent but the unlawful and inhuman country destroying rate of 3 per cent a month, some going still farther and charging 50 per cent per annum. We are cursed, many of us financially, beyond redemption, not by the hot winds so much as by the swindling game of the bankers and money loaners, who have taken the money and now are after the property, leaving the farmer

moneyless and homeless. . . . I have borrowed for example $1,000. I pay $25 besides to the commission man. I give my note and second mortgage of 3 per cent of the $1,000 which is $30 more. Then I pay 7 per cent on the $1,000 to the actual loaner. Then besides all this I pay for appraising the land, abstract, recording, etc., so when I have secured my loan I am out the first year $150. Yet I am told by the agent who loans me the money, he can't stand to loan at such low rates. This is on the farm, but now come the chattel loan. I must have $50 to save myself. I get the money; my note is made payable in thirty or sixty days for $35, secured by chattel of two horses, harness and wagon about five times the value of the note. The time comes to pay, I ask for a few

days. No I can't wait; must have the money. If I can't get the money, I have the extreme pleasure of seeing my property taken and sold by this iron handed money loaner while my family and I suffer.

"W. M. Taylor to editor, Farmer's Alliance (Lincoln), January 10, 1891," Nebraska Historical Society, reprinted in Robert D. Marcus and David Burner, eds., America Firsthand, Vol. II (New York: St. Martin's Press, 1992), p. 90.

THINKING CRITICALLY

How does President Cleveland justify his veto of the "Texas Seed Bill"? What, in his view, is the role of the federal government in times of disaster? What problems does the farmer face? How would President Cleveland have responded to the farmer's letter?

stimulated it by providing needed credit. As alarm and unemployment spread, Cleveland's popularity plummeted. Democrats were buried in the congressional elections of 1894. Dropping moralistic reforms and stressing national activism, Republicans won control of both the House and the Senate.

With the Democrats confined to the South, the politics of stalemate was over. All that remained for the Republican Party was to capture the White House in 1896.

The Battle of the Standards >> The campaign of 1896 quickly became a "battle of the standards." Both major parties obsessed over whether gold alone or gold and silver should become the monetary standard. Most Republicans saw gold as the stable base for building business confidence and economic prosperity. They adopted a platform calling for "sound money" supported by gold. Their candidate, Governor William McKinley of Ohio, cautiously supported the gold plank and firmly believed in high tariffs to protect American industry.

Silverites campaigned for "free and independent" coinage of silver, in which the Treasury freely minted all the silver presented to it, independent of other nations. Sixteen ounces of silver would equal one ounce of gold. Silverites believed increasing the supply of money would aid debtors, especially farmers, by raising the prices of their commodities, lowering the interest rates they paid, and bringing about economic recovery, or so their theory went. But the free silver movement was more than a monetary theory. It was a symbolic protest of region and class—of the agricultural South and West against the commercial Northeast, of debt-ridden farm folk against industrialists and financiers, of have-nots against haves.

At the Democratic National Convention in Chicago, William Jennings Bryan of Nebraska was ready to fight as well. Just 36 years old, Bryan looked "like a young divine," with a booming voice that could fill a hall before electronic amplification. He had served two terms in Congress and worked as a journalist. He favored low tariffs, opposed the pro-gold Cleveland, and came out belatedly for free silver. Systematically, he coordinated a quiet fight for his nomination.

Silverites controlled the convention from the start. They paraded with silver banners, wore silver buttons, and wrote a plank into the anti-Cleveland platform calling for free and unlimited coinage of the metal. The high point came when Bryan stepped to the lectern and offered himself to "a cause as holy as the cause of liberty—the cause of humanity." The crowd was in a near frenzy as he reached the dramatic climax and spread his arms in mock crucifixion: "You shall not crucify mankind upon a cross of gold." No condemnation of the gold standard could have been stronger. The next day, in the wake of his "Cross of

Gold" speech, the convention nominated him for the presidency.

Populists were in a quandary. They expected the Democrats to stick with Cleveland and gold and counted on unhappy silverites flocking to their camp. Instead, the Democrats endorsed silver and nominated Bryan. "If we fuse [with the Democrats] we are sunk," complained one Populist. "If we don't fuse, all the silver men we have will leave us for the more powerful Democrats." At a bitter convention, those who wanted to join with the Democrats nominated Bryan for president. The best the opposition could do was to nominate a vice presidential candidate, Tom Watson, the agrarian firebrand from Georgia.

Campaign and Election >> Bryan knew he faced an uphill battle. Mounting an aggressive campaign that would be imitated in the future, he traveled 18,000 miles by train, gave as many as 30 speeches a day, and reached perhaps 3 million people in 27 states. The nomination of the People's Party actually did more harm than good by labeling Bryan a Populist (which he was not) and a radical (which he definitely was not). Devoted to the "plain people," the Great Commoner spoke for rural America and Jeffersonian values— small farmers, small towns, small government—and put them all on a silver platter.

McKinley knew he could not match Bryan's barnstorming. He contented himself with sedate speeches from his front porch in Canton, Ohio. The folksy appearance of the campaign belied its reality. From the beginning, campaign strategist Marcus Alonzo Hanna, a talented Ohio industrialist, relied on modern techniques of organization and marketing. The well-financed campaign brought tens of thousands to Canton. They cheered McKinley's promises of the return of prosperity and a "full dinner pail." Hanna saturated the

⌃ William Jennings Bryan made the first of his three presidential bids in 1896, when he ran on both the Democratic and Populist tickets. Passionate in his convictions and devoted to the "plain people," the "Great Commoner" is depicted in this hostile cartoon as a Populist snake devouring the Democratic Party.
Source: Library of Congress, Prints and Photographs Division

country with millions of leaflets, along with 1,400 speakers attacking free trade and free silver. McKinley won in a landslide, with the first majority of the popular vote since Ulysses S. Grant in 1872.

The election proved to be one of the most critical in the Republic's history.[1] Over the previous three decades, political life had been characterized by more noise than substance, slim party margins, high voter turnout, and low-profile presidents. The election of 1896 signaled a new era of shrinking party loyalties and voter turnout, stronger presidents, and Republican rule.

McKinley's victory broke the political stalemate and forged a powerful coalition that dominated politics for the next 30 years. It rested on the industrial cities of the Northeast and Midwest and combined old support from businesses, farmers, and Union army veterans with broader backing from industrial wage earners. The Democrats controlled little but the South. And the Populists virtually vanished, but not

Candidate (Party)	Electoral Vote (%)	Popular Vote (%)
William McKinley (Republican)	271 (61)	7,108,480 (52)
William Jennings Bryan (Democrat)	176 (39)	6,511,495 (48)
Nonvoting territories		

MAP 21.1: ELECTION OF 1896

The critical election of 1896 established the Republicans as the majority party, ending two decades of political gridlock with a new political realignment. Republican victor William McKinley dominated the large industrial cities and states, as the returns of the Electoral College show.

[1] Five elections, in addition to the contest of 1896, are often cited as critical shifts in voter allegiance and party alignments: the Federalist defeat of 1800, Andrew Jackson's rise in 1828, Lincoln's Republican triumph of 1860, Al Smith's Democratic loss in 1928, and—perhaps—Ronald Reagan's conservative tide of 1980.

before serving as a catalyst for political change, an impetus for federal action, and a prelude to a new age of reform.

The Rise of Jim Crow Politics >> In 1892, despite the stumping of Populists, African Americans cast their ballots for Republicans, when they could vote at all. Increasingly, their voting rights were being erased across the South.

As the century drew to a close, long-standing racialism—categorizing people on the basis of race—deepened. The arrival of "new" immigrants from eastern and southern Europe and the acquisition of new overseas colonies, often populated by people of color, encouraged prejudices that championed white supremacy, segregation, and other forms of racial control.

In the South, the white supremacy campaign launched a drive to deprive poor southerners, Black and white, of their right to vote. Ostensibly directed at African Americans, these campaigns had the broader aim of quashing rebellion from below.

Mississippi, where Democrats had led the move to "redeem" their state from Republican Reconstruction, took the lead in disfranchising or depriving African Americans of the right to vote. In 1890 a new state constitution required voters to pay a poll tax and pass a literacy test, which eliminated the great majority of Black voters. Conservative Democrats favored the plan, because it also reduced the voting of poor whites, who were likely to join opposition parties. Before the new constitution went into effect, Mississippi contained more than 250,000 eligible voters. By 1892, after its adoption, there were fewer than 77,000. Between 1895 and 1908, white supremacy and disfranchisement campaigns won out in every southern state, barring many poor whites from voting as well as Blacks.

The white supremacy and disfranchisement campaigns had one final consequence. They split rebellious whites from Blacks, as the fate of Tom Watson demonstrated. Only a dozen years after his biracial campaign of 1892, Watson was promoting Black disfranchisement in Georgia. Like other southern Populists, Watson returned to the Democrat Party still hoping to help poor whites. Only by playing a powerful race card could he hope to win election. "What does civilization owe the negro?," he asked bitterly. "Nothing! Nothing!! NOTHING!!!" In 1920, after a decade of baiting Blacks (as well as Catholics and Jews), the Georgia rebel was elected to the Senate. Watson, who began with such high racial ideals, gained power by abandoning them.

The African American Response >> To mount a successful crusade for disenfranchisement, white conservatives inflamed racial passions. They staged "White Supremacy Jubilees" and peppered newspaper editorials with complaints of "bumptious" and "impudent" African Americans. The number of Black lynchings by whites peaked during the 1890s, averaging over a hundred a year for the decade. Most took place in the South.

Under such circumstances African Americans worked out their own responses to racial intolerance. Ida B. Wells, a

^ This black-and-white photo of the charismatic African American activist and educator Booker T. Washington highlights his piercing gray eyes, nearly luminous against what one observer described as his "reddish" complexion. Born into slavery, Washington sits here with his legs casually crossed, a literate, well-to-do free man in a suit and tie. (Note the reading material in his lap.) "He wasn't dark and he wasn't light," wrote the composer Zenobia Powell Perry. "I'll never forget those eyes." In many ways Washington served as a bridge between white and Black worlds and his "in between" complexion may have advanced that role.
Library of Congress, Prints and Phototgraphs Division(LC-USZ62-49568)

Black woman born into slavery, launched a nationwide campaign against lynching when a friend and two of his partners in the People's Grocery were brutally murdered after a fight with a white competitor in 1892. Wells dedicated much of her time to educating Americans about the use of lynching and other forms of mob violence to terrorize African Americans. Though her lobbying failed to produce a federal antilynching law, Wells did help organize Black women, eventually into the National Association of Colored Women in 1896. This group supported wide-ranging reforms, including education, housing, health care, and, of course, antilynching laws.

Wells's campaign focused on stopping mob violence, but Booker T. Washington, another formerly enslaved African American, emphasized the need for working within the prevailing framework of race relations for the time being. In a speech in Atlanta in 1895, he conceded that white prejudice existed throughout the South but counseled African Americans to work for their economic betterment through manual labor. Every laborer who learned a trade, every farmer who tilled the land could increase his or her savings. Those earnings amounted to "a little green ballot" that "no one will throw out or refuse to count." Toward that end, the ever-practical Washington founded the Tuskegee Institute in Alabama in 1881. It stressed vocational skills for farming, manual trades, and industrial work.

Many white Americans hailed what one Black critic called Washington's "Atlanta Compromise," for it struck the note of patient humility they were eager to hear. For African Americans, it made the best of a bad situation. Washington, a practical politician, discovered that philanthropists across the nation were eager to support Tuskegee. He was the guest of Andrew Carnegie at his imposing Skibo Castle in Scotland. California railroad magnate Collis Huntington became his friend, as did other business executives eager to discuss "public and social questions."

Throughout, Washington preached accommodation to the racial caste system. He accepted segregation (as long as separate facilities were equal) and qualifications on voting (if they applied to white citizens as well). Above all, Washington sought economic self-improvement for common Black folk in fields and factories. In 1900 he organized the National Negro Business League to help establish Black business executives as the leaders of their people. The rapid growth of local chapters (320 by 1907) extended his influence across the country.

McKinley in the White House >> In William McKinley, Republicans found a skillful chief with a national agenda and personal charm. He cultivated news reporters and openly walked the streets of Washington. He courted the public with handshakes and flowers plucked from his lapel. Firmly but delicately, he curbed the power of state bosses. When necessary, he even prodded Congress to action. In all these ways, he foreshadowed "modern" presidents, who would act as party leaders rather than as executive caretakers.

Fortune at first smiled on McKinley. When he entered the White House, the economy had already begun its recovery. Factory orders were slowly increasing, and unemployment dropped. Farm prices climbed. New discoveries of gold in Alaska and South Africa expanded the supply of money without causing "gold bugs" to panic that the economy was being destabilized by silver.

Freed from the burdens of the economic crisis, McKinley called a special session of Congress to increase the tariff, as he had promised during his campaign. In 1897 the Dingley Tariff raised protective rates to their highest levels in history, but again added a provision for reciprocity as a concession to opponents. McKinley also sought a solution for resolving railroad strikes before they turned violent. The Erdman Act of 1898 set up machinery for government arbitration of labor disputes with railroads. McKinley even began laying plans for stronger regulation of trusts.

The same expansiveness that had pushed an industrial nation across the continent, displayed its wares at Chicago's world's fair, and shipped grain and cotton abroad was also drawing the country into a race for empire and a war with Spain. Regulation—and an age of reform—would have to wait.

✓ **REVIEW**

How did the election of 1896 resolve the "politics of stalemate" of the late nineteenth century?

VISIONS OF EMPIRE

It took a war with Spain to turn American attention abroad. Underlying the conflict were larger forces linking the United States to the world economy and international events. By the 1890s, southern farmers were exporting half their cotton crop to factories worldwide. Wheat farmers earned some 30 to 40 percent of their income from foreign markets. John D. Rockefeller's Standard Oil Company shipped about two-thirds of its refined products overseas, and Cyrus McCormick supplied Russian farmers with his famous reaper for harvesting crops.

More than commerce turned American eyes overseas. Since the 1840s, expansionists had spoken of a divine destiny to overspread the North American continent. Some Americans still cast covetous eyes at Canada to the north and Mexico and Cuba to the south. The boldest dreamed of empire in more-distant lands to match the empires of other great world powers.

Imperialism, European and American

Style >> The scramble for colonies, resources, and markets was well under way by the time the Americans, Japanese, and Germans entered the race in the late nineteenth century. Spain and Portugal still clung to the remnants of their seventeenth-century empires. Meanwhile, Great Britain, France, and Russia accelerated their drive to control foreign peoples and lands. The late nineteenth century be-

imperialism acquisition of control over the government and the economy of another nation, usually by conquest.

came the new age of **imperialism** because weapons technology and modern networks of communication, transportation, and commerce brought the prospect of truly global empires within reach.

The speed and efficiency with which Europeans took over in the Niger and Congo basins of Africa in the 1880s prompted many Americans to argue for this European-style imperialism of conquest and possession. Other Americans preferred a more indirect imperialism that exported products, ideas, and influence. To them, this American-style imperialism seemed somehow purer. Under it, Americans could position themselves as bearers of long-cherished values of democracy, free-enterprise capitalism, and Christianity. In return they would gain new markets and cheap natural resources.

While Americans justified imperial control in the name of such values, social, economic, and political forces were drawing the nation into a hard-knuckled race for a more traditional empire. The growth of industrial networks linked the United States to international markets as never before. With economic systems more tightly knit and political systems more responsive to industrialists and financiers, a rush for control of distant markets and lands was perhaps unavoidable.

The Shapers of American Imperialism >>

Although expansion and imperialism had wide appeal at the end of the nineteenth century, the small farmer or steelworker cared little about how the United States advanced its goals abroad. It was an elite group of Christian missionaries, intellectuals, business leaders, and commercial farmers, joined with navy officers, who shaped American imperialism. They lobbied the White House and Congress, where foreign policy was made, and the State and War Departments, where it was carried out.

In 1880 the U.S. Navy ranked twelfth in the world, behind Denmark and Chile. The United States had a coastal fleet but no functional group of vessels to protect its interests abroad.

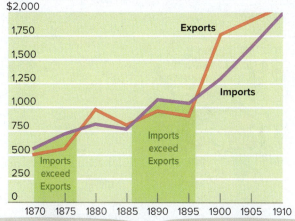

BALANCE OF U.S. IMPORTS AND EXPORTS, 1870–1910

After the depression of 1893 both imports and exports rose sharply, suggesting one reason why the age of imperialism was so closely linked with the emerging global industrial economy.
Photo: James Steidl/iStockphoto

IMPERIALIST EXPANSION, 1900

The race for colonies accelerated in the late nineteenth century as European nations scrambled for empire. New world powers—in particular Germany, Italy, Japan, and the United States—expanded their holdings. A comparison of Africa in 1878 (inset) and 1900 shows how quickly Europeans extended their colonial empires. Often resource-poor countries like Japan and England saw colonies as a way to acquire raw materials: diamonds from South Africa or tin from Southeast Asia. A closer look reveals that four of the most rapidly industrializing countries—Germany, Japan, Russia, and the United States—had few if any overseas possessions, even in 1900. And while China appears to be undivided, all the major powers had established spheres of influence there.

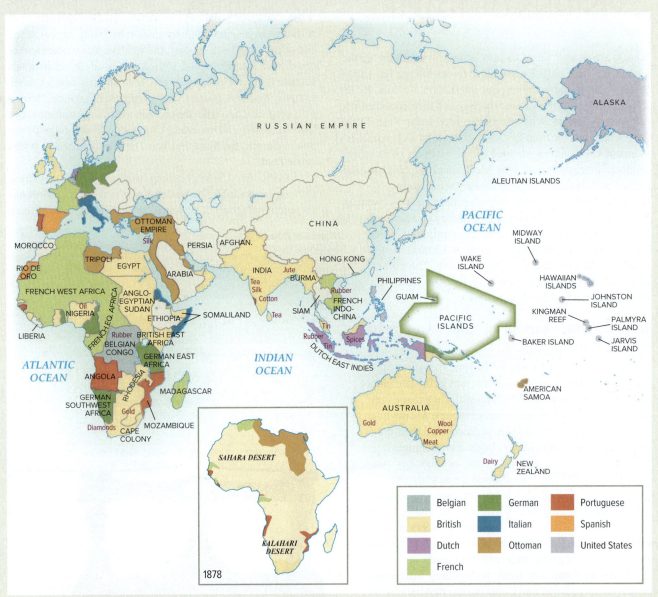

MAP READING

1. What is the biggest U.S. possession on the map? The next biggest?
2. What raw materials were imperial nations seeking in Africa? In India and Southeast Asia? In Australia and New Zealand?
3. Which European nation appears to possess the most geographically widespread empire

MAP INTERPRETATION

1. Which countries were winning the race for empire by 1900? On what grounds should we make that judgment?
2. What geographic factors explain the location of U.S. possessions?
3. Why did rapidly industrializing nations such as Germany, Japan, Russia, and the United States have so few overseas possessions?

Unhappy naval officers combined with trade-hungry business leaders to press Congress for a modern navy. Alfred Thayer Mahan, a navy captain and later admiral, formulated their ideas into a widely accepted theory of **navalism**. In *The Influence of Sea Power upon History* (1890), Mahan argued that all great nations were seafaring powers that relied on foreign trade for wealth and might. The only way to protect foreign markets was with large cruisers and battleships. Operating far from American shores, the new navy would need coaling stations and other facilities for resupply throughout the world.

navalism theories of warfare and trade that rely on a nation's navy as a principal instrument of policy.

Mahan's logic was so persuasive and the potential profits to be reaped from overseas sales so great that Congress finally acted. It launched a program to rebuild the old wood-and-sail navy with steam vessels made of steel. By 1900 the U.S. Navy ranked third in the world and finally had the means to become an imperial power.

Protestant missionaries provided a spiritual rationale that complemented Mahan's navalism. Although overseas missionaries often encountered people whose cultural differences made them unreceptive to Christianity, many thought that adequate exposure to Western culture could turn them into true believers. Missionaries introduced Western goods, education, and systems of government administration—any "civilizing medium," as one minister remarked. They harbored no territorial ambitions and opposed direct military or political intervention, but fancied themselves agents of cultural advancement. With great enthusiasm, they took up what the British poet and imperial apologist Rudyard Kipling called the "white man's burden" of civilizing the lesser, "colored" races of the world.

From scholars, academics, and scientists came racial theories to justify expansion. Charles Darwin's *On the Origin of Species* (1859) had popularized the notion that among animal species the fittest survived through a process of natural selection. Social Darwinists argued that the same laws of survival governed the social order. When applied aggressively, social Darwinism justified theories of white supremacy as well as the slaughter and enslavement of those who resisted conquest.

Perhaps more compelling than either racial or religious motives was the need for trade. The business cycle of boom and bust reminded Americans of the unpredictability of their economy. In hard times people sought salvation wherever they could, and one obvious road to economic redemption lay in markets abroad. The National Association of Manufacturers explained that, with American companies outgrowing the home market, "expansion of our foreign trade is [the] only promise of relief."

⌃ Missionaries often viewed the Chinese as uncivilized "heathen," whose souls needed saving and whose culture needed civilizing. This cartoon, published around 1900, pokes fun at the common stereotype by suggesting what the Chinese must think of the American "heathen." "Contributions Received Here to Save the Foreign Devils," reads the sign of the Chinese "preacher," who laments the uncivilized behavior of corrupt American city governments, feuding backwoodsmen, rioting laborers, and mobs tormenting Chinese and Black Americans.
Library of Congress, Prints and Photographs Division [LC-USZC2-1029]

Dreams of a Commercial Empire >> No one did

more to initiate the idea of a "New Empire" of commerce than William Henry Seward, secretary of state under Abraham Lincoln and Andrew Johnson. Seward believed that "empire has . . . made its way constantly westward." He believed that the United States must be prepared to assert supremacy all the way to Asia—not by acquiring colonies or sending troops but by pursuing commerce. Equal access to foreign markets, often called the "open door," guided U.S. policy in Asia and made Seward's strategy truly revolutionary.

Seward simultaneously pursued ties to Japan, Korea, and China, along with a transcontinental railroad at home and a canal across the Central American isthmus. Link by link, he was trying to connect eastern factories to western ports in the United States and, from there, to markets in Asia. In pursuit of these goals Seward made two acquisitions in 1867: Midway Island in the Pacific and Alaska. Midway was unimportant by itself; its value lay in being a way station across the ocean not far from Hawai'i, where missionary planters were already establishing an American presence. Critics called Alaska "Seward's Folly," but folly turned out to be a fortune. He paid roughly 2 cents an acre for a mineral-rich territory twice the size of Texas.

Seward's conviction that the future of the United States lay in the Pacific and Asia flourished in the 1890s. By then, Mahan's naval theory had won powerful supporters, and the vanishing American frontier supplied an economic rationale for extending Manifest Destiny beyond continental borders.

Hawai'i was the crucial link in expansionist hopes to extend trade across the Pacific to China, affording a fine naval base and a refueling station. In 1893 U.S. sugar planters overthrew the recently enthroned Queen Liliuokalani, a Hawaiian nationalist eager to rid the island of American influence. The planters' success was ensured when a contingent of U.S. marines landed on the pretext of protecting American lives.

Eager to avoid the McKinley Tariff's new tax on sugar imported into the United States, planters lobbied for the annexation of Hawai'i. President Cleveland refused. He was no foe of expansion but was, as his secretary of state noted, "unalterably opposed to stealing territory, or of annexing people against their consent, and the people of Hawai'i do not favor annexation." The idea of incorporating the nonwhite population also troubled Cleveland. President William McKinley had no such qualms. When the provisional government in Hawai'i continued to press for annexation, McKinley offered little resistance. In 1898, under a congressional resolution, Hawai'i officially became a territory of the United States.

✔ REVIEW

What social, economic, and cultural factors drew the United States into the race for empire?

THE IMPERIAL MOMENT

In 1895, after almost 15 years of planning from exile in the United States, José Martí returned to Cuba to renew the struggle for independence from Spain. With cries of *Cuba libre* ("free Cuba"), Martí and his rebels cut railroad lines, destroyed sugar mills, and set fire to cane fields. Within a year rebel forces controlled more than half the island.

The Spanish overlords struck back at the rebels with brutal violence. Governor-General Valeriano Weyler herded a half-million Cubans from their homes into fortified camps, where filth, disease, and starvation killed perhaps 200,000. Outside these "reconcentration" camps, Weyler chased the rebels across the countryside, polluting drinking water, killing farm animals, and burning crops. Such brutal tactics outraged some Americans.

Mounting Tensions >> President Cleveland had little

sympathy for the Cuban revolt. He doubted that the mostly Black population was capable of self-government and feared that independence from Spain might lead to chaos on the island. Already the revolution had destroyed American-owned property. In the end, the president settled on a policy that favored neither the Spanish nor the rebels: opposing the rebellion, but pressing Spain to grant Cuba some freedoms.

ᐱ When Thomas Edison invented the phonograph in 1877, few people would have thought of it as a weapon of conquest. But when Americans and Europeans brought the machine to less technologically advanced societies, native peoples were awestruck by the sounds it made and sometimes cowed by those who controlled it. These white men, it appeared, had the power to conjure up the voices of invisible speakers and summon music from the air.
Comstock Images/Alamy Stock Photo

In the Republican Party, expansionists such as Theodore Roosevelt and Massachusetts senator Henry Cabot Lodge called for recognition of Cuban independence. If taken, the step would likely provoke war with Spain. When Republican William McKinley entered the White House, his supporters were surprised to find only a moderate expansionist. Cautiously and privately he lobbied Spain to stop cracking down on the rebels and destroying American property.

In 1897 the Spanish government promised to remove the much-despised Weyler, end reconcentration, and offer Cuba greater autonomy. The shift encouraged McKinley to resist pressure at home for more belligerent action. The leaders of the Spanish army in Cuba, however, had no desire to compromise. Although Weyler was removed, the military renewed efforts to crush the rebels and stirred pro-army riots in Havana. Early in 1898 McKinley sent the battleship *Maine* to show that the United States meant to protect its interests and its citizens.

In February 1898 the State Department received a stolen copy of a letter to Cuba sent by the Spanish minister in Washington, Enrique Dupuy de Lôme. So did publisher William Randolph Hearst. Hearst was a pioneer of sensationalist, or **"yellow," journalism**. His

yellow journalism brand of newspaper reporting that stresses excitement and shock over even-handedness and facts.

New York Journal was on the cutting edge of a new journalism that used bold, eye-catching and often salacious headlines to capture readers' attention. Stories traded in shock, scandal, exaggeration, and outright lies. Lurid images often accompanied them. Facts mattered less than the strong emotions they stirred and the sales they boosted.

Hearst saw a war with Spain as a way to boost sales. "WORST INSULT TO THE UNITED STATES IN ITS HISTORY," screamed the headline of the *Journal,* referring to the de Lôme letter. What had the minister actually written? After referring to McKinley as a "would-be politician," the letter admitted that Spain had no intention of changing its policy of crushing the rebels. Red-faced Spanish officials immediately recalled de Lôme, but most Americans believed, as Hearst intended, that Spain had deceived the United States.

On February 15, 1898, as the *Maine* lay at anchor in Havana Harbor, explosions ripped through the hull. Within minutes the ship sank, killing some 260 American sailors. Much later an official investigation concluded that the explosion was the result of spontaneous combustion in a coal bunker aboard ship. Americans at the time, inflamed by the hysterical and unsubstantiated news accounts of Hearst and other yellow journalists, concluded that Spanish agents had sabotaged the ship.

⌄ The grisly depiction of the explosion that sank the battleship *Maine* in Havana Harbor in 1898, complete with a panel titled "Recovering the Dead Bodies" (*upper right*). Illustrations such as this one helped jingoists turn the event into a battle cry, "Remember the *Maine*."
Glasshouse Images/Alamy Stock Photo

Pressures for war proved too great to resist, and on April 11, McKinley asked Congress to authorize "forceful intervention" in Cuba. A week later, Hearst took credit for it. "How do you like the *Journal*'s war?" read the headline of his newspaper. As it turned out, New York papers like Hearst's had little influence outside of the city, but his innovative techniques laid the foundation for the use of "fake news" to manipulate public opinion a century later.

Congress quickly recognized Cuban independence, insisted on the withdrawal of Spanish forces, and gave the president authority to use military force. In a flush of idealism, Congress also adopted the Teller Amendment, surrendering any claim to annex Cuba. Certainly both idealism and moral outrage led many Americans down the path to war. But in the end, what Secretary of State John Hay called the "splendid little war" came as a result of less lofty ambitions: empire, trade, glory.

The Imperial War >>
For the 5,462 men who died, there was little that was splendid about the Spanish-American War. Only 379 gave their lives in battle. The rest succumbed to accidents, disease, and the mismanagement of an unprepared army. Troops were issued winter woolens rather than tropical uniforms and sometimes fed on rations that were diseased, rotten, or poisoned. Some soldiers found themselves fighting with weapons from the Civil War.

The navy fared better. Decisions in the 1880s to modernize the fleet paid handsome dividends. Naval battles largely determined the outcome of the war. At the outbreak of war, Admiral George Dewey ordered his Asiatic battle squadron from China to the Philippines. Just before dawn on May 1, he opened fire on the Spanish ships in Manila Bay. Spanish coastal defenses and ships were no match for a modern navy. Guarding Manila Harbor, for example, was muzzle-loading artillery invented in the eighteenth century.

Five hours later the entire Spanish squadron lay at the bottom of the bay. Dewey had no plans to follow up his stunning victory with an invasion. His fleet carried no marines with which to take Manila. So ill prepared was President McKinley for war that only after learning of Dewey's success did he order 11,000 U.S. troops to the Philippines to fight the Spanish and capture the city.

Halfway around the globe, another Spanish fleet had slipped into Santiago harbor in Cuba just before the arrival of the U.S. Navy. The navy blockaded the island, expecting the Spanish to flee under the cover of darkness. Instead, in broad daylight on July 3, the Spanish made a desperate dash for open water. So startled were the Americans that several of their ships nearly collided as they rushed to attack their exposed foes. All seven Spanish ships were sunk. With Cuba cut off from Spain, the war was virtually won.

Without a fleet for cover or any way to escape, the Spanish garrison surrendered on July 17. In the Philippines, a similar brief battle preceded the fall of Manila on August 13. The "splendid little war" had ended in less than four months.

Peace and the Debate over Empire >>
Conquering Cuba and the Philippines proved easier than deciding what to do with them. The Teller Amendment had renounced any U.S. claim to Cuba. But clearly the United States had not freed the island to see chaos reign or American business and military interests excluded. And what of the Philippines and Spanish Puerto Rico, which American forces had taken without a struggle? Powerful public and congressional sentiment pushed McKinley to claim empire as the fruits of victory.

Even the president favored such a course. The battle in the Pacific highlighted the need for naval bases and coaling stations. "To maintain our flag in the Philippines, we must raise our flag in Hawaii," the *New York Sun* insisted. It was then, on July 7, that McKinley signed the joint congressional resolution annexing Hawai'i, as planters had wanted for nearly a decade.

The Philippines presented a more difficult problem. Filipinos had greeted Americans as liberators, not colonizers. The popular leader of the rebel forces fighting Spain, Emilio Aguinaldo, had even returned to the islands on an American ship. To the rebels' dismay, McKinley insisted that the islands were under American authority until the peace treaty settled matters.

Many influential Americans—former president Grover Cleveland, steel baron Andrew Carnegie, novelist Mark Twain—opposed annexation of the Philippines. Yet such "anti-imperialists" nonetheless favored expansion, if only in the form of trade. Business leaders especially believed that the country could enjoy the economic benefits of the Philippines without the expense of maintaining the islands as a colony. Annexation would also mire the United States in the quicksands of Asian politics, they argued. More important, a large fleet to defend the islands would only add to costs. To imperialists that was the point. A fleet was key to a powerful commercial nation whatever the price.

Racist ideas shaped both sides of the argument. Imperialists believed that the racial inferiority of nonwhites made occupation of the Philippines necessary. They were ready to assume the "white man's burden" and govern. Gradually, they argued, Filipinos would be taught the virtues of Western civilization, Christianity,[2] democracy, and self-rule. For their part, anti-imperialists feared racial intermixing and the possibility that Asian workers would flood the American labor market. They shared a common skepticism that dark-skinned people could ever develop the capacity for self-government. U.S. authority in the Philippines could be sustained only at the point of bayonets—yet the U.S. Constitution made no provision for governing people without representation or equal rights. Such a precedent, the anti-imperialists warned, might one day threaten American liberties at home.

When the Senate debated the Treaty of Paris ending the Spanish-American War in 1898, the imperialists had the support of the president, most of Congress, and the majority of public opinion. Even such a staunch anti-imperialist as William Jennings Bryan supported the treaty. Spain surrendered title to Cuba, ceded Puerto Rico and Guam to the

---

[2] In point of fact, most Filipinos were already Catholic after many years under Spanish rule.

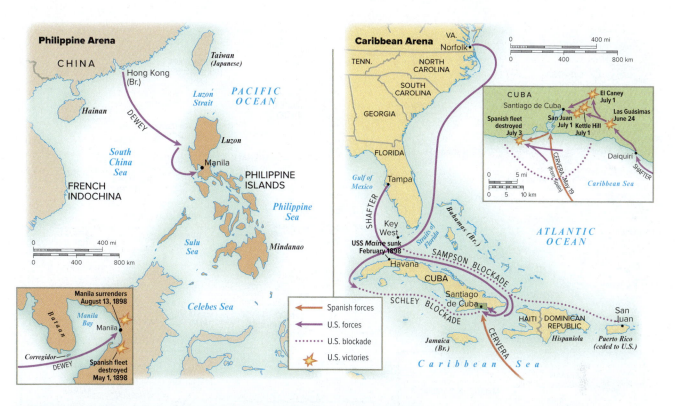

Philippine Arena

CHINA
Taiwan (Japanese)
Hong Kong (Br.)
Hainan
Luzon Strait
PACIFIC OCEAN
South China Sea
DEWEY
Luzon
Manila
FRENCH INDOCHINA
PHILIPPINE ISLANDS
Philippine Sea
Sulu Sea
Mindanao
Celebes Sea

0   400 mi
0 400 800 km

Manila surrenders August 13, 1898
Bataan
Manila Bay
Manila
Corregidor
DEWEY
Spanish fleet destroyed May 1, 1898

Caribbean Arena

VA.
Norfolk
TENN.   NORTH CAROLINA
SOUTH CAROLINA
GEORGIA
FLORIDA
Gulf of Mexico
Tampa
SHAFTER
Key West
Straits of Florida
USS *Maine* sunk February 1898
Havana
CUBA
SAMPSON BLOCKADE
SCHLEY BLOCKADE
Santiago de Cuba
CERVERA
Jamaica (Br.)
Bahamas (Br.)
ATLANTIC OCEAN
HAITI   DOMINICAN REPUBLIC
Hispaniola
San Juan
Puerto Rico (ceded to U.S.)
Caribbean Sea

0   400 mi
0   400   800 km

CUBA
Santiago de Cuba
Spanish fleet destroyed July 3
San Juan July 1
Kettle Hill July 1
El Caney July 1
Las Guásimas June 24
CERVERA–May 19 (from Spain)
Daiquirí
SHAFTER
Caribbean Sea

0   5 mi
0 5 10 km

Spanish forces
U.S. forces
U.S. blockade
U.S. victories

MAP 21.2: THE SPANISH-AMERICAN WAR

Had the Spanish-American war depended largely on ground forces, the ill-prepared U.S. Army might have fared poorly. But the key to success, in both Cuba and the Philippines, was naval warfare, in which the recently modernized American fleet had a critical edge. Proximity to Cuba also gave the United States an advantage in delivering troops and supplies and in maintaining a naval blockade that isolated Spanish forces. *What role did the U.S. Navy play in winning the Spanish-American War?*

United States, and in return for $20 million turned over the Philippines as well.

From Colonial War to Colonial Rule >>

Managing an empire turned out to be more devilish than acquiring one. As the Senate debated annexation of the Philippines in Washington in 1899, rebels clashed with an American patrol outside Manila, igniting a guerrilla war. The Philippine-American War lasted for more than three years. When it ended in 1902, nearly 5,000 Americans, 25,000 rebels, and perhaps as many as 200,000 civilians lay dead.

After a series of conventional battles ended in their defeat, Filipino *insurrectos* quickly learned to take advantage of the mountainous, jungle terrain of the Philippine archipelago. From his hideaway in the mountains of Bayombong, Aguinaldo ordered his troops to employ *guerrilla* ("little war" in Spanish) tactics. Hit-and-run ambushes by lightly armed rebels perfectly suited the dense landscape. As *insurrectos* melted into tropical forests and friendly villages, Americans could barely distinguish between enemies and friends. It was the first instance of jungle warfare the United States had ever encountered.

The United States's decision to occupy the Philippines rather than give it independence compelled Filipino nationalists like these to fight U.S. troops, as they had already been fighting the Spanish since 1896. Sporadic, bloody guerrilla fighting continued until 1902, and other incidents persisted until 1906. Here General Emilio Aguinaldo, leader of the nationalists, sits astride a horse with a portion of his army.
Bettmann/Getty Images

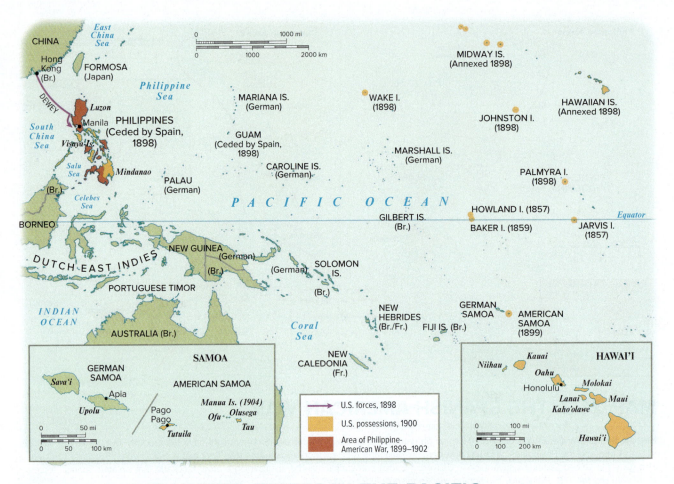

MAP 21.3: THE UNITED STATES IN THE PACIFIC

In the late nineteenth century Germany and the United States emerged as Pacific naval powers and contestants for influence and trade in China. The island groups of the Central and Southwest Pacific were of little economic value but had great strategic worth as bases and coaling stations along the route to Asia.

In what year did the United States gain more Pacific possessions than in any other? Which islands were its earliest acquisitions?

Jungle warfare aggravated racial antagonisms and spurred savage fighting on both sides. Rebel resistance to foreign occupation was accompanied by reports of *insurrectos* treating American prisoners in "fiendish fashion," burying some alive, dismembering others, and slaughtering Filipinos who opposed them. American soldiers dismissed Filipinos as nearly subhuman. "The only good Filipino is a dead one," declared one U.S. soldier, echoing the infamous anti-native cry of the American West.

To combat the insurgents, General Arthur MacArthur imposed a brutal campaign of "pacification" late in 1899. Filipinos were herded into concentration camps for their protection. Food and crops were seized or torched to starve the rebels into surrender. The strategy was embarrassingly reminiscent of "Butcher" Weyler in Cuba. Only after the capture of Aguinaldo and the last gasps of rebel resistance did the war finally come to a close in 1902. It marked the end of the westward march of American empire that began with the Louisiana Purchase in 1803.

Despite the bitter guerrilla war, the United States ruled its new island territory with relative benevolence. Under William Howard Taft, the first civilian governor, the Americans built schools, roads, sewers, and factories and inaugurated new farming techniques. The aim, said Taft, was to prepare the Philippines for independence, and to prove it he granted great authority to local officials. These advances—social, economic, and political—benefited the Filipino elite and thus earned their support. Ordinary Filipinos, who had fought so hard for freedom and sovereignty, fared less well, and all had to wait until July 4, 1946, for their country to receive independence.

The United States played a similar role in Puerto Rico. As in the Philippines, executive authority resided in a governor appointed by the U.S. president. Under the Foraker Act of 1900, Puerto Ricans received a voice in their government as well as a nonvoting representative in the U.S. House of Representatives and certain tariff advantages. All the same, many Puerto Ricans chafed at the idea of such second-class

museums. They smashed the windows of department stores, broke up political meetings, and even burned the houses of Parliament members. British authorities arrested these militant suffragists and threw them in jail. When the women went on hunger strikes, wardens tied them down, held their mouths open with wooden clamps, and fed them through tubes down their throats and noses. Rather than permit the protesters to die as martyrs, Parliament passed the Cat and Mouse Act. The statute (of doubtful legality) allowed officials to release starving prisoners, then rearrest them once they returned to health.

Among the British suffragists was a determined American. In 1907, barely out of her teens, Alice Paul had gone to Britain to join the suffrage crusade. When asked why she had enlisted, Paul credited her Quaker upbringing. "One of their principles . . . is equality of the sexes," she explained. After marching arm in arm with British suffragists, Paul brought a more militant brand of protest to the United States in 1910. Three years later, Paul organized 5,000 women to parade in protest at President Woodrow Wilson's inauguration. Wilson, who was skeptical of women voting, favored a state-by-state approach. Half a million people watched as a near-riot ensued. Paul and other suffragists were hauled to jail, stripped naked, and thrown into cells with prostitutes.

In 1914 Paul broke with the more moderate National American Woman Suffrage Association and formed the Congressional Union. The Union was dedicated to enacting national woman suffrage through a constitutional amendment. She allied her organization with western women

⌃ Alice Paul, pictured here, made use not only of militant protests but also of the latest technology. Here she employs a telephone to connect with other suffragists. Such innovations in communications allowed activists to create nationwide networks to press for voting rights.
Universal History Archive/Getty Images

voters in the more combative National Woman's Party in 1917. That fall, Paul was arrested at the gates of the White House for protesting in favor of an amendment. Guards dragged her off to a cell block in the Washington, D.C., jail, where she and others refused to eat. Prison officials declared her insane, but a public outcry over her treatment soon led to her release.

Such repression widened public support for woman suffrage in the United States and elsewhere. So did the many contributions of women to World War I (see Chapter 23). After the war, Great Britain granted women over 30 the vote in 1918, Germany and Austria in 1919, and the United States in 1920 through the Nineteenth Amendment. The number of eligible voters in the country doubled.

 REVIEW

Why were women so deeply involved in the "search for the good society," and what were some of their chief accomplishments? Why did it take so long for women to win the vote?

CONTROLLING THE MASSES

"Observe immigrants," wrote one American in 1912. "You are struck by the fact that from ten to twenty percent are hirsute, low-browed, big-faced persons of obviously low mentality." The writer was neither an uneducated fanatic nor a stern opponent of change. He was Professor Edward A. Ross, a progressive who prided himself on his scientific study of sociology.

Faced with the chaos of urban life, more than a few progressives feared they were losing control of their country. Saloons and dance halls lured youngsters and impoverished laborers; prostitutes walked the streets; vulgar amusements pandered to the uneducated. And worse—strange, foreign cultures clashed with "all-American" customs, while races jostled uneasily. The city challenged middle-class reformers to convert this riot of diversity into a more uniform society, at least as they saw it. To maintain control they sometimes moved beyond education and regulation and sought restrictive laws to define and control the "social vices" of the new masses.

Stemming the Immigrant Tide >> A rising tide of new immigrants from southern and eastern Europe with darker complexions and non-Protestant religions worried some native-born Americans, including progressive reformers. They were anxious about the changing ethnic makeup of the country. In northern cities, progressives often succeeded in reducing the voting power of these new immigrants by increasing residency requirements.

The now-discredited science of "eugenics" lent respectability to the idea that the newcomers were biologically inferior. Eugenicists believed that heredity determined everything. They advocated selectively breeding human beings (or sterilizing those deemed unworthy) to improve the species or rid it of unwanted traits. By 1914 magazine articles discussed eugenics more often than slums, tenements, and living standards combined.

In *The Passing of the Great Race* (1916), amateur zoologist Madison Grant helped popularize the notion that the "lesser breeds" threatened to "mongrelize" the United States by weakening the gene pool. So powerful was the pull of eugenics that it captured the support of some progressives, including birth control advocate Margaret Sanger. She saw contraception as a way of reducing birthrates among those deemed physically and mentally "unfit." Thirty states enacted forced sterilization laws, deemed constitutional by the Supreme Court in *Buck v. Bell* (1927).

Most progressives believed in the shaping power of environment and so favored either assimilating immigrants into U.S. society or restricting their entry. Jane Addams stressed the "gifts" immigrants brought: folk rituals, dances, music, and handicrafts. With characteristic paternalism, she and other reformers hoped to "Americanize" the foreign-born by teaching them middle-class ways. Education was one key. Progressive educator Peter Roberts developed a lesson plan for the Young Men's Christian Association that taught immigrants how to dress, tip, buy groceries, and vote.

Less tolerant citizens, often native-born and white, sought to restrict immigration as a way of reasserting control and achieving social harmony. Although usually not progressives themselves, they employed progressive methods of organization, investigation, education, and legislation. Active since the 1890s, the Immigration Restriction League pressed Congress in 1907 to require a literacy test for admission into the United States. Presidents Taft and Wilson vetoed it, but Congress overrode Wilson's second veto in 1917, as war fever raised fears of foreigners.

The Curse of Demon Rum >>
Tied closely to concern over immigrants, many of whom came from drinking cultures, was an attack on saloons. Part of a broader crusade to clean up cities, the antisaloon campaign drew strength from the century-old drive to lessen the consumption of alcohol.

Women made up a disproportionate number of alcohol reformers. In some ways, the temperance movement reflected their growing campaign to storm male domains, in this case the saloon, and to stop male violence associated with drinking, particularly wife and child abuse. The "Demon Rum," as some reformers called liquor, had to be exorcised from the home as well as the street corner.

Reformers considered a national ban on drinking unrealistic and intrusive. Instead, they concentrated on prohibiting the sale of alcohol at local and state levels. The Anti-Saloon

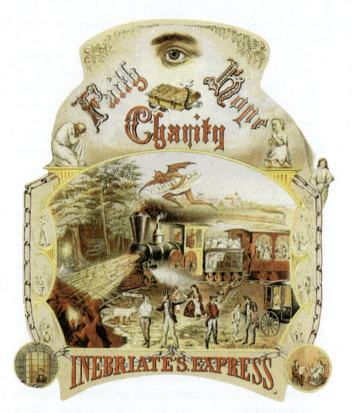

^ The "Inebriate's Express," loaded with drunken riders, is heading straight for hell. This detail from a chromolithograph, published around 1900, was typical of Victorian era responses to the problems posed by alcohol. To the all-seeing eye of the omnipotent God, faith, hope, charity, and the Bible are sufficient to cure the problems of drinking.
Library of Congress, Prints and Photographs Division

League (1893) led a massive publicity campaign that bombarded citizens with pamphlets and advertisements. Doctors cited scientific evidence linking alcohol to cirrhosis, heart disease, and insanity. Social workers connected drink to the deterioration of the family; employers, to accidents on the job and lost efficiency; and political reformers, to corrupt political machines that were often housed in saloons.

By 1917, three out of four Americans lived in dry counties. Nearly two-thirds of the states had taken the "local option" by outlawing the manufacture and sale of alcoholic beverages through county and municipal action. Not all progressives were prohibitionists, but those who were believed curtailing the liquor trade had taken some of the profit out of human pain and corruption. An even broader assault in the form of a constitutional amendment to prohibit the manufacture, sale, transportation, and importation of all liquor gained popular support.

Prostitution >>
Immigration restriction and prohibition calmed fears about newcomers by promising to contain their numbers and their vices, but no vice worried reformers more than prostitution. In their eyes it was a "social evil" that threatened young women, the purest and most vulnerable among them. The Chicago Vice Commission of 1910 estimated

Mementos of Murder

Jesse William Stanley

Could this be "Joe"?

Men face the camera without making any effort to mask their faces

Young boys present

Katy Electric Studio Temple Texas H. Lippe Prop.

No stamp or postmark indicating that the card was sent. Did "Joe" keep it?

"This is the Barbecue we had last night[.] My picture is to the left with a cross over it[.] your son, Joe."

©National Center for Civil and Human Rights, Atlanta, GA, USA

Not all historians need be professionals. Even amateurs can help us see the past in a new light. James Allen described himself as a "picker," rummaging through other people's junk for things he might sell. Postcards hadn't much interested him until he came across one that bore the photograph of a lynching. "It wasn't the corpse that bewildered me but the canine-thin faces of the pack," he recalled. Collected and later published by Allen, postcards memorializing lynchings were part of a larger postcard industry that flourished in the late nineteenth and early twentieth centuries. For a penny in postage, the cards—of hotels, city streets, or even just photos of individuals taken by photographers—could be sent to friends and relatives as souvenirs. But the cards Allen came across over the years were of a different order: grisly mementos of ritualized murder. The one above—of the lynching and burning of an African American named Jesse William Stanley in 1915—appears not to have been mailed.

THINKING CRITICALLY

Why might people have their photographs taken at lynchings and then send postcards of those photographs to friends and relatives? What does that tell us about the racial environment in which such events occurred?

that 5,000 full-time and 10,000 occasional prostitutes plied their trade in the city. Other cities, small and large, reported similar findings.

An unlikely group of reformers united to fight the vice: feminists who wanted husbands to be as chaste as their wives, social hygienists who worried about the spread of sexually transmitted diseases, and immigration restrictionists who regarded the growth of prostitution as yet another sign of corrupt newcomers. Progressives condemned prostitution but saw the problem in economic and environmental terms. "Poverty causes prostitution," concluded the Illinois Vice Commission in 1916.

As real abuses blended with sensationalist reports, Congress passed the Mann Act (1910), prohibiting the interstate transport of women for immoral purposes. By 1918 reformers succeeded in banning previously tolerated **red-light districts** in most cities, where prostitutes plied their trade. As with liquor, progressives went after those who made money from misery.

red-light district area in cities reserved for prostitutes. The term, first employed in the United States, resulted from the use of red lights to show that prostitutes were open for business.

"For Whites Only" >> Most progressives paid little attention to the suffering of African Americans. The 1890s had been a point so low for Black citizens that historians have called it "The Nadir." Across the region, the lynching of African Americans increased, as did restrictions on Black voting and the use of segregated facilities. Signs decreeing "For Whites Only" appeared on drinking fountains and restrooms and in other public places.

A few progressives condemned racial discrimination, but most ignored it or used it to political advantage. Throughout the South, white progressives and old-guard politicians used the rhetoric of reform to support white supremacy. Such "reformers" won office by promising to disenfranchise African Americans in order to break the power of corrupt political machines, which marshaled the Black vote in the South, much as northern machines did with immigrant voters.

In the face of such discrimination African Americans fought back. After the turn of the century, some Black critics rejected the accommodationist approach of Booker T. Washington's "Atlanta Compromise," which counseled African Americans to accept segregation, learn a trade, and work their way up the economic ladder. W.E.B. Du Bois, a professor at Atlanta University, leveled the most stinging attack in *The Souls of Black Folk* (1903). He saw no benefit in sacrificing intellectual growth for narrow vocational training. Nor was he willing to accept the stigma of inferiority imposed by segregation in the South. A better future could be had only if Black citizens achieved unrestricted suffrage and equal rights.

Instead of exhorting African Americans to pull themselves up slowly from the bottom, Du Bois called on the "talented tenth," a cultured Black vanguard, to blaze the trail. In 1905 he founded the Niagara Movement for political and economic equality. Four years later, a coalition of Back and white reformers transformed the Niagara Movement into the National Association for the Advancement of Colored People (NAACP). Its formation followed an ugly race riot in Springfield, the capital of Illinois, in 1908.

As with other progressive organizations, its membership was largely limited to the middle class. The NAACP raised legal challenges to segregation and bigotry and promoted legislation to encourage tolerance and equal opportunity in a color-blind society. By 1919 the NAACP had some 90,000 members in 300 branches across the country. Accommodation was giving way to combative organizations and new forms of protest.

✓ **REVIEW**

Which "masses" did progressives want to control, why did they want to control them, and what instruments did they employ?

THE POLITICS OF MUNICIPAL AND STATE REFORM

Reform the system. In the end, so many urban problems came back to overhauling government. Jane Addams learned as much outside the doors of her beloved Hull House in Chicago. For months during the early 1890s, garbage piled up in the streets around the settlement house. The filth and stench drove Addams and her fellow workers to city hall in protest—700 times in one summer—but to no avail. In Chicago, as elsewhere, corrupt city bosses turned garbage into a profitable business for the company that paid the most for a contract to haul it away.

In desperation Addams submitted a bid to collect the garbage herself. When it was thrown out on a technicality, she won an appointment as garbage inspector. For a year she dogged collection carts, but boss politics kept things dirty. So Addams ran candidates in 1896 and 1898 against the local ward boss. They lost, but Addams kept up the fight for honest government and social reform. Politics turned out to be the only way to clean things up.

The Reformation of the Cities >> In the smokestack cities of the Midwest, where the frustrations of the industrial and agricultural United States fed each other, the urban battleground furnished the middle class with the first test of political reform. Colorful and independent mayors showed that cities could be run honestly and humanely without changing the structure of government. Other cities across the country experimented with new forms of governing.

In Detroit, shoe magnate Hazen Pingree became one of the first mayors to enact a reform program when elected in 1889. By the end of his fourth term, Detroit had new parks and public baths, fairer taxes, public ownership of the local lighting plant, and a work-relief program for victims of the depression of 1893. In 1901, Cleveland mayor Tom Johnson launched a similar reform campaign. Before he was through, municipal franchises had been limited to a fraction of their previous 99-year terms, and the city ran the utility company. By 1915 nearly two out of every three cities had copied some form of this "gas and water socialism" to control the runaway prices of utility companies.

Tragedy sometimes dramatized the need to alter the structure of government. On a hot September night in 1900,

^ Detroit's Hazen S. Pingree was a reforming mayor who, during the hard times of 1893, hired unemployed laborers for public-works projects that, among other things, turned the city's Belle Isle into a popular island park along the Detroit River. "Old Ping," as the mayor was known, was plump, short, bald, bearded, and determined. During the depression, he mobilized vacant land in the city as "potato patches," where food was grown to tide over the urban poor.
Library of Congress, Prints and Photographs Division

a tidal wave from the Gulf of Mexico swept through Galveston, Texas. The giant swell and the hurricane that followed destroyed two-thirds of the city, killed between 6,000 and 12,000 people on Galveston Island and the mainland, and left 10,000 homeless. The city sank into confusion. Business leaders stepped in with a new charter that replaced the mayor and city council with a powerful commission. Each of the five commissioners controlled a municipal department, and together they ran the city. Nearly 400 cities had adopted this plan by 1920. Expert commissioners enhanced efficiency and helped check party rule in municipal government.

In still other cities, elected officials appointed an outside expert or "city manager" to run things, the first in Staunton, Virginia, in 1908. Within a decade, 45 cities had managers and commissioners. Experts took charge of services: engineers, utilities; accountants, finances; doctors and nurses, public health; specially trained firefighters and police, the safety of citizens.

Progressivism in the States >> "Whenever we try to do anything, we run up against the charter," complained one reform-minded mayor. Charters granted by state governments defined the powers of cities. Since rural interests dominated state legislatures, they rarely gave cities adequate authority to levy taxes, set voting requirements, draw up budgets, or enact reforms. Reformers therefore tried to place their candidates where they could do some good: in the governor's mansion.

State progressivism, like urban reform, enjoyed its earliest success in the Midwest, under the leadership of Robert La Follette of Wisconsin. La Follette first won election to Congress in 1885 by toeing the Republican line of high tariffs and the gold standard. When a Republican boss offered him a bribe in a railroad case, La Follette pledged to break "the power of this corrupt influence." In 1900 he won the governorship of Wisconsin as an uncommonly independent Republican.

Over the next six years, "Battle Bob" La Follette made Wisconsin, in the words of Theodore Roosevelt, "the laboratory

Wisconsin idea series of progressive reforms at the state level promoted by Robert La Follette during his governorship of Wisconsin (1901–1906). They included primary elections, corporate property taxes, regulation of railroads and public utilities, and supervision of public resources in the public interest.

of democracy." La Follette's **"Wisconsin idea"** produced the most comprehensive set of state reforms in American history. New laws regulated railroads, controlled corruption, and expanded the civil service. The direct primary weakened the hold of party bosses by transferring nominations from the party to the voters. La Follette's Wisconsin created the first state income tax, the first state commission to oversee factory safety and sanitation, and the first Legislative Reference Bureau—at the University of Wisconsin. University-trained experts poured into state government.

Other states copied the Wisconsin idea or hatched their own. All but three had enacted direct primaries by 1916. No reform gave voters more power in choosing candidates. To cut the influence of party organizations and make politicians directly responsible to the public, progressives worked for three additional reforms: initiative (voter introduction of legislation), referendum (voter enactment or repeal of laws), and recall (voter-initiated removal of elected officials). In 1913 the Seventeenth Amendment to the Constitution permitted the direct election of senators. Previously they had been chosen by state legislatures, where rural political machines and corporate lobbyists controlled the selections.

In the West, progressivism thrived. Western states were the nation's first to grant women the right to vote. To protect their health, the Oregon legislature was the first to limit the number of hours women could work. That particular reform was a paternal brand of progressivism, designed to take care of women rather than empowering women to take care of themselves, as the right to vote did. In California, the urban middle class supported progressive Hiram Johnson's drive to oust political machines from cities and the statehouse. Colorado Governor John Shafroth fought the local political machine and pressed a balky legislature to regulate railroad rates, insure commercial bank deposits, and create a public service commission. He also supported the direct primary.

Almost every state established regulatory commissions with the power to hold public hearings, examine company books, and question officials. Some could set maximum prices and rates. Yet it was not always easy to define, let alone serve, the "public good." Often commissioners found themselves refereeing battles within industries rather than between what progressives called "the bad interests" and "the good people." Regulators also had to rely on the advice of experts drawn from the business community itself. The commissions created to restrain corporations often fell under the influence of their experts and lobbyists. "Capture," much more than corruption, turned regulation industry's way.

Social welfare received special attention from the states. The lack of workers' compensation for injury, illness, or death on the job had long drawn fire from reformers and labor leaders. U.S. courts still operated on the common-law assumption

that employees accepted the risks of work. Workers or their families could collect damages only if they proved employer negligence. Most accident victims received nothing. In 1902, Maryland adopted the first workers' compensation act. By 1916 most states required insurance for factory accidents. Over half had employer liability laws. Thirteen states provided pensions for widows with dependent children.

Such working-class reforms found advocates among women's associations, especially those concerned with mothers, children, and workingwomen. The Federation of Women's Clubs opened a crusade for mothers' pensions (a forerunner of Aid to Mothers with Dependent Children). When the National Consumers' League and other women's groups succeeded in establishing the Children's Bureau in 1912, it was the first federal welfare agency and the only female-run national bureau in the world. Even before women won the vote, they sowed the seeds of the welfare state.

✓ **REVIEW**

What reforms did cities and states enact, and how did those reforms address the problems they faced?

PROGRESSIVISM GOES TO WASHINGTON

On September 6, 1901, at the Pan-American Exposition in Buffalo, New York, Leon Czolgosz stood nervously in line. He was waiting to meet President William McKinley. Unemployed and bent on murder, Czolgosz shuffled toward McKinley. As the president reached out, Czolgosz fired two bullets into his chest. McKinley slumped into a chair. Eight days later, the president was dead.

The mantle of power passed to Vice President Theodore Roosevelt. At 42 he became the youngest president ever to hold the office. His succession was a political accident. Party leaders had seen the weak vice presidency as a way of isolating him from power, but the tragedy in Buffalo foiled their plans. Surely progressivism would have come to Washington without TR, and while there, he was never its most daring advocate. In many ways he was quite conservative. He saw reform as a way to avoid radical change.

TR >> TR, as so many Americans called him, was the scion of seven generations of wealthy, aristocratic New Yorkers. A sickly boy, he built his body through rigorous exercise, sharpened his mind through constant study, and pursued a life so strenuous that few could keep up. He learned to ride and shoot, roped cattle in the Dakota Badlands, and mastered judo. Later in life he climbed the Matterhorn, hunted African game, and explored the Amazon.

Library of Congress, Prints and Photographs Division

⌃ Bullnecked and barrel-chested, Theodore Roosevelt was "pure act," said one admirer. Critics, less enthused with his perpetual motion, charged him with having the attention span of a golden retriever.
National Park Service via Theodore Roosevelt Digital Library, Dickinson State University

In 1880, driven by an urge to lead and serve, Roosevelt won election to the New York State Assembly. In rapid succession, he became a civil service commissioner in Washington, New York City police commissioner, assistant secretary of the navy, and the Rough Rider hero of the Spanish-American War. At the age of 40, he won election as reform governor of New York. Two years later he became vice president and barely a year after that president.

As president, Roosevelt brought to the Executive Mansion (he renamed it the "White House") a passion for order, a commitment to the public, and a sense of presidential possibilities. Most presidents believed that the Constitution set limits on their power. Roosevelt thought that the president could do anything the Constitution did not expressly forbid. Recognizing the value of publicity, he created the first press

room in the White House for reporters and provided them constant newsworthy material. He was the first president to ride in an automobile, fly in an airplane, and dive in a submarine—and everyone knew it.

To dramatize racial injustice Roosevelt invited Black educator Booker T. Washington to lunch at the White House in 1901. White southern journalists called such race mingling treason, but for Roosevelt the gesture served both principle and politics. His lunch with Washington was part of a "Black and tan" strategy to build a biracial coalition among southern Republicans. He denounced lynching and appointed Black southerners to important federal offices in Mississippi and South Carolina.

Sensing the limits of political feasibility, Roosevelt went no further. Perhaps his own racial narrowness stopped him, too. He held to the common belief in the superiority of the white race and acted on it. In 1906, when Atlanta exploded in a race riot that left 12 people dead, he said nothing. Later that year he discharged "without honor" three entire companies of Black troops, because some of the soldiers were unjustly charged with having "shot up" Brownsville, Texas. All lost their pensions, including six winners of the Medal of Honor. The act stained Roosevelt's record. Congress admitted the wrong in 1972 by granting the soldiers postmortem, honorable discharges.

A Square Deal >> By temperament, Roosevelt could not long follow the cautious course McKinley had charted. He had more energetic plans in mind for the country. He accepted growth—whether of business, labor, or agriculture—as natural. In his pluralistic system, big labor would counterbalance big capital, big farm organizations would offset big food processors, and so on. Standing astride them all, a big government would ensure fairness. As he campaigned for a second term in 1904, Roosevelt named his program the "Square Deal."

In a startling display of presidential initiative, in 1902 Roosevelt intervened in a strike that idled 140,000 miners and paralyzed the anthracite (hard) coal industry. As winter approached, public resentment against the operators mounted when they refused even to recognize the miners' union, let alone negotiate. Roosevelt summoned both sides to the White House. John A. Mitchell, the young president of the United Mine Workers, agreed to arbitration, but mine owners balked. Roosevelt leaked word to Wall Street that the army would take over the mines if management did not yield.

Seldom had recent presidents acted so decisively, and never on behalf of strikers. In late October 1902, the owners settled by granting miners a 10 percent wage hike and a nine-hour day, in return for increases in coal prices and no recognition of the union. Roosevelt was equally prepared to intervene on the side of management, as he did when he sent federal troops to end strikes in Arizona in 1903 and Colorado in 1904. His aim was to establish a vigorous presidency ready to deal squarely with both sides.

One issue Roosevelt especially needed to face was economic concentration. Financial power had become consolidated in giant trusts following a wave of mergers at the end of the century. Government investigations revealed rampant corporate abuses: rebates, collusion, **watered stock**, payoffs to government officials. The conservative courts showed little willingness to break up the giants or blunt their power. In *United States* v. *E. C. Knight* (1895), the Supreme Court had crippled the Sherman Antitrust Act by ruling that the law applied only to commerce that crossed state lines and not to manufacturing, even when products were sold in another state. The decision left the American Sugar Refining Company in control of 98 percent of the nation's sugar factories.

watered stock stock issued in excess of the assets of a company. The term derived from the practice of some ranchers who made their cattle drink large amounts of water before weighing them for sale.

In his first State of the Union message, Roosevelt told Congress that he did not oppose trusts. As he saw it, large corporations were not only inevitable but also more productive than smaller operations. He did want to regulate them to make them fairer and more efficient. Only then would the economic order be humanized, its victims protected, and class violence avoided. Like individuals, trusts had to be held to strict standards of morality. Conduct, not size, was the yardstick TR used to distinguish "good" from "bad" trusts.

With a progressive's faith in the power of publicity and a regulator's need for the facts, Roosevelt moved immediately to strengthen the federal power of investigation. He called for the creation of a Department of Labor and Commerce with a Bureau of Corporations that could force companies to hand over their records. Congressional conservatives shuddered at the prospect of putting corporate books on display. Finally, after Roosevelt charged that John D. Rockefeller was orchestrating the opposition, Congress enacted the legislation and provided the Justice Department with additional staff to prosecute antitrust cases.

In 1902, to demonstrate the power of government, Roosevelt had his attorney general file an antitrust suit against the Northern Securities Company. The mammoth holding company used its near monopoly over railroads in the Northwest to set high freight rates while ignoring local protests. Here was a symbol of a "bad" trust. A trust-conscious nation cheered as the Supreme Court ordered the company to dissolve in 1904. Ultimately the Roosevelt administration brought suit against 44 giants.

Despite his reputation for trust-busting, Roosevelt preferred controlling monopolies through regulation. The problems of the railroads, for example, were underscored by a fresh round of mergers and acquisitions that again contributed to higher freight rates. In 1903 Roosevelt pressed Congress to pass the Elkins Act, which gave the ineffective **Interstate Commerce Commission (ICC)** power to end rebates, the costly practice of granting special reductions to large shippers. Even the railroads cheered.

Interstate Commerce Commission (ICC) federal agency charged with regulating trade in goods that cross state lines.

By the election of 1904 the president's initiatives had won him broad popular support. He trounced his two rivals, Democrat Alton B. Parker, a jurist from New York, and Eugene V. Debs of the Socialist Party. No longer was he a "political accident," Roosevelt boasted.

Conservatives in his own party opposed Roosevelt's meddling in the private sector. But progressives demanded still more regulation of the railroads. In 1906 the president finally reached a compromise typical of his restrained approach to reform. The Hepburn Railway Act allowed the ICC to set maximum rates and to regulate sleeping-car companies, ferries, bridges, and terminals. Progressives did not gain the provision for disclosure of company value or service costs they sought, but the Hepburn Act drew Roosevelt nearer to his goal of broad regulation of business.

Bad Food and Pristine Wilds >>

Extending the umbrella of federal protection to consumers, Roosevelt belatedly threw his weight behind campaigns for healthy foods and drugs. Several pure food and drug bills had already died at the hands of lobbyists. The appearance in 1906 of Upton Sinclair's book *The Jungle* about the meatpacking industry spurred Congress to finally act. The novel contained a brief but dramatic description of the slaughter of cattle infected with tuberculosis, of meat covered with rat dung, and of workers falling into cooking vats. Readers paid scant attention to the workers, the true object of Sinclair's sympathy, but they gagged at what they might be eating for dinner. The Pure Food and Drug Act of 1906 sailed through Congress, and the Meat Inspection Act soon followed.

Roosevelt came late to the cause of consumer protection, but on conservation he led the nation. An outdoors enthusiast, he galvanized public concern over the reckless use of natural resources. His chief forester, Gifford Pinchot, persuaded him that planned management under federal guidance was needed to protect the natural domain. Cutting trees must be synchronized with tree planting, oil should be pumped from the ground under controlled conditions, and so on.

In most of the western states, water was the problem. Economic growth, even survival, depended on it. Uneven local and state water policies sparked controversy, violence, and waste. Progressives campaigned for a federal program to replace the chaotic web of rules. The Reclamation Act of 1902 set aside proceeds from the sale of public lands for irrigation projects under the control of the new federal Bureau of Reclamation. Its creation signaled another progressive step toward the conservationist goal of rational resource development.

Conservation, the form of environmental protection most appealing to progressives, often came into conflict with the more radical vision of preservationists who wanted wilderness left untouched. In *Man and Nature* (1864), naturalist George Perkins Marsh had sounded an early alarm about the damage human action could inflict on the planet. Already, he wrote, the agricultural and industrial revolutions had begun to erode soil, deforest timberland, dry up watersheds, and endanger plants and animals.

^ Long a target of reformers, patent medicines made wild curative claims, ranging from restoring hair and cleaning the blood to ridding invalids of worms, as this Tonic Vermifuge advertised in 1889. The Pure Food and Drug Act finally placed patent medicines under federal regulation.
Library of Congress, Prints and Photographs Division

Another naturalist, the wilderness philosopher John Muir, took Marsh's call a step further. Muir, a Scot, had emigrated to the United States with his family as a boy. Trained as an engineer, he nearly lost his sight when a sharp file punctured his right eye. His sight miraculously returned and he vowed to be true to himself by following his passion: the study of the wild world. Study turned to activism in 1892 when Muir cofounded the Sierra Club. He hoped to keep such natural wonders as the Hetch Hetchy valley in his beloved Yosemite National Park "forever wild" to benefit future generations. "When we try to pick out anything by itself," Muir wrote, "we find it hitched to everything else in the universe." Many conservationists saw such valleys only as sites for dams and reservoirs to manage and control water.

Controversy flared when San Francisco announced plans to create a city reservoir by flooding the Hetch Hetchy valley in 1900. For 13 years Muir waged a publicity campaign against the reservoir. Pinchot enthusiastically backed San Francisco's claim. Roosevelt, torn by his friendship with Muir, did so less loudly. Not until 1913 did President Woodrow Wilson finally decide the issue in favor of San Francisco. Conservation had triumphed over preservation.

But this was not always the outcome. Over the protests of cattle and timber interests, Roosevelt added nearly 200 million acres to government forest reserves; placed coal and mineral lands, oil reserves, and water-power sites in the public domain; and enlarged the national park system. When Congress balked, Roosevelt appropriated another 17 million acres of forest before the legislators could pass a bill limiting him. Roosevelt set in motion national congresses and commissions on conservation and mobilized governors across the country. Like a good progressive, he sent hundreds of experts to work applying science, education, and technology to environmental problems.

The Troubled Taft

The Troubled Taft >> On March 4, 1909, as snow swirled outside the White House, William Howard Taft readied himself for his inauguration. Over breakfast with Roosevelt, he basked in the glow of recent Republican victories. Roosevelt's handpicked successor, Taft had beaten Democrat William Jennings Bryan in the "Great Commoner's" third and last bid for the presidency. Republicans retained control of Congress as well as many northern legislatures. Reform was at high tide, and Taft was eager to continue the Roosevelt program.

"Will," as Roosevelt liked to call him, was a distinguished jurist and public servant, the first American governor-general of the Philippines, and Roosevelt's secretary of war. Taft had great administrative skill and personal charm but disliked political maneuvering. He preferred conciliation to confrontation, judicious reasoning to emotional eruptions, argumentation to decision making.

Trouble began early when progressives in the House moved to curb the near-dictatorial power of conservative Speaker Joseph Cannon. Taft waffled, first supporting and then abandoning them to preserve the tariff reductions he was seeking. When progressives later broke Cannon's power without Taft's help, they abandoned the president. Taft's compromise was wasted. Senate protectionists peppered the tariff bill with so many amendments that rates jumped nearly to their old levels.

Late in 1909 the rift between Taft and progressives reached the breaking point in a dispute over conservation. Taft had appointed Richard Ballinger secretary of the interior over the objections of Roosevelt's old friend and mentor, Chief Forester Pinchot. When Ballinger opened a million acres of public coal lands in Alaska for sale, Pinchot charged that shady dealings led the secretary to transfer Alaskan public coal lands to a syndicate that included J. P. Morgan. Early in 1910 Taft fired Pinchot for insubordination. Angry progressives saw the Ballinger-Pinchot controversy as another betrayal by Taft. They began to look longingly across the Atlantic, where TR was stalking big game in Africa.

⌃ The Sierra Club, founded by naturalist John Muir (*center, with beard*), believed in the importance of preserving wilderness in its natural state. "In God's wildness," Muir wrote in 1890, "lies the hope of the world—the great fresh unlighted, unredeemed wilderness." In front of this giant redwood tree, Theodore Roosevelt stands to the left of Muir, who persuaded the president to double the number of national parks.
RBM Vintage Images/Alamy Stock Photo

Despite his failures Taft was no conservative pawn. For the next two years he pushed Congress to enact a progressive program regulating safety standards for mines and railroads. He created a federal children's bureau, and set an eight-hour workday for federal employees. Taft's support of an income tax—sometimes heated, sometimes tepid—was finally decisive. Early in 1913. the Sixteenth Amendment created the first federal income tax. Historians view it as one of the most important reforms of the century, for it eventually generated the revenue that allowed the government to assume new responsibilities.

The Election of 1912 >> In June 1910 Roosevelt came home, laden with hunting trophies and as exuberant as ever. He found Taft unhappy and progressive Republicans threatening to defect. Party loyalty kept Roosevelt quiet through most of 1911, but in October Taft pricked him personally on the sensitive matter of busting trusts. Like TR, Taft accepted trusts as natural, but demanded that all

trusts—whether "good" or "bad"—be prevented from restraining trade. In four years as president, Taft had brought nearly twice the antitrust suits Roosevelt had in seven years.

In October 1911 the Justice Department charged U.S. Steel with having violated the Sherman Antitrust Act by acquiring the Tennessee Coal and Iron Company. Roosevelt regarded the action as a personal rebuke, since he himself had allowed U.S. Steel to proceed with the acquisition. Taft, complained TR, "was playing small, mean, and foolish politics."

In a speech at Osawatomie, Kansas, in 1910, Roosevelt had begun to sharpen his differences with Taft by outlining a program of sweeping national reform called the "New Nationalism." He had already recognized the value of consolidation in the economy—whether in the growth of big business or big labor—and insisted on protecting the interests of individuals through big government. The New Nationalism went much further: it stressed planning and efficiency under a powerful executive as "steward of the public welfare." It promised new taxes on incomes and inheritances and greater regulation of industry. And it promoted social justice, specifically workers' compensation for accidents, minimum wages and maximum hours, child labor laws, and "equal suffrage"—a nod to women and loyal Black Republicans. Roosevelt, a cautious reformer as president, grew bold campaigning for the White House.

"My hat is in the ring!" Roosevelt announced in February 1912. The enormously popular former president won most of the primaries; but by the time Republicans met in Chicago in June 1912, Taft had used presidential patronage and promises to secure the nomination. A frustrated Roosevelt bolted and took progressive Republicans with him. Two months later, amid choruses of "Onward Christian Soldiers," delegates to the newly formed Progressive Party nominated Roosevelt for the presidency. "I'm feeling like a bull moose!" he bellowed. Progressives had a symbol for their new party.

The Democrats met in Baltimore, jubilant over the prospect of a divided Republican Party. Delegates chose as their candidate Woodrow Wilson, the progressive governor of New Jersey. Wilson wisely concentrated his fire on Roosevelt. He countered the New Nationalism with his "New Freedom." It rejected the economic consolidation that Roosevelt accepted. Bigness was a sin, crowding out competition, promoting inefficiency, and reducing opportunity. Only by strictly limiting the size of businesses could the free market be preserved. And only by keeping government small could individual freedom be preserved. "Liberty," Wilson cautioned, "has never come from government," only from the "limitation of governmental power."

In an age of reform, even the Socialists made gains. Better led, financed, and organized than ever, the Socialist Party had increased its membership to nearly 135,000 by 1912. The party also had an appealing candidate in Eugene V. Debs, the Indiana-born labor leader. He had won 400,000 votes for president in 1904. Now, in 1912, he summoned voters to make "the working class the ruling class." Voters found Taft beside the point.

On Election Day they gave progressivism a resounding endorsement. Wilson won 6.3 million votes; Roosevelt, 4.1 million; Taft, just 3.6 million; and Debs almost a million. Together the two progressive candidates amassed a three-to-one margin. But the Republican split broke the party's hold on national politics. For the first time since 1896, a Democrat would sit in the White House, and his party would control Congress.

✓ REVIEW
How did President Roosevelt's reform agenda reflect his promise of a "Square Deal" for Americans?

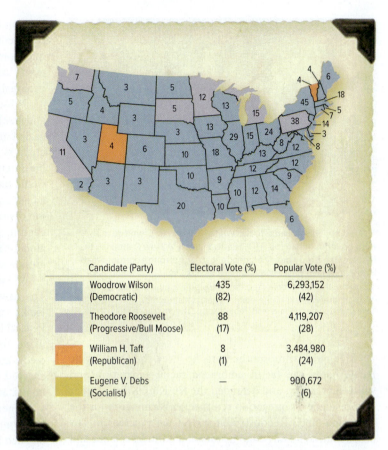

Candidate (Party)	Electoral Vote (%)	Popular Vote (%)
Woodrow Wilson (Democratic)	435 (82)	6,293,152 (42)
Theodore Roosevelt (Progressive/Bull Moose)	88 (17)	4,119,207 (28)
William H. Taft (Republican)	8 (1)	3,484,980 (24)
Eugene V. Debs (Socialist)	—	900,672 (6)

MAP 22.2: ELECTION OF 1912

WOODROW WILSON AND THE POLITICS OF MORALITY

Soon after the election, Woodrow Wilson made a proud if startling confession to the chair of the Democratic National Committee: "God ordained that I should be the next President of the United States." Wilson brought a sense of destiny and a passion for reform to the White House. He always believed he was meant to accomplish great things, and he did. Under him, progressivism peaked, magnifying its strengths and liabilities, as well as his own.

Early Career >> From the moment of his birth in 1856, Woodrow Wilson felt he could not escape destiny. It was all around him. In his family's Presbyterian faith, in the sermons of his minister father, in dinnertime talk ran the unbending belief in a world predetermined by God and ruled by saved souls, an "elect." Wilson ached to be one of them and behaved as though he were.

⌃ Woodrow Wilson came to the White House with promises to reform government. In this 1913 cartoon titled "A New Captain in the District," the newly elected president strides through corrupt Washington, ready to police such abuses as easy land grants and pork barreling, the much-criticized congressional practice of voting for projects that benefit home districts and constituents.
Library of Congress, Prints and Photographs Division

Like most white southerners, he loved the Democratic Party, hated the tariff, embraced racial separation and white supremacy, and defended the Ku Klux Klan. (Under his presidency, segregation returned to Washington for the first time since Reconstruction.) An early career in law bored him, so he turned to history and political science and became a professor. His studies persuaded him that a modern president must act as a "prime minister," directing and uniting his party, molding legislation and public opinion, exerting continuous leadership. In 1910, after his stormy tenure as head of Princeton University, Democratic Party bosses helped Wilson win the New Jersey governorship. In 1912 they helped him again, this time to the presidency of the country.

The Reforms of the New Freedom >> As governor, Wilson had led New Jersey on the path of progressive reform. As president, he was a model of progressive leadership. He went to Congress to let members know he intended to work personally with them. He kept party discipline tight and mobilized public opinion when Congress refused to act. More than Roosevelt, he shaped policy and legislation.

Progressives had long attacked the tariff as another example of the power of trusts. Lowering the high tariff became Wilson's first order of business. By protecting American manufacturers, Wilson argued, high tariffs weakened the competition he cherished and created anything but a free market. When the Senate threatened to raise rates, the new president appealed directly to the public. "Industrious" and "insidious" lobbyists were blocking reform, he cried to reporters.

The Underwood-Simmons Tariff of 1913 marked the first downward revision in 19 years and the biggest since before the Civil War. To compensate for lost revenue, Congress enacted a graduated income tax under the new Sixteenth Amendment. It applied solely to corporations and the tiny fraction of Americans who earned more than $4,000 a year. It nonetheless began a momentous shift in government revenue from its nineteenth-century base—public lands, alcohol taxes, and customs duties—to its twentieth-century base of personal and corporate incomes.

Wilson turned next to the perennial problems of money and banking. Early in 1913 a congressional committee revealed that a few powerful banks controlled the nation's credit system. They could choke Wilson's free market by raising interest rates or lowering the supply of money. Either would tighten the money available for loans to businesses. As a banking reform bill moved through Congress in 1913, opinion divided over the locus of control. Conservatives wanted centralized and private control. Rural Democrats wanted regional banks with local bankers in charge. Populists and progressives wanted government in the driver's seat.

Wilson compromised in the Federal Reserve Act of 1913. The new Federal Reserve System consisted of 12 regional banks scattered across the country. It also featured a central Federal Reserve Board in Washington, appointed by the president, to supervise the system. The board could regulate credit and the money supply by setting the interest rate it charged member banks, by buying or selling government bonds, and by issuing paper currency.

When Wilson finally took on the central issue of his New Freedom, the trusts, he inched toward the New Nationalism of Theodore Roosevelt. The Federal Trade Commission Act of 1914 created a bipartisan executive agency to oversee the activities of businesses, large and small. The end—to enforce orderly competition—was distinctly Wilsonian, but the means—an executive commission to regulate commerce—were pure Roosevelt.

Roosevelt would have stopped there, but Wilson made good on his campaign pledge to attack trusts. In 1914, the new Clayton Antitrust Act barred some of the worst corporate practices: price discrimination, holding companies, and interlocking directorates (directors of one corporate board sitting on others). But despite Wilson's bias against size, the advantages of large-scale production and distribution were inescapable. In practice, his administration chose to regulate rather than break up bigness. Under Wilson, the Justice Department filed fewer antitrust suits than under the Taft administration.

Labor and Social Reform >> For all of Wilson's impressive accomplishments, voters seemed uninspired by the New Freedom. Off-year election losses in 1914 pushed Wilson toward the social reforms of the New Nationalism. Earlier, he had criticized them as paternalistic and unconstitutional. In 1916, as his reelection approached, he signaled a change when he nominated his close adviser Louis D. Brandeis to the Supreme Court. The progressive Brandeis had fought for the social reforms lacking from Wilson's legislative agenda. His appointment also broke the tradition of anti-Semitism that had previously kept Jews such as Brandeis off the Court.

Justice Louis Brandeis, who dropped his corporate law practice to become "the people's lawyer," continued to apply progressive principles after Wilson appointed him to the Supreme Court in 1916. Library of Congress, Prints and Photographs Division

promoted racial bias and discrimination. The results of all their efforts, however mixed, set the agenda of reform for the twentieth century.

THEN&NOW

Over a hundred years ago, four progressive amendments to the Constitution enacted in less than a decade changed American life forever. Ratified in 1913, the Sixteenth Amendment gave government the power to tax incomes. Today, all Americans are subject to it. The Seventeenth Amendment (1913) moved the election of U.S. senators from state legislators and to voters through direct elections. Democracy thus spread to another high office and has stayed there. The Eighteenth Amendment (1918) banned the manufacture, sale, importation, and transportation of alcohol. It set off more than a decade of prohibition, fed organized crime, reshaped drinking habits, and provided a model for laws outlawing drugs deemed dangerous ever since. Perhaps most consequential, the Nineteenth Amendment, passed in 1920, established woman suffrage. As a result, women have become an even greater part of American political life, often determining elections and today holding positions of authority throughout government, including the election of Kamala Harris as the first woman vice president in 2020.

 REVIEW

Compare and contrast Theodore Roosevelt's approach to reform with that of Woodrow Wilson.

In other ways, Wilson showed a new willingness to pursue progressive reforms for workers and farmers previously absent from his agenda. He pressed for laws improving the working conditions of merchant seamen and setting an eight-hour day for interstate railroad workers. He supported the Keating-Owen Child Labor Act (1916) that restricted the sale of items made by children and sold across state lines. Farmers benefited from legislation providing them with low-interest loans. And just before the election of 1916, Wilson intervened to avert a nationwide strike of rail workers. These actions reflected a turn toward the progressive goals of social justice and social welfare.

Wilson's administration capped a decade and a half of heady reform. Seeing chaos in the modern industrial city, progressive reformers worked to reduce the damage of poverty and the hazards of industrial work, control rising immigration, and spread a middle-class ideal of morality. In city halls and state legislatures, they tried to break the power of corporate interests and entrenched political machines. In Washington, they enlarged government and broadened its mission from caretaker to promoter of public welfare. But they were frequently blind to issues of color and too often

History in Global Context >> The United States did not pioneer progressive reforms. The machine age triggered a wave of reform across the industrialized world. Early in the nineteenth century, movements for social justice and social welfare sprang up first in Great Britain, where the Industrial Revolution began. British reformers publicized the plight of women and children in factories and mines beginning in the 1820s. The resulting Factory Act of 1833 outlawed child labor in textile mills for those under 9. The Mines Act of 1842 made it illegal to employ women as well as children younger than 10 in work underground. In 1884 Toynbee Hall, the world's first settlement house, opened in London's East End to minister to the needs of the poor. It inspired Jane Addams's Hull House.

In political reforms the world sometimes lagged behind the United States, particularly on the issue of woman suffrage. Except in Scandinavia, most European women did not receive the vote until after World War I. Despite the democratic revolutions that swept across Latin America in the nineteenth century, national woman suffrage was opposed by the Catholic Church and did not come to Ecuador until 1929 and El Salvador until 1939. Asia was slower still, often because colonial rulers denied or limited suffrage or because patriarchal Asian societies looked down on women. Only in 1950, after India achieved independence, did Indian women achieve the right to vote.

CHAPTER SUMMARY

Progressivism embraced a broad-based set of reforms and became the first truly national reform movement in American history.

- Progressive reform sprang from many impulses:
  - ► Desires to curb the advancing power of big business and to end political corruption.
  - ► Efforts to bring order and efficiency to economic and political life.
  - ► Attempts by new interest groups to make business and government more responsive to the needs of ordinary citizens.
  - ► Moralistic urges to rid society of industries such as the liquor trade and prostitution, to bridge the gap between immigrants and native-born Americans, and to soften the consequences of industrialization through social justice and social welfare.
- Led by members of the urban middle class, progressives were moderate modernizers, embracing such traditional American values as democracy, Judeo-Christian ethics, individualism, and the spirit of public service, while employing new techniques of management and planning, coordinated systems, and bureaucracies of experts.
- Progressive women extended their traditional sphere of home and family to become "social housekeepers" and crusaders for women's rights, especially the right to vote.
- Progressivism animated politics, first at the local and state levels, then in the presidencies of Theodore Roosevelt and Woodrow Wilson.
- In the end, the weaknesses of progressivism—its fuzzy conception of the public interest, its exclusion of minorities, and the ease with which its regulatory mechanisms were "captured" by those being regulated—were matched by its accomplishments in establishing the modern activist state.

Digging Deeper

The long debate over what progressivism was and who was progressive has several benchmarks, among them George Mowry, *The California Progressives* (1951); and Richard Hofstadter, *The Age of Reform* (1955), both of whom see progressives as a small elite seeking to recapture its fading status. Michael McGerr's *A Fierce Discontent: The Rise and Fall of the Progressive Movement* (2003) depicts progressivism as a daring middle-class movement to transform society. David Traxel sees both reforming progressives and World War I as spawning a *Crusader Nation* (2006). Finally, Jackson Lears, *Rebirth of a Nation* (2009), places progressivism in the context of an enduring search for regeneration in the decades after the Civil War.

The social history of progressivism is the focus of Steven J. Diner's *A Very Different Age* (1998). Daniel Okrent's *The Guarded Gate: Bigotry, Eugenics and the Law That Kept Two Generations of Jews, Italians, and Other European Immigrants Out of America* (2019) traces of the dangerous combination of eugenics and immigration restriction. On the drive for pure foods and drugs see Deborah Blum's *The Poison Squad: One Chemist's Single-Minded Crusade for Food Safety at the Turn of the Century* (2018). In *Illiberal Reformers: Race, Eugenics, and American Economics in the Progressive Era* (2016), Thomas Leonard examines "economic Progressives" and the roots and consequences of their ambivalence on race and ethnicity. Elaine Weiss's *The Woman's Hour: The Great Fight to Win the Right to Vote* (2019) gives a vivid account of the battle for woman suffrage. Eric Rauchway's *Murdering McKinley: The Making of Theodore Roosevelt's America* (2003) presents a fresh account of the era; while James Chace recounts its turning point in *1912: Wilson, Roosevelt, Taft, and Debs and the Election That Changed the Country* (2004).

John M. Blum, *The Republican Roosevelt* (1954), remains the most incisive rendering of TR; and H. W. Brands, *TR: The Last Romantic* (1997), is the best single-volume biography. Ian Tyrrell's *The Crisis of the Wasteful Nation: Conservation and Empire in Theodore Roosevelt's America* (2015) places the progressive conservation movement in a global context. Unsurpassed in detail and depth is Arthur Link, *Woodrow Wilson*, 5 vols. (1947–1965). Robert Crunden, *Ministers of Reform* (1982), emphasizes the cultural aspects of progressivism; and Ellen Chesler, *Woman of Valor* (1992), offers a feminist perspective on Margaret Sanger. Melvyn Urofsky's *Louis D. Brandeis* (2009) is admiring and authoritative. In *Triangle: The Fire That Changed America* (2004), David Von Drehle presents the fullest account yet of that calamity.

23 The United States and the Collapse of the Old World Order

1901–1920

The ironically titled *Paths to Glory* (1917) was painted by C. R. W. Nevinson, a British artist and volunteer ambulance driver in World War I. He experienced firsthand the pockmarked, muck-filled hell of trench warfare. What is the artist trying to say with this realistic painting?

Photo12/Universal Images Group/Getty Images

>> An American Story

"A PATH BETWEEN THE SEAS"

In 1898, as eager young Americans signed up to kill Spaniards in Cuba, the USS *Oregon* left San Francisco Bay to take up its battle station in the Caribbean. It headed south through the Pacific, passing and leaving Central America thousands of miles behind. In the narrow Strait of Magellan at South America's tip, the ship encountered a gale so ferocious that the shore

MAP 23.1: PANAMA CANAL—OLD AND NEW TRANSOCEANIC ROUTES

Tropical forests cover three-fourths of Panama, including the Canal Zone. Vegetation is denser at high elevations but tightly packed even below 1,000 feet. The terrain is rugged, but the distance saved by the canal (nearly 8,000 miles) convinced Roosevelt and other American leaders that the ordeal of construction and the loss of lives were worthwhile in the long run.

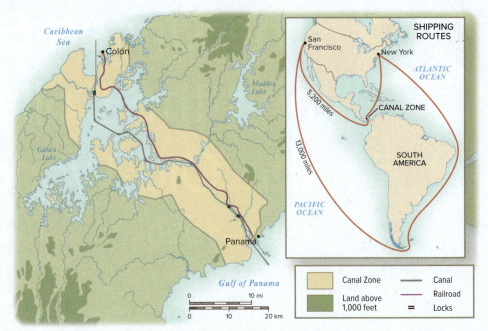

disappeared from sight. The *Oregon* survived and steamed north into the Atlantic. Finally, after 68 days and 13,000 miles at sea, it reached Cuba and helped win the Battle of Santiago Bay and the Spanish-American War.

The daring voyage electrified the nation but worried its leaders. Since the defeat of Mexico in 1848, the United States had stretched from the Atlantic to the Pacific without enough navy to go around. As an emerging power, the country needed a passageway between the seas. A canal across the narrow isthmus of Colombia's Panamanian province in Central America would enable the United States to defend itself from coast to coast and promote its growing trade.

"I took the isthmus," President Theodore Roosevelt later told a cheering crowd. In a way he did. In 1903 he reached an agreement with Colombia to lease the needed strip of land. Hoping for more money and greater control over the canal, the Colombian senate refused to ratify the pact.

Privately TR talked of seizing Panama. But when he learned of a budding independence movement there, he let it be known that he welcomed a revolt. On schedule and without bloodshed, the Panamanians rebelled late in 1903. The next day a U.S. cruiser dropped anchor offshore to prevent Colombia from landing troops. The United States quickly recognized the Republic of Panama and concluded a treaty for a renewable lease on a canal zone 10 miles wide. Panama received $10 million plus a yearly fee of $250,000. Critics called it "a rough-riding assault upon another republic."

The Panama Canal embodied Roosevelt's muscular diplomacy backed by military strength. TR modernized the army and tripled its size. He enlarged the navy, created a general staff for planning and mobilization, and established the Army War College. As a pivot point between the two hemispheres, his canal allowed the United States to flex its strength across the globe.

These expanding horizons came about largely as an outgrowth of American commercial and industrial expansion. The empires of Great Britain, France, Germany, Russia, and Japan reflected the spread of the same industrial and commercial might. But many Americans, steeped in democratic ideals, were uncomfortable with the naked ambitions of European empire-builders. Roosevelt's embrace of the canal, however, showed how far some Americans, especially progressives, would go to shape the world in their interests. They would intervene abroad if they believed American affairs required it.

Expansionist diplomats assured each other that global order could be maintained by balancing power through a set of carefully crafted alliances, spheres of influence and colonial holdings. But the scramble for empire bred conflict. In 1914, the year the Panama Canal opened, a terrible war erupted and shattered the old world order forever. <<

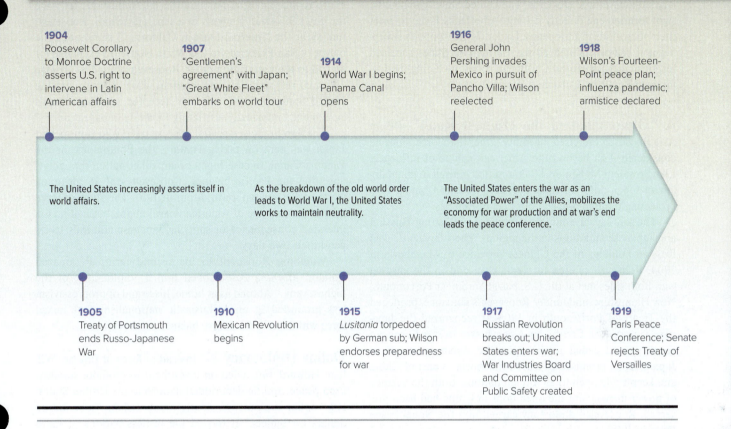

1904 Roosevelt Corollary to Monroe Doctrine asserts U.S. right to intervene in Latin American affairs

1907 "Gentlemen's agreement" with Japan; "Great White Fleet" embarks on world tour

1914 World War I begins; Panama Canal opens

1916 General John Pershing invades Mexico in pursuit of Pancho Villa; Wilson reelected

1918 Wilson's Fourteen-Point peace plan; influenza pandemic; armistice declared

The United States increasingly asserts itself in world affairs.

As the breakdown of the old world order leads to World War I, the United States works to maintain neutrality.

The United States enters the war as an "Associated Power" of the Allies, mobilizes the economy for war production and at war's end leads the peace conference.

1905 Treaty of Portsmouth ends Russo-Japanese War

1910 Mexican Revolution begins

1915 *Lusitania* torpedoed by German sub; Wilson endorses preparedness for war

1917 Russian Revolution breaks out; United States enters war; War Industries Board and Committee on Public Safety created

1919 Paris Peace Conference; Senate rejects Treaty of Versailles

PROGRESSIVE DIPLOMACY

Progressive diplomacy took shape while the Panama Canal was being built. Like progressive politics, it stressed moralism and order. Expanded executive power would make possible the flexibility to mold the international environment. At the core of this mission lay a belief in the superiority of Anglo-American values and institutions and the need to spread them. All Western leaders assumed that northern Europeans were racially superior, with a responsibility to uplift the "lesser peoples" of the tropical zones.

Economic expansion underlay the commitment to this civilizing mission. The depression of 1893 encouraged American manufacturers and farmers to look overseas for markets, and that expansion continued after 1900. Every administration that followed committed itself to opening doors of trade and keeping them open. Whatever civilizing mission Americans cited for expansion, the desire to secure markets for manufacturers and farmers lay at the root.

Big Stick in the Caribbean >> Theodore Roosevelt liked to invoke the old African proverb "Walk softly and carry a big stick." In the Caribbean, he moved loudly and mightily. The Panama Canal gave the United States a commanding position in the Western Hemisphere. Its importance required the country to "police the surrounding premises," explained Secretary of State Elihu Root. Before granting Cuba its independence in 1902, for example, the United States reorganized its finances and wrote the Platt Amendment into the Cuban constitution. It gave the United States the right to intervene if Cuban independence or internal order were threatened. Asserting that power, U.S. troops occupied the island twice between 1906 and 1923.

In looking to enforce a favorable environment for trade in the Caribbean, Roosevelt worried about European intentions. The Monroe Doctrine of 1823 declared against further European colonization of the Western Hemisphere, but in the early twentieth century the rising debts of Latin Americans to Europeans invited intrusion. "If we intend to say hands off to the power of Europe, then sooner or later we must keep order ourselves," TR warned.

Going well beyond Monroe's concept of resisting foreign penetration, Roosevelt asserted American command of the

Caribbean, more like an imperialist than a protector of Latin American independence. In 1904, when the Dominican Republic defaulted on its debts, he added the "Roosevelt Corollary" to the Monroe Doctrine. The United States claimed the right to intervene directly if Latin Americans failed to meet their obligations to Europeans. Under the new policy's sweeping and self-proclaimed power, the United States assumed responsibility for several Caribbean states, including the Dominican Republic, Cuba, and Panama.

A "Diplomatist of the Highest Rank" >> In Asia Roosevelt exercised ingenuity rather than force, since he considered Asia beyond the American sphere of influence. Like President McKinley, TR committed himself to maintaining an "open door" of equal access to trade in China and to protecting the Philippines, "our heel of Achilles."

The key lay in counterbalancing or offsetting Russian and Japanese ambitions in the region. When Japan attacked Russian holdings in the Chinese province of Manchuria in 1904, Roosevelt offered to mediate an end to the ensuing war. Both sides met at the U.S. Naval Yard near Portsmouth, New Hampshire, and, under Roosevelt's guidance, produced the Treaty of Portsmouth in 1905. It recognized the Japanese victory (the first by an Asian power over a European country) and ceded territory on the Asian mainland to Japan. Japan promised to leave Manchuria as part of China and keep trade open to all foreign nations. Both the balance of power in Asia and the open door in China had been preserved. Roosevelt's diplomacy earned him the Nobel Peace Prize in 1906.

⌃ Sailors from the Japanese torpedo boat *Sazanami* board a Russian torpedo boat during a heated sea battle off Port Arthur during the Russo-Japanese War. Japan's victory, the first of an Asian over a European power, signaled Japan's new status as a great world power, as well as the country's success in "modernizing" along Western lines.
Library of Congress, Prints and Photographs Division

Some Japanese nationalists resented the peace treaty for curbing Japan's ambitions in Asia. Their anger surfaced in a protest lodged against the San Francisco school board. In 1906, rising Japanese immigration led authorities to place the city's 93 Asian students in a separate school. Roosevelt, fuming at the "infernal fools in California," summoned the mayor of San Francisco to the White House. In exchange for an end to the segregation order, Roosevelt offered to arrange a mutual restriction of immigration between Japan and the United States. In 1907 all sides accepted his "gentlemen's agreement," informally restricting Japanese immigration.

The San Francisco school crisis sparked wild rumors that Japan was bent on taking Hawai'i, the Philippines, or the Panama Canal. In case Japan or any other nation thought of upsetting the Pacific balance, Roosevelt sent 16 gleaming white battleships on a world tour in 1907. The show of force heralded a new age of American naval might, but had an unintended consequence of spurring Japanese admirals to expand their own navy.

Watching Roosevelt in his second term, an amazed London *Morning Post* dubbed him a "diplomatist of the highest rank." Abroad as at home, his brand of progressivism was grounded in an enthusiastic nationalism that mixed force with finesse to achieve balance and order.

Dollar Diplomacy >> Instead of force or finesse, William Howard Taft relied on investment to promote stability, keep peace, and tie debt-ridden nations to the United States. His "dollar diplomacy" simply amounted to "substituting dollars for bullets." It treated the restless nations of Latin America like struggling businesses, injecting capital and reorganizing management. When Taft left office in 1913, half of all American investments abroad lay in Latin America, often relying on Roosevelt's Corollary as a foundation.

Failure dogged Taft overseas as it did at home. In the Caribbean, his dollar diplomacy was linked so closely with unpopular governments, corporations, and banks that Woodrow Wilson rejected it as soon as he entered the White House. In 1912, a revolution in Nicaragua led Taft to dispatch 2,000 marines to protect American lives and property. Sporadic U.S. interventions in the nation lasted more than a dozen years.

Taft's efforts to strengthen China with investments and trade only intensified rivalry with Japan and made China more suspicious of all foreigners. In 1911, dollar diplomacy was a factor in fomenting a rebellion in the southern Chinese provinces against foreign intrusion that eventually overthrew the Chinese monarchy. Only pressure from the White House kept dollar diplomacy alive in Asia. In the end, no brand of progressive diplomacy could achieve stability as the old imperial order lurched toward war.

REVIEW

How did Theodore Roosevelt's policies in Latin America and Asia differ from William Howard Taft's?

WOODROW WILSON AND MORAL DIPLOMACY

The Lightfoot Club had been meeting in Reverend Wilson's hayloft for months when the question arose of whether the pen was mightier than the sword. Young Tommy Wilson, who had organized the debating society, jumped at the chance to argue that words were more powerful than armies. When the boys drew lots, Tommy ended up on the other side. "I can't argue for something I don't believe in," he protested.

Thomas Woodrow Wilson eventually dropped his first name but never abandoned his conviction that morality, at least as he defined it, should guide conduct. To order, force, and finance, Wilson added a missionary zeal for spreading capitalism, democracy, and the progressive values of harmony and cooperation, all moral components of his approach to diplomacy.

Missionary Diplomacy >> As president, Woodrow Wilson revived and enlarged Jefferson's notion of the United States as a beacon of freedom. "We are chosen, and prominently chosen, to show the way to the nations of the world how they shall walk in the paths of liberty," he said. Such paternalism only thinly masked Wilson's assumption of Anglo-American superiority. It also veiled Wilson's willingness to export Western-style democracy, capitalism, and morality, all in line with progressive values, through force if need be.

Wilson's missionary diplomacy had a practical side. American industries "will burst their jackets if they cannot find free outlets in the markets of the world," he cautioned in 1912. Wilson's genius lay in reconciling commercial self-interest with global idealism. In his eyes, exporting American democracy and capitalism would promote stability and progress throughout the world.

In Asia, Wilson moved to put "moral and public considerations" ahead of the "material interests of individuals." He pulled American bankers out of a six-nation railroad project in China backed by President Taft. The United States became the first major power to recognize the new Republic of China after a revolution in 1911 and in 1915 strongly opposed Japan's "21 Demands" for territorial and commercial privileges there.

In the Caribbean and Latin America, Wilson discovered that interests closer to home could not be pursued through

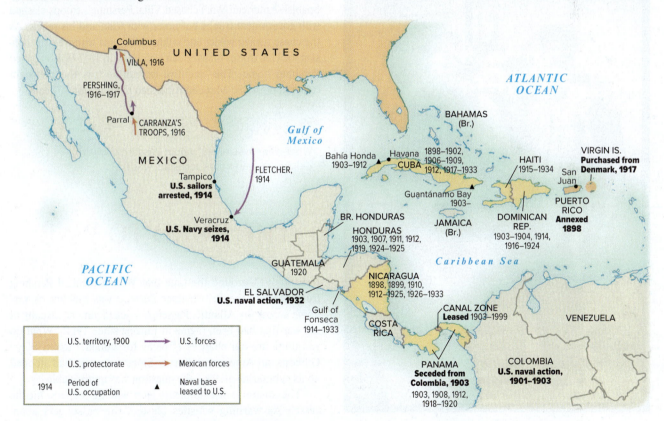

MAP 23.2: AMERICAN INTERVENTIONS IN LATIN AMERICA AND THE CARIBBEAN, 1898–1930

In the first three decades of the twentieth century, armed and unarmed interventions by the United States virtually transformed the Caribbean into an American lake.
In which nations did the United States intervene for the longest time?

principles alone. In August 1914 he convinced Nicaragua, already occupied by American troops, to yield control of a naval base and grant the United States an alternative canal route. Upheavals in Haiti and the Dominican Republic brought in the U.S. Marines. By the end of his administration, American troops were still stationed there and also in Cuba. Missionary diplomacy, it turned out, could spread its gospel with arms as well as cash.

Intervention in Mexico >> In Mexico a lingering crisis made a mockery of Wilson's "moral diplomacy." A common border, 400 years of shared history, and millions of dollars in investments gave the United States a vested interest in what happened in Mexico. In 1910 a revolution plunged Mexico into turmoil. Just as Wilson entered the White House in 1913, the ruthless general Victoriano Huerta emerged as

⌃ General John J. "Black Jack" Pershing led U.S. forces into Mexico to catch rebel leader Pancho Villa "dead or alive." Villa (pictured here with his wife, María Luz Corral) eluded the Americans for several months before they abandoned the expedition. Audacious and ruthless, he was worshiped by Mexican peasants, who extolled his exploits in folktales and ballads after his assassination in 1923 by Mexican political rivals.
Library of Congress, Prints and Photographs Division

head of the government. Wealthy, upper-class landowners and foreign investors endorsed Huerta, who was likely to protect their holdings. Soon a bloody civil war was raging.

Unlike most European leaders, Wilson refused to recognize Huerta and his immoral "government of butchers." (Huerta had murdered the popular leader Francisco Madero.) Instead, he backed rebel leader Venustiano Carranza. When a bankrupt Huerta resigned in 1914, Carranza formed a new constitutionalist government but refused to follow Wilson's guidelines. Wilson threw his support to Francisco "Pancho" Villa, a wily, peasant-born general who had broken with Carranza. Together with Emiliano Zapata, another peasant leader, Villa kept rebellion flickering.

A year later, when Wilson finally recognized the Carranza regime, Villa turned against the United States in protest. In January 1916 he abducted 18 Americans from a train in Mexico and slaughtered them. In March he galloped into Columbus, New Mexico, killed 19 people, and left the town in flames. Wilson ordered 6,000 troops into Mexico to capture Villa. In the aftermath, a reluctant Carranza agreed to the American incursion.

For nearly two years, General John "Black Jack" Pershing (nicknamed for the all-Black unit he had commanded in the Spanish-American War) chased Villa. Pershing's troops clashed with government troops but never with Villa and his rebels. As the chase turned wilder and wilder, Carranza withdrew his consent for U.S. troops on Mexican soil. Early in 1917 Wilson called Pershing home. The "punitive expedition," as the president called it, poisoned Mexican-American relations for 30 years.

✓ **REVIEW**

What was "missionary" about Woodrow Wilson's diplomacy, and how successful was he?

THE ROAD TO WAR

In early 1917, around the time that Wilson recalled Pershing from Mexico, the British liner *Laconia* was making its way home across the Atlantic. Passengers talked almost casually of the war that had been raging in Europe since 1914. "What do you think are our chances of being torpedoed?" asked Floyd Gibbons, an American reporter. Since Germany had stepped up its submarine attacks, the question was unavoidable.

The answer came moments later when a torpedo hit the vessel. As warning whistles blasted, the passengers abandoned ship. From lifeboats, they watched a second torpedo send the *Laconia* to a watery grave. After a miserable night spent bobbing in the waves, Gibbons was rescued. But by 1917, other citizens of the neutral United States had already lost their lives to German torpedoes. Despite the best efforts of its leaders, the country soon found itself in a war that few Americans wanted, not least the president who led them into it.

The Guns of August >> For a century profound strains had pushed Europe toward war. Its population tripled, its middle and working classes swelled, and discontent with industrial society mushroomed. Nationalism surged and with it militarism and imperialism. Eager for empire, Germany allied with Turkey and Austria-Hungary. Great Britain and France, looking to contain Germany, supported its Russian foe. By the summer of 1914, Europe bristled with weapons, troops, and armor-plated navies, all linked through diplomatic and military alliances ready to fight the moment something set them in motion.

That moment came on June 28, 1914, in the streets of Sarajevo, the provincial capital of Bosnia in southwestern Austria-Hungary. There, a young assassin belonging to the Black Hand, gunned down the heir to the Austro-Hungarian throne, Archduke Franz Ferdinand, and his wife. The Black Hand terrorists had vowed to reunite Bosnia with Serbia and create another Slavic nation on Austria-Hungary's border.

Austria-Hungary troops marched into Serbia in response. Russia, Germany's main rival in Europe, mobilized its 6-million-troop army to aid the Serbs. Germany joined with Austria-Hungary, France with Russia. On July 28, after a month of insincere demands for apologies, Austria-Hungary attacked Serbia to punish it for the death of Archduke Ferdinand. Germany declared war on Russia on August 1 and, two days later, on France.

The guns of August heralded the first global war. Like so many dominoes, nations fell into line. Britain, Japan, Romania, and later Italy rushed to the side of "Allies" France and Russia; Bulgaria and Turkey to the "Central Powers" of Germany and Austria-Hungary. Armies fought from the deserts of North Africa to the plains of Flanders. Fleets battled off the coasts of Chile and Sumatra.

Neutral but Not Impartial >> The outbreak of war in Europe shocked most Americans. Few knew Serbia as anything but a tiny splotch on a map. Fewer still were prepared to go to war in its defense. President Wilson issued a declaration of neutrality and approved a plan for evacuating Americans stranded in Belgium.

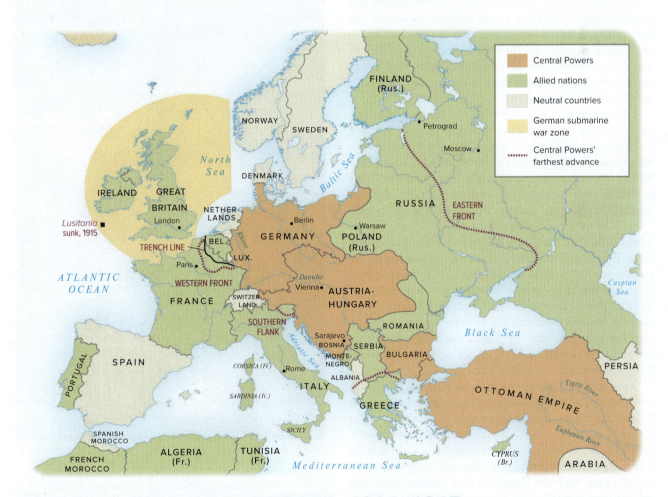

MAP 23.3: THE WAR IN EUROPE, 1914–1917

When World War I erupted, few countries in Europe remained neutral. The armies of the Central Powers penetrated as far west as France and as far east as Russia. By 1917 the war in Europe had settled into a hideous standoff along a deadly line of trenches on the Western Front. *In which nation did the Western Front remain for most of the war? In which nation did the Eastern Front remain until 1917?*

Wilson believed a neutral United States could take the moral high ground and lead warring nations to "a peace without victory." There would be none of the territorial concessions or monetary reparations that accompanied past wars. Instead Wilson hoped to inspire a new world order in which selfish nationalism gave way to cooperative internationalism; power politics to collective security. Nations would join together to ensure the safety of all by isolating aggressors and keeping the peace. Progressive faith in reason would triumph over violence. Everything hinged on maintaining neutrality. Only if the United States remained "impartial in thought as well as action" could Wilson's missionary diplomacy triumph and a new world order emerge.

In a country as ethnically diverse as the United States, true impartiality was impossible. Americans of German and Austrian descent naturally sympathized with the Central Powers, as did Irish Americans, who resented Britain's centuries-old domination of Ireland. Yet, the bonds of language, culture, and history tied most Americans to Great Britain. And gratitude for French aid during the American Revolution still lived.

Germany aroused mixed sentiments. Although some progressives admired German social reforms, a majority saw Germany as an iron military power bent on conquest. British propaganda pictured spike-helmeted "Huns" raping Belgian women, bayoneting their children, and pillaging their towns. Some stories were true, some embellished, some utterly false, but all worked to antagonize Americans against Germany.

Longstanding U.S. economic ties to Britain and France also created a financial stake in Allied victory. New war orders created an economic boom. Between 1914 and 1916, Allied trade rocketed from $800 million to $3 billion. The Allies borrowed more than $2 billion from American banks to finance their purchases. In contrast, a British blockade reduced American war-goods trade with the Central Powers.

The Diplomacy of Neutrality >> Wilson had admired

Great Britain all his life and could not contain his British sympathies. Although he insisted that all warring powers respect the right of neutrals to trade with any nation, he hesitated to retaliate against Britain's blockade of Germany. Its powerful navy was Britain's key to victory over Germany, a land power. By the end of 1915, the United States had all but accepted the blockade, while American supplies continued to flow to Britain. True neutrality was dead.

Early in 1915, Germany loosed a dreadful new weapon to even the odds at sea. It mounted a counterblockade of Great Britain with two dozen submarines, or *Unterseeboote,* called U-boats. Unlike surface ships, submarines attacked without warning and spared no lives. Invoking international law and national honor, Wilson threatened to hold Germany to "strict accountability" for any American losses. Germany promised not to sink any American ships, but soon a new issue grabbed the headlines: the safety of American passengers on vessels of nations at war.

On the morning of May 7, 1915, the British passenger liner *Lusitania* appeared out of a fog bank off the coast of Ireland on its way from New York to Southampton. The commander of a German U-20 fired a single torpedo. A tremendous roar followed as one of the *Lusitania*'s main boilers exploded. The ship listed so badly that lifeboats could barely be launched before the vessel sank. Nearly 1,200 men, women, and children perished, including 128 Americans.

Wilson, though horrified, did little more than send notes of protest to Germany. Secretary of State William Jennings Bryan, an advocate of what he called "real neutrality," supported a more measured response, with equal protests lodged against German submarines and British blockaders. He suspected that the *Lusitania* was carrying munitions and was thus a legitimate target. (Much later, evidence proved him right.) Relying on passengers for protection against attack, Bryan argued, was "like putting women and children in front of an army." Rather than endorse Wilson's policy, Bryan resigned.

As its desperation rose, Germany declared unrestricted submarine warfare against all armed vessels. More ships with American passengers came under attack. Wilson responded

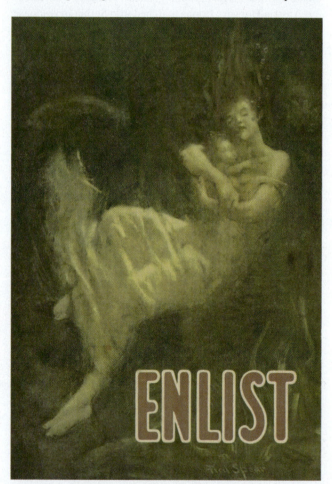

⌃ This American poster, drawn by Fred Spear and issued by the Boston Public Safety Committee during the Preparedness Campaign in 1916, employs a common trope of war propaganda—endangered women and children—to inspire support for United States's involvement in the conflict and to inspire young men to join the armed services. A drowned woman passenger from the *Lusitania* holds an infant as both sink to the bottom of the sea. "Enlist" is the simple one-word message.
Everett Collection Inc/Alamy Stock Photo

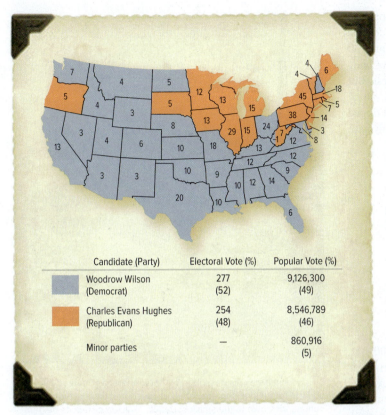

MAP 23.4: ELECTION OF 1916

Candidate (Party)	Electoral Vote (%)	Popular Vote (%)
Woodrow Wilson (Democrat)	277 (52)	9,126,300 (49)
Charles Evans Hughes (Republican)	254 (48)	8,546,789 (46)
Minor parties	—	860,916 (5)

with an ultimatum in mid-April 1916: if Germany refused to stop sinking nonmilitary vessels, the United States would break off diplomatic relations. War would surely follow. Without enough U-boats to control the seas, Germany agreed to Wilson's terms, all but abandoning its counterblockade. This *Sussex* pledge gave Wilson a major victory but carried a grave risk. If German submarines resumed unrestricted attacks, the United States would have to go to war.

Peace, Preparedness, and the Election of 1916 >>

While hundreds of pro-Allied Yanks slipped across the border to enlist in the Canadian army, most Americans agreed that neutrality was the wisest course. Pacifists condemned the war, but Republicans and corporate leaders argued that keeping the nation at peace required military strength. The army numbered only 80,000 troops in 1914; the navy, just 37 battleships and a handful of new "dreadnoughts," or supercruisers. Advocates of "preparedness" called for a navy larger than Great Britain's, an army of millions of reservists, and universal military training.

By the end of 1915, frustration with German use of submarines led Wilson to join the cause of preparedness. He toured the country promising a "navy second to none." In Washington, he pressed Congress to double the army, increase the National Guard, and begin construction of the largest navy in the world.

Preparedness had political power, too, as the Democrats discovered early in the presidential campaign of 1916. At the Democratic National Convention in June, the keynote speaker began what he expected to be a dull recitation of Wilson's recent diplomatic maneuvers—only to have the crowd roar back in each case, "What did we do?" The speaker knew the answer and shouted it back: "We didn't go to war!" The next day Wilson was renominated by acclamation. "He Kept Us Out of War" became his campaign slogan.

The Republicans had already nominated Charles Evans Hughes, the former governor of New York. Also wanting to avoid war, he endorsed "straight and honest" neutrality and peace. Despite his moderate stand, Democrats succeeded in painting him as a warmonger. By the time the polls closed, Wilson had squeaked out a victory, carried again to the presidency on a tide of prosperity, progressive reform, and promises of peace.

Wilson's Final Peace Offensive >>

Twice since 1915 Wilson had sent his trusted adviser Edward House to Europe to negotiate an end to the war, and twice House failed. With the election over, Wilson opened his final peace offensive. When he asked the warring powers to state their terms for a cease-fire, none responded. Frustrated and fearful, Wilson called for "a peace among equals" in January 1917.

As the president spoke, a fleet of U-boats was cruising toward the British Isles. Weeks earlier, German military leaders had decided to take one last gamble to starve the Allies into submission. On January 31, 1917, the German ambassador in Washington announced that unrestricted submarine warfare would resume the next day.

Wilson's dream of neutrality collapsed. He asked Congress for authority to arm merchant ships and severed relations with Germany. Then British authorities handed him a bombshell—an intercepted telegram from the German foreign secretary, Arthur Zimmermann, to the kaiser's ambassador in Mexico. In case the United States went to war with Germany and Mexico joined the Central Powers, the ambassador was instructed to offer Mexico guns, money, and its "lost territory in Texas, New Mexico, and Arizona." An angry Wilson released the Zimmermann telegram to the press. Soon after, he ordered gun crews aboard merchant ships and directed them to shoot U-boats on sight.

Those policies now combined with events abroad to propel a reluctant Wilson toward war. On March 12, U-boats torpedoed the American merchant vessel *Algonquin*. On March 15, a revolution in Russia toppled Czar Nicholas II, crippling a key ally from within. By the end of the month U-boats had sunk nearly 600,000 tons of Allied and neutral shipping. For the first time, reports came to Washington of cracking morale in the Allied ranks.

On April 2, 1917, Wilson trudged up the steps of the Capitol and delivered a stirring war message to Congress. He called "for democracy, for the right of those who submit to authority to have a voice in their own governments, for the rights and liberties of small nations." Six senators and 50 House members opposed the war resolution, including Jeannette Rankin of Wyoming, the first woman in Congress. But cultural, economic, and historical ties to the Allies, along with the German campaign of submarine warfare, had tipped the country toward war. Now the battlefield was the only path to the higher peace Wilson sought.

 REVIEW

What steps did Woodrow Wilson take to avoid World War I, and why did they fail?

WAR AND SOCIETY

In 1915 the German zeppelin LZ-38, hovering at 8,000 feet, dropped a load of bombs that killed seven Londoners. For the first time in history, civilians died in an air attack. Few aerial bombardments occurred during World War I, but they signaled the growing importance of the home front in modern combat. Governments not only fielded armies but also mobilized industry, controlled labor, even rationed food. In the United States, traditions of cooperation and volunteerism helped the war effort at home and abroad, often in ways that were distinctly progressive.

The Slaughter of Stalemate >> While the United States debated entry into World War I, the Allies were close to losing it. Following the initial German assault in 1914, the war had settled into a grisly stalemate. A stationary battlefront stretched south from Flanders in Belgium to Switzerland. Troops dug ditches, six to eight feet deep and four to five feet wide, to escape bullets, grenades, and artillery. Twenty-five thousand miles of these "trenches" slashed a muddy scar across Europe. Troops lived in them for years, prey to disease, trench-foot, lice, and rats.

War in the machine age gave the advantage to the defense. When soldiers bravely charged "over the top" of the trenches, they were shredded by machine guns that fired 600 rounds a minute. Poison gas choked them in their tracks. Giant howitzers lobbed shells on them from positions too distant to see. In the Battle of the Somme River in 1916, a million soldiers were killed in just four months of fighting. Only late in the war did new armored "landships"—code-named "tanks"—return the advantage to the offense. Their caterpillar treads propelled steel chassises over obstacles in their path.

As stalemate lingered on the Western Front, Vladimir Lenin sped home to Russia from exile in Switzerland. Food riots, coal shortages, and protests against the government had triggered a revolution in his homeland. Upon his return,

^ Trench warfare was described by one general as "marked by uniform formations, the regulation of space and time by higher commands down to the smallest details . . . fixed distances between units and individuals." The reality was something else.
Chronicle/Alamy Stock Photo

Lenin led his Bolshevik Party to power in November 1917. A separate peace with Germany soon followed. A million German soldiers who had been occupied with fighting the Russians marched to the Western Front for the coming spring offensive.

"You're in the Army Now" >> The Allies' plight drove the U.S. army into a desperate bid to send a million soldiers of its own to Europe by the spring of 1918. When Congress declared war, the United States had barely 180,000 soldiers in uniform. To raise the force, Congress passed the Selective Service Act in May 1917. Feelings against the draft ran high. One critic saw little difference between a "conscript and a convict." Progressives were more inclined to see military service as an opportunity to unite the United States and promote democracy by breaking down class differences. "Universal [military] training will jumble the boys of America all together, . . . smashing all the petty class distinctions that now divide, and prompting a brand of real democracy," predicted one.

On July 20, 1917, Secretary of War Newton Baker tied a blindfold over his eyes, reached into a huge glass bowl, and drew the first number in the new draft lottery. Some 24 million men were registered. Almost 3 million were drafted; another 2 million volunteered. Most were white, and all were young, between the ages of 21 and 31. Several thousand women served as military clerks, telephone operators, and nurses.

In a nation of immigrants, nearly one draftee in five had been born in another country. Training often aimed at educating and Americanizing these recruits. In special units called "development battalions," drill sergeants barked out marching orders while volunteers from the YMCA taught American history and English.

Mexican Americans and African Americans volunteered in disproportionately high numbers. While Mexican Americans were integrated into regular army units, African Americans remained segregated. They quickly filled the four all-Black army and eight National Guard units already in existence. Abroad, where 200,000 Black troops served in France, only about a fifth were permitted in combat. Southern Democrats in Congress had opposed combat training for African Americans, fearful of putting "arrogant, strutting representatives of Black soldiery in every community." Four regiments of the all-Black Ninety-Third Division, brigaded with the French army, were nonetheless among the first Americans in the trenches and among the most decorated units in the U.S. Army.

Racial violence sometimes flared among the troops. The worst episode occurred in Houston in the summer of 1917. Harassed by white soldiers and the city's Jim Crow laws, seasoned Black regulars fought back and ended up killing 17 white civilians. Their whole battalion was arrested, disarmed, and sent to New Mexico. Thirteen troopers were condemned to death and hanged within days, too quickly for appeals even to be filed.

Progressive reformers did not miss the opportunity to put the social sciences to work in the army. Most recruits had fewer than seven years of education, yet they had to be classified and assigned quickly to units. Psychologists saw the chance to use new intelligence tests to help the army and prove their own theories about the value of "IQ" (intelligence quotient) in measuring brainpower. In fact, these new "scientific" IQ tests often measured little more than class origins. The army stopped the testing program in January 1919, but schools across the country adopted it after the war, reinforcing many ethnic and racial prejudices.

Mobilizing the Economy >>
Clothed, armed, and drilled, the doughboys sailed on "Atlantic ferries"—the ships that conveyed them to Europe. (Infantrymen were called "doughboys," most likely because of the clay dough used by soldiers in the 1850s to clean their brass belt buckles.) To equip, feed, and transport an army of nearly 5 million required a national effort.

national debt cumulative total of all previous annual federal deficits or budget shortfalls incurred each year and owed by the federal government.

At the Treasury Department, Secretary William Gibbs McAdoo fretted over how to finance the war, which finally cost $32 billion. At the time, the entire **national debt** ran to only $2 billion. New taxes paid about a third of the war costs. The rest came from loans financed through "Liberty" and "Victory" bonds and war savings certificates. By 1920 the national debt had climbed to $20 billion.

⌃ Regardless of their race or ethnicity, Americans supported the war by buying war bonds. Some groups, like African Americans, bought bonds in numbers greater than their proportion of the population, often to demonstrate their love of country despite the hardships they faced. Here a Chinese American man is surrounded by a biracial committee as he signs up to purchase some of the second issue of government "Liberty Bonds" in 1918.
FPG/Archive Photos/Getty Images

With sweeping grants of authority provided by Congress, President Wilson constructed a massive bureaucracy to mobilize the home front. What emerged was a **managed economy** similar to the New Nationalism envisioned by Theodore Roosevelt. No industries were actually nationalized. Instead, new executive agencies regulated and supervised the private sector by rewarding rather than punishing businesses.

managed economy economy directed by the government with power over prices, allocation of resources, and marketing of goods.

A War Industries Board (WIB) coordinated production through networks of industrial and **trade associations**. Rather than order firms to comply and risk lawsuits against the government, the WIB relied on persuasion through publicity and "cost-plus" contracts. The formula covered all production costs and guaranteed a profit. Antitrust suits, which might have prevented business cooperation, were simply put "to sleep," recalled one official. Corporate profits tripled, and production soared.

trade association organization of individuals and firms in a given industry that provides lobbying and other services to members.

The Food Administration encouraged farmers to grow more and citizens to eat less wastefully. Publicity campaigns promoted "wheatless" and "meatless" days and exhorted families to plant their own vegetables, called "victory gardens." Spurred by rising prices, farmers brought more marginal lands into cultivation as their real income jumped 25 percent.

A Fuel Administration met the army's energy needs by increasing production and limiting domestic consumption. The U.S. Railroad Administration simply took over rail lines for the duration of the war. Government coordination, together with a new system of permits, got freight moving and kept workers happy. Rail workers saw their wages rise by $300 million. Railroad unions won recognition, an eight-hour day, and a grievance procedure. For the first time in decades, labor unrest on the rail lines subsided and the trains ran on time.

bureaucratic state government run by administrative bureaus and staffed by nonelected officials.

The modern **bureaucratic state** received a big boost during the 18 months the United States was at war. Some 5,000 new federal agencies centralized authority, managed the economy, and cooperated with business and labor. The number of federal employees more than doubled between 1916 and 1918 to over 850,000. Although the wartime bureaucracy was quickly dismantled, it spurred the trend toward big government.

THEN&NOW

World War I represented the first national effort to wage a truly global conflict. After years of tension over regulation and antitrust, government and business forged a partnership based on mutual needs. The partnership produced new executive agencies that strengthened the presidency and gave the government and the private sector more power over the economy. During the New Deal, some of these executive agencies were retooled to fight the Great Depression. And in the Cold War, business-government cooperation in research, production, policy, and execution followed the precedent established during World War I. Over the years, that cooperation produced what President Dwight Eisenhower called the "military-industrial complex." He warned against its capacity to consume resources and create a garrison state, always at war or on its cusp. For good and ill, the military-industrial complex still exists, as do the dangers it poses.

War Work >> The war benefited workingmen and workingwomen, though not as much as their employers. Government contracts guaranteed high wages, an eight-hour day, and equal pay to men and women for comparable work. To encourage people to stay on the job, federal contracting agencies set up special classes to teach employers the new science of personnel management to supervise workers more effi-

welfare capitalism business practice of providing welfare—in the form of pension and profit-sharing programs, subsidized housing, personnel management, paid vacations, and other services and benefits—for workers.

ciently and humanely. American industry moved one step closer to the **welfare capitalism** of the 1920s, with its profit sharing, company unions, and personnel departments to forestall worker discontent.

Personnel management was not always enough to guarantee industrial peace. In 1917 American workers called over 4,000 strikes, the most in American history. To keep factories running, President Wilson created the National War Labor Board (NWLB) early in 1918. The NWLB arbitrated more than 1,000 labor disputes during the war, helped increase wages, and established overtime pay. In return for no-strike pledges, the board guaranteed the rights of unions to organize and bargain collectively. Prewar membership in the American Federation of Labor almost doubled by 1919.

Wartime demand for workers brought nearly a million more women into the labor force. Most were young and single. Some took over jobs once held by men, such as railroad engineers, drill-press operators, and electric-lift truck drivers. The prewar trend toward higher-paying jobs for women intensified, though most women still earned less than the men they replaced. And some of the most spectacular gains evaporated after the war as male veterans returned and the country demobilized.

War work nonetheless helped energize several women's causes and organizations. Radical suffragist Alice Paul and others who had protested against the war now argued for women's rights, including the right to vote, on the basis of it. Positions alongside men in wartime factories and offices or on the front provided a basis for claims for economic and political equality. One step in that direction came after the war with the ratification of the Nineteenth Amendment in 1920, guaranteeing women the right to vote.

^ The constraints of war brought more women than ever into the job market. These women work in an armament factory slotting fuses. Like in many factories of the day, the whirring belts turning machinery could prove hazardous if they caught a stray hand or clothing.
Corbis/Getty Images

Great Migrations >> War work sparked massive migrations of laborers. As the fighting abroad choked off immigration and the draft depleted the workforce, factory owners scoured the country for workers. Industrial cities, no matter how small, soon swelled with newcomers. Between 1917 and 1920 some 150,000 Mexicans crossed the border into the Southwest. Some Mexican Americans left segregated barrios in western cities for war plants in Chicago, Omaha, and other northern cities, pushed out by cheaper labor from Mexico and seeking higher-paying jobs. But most worked on farms and ranches, freed from military service by the deferment granted to agricultural laborers.

Northern labor agents fanned out across the rural South to recruit young African Americans, while Black newspapers like the *Chicago Defender* summoned them to the "Land of Hope." During the war, over 400,000 moved to northern industrial cities. Largely unskilled and semiskilled, they worked in the steel mills of Pennsylvania, the war plants of Massachusetts, and the brickyards of New Jersey. Southern towns were decimated by the drain.

African American migrations—into the army as well as into the city—aggravated racial tensions. Lynching parties murdered 38 Black southerners in 1917 and 58 in 1918. In 1919, after the war ended, more than 70 were murdered, some still in uniform. Housing shortages and job competition contributed to race riots across the North. In almost every city, Black citizens, stirred by war rhetoric of freedom and democracy, showed new militancy. During the bloody "red summer" of 1919, race wars broke out in Washington, D.C., Omaha, Nebraska, New York City, and Chicago, where thousands of African Americans were burned out of their homes and hundreds injured as they fought white mobs.

Propaganda and Civil Liberties >> "Once lead this people into war," President Wilson warned before American entry into the conflict, "and they'll forget there ever was such a thing as tolerance." Americans succumbed to a ruthless hysteria during World War I, encouraged in part by the very president who decried it. Wilson knew how reluctant Americans had once been to enter the war. In 1917 he created the Committee on Public Information (CPI) to rouse their support.

Under George Creel, a California journalist, the CPI launched a vigorous publicity campaign that produced colorful war posters, 75 million pamphlets, and patriotic "war expositions" in two dozen cities. An army of 75,000 fast-talking "Four-Minute Men" invaded theaters, schools, and churches to keep patriotism at "white heat" with four-minute war tirades. The CPI organized "Loyalty Leagues" in ethnic communities and sponsored rallies, including an immigrant "pilgrimage" to Washington's birthplace.

As the CPI campaign intensified, simple patriotism transformed into a more virulent "100 percent Americanism." Beyond patriotic fervor, it bred distrust and intolerance of all aliens, radicals, pacifists, and dissenters. German Americans became special targets. In Iowa the governor made it a crime to speak German in public. When a mob outside St. Louis lynched a German American who had tried to enlist in the navy, a jury found the leaders not guilty.

Passage of the Espionage and the Sedition Acts of 1917 and 1918 outlawed any act deemed unpatriotic or detrimental to the war effort. **Sedition** includes words or actions that incite revolt against the law or duly constituted government. The penalties were severe. Following passage, 1,500 citizens were arrested for offenses that

> **sedition** words or actions that incite revolt against the law or duly constituted government.

included denouncing the draft, criticizing the Red Cross, and complaining about wartime taxes.

Treatment of radicals was even harsher. The Industrial Workers of the World (IWW), a militant union centered in western states, saw the war as a battle waged by capitalists at the expense of workers. The union threatened to strike mining and lumber companies in protest. In response, federal agents raided the IWW Chicago headquarters and arrested 113 members. The crusade destroyed the union.

Since the Socialist Party opposed the war on grounds similar to the IWW. the postmaster general banned a dozen Socialist publications from the mail, even though the party was a legal organization that had elected mayors, municipal officials, and members of Congress. In 1918 government agents arrested Eugene V. Debs, the Socialist candidate for president in 1912, for an antiwar speech. A jury found him guilty of sedition for opposing the draft and sentenced him to 10 years in jail.

The Supreme Court endorsed such actions. In *Schenck v. United States* (1919) the Court unanimously affirmed the conviction under the Espionage Act of a Socialist Party officer for mailing pamphlets urging resistance to the draft. The pamphlets, wrote Justice Oliver Wendell Holmes, created "a clear and present danger" to a nation at war. Under the Espionage Act, free speech was neither free nor unrestricted.

Over There >> The first American doughboys landed in France in June 1917, but few saw battle. General John Pershing held back his raw troops until they received more training. He also separated them in the American Expeditionary Force to preserve their identity and avoid Allied disagreements over strategy.

In the spring of 1918, as the Germans pushed toward Paris, Pershing rushed 70,000 American troops to the front. American units helped block the Germans at the town of Château-Thierry and at Belleau Wood. Two more German attacks, one at Amiens and the other just east of the Marne River, ended in costly German retreats. In September 1918, half a million American soldiers and a smaller number of French troops took just four days to overrun the German stronghold at Saint-Mihiel.

Many HISTORIES

THE LIMITS OF FREE SPEECH

When the Socialist Party printed and distributed 15,000 leaflets attacking the Conscription Act (1917), authorities charged the party's secretary general Charles Schenck with having violated the newly enacted Espionage Act by opposing conscription (drafting men into military service). In ruling against Schenck, Justice Oliver Wendell Holmes, writing for the majority of the Supreme Court, outlined the limits of free speech in wartime.

DOCUMENT 1
Flyer Distributed by Socialist Party

ASSERT YOUR RIGHTS!

The Constitution of the United States is one of the greatest bulwarks of political liberty. It was born after a long, stubborn battle between king-rule and democracy. . . . In this battle the people of the United States established the principle that freedom of the individual and personal liberty are the most sacred things in life. Without them we become slaves. . . .

The Thirteenth Amendment of the Constitution of the United States . . . embodies this sacred idea. The Socialist Party says this idea is violated by the Conscription Act. When you conscript a man and compel him to go abroad to fight against his will, you violate the most sacred right of personal liberty, and substitute for it what Daniel Webster called "despotism of the worst form."

A conscript is little better than a convict. He is deprived of his liberty and of his right to think and act as a free man. A conscripted citizen is forced to surrender his right as a citizen and become a subject. He is forced into involuntary servitude. He is deprived of the protection given him by the Constitution of the United States. He is deprived of all freedom of conscience in being forced to kill against his will. . . .

In a democratic country each man must have the right to say whether he is willing to join the army. Only in countries where uncontrolled power rules can a despot force his subjects to fight. Such a man or men have no place in a democratic republic. This is tyrannical power in its worst form. It gives control over the life and death of the individual to a few men. There is no man good enough to be given such power.

Conscription laws belong to a bygone age. Even the people of Germany, long suffering under the yoke of militarism, are beginning to demand the abolition of conscription. Do you think it has a place in the United States? Do you want to see unlimited power handed over to Wall Street's chosen few in America? If you do not, join the Socialist Party in its campaign for the repeal of the Conscription Act. Write to your congressman and tell him you want the law repealed. Do not submit to intimidation. You have a right to demand the repeal of any law. Exercise your rights of free speech, peaceful assemblage and petitioning the government for a redress of grievances. Come to the headquarters of the Socialist Party . . . and sign a petition for the repeal of the Conscription Act. Help us wipe out this stain upon the Constitution!

> Help us re-establish democracy in America. Remember, "eternal vigilance is the price of liberty."
> Down with autocracy!
> Long live the Constitution of the United States!
> Long live the Republic!

Cornwell, Nancy, *Freedom of the Press: Rights and Liberties under the Law*, Santa Barbara: CA, ABC-CLIO, 2004, pp. 281–285.

DOCUMENT 2
Justice Oliver Wendell Holmes on Free Speech in Wartime

We admit that, in many places and in ordinary times, the defendants, in saying all that was said in the circular, would have been within their constitutional rights. But the character of every act depends upon the circumstances in which it is done. The most stringent protection of free speech would not protect a man in falsely shouting fire in a theatre and causing a panic. It does not even protect a man from an injunction against uttering words that may have all the effect of force. The question in every case is whether the words used are used in such circumstances and are of such a nature as to create a clear and present danger that they will bring about the substantive evils that Congress has a right to prevent. It is a question of proximity and degree. When a nation is at war, many things that might be said in time of peace are such a hindrance to its effort that their utterance will not be endured so long as men fight, and that no Court could regard them as protected by any constitutional right. It seems to be admitted that, if an actual obstruction of the recruiting service were proved, liability for words that produced that effect might be enforced. The statute of 1917, in §4, punishes conspiracies to obstruct, as well as actual obstruction. If the act (speaking, or circulating a paper), its tendency, and the intent with which it is done are the same, we perceive no ground for saying that success alone warrants making the act a crime. Indeed, that case might be said to dispose of the present contention if the precedent covers all *media concluded*. But, as the right to free speech was not referred to specially, we have thought fit to add a few words.

It was not argued that a conspiracy to obstruct the draft was not within the words of the [Conscription] Act of 1917. The words are "obstruct the recruiting or enlistment service," and it might be suggested that they refer only to making it hard to get volunteers. Recruiting heretofore usually having been accomplished by getting volunteers, the word is apt to call up that method only in our minds. But recruiting is gaining fresh supplies for the forces, as well by draft as otherwise. It is put as an alternative to enlistment or voluntary enrollment in this act.

Schenck v. United States, 249 U.S. 47 (1919).

THINKING CRITICALLY

What actions does the leaflet call for and on what grounds? According to Justice Holmes, what are the limits of free speech in peacetime and wartime? Why are they different? Do you think that there are ever instances in war when citizen protest is permissible under the Constitution?

One group of some 223 Americans were often close to the trenches but never took up arms. These were the women who served in the U.S. Army Signal Corps. Called "Hello Girls" for the greeting they gave callers, they operated telephone switchboards and relayed vital information to the front lines, sometimes while under fire. Their patience, eye for detail, composure, and efficiency proved vital to the war effort. After the war, their performance helped women win the vote by challenging the stereotype of female weakness under pressure.

Late in 1918, with their army in retreat and civilian morale low, Germany's leaders sought an **armistice**. They hoped to negotiate terms along the lines laid out by Woodrow Wilson in a speech to Congress in January. His bright vision had encompassed 14 points. The key provisions called for open diplomacy, free seas and free trade, disarmament, and democratic self-rule. Most important was the 14th point: an

armistice mutually agreed-on truce or temporary halt in the fighting of a war so that the combatants may discuss peace.

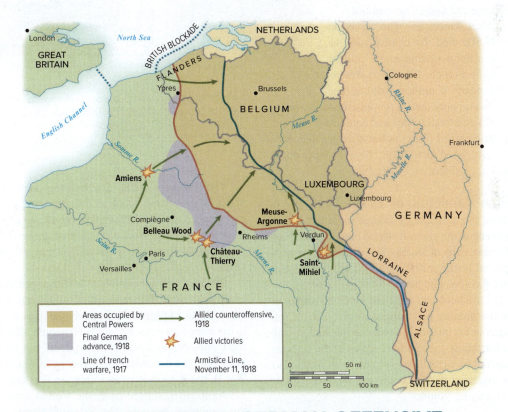

MAP 23.5: THE FINAL GERMAN OFFENSIVE AND ALLIED COUNTERATTACK, 1918

On the morning of March 21, 1918, over 60 German divisions sliced through Allied lines. They then plunged within 50 miles of Paris before being stopped at the Marne River in July. The Allied counterattack was marked by notable American victories at Château-Thierry, Belleau Wood, Saint-Mihiel, and Meuse-Argonne.
Into which country did the Allied counteroffensive advance during 1918? Which Allied nation does the text indicate had the largest number of troops at the victory at Saint-Mihiel?

"association of nations" to resolve differences diplomatically and to guarantee security collectively. It was a new world order to end selfish nationalism, imperialism, and war.

Wilson's idealistic platform was also designed to save the Allies embarrassment. Almost as soon as it came to power in 1917, the new Bolshevik government in Russia began publishing secret treaties from the czar's archives. They revealed that the Allies had gone to war with hopes of gaining territory and colonies. Wilson's Fourteen Points cloaked their cause in a more noble purpose.

Wilson's ideals also appealed to German liberals, who found in the proposals the promise of an honorable truce. On October 6, Wilson received a telegram from Berlin requesting an immediate end to the fighting on the basis of the Fourteen Points. Within a month, Turkey and Austria-Hungary surrendered. Early in November, Kaiser Wilhelm II, Germany's monarch, was overthrown and fled to neutral Holland. On November 11, 1918, German officers filed into Allied headquarters in a converted railroad car in France and signed the armistice.

Of the 2 million Americans who served in France, some 116,500 died. By comparison, the war claimed 2.2 million Germans, 1.7 million Russians, 1.4 million French, 1.2 million Austro-Hungarians, and nearly a million Britons. The American contribution nonetheless proved crucial, providing vital convoys at sea and fresh troops and equipment on land. The United States emerged from the war stronger than ever. In contrast, Europe looked forward, as one newspaper put it, only to "Disaster . . . Exhaustion . . . Revolution."

Die spanische Krankheit

Der Friedensengel: „Und dieses scheußliche Frauenzimmer hat überall Zutritt!"

ᐱ A grim specter representing the influenza virus overtakes the angel of peace in this German cartoon from 1918. Deaths from the pandemic worldwide far exceeded deaths from the war. Chronicle/Alamy Stock Photo

The Influenza Pandemic of 1918–1919 >> In the months before the armistice, a scourge more lethal than war had begun to engulf the globe. It started innocently enough at Fort Riley, Kansas, early in March 1918, when a young company cook reported to the infirmary. His head and muscles ached, his throat was sore, and he had a low-grade fever.

By noon, 107 soldiers had reported similar symptoms. Within a week the number had jumped to over 500. It was influenza, dangerous for infants and older people but ordinarily no problem for robust young adults. Cases of the flu were soon being reported in virtually every state, even on the isolated island of Alcatraz in San Francisco Bay. And hardy young adults were dying from it.

The first wave of flu produced few deaths in the United States. As the virus mutated over the next year, its victims experienced more-distressing symptoms: vomiting, dizziness, labored breathing. More of them died, drowning in their own body fluids from the pneumonia that accompanied the virus.

Soldiers and others living in close quarters were especially vulnerable. For reasons still unknown, so were young adults 20 to 34 years old, precisely the ages of most of those in the armed services. For every 50 people infected, 1 died. In the United States alone, the final death toll rose to 675,000, more than the American battle deaths in World War I, World War II, the Korean War, and Vietnam War combined.

Although it started here, the United States was among the countries least affected by this worldwide epidemic, called a **pandemic**. American soldiers seem to have carried the disease to Europe, where it jumped from one country to another in the spring and summer of 1918. French troops and civilians soon suffered from it, then British and German. General Eric von Ludendorff counted the flu as one of the causes of the failure of the final German offensive in 1918.

> **pandemic** broad outbreak of disease spreading across national boundaries.

Make a Case

Should the United States have fought in World War I? What did the United States gain and what did it lose by going to war?

THE FLU PANDEMIC OF 1918–1919

Maps have long charted the progress of battles and wars, portraying strategies and troop movements. But tracking the progress of an influenza pandemic also provides revealing information to historians. This map depicts the spread of the second stage of the virus, when a more virulent strain began spreading, first from France in August 1918. Study the movements of the disease and the statistics that accompany the map.

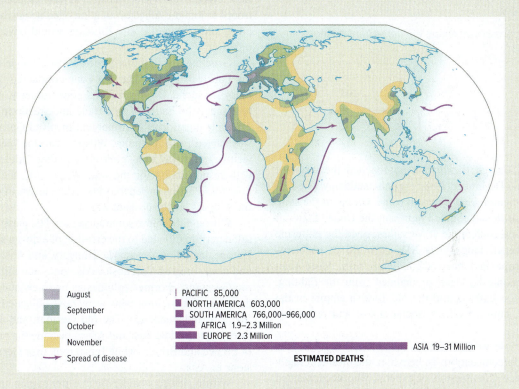

| August |
| September |
| October |
| November |
| → Spread of disease |

| PACIFIC 85,000 |
| NORTH AMERICA 603,000 |
| SOUTH AMERICA 766,000–966,000 |
| AFRICA 1.9–2.3 Million |
| EUROPE 2.3 Million |
| ASIA 19–31 Million |

ESTIMATED DEATHS

MAP READING

1. *How many months does the map cover? In what year?*
2. *Which continent experienced the greatest number of deaths?*
3. *Rearrange the list of continents below in the rough order in which cases of the flu spread from one continent to the next. (The new strain appears first in France.)* **Africa Antarctica Asia Australia Europe North America South America**
4. *Which of the seven continents had no significant number of cases? Why?*

MAP INTERPRETATION

1. *How did the pandemic spread geographically within continents?*
2. *Can you suggest reasons it did not spread in certain areas, such as northwestern Canada and many parts of Russia? Why are there no deaths shown for Antarctica?*
3. *What reasons might explain the much higher number of deaths in Asia?*

With steamships and railroads carrying people all over the globe, virtually no place was safe. By the summer of 1918, the virus had leapt from North America and Europe to Asia and Japan; by fall, to Africa and South America. As far north as the Russian city of Archangel, officials were reporting 30 influenza deaths a day in October 1918.

After the milder outbreak in the spring of 1918, a more deadly form of influenza spread outward from the coast of France at the beginning of August. The worldwide transportation system quickly dispersed this strain of the disease, sending it first to the western coast of Africa (beginning at Freetown, Liberia) and the eastern coast of North America (at Boston). The disease reached virtually all continents, although Australia's strict quarantine delayed entrance of the flu there until 1919. By far, the continent hardest hit was Asia, where anywhere from 12 to 20 million died in India alone.

Sixteen months after it appeared, the flu vanished. Conservative estimates placed the number of dead worldwide at over 50 million, making the influenza pandemic of 1918–1919 the most lethal outbreak of disease on an annual basis in human history. Global war helped spread the disease, but improvements in transportation and two centuries of global migrations also played a part. As automobiles and airplanes continued to shrink the globe, pandemics continued to threaten humankind. In 2020, more than a century later, the COVID-19 virus shot across the globe within months, leaving a trail of illness and death in its wake.

REVIEW

How did progressivism shape the home front during World War I?

THE LOST PEACE

As the USS *George Washington* approached the coast of France in mid-December 1918, the mist suddenly lifted. It seemed an omen of good things to come. On board the ship, Woodrow Wilson had come to represent the United States at the Paris peace conference at Versailles, once the glittering palace of French king Louis XIV. A world of problems awaited. Europe had been shelled into ruin. More than 37 million people lay dead or maimed from the fighting. Throughout the Balkans and the old Turkish empire in the Middle East, ethnic rivalries, social chaos, and revolution loomed.

With the old world order in shambles, Wilson felt the need to take forceful action. To help him, the president hand-picked a Peace Commission of experts, who accompanied him. It included economists, historians, geographers, and political scientists—but not a single member of the Republican-controlled Senate. The commission of experts, called "The Inquiry," provided advice to make peace negotiations easier but created a crippling liability in Washington. There, Republicans, having been cut out of the peace process, were none too eager to accept its results.

The Treaty of Versailles >> Everywhere Wilson went, crowds cheered him. In Paris, 2 million people showered him with flowers. In Italy they hailed him as the "peacemaker from America." And Wilson believed what he heard, unaware of how determined the victors were to punish the vanquished. David Lloyd George of Britain, Georges Clemenceau of France, Vittorio Orlando of Italy, and Wilson constituted the "Big Four" at the conference that included some 27 nations. War had united them; peacemaking threatened to tear them apart.

Wilson's sweeping reforms had taken Allied leaders by surprise. Hungry for new colonies, eager to see Germany crushed and disarmed, they had already adopted in secret treaties that divided the territories of the Central Powers. Germany surrendered on the basis of Wilson's Fourteen Points, but the Allies refused to accept them. When Wilson threatened to negotiate peace on his own, Allied leaders finally agreed to his terms—but only for the moment.

Absent when the peace conference convened in January 1919 were the Russians. None of the Western democracies had recognized the Bolshevik regime in Moscow, out of fear that the communist revolution might spread. Instead, France and Britain were helping finance a civil war to overthrow the Bolsheviks. Even Wilson had sent several thousand American troops to join the Allied occupation of some northern Russian ports and to Siberia. The Russians would never forget this intrusion.

Grueling negotiations forced Wilson to yield several of his Fourteen Points. The Big Four conducted "open diplomacy" in secret. Britain, with its powerful navy, refused even to discuss the issues of free trade and freedom of the seas. The only mention of disarmament involved Germany, which was barred from rearming. Wilson's call for "peace without victory" gave way to a "guilt clause" that saddled Germany with responsibility for the war. Worse still, the victors imposed $33 billion in reparations on the losers to compensate the winners for the costs of war.

Wilson did achieve some successes. His pleas for national self-determination led to the creation of a dozen new states in Europe, including Yugoslavia, Hungary, and Austria. (Poland and newly created Czechoslovakia contained millions of ethnic Germans.) Former colonies gained new status as "mandates" of the victors, who were now obligated to prepare them for independence. The old German and Turkish Empires in the Middle East and Africa became the responsibility of France and Britain, while Japan took over German possessions in Asia.

Wilson yielded what he did in order to gain his main goal: a league of nations. This new world organization, he believed, would correct any mistakes in the peace treaty. Members promised to submit all war-provoking disagreements to arbitration and to isolate aggressors by cutting off commercial and military trade. Article X (Wilson called it "the heart" of the agreement) bound members to respect one another's independence and territory and to join together against attack. In that way, war would end or be quickly contained. Negotiation, arbitration and diplomacy would replace violence, at least as Wilson saw it.

The Battle for the Treaty >> Growing opposition in Congress forced Wilson to return home. In the off-year elections of 1918, voters, unhappy with wartime controls, new taxes, and attacks on civil liberties, gave Republicans control in both the Senate and the House of Representatives. The Republican majority in the Senate chose Wilson's arch rival, Henry Cabot Lodge of Massachusetts, to chair the all-important Foreign Relations Committee.

Although most of the country favored the treaty, Lodge opposed it. He had long fought to preserve American freedom of action in international affairs and worried that the League would subject the country to "the will of other nations." Its war-making power could be lost if the League saw

MAP 23.6: EUROPE AND THE MIDDLE EAST AFTER WORLD WAR I

The face of Europe and the Middle East changed after World War I, as these two maps indicate. In Europe new countries were carved out of Russia, Germany, and the old Austro-Hungarian Empire, while "mandates" created by the Treaty of Versailles and destined for eventual independence in the Middle East were formed from the old Turkish Empire.

Which of the changes on this map reflect the influence of Wilson's Fourteen Points?

^ "IF WE WERE IN THE LEAGUE OF NATIONS," warns this cartoon ominously, the United States would see more wounded and dead soldiers coming home by the boatload. Uncle Sam watches silently as the remnants of the American army return, including a flag-draped coffin in the background, while "J[ohn] Bull" (symbol of Great Britain) shouts: "Send over a new army!"
Library of Congress, Prints and Photographs Division

fit to take it. Lodge certainly did not want Democrats to win votes by taking credit for the treaty. He secured enough support to block the treaty and offered a "round robin" resolution against the League early in March 1919.

Wilson's only hope of winning the necessary two-thirds majority lay in compromise, but he stubbornly refused any changes. Despite his failing health, Wilson took his case to the people in a monthlong campaign across the nation in 1919. In Pueblo, Colorado, a crowd of 10,000 heard him speak of American soldiers killed in France and American boys whom the League one day would spare from death. Listeners wept openly.

That evening, utterly exhausted, Wilson collapsed in a spasm of pain. On October 2, four days after being rushed back to the White House, he fell to the bathroom floor, knocked unconscious by a stroke. He recovered slowly but never fully. Increasingly the battle for the treaty consumed his fading energies and his wife Edith ran the day-to-day business of the presidency.

Late in 1919, Lodge finally reported the treaty out of committee with 14 "reservations" (mimicking Wilson's Fourteen Points). They limited American responsibilities and asserted American rights under the treaty. The most important declared that the United States assumed no obligation to aid

League members unless Congress consented. Wilson refused to compromise and asked Senate Democrats to vote down the amended treaty.

When the Senate vote was tallied in March 1920, enough Democrats broke from the president to produce a majority in favor—but not the required two-thirds for passage. The treaty was dead in America. Not until July 1921 did Congress enact a joint resolution ending the war. The United States, which had fought separately from the Allies, made a separate peace as well.

Red Scare >> Peace abroad did not bring peace at home.

On May Day 1919, six months after the war ended, mobs in a dozen cities broke up Socialist parades, injuring hundreds and killing three people. Later that month, when a spectator at a Victory Loan rally in Washington refused to stand for the national anthem, a sailor shot him in the back. The stadium crowd cheered.

This spontaneous violence and extremism erupted because Americans believed they were under attack, not by an enemy from abroad but by homegrown and foreign-sponsored radicals. When a rapid end to wartime controls brought skyrocketing prices and unemployment grew as millions of veterans returned, a wave of labor unrest swept the country. Even the Boston police went on strike for higher pay. In Seattle, a general strike paralyzed the city for five days in January 1919. Mayor Ole Hanson blamed radicals, while Congress ascribed the national ills to Bolshevik agents, inspired by the Russian Revolution.

The menace of radicalism was overblown. With Socialist Eugene Debs in prison, his dwindling party numbered only about 30,000. Left-wing radicals at first hoped that the success of the Russian Revolution would help reverse their fortunes in the United States. But most Americans found the prospect of "Bolshevik" (the name of the party that fomented the revolution) agitators threatening. In March 1919, the new Russian government added to those fears by forming the "Comintern" to spread revolution abroad. Furthermore, the Left in the United States splintered. Dissent Socialists formed the more radical Communist Labor Party, while a group of mostly ethnic Slavs created a separate Communist Party. The two organizations together could count no more than 40,000 members.

On April 28, Seattle Mayor Hanson received a small brown parcel, evidently another present from an admirer of his tough patriotism. It was a homemade bomb. Within days, 20 such packages were discovered, including ones sent to John D. Rockefeller, Supreme Court justice Oliver Wendell Holmes, and the postmaster general. On June 2, bombs exploded simultaneously in eight different cities. One of them demolished the front porch of A. Mitchell Palmer, attorney general of the United States. The bomber was blown to bits, but enough remained to identify him as an Italian anarchist from Philadelphia. Edgy over Bolshevism and labor militancy, many Americans assumed that a conspiracy of radicals was to blame for the bombings and planning to overthrow the government.

<< In September 1919 some 300,000 steelworkers struck for higher wages, recognition of their union, and a reduction in the 70-hour workweek. In Gary, Indiana, women in sympathy with the strike prepare to picket the plant. Library of Congress, Prints and Photographs Division

Palmer, a Quaker and a progressive, hardened in the wake of the bombings. In November 1919 and again in January 1920, he launched raids in over 30 cities. Government agents invaded private homes, meeting halls, and pool parlors. They took thousands of alleged communists into custody without warrants and beat those who resisted. Prisoners were marched through streets in chains, crammed into dilapidated jails, held without hearings. Over 200 aliens, most of whom had no criminal records, were deported to the Soviet Union.

Such abuses of civil liberties provoked a backlash. After the New York legislature expelled five Socialists in 1919, responsible politicians there denounced the action. The "deportation delirium" ended early in 1920, when Palmer finally overreached himself by predicting a revolutionary uprising for May 1. Nothing happened. In the fall of 1920, a wagonload of bombs exploded on Wall Street, killing 35 people and injuring over 200. Palmer blamed a Bolshevik conspiracy, but most Americans saw it as the work of a few demented radicals (which it probably was) and went about business as usual. The Red Scare was over.

 REVIEW

What were the results of the Paris Peace Conference and the Treaty of Versailles?

History in Global Context >> In early August 1914 the Panama Canal opened without fanfare, but no one could miss the significance: the new American empire now spanned

the globe, stretching from the Caribbean to the Pacific and linked by a waterway between the seas. There were plans for a tremendous celebration in which the battleship *Oregon*, whose 1898 "race around the Horn" had inspired the idea of an American-owned canal, would lead a flotilla of ships through the locks. But the plans had to be scrapped, for in that fateful month of August, the old world order collapsed into a world war.

World War I was rightly named "the Great War" by Europeans, because it transformed the continent and left a bitter legacy that shaped the twentieth century. In Europe, France and Great Britain triumphed, only to find their economies enfeebled, their people dispirited, their empires near collapse, and a generation of young men dead. Two other empires—of vanquished Austria-Hungary and Turkey—were dismembered. Germany's kaiser abdicated and revolution toppled the once-mighty czars of Russia. The Soviet Union emerged from the ashes of the Russian Empire. Eventually it fell under the brutal dictatorship of Joseph Stalin. Germany suffered defeat, humiliation, and a crushing burden of debt, which paved the way for Adolf Hitler and his Nazi Party.

Elsewhere, a victorious Japan left the Paris peace table shamed by what it regarded as paltry spoils of war and determined to rise to global greatness. Its infant democracy soon died at the hands of militarists and emperor worshipers. In the Middle East, in Africa, and on the Indian subcontinent, the unfulfilled promises of a world made "safe for democracy" sparked nationalist and anticolonial movements. The twentieth century of global change and violence was forged in World War I.

CHAPTER SUMMARY

World War I marked the beginning of the end of the old world order of colonial imperialism, military alliances, and balances of power; it also marked a failed effort to establish a new world order based on the progressive ideals of international cooperation and collective security.

- Progressive foreign policy—whether through Theodore Roosevelt's big stick diplomacy, William Taft's dollar diplomacy, or Woodrow Wilson's missionary diplomacy—stressed moralism and order, championed "uplifting" nonwhites, and stretched presidential authority to its limits.
- With the outbreak of World War I in 1914, Woodrow Wilson saw an opportunity for the United States to lead the world to a higher period of international cooperation by remaining neutral and brokering the peace settlement.
- American sympathy for the Allies, heavy American investments in the Allies, and the German campaign of unrestricted submarine warfare finally drew the country into the war in 1917.
- Progressive faith in government, planning, efficiency, and publicity produced a greatly expanded bureaucratic state that managed the war effort on the home front.
- The darker side of progressivism also flourished as the war transformed progressive impulses for assimilation and social control into campaigns for superpatriotism and conformity that helped produce a postwar Red Scare in 1919 and 1920.
- Meanwhile, changes already under way, including more women in the labor force and migrations of African Americans and Mexican Americans from rural to urban America, vastly accelerated with the expansion of opportunities for war work and for racial conflict.
- When the war ended, Wilson's idealistic hopes for "peace without victory" and a new world order, embodied in his Fourteen Points, were dashed when his European allies imposed a harsh settlement on Germany and the U.S. Senate failed to ratify the Treaty of Versailles.

Digging Deeper

Why did the United States enter World War I? Early revisionist accounts emphasizing a financial conspiracy to bring the nation to war include Charles Beard, *The Open Door to War* (1934); and Charles C. Tansill, *America Goes to War* (1938). George Kennan, from the school of realism, is critical of Wilson's moral motives in *American Diplomacy, 1900-1950* (rev. ed., 1971). Christopher Clark's *The Sleepwalkers: How Europe Went to War* (2014) sees the war in Europe as the result of human foibles. David M. Kennedy, *Over Here: The First World War and American Society* (1980), surveys mobilization and the home front. Lynn Dumenil stresses the changes brought by and for women during the war in *The Second Line of Defense: American Women and World War I* (2017); see also Maurine W. Greenwald, *Women, War, and Work* (1980); and Kathleen Kennedy, *Disloyal Mothers and Scurrilous Citizens: Women and Subversion during World War I* (1999). Elizabeth Cobb tells the story of the vital role played by female telephone operators overseas in *The Hello Girls: America's First Women Soldiers* (2017). Richard S. Faulkner's *Pershing's Crusaders: The American Soldier in World War I* (2016) provides the best account of the experiences of American soldiers.

Isabel Wilkerson provides a riveting portrait of the Great Migration in *The Warmth of Other Suns* (2010) that upsets many stereotypes of those who journeyed north. Mark Ellis, *Race, War, and Surveillance: African Americans and the United States Government during World War I* (2001); and Mark Robert Schneider, *"We Return Fighting": The Civil Rights Movement in the Jazz Age* (2001), look at the effects of the war on African American civil rights. Jennifer D. Keene, *Doughboys, the Great War, and the Remaking of America* (2001), examines the impact of the war on soldiers and on the country. For African Americans on the battlefront, see Chad L. Williams, *Torchbearers of Democracy: African American Soldiers in the World War I Era* (2013).

Robert Ferrell, *Woodrow Wilson and World War I* (1985), analyzes Wilson's wartime diplomacy, the peace negotiations, and the fate of the Treaty of Versailles. For the influenza pandemic, see John M. Barry's *The Great Influenza: The Epic Story of the Deadliest Plague in History* (2004). For a colorful, thorough, and thoughtful account of the Paris Peace Conference, see Margaret Macmillan and Richard Holbrooke, *Paris, 1919: Six Months That Changed the World* (2001). Beverly Gage's *The Day Wall Street Exploded: A Story of America in Its First Age of Terror* (2009) takes a fresh look at the 1920 bombing within the context of class warfare and labor radicalism following World War I.

24 The New Era

1920–1929

The 1920s seemed like a "New Era" for many reasons. There were new ways of dressing, including shorter skirts and the lack of bulky petticoats for women, and patent leather dance shoes for men. New styles of dancing included the "Charleston," a jazz tune created by two African Americans, Jimmy Johnson and Cecil Mack, whose sheet music for the song is shown here. The tune (by Johnson) was inspired by the music of South Carolina dockworkers and first premiered in a Broadway musical, *Runnin' Wild* (1923). More traditional Americans agreed with that title, condemning the "wriggling movement and sensuous stimulation of the abominable jazz orchestra."

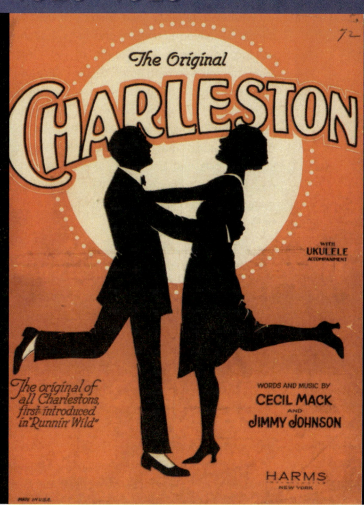

The Advertising Archives/Alamy Stock Photo

>> An American Story

YESTERDAY MEETS TODAY IN THE NEW ERA

Just before Christmas 1918, the "Gospel Car" pulled into Los Angeles. Bold letters on the side announced: "JESUS IS COMING—GET READY." Aimee Semple McPherson, the ravishing redheaded driver, had just completed a cross-country trip to seek her evangelical future.

471

↑ Sister Aimee Semple McPherson, billed as the "world's most pulchritudinous evangelist," in her robes.
Bettmann/Getty Images

After three years of wandering California, "Sister Aimee," as she was now known, landed in San Diego. The city had the state's highest rates of illness and suicide. It was perfect for preaching her healing message of the "Foursquare Gospel." Sister's revival attracted 30,000 people. They witnessed her first miracle: a paraplegic walked.

On New Year's Day 1923, to the blare of trumpets, Sister unveiled the $1.5 million Angelus Temple. It sat 5,300 people and was soon capped by a 75-foot rotating neon cross. Her lively sermons, broadcast over her own radio station,

promoted the spirit of what people were calling the "New Era" of productivity and consumerism. While country preachers menaced their congregations with eternal damnation, Sister Aimee, wrote a reporter, offered "flowers, music, golden trumpets, red robes, angels, incense, nonsense, and sex appeal."

Whatever its glitzy style, Sister's ministry survived scandals, one involving an alleged kidnapping of Sister herself, and hard times. Sister fared less well. Though her popularity continued to rise, her health suffered. She died at the age of 53 from an accidental overdose of sleeping pills. But her legacy lived on, inspiring preachers of Charismatic Christianity and a generation of modern televangelists.

Modernizing the gospel was only one change ushered in by the New Era. Writing in 1931, journalist Frederick Lewis Allen found the transformations so dizzying that it hardly seemed possible 1919 was "only yesterday," as he titled his best-selling book. To demonstrate the transformation, Allen followed an average American couple, the fictitious "Mr. and Mrs. Smith," through the decade.

Women's fashions and behavior were only the most obvious changes. Mrs. Smith's hemline jumped from her ankle to her knee.

With Prohibition in full force, she and other women could walk into illegal "speakeasy" saloons as easily as men. Earlier they had been denied entry. The Smiths danced to jazz and sprinkled their conversations with talk of "repressed sexual drives." The most striking change was one visible in their address: these "average" Americans were urbanites. For the first time, over half the population lived in cities.

Yet the city-dwelling Smiths of Frederick Allen's imagination were hardly average. Nearly as many Americans lived on isolated farms and in villages and clung to the small-town values of an earlier America. In tiny Hyden, Kentucky, along the Cumberland Plateau, Main Street remained unpaved. God-fearing Baptists still repaired to the Middle Fork of the Kentucky River for an open-air baptism when they declared their new birth in Christ. They would have nothing to do with jazz or the showy miracles of Aimee McPherson.

As much as some Americans resisted the transforming forces of modern life, the New Era could not be walled out. Whether Americans embraced or condemned it, modern life came nonetheless, in the form of a mass-produced consumer economy, a culture shaped by mass media, and a more materialistic society. <<

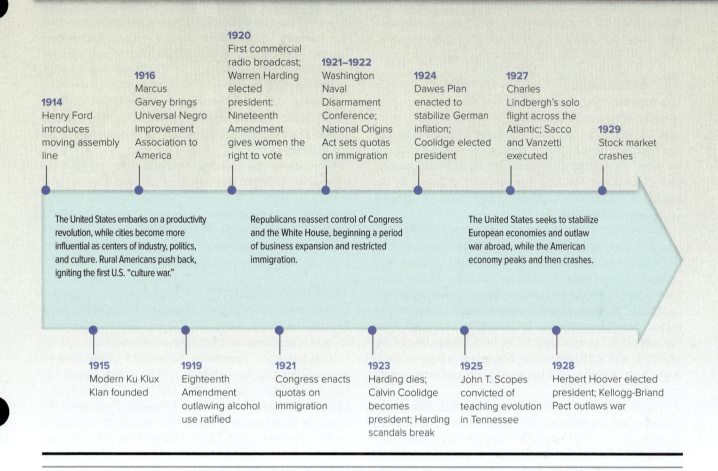

1914 Henry Ford introduces moving assembly line

1916 Marcus Garvey brings Universal Negro Improvement Association to America

1920 First commercial radio broadcast; Warren Harding elected president; Nineteenth Amendment gives women the right to vote

1921–1922 Washington Naval Disarmament Conference; National Origins Act sets quotas on immigration

1924 Dawes Plan enacted to stabilize German inflation; Coolidge elected president

1927 Charles Lindbergh's solo flight across the Atlantic; Sacco and Vanzetti executed

1929 Stock market crashes

The United States embarks on a productivity revolution, while cities become more influential as centers of industry, politics, and culture. Rural Americans push back, igniting the first U.S. "culture war."

Republicans reassert control of Congress and the White House, beginning a period of business expansion and restricted immigration.

The United States seeks to stabilize European economies and outlaw war abroad, while the American economy peaks and then crashes.

1915 Modern Ku Klux Klan founded

1919 Eighteenth Amendment outlawing alcohol use ratified

1921 Congress enacts quotas on immigration

1923 Harding dies; Calvin Coolidge becomes president; Harding scandals break

1925 John T. Scopes convicted of teaching evolution in Tennessee

1928 Herbert Hoover elected president; Kellogg-Briand Pact outlaws war

THE ROARING ECONOMY

In the 1920s the United States was in the midst of a production boom. Manufacturing rose 64 percent; output per work hour, 40 percent. The sale of electricity doubled; fuel oil purchases more than doubled. Between 1922 and 1927, the economy grew by 7 percent a year—the largest peacetime growth rate ever. If anything roared in the "Roaring Twenties," it was production and consumption.

Technology, Consumer Spending, and the Boom in Construction >> Technology was partly responsible for the upsurge. Steam turbines and shovels, electric motors, belt and bucket conveyors, and countless other new machines became commonplace at work sites. They replaced 200,000 workers each year, and a new phrase—"technological unemployment"—entered the vocabulary.

Even so, demand kept the labor force growing at a rate faster than that of the population.

Consumer goods, the product of a maturing industrial economy, fueled rising demand. Cigarette lighters, wristwatches, radios, and other new merchandise disappeared from store shelves almost as quickly as they were stocked. The improvement in productivity helped keep down prices. Meanwhile, the purchasing power of wage earners jumped by 20 percent. Even so, a dangerous imbalance was developing. Most Americans saved little, and personal debt was rising two and a half times faster than personal income. Buying on credit allowed consumers to spend money they did not have.

Along with technology and consumer spending, new "boom industries" promoted economic growth. In a rebound after the war, residential building doubled as suburban populations soared. Beverly Hills, on the edge of Los Angeles, grew by 2,500 percent. New roads made suburban life possible and pumped millions of dollars into the economy. In 1919, Oregon, New Mexico, and Colorado hit on a novel idea for financing roads: a tax on gasoline. Within a decade every state had one.

Construction stimulated other businesses: steel, concrete, lumber, home mortgages, and insurance. It even helped change the nation's eating habits. The limited storage space of small "kitchenettes" boosted supermarket chains and the canning industry. As shipments of fresh fruits and vegetables sped across new roads, interest in nutrition grew. Vitamins, publicized with new zeal, began to appear on breakfast tables.

The Automobile >> No industry boomed more than auto manufacturing. Although cars first appeared at the turn of the century, they remained expensive toys. By 1920 there were 10 million in the United States. By 1929 the total had almost tripled to one for every 5 people (compared with one for every 43 in Britain). Automakers bought more rubber, plate glass, nickel, and lead than any other industry. By the end of the decade, one American in four somehow earned a living from automobiles.

Henry Ford made it possible. He pushed standardization and mass production to such ruthless extremes that automobiles became affordable. Trading on his fame as a race-car manufacturer, he founded the Ford Motor Company in 1903 with the dream of making a "motor car for the multitude." He believed that the way to reach his goal was to reduce manufacturing costs by making all cars alike, "just like one pin is like another pin." In 1908 Ford perfected the Model T, with a 20-horsepower engine and a body of steel. It was high enough to ride the worst roads and came in only one color: black.

Priced at $845, the Model T was cheap by industry standards but still too costly and too time-consuming to build. To bring down costs and increase efficiency, Ford engineers copied a practice of Chicago meatpacking houses, in which beef carcasses were carried on moving chains past meat dressers. In 1914 Ford introduced the moving assembly line. A conveyor belt, positioned waist high to eliminate bending or walking, propelled the chassis past stationary workers who put the cars together. The process cut assembly time in half. In 1925 a new Model T was rolling off the lines every 10 seconds. At $290, almost anybody could buy one. Ford provided credit to those who couldn't.

Ford was also a social innovator. Breaking with other manufacturers, he preached a "doctrine of high wages." According to it, workers with extra money in their pockets would buy enough to sustain prosperity. In keeping with this philosophy, in 1915 Ford's Dearborn plants established the "Five-Dollar Day," twice the wage rate in Detroit. He also reduced working hours from 48 to 40 a week and cut the workweek to five days.

Yet many Ford workers were unhappy. Ford admitted that the repetitive operations on his assembly line made it almost impossible for a worker "to continue long at the same job." The Five-Dollar Day was designed, in part, to reduce turnover rates of 300 percent a year at Ford plants. Ford recouped his profits by speeding up the assembly line and enforcing stringent work practices. Ford workers could not sit or talk on the job, communicating only in the "Ford Whisper,"

accomplished without moving their lips. A "sociological department" spied on workers at home.

By making automobiles available to nearly everyone, the industry changed the face of the United States. The spreading web of paved roads fueled urban sprawl and a new roadside economy of restaurants, service stations, and motels. The expanding roadways and affordability of new cars fed real estate booms, especially in California and Florida. Thousands of "auto camps" opened to provide tourists with tents and crude toilets. The growing number of people traveling across the nation by automobile had social consequences: it broke down rural isolation and advanced common dialects and manners.

Throughout the country, the automobile also gave the young unprecedented freedom from parental control. After hearing 30 cases of "sex crimes" (19 had occurred in cars), an exasperated juvenile court judge labeled the automobile "a house of prostitution on wheels." It was, of course, much more: a catalyst for economic growth, a transportation revolution, and a symbol of modernization.

The Future of Energy >> The automobile also helped ensure that the future of energy would be written in oil. Never foreordained, it was the result of several factors—some natural, others economic, and still others corporate.

One factor was abundance. Beginning with the great oil strike at Titusville, Pennsylvania, in 1859, drillers tapped into huge pools of petroleum in Ohio, Indiana, Illinois, and other states in the South and the West. Following a mammoth discovery in southeastern Texas in 1901, the price of crude or unrefined oil dropped to 3 cents a barrel. Coal-driven railroad and steamship companies jumped at the chance to buy a new energy source that reduced their costs.

Chemistry abetted abundance. Chemists found that "cracking," or breaking the string of carbon molecules in oil, more than doubled the gasoline squeezed from a barrel of unrefined petroleum. In the early 1920s, engineers at General Motors discovered that adding certain compounds, including tetraethyl lead, could raise the energy level of this "high-octane" gasoline.

Among other additives was alcohol. Alcohol from fermented plants could also power engines. By 1925 Henry Ford was calling alcohol "the fuel of the future." Hydrocarbons were bound to run out, leaving the United States dependent on foreign reserves and eventually the planet without its most precious source of fuel. But as long as plants grew, alcohol was endlessly renewable and to Ford the energy of tomorrow.

For a time in the 1920s, other automobile manufacturers as well as engineers and chemists agreed, but in the end alcohol lost out. For one thing, alcohol provided 30 percent less energy than gasoline. Alcohol was more expensive to produce when growing, harvesting, distilling, and transporting were taken into account. New oil discoveries drove crude oil prices down to 2 cents a barrel by 1931. Finally, gasoline provided more power for the bigger cars with quicker acceleration that American drivers preferred.

Cancel distance & conquer weather

The woman who drives her own Ford Closed Car is completely independent of road and weather conditions in any season.

It enables her to carry on all those activities of the winter months that necessitate travel to and fro—in or out of town. Her time and energy are conserved; her health is protected, no matter how bitterly cold the day, or how wet and slushy it is underfoot.

A Ford Sedan is always comfortable—warm and snug in winter, and in summer with ventilator and windows open wide, as cool and airy as an open car.

This seasonal comfort is combined with fine looks and Ford dependability; no wonder there is for this car so wide and ever-growing a demand.

FORD MOTOR COMPANY, DETROIT, MICHIGAN

TUDOR SEDAN, $580 ∴ FORDOR SEDAN, $660
COUPE, $520 ∴ ALL PRICES F. O. B. DETROIT

CLOSED CARS

⌃ In the 1920s, the Ford Motor Company began marketing its cars to women. It was a sign of their new-found buying power and their new independence. This ad played on the notion of growing female autonomy, touting "the woman who drives her own Ford Closed Car" as "independent of road or weather conditions in any season."
Fotosearch/Getty Images

The long-term price paid for energy dependence on oil and leaded gasoline told over time. Half a century later, long lines at gas stations and high prices at the pump testified to the power of foreign oil suppliers to vex American consumers and threaten national security. Even earlier, minute flecks of lead in oil refineries were poisoning workers, while lead-laden emissions from automobiles contaminated soil and water. Federal regulations finally began to phase out the metal from gasoline and other products in the 1970s. Another problem was the smog, thickened by emissions from gasoline-driven automobiles, that blanketed cities such as Los Angeles in a choking haze. Led by California, new regulations set limits on harmful auto emissions in the 1960s and 1970s.

The Business of the United States >> "The chief business of the American people," President Calvin Coolidge declared in 1925, "is business." A generation earlier, progressives had criticized business for its social irresponsibility. But the wartime contributions of business managers and the return of prosperity in 1922, following a short-lived recession, gained them renewed respect.

Encouraged by federal permissiveness, a wave of mergers swept the economy. Oligopolies (whereby a few firms dominated whole industries) grew in steel, meatpacking, cigarettes, and other businesses. National chains replaced local "mom-and-pop" stores. By 1929, 1 bag of groceries in 10 came from the 15,000 red-and-gold markets of the Great Atlantic and Pacific Tea Company, known as A&P. Sears, Roebuck opened stores accessible by automobile.

Expansion and consolidation meant that national wealth was being controlled not by affluent individuals but by corporations. The model of modern business was an enterprise in which those who actually ran the company, the managers, had little to do with the stockholders who owned it. A salaried bureaucracy of elite executives and plant managers learned the techniques of **scientific management** through new schools of business, as well as new professional societies and consulting firms. They used their earnings to expand their companies, build factories, and carry on research. By 1929, 100 corporations earned half of all industrial income.

scientific management system of factory production that stresses efficiency, pioneered by American engineer Frederick Winslow Taylor.

Welfare Capitalism >> The new scientific management also stressed good relations between managers and employees. A rash of postwar strikes left business leaders suspicious of labor unions and determined to find ways to limit their influence.

Some tactics were more strong-arm than scientific. In 1921 the National Association of Manufacturers, the Chamber of Commerce, and other employer groups launched the "American Plan," aimed at ending "closed shops," factories where only union members could work. Employers made workers sign agreements disavowing union membership. Companies infiltrated unions with spies, locked union members out of factories, and boycotted firms that hired union labor.

The benevolent side of the American Plan involved the social innovation called welfare capitalism. Companies such as General Electric and Bethlehem Steel pledged to care for their employees and give them incentives for working hard. They built clean, safe factories, installed cafeterias, hired trained dietitians, and formed baseball teams and glee clubs. Several hundred firms encouraged perhaps a million workers to buy company stock and even more to enroll in company unions. Called "Kiss-Me Clubs" for their lack of power, they nonetheless offered what few independent unions could match: health and safety insurance, a grievance procedure, and representation for minorities and women.

Most companies cared more for production than for contented employees. Welfare capitalism affected barely 5 percent of the workforce and often gave benefits only to skilled laborers, the hardest to replace. In the 1920s, a family of four could live in "minimum health and decency" on $2,000 a year. The average annual industrial wage was $1,304. Thus working-class families often needed more than one wage earner just to get by. Over a million children aged 10 to 15 still worked full-time in 1920.

In 1927, 2,500 mill hands in the textile town of Gastonia, North Carolina, left their jobs in the most famous strike of the decade. Even strikebreakers walked out. Eventually, authorities broke the strike, foreshadowing a national trend. A year later there were only 629 strikes, a record low. Union membership sank from 5 million in 1921 to less than 3.5 million in 1929.

The Consumer Culture >> During the late nineteenth century the economy had boomed, too, but much of its growth went into nonconsumer goods: steel factories and rails, telephone and electric networks. By World War I, these industrial networks penetrated enough of the country to create mass markets. With the industrial infrastructure already built and population concentrating in cities, production increasingly went into consumer goods, and prosperity hinged on their purchase. If consumers bought more goods, factories would hum and high-volume sales would bring down costs. Low cost would lift sales still higher, expanding employment, and repeating the cycle, theoretically forever.

Consumption was the key, and increasing it relied on two innovations: advertising to encourage people to buy and credit to help them pay. Around the turn of the century, advertisers began a critical shift from emphasizing products to stressing the underlying desires of consumers for health, popularity, and social prestige. Albert Lasker, the owner of Chicago's largest advertising firm, Lord and Thomas, created modern advertising in the United States. His eye-catching ads were hard-hitting, positive, and often preposterous. To expand the sales of Lucky Strike cigarettes, Lord and Thomas advertisements claimed that smoking made people slimmer and more courageous. "Lucky's" became one of the most popular brands in the country.

Advertisers encouraged Americans to borrow against tomorrow so that they could purchase what advertising convinced them they wanted today. Installment buying on credit had once been confined to sewing machines and pianos. In the 1920s it grew into the tenth-biggest business in the country. In 1919 automaker Alfred Sloan created millions of new customers by establishing the General Motors Acceptance Corporation, the nation's first consumer credit organization. By 1929 Americans were buying most of their cars, radios, and furniture on the installment plan. Such credit purchases had an unfortunate consequence. Across the decade, consumer debt jumped 250 percent to $7 billion, almost twice the federal budget.

✓ **REVIEW**

What factors produced unprecedented economic growth in the 1920s?

A MASS SOCIETY

In the evening, after a day's work in the fields—perhaps in front of an adobe house built by one of the western sugar beet companies—Mexican American workers might gather to chat or sing a *corrido* or two. The *corrido*, or ballad, was a Mexican folk tradition. The subjects changed over time to match the concerns of composers. One *corrido* during the 1920s told of a field laborer distressed over his family's abandonment of Mexican culture and embrace of American customs. His wife, he sang, wore makeup and went about "painted like a piñata." His children spoke English, not Spanish, and loved the latest dance crazes.

For Americans from all backgrounds the New Era brought "a vast dissolution of ancient habits," per a comment by columnist Walter Lippmann. Mass marketing and mass distribution led to a higher standard of living but also the loss of diverse regional cultures. In place of moral standards set by local communities and churches came "modern" styles and attitudes, spread by the new mass media of movies, radio, and magazines. In the place of "ancient habits" came the modern forces of change: independent women, more-open sexuality, standardized culture, urban energy and impersonality, and growing alienation.

A "New Woman" >> During the tumultuous 1890s a "New Woman" had appeared, one more assertive, athletic, and independent than her Victorian peers. By the 1920s more-modern versions of this New Woman were leading what Frederick Lewis Allen called the "revolution in manners and morals." The most flamboyant of them wore makeup, close-fitting felt hats, long-waisted dresses, and strings of beads.

>> Not all women conformed to the rambunctious image of the flapper. Pictured here is Margaret Gorman of Washington, D.C., crowned in 1921 as the first Miss America. She represented the wholesome and athletic aspects of the New Woman. Library of Congress, Prints and Photographs Division

Cocktail in hand, footloose, and economically free, they called themselves "flappers." They became a symbol of liberation to some, of decadence to others.

World War I served as a powerful social catalyst, continuing the prewar trend toward increasing the percentage of women in the workforce and changing many attitudes. Before the war, women could be arrested for smoking cigarettes openly, using profanity, or driving automobiles without men. Wartime America ended many of these restrictions. With women bagging explosives and running locomotives, the old taboos seemed silly.

Disseminating birth control information by mail had also been a crime before the war. By the armistice, there was a birth control clinic in Brooklyn, a National Birth Control League, and later an American Birth Control League led by Margaret Sanger. By the 1920s her message had found a receptive middle-class audience. Within a decade, nearly 90 percent of college-educated couples reported practicing contraception.

In 1909 Sigmund Freud had come to America to lecture on his theories of coping with the unconscious and overcoming harmful repressions. Some of Freud's ideas, specifically his emphasis on childhood sexuality, shocked Americans, while most of his complex theories sailed over their heads. As popularized in the 1920s, Freudian psychology stamped sexuality as a key to health.

Once they were able to limit pregnancy, women felt less guilt about enjoying sex. Sexual satisfaction became more important in the new model of marriage emerging during the decade. No longer were married couples duty-bound to join for procreation alone and to keep to separate male and female spheres. As old conventions crumbled and women became more assertive, love replaced duty as the bond holding a couple together. Companionship—spending time with each other and sharing interests (including sex)—became the key to

^ In 1929 Margaret Sanger discovered that she had been banned from making a speech about birth control in Boston. She decided to take advantage of the resulting publicity and had herself gagged in protest. The evening's festivities included actors performing a skit, "The Suppressed Bookshop," condemning the practice of censorship, during which the bookseller sprayed some of the banned books with disinfectant. Sanger handed a copy of her speech to Harvard historian Arthur Schlesinger, who read it for her: "I have been gagged, I have been suppressed, I have been arrested, I have been hauled off to jail. Yet every time, more people have listened to me, more have protested, more have lifted their own voices, more have responded with courage and bravery." Bettmann/Getty Images

cosmeticians. "Women's fields" carved out by progressive reformers expanded opportunities in education, libraries, and social welfare. Women earned a higher percentage of doctoral degrees (from 10 percent in 1910 to 15.4 percent in 1930) and held more college teaching posts than ever (32 percent). But in most areas professional men resisted the "feminization" of the workforce. The number of female doctors dropped by half during the decade. Medical schools imposed restrictive quotas, and 90 percent of all hospitals rejected female interns.

Politics was just as restricted. In 1924 only two women—Nellie Ross in Wyoming and Miriam ("Ma") Ferguson in Texas—were elected governors, the first female chief executives. Women continued to be marginalized in party politics while remaining widely involved in educational and welfare programs. Operating outside male-dominated political parties, women activists succeeded in winning passage of the Sheppard-Towner Federal Maternity and Infancy Act in 1921, which established rural prenatal and baby care centers to fight high rates of infant mortality. It was the first federal welfare statute. Yet by the end of the decade the Sheppard-Towner Act had lapsed.

In the wake of winning the vote, feminists splintered. The National Woman Suffrage Association disbanded in 1920. The new League of Women Voters took its place and campaigned to encourage informed voting. For the more militant Alice Paul and her allies, that was not enough. Their National Woman's Party pressed for a constitutional Equal Rights Amendment (ERA). Social workers and others familiar with the conditions under which women labored opposed it. Death and injury rates for women were nearly double those for men. To them, the ERA meant losing the benefits women derived from mothers' pensions and maternity insurance. Joined by most men and a majority of Congress, they fought the amendment to a standstill.

Mass Media >> The climate in sunny Southern California allowed the film industry to make movies year-round. Some called Hollywood a "dream factory" that portrayed the New Woman as a temptress and trendsetter. When sexy actress Theda Bara appeared in *The Blue Flame* in 1920, crowds mobbed theaters. And just as Hollywood dictated standards of physical attractiveness, it became the standard of taste and fashion in countless other ways. Motion pictures were a universal medium. The black-and-white images required nothing of viewers but their eyesight. It didn't matter whether audiences could speak English, let alone read it. In this "silent era," the power of the moving picture alone was enough to tell a story and set trends nationwide.

Motion pictures, invented in 1889, had first been shown in tiny neighborhood theaters called "nickelodeons." For only a nickel, patrons watched a silent screen flicker with pictures as an accompanist played music on a tinny piano. After the first feature-length film, *The Great Train Robbery* (1903), productions became rich in spectacle, attracted middle-class audiences, and turned into

marital bliss. This new "companionate" marriage afforded women greater freedom and equality by breaking down gendered spheres and strengthening ties between husbands and wives. Without the money and leisure often needed for companionate marriages, the working class and working poor continued to play more traditional married roles.

Such changes in the social climate were real enough, but the life of a flapper hardly mirrored the experiences of most American women. During the 1920s the female labor force grew by only 1 percent, slowing the prewar and wartime trends of greater employment of women. As late as 1930, nearly 60 percent of all workingwomen were African American or foreign-born and generally held low-paying jobs in domestic service or the garment industry.

The New Era did spawn new careers for women. The consumer culture capitalized on a preoccupation with appearance and led to the opening of some 40,000 beauty parlors staffed by hairdressers, manicurists, and

America's favorite form of entertainment. By 1926 more than 20,000 movie houses offered customers lavish theaters with overstuffed seats, live music, and a celluloid dream world. At the end of the decade, they were drawing in over 100 million people a week, roughly the equivalent of the national population.

In the spring of 1920 Frank Conrad of the Westinghouse Company in East Pittsburgh rigged up a radio research station in his barn and started transmitting phonograph music and baseball scores to local, mostly male operators of wireless receivers. Six months later, Westinghouse officials opened the first licensed broadcasting station in history, KDKA, to stimulate sales of their supplies. By 1922 the number of licensed stations had jumped to 430, and by the end of the decade nearly one home in three had a radio ("furniture that talks," comedian Fred Allen called it).

At first radio was seen as a civilizing force. "The air is your theater, your college, your newspaper, your library," exalted one ad in 1924. With the growing number of sets came commercial broadcasting, catering to common tastes. Advertisers produced programs on which they sold their products. At night, families gathered around the radio instead of the fireplace, listening to a concert, rather than going out to hear music. Linked by nothing but airwaves, Americans were finding themselves part of a vast new community of listeners.

Print journalism also broadened its audience during the 1920s. In 1923 former Yale classmates Henry R. Luce and Briton Hadden rewrote news stories in a snappy style, mixed them with photographs, and created the country's first national weekly, *Time* magazine. Fifty-five giant newspaper chains distributed 230 newspapers with a combined circulation of 13 million by 1927. Though they controlled less than 10 percent of all papers, the chains pioneered modern mass news techniques. Editors relied on central offices and syndicates to prepare editorials, sports, gossip, and Sunday features for a national readership.

The Cult of Celebrity >>
In a world where Americans were rapidly being reduced to anonymous parts in a vast industrialized society, media offered a chance to identify with individuals who inhabited a world of celebrities and heroes. Sports figures such as Babe Ruth, business executives like Henry Ford, and movie stars led by Latin heart throb Rudolf Valentino found their exploits splashed across front pages of newspapers. Millions more followed them on radio, hungry for thrills and eager to project their own dreams onto others.

No celebrity attracted more attention than a shy, reed-thin youth named Charles Lindbergh. Early on May 20, 1927, "Lucky Lindy" rose into the skies above Long Island in a silver-winged monoplane called the *Spirit of St. Louis* and headed east. Thirty-three hours and 30 minutes later he landed just outside Paris, the first flier to cross the Atlantic alone. An ecstatic mob nearly tore his plane to pieces in search of souvenirs.

^ Charles A. Lindbergh, with the *Spirit of St. Louis* in the background, May 31, 1927.
Library of Congress, Prints and Photographs Division

Lindbergh returned with his plane aboard the warship USS *Memphis*. In New York City, at various ceremonies and parades, nearly 4 million cheering fans greeted him. The mass media cheered him as an individual who mastered a machine completely and conquered nature courageously. To Americans ambivalent about mass society and anxious over being subordinated to bureaucracy and controlled by technology, he was an answer. Perhaps like Lindbergh they could master the New Era without surrendering their cherished individualism.

"Ain't We Got Fun?" >>
"Ev'ry morning, ev'ry evening, ain't we got fun?" ran the 1921 hit song. The average hours on the job each week decreased from 47.2 in 1920 to 42 in 1929. Spending on recreation shot up 300 percent as spectator sports came of age. In 1921, 60,000 fans paid $1.8 million to see Jack Dempsey, the "Manassas Mauler," knock out French champion Georges Carpentier. Millions more listened on radio for the first time in sports history. Universities constructed huge stadiums for football, such as Ohio State's 64,000-seater. By 1930 college football games were outdrawing major league baseball.

Baseball remained the national pastime, but became a bigger business. An ugly World Series bribing scandal in 1919 led owners to appoint Judge Kenesaw Mountain

Landis "czar" of the sport early in the next decade. His strict rule reformed the game. In 1920 a grandson of German immigrants revolutionized it. George Herman "Babe" Ruth hit 54 home runs and made the New York Yankees the first club to attract a million fans in one season. His legendary drinking and womanizing also made him baseball's bad boy. But under the guidance of the first modern sports agent, Christy Walsh, Ruth became the highest-paid player in the game and made a fortune endorsing everything from automobiles to clothing.

From turn-of-the-century brothels and gaming houses in New Orleans, Memphis, and St. Louis a new, compelling music swept into nightclubs and over the airwaves. The rhythmic style soon stamped the age with its name: jazz. Jazz was a remarkably complex blend of several older African American musical traditions, combining the soulfulness of the blues with the syncopated rhythms of ragtime music. Jazz band musicians improvised as they embellished melodies and played off one another. The style spread when the Original Dixieland Jazz Band (hardly original but possessing the commercial advantage of being white) recorded several pieces for the phonograph.

The music business, dominated by white publishers, recording studios, and radio stations, seized on the new sound as jazz swept the country. Black New Orleans stalwarts like Joe "King" Oliver's Creole Jazz Band began touring, and in 1924 Paul Whiteman inaugurated respectable "white" jazz in a concert at Carnegie Hall. When self-appointed guardians of good taste denounced such music as "intellectual and spiritual debauchery," Whiteman disagreed: "Jazz is the folk music of the machine age."

The Art of Alienation >> Before World War I, a generation of young writers had begun rebelling against Victorian purity. The savagery of the war drove many of them even further from faith in reason or progress. Instead, they embraced a "nihilism" that denied all meaning in life. When the war ended, they turned their resentment inward against their own country, especially its small towns, big businesses, conformity, and materialism.

Some led unconventional lives in New York City's Greenwich Village. Others, called **expatriates,** left the country for the artistic freedom of London and Paris. Their alienation helped produce a literary outpouring unmatched in American history. At home, Minnesota-born Sinclair Lewis, the first American to win a Nobel Prize in Literature, sketched a scathing vision of midwestern small-town life in *Main Street* (1920). The book portrayed "savorless people . . . viewing themselves as the greatest race in the world."

> **expatriates** people who leave the country of their birth or citizenship to live in another, often out of a sense of alienation.

A "New Negro" >> As World War I seared white intellectuals, it also galvanized Black Americans. Wartime labor shortages spurred a migration of half a million African Americans from southern farms and small towns to northern cities and factories (see Mapping the Past). Postwar unemployment and racial violence quickly dashed Black hopes for equality and thwarted their progress. Common folk in these urban enclaves found an outlet for their own alienation in a charismatic nationalist from Jamaica named Marcus Garvey.

Garvey brought his organization, the Universal Negro Improvement Association (UNIA), to the United States in 1916 in hopes of restoring Black pride by ending colonialism and returning Africans to Africa. When Garvey spoke at the first national UNIA convention in 1920, over 25,000 supporters jammed into Madison Square Garden in New York. Even his harshest critics admitted there were at least half a million members in more than 30 branches of his organization. It was the first mass movement of African Americans in history. But in 1925 Garvey's dream shattered. He was convicted of mail fraud for having oversold stock in his Black Star Line, the steamship company founded to return African Americans to Africa.

As Garvey rose to prominence, an outpouring of Black literature, painting, and sculpture bloomed in

⋏ This mural still appears in the Edison Hotel, which opened in midtown New York in 1931. The wall painting features the famous Cotton Club of Harlem, where white and Black patrons heard the latest jazz acts. One of the club's most renowned performers (*center*) was Cab Calloway, a bandleader and jazz singer who pioneered "scat"—a style of vocalizing that used syllables rather than words to deliver a vibrant, improvised complement to the instruments of the band. Duke Ellington, another of the era's most prominent bandleaders and jazz composers, is pictured at the left.
Randy Duchaine/Alamy Stock Photo

Make a Case

Had Martin Luther King been active during the 1920s, could the modern civil rights movement have begun decades earlier than the 1950s? What factors should you take into account in making your case?

Harlem. The first manifestations of what came to be called the "Harlem Renaissance" struck a strident tone. In 1922, Claude McKay, another Jamaican immigrant, published a book of poems titled *White Shadows.* In his most famous poem, "If We Must Die," McKay mixed defiance and dignity: "Like men we'll face the murderous, cowardly pack / Pressed to the wall, dying but fighting back!" Often supported by white patrons, or "angels," young Black writers and artists found their subjects in the sinews of Black life: the culture of city streets, the folkways of the rural South, and the

Marcus Garvey, seated at his desk, was an early Black nationalist and separatist. His charisma and his writings attracted a range of followers. Among them was Earl Little, the father of Malcolm X, who would later embrace a militant form of Black nationalism and separatism.
Library of Congress, Prints and Photographs Division

primitivism of preindustrial societies. Poet Langston Hughes reminded his readers of the ancient heritage of African Americans in "The Negro Speaks of Rivers," and Zora Neale Hurston collected folktales, songs, and prayers of Black southerners.

Though generally not a racial protest, the Harlem Renaissance drew on the growing assertiveness of African Americans as well as on the alienation of white intellectuals. In 1925 Alain Locke, a Black professor from Howard University, collected a sampling of their works in *The New Negro.* The title reflected not only an artistic movement but also a new racial consciousness.

✓ REVIEW

How did mass media and mass culture reshape American life in the 1920s?

DEFENDERS OF THE FAITH

As mass society rocketed Americans into a future of machines, organization, middle-class living, ethnic diversity, and cosmopolitan culture, not everyone approved. Dr. and Mrs. Wilbur Crafts, the authors of *Intoxicating Drinks and Drugs in All Lands and Times,* cataloged the sins that tempted young people in this modern "age of cities": "Foul pictures, corrupt literature, leprous shows, gambling slot machines, saloons, and Sabbath breaking. . . . We are trying to raise saints in hell."

The modern values of the New Era especially threatened people like the Crafts. Their deeply held convictions reflected the rural roots of so many Americans and what they regarded as "traditional beliefs": small communities; neighborliness; sameness in race, religion, and ethnicity; and a reliance on localities rather than on state or federal government. Such "traditionalism" flourished among country folk, where more insular living made it easier to cling to the past. It also survived among rural migrants to cities and an embattled Protestant elite who found their influence in American culture waning in the more secular society of the New Era.

All were determined to defend their older faiths against the modern age. They resisted urban scale and anonymity, with its moral fluidity, diverse races and ethnicities, and religious pluralism. In the 1920s a full-scale culture war erupted, pitting these traditionalists against the apostles of modern life.

Nativism and Immigration Restriction >> In 1921 two Italian aliens and admitted anarchists, Nicola Sacco and Bartolomeo Vanzetti, were sentenced to death for a shoe company robbery and murder in South Braintree, Massachusetts. Critics charged that they were innocent and convicted

^ Sacco and Vanzetti, dressed in suits and handcuffed for their court appearance.
New York Public Library/Science Source

only of being foreign-born radicals. During the trial, the presiding judge had scorned them in private as "anarchist bastards." Appeals raised doubts about their guilt, but in 1927 Massachusetts executed them. Protests erupted around the world.

By then, nativism—a rabid hostility to foreigners—had produced the most restrictive immigration laws in American history. In the aftermath of World War I, immigration returned almost to prewar levels, close to 1 million people a year, Most came from eastern and southern Europe and from Mexico; the majority were Catholics and Jews. Alarmed native-born Protestants warned that if the flood continued Americans might become "a hybrid race of people as worthless and futile as the good-for-nothing mongrels of Central America and Southeastern Europe." Appreciating the potential for higher wages in a shrunken labor pool, the American Federation of Labor also supported restriction.

In the Southwest, Mexicans and Mexican Americans became a special target of concern. By 1900 about 300,000 Mexican Americans lived in the United States, some with ancestors who had inhabited the region for nearly 400 years. In the following decade, widespread poverty and revolution in Mexico pushed more Mexicans across the border. The Latino population of Texas and New Mexico almost doubled. In California it quadrupled. During World War I, labor shortages led to relaxed immigration laws, and in the 1920s American farmers opened a campaign to attract low-wage Mexican farmworkers.

Pushed out by the new arrivals, tens of thousands of Mexican Americans found homes in northern industrial cities. Thriving communities of Mexicans, called *barrios,* provided Spanish-speaking newcomers with a life of family and festivals, churchgoing, hard work, and slow adaptation. By 1930, the census listed nearly 1.5 million Mexicans living in the United States, not including an untold number who entered the country illegally.

The surge worried nativists, but Mexicans were just one target of the new National Origins Act, first enacted in 1921. It capped all immigration at 350,000 and admitted a quota of up to 3 percent of each nationality living in the United States as of the census of 1910. The system of quotas favored European "races" commonly believed to be superior—"Nordics" (from northern and western Europe)—over those considered inferior—"Alpines" and "Mediterraneans" (from southern and eastern Europe). In 1924 proponents of immigration went further. A second National Origins Act slashed the total admitted to 150,000, reduced the percentage to 2, and pushed the base year back to 1890, before the bulk of southern and eastern Europeans had arrived.

The National Origins Acts fixed patterns of entry for the next four decades. Immigration from southern and eastern Europe was reduced to a trickle. The free flow of Europeans to America, a migration of classes and nationalities that had been unimpeded for 300 years, came to an end.

The "Noble Experiment" >> For nearly a hundred years, reformers had tried with sporadic success to reduce the consumption of alcohol. Their most ambitious campaign climaxed in January 1920, when the Eighteenth Amendment went into effect. Its ban on liquor was not total: private citizens could still drink. They simply could not manufacture, sell, transport, or import any "intoxicating beverage" containing more than 0.5 percent alcohol. Despite underfunded and ineffective enforcement, the effort reduced alcohol consumption by as much as half.

From the start, Prohibition enjoyed wide backing. Science taught that alcohol was bad for health; social science, that it corroded family life and weakened society. Corporate executives and labor leaders supported Prohibition to promote a sober, efficient workforce. Even some Catholics, normally the target of prohibitionists, favored it. They saw the road to perdition paved with liquor bottles. Finally, the liquor industry hurt itself with a terrible record of bribing legislatures and corrupting minors, who were targets of campaigns to recruit young drinkers.

Many of the consequences of so vast a social experiment were unexpected. Before Prohibition, drinkers preferred beer and wine to spirits, but the Eighteenth Amendment reversed the trend. Hard liquor became more available because it was easier and more profitable for bootleggers to

POPULATION GROWTH AND AFRICAN AMERICAN MIGRATION, 1920

In the 1920s the population of urban America grew by some 15 million people, at the time the greatest 10-year jump in American history. For the first time, more people lived in urban than rural areas. Spurred first by the industrial demands of World War I and then by declining farm income, cities grew largely by depopulating farms and small towns. In the most dramatic manifestation of the overall trend, more than a million African Americans migrated from the rural South to the urban North.

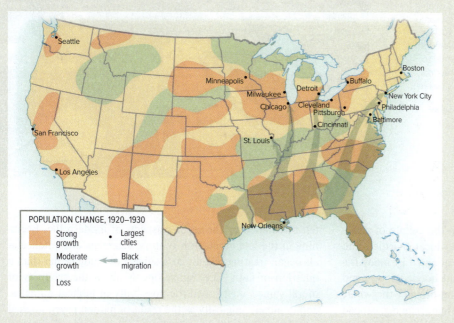

MAP READING

1. Which regions of the country experienced the biggest gains in population? Which regions experienced the biggest declines?
2. From which region of the country did African Americans depart? To what sort of areas did they migrate?
3. Which cities were located in the areas of greatest growth?

MAP INTERPRETATION

1. What economic and social factors might have prompted people to leave their homes and move to other parts of the country?
2. What might have led African Americans to move from farms and towns in the South to cities in the North?
3. How would the popularity of the automobile have affected social mobility and migration?

---

make it. The "Noble Experiment" also helped turn gangsters, including "Scarface" Al Capone, into wealthy celebrities. And it inadvertently advanced women's rights. While licensed saloons had discriminated against "ladies" by having them enter through a separate door or barring any but prostitutes, "speakeasies"—taverns operating undercover—welcomed them. Unintentionally, the alcohol ban leveled this social playing field.

Prohibition can best be understood as cultural and class legislation. Support ran deepest in Protestant churches, especially the evangelical Baptists and Methodists, who worried that non-Protestants like Catholics and Jews might take over. There had always been a strong antiurban and anti-immigrant bias among reformers, who saw alcohol fueling political corruption and social chaos among the new arrivals. As it turned out, the steepest decline in drinking during Prohibition occurred among these working-class ethnics. Traditionalists typically celebrated the triumph of the Noble Experiment, but modern urbanites either ignored or resented it.

KKK >> On Thanksgiving Day 1915, just outside of Atlanta, Georgia, 16 men trudged up a rocky trail to the crest of Stone Mountain. As night fell, they set ablaze a huge wooden cross and swore allegiance to the Invisible Empire, Knights of the Ku Klux Klan. An old scourge was reborn.

While the modern Klan was a throwback to the hooded order of Reconstruction days, it had clear differences as well. The old Klan terrorized African Americans, but the new Klan reflected the insecurities of many traditionalists over multiple changes in modern society. They attributed new ways not only to African Americans but also to the rising tide of immigrants, to newly independent "uppity women," and to Jews. Whereas any white man could join the Klan of old, the new one admitted only "native born, white, gentile [Protestant] Americans." Unlike the old hooded night riders, the reborn Klan was not confined to the rural South. Its capital was Indianapolis, Indiana. Over half its leadership and a third of its members came from cities of more than 100,000 people.

>> The Ku Klux Klan grew in influence after World War I and race riots erupted in over 25 cities beginning in 1919, including Chicago; Longview, Texas; Knoxville, Tennessee; and Omaha, Nebraska. More than 70 African Americans were lynched in the first year after the end of the war, and 11 were burned alive. Many Blacks fought back, their experience in World War I having made them determined to resist repression. In late May and early June 1921, a riot exploded in Tulsa, Oklahoma. As the billowing smoke in this photograph indicates, white mobs burned down 35 square blocks of the African American Greenwood district. Known as the "Black Wall Street," it was the wealthiest Black neighborhood in the country. Confirmed deaths were listed as 26 Blacks and 10 whites, though some estimates put the number as anywhere from 100 to 300 dead. Some 10,000 African Americans were left homeless, and Black property damage amounted to $1.5 million with an additional $750,000 in personal effects (or a total of over $32 million in today's dollars). The National Guard was called out to reestablish order.
©Research Division of the Oklahoma Historical Society

The new Klan nonetheless drew on the culture of small-town America. It was patriotic, gave to local charities, and boasted the kind of outfits and rituals adopted by many fraternal lodges. Klansmen still wore white-hooded sheets and satin robes, but now a typical gathering brought the whole family to a barbecue with fireworks and hymn singing, capped by the burning of a giant cross. Members came mostly from the middle and working classes: small businesspeople, clerical workers, independent professionals, farmers, and laborers with few skills. The Klan offered them status, security, and the promise of restoring an older America where white supremacy, chastity, and Protestantism reigned. When boycotts and whispering campaigns failed to cleanse communities of those who offended their social code, the Klan sometimes resorted to floggings, kidnappings, acid mutilations, and murder.

Behind the scenes, two professional fund-raisers used modern methods of promotion and an army of 1,000 salesmen to attract new members and sell Klan paraphernalia. They enrolled perhaps 3 million dues-paying members by the early 1920s. Moving into politics, Klan candidates captured legislatures in Indiana, Texas, Oklahoma, and Oregon. The organization helped elect six governors, three senators, and thousands of local officials. In the end, like Aimee Semple McPherson, the Klan was undone by the personal excesses of its leaders. Its political power waned after 1925, when the grand dragon of the Indiana Klan was sentenced to life imprisonment for rape and second-degree murder.

Fundamentalism versus Darwinism >>

Although Aimee Semple McPherson embraced the fashions of the New Era, many Protestants, especially in rural areas, felt threatened by the secular aspects of modern life. Beginning in the late nineteenth century, scientists and intellectuals began treating religion as a subject of study rather than a question of faith. They spoke openly about the relativity of moral values, questioned the possibility of biblical miracles, and depicted religiosity as the result of hidden psychological needs and the Bible as mere literature. Darwinism, pragmatism, and other modern theories exposed traditional religious teachings to skepticism and scorn.

Reflecting these secular beliefs, liberal Protestants in the 1870s sought to make Christianity more relevant to contemporary life through a movement known as "Modernism." One leader defined it as "the use of scientific, historical and social methods in understanding and applying evangelical Christianity to the needs of living persons." The power of faith, a belief in miracles, and the sheer wonder of religion seemed to be left out.

Conservative Protestants disagreed with this updating of orthodoxy. Between 1910 and 1915, two wealthy oil executives from Los Angeles subsidized the publication of some 3 million copies of a series of pamphlets called *The Fundamentals.* They advocated a return to what they considered the fundamentals of Christian faith, among them the virgin birth, the resurrection of Jesus, and a literal reading of Scripture. After 1920 a variety of conservative Protestants began calling themselves "Fundamentalists."

The movement grew dramatically in the first two decades of the twentieth century. Nothing disturbed Fundamentalists more than Darwinian theories of evolution that challenged the divine origins of humankind. In 1925 what began as an in-house fight among Protestants became a national brawl when the Tennessee legislature made it illegal to teach that "man has descended from a lower order of animals."

In 1925, encouraged by the newly formed American Civil Liberties Union, religious skeptics in the town of Dayton, Tennessee, decided to test the law. They put a bespectacled biology teacher named John T. Scopes on trial for teaching evolution. Behind the scenes, Scopes's sponsors saw his trial as a way to give Dayton a commercial boost with all the attention the trial might bring.

The results exceeded their wildest expectations. When the court convened in July, millions listened over the radio to the first trial ever broadcast. Inside the courtroom Clarence Darrow, the renowned defense lawyer from Chicago and a professed agnostic, acted as co-counsel for Scopes. Serving as co-prosecutor was William Jennings Bryan, the three-time presidential candidate who had recently joined the antievolution crusade. It was urban Darrow against rural Bryan in what Bryan described as a "duel to the death" between Christianity and evolution.

As the trial opened, the presiding judge ruled scientists' testimony "hearsay" because none had been present at the Creation. Without scientific testimony, the defense virtually collapsed, until Darrow called Bryan to the stand as an "expert on the Bible." Under withering cross-examination, Bryan admitted that the Earth might not have been made "in six days of 24 hours." Even so, the Dayton jury took only eight minutes to find Scopes guilty and fine him $100.

By then the excesses of the Scopes trial had transformed it into more of a national circus than a confrontation between darkness and light. But the debate over evolution raised a larger question that continued to reverberate throughout the twentieth century. As scientific, religious, and cultural standards clashed, how much should religious beliefs and local standards influence public education?

THEN&NOW

The culture wars of the twenty-first century are nothing new. On January 17, 1920, the successful enactment of Prohibition opened the nation's first culture war. Among its aims was controlling the behavior of new immigrants. The alcohol ban was followed a year later by new legislation that imposed the first caps and quotas in immigration history. Later in the decade, in Dayton, Tennessee, Darwin's theory of evolution went on trial and lost to a rising tide of religious Fundamentalism that challenged the right of science to contradict the Bible. A new wave of white supremacy and xenophobia reignited the Ku Klux Klan, which now targeted immigrants, Catholics, Jews, and independent women in addition to African Americans and other people of color. The Great Depression and World War II partially submerged those cultural conflicts, only to have them bubble to the surface in the twenty-first century. Mobilized by the same fears and fought over the same ground, the culture wars of today divide politics as sharply now as then.

REVIEW

Along what fronts did traditionalists fight the culture war of the 1920s and with what weapons?

REPUBLICANS ASCENDANT

"The change is amazing," wrote a Washington reporter after the inauguration of Warren G. Harding in March 1921. Wilson's sentries disappeared from the gates of the White House, tourists again walked the halls, and reporters freely questioned the president for the first time in years. The reign of "normalcy," which Harding misread for "normality," had begun. "By 'normalcy,'" he explained, "I mean normal procedure, the natural way, without excess."

The Politics of "Normalcy" >> *Normalcy* turned out to be anything but normal. After eight years of Democratic rule, Republicans gained control of the White House and both houses of Congress. Fifteen years of reform gave way to eight years of cautious governing. The presidency, strengthened by Wilson, fell into weak hands. The cabinet and Congress set the agenda.

Harding and his successor, Calvin Coolidge, chose to delegate power, in Harding's case to a cabinet of what he called "the best minds." Harding appointed some men of quality: the respected jurist Charles Evans Hughes as secretary of state; Henry C. Wallace, a farmer himself, as secretary of agriculture; and Herbert Hoover as secretary of commerce. Hoover had built a reputation as a master organizer and engineer, a business executive, and a philanthropist.

Harding also made, as one critic put it, "unspeakably bad appointments": his old crony Harry Daugherty as attorney general and New Mexico senator Albert Fall as interior secretary. Daugherty sold influence for cash and resigned in 1923. In 1922, Fall accepted bribes of more than $400,000 for secretly leasing naval oil reserves at Elk Hill, California, and Teapot Dome, Wyoming, to private oil companies. In 1929, he became the first cabinet member ever to be convicted of a felony.

Harding died suddenly in August 1923, before most of the scandals came to light. Although he would be remembered as passive and weak-kneed, his tolerance and moderation had a calming effect on the strife-ridden nation in the aftermath of World War I. Slowly he had even begun to lead. In 1921 he created a Bureau of the Budget that brought modern accounting techniques to the management of federal revenues. Toward the end of his administration, he cleared an early scandal from the Veterans' Bureau and set an agenda for Congress that included expanding the merchant marine.

To his credit, Calvin Coolidge handled Harding's troubled legacy with skill and dispatch. He created a special investigatory commission, prosecuted wrongdoers, and restored the confidence of the nation. Decisiveness, when he chose to exercise it, was one of Coolidge's hallmarks. But he rarely did. He believed in small-town democracy and minimalist government. "One of the most important accomplishments of my administration has been minding my own business," he boasted. Above all Coolidge worshiped wealth. "Civilization and profits," he once said, "go hand in hand."

The Policies of Mellon and Hoover >> Coolidge retained most of Harding's cabinet, including his powerful treasury secretary, Andrew Mellon. A banker and former head of Aluminum Corporation of America, Mellon believed that prosperity "trickled down" from rich to poor through investment, which raised production, employment, and wages. In 1921 Mellon persuaded Congress to repeal the excess-profits tax on corporations. Under Coolidge, he convinced legislators to end all gift taxes, to halve estate and income taxes, and to reduce corporation and consumption taxes even further. In 1922 he endorsed the protective Fordney-McCumber Tariff, raising rates on manufactured and farm goods. Everything Mellon supported profited American businesses and the wealthy.

Unlike Mellon, Commerce Secretary Herbert Hoover (also a Harding holdover) was not a traditional business conservative. Instead, he promoted a progressive brand of capitalism called "associationalism." It aimed at aiding businesses directly by spreading a new gospel of efficiency and productivity through trade associations, groups of private companies organized industry by industry. The role of government, as Hoover saw it, was to encourage voluntary cooperation among businesses. In his view, government agencies should provide advice, statistics, and forums where business leaders could exchange ideas, set industry standards, and develop markets. Such cooperation meant increased power for businesses.

Both Hoover and Mellon placed government in the service of business. As a result, the impact of government on the economy grew. So did its size, by more than 40,000 employees between 1921 and 1930. Building on their wartime partnership, government and business dropped all pretense of a laissez-faire economy. Efficiency increased, production soared, and prosperity reigned. At the same time, however, Mellon's tax policies helped concentrate wealth in the hands of fewer individuals and corporations, while Hoover's associationalism helped them consolidate their power. Competition among businesses decreased, and consumer groups were largely ignored. By the end of the decade, 200 giant corporations controlled almost half the corporate assets in America.

Crises at Home and Abroad >> Some groups remained outside the magic circle of prosperity. Ironically, among them were those people who made up the biggest business in America: farmers. In 1920, agriculture still had an investment value greater than manufacturing, all utilities, and all railroads combined. Yet farmers' portion of the national income shrank by almost half during the 1920s.

The reasons for the decline were complex and the results devastating. At the end of the war, the government had quickly withdrawn price supports for wheat and ended its practice of feeding refugees. As postwar European agriculture revived, the demand for American exports dropped. And new dietary habits meant that Americans were eating 75 fewer pounds of food annually than they had in 1910. Meanwhile, new synthetic fibers drove down demand for wool and cotton.

For the five years that Coolidge ran a "businessman's government," workers were another group that realized few gains. Wages, purchasing power, and bargaining rights stagnated. Although welfare capitalism promised benefits to workers, only a handful of companies put it into practice. Those that did often used it to weaken independent unions. As dangerous imbalances in the economy developed, Coolidge ignored them.

One sign of crisis could not be ignored: the Great Mississippi Flood of 1927. After years of deforestation and months of heavy rain, the Mississippi River burst through its levees, rampaging from southern Missouri to Louisiana, affecting an immense area roughly the size of New England. Floodwaters reached 100 feet in some places and did not recede for three months.

A network of private agencies was quickly knit together and placed under Commerce Secretary Herbert Hoover. With Hoover in charge, an army of local citizens, many of them Black and some conscripted at gunpoint, erected refugee camps to cope with the 700,000 people displaced by the flood. Nearly 250 people died, and 130,000 homes were destroyed. Property damage ran to $350 million ($5 billion in today's dollars). Before the end of 1928, half the African American population of the Mississippi Delta's Black Belt had fled the region. For the rest of the decade, commerce throughout the central United States suffered. A bright spot lay in the new federal legislation that finally gave responsibility to the federal government for controlling such disasters along the Mississippi.

Most Americans paid little attention to the Great Flood and other crises at home. They utterly ignored economic unrest abroad. At the end of World War I, Europe's victors had forced Germany to take on $33 billion in war costs or reparations, partly to repay their own war debts to the United States. When Germany defaulted in 1923, French forces occupied the Ruhr valley in Germany's industrial heartland, depriving it of a valuable asset. Germany struck back by printing more money to keep its economy afloat and to dramatize the crushing burden of its debt. The resulting inflation wiped out the savings of the German middle class, shook confidence in the new Weimar Republic, and soon threatened the economic stability of Europe.

In 1924 American business leader Charles G. Dawes tried to solve the problem by persuading the victorious Europeans to lower reparations. In return, the United States

MAP 24.1: THE GREAT FLOOD OF 1927

Hurricane Katrina (2005), the costliest storm in U.S. history, devastated parts of four states. By comparison the Great Mississippi Flood of 1927 swamped parts of 11 states and covered some 27,000 square miles. It sparked a massive migration of tens of thousands of African Americans from the affected areas to northern cities, such as Chicago.

promised to help stabilize the German economy. Encouraged by the State Department, American bankers made large loans to Germany, with which the Germans paid their reparations to the European victors, who then used the funds to repay their debts to the United States. It amounted to taking money from one American pocket and placing it in another. To help further, the United States reduced European war debts in 1926. Canceling them would have done more good.

Despite Europe's debts, a costly arms race continued to drain the great powers. Two grand diplomatic gestures united the complementary desires for peace and belt-tightening. In 1921, following the lead of the United States, the world's sea powers gathered at the Washington Naval Disarmament Conference. There they agreed to freeze battleship construction for 10 years and to set ratios on the tonnage of each navy. The Five-Power Agreement was the first disarmament treaty in modern history.

A more ambitious gesture followed seven years later. In 1928, the major nations of the world (except the Soviet Union) signed an agreement outlawing war, the Kellogg-Briand Pact. It was named for its sponsors, French foreign minister Aristide Briand and U.S. secretary of state Frank Kellogg. "Peace is proclaimed," Kellogg declared as he signed the document with a foot-long gold pen.

The two pacts proved to be little more than that good intentions. The French and Japanese, among others, resented the lower limits on their battleships and began building smaller vessels such as submarines, cruisers, and destroyers in their place. The arms race now continued, now concentrated on these vessels. And the Kellogg-Briand Pact remained a toothless proclamation with no means of enforcement and no impact.

The Election of 1928 >> On August 2, 1927, in a small classroom in Rapid City, South Dakota, Calvin Coolidge handed a terse typewritten message to reporters: "I do not choose to run for President in nineteen twenty-eight." Republicans honored the request and nominated Herbert Hoover. Hoover was not a politician but a business executive and government administrator. He had never once campaigned for public office. It didn't matter. Republican prosperity made it difficult for any Democrat to win. Hoover's reputation as perhaps the most admired public servant in America made it nearly impossible.

The Democratic Party continued to split between its rural supporters in the South and West and urban laborers in the Northeast. By 1928 the shift in population toward cities gave the party's urban wing an edge. Former New York governor Al Smith won the nomination on the first ballot, even though his handicaps were evident. When the New York City–bred Smith spoke "poisonally" on the "rhadio," his accent made voters wince. Though he pledged to enforce Prohibition, he campaigned against it and even took an occasional drink. Most damaging, he was Catholic, at a time when anti-Catholicism remained strong in many areas of the country.

MAP 24.2: ELECTION OF 1928

Candidate (Party)	Electoral Vote (%)	Popular Vote (%)
Herbert Hoover (Republican)	444 (84)	21,437,277 (58)
Alfred Smith (Democratic)	87 (16)	15,007,698 (41)
Minor parties	—	337,115 (1)

• Dots indicate the 12 largest cities in the nation.

In the election of 1928, nearly 60 percent of eligible voters turned out to give all but eight states to Hoover. Party loyalties faded. The solidly Democratic South for the first time voted for a Republican. Another development involved the 12 largest cities. They had gone to the Republican candidate in 1924, but in 1928 the Democrats won them. A major political realignment was underway. Democrats were becoming the party of the cities and of their working-class ethnic voters. Around this core, they would build the most powerful political coalition of the twentieth century.

 REVIEW

What public policies did Presidents Harding and Coolidge pursue during the 1920s and why did they pursue them?

THE GREAT BULL MARKET

Strolling across the felt-padded floor of the New York Stock Exchange, Superintendent William Crawford greeted the New Year with swaggering confidence. The rampaging "bulls," or buyers of stock, had routed the hibernating "bears," those who sell. It was the greatest "bull market" in history, as eager purchasers drove prices to new highs. At the end of the last business day of 1928, Crawford declared flatly, "The millennium's arrived."

Veteran financial analyst Alexander Noyes had doubts. Speculation—buying and selling purely on the expectation that prices will rise and yield quick gains—had turned the stock market into a gambling casino. "Something has to give," said Noyes in September 1929. Less than a month later, the Great Bull Market collapsed in a heap.

The Rampaging Bull >> No one knows exactly what caused the wave of speculation that boosted the stock market to dizzying heights. Driven alternately by greed and fear, the market was dominated by greed in a decade that considered it a virtue. Plentiful money and credit fueled the market's rise. Nearly $900 million worth of overseas gold expanded the money supply by $6 billion, Corporate profits grew 80 percent. With interest rates as high as 25 percent, more could be made from lending money to brokers than from constructing new factories. Brokers then lent the money to their stock-buying clients. By 1929, these "brokers' loans" had almost tripled from what they were two years earlier.

"Margin requirements," the cash actually put down to purchase stock, hovered around 50 percent for most of the decade. Thus buyers had to come up with only half the price of a share. The rest came from brokers' loans. As trading reached record heights in August 1929, the Federal Reserve Board tried to deter speculation by raising interest rates. Higher interest rates made borrowing of all kinds more expensive and, authorities hoped, would rein in the galloping bull market. They were wrong. It was already too late.

The Great Crash >> At the opening bell on Thursday, October 24, 1929, a torrent of orders to sell flooded the exchange. Nervous speculators were worried about a decline. Prices plunged as panic set in. By the end of "Black Thursday," nearly 13 million shares had been traded—a record. Losses stood at $3 billion, another record. Thirty-five of the largest brokerage houses on Wall Street issued a joint statement of reassurance: "The worst has passed."

The worst had just begun. Prices rallied for the rest of the week, buoyed by a bankers' buying pool. But the following Tuesday, October 29, 1929, the bubble burst. Stockholders lost $10 billion in a single day. Within a month, industrial stocks dropped half their value. At their peak in 1929, stocks had been worth $87 billion. The sickening slide in stock prices that began on Black Thursday continued for four years. In 1933, stocks bottomed out at $18 billion.

The Great Crash did not cause the Great Depression, but it did damage the economy and broke the unbounded optimism of the New Era. Although only about 500,000 people were actually trading stocks in 1929, their investments helped sustain prosperity and business confidence. Commercial banks—some loaded with corporate stocks, others financing brokers' loans—reeled in the wake of the market's collapse. When thousands of wealthy investors saw their fortunes disappear, the hard-earned savings of middle-class stockholders vanished, too, and with them their futures. The Great Crash signaled the start of the greatest depression in history. In the United States, the gains of the 1920s were wiped out in a few years. By 1933, national income had fallen by half, factory wages by almost half. By some estimates 85,000 businesses failed.

Although the Great Depression was neither as deep nor as prolonged in the United States as in other countries, the shock waves from the United States rippled around the globe. American loans, investments, and purchases had supported European economies since the end of World War I. When those revenue sources dwindled, European governments defaulted on war debts. More of their banks failed; more of their businesses collapsed; and unemployment surged to at least 30 million worldwide by 1932.

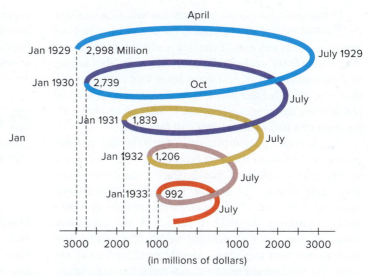

DECLINING WORLD TRADE, 1929–1933

As the Great Depression deepened, world trade spiraled downward. Here the imports of 75 countries are tracked from 1929 to 1933. (The amounts are measured in millions of U.S. gold dollars.) The greatest annual decline occurred between 1930 and 1931, as production plummeted and nation after nation began to erect high tariff barriers to protect their domestic markets from cheaper imports. Over the four-year period, world import trade fell by almost two-thirds, only underscoring the growing interdependence of the global economy.

TAIL HOLT

^ A desperate investor, money flying from his pockets, hangs on to the galloping "Bear Market," as buildings sag in a collapsing Wall Street. Signs of the looming disaster must have been visible to artist Rollin Kirby, who drew this cartoon three weeks *before* the "Black Friday" stock market crash of October 29, 1919.
Everett Collection Historical/Alamy Stock Photo

Europeans scrambled to protect themselves. Led by Great Britain in 1931, 41 nations abandoned the gold standard to give themselves more monetary flexibility. Foreign governments hoped to devalue their currencies by expanding their supplies of money. Conventional wisdom taught that exports would be cheaper and foreign trade would increase. But several countries did so all at once, while each country also raised tariffs to protect itself from foreign competition. Devaluation failed, and the resulting trade barriers only deepened the crisis by choking off world trade.

In the United States, declining sales abroad sent crop prices to new lows. Farm income dropped by more than half. Spurred by defaults on farm mortgages, an epidemic of rural bank failures spread to the cities. Nervous depositors rushed to withdraw their cash. Even healthy banks could not bear the strain. Between 1929 and 1933, collapsing banks took more than $20 billion in assets with them.

Causes of the Great Depression >> What, then, caused the Great Depression in the United States? In the months before the crash, with national attention riveted on the booming stock market, hardly anyone paid attention to existing defects in the economy. By 1928, the booming construction and automobile industries had begun to lose vitality as demand sagged. Increases in consumer spending had slowed to a lethargic 1.5 percent for 1928–1929. Warehouses began to fill as sales fell.

In one sense, businesses had done too well. Corporations had boosted their profits by keeping the cost of labor and raw materials low as well as by increasing productivity (producing more, using fewer workers). But without strong labor unions or government support, real wages never kept pace with productivity, which led to a paradox. As consumers, workers did not have enough money to buy the products they were making more efficiently and at lower cost than ever.

People made up the difference between earnings and purchases by borrowing. Shoppers bought "on time," paying for merchandise a little each month. During the decade, consumer debt rose by 250 percent. Few could afford to keep spending at that rate. Nor could the distribution of wealth sustain prosperity. By 1929, 1 percent of the population owned 36 percent of all personal wealth. The wealthy had more money than they could possibly spend and saved too much. The working and middle classes had not enough money to keep the economy growing, spend though they might.

Another problem lay with the banking system. Mismanagement, greed, and the emergence of a new type of executive—half banker, half broker—led banks to divert more funds into speculative investments. The decentralized American banking system offered no way to compensate for a failed bank. By the end of the 1920s, half of the 25,000 banks in America lay outside the Federal Reserve System, whose controls over even its members were weak. During the decade, 6,000 banks had already failed, taking depositors' savings with them.

A shaky corporate structure made matters worse. No government agency monitored the stock exchanges, while big business operated largely free from government regulation. Insider stock trading, shady stock deals, and outright fraud were rampant. Meanwhile, public policy enabled corporate consolidation and control by filing fewer antitrust suits. High profits and the Mellon tax program under Coolidge left many corporations relatively immune to fluctuating prices and helped make them wealthy enough to avoid borrowing. Changes in interest rates—over which the Federal Reserve exercised some control—had little influence on them. Strong profits and weak government regulation allowed huge corporations to rule the economy with a relatively free hand. And they ruled badly.

In a sign of growing softness in the economy, unemployment began to increase as early as 1927. By the fall of 1929, some 2 million people were out of work. Many of them had worked in textiles, coal mining, lumbering, and railroads. These had been "sick" industries during the decade, suffering from overexpansion, weak demand, and weak management.

Finally, plain economic ignorance contributed to the calamity. High tariffs protected American industries but discouraged European businesses from selling to the world's most profitable market. Only American loans and investments supported demand abroad. When the American economy collapsed, those disappeared and with them American foreign trade. Furthermore, the Federal Reserve had been stimulating the economy by expanding the money supply and lowering interest rates. Those moves only fed the speculative fever by furnishing investors with cheap money. A decision to finally raise interest rates in 1929 to stem speculation ended up speeding the slide by making it more expensive to borrow when borrowing might have slowed the decline.

✓ REVIEW

What caused the Great Depression, and what role did the Great Crash play in it?

History in Global Context >> The mix of exuberance, hedonism, and anxiety that characterized the United States in the 1920s took root in other nations as did Woodrow Wilson's dream of a world made safe for democracy. Germany, once ruled by Hohenzollern monarchs, became the Weimar Republic. Its constitution provided universal suffrage and a bill of rights. The nations carved out of the old Russian and Austro-Hungarian Empires attempted to create similarly democratic governments. In Turkey, Kemal Ataturk abolished the sultanate and established the Turkish Republic. Mohandas Gandhi's Congress Party pressed the British for greater representation and independence in India.

The Great Crash and the Great Depression weakened these fragile democracies. Weimer Germany gave way to a totalitarian state, while foundering economies strengthened dictators in Italy and the Soviet Union. Japan abandoned its peaceful parliamentary path and embraced militarism, emperor worship, and foreign expansion. No one—not the brokers of Wall Street or the captains of industry or the diplomats at the League of Nations—could predict the future, let alone control it.

CHAPTER SUMMARY

The New Era of the 1920s brought a booming economy and modern times to America, vastly accelerating the forces of change—bureaucracy, productivity, technology, advertising and consumerism, mass media, and suburbanization. Urban-rural tensions peaked with shifts in population that gave cities new power but split the country in its first culture war. As the decade wore on, weaknesses in the economy and a new ethos of getting and spending proved to be the New Era's undoing.

- Technology, advertising and consumer spending, and such boom industries as automobile manufacturing and construction fueled the largest peacetime economic growth in American history to that date.
- Key features of modern life—mass society, mass culture, and mass consumption—took hold, fed by mass media in the form of radio, movies, and mass-circulation newspapers and magazines.

- Modern life unsettled old ways and eroded social conventions that had limited opportunities, especially for women, leading to the emergence of a New Woman.
- Great migrations of African Americans from the rural South to the urban North and of Latinos from Mexico to the United States reshaped the social landscape and ignited racial strife.
- Traditional culture, centered in rural America, hardened and defended itself against change through immigration restriction, Prohibition, Fundamentalism, and a reborn Ku Klux Klan.
- A galloping bull market in stocks reflected the commitment of government to big business and economic growth.
- When the stock market crashed in 1929, weaknesses in the economy—overexpansion, declining purchasing power, uneven distribution of wealth, weak banking and corporate structures, "sick" industries, and economic ignorance—finally brought down the economy, and with it the New Era came to a close.

Digging Deeper

For years, Frederick Lewis Allen, *Only Yesterday: An Informal History of the 1920s* (1931), shaped the stereotyped view of the decade as a frivolous interlude between World War I and the Great Depression. William Leuchtenburg, *The Perils of Prosperity, 1914-1932* (1958), began an important reconsideration by stressing the serious conflict between urban and rural America and the emergence of modern mass society. Lynn Dumenil updates Leuchtenburg in her excellent *The Modern Temper: American Culture and Society in the 1920s* (1995). Ann Douglas, *Terrible Honesty: Mongrel Manhattan in the 1920s* (1995), puts Manhattan at the center of the cultural transformation. On immigration restriction, see Roger Daniels, *Guarding the Golden Door: American Immigration Policy and Immigrants since 1882* (2004). Daniel Okrent, *The Guarded Gate: Bigotry, Eugenics and the Law That Kept Two Generations of Jews, Italians, and Other European Immigrants Out of America* (2019), discusses the influence of eugenics.

On the Scopes trial, see Edward J. Larson, *Summer for the Gods: The Scopes Trial and America's Continuing Debate over Science and Religion* (1997). Lisa McGirr's *The War on Alcohol: Prohibition and the Rise of the American State* (2015) takes a new look at the anti-alcohol crusade as a means of growing the penal power of government. Linda Gordon, *The Second Coming of the KKK: The Ku Klux Klan of the 1920s and the American Political Tradition* (2017), traces the origins and instruments of the new Klan of the 1920s.

Roland Marchand, *Advertising the American Dream: Making Way for Modernity, 1920-1940* (1985), analyzes the role of advertising in shaping mass consumption, values, and culture; and Ellis Hawley, *The Great War and the Search for a Modern Order* (1979), emphasizes economic institutions. For women in the 1920s, see Kathleen M. Blee, *Women of the Klan: Racism and Gender in the 1920s* (1991); and Virginia Scharff, *Taking the Wheel: Women and the Coming of the Motor Age* (1991). In a penetrating and gendered discussion of Garveyism and of the Harlem Renaissance, Martin Summers profiles evolving notions of what it meant to be a Black man in *Manliness and Its Discontents: The Black Middle Class and the Transformation of Masculinity, 1900-1930* (2004).

The most thorough and readable examination of the stock market's relation to the economy and public policy is still Robert Sobel, *The Great Bull Market: Wall Street in the 1920s* (1968). For the run-up to the crash, see Maury Klein, *Rainbow's End: The Crash of 1929* (2001). In *Lords of Finance: The Bankers Who Broke the World* (2010), Liaquat Ahamed finds the roots of the financial crisis in policies pursued by four key bankers in the United States, Great Britain, France, and Germany. For an analysis of the Great Depression from the perspective of Keynesian economics, see John Kenneth Galbraith, *The Great Crash* (rev. ed., 1988). For the argument of monetarists, who see the roots of the Depression in the shrinking money supply, see Peter Temin, *Did Monetary Forces Cause the Great Depression?* (1976). John M. Barry, *Rising Tide: The Great Mississippi Flood of 1927 and How It Changed America* (1997), is especially good on the fate of African Americans and the failure of government and private aid organizations.

25 The Great Depression and the New Deal

1929–1939

Homesteaders Jack and Edith Whinery lived with their five children in Pie Town, New Mexico. The effects of the Great Depression lingered there well into 1940, when Russell Lee snapped this slide. It is part of a larger series of color images captured by government photographers at sites across the country. What details emerge of their home life from this still photograph? Does the use of color affect our view of the past?

Library of Congress, Prints and Photographs Division

>> An American Story

LETTERS FROM THE EDGE

Winner, South Dakota, November 10, 1933. "Dammit, I don't WANT to write to you again tonight. It's been a long, long day, and I'm tired." All the days had been long since Lorena Hickok began her cross-country trek. Four months earlier Harry Hopkins, the new federal relief administrator, had hired the journalist to report on the human impact of the New Deal in its fight against the Great Depression. "Talk with the unemployed," he told her, "and when you talk to them, don't ever forget that but for the grace of God you, I, any of our friends might be in their shoes."

In 1933 and 1934 Hickok found that Roosevelt's relief, or public assistance, programs were falling short. Its most ambitious effort, a half-billion-dollar subsidy to states, localities, and charities, was leaving out too many Americans, like the sharecropper Hickok discovered near Raleigh, North Carolina. He and his daughters had been living in a tobacco barn for two weeks on little more than weeds and table scraps. "Seems like we just keep goin' lower and lower," said a 16-year-old daughter. To her surprise, hope still flickered in the teenager's eyes. Hickok couldn't explain it until she noticed a pin on her chest. It was a campaign button from the 1932 election—"a profile of the President." Hope sprang from Franklin D. Roosevelt, the man in the White House.

Before Roosevelt and the New Deal, the White House was far removed from ordinary citizens. The only federal agency in sight was the post office, and as the Depression began, it usually delivered bad news to a sullen nation.

As Hickok traveled across the country in 1933, she detected a change. People were talking about government programs. Perhaps it was long-awaited contributions to relief or maybe reforms of the stock market and the banks or the new recovery programs for industry and agriculture. Just as likely, they were talking about Franklin Roosevelt. People, she wrote, were "for the President."

The message was clear: Roosevelt and the New Deal had begun to restore national confidence. The

˄ In the shantytowns or "Hoovervilles" that sprang up during the Great Depression, housing was makeshift, with the homeless living in crude tin and wood shacks or tents. This young girl uses an abandoned tire as a makeshift seat.
Library of Congress, Prints and Photographs Division

New Deal never brought full recovery, which would have to await the massive spending of World War II. But it did improve the economy and provide aid to millions. It reformed the financial system, broadened business regulation, and committed the federal government to managing economic ups and downs.

The New Deal extended the progressive drive to soften industrialization and translated decades of mounting concern for the disadvantaged into federal aid programs. For the first time, Americans believed Washington would help them through a terrible crisis. The liberal state came of age in Roosevelt's New Deal—active, interventionist, and committed to regulated capitalism and social justice. The New Deal did have limits. It failed to achieve recovery or lift the poor from impoverishment. It never crossed the color line of segregation that continued to favor whites. Despite charges of "socialism," New Deal liberalism turned out to be a relatively conservative response to the perceived failure of capitalism and to calls for more radical action across the nation and the globe. ≪

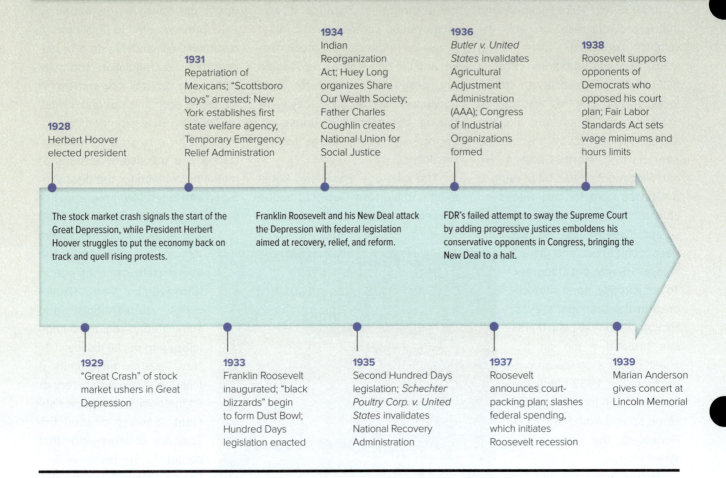

1928
Herbert Hoover elected president

1931
Repatriation of Mexicans; "Scottsboro boys" arrested; New York establishes first state welfare agency, Temporary Emergency Relief Administration

1934
Indian Reorganization Act; Huey Long organizes Share Our Wealth Society; Father Charles Coughlin creates National Union for Social Justice

1936
Butler v. United States invalidates Agricultural Adjustment Administration (AAA); Congress of Industrial Organizations formed

1938
Roosevelt supports opponents of Democrats who opposed his court plan; Fair Labor Standards Act sets wage minimums and hours limits

The stock market crash signals the start of the Great Depression, while President Herbert Hoover struggles to put the economy back on track and quell rising protests.

Franklin Roosevelt and his New Deal attack the Depression with federal legislation aimed at recovery, relief, and reform.

FDR's failed attempt to sway the Supreme Court by adding progressive justices emboldens his conservative opponents in Congress, bringing the New Deal to a halt.

1929
"Great Crash" of stock market ushers in Great Depression

1933
Franklin Roosevelt inaugurated; "black blizzards" begin to form Dust Bowl; Hundred Days legislation enacted

1935
Second Hundred Days legislation; *Schechter Poultry Corp. v. United States* invalidates National Recovery Administration

1937
Roosevelt announces court-packing plan; slashes federal spending, which initiates Roosevelt recession

1939
Marian Anderson gives concert at Lincoln Memorial

THE HUMAN IMPACT OF THE GREAT DEPRESSION

Long breadlines snaked around street corners. Vacant-eyed apple-sellers stood shivering in the wind. Men with hats in their hands came to back doors asking for food in exchange for work. Women, desperate to help their families, took in any boarder who could pay. Between 1929 and 1932 an average of 100,000 people lost their jobs every week until some 13 million Americans, 1 out of 4, were unemployed. For the first time in American history, the number of people leaving the country exceeded the number entering, because jobs were so scarce in the United States.

The Great Depression acted as a great leveler that reduced differences in the face of common want. It often provoked the same human responses regardless of the circumstances. The New York seamstress without enough piecework to pay her rent felt the same pinch of frustration, anger, and insecurity as the UC Berkeley student whose college education was cut short when the bank let her father go. But not everyone was devastated; most Americans survived by scrimping to make ends meet. As one Depression-era survivor recalled, "We lived lean."

Hard Times >> Hard times lasted for a decade. Even before the Great Crash of 1929 many Americans struggled to make a living. In 1929 a family of four required $2,000 a year for the barest necessities. That was more than what 60 percent of American families earned. Between 1929 and 1933 living costs dropped 25 percent, but family incomes tumbled an average of 40 percent.

Unable to pay mortgages or rent, many families lived off the generosity of forgiving landlords. Some traded down to smaller quarters or simply lost their homes. By 1932 between 1 and 2 million Americans were homeless wanderers, among them an estimated 25,000 families. Despite official claims that no one died of hunger, the New York City Welfare Council reported 29 victims of starvation and 110 deaths from malnourishment in 1932 alone.

Marriages and births, symbols of faith in the future, decreased. For the first time in three centuries the curve of population growth began to level as many young couples postponed having children. Experts worried about an impending "baby crop shortage." For those who were married, strong families hung together and grew closer; weak ones languished or fell apart. Although divorce declined, desertion—the "poor man's divorce"—mushroomed. Under the strain, rates of mental illness and suicide rose as well.

Many fathers, whose lives had been defined by work, suddenly had nothing to do. They grew listless and depressed. Most mothers stayed home and found their traditional roles as nurturer and household manager less disrupted and more highly valued than the breadwinning roles of their husbands.

Homemakers watched household budgets with a closer eye than ever. They canned more food and substituted less expensive fish for meat. When they earned extra money, they often did so within the confines of the "woman's sphere" by taking in boarders, laundry, and sewing; opening beauty parlors in their kitchens; and selling baked goods from their own ovens.

For those women who worked outside the home, prejudice often relegated them to so-called women's work. Over half the female labor force continued to work in domestic service or the garment trades, while others found traditional employment as schoolteachers, social workers, and secretaries. Only slowly did the female proportion of the workforce reach pre-Depression levels, until it rose finally to 25 percent by 1940, largely because women were willing to take almost any job.

The Great Depression shook many Americans and left a legacy of self-doubt, pessimism, and shame. People blamed themselves for their misfortune. "I would go stand on the relief line [and] bend my head low so nobody would recognize me," recalled one man. Humiliation and fear—that you had caused your own downfall; that the bottom would drop out again—was what one writer called an "invisible scar."

The Golden Age of Radio and Film >> By the end of the 1930s, almost 9 out of 10 families owned radios. People depended on them for nearly everything—news, sports, and weather; music and entertainment; advice on how to bake a cake or find God. Some programming helped change national habits. When *The Sporting News* conducted a baseball poll in 1932, editors were surprised to discover that a "new crop of fans has been created by radio . . . the women." Many women were at home during the day when most games were played and had begun to tune in. Night games soon outran day games in attendance, in part because husbands began taking wives and daughters. Having listened on the radio, they wanted to see games in person.

Radio entered a golden age of commercialism. Advertisers hawked their products on variety programs like Major Bowes's *Amateur Hour* and on comedy shows with entertainers such as George Burns and Gracie Allen. Daytime melodramas (called "soap operas" because they were sponsored by soap companies) aimed at women, featuring stories of the personal struggles of ordinary folk.

Radio continued to bind the country together. A teenager in Splendora, Texas, could listen to the same wisecracks from Jack Benny and the same music from Guy Lombardo as kids in New York City and Los Angeles. In 1938 Orson Welles created a near-nationwide panic when he broadcast H. G. Wells's classic science fiction tale *The War of the Worlds* as if it where really happening. Americans everywhere listened to its breathless reports of an "invasion from Mars." Bombarded with news of impending war in Europe and accustomed to responding to radio advertising, they were prepared to believe almost anything, including reports of Martian invaders.

In Hollywood an efficient but autocratic studio system churned out a record number of feature films. Eight motion picture companies produced more than two-thirds of them. Color, first introduced to feature films in *Becky Sharp* (1935),

⌃ The artist Reginald Marsh, famous for his Depression-era drawings, depicts a long line of hungry men, waiting for food at a soup kitchen in New York around 1930. The line seems to go on forever. Marsh's subjects often have their hands in their pockets, eyes downcast, and shoulders hunched over. What does the drawing convey that a photograph might not?
MPI/Archive Photos/Getty Images

Wonder Woman, Women's Rights, and Birth Control

Peters's note to Marston complains that Wonder Woman's shoes look like "a stenographer's." How might changing her shoes–to near knee-length boots as eventually occurred–change Wonder Woman's image?

Artist Harry G. Peters made these preliminary sketches of Wonder Woman for William M. Marston, the character's creator.

Marston's reply tells Peters he thinks the woman "very cute" but wants a belt to cover her bare waist and something "more like a crown" to cover her head. Why might these be necessary?

Comic book superheroes may appear to be little more than child's play, but historians can also use them to penetrate the complexities of culture, just as they do radio programs and films. In 1941 a new superhero leapt from the pages of DC comics: "Wonder Woman," the warrior-princess of a lost tribe of man-hating Amazons. She looked like a movie star, with jet-black hair, a gold tiara, and ruby-red lipstick. Rivaling the strength of Superman, she flew an invisible plane, wore bullet-deflecting bracelets, and carried a magic lasso that forced all whom it touched to tell the truth.

Wonder Woman was the brainchild of the remarkable William Moulton Marston, a free-thinking renegade psychologist who had gained earlier notoriety for inventing a "lie detector" machine meant to aid in the prosecution of criminals. As an adviser to DC Comics, Marston created a character designed to "set up a standard among children and young people of strong, free, courageous womanhood; to combat the idea that women are inferior to men." He took inspiration for his character not only from the strong female figures of Greek mythology, but also from Margaret Sanger, who, as it happened, was the aunt of Marston's long-term mistress. The birth control and women's rights advocate represented the unflinching, independent woman Marston hoped would rule the world someday.

THINKING CRITICALLY

Over 75 years later, Wonder Woman remains the most popular female superhero ever created. Why? What does the character tell us about the 1930s and 1940s? About our own day? Can you think of other superheroes who reflect their culture at the moment of their creation? How might their changes over time have mirrored broader changes in society?

Peter Marsten/DC Entertainment

soon complemented sound, which had debuted in the 1927 version of *The Jazz Singer*. Neither innovation could keep movie theaters full, though. As attendance dropped early in the Depression, big studios such as Metro-Goldwyn-Mayer (MGM) and Universal lured audiences back with films that shocked, titillated, and just plain entertained.

By the mid-1930s more than 60 percent of Americans went to the movies at least once a week. In the face of growing criticism of the content of their films, the studios began to regulate themselves to avoid federal intervention. In 1933 the Catholic Church created the Legion of Decency to monitor features. To avoid censorship and boycotts, studios prohibited the depiction of homosexuality, abortion, drug use, and sex. (Even the word *sex* was banned, as was all profanity.) Middle-class morality reigned on the screen, and most Depression movies, like radio and other instruments of popular culture, preserved traditional values of family, faith, community, and country.

In Europe the "mass aspects" of media turned radio into an instrument of politics as well as entertainment. While Hollywood produced films that affirmed popular faith in democratic government, a capitalist economy, and the success ethic, totalitarian Nazi Germany broadcast the fiery rallies and speeches of Adolf Hitler. Leaders as different as Hitler and Franklin Roosevelt could now reach broad audiences and shape a national political culture. Movies were even more powerful. In *Triumph of the Will* (1935), German director Leni Riefehstahl combined myth and symbol to depict Hitler as the savior of Germany.

"Dirty Thirties": An Ecological Disaster >>

Each year between 1932 and 1939 an average of nearly 50 dust storms, or "black blizzards," turned 1,500 square miles between the Oklahoma panhandle and western Kansas into a gigantic "Dust Bowl." Its baleful effects were felt as far north as the Dakotas and as far south as Texas. It was one of the worst ecological disasters in modern history.

Nature played its part, scorching the earth with years of drought and whipping the winds into gales. But the "dirty thirties" were mostly made by people. The semiarid lands west of the 98th meridian were not suitable for agriculture or livestock. Sixty years of intensive farming and grazing had stripped the prairie of its natural vegetation and rendered it defenseless against the elements. When the dry winds blew, they carried away a third of the Great Plains soil, sometimes taking it thousands of miles from home.

^ "Black blizzards" dwarfed the landscape and everything human in it. The drought that helped bring them about lasted from 1932 to 1936. In a single day in 1934, dust storms dumped 12 million tons of western dirt on Chicago. This automobile flees the approaching clouds on a road stretching across the Texas panhandle.
Library of Congress, Prints and Photographs Division

Some 3.5 million people abandoned or were driven off their farms in the plains. As in industrial America, the strategy in agriculture was to consolidate, control, and mechanize. Landowners and corporations forced off about half of tenants and sharecroppers as commercial farming spread into the country's heartland. Such large-scale operations were more common in California, where 10 percent of the farms grew more than 50 percent of all crops. In most Dust Bowl counties people owned less than half the land they farmed. American agriculture was transforming from a way of life into an industry, turning independent farmers into agricultural workers. And as the economy contracted, owners cut costs by cutting their labor force.

THEN&NOW

The storms that rolled across the Great Plains in the 1930s ruined crops, killed livestock, and produced one of the largest mass migrations in American history. Scientific consensus places considerable blame on human activity—too much attention to production and too little to ground cover, tree stands, and soil quality. The New Deal responded with a web of executive agencies to preserve the natural environment and conserve resources. Now the climate is changing on a global scale, and humans again bear some responsibility. In 2019, for example, the United Nations reported that within a decade, one-quarter of the Earth's population will face a water shortage. Poor water management lies among the causes. Accompanying this new ecological crisis are calls for a "Green New Deal" of large-scale government action that point the way to the future by drawing on the past.

Relief offices around the country reported a change in migrant families. Rather than Black or brown, more and more were white and native-born, typically a young married couple with one child. Long-distance migrants from Oklahoma, Arizona, and Texas usually set their sights on California. If they were like the Joad family in John Steinbeck's masterly novel *The Grapes of Wrath* (1939), they drove west along Route 66 through Arizona and New Mexico, their belongings piled high atop a rickety jalopy, heading for the West Coast and the promise of jobs picking fruit and harvesting vegetables.

More than 350,000 Oklahomans migrated to California—so many that "Okie" came to mean any Dust Bowler, even though most of Oklahoma lay outside the Dust Bowl. According to one government study, between 1935 and 1940 only a third of migrants from the Southwest to California had lived on farms before leaving. More than half had resided in cities. Like the Joads, most ended up in one California city or another.

Wherever they landed, only one in two or three migrants actually found work. The labor surplus allowed growers to cut wages to less than a third the subsistence level. Families that did not work formed wretched enclaves called "little Oklahomas." The worst were located in the fertile Imperial Valley.

Mexican Americans and Repatriation >> The

Chávez family lost their farm in Arizona in 1934. César, barely six years old at the time, remembered disjointed images of their departure: a "giant tractor" leveling the corral; the loss of his room and bed; a beat-up Chevy hauling the family west; his father promising to buy another farm. The elder Chávez could never keep his promise. Instead, he and his family "followed the crops" in California, year after year.

Moving so often, the children of migrants struggled to get an education, and with so many pickers looking for work, it was just as difficult for their parents to earn a decent living. In eight years César went to 37 schools. When they found work, his family earned less than $10 a week. His father joined strikers in the Imperial Valley in the mid-1930s, only to have the strikes crushed. "Some people put this out of their minds," said César Chávez years later. "I don't." Thirty years later he founded the United Farm Workers of America, the first union of migratory workers in the country.

A deep ambivalence had always characterized American attitudes toward Mexicans and Mexican Americans like the Chávezes, but the Great Depression turned most Anglo communities against them. Cities such as Los Angeles, fearing the burden of relief, found it cheaper to ship Mexicans home. Some migrants left voluntarily. Frustrated officials or angry neighbors drove out others. Beginning in 1931 the federal government launched a series of deportations, or **repatriations**, of Mexicans back to Mexico. These deportations included the Mexicans' American-born children, who by law were citizens of the United States.

> **repatriation** act of returning people to their nation of origin. The term often refers to the act of returning soldiers or refugees to their birth country.

During the 1930s the Latino population of the Southwest dropped by 500,000. In Chicago, the Mexican American community shrank by almost half. Staying in the United States often turned out to be as difficult as leaving, with families living from hand to mouth, as so many did even in good times. In the mid-1930s, the average income of Mexican American families in the Rio Grande valley of Texas was $506 a year.

For Americans of Mexican descent, the Great Depression deepened anxiety over identity. Were they Mexicans, as many Anglos regarded them, or were they Americans, as they regarded themselves? In the 1920s, several groups organized to assert the American identity of native-born and naturalized Mexican Americans and to pursue their civil rights. In 1929, on the eve of the Depression, many of them consolidated into the League of United Latin American Citizens (LULAC). By the early 1940s, "Flying Squadrons" of LULAC organizers had founded 80 chapters nationwide, making it the largest Mexican American civil rights association in the country.

LULAC permitted only Latinos who were U.S. citizens to join, excluding hundreds of thousands of ethnic Mexicans who nonetheless regarded the United States as their home. It pointedly conducted meetings in English. An assimilated middle class provided its leadership and stressed desegregation of public schools, voter registration, and an end to discrimination in public facilities and on juries.

African Americans in the Depression >> Hard
times were nothing new to African Americans. Slavery and the era of Jim Crow politics left a legacy of racial bigotry, discrimination, and white supremacy. "The Negro was born in depression," opined one Black man, reflecting on that history. "It only became official when it hit the white man." In the face of the Great Depression, Black unemployment surged to 50 percent by 1932, twice the national level. By 1933 several cities reported between 25 and 40 percent of their Black residents had no support except relief payments. Meanwhile, the average income for Black cotton farmers was less than $200 a year.

Like many African Americans, George Baker refused to be victimized by the Depression. Baker had moved from Georgia to Harlem in 1915. He changed his name to M. J. Divine and founded a religious movement that promised followers an afterlife of full equality. In the 1930s "Father Divine" preached economic cooperation and opened shelters, or "heavens," for regenerate "angels," Black and white. In Detroit Elijah Poole began calling himself Elijah Muhammad and in 1931 established the Black Muslims, a blend of Islamic faith and Black nationalism. He exhorted African Americans to celebrate their African heritage, to live lives of self-discipline and self-help, and to strive for a separate all-Black nation.

The Depression inflamed age-old racial prejudice that had erupted in violence and a reenergized Ku Klux Klan only a decade earlier. Lynchings tripled between 1932 and 1933. In 1932 the Supreme Court ordered a retrial in the most celebrated racial case of the decade. A year earlier, nine Black teenagers had been accused of raping two white women on a train bound for Scottsboro, Alabama. Within weeks all-white juries sentenced eight of them to death. The convictions rested on the testimony of the women, one of whom later admitted that the boys had been framed. Appeals kept the case alive for almost a decade. In the end, charges against four of the "Scottsboro boys" were dropped. The other five received substantial prison sentences.

REVIEW
What were the human costs of the Great Depression for Anglos, Latinos, and African Americans? How and why were they similar? How and why were they different?

^ "Juke joints" like this one in Belle Glade, Florida, provided a temporary haven, and sometimes living quarters, for migratory African American workers who came to drink and dance to the songs played on a jukebox.
Library of Congress, Prints and Photographs Division

THE TRAGEDY OF HERBERT HOOVER

The presidency of Herbert Hoover began with great promise. A master organizer, engineer, and business executive who had run the powerful Commerce Department for eight years was now in charge. No one seemed better equipped to run things. All too soon, the worst economic depression in the nation's history turned the bright promise of a Hoover presidency into the biggest nightmare of Hoover's life.

"I have no fears for the future of our country," the new president announced at his inauguration in March 1929. Within seven months a "depression" struck. (Hoover used the word, instead of the traditional "panic," to downplay the emergency.) Despite making more effort than any of his predecessors to restore a damaged economy and national morale, Herbert Hoover failed. Angry unemployed citizens cursed his name.

For all of Hoover's promise and innovative intelligence, he served as a transitional figure. He represented an important break from the do-nothing policies of past depression presidents and was the herald of modern, engaged presidents to come. Even so, his rigid commitment to preserving limited government and American individualism doomed his presidency and tarnished his reputation for generations.

The Failure of Relief >> By the winter of 1931–1932
the picture was bleak: aid organizations had too little money and too few resources to make headway against the Depression. Private charity dwindled to 6 percent of all relief funds.

Ethnic charities tried to stave off disaster for their own communities. Groups historically subjected to racial discrimination, such as Mexicans, Puerto Ricans, and Chinese Americans, received no help from the government and little

^ Cities provided little or no aid to those in need, as the Depression had depleted their treasuries, and many residents could not afford to pay taxes. Buildings often showed signs of wear and Depression-bred neglect. This section of tenements was located in Brockton, Massachusetts.
Library of Congress, Prints and Photographs Division

but scorn from their fellow citizens. Latinos turned for support to *mutualistas*, traditional societies that provided members with social support, life insurance, and sickness benefits. In San Francisco, the Chinese Six Companies offered food and clothing to those in need in Chinatown.

As the head of the Federation of Jewish Charities warned, private efforts were failing. The government would be "compelled, by the cruel events ahead of us, to step into the situation and bring relief on a large scale." But government was not equal to the task. In Philadelphia, for example, relief payments to a family of four totaled $5.50 a week, and this was the highest rate in the country. Some cities gave nothing to unmarried people or childless couples, no matter how impoverished they were.

Cities clamored for help from state capitals, but after a decade of extravagant spending and sloppy bookkeeping, many states were already in debt. As businesses and property values collapsed, tax bases shrank and with them state revenues. Until New York established its Temporary Emergency Relief Administration (TERA) in 1931, no state had any agency to handle the unemployed, whatever their race or ethnicity.

The Hoover Depression Program >> Beginning
in 1930 President Hoover assumed leadership in combating the Depression. He demonstrated more vigor and compassion than any other executive before him. It was a mark of his character. Orphaned at 9, he became one of Stanford University's first graduates. Before turning 40, he was the millionaire head of one of the most successful mine engineering firms in the world.

Hoover's Quaker upbringing taught him the importance of balancing private gain with public service and neighborly cooperation. After war broke out in Europe in 1914, he worked 14 hours a day without pay to save starving Belgian refugees. Marshaling resources outside of governments, he convinced private organizations and businesses to donate food, clothing, and other necessities and distributed them with efficiency and effectiveness. In his honor, Finns created a new word: to "hoover" meant to help.

When the Depression struck, Hoover was no passive figurehead. Past presidents had feared that government intercession would upset the natural workings of the economy. The sole responsibility of government, economic orthodoxy taught, was to balance its budget. A more forward-thinking Hoover understood the vicious cycle in which rising unemployment drove down consumer demand, requiring investment to stimulate the economy.

To encourage investment, Hoover set in motion an unprecedented program of government activism, but every step forward turned out to be a step too far for him. His ideological rigidity trumped simple practicality. He believed in the need for what he called "American individualism" and believed that a heavy dose of self-reliance, bolstered by Quaker neighborliness and cooperation among people and private organizations, would solve all problems. Anything more risked destroying the self-esteem, confidence, and innovation on which American success rested. Worse still, anything more enlarged government and enhanced the power of the state at a time when democratic institutions were under assault in Germany, Italy, and Japan.

Still, Hoover acted, however haltingly. At first, he rallied business leaders, who pledged to maintain employment, wages, and prices—only to back down as the economy sputtered. In 1930, he pushed a tax cut through Congress in order to put more money in people's hands and increase their purchasing power. When the cuts unbalanced the federal budget, Hoover reversed course and raised taxes. That only soaked up money that might have been spent or invested. Without consumption and capital there could be no recovery.

Equally disastrous, the president endorsed the Smoot-Hawley Tariff (1930) to protect the United States from cheap foreign goods. The tariff brought a wave of retaliation from countries abroad, which only made matters worse. World trade shrank, as did American sales overseas. Even the $1 billion Hoover spent on **public works**— more than the total spent by all his predecessors combined—did not approach the $10 billion

> **public works** government-financed construction projects, such as highways and bridges, for use by the public.

needed to employ only half the jobless. Spending such huge sums might have begun a recovery, but creating such an enormous deficit scuttled it. At the time, the entire federal budget was only $3.2 billion.

Under pressure from Congress, Hoover took his boldest action to save the banks. Between 1930 and 1932 some 5,100 banks failed as panicky depositors withdrew their funds. Without loans from sound banks for investment, capitalism really would grind to a halt. Hoover agreed to the creation of the Reconstruction Finance Corporation (RFC) in 1932 to lend money to banks. Modeled on an executive agency created during World War I, the

RFC had a capital stock of $500 million and the power to borrow four times that amount. Within three months, bank failures dropped from 70 a week to 1 every two weeks.

Critics charged that Hoover rescued banks but not people. From the start he rejected the idea of a "dole," or giveaway program, for fear it would damage the initiative of recipients, perhaps even producing a permanent underclass. The bureaucracy that would be needed to police recipients, moreover, would inevitably meddle in their private lives and bring a "train of corruption and waste."

As unemployment rose, Hoover softened his opposition to federal aid. In 1932 he allowed Congress to pass the Emergency Relief and Construction Act. It authorized the RFC to lend up to $1.5 billion for "reproductive" public works—large construction projects like toll bridges that paid for themselves. Another $300 million went to states as loans for direct payments to the unemployed. It barely mattered. Too few public works were ready to go, and too little money was ready for dispersal. When the governor of Pennsylvania requested loans to furnish the destitute with 13 cents a day for a year, the RFC sent only enough for 3 cents a day. The programs, well intentioned as they were, turned out to be wholly inadequate.

Stirrings of Discontent >> Despite unprecedented action, Hoover could not stem rising discontent. "The word revolution is heard at every hand," one writer warned in 1932. Some wondered if capitalism itself had gone bankrupt.

In 1932 anger erupted into violence. Wisconsin dairy farmers overturned tens of thousands of milk cans in a fruitless effort to create a shortage and increase prices. A 48-mile-long "Coal Caravan" of striking miners drove through southern Illinois in protest. Three thousand marchers stormed Henry Ford's plant in Dearborn, only to have Ford police turn power water hoses and guns on them. When it was over, 4 marchers lay dead and more than 20 wounded.

For all the stirrings of discontent, revolution was never a real danger. The Communist Party of the United States (CPUSA) had just 20,000 members in 1932. That was up from 6,500 only three years earlier, but hardly enough to constitute a political threat. Its support of labor, social justice, and civil rights, including an end to segregation, drew intellectuals, the working class, and some African Americans to its ranks. The CPUSA organized unions, held rallies and protests, and spearheaded the defense of the Scottsboro boys. It became the first political party to integrate white and Black members.

⌃ In the early years of the Depression, demonstrations by the unemployed, some organized by Communists and other radicals, broke out all over the country. On March 6, 1930, a Communist-led protest at Union Square in New York City turned into an ugly riot. In 1935 Communist parties, under orders from Moscow, allied with democratic and socialist groups against fascism, proclaiming in the United States that "Communism is twentieth-century Americanism."
ASSOCIATED PRESS/AP images

Deeply suspicious of its Marxist doctrine, most Americans were deaf to the party's cries for collectivism and an end to capitalism. The CPUSA's appeal grew when it adopted a cooperative approach to containing Adolf Hitler, his Nazi Party, and German expansion. After Hitler and the Nazis won control of Germany in 1933, he embarked on an aggressive policy of expansion. Two years later, the Soviet Union sought to form a "popular front" against Nazism. Russian Premier Joseph Stalin ordered Communist parties in Europe and the United States to join with liberal politicians. Party membership in the United States soared to a peak of perhaps 80,000. Disillusioned by the rigidity of party practices and the brutality of the Soviet regime, most quit by the end of the decade, Stalin's brutal purges against political rivals drove out others and splintered the party.

The Bonus Army >>

Hoover sympathized with the discontented, but as the "Bonus Army" learned in the summer of 1932, only to a point. The army, a scruffy collection of World War I veterans, was hungry and looking to cash in certificates, due in 20 years, that promised them a bonus payment for wartime service. By the time they reached Washington, D.C., in June 1932, their numbers had swelled to nearly 20,000, the largest protest in the city's history. Hoover dismissed them as a special-interest lobby and refused to see their leaders.

When the Senate blocked the bonus bill, some 2,000 marchers stayed to dramatize their plight, camping with their families and parading peaceably. Despite eviction orders, the protesters refused to leave. By the end of July, the president had had enough. He called in the U.S. Army under the command of Chief of Staff General Douglas MacArthur. MacArthur arrived with saber-brandishing cavalry, six tanks, and a column of infantry with fixed bayonets. By the time the smoke cleared the next morning, only 300 wounded veterans remained.

Though he had intended that the army only assist the police, Hoover accepted responsibility for the action. The sight of American troops assaulting unarmed and unemployed veterans soured most Americans, who now saw Hoover as unsympathetic to the plight of those in need. In Albany, New York, Governor Franklin D. Roosevelt exploded at the president's failure: "There is nothing inside the man but jelly."

The Election of 1932 >>

In 1932 Republicans stuck with Hoover and endorsed his Depression program. Democrats countered with New York governor Franklin D. Roosevelt. As a sign of change, Roosevelt broke precedent by flying to Chicago and addressing the delegates in person. "I pledge you, I pledge myself to a new deal for the American people," he told them.

Roosevelt zigged and zagged in an effort to appeal to build a national bloc of voters. One minute he called for a balanced budget, the next for costly public works and aid to the unemployed. He promised to help business, then spoke of remembering the "forgotten man" and "distributing wealth and products more equitably." His progressive record as governor was a valuable asset. For his part, Hoover denounced

⌃ In the wake of the attack on the Bonus Army, General Douglas MacArthur and his second in command, Colonel Dwight Eisenhower, surveyed the results. In a highly unusual move, MacArthur personally took charge of field operations, allegedly against Eisenhower's advice. Eisenhower would later command Allied forces in Europe during the World War II and later still, serve two terms as president. Bettmann/Getty Images

Roosevelt's New Deal as a "dangerous departure" from time-honored traditions that would destroy American values and institutions. This New Deal, he said, would "build a bureaucracy such as we have never seen in our history."

On Election Day, Roosevelt captured a thundering 58 percent of the popular vote and carried large Democratic majorities into Congress. Industrial workers in the North, poor farmers in the South and West, immigrants and big-city dwellers from every region were galvanizing into a broad new coalition. They had experienced firsthand the savage effects of the boom-and-bust business cycle, wanted change, and put their faith in Roosevelt and the Democrats. With the election of 1932, over 30 years of nearly unbroken Republican rule came to an end.

 REVIEW

What were the shortcomings of Herbert Hoover's Depression program? What actions would you have recommended? Why?

Candidate (Party)	Electoral Vote (%)	Popular Vote (%)
Franklin D. Roosevelt (Democratic)	472 (89)	22,829,501 (57)
Herbert Hoover (Republican)	59 (11)	15,760,684 (40)
Minor parties	—	1,160,615 (3)

MAP 25.1: ELECTION OF 1932

THE EARLY NEW DEAL (1933–1935)

On March 4, 1933, as the clocks struck noon, Eleanor Roosevelt wondered if it were possible to "do anything to save America now." She looked at her husband, who had just been sworn in as the thirty-second president of the United States. Franklin Roosevelt radiated confidence as he faced the crowd of over 100,000. "The only thing we have to fear is . . . fear itself," he thundered. Heeding the nation's call for "action, and action now," he promised to exercise "broad Executive power to wage a war against the emergency." The crowd cheered. Eleanor was terrified: "One has the feeling of going it blindly because we're in a tremendous stream, and none of us knows where we're going to land."

The early New Deal unfolded in the spring of 1933 with a chaotic 100-day burst of legislation. It stressed recovery through planning and cooperation with business but also aid for the unemployed and reform of the economic system. Above all, the early New Deal broke the cycle of despair. With Roosevelt in the White House, most Americans believed that they were in good hands, wherever they landed.

The Democratic Roosevelts >> From the moment they entered it in 1933, Franklin and Eleanor—the Democratic Roosevelts—transformed the White House. No more seven-course meals as Hoover had served in an effort to show that nothing was wrong. Instead, visitors got fare fit for a boardinghouse. The gesture was symbolic, but it made the president's point of ending business as usual.

Such belt-tightening was new to Franklin Roosevelt. Born of an old Dutch family in New York, he grew up rich and pampered. He idolized his Republican cousin Theodore Roosevelt and mimicked his career, except as a Democrat. Like Theodore, Franklin graduated from Harvard University (in 1904), won a seat in the New York State legislature (in 1910), secured an appointment as assistant secretary of the navy (in 1913), and ran for the vice presidency (in 1920). Then disaster struck. On vacation in the summer of 1921, Roosevelt fell ill with poliomyelitis. The disease paralyzed him from the waist down for the rest of his life.

Roosevelt emerged from the ordeal a more compassionate person. As governor of New York, he created the first state relief agency in 1931, the Temporary Emergency Relief Administration. Aid to the jobless "must be extended by Government, not as a matter of charity, but as a matter of social duty," he explained. He considered himself a progressive, but moved well beyond the cautious federal activism of most progressives. He adopted no single ideology. He cared little about economic principles. What he wanted were results. Experimentation and pragmatism became the hallmarks of the New Deal.

⌃ Franklin Roosevelt contracted polio in 1921 and remained paralyzed from the waist down for the rest of his life. Out of respect for his politically motivated wishes, photographers rarely showed him wearing heavy leg braces or sitting in a wheelchair. This photograph, snapped outside his New York City brownstone in September 1933 during his first year as president, is one of the few in which Roosevelt's braces are visible (just below the cuffs of his trousers). Note the wooden handrails constructed especially to help hold him up.
Martin McEvilly/New York Daily News/Getty Images

TWO VIEWS OF THE "FORGOTTEN MAN"

When President Franklin Roosevelt promised to help the "forgotten man" during the Great Depression, not everyone agreed that poverty-stricken Americans deserved help. Two views of forgotten men and women follow, one from an Indiana farm woman critical of any form of assistance (Document 1), the other from a reporter stressing the necessity for more aid and the danger of failing to provide it (Document 2).

DOCUMENT 1
Aid Rewards the "Shiftless"

We have always had a shiftless, never-do-well class of people whose one and only aim in life is to live without work. I have been rubbing elbows with this class for nearly sixty years and have tried to help some of the most promising and have seen others try to help them, but it can't be done. We cannot help those who will not try to help themselves and if they do try, a square deal is all they need, and by the way that is all this country needs or ever has needed, a square deal for all and then, let each paddle their own canoe, or sink. . . .

The women and children around here have had to work at the fields to help save the crops and several women fainted while at work and at the same time we couldn't go up or down the road without stumbling over some of the reliefers, moping around

carrying dirt from one side of the road to the other and back again, or else asleep. I live alone on a farm and have not raised any crops for the last two years as there was no help to be had. I am feeding the stock and have been cutting the wood to keep my home fires burning. There are several reliefers around here now who have been kicked off relief, but they refuse to work unless they can get relief hours and wages, but they are so worthless no one can efford [sic] to hire them.

As for the clearance of the real slums, it can't be done as long as their inhabitants are allowed to reproduce their kind. I would like for you to see what a family of that class can do to a decent house in a short time. Such a family moved into an almost new, neet, four-room house near here last winter. They even

cut down some of the shade trees for fuel, after they had burned everything they could pry loose. . . . I will not try to describe their filth for you would not believe me. They paid no rent while there and left between two suns [sic] owing everyone from whom they could get a nickels worth of anything. They are just a fair sample of the class of people on whom so much of our hard earned tax money is being squandered and on whom so much sympathy is being wasted. . . .

Is it any wonder the taxpayers are discouraged by all this penalizing of thrift and industry to reward shiftlessness, or that the whole country is on the brink of chaos?

"Minnie A. Hardin (Columbus, Ind.) to Mrs. F. D. Roosevelt, December 14, 1937," reprinted in Carroll, Andrew, ed., *Letters of a Nation: A Collection of Extraordinary American Letters, New York*, 1997, pp. 196–199.

DOCUMENT 2
Aid Helps the Truly Needy

One hears a good deal about "relief psychology" these days—that if it were all direct relief, with no work, thousands would never apply. No social worker out in the field would deny this. Through work the stigma has to some extent been removed from relief. Into every relief office in the country have come applicants, not for relief, but for jobs. More of them than you would perhaps believe have shaken their heads and turned away when informed that it was really relief. Without doubt there are many thousands of families on work relief in this country who would not have applied had they not been able to call it—to themselves at any rate—a "job." But when one hears the testimony of clinical doctors, school nurses, teachers, and social workers that the "marginal families"—those who haven't yet come on relief—are really worse off than those on relief, one wonders how long these people could have held out after all. . . . This from a doctor in a mental hygiene clinic in Providence, R. I.: "most people we see are not on relief, but are

starving. Many of these are white collar people and people in the skilled labor class who avoid relief, whose pride remains stronger than hunger. The result on the children is malnutrition and a neurotic condition produced by hearing and being constantly part of parental fear. The child grows obsessed with the material problems of the home and mentally shoulders them, and the nervous system cracks.". . .

. . . [A] FERA (Federal Emergency Relief Administration) investigator a few weeks ago sent this poem from a town in Ohio. It was written by an 18-year-old boy:

Prayer of Bitter Men
We are the men who ride the swaying
    freights,
We are the men whom Life has beaten
    down,
Leaving for Death nought but the final pain
Of degradation, Men who stand in line
An hour for a bowl of watered soup,
Grudgingly given, savagely received.
We are the Ishmaels, outcasts of the earth,

Who shrink before the sordidness of Life
And before the filthiness of Death.
Will there not come a great, a Man,
A radiant leader with a heavier sword
To crush to earth the enemies who crush
Those who seek food and freedom on the
    roads?
We care not if their flag be white or red,
Come, ruthless Savior, messenger of God,
Lenin or Christ, we follow Thy bright sword.

Report Summary, "Lorena Hickok to Harry Hopkins, January 1, 1935," reprinted in Lowitt, Richard and Beasley, Maurine, eds. *One Third of a Nation: Lorena Hickok Reports on the Great Depression*, Urbana: IL, 1981, pp. 351–365.

THINKING CRITICALLY

What complaints does the woman in the first letter make to the First Lady, and why does she make them? What picture emerges from the field report including the poem of the young man appended to the end of the report? How do you account for the differences between the two views?

Eleanor Roosevelt redefined what it meant to be First Lady. Never had a president's wife been so visible, so much of a crusader, so cool under fire. She was the first First Lady to hold weekly press conferences. Her column, "My Day," appeared in 135 newspapers, and her twice-weekly broadcasts made her a radio personality rivaling her husband. She became his eyes, ears, and legs, traveling 40,000 miles a year. Secret Service agents code-named her "Rover."

Eleanor believed she was only a spur to presidential action. But she was active in her own right, as a teacher and social reformer before Franklin became president and afterward as a tireless advocate of the underdog. In the White House, she pressed him to hire more women and minorities, supported antilynching and anti-poll-tax measures, when he would not, and experimental towns for homeless people. By 1939 more Americans approved of her than her husband.

Saving the Banks >> Before the election, Roosevelt had gathered a group of economic advisers called the "Brains Trust." Out of their recommendations came the early, or "first," New Deal committed to planning, intervention, and experimentation. Although Brains Trusters disagreed over the means, they agreed over ends: economic recovery, relief for the unemployed, and sweeping reform to ward off future depressions. The first step was to save the banks. By the eve of the inauguration, governors in 38 states had temporarily closed their banks to stem the withdrawal of deposits. Without a sound credit structure, there could be no recovery.

On March 5, the day after his inauguration, Roosevelt ordered every bank in the country closed for four days. He shrewdly called it a "bank holiday," lending a festive air to a serious policy decision. On March 9, the president introduced emergency banking legislation. The House passed the measure, sight unseen, and the Senate endorsed it later in the day. Roosevelt signed it that night.

Rather than nationalizing the banks as radicals wanted, the Emergency Banking Act followed the modest course of extending federal assistance to them. Sound banks would reopen immediately with government support. Troubled banks would be handed over to federal "conservators," who would guide them to solvency. In plain and simple language, Roosevelt explained what was happening in the first of his many informal "fireside chat" radio broadcasts. When banks reopened the next day, deposits exceeded withdrawals.

To guard against another stock market crash, financial reforms gave government greater authority to manage the currency and regulate stock transactions. In April 1933 Roosevelt dropped the gold standard and began experimenting with the value of the dollar to boost prices. Later that spring the Glass-Steagall Banking Act restricted speculation by banks and, more importantly, created federal insurance for bank deposits of up to $2,500. Despite Roosevelt's objections that the Federal Deposit Insurance Corporation would preserve weak banks at the expense of strong ones, fewer banks failed for the rest of the decade than had failed in more than a decade. The Securities Exchange Act (1934) established a new federal agency, the Securities and Exchange Commission (SEC), to oversee the stock market.

Relief for the Unemployed >> Saving the banks and financial markets meant little if human suffering continued. Mortgage relief for the millions who had lost their homes came eventually in 1934 with the Home Owners' Loan Act, but the more urgent need to alleviate starvation led Roosevelt to propose a bold new giveaway program almost right away. The Federal Emergency Relief Administration (FERA) opened its door in May 1933. Sitting amid unpacked boxes, gulping coffee and chain-smoking, former social worker Harry Hopkins spent $5 million in his first two hours as head of the new agency. In its two-year existence, FERA furnished more than $1 billion in grants of money and food to states, localities, and private charities.

Hopkins persuaded Roosevelt to expand relief with an innovative shift from government giveaways to a work program for the winter of 1933–1934. Paying someone "to do something socially useful," Hopkins explained, "preserves a man's morale." The Civil Works Administration (CWA) employed 4 million Americans. Alarmed at the high cost of the program, Roosevelt disbanded it in the spring of 1934. It nonetheless furnished a new weapon against unemployment and an important precedent for future aid.

Another work-relief program established in 1933 proved even more creative. The Civilian Conservation Corps (CCC) was Roosevelt's pet project. It combined his concern for conservation with compassion for young people. The CCC took unmarried 18- to 25-year-olds from relief rolls and sent them into the woods and fields to plant trees, build parks, and fight soil erosion. During its 10 years, the CCC provided 2.5 million young men with jobs, including nearly a quarter of a million African Americans serving in segregated camps. Southern field administrators ensured that many more whites than Blacks would be enrolled. Rarely were African Americans placed in supervisory positions. Their complaints of discrimination produced no changes. Chanting "where's the she, she, she," critics of the all-male program got the same snub.

New Dealers intended relief programs to last only through the crisis. But the Tennessee Valley Authority (TVA)—a massive public-works project created in 1933—made a continuing contribution to regional planning and revealed the power of federal spending to alter whole sections of the country. For a decade, planners had dreamed of transforming the flood-ridden basin of the Tennessee River, one of the poorest areas of the country. They proposed a program for regional development and social engineering. The TVA constructed a series of dams along the seven-state basin to control flooding, improve navigation, and generate cheap electric power. In cooperation with state and local officials, it also launched social programs to stamp out malaria, provide library bookmobiles, and create recreational lakes.

>> MAPPING THE PAST <<

UNEMPLOYMENT RELIEF, 1934

Under Franklin Roosevelt's New Deal, the federal government took responsibility for providing "relief" or public assistance to the unemployed for the first time. Beginning in 1934, through the new Federal Emergency Relief Administration, states received grants of food and money to distribute as they saw fit. Different states had different needs and different resources, both public and private, on which to draw. The percentage of those receiving unemployment relief differed markedly throughout the nation.

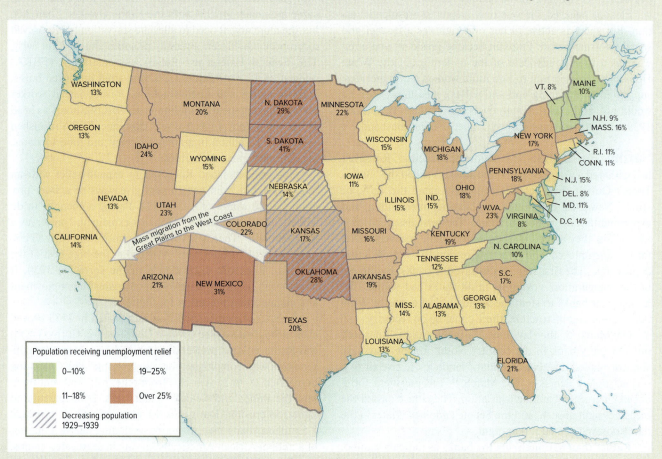

MAP READING

1. Which state had the highest percentage of its population receiving unemployment relief? Which states had the lowest?
2. Which states lost population from 1929 to 1939?
3. Which state does the map indicate received the most migrants from those states that lost population?

MAP INTERPRETATION

1. Which regions of the country were hardest hit by the Depression, based on these relief figures? Which regions seem to have been least hit?
2. What factors might have contributed to South Dakota having the highest percentage of those receiving unemployment relief and Vermont and Virginia being among the lowest?
3. Why might Americans have migrated to the West Coast, and what impact might the migrants have had on states receiving them? For those losing them?

Like many New Deal programs, the TVA produced a mixed legacy. It saved 3 million acres from erosion, multiplied the average income in the valley 10-fold, and repaid its original investment in federal taxes. Its cheap electricity helped bring down the rates of private utility companies. But the experiment in regional planning also pushed thousands of families from their land, failed to end poverty, and created an agency that decades later became one of the worst coal-burning polluters in the country.

Planning for Industrial Recovery >> Many New Dealers viewed planning, not just for specific regions but for

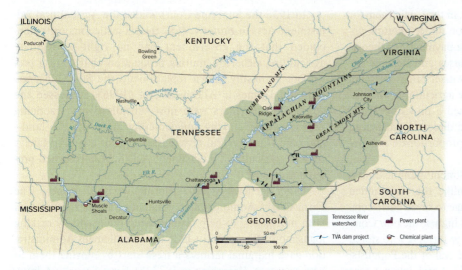

MAP 25.2: THE TENNESSEE VALLEY AUTHORITY

The Tennessee River basin encompassed parts of seven states. Rivers honeycombed the area, which received some of the heaviest rainfall in the nation. A longtime dream of Senator George Norris, the Tennessee Valley Authority, created in 1933, constructed some 20 dams and improved 5 others over the next 20 years to control chronic flooding and erosion and to produce cheap hydroelectric power and fertilizers.
Why involve the federal government in such a project?

the whole economy, as the key to recovery. If businesses planned and cooperated with one another, the ruthless competition that drove down prices, wages, and employment could be controlled and the riddle of recovery solved. Business leaders had been urging such a course since 1931, and in his fashion Hoover had tried to do as much. In June 1933, under the National Industrial Recovery Act (NIRA), Roosevelt put planning to work for industry.

The legislation created two new agencies. The Public Works Administration (PWA) was designed to boost industrial activity and consumer spending with a $3.3 billion public-works program. Employment and economic stimulation would be the immediate results, an inventory of capital improvements the long-term legacy. Harold Ickes, the prickly interior secretary who headed the PWA, built the Triborough Bridge and the Lincoln Tunnel in New York City, the port city of Brownsville, Texas, and two aircraft carriers. But he worried so much about waste and corruption that he never spent enough money quickly enough to jump-start the economy.

A second federal agency, the National Recovery Administration (NRA), aimed directly at controlling competition. Under NRA chief Hugh Johnson, representatives from government and business (and also from labor and consumer groups) drew up "codes of fair practices." Industry by industry, the codes established minimum prices, minimum wages, and maximum hours. The NRA also required business to accept key demands of labor, including union rights to organize

and bargain with management (thus ensuring that if prices jumped, so, too, might wages). And each code promised improved working conditions and outlawed practices such as child labor and sweatshops.

No business was forced to comply because New Dealers feared that government coercion might be ruled unconstitutional. The NRA relied on voluntary participation, but with more than a gentle shove from the government. A publicity campaign featuring parades, posters, and public pledges exhorted businesses to join the NRA and consumers to buy only NRA-sanctioned products. More than 2 million employers eventually signed up. In store windows and on merchandise, shiny decals with blue-eagle crests alerted customers that "We Do Our Part."

For all the hoopla, the NRA failed to bring recovery. Big businesses shaped the codes to their advantage and frequently limited production to maintain or even raise prices. Not all businesses joined, and those that did often found the codes too complicated or costly to follow. Big businesses, in control of the code-making process, fared better than small ones. With no means of enforcing its guarantees of union rights, NRA support for labor tottered. Business survived under the NRA, but without any incentives for the expansion and new investment needed to end hard times. The NRA was soon spawning little but evasion and criticism.

On May 27, 1935, the Supreme Court, in *Schechter Poultry Corp.* v. *United States,* struck down the floundering agency. The justices unanimously ruled that the NRA had exceeded federal power over commerce among the states by regulating the Schechter brothers, who did business in a single state, New York. Privately, Roosevelt was relieved to be rid of the NRA. But he and other New Dealers were plainly shaken by the grounds of the decision. Their broad view of the commerce clause to fight the Depression suffered a grave blow. Distress inside the administration only grew when Justice Benjamin Cardozo added a chilling afterthought: the NRA's code-making represented "an unconstitutional delegation of legislative power" to the executive branch. Without the ability to make rules and regulations, all the executive agencies of the New Deal might flounder.

Planning for Agriculture >> Like planning for industry, New Deal planning for agriculture relied on private interests—the farmers—to act as the principal planners. Under the Agricultural Adjustment Act of 1933, farmers limited

their own production. The government, in turn, paid them for leaving their fields fallow, while a tax on millers, cotton ginners, and other processors financed the payments. In theory, production limits would reduce surpluses and demand for scarcer commodities would rise, and with it prices. Agriculture would recover but not necessarily agricultural workers. Southern members of Congress blocked a provision in the bill to send a portion of the payments directly to displaced farmworkers and sharecroppers, a disproportionate number of them Black.

In practice, the Agricultural Adjustment Administration (AAA) did help increase prices. Unlike the code-ridden NRA, the AAA wisely confined coverage to seven basic commodities. As a way to push prices even higher, the new Commodity Credit Corporation gave loans to farmers who stored their crops rather than sold them—a revival of the Populists' old subtreasury plan (see Chapter 21). Farm income rose from $5.5 billion in 1932 to $8.7 billion in 1935.

Not all the gains were the result of government actions or free from problems. In the mid-1930s dust storms, droughts, and floods helped reduce harvests and push up prices. The AAA, moreover, failed to distribute its benefits equally. Large landowners controlled decisions over which plots would be left fallow. In the South, these decisions frequently meant cutting the acreage of tenants and sharecroppers, often Black, or forcing them out. Even when they reduced the acreage that they themselves plowed, big farmers could increase yields through intensive cultivation.

In 1936 the Supreme Court voided the Agricultural Adjustment Act. In *Butler* v. *U.S.,* the six-justice majority concluded that the government had no right to regulate agriculture, either by limiting production or by taxing processors. A hastily drawn replacement, the Soil Conservation and Domestic Allotment Act (1936), addressed the complaints. Farmers were now subsidized for practicing "conservation"—taking soil-depleting crops off the land—and paid from general revenues instead of a special tax. A second Agricultural Adjustment Act in 1938 returned production quotas.

Other agencies tried to help impoverished farmers. The Farm Credit Administration refinanced about a fifth of all farm mortgages, to help farmers keep their land by making loans more affordable. In 1935 the Resettlement Administration gave marginal farmers a fresh start by moving them to better acreage. Beginning in 1937 the Farm Security Administration furnished low-interest loans to help tenants buy a farm. There was never enough money. Fewer than 5,000 families were resettled, and less than 2 percent of tenant farmers received loans.

 REVIEW

What measures did the early New Deal take to relieve the Depression, and how successful were they?

˄ "Look in her eyes" read the caption of the photograph on the left, snapped by photojournalist Dorothea Lange in 1936. Titled *Migrant Mother,* the photo became an icon of the era, depicting the anxiety and desperation of so many Americans as well as the perseverance of 32-year-old peapicker Florence Thompson. Her worry-worn face is framed by her children as they turn away from the camera and lean on their mother for support. Other poses were less haunting, as seen in the photo on the right where one child smiles into the camera. The Farm Security Administration, a New Deal agency that commissioned the photographs, chose the more moving image to show the human costs of the Depression and to justify government programs to help those who were dispossessed.
(*left*): Library of Congress Prints and Photographs Division [LC-DIG-fsa-8b29516]; (*right*): Fotosearch/Archive Photos/Getty Images

A SECOND NEW DEAL (1935–1936)

"Boys—this is our hour," crowed the president's adviser, Harry Hopkins, in the spring of 1935. A year earlier, voters broke precedent by returning the party in power to Congress, giving the Democrats their largest majorities in decades. With the presidential election only a year away, time was short. "We've got to get everything we want," Hopkins declared, "a works program, social security, wages and hours, everything—now or never."

In 1935 politics, swept along by a torrent of protest, led to a "second hundred days" of lawmaking and a "Second New Deal." The emphasis shifted from planning and cooperation with business to greater regulation of business, broader relief, and bolder reform. A limited welfare state emerged in which the government was finally committed, at least symbolically, to guaranteeing the material well-being of Americans in need.

Dissent from the Deal >>

In 1934 a mob of 6,000 stormed the Minneapolis city hall, demanding more relief and higher pay for government jobs. In San Francisco, longshore workers walked off the job, setting off a citywide strike. By year's end, 1.5 million workers had joined in 1,800 strikes throughout the country. Conditions were improving but not quickly enough, and across the country dissent gathered strength.

From the right, wealthy business executives and conservatives charged that Roosevelt was an enemy of private property, a radical socialist, and a dictator in the making. In August 1934 they founded the American Liberty League. Despite spending $1 million in anti–New Deal advertising, the league won little support and only helped convince the president that cooperation with business was failing.

In California, discontented voters took over the Democratic Party and turned sharply to the left by nominating novelist Upton Sinclair, a Socialist, for governor. Running to "End Poverty in California" (EPIC), Sinclair proposed that the government confiscate idle factories and land and permit the unemployed to use them to produce for their own use. Republicans mounted a no-holds-barred counterattack, including fake newsreels depicting Sinclair as a Bolshevik, atheist, and free-lover. He lost the election, but won nearly a million votes.

Huey P. Long, a flamboyant senator from Louisiana, had ridden to power on a wave of rural discontent against banks, corporations, and political machines. As governor of Louisiana, he pushed through reforms regulating utilities, building roads and schools, and even distributing free schoolbooks. Opponents labeled him "dictator"; most Louisianans simply called him the "Kingfish." Breaking with Roosevelt in 1933, Long pledged to bring about recovery by making "every man a king." "Share Our Wealth" was a drastic but simple plan: the government would limit the size of all fortunes and confiscate the rest. Every family would receive an annual income of $2,500 and an estate of $5,000, enough to buy a house, an automobile, and a radio, over which Long had already built a national following.

By 1935, one year after its founding, Long's Share Our Wealth organization boasted 27,000 clubs with files containing nearly 8 million names. Democratic National Committee members shuddered at polls showing that the Kingfish might capture up to 4 million votes in 1936, enough to put a Republican in the White House. Late in 1935, in the corridors of the Louisiana Capitol, a disgruntled constituent whose family had been wronged by the Long political machine ended the threat by assassinating him.

Father Charles Coughlin was Long's urban counterpart. Where Long explained the Depression as the result of bloated fortunes, Coughlin blamed the banks. In weekly broadcasts from the Shrine of the Little Flower in suburban Detroit, the "Radio Priest" told his working-class, largely Catholic audience about the international bankers who had toppled the world economy by manipulating gold-backed currencies. The anti-Semitic tropes of international monetary conspiracies on which he based his message rippled just beneath its surface.

Coughlin promised to end the Depression with simple strokes: nationalizing banks, inflating the currency with silver, spreading work. (None would have succeeded, because each would have dampened investment, the key to recovery.) Across the urban North, 30 to 40 million Americans—the largest audience in the world—huddled around their radios to listen. In 1934 Coughlin organized the National Union for Social Justice to pressure both parties. As the election of 1936 approached, the union loomed on the political horizon, and Coughlin edged closer to the outright anti-Semitism that characterized his later attacks on money and banking.

A less ominous challenge came from Dr. Francis Townsend. The 67-year-old physician had recently retired in California from the public health service. Moved by the plight of older Americans without pension plans or medical insurance, Townsend set up Old Age Revolving Pensions, Ltd., in 1934. He proposed to have the government pay $200 a month to those 60 years or older who quit their jobs and spent the money within 30 days. By 1936, Townsend clubs counted 3.5 million members, most of them small-business owners and farmers at or beyond retirement age.

For all their differences, Sinclair, Long, Coughlin, Townsend, and other critics struck similar chords. The solutions they proposed were simplistic and unworkable, but the problems they addressed were real and serious: a maldistribution of goods and wealth, inadequacies in the money supply, the plight of older people. They attacked the growing control of corporations, banks, and government over individuals and communities. And they created mass political movements based on social as well as economic dissatisfaction.

The Second Hundred Days >>

By the spring of 1935, Congress joined the forces of discontent in pushing

Roosevelt to more action. With Democrats accounting for more than two-thirds of both houses, they were prepared to extend the New Deal. A "second hundred days" produced a burst of legislation that moved the New Deal toward Roosevelt's ultimate destination—"a little to the left of center." That elusive spot was where government could soften the impact of industrialism, protect people in need, and compensate for the boom-and-bust business cycle without sacrificing basic freedoms.

To help the many Americans who were still jobless, Roosevelt proposed the Emergency Relief Appropriation Act of 1935, with a record $4.8 billion for relief and employment. It was the largest peacetime appropriation to that date. Some of the money went to the new National Youth Administration (NYA) for more than 4.5 million jobs for young people. The lion's share went to the new Works Progress Administration (WPA), where Harry Hopkins mounted the largest work-relief program in history.

Before its end in 1943, the Works Progress Administration employed at least 8.5 million people. Constrained from competing with private industry and committed to spending 80 percent of his budget on wages, Hopkins showed remarkable ingenuity. WPA workers taught women to sew in West Virginia and psychiatric patients to draw in Cincinnati. They built the Griffith Observatory in California, and erected the spectacular Timberline Lodge, near the peak of Mount Hood in Oregon, log by log.

The ambitious Social Security Act, passed in 1935, sought to help those who could not help themselves: the aged poor, the infirm, and dependent children. This commitment to the destitute laid the groundwork for the modern welfare state. But Social Security also acted as an economic stabilizer by putting money in people's hands when they needed it most. It furnished pensions for retirees and insurance for those who lost their jobs. A payroll tax on both employer and employee underwrote pensions after age 65, while an employer-financed system of insurance made possible government payments to unemployed workers.

Social Security marked a historic reversal in American political values. A new social contract between the government and its citizens replaced the gospel of self-help and the older policies of laissez faire. At last government acknowledged a broad responsibility to protect social and economic rights. The welfare state, foreshadowed in the aid given veterans and their families after the Civil War, was institutionalized, though its coverage was limited. To win the votes of southern members of Congress hostile to African Americans, the legislation excluded farmworkers and domestic servants, doubtless among the neediest Americans but often Black and disproportionately southern.

Roosevelt had hoped for social insurance that would cover Americans "from cradle to grave." Congress whittled down his plan to far more conservative dimensions, but its labor legislation pushed the president well beyond his goal of providing paternalistic aid for workers. Pension plans and unemployment insurance were what Roosevelt had in

△ Social Security poster, 1935.
Library of Congress, Prints and Photographs Division

mind. New York senator Robert Wagner, the son of a janitor, saw things differently. He wanted workers to fight their own battles.

When the Supreme Court declared the NRA unconstitutional in 1935, Wagner introduced what became the National Labor Relations Act. So important had labor support become to Roosevelt that the president gave the bill his belated blessing. The "Wagner Act" created a National Labor Relations Board (NLRB) to supervise the election of unions and ensure union rights to bargain. Most vitally, the NLRB had the power to enforce these policies. By 1941 the number of unionized workers had doubled, but not among disproportionately Black and Latino agricultural workers. Southerners again succeeded in excluding them from coverage

Roosevelt responded to the growing hostility of business by turning against the wealthy and powerful in 1935. The popularity of Long's tirades against the rich and Coughlin's attacks on banks sharpened his attack. The Revenue Act of 1935 (called the "Wealth Tax Act") threatened to "soak the rich." By the time it worked its way through Congress, however, it levied only moderate taxes on high incomes and inheritances. The Banking Act of 1935 centralized authority over the money market in the Board of Governors of the Federal Reserve System. Controlling the money supply and interest rates, as the Board did, increased the government's ability to compensate for swings in the economy. The Public Utilities Holding Company Act (1935) limited the size of utility empires. Long the target of progressive reformers, the giant holding companies produced nothing but higher profits for speculators and higher prices for consumers. Diluted like the wealth tax, the utility law was still a political victory for New Dealers.

The Election of 1936 >>
In June 1936 Roosevelt traveled to Philadelphia to accept the Democratic nomination for a second term as president. "This generation of Americans has a rendezvous with destiny," he told a crowd of 100,000. Whatever destiny had in store for his generation, Roosevelt knew that the coming election would turn on a single issue: "It's myself."

Roosevelt ignored his Republican opponent, Governor Alfred Landon of Kansas. Despite a bulging campaign chest of $14 million, Landon lacked luster as well as issues. He favored the regulation of business, a balanced budget, and much of the New Deal. For his part Roosevelt turned the election into a contest between haves and have-nots. The forces of "organized money are unanimous in their hate for me," he told a roaring crowd at New York's Madison Square Garden, "and I welcome their hatred."

The strategy deflated Republicans, discredited conservatives, and stole the thunder of the newly formed Union Party of Townsendites, Coughlinites, and old Long supporters. The election returns shocked even experienced observers. Roosevelt won the largest Electoral College victory ever—523 to 8—and a whopping 60.8 percent of the popular vote. The margin of victory came from those at the bottom of the economic ladder, grateful for help furnished by the New Deal.

A dramatic political realignment was now clearly in place, as important as the Republican rise to power in 1896. The "Roosevelt coalition" rested on three pillars: traditional Democratic support in the South; citizens of the big cities, particularly ethnics and African Americans; and labor, both organized and unorganized. The Democrats reigned as the new majority party for the next 30 years. The minority Republicans became the party of big business and small towns.

REVIEW

What were the differences between the "first" and "second" New Deals? Can we understand these two phases of the New Deal as part of a larger reform effort to resolve systemic problems?

THE NEW DEAL AND THE AMERICAN PEOPLE

Before 1939 farmers in the Hill Country of Texas spent their evenings in the light of 25-watt kerosene lamps. Farm wives washed eight loads of laundry a week, all by hand. Every day each woman hauled home 200 gallons—about 1,500 pounds—of water from a nearby well. Farms had no milking machines, no washers, no automatic pumps or water heaters, no refrigerators, and no radios. The reason for this limited technology was simple: the Hill Country had no electricity.

No agency of the Roosevelt administration changed the way people lived more dramatically than the Rural Electrification Administration (REA), created in 1935. At the time less than 10 percent of American farms had electricity. Six years later 40 percent did, and by 1950, 90 percent. Electric power brought Hill Country Texans into the twentieth century.

The New Deal did not always have such a marked impact, and its overall record was mixed. But time and again it changed the lives of ordinary people as government never had before.

The New Deal and Western Water >>
In September 1936 President Roosevelt pushed a button in Washington, D.C., and sent electricity pulsing westward from the towering Hoover Dam in Nevada to cities as far away as Los Angeles. Begun during the Hoover administration, the dam diverted waters that irrigated 2.5 million acres, while its floodgates protected millions of people in Southern California, Nevada, and Arizona. In its water management programs, the New Deal further extended federal power, literally across the country.

The Hoover Dam was one of several multipurpose dams completed under the New Deal in the arid West. The aim was simple: to control whole river systems for regional use. Buchanan Dam on the lower Colorado River, the Bonneville and Grand Coulee Dams on the Columbia, and many smaller versions curbed floods, generated cheap electricity, and developed river basins from Texas to Washington State. Beginning in 1938, the All-American Canal channeled the Colorado River to irrigate the lush Imperial Valley in California.

Environmental degradation often accompanied human intervention. The once-mighty Columbia River, its surging waters checked by dams, now flowed sedately from one human-made lake to another, without habitat for salmon. Their spawning runs were also checked. Blocked by the All-American Canal from its path to the sea, the Colorado River slowly turned salty. By 1950 its waters were unfit for drinking or even irrigation.

The Limited Reach of the New Deal >>
In the spring of 1939, the Daughters of the American Revolution

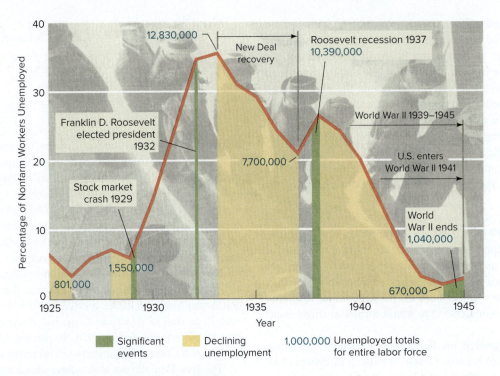

UNEMPLOYMENT, 1925–1945

Unemployment mushroomed in the wake of the stock market crash of 1929. It did not drop to 1929 levels until American entry into the World War II in 1941. The yellow bands indicate periods of declining unemployment. Note that unemployment begins to rise in 1945 as the military services begin to stand down, wartime industries begin the slow shift to peacetime production, and returning veterans begin to flood the labor force.

(Background photo) Library of Congress, Prints and Photographs Division

refused to permit the Black contralto Marian Anderson to sing at Constitution Hall in Washington, D.C. Eleanor Roosevelt quit the DAR in protest, and Interior Secretary Harold Ickes began looking for another site. On a nippy Easter Sunday, in the shadow of the Lincoln Memorial, Anderson finally stepped to the microphone and sang to a crowd of 75,000. Lincoln himself would not have missed the irony.

In 1932 most African Americans cast their ballots as they had since Reconstruction—for Republicans, the party of Abraham Lincoln and emancipation. But disenchantment with decades of broken promises was spreading, and by 1934 African Americans were voting for Democrats. "Let Jesus lead you and Roosevelt feed you," a Black preacher told his congregation on the eve of the 1936 election. When the returns were counted, three of four Black voters had cast their ballots for Roosevelt.

The New Deal accounted for this voting revolution. Sympathetic to but never a champion of African American rights, Roosevelt regarded African Americans as one of many groups whose interests he brokered. This was an improvement over recent administrations. Federal offices had been segregated since Woodrow Wilson's day, and in the 1920s Black leaders called Hoover "the man in the lily-White House." Under Roosevelt, racial integration slowly returned to government. Supporters of civil rights such as Eleanor Roosevelt and Harold Ickes brought economist Robert C. Weaver and other

African American advisers into the administration, forming a "Black Cabinet" to help design federal policy. Mary McLeod Bethune, a sharecropper's daughter and founder of Bethune-Cookman College, ran a division of the National Youth Administration.

Outside of government the Urban League continued to lobby for economic advancement, and the NAACP pressed to make lynching a federal crime. In a pattern typical of his cautious approach to civil rights, Roosevelt refused to make antilynching "must" legislation for fear of losing the support of white southern members of Congress, even though he privately favored the bill.

Seeing the unwillingness of New Dealers to confront white supremacists, African Americans acted on their own. In 1933, the Reverend John H. Johnson organized the Citizens' League for Fair Play in Harlem to persuade white merchants to hire Black clerks. After picketers blocked storefronts, hundreds of African Americans got jobs with retailers and utility companies. Racial tension over employment and housing continued to run high, and in 1935 Harlem exploded in the only race riot of the decade.

Discrimination persisted under the New Deal. Black newspapers reported hundreds of cases of NRA codes resulting in jobs lost to white workers or wages for Blacks lower than white rates of pay. Disgusted editors renamed the agency "Negroes Ruined Again." Federal efforts to promote grassroots democracy often gave control of New Deal programs to local governments, where discrimination went unchallenged. New Deal showplaces like the TVA's model town of Norris, Tennessee, and the homestead village of Arthurdale, West Virginia, excluded African Americans.

African Americans reaped benefits from the New Deal nonetheless. The WPA hired Black workers for almost 20 percent of its jobs, even though African Americans made up less than 10 percent of the population. When it was discovered that the WPA was paying Black workers less than whites, Roosevelt issued an executive order to halt the practice. Public Works administrator Ickes established the first quota system for hiring Black Americans. By 1941 the percentage of African Americans working for the government exceeded their proportion of the population.

Civil rights never became a serious aspect of the New Deal, and like African Americans, the nearly 1 million Mexican Americans in the United States were never a target of relief or of any efforts to support their rights as citizens. They received even less help than African Americans. Latino culture sometimes frustrated federal efforts. Mexican folk traditions of self-help inhibited some from seeking aid, while others remained unfamiliar with claim procedures. Still others failed to meet residency requirements. Meanwhile, low voter turnout hampered their political influence, and discrimination limited economic advancement.

In the Southwest and California, the Civilian Conservation Corps and the Works Progress Administration furnished some jobs to Latinos, though fewer of them and for less pay than whites. On Capitol Hill, Dennis Chávez of New Mexico, the only Mexican American in the Senate, channeled what funds he could into Spanish-speaking communities. The many Mexican Americans who worked the fields as migratory laborers lay outside the reach of most New Deal programs.

Tribal Rights >> The New Deal
renewed federal interest in Native Americans. Among the most disadvantaged Americans, families on reservations rarely earned more than $100 a year. Their infant mortality rate was the highest in the country, their life expectancy the shortest, and their education level the lowest. Their rate of unemployment was three times the national average.

In the 1930s Native Americans had no stronger friend in Washington than John Collier. For years he had fought as a social worker among the Puebloans to restore tribal culture. As the new commissioner of Native American affairs, he reversed the decades-old policy of assimilation and promoted tribal life. Under the Indian Reorganization Act of 1934, elders were urged to celebrate festivals, artists to work in native styles, and children to learn the old languages. A special Court of Indian Affairs removed Native Americans from the jurisdictions of the states in which they lived. Tribal governments ruled reservations. Perhaps most important, tribes regained control over Native American land. Since the Dawes Act of 1887, the land had been allotted to individual Native Americans, who were often forced by poverty to sell to whites. By the end of the 1930s, under Collier's direction, Native American landholding had increased for the first time in years.

Native Americans split over Collier's policies. The Puebloans, with a strong communal spirit and functioning communal societies, favored them. The tribes of Oklahoma and the Great Plains tended to oppose them. Individualism, the profit motive, and an unwillingness to share property with other tribe members fed resistance. So did age-old suspicion of all government programs. Some Native Americans, such as the Navajo, genuinely desired assimilation and saw tribal government as a step backward.

A New Deal for Women >> As the tides of change
washed across the country, a new deal for women was unfolding in Washington. The New Deal's welfare agencies offered unprecedented opportunity for social workers, teachers, and other women who had spent their lives helping the downtrodden. Several were friends with professional ties, and together they formed a network of activists promoting women's interests and social reform. Women received federal appointments

^ John Collier (*right*) was the Roosevelt administration's chief advocate for Native American affairs. Here he sits with Hopi chiefs Loma Haftowa and Kol Chaf Towa in a ceremony held at the new Interior Department building.
George Rinhart/Corbis Historical/Getty Images

in unprecedented numbers. They served on the consumers' advisory board of the NRA, helped administer the relief program, and won positions on the new Social Security Board.

Women became part of the Democratic Party machinery. Under the leadership of social worker Mary W. "Molly" Dewson, the Women's Division of the Democratic National Committee played a critical role in the election of 1936. Thousands of women mounted a "mouth-to-mouth" campaign and traveled door to door to drum up support for Democrats. When the ballots were tallied, women formed an important part of the new Roosevelt coalition.

Federal appointments and party politics broke new ground for women, but the New Deal largely abided by existing social standards. Gender equality, like racial equality, was never high on its agenda, and women never came close to achieving it. One-quarter of all NRA codes permitted women to be paid less than men for comparable work. WPA wages averaged $2 a day more for men than for women. Despite impressive appointments, the New Deal gave few jobs to women. When it did, they were often in gender-segregated trades such as sewing. Government employment patterns fell below even those in the private sector. Women workers fared better in the Progressive Era.

Reflecting old conceptions of reform, New Dealers placed greater emphasis on aiding and protecting women—and most of those it helped—than on employing them. The Federal Emergency Relief Administration built 17 camps for homeless women in 11 states. Social Security furnished subsidies to mothers with dependent children, and the WPA established emergency nursery schools, the government's first foray into early childhood education. Federal protection usually fell short. Social Security, for example, did not cover domestic servants, most of whom were women.

The Rise of Organized Labor >> Although women and minorities discovered the New Deal's limitations, a powerful union movement arose in the 1930s by taking full advantage of the new climate. At the outset of the Depression, barely 6 percent of the labor force belonged to unions. By the end of the decade, nearly 30 percent were members.

Though the New Deal left farmworkers outside its coverage, its promises encouraged them to act on their own. In California, where large agribusinesses employed migrant laborers to pick crops, some 37 strikes involving over 50,000 workers swept the state after Roosevelt took office. The most famous broke out in the cotton fields of the San Joaquin Valley under the auspices of the Cannery and Agricultural Workers Industrial Union (CAWIU). Most of the strikers were Mexican, supported by a complex network of families, friends, and coworkers more than by the weak CAWIU. The government finally stepped in to arbitrate a wage settlement. The strike ended but at a fraction of the pay the workers sought.

Government support was not enough to embolden the cautious American Federation of Labor (AFL), the nation's premier union. Historically bound to skilled labor and organized on the basis of crafts, the AFL paid no attention to unskilled workers, who made up most of the industrial labor force, and virtually ignored women and Black workers. The union also avoided major industries such as rubber,

∧ During the wave of agricultural strikes in California in 1933, Mexican and Mexican American laborers who had been evicted from their homes settled in camps such as this one in Corcoran. The camp held well over 3,000 people, each family providing an old tent or burlap bags for habitation. Makeshift streets were named in honor of Mexican towns and heroes. By chance, a Mexican circus, the Circo Azteca, had already set up camp in the field, and it provided nightly entertainment.
Library of Congress, Prints and Photographs Division

automobiles, and steel. They had long been hostile to organized labor and employed many unskilled workers.

In 1935 John L. Lewis of the United Mine Workers and the heads of seven other AFL unions announced the formation of the Committee for Industrial Organization (CIO) to organize industrial workers. The AFL suspended the rogue unions in 1936. The CIO, later rechristened the Congress of Industrial Organizations, turned to unskilled workers. CIO representatives succeeded in unionizing the mighty steel industry, which had clung to the "open," or nonunion, shop since 1919. The new union gave unskilled and semiskilled industrial workers a powerful voice at the bargaining table.

In other industries the rank and file did not wait. Fortified by the recent passage of the Wagner Act, a group of rubber workers in Akron, Ohio, employed a new strategy in 1936. They simply sat down on the job. Since the strikers occupied the plants, managers could not replace them with strikebreakers. Nor could the rubber companies call in the military or police without risk to their property. When the Goodyear Tire & Rubber Company laid off 70 workers, 1,400 rubber workers struck on their own. An 11-mile picket line sprang up outside the plant. Eventually, Goodyear recognized the union and accepted its demands on wages and hours.

The biggest strikes erupted in the automobile industry. A series of spontaneous strikes at General Motors plants in Atlanta, Kansas City, and Cleveland spread to Fisher Body No. 2 in Flint, Michigan, late in December 1936. Workers took over the plant while wives, friends, and fellow union members handed supplies through windows. Police tried to break up supply lines, only to be driven off by a hail of nuts, bolts, coffee mugs, and bottles.

In the wake of this "Battle of Running Bulls" (a reference to the retreating police), Michigan governor Frank Murphy called out the National Guard, not to arrest but to protect strikers. General Motors surrendered in February 1937. Less than a month later, U.S. Steel capitulated without a strike. By the end of the year every automobile manufacturer except Henry Ford had negotiated with the United Auto Workers.

Bloody violence accompanied some drives. On Memorial Day 1937, 10 strikers lost their lives when Chicago police fired on them as they marched peacefully toward the Republic Steel plant. And sit-down strikes often alienated an otherwise sympathetic middle class. (In 1939 the Supreme Court outlawed the tactic.) Yet a momentous transfer of power had taken place. Union membership swelled, and the unskilled now had powerful representation in the CIO. Women's membership in unions tripled between 1930 and 1940, and African Americans also made gains. Independent unions had become a significant part of industrial America.

"Art for the Millions" >> No agency of the New Deal touched more Americans than Federal One, the bureaucratic umbrella of the WPA's arts program. For the first time, thousands of unemployed writers, musicians, painters, actors, and photographers went on the federal payroll. Public projects—from massive murals to tiny guidebooks—would make "art for the millions."

⌃ The wives of workers at a General Motors auto plant in Flint, Michigan, march past windows broken in a battle the day before. The windows were smashed not by the strikers inside the plant but by women who had established an "Emergency Brigade." Rumors had spread that the men inside were being gassed. Women played a vital role in supporting the strikes, collecting and distributing food to strikers and their families, setting up a first-aid station, and furnishing day care. Women of the Emergency Brigade wore red tams and armbands with the initials "EB" as shown here.
(red tam): ©Walter P. Reuther Library/Wayne State University; (bottom): Bettmann/Getty Images

The Federal Writers Project (FWP) produced about a thousand publications. Its 81 state, territorial, and city guides were so popular that commercial publishers happily printed them. Interest in American history peaked during the Depression as people looked to the past for signs of resilience. The FWP collected folklore, studied ethnic groups, and recorded the reminiscences of 200 men and women freed from slavery. The Federal Music Project (FMP) employed some 15,000 out-of-work musicians. In the Federal Art Project (FAP), artists taught sculpture, painting, and carving. Watercolorists and drafters painstakingly prepared the Index of American Design with elaborate illustrations of American material culture, like skillets and cigar-store native people.

The most notable contribution of the FAP was its murals. Under the influence of Mexican muralists Diego Rivera and José Clemente Orozco, American artists covered the walls of thousands of airports, post offices, and other government buildings with wall paintings glorifying local life, history, and work. Its rare treatment of class conflict opened the FAP to charges of communist infiltration, but most of the murals stressed enduring institutions that bound Americans together: family, work, community.

The Federal Theater Project (FTP) reached the greatest number of people—some 30 million—and aroused the most controversy. *Living Newspapers,* ripped from the headlines, covered contentious subjects such as poverty and the Dust Bowl. Occasionally frank depictions of class conflict riled congressional conservatives, and beginning in 1938, the House Un-American Activities Committee investigated the FTP as "a branch of the Communistic organization." A year later Congress slashed its budget and brought government-sponsored theater to an end.

The documentary impulse to record life permeated the arts in the 1930s. Novels such as Erskine Caldwell's *Tobacco*

Make a Case

Historians rank Franklin D. Roosevelt among the three greatest presidents in American history. (Can you guess the other two?) Based only on his responses to the Great Depression, would you say Roosevelt deserves the honor? How might FDR have ranked if he had not been president during the Great Depression and World War II? What standards would you use to test presidential greatness in making your case?

Road, feature films such as John Ford's *The Grapes of Wrath,* and such federally funded documentaries as Pare Lorentz's *The River* stirred the social conscience of the country. Photographers produced a graphic record of the Great Depression. Their raw and haunting photographs turned history into both propaganda and art. New Dealers had practical motives for promoting documentary realism: they wanted to blunt criticism of New Deal relief measures by literally picturing the distress so everyone could see it.

 REVIEW

How did the New Deal help minorities and workers? Why did the New Deal fail to do more?

>> California's multiethnic workforce is captured in this detail from one of the murals that adorn Coit Tower, built in 1933 on San Francisco's Telegraph Hill and commissioned by the Public Works of Art Project of the Treasury Department. Like other American muralists, John Langley Howard drew on the work of Mexican artists such as Diego Rivera and David Alfaro Siqueiros to paint murals and frescoes with political themes. Here, Howard shows resolute workers rallying on May Day, an international labor holiday commemorating, among other things, the Haymarket Square Riot of 1886.
Spencer Grant/agefotostock/SuperStock

THE END OF THE NEW DEAL (1937–1940)

"I see one-third of a nation ill-housed, ill-clad, ill-nourished," the president lamented in his second inaugural address on January 20, 1937. Industrial output had doubled since 1932; farm income had almost quadrupled. But full recovery remained elusive. More than 7 million Americans were still out of work, and national income was only half again as large as it had been in 1933, when Roosevelt took office.

Now at the height of his popularity, with wide majorities in Congress, Roosevelt planned to expand the New Deal. Within a year, those plans floundered. The New Deal was largely over, drowned in a sea of economic and political troubles—many of them Roosevelt's own doing.

Packing the Courts >>

As Roosevelt's second term began, only the Supreme Court clouded the political horizon. A conservative majority spearheaded a new judicial activism. It rested on a narrow view of the constitutional powers of Congress and the president.

As the New Deal broadened those powers, the Supreme Court let loose a torrent of rulings declaring important parts of Roosevelt's program unconstitutional. In 1935 the Court wiped out the NRA. A year later, it voided the AAA. In *Moorehead* v. *Tipaldo* (1936) the Court ruled a New York minimum-wage law invalid because it interfered with the right of workers to negotiate a contract. A frustrated Roosevelt complained that the rulings had created a "'no-man's land,' where no government—State or Federal"—could act.

Roosevelt's frustration only grew when none of the aged justices, most of them hostile to his programs, seemed ready to resign his lifetime appointment. Among federal judges, Republicans outnumbered Democrats by more than two to one in 1933. Roosevelt intended to redress the balance with legislation that added new judges to the federal bench, including the Supreme Court. Overburdened federal courts had too many "aged or infirm" judges, he declared in February 1937. He proposed to "vitalize" the judiciary with new members. When a 70-year-old federal judge with 10 years on the bench failed to retire, the president could add another, up to 6 justices to the Supreme Court and 44 judges to the lower federal courts.

Roosevelt regarded courts as political, not sacred, institutions and had ample precedent for altering even the Supreme Court. As recently as 1869, Congress had increased its size to nine. But in the midst of the Depression-spawned crisis, most Americans clung to the courts as symbols of stability. Few accepted Roosevelt's efficiency argument, and no one on Capitol Hill—with its share of 70-year-olds—believed that seven decades of life made one too infirm to work. Worse still, the proposal split Roosevelt's own party, where many conservative Democrats abandoned him.

Suddenly, the Court reversed itself. In April, *N.L.R.B.* v. *Jones and Laughlin Steel Corporation* upheld the Wagner Act by one vote. A month later the justices sustained the Social Security Act as a legitimate exercise of the commerce power. And when Justice Willis Van Devanter, the oldest and most conservative justice, retired later that year, Roosevelt at last made his first appointment to the Supreme Court.

With Democrats deserting him, the president accepted a watered-down version of his original court bill. It completely ignored his proposal to appoint new judges. Roosevelt nonetheless claimed victory, for he had gotten what he really wanted: a sympathetic Court majority. Eventually, in an ironic twist of fate, Roosevelt ended up appointing nine Supreme Court justices.

Victory came at a price. Roosevelt had undermined the momentum of the 1936 election, along with the unity of the Democratic Party. Opponents sensed that Roosevelt could be beaten. More politically damaging, a conservative coalition of Republicans and rural Democrats had come together around the first of what would be several anti–New Deal causes.

The Demise of the Deal >>

As early as 1936 Secretary of the Treasury Henry Morgenthau had begun to plead for fiscal restraint. With productivity rising and unemployment falling, he argued that it was time to reduce spending, balance the budget, and permit business to lead the recovery. "Strip off the bandages, throw away the crutches," and let the economy "stand on its own feet," he said.

Morgenthau was preaching to the converted. Although the president had been willing to run budget deficits in the crisis, he was never comfortable with them. Still, some experts believed he was on the right track. In a startling new theory, British economist John Maynard Keynes called on government not to balance the budget but to spend its way out of depression, even if it meant running up deficits. When prosperity returned, Keynes argued, government could pay off its debts through tax increases. This deliberate policy of "countercyclical" action (spending in bad times, taxing in good) would compensate for swings in the economy.

Keynes's theory was precisely the path chosen by several industrial nations that recovered more quickly than the United States. Germany built its rapid recuperation on spending. When Adolf Hitler and his National Socialist (Nazi) Party came to power in 1933, they went on a building spree, constructing huge highways called *Autobahns* and other public works. Rebuilding the German military for war added to the deficits. Germans paid dearly in lost freedoms, but by 1936, their depression was over.

Not all nations relied on military spending. Many of them, such as Great Britain and France, had missed out on the economic boom of the 1920s, which meant that their economies were a shorter distance from pre-Depression levels. Yet spending of one kind or another helped produce recovery in country after country. In Great Britain, for example, low interest rates plus government assistance to those in need

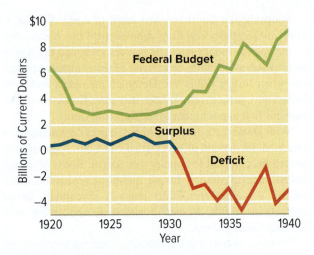

FEDERAL BUDGET AND SURPLUS/DEFICIT, 1920–1940

During the 1920s the federal government ran a modest surplus as spending dropped sharply after World War I. Deficits grew steadily as Franklin Roosevelt's New Deal spent boldly and as revenues from taxes and tariffs continued to sink. In 1937 federal spending cuts to balance the budget reduced the deficit but brought on a recession that was quickly followed by renewed federal spending and increasing deficits.

sparked a housing boom. Government subsidies to the auto industry and to companies willing to build factories in depressed areas slowed the slide. By 1937 Britain had halved unemployment.

In the United States, bucking Keynesian wisdom, Roosevelt cut spending early in 1937. Within six months, the economy sputtered. At the end of the year, unemployment stood at 10.5 million as the "Roosevelt recession" deepened. Finally, spenders convinced him to propose a $3.75 billion omnibus measure in April 1938. Facing an election, Congress happily complied, quadrupling farm subsidies, and embarking on a new shipbuilding program. The economy revived but never recovered. Keynesian economics was vindicated, though a decade passed before it became widely accepted.

With Roosevelt vulnerable, conservatives in Congress struck, trimming public housing programs and minimum-wage guarantees in the South. The president's few successes came where he could act alone, principally in a renewed attack on big business. At his urging the Justice Department opened investigations of corporate concentration. Even Congress responded by creating the Temporary National Economic Committee to examine corporate abuses and recommend revisions in the antitrust laws. These were small consolations. The president wrote Interior Secretary Ickes in August 1938, "is punch drunk from the punishment."

Vainly Roosevelt fought back in the arena of campaign politics. In the off-year elections of 1938, he tried to purge Democrats who had deserted him. The five senators he targeted for defeat all won. Republicans posted gains in the House and Senate and won 13 governorships. Democrats still held majorities in both houses, but conservatives now had the votes to block new programs. The New Deal passed into history.

The Legacy of the New Deal >> The New Deal lasted only five years, from 1933 to 1938, and it never spent enough to end the Depression. Though it pledged itself to the "forgotten" Americans, it failed to help the neediest among them: sharecroppers, tenant farmers, migrant workers. In many ways, it was quite conservative. It left capitalism intact and overturned few cultural or economic conventions. Even its reforms followed the old progressive formula of softening industrialism by strengthening the state, often with the same paternalism as progressives.

Yet for all its conservatism and continuities, the New Deal left a legacy of change. Under it, government assumed a broader role in the economy. To regulation was now added the complicated task of maintaining economic stability by compensating for swings in the business cycle. In its securities and banking regulations, unemployment insurance, and requirements for wages and hours, the New Deal provided a measure of security to workers and the elderly and stabilizers to soften future downturns.

Franklin Roosevelt modernized the presidency. He turned the White House into the heart of government. Americans looked to the president to set the public agenda, spread new ideas, initiate legislation, and assume responsibility for the nation. The power of Congress shrank, but the scope and size of government ballooned. In 1932 there were 605,000 federal employees; by 1939 there were nearly a million. The New Deal touched ordinary Americans as government never had before, making them more secure, bolstering the middle class, and forming the outlines of the new welfare state.

At a time when dictators and militarists came to power in Germany, Italy, Japan, and Russia, the New Deal strengthened democracy in America. Roosevelt acted as a political broker, responding first to one group, then to another. He embraced groups previously spurned: unions, farm organizations, ethnic minorities, women. In the 1930s the United States found a middle way, avoiding the extremes of communism and fascism. The broker state did have limits. The unorganized, whether in city slums or in sharecroppers' shacks, often found themselves ignored.

Under the New Deal the Democratic Party dominated politics. In a quiet revolution, African Americans came into the party's fold, as did workers and farmers. Political attention shifted to bread-and-butter issues. In 1932 people had argued about Prohibition and European war debts. By 1935 they were debating social security, labor relations, tax reform, public housing, and the TVA. Most important, Americans now assumed that in hard times government would come to their aid. With remarkable speed, the New Deal became a vital part of American life.

What the New Deal Did . . .

	Relief	Recovery	Reform
For the Farmer	Rural Electrification Administration (1936) Farm Security Administration (1937)	Agricultural Adjustment Act (1933)	
For the Worker		National Industrial Recovery Act (1933)	National Labor Relations Act (1935) Fair Labor Standards Act (1938)
For the Middle Class	Home Owners' Loan Act (1934)		Revenue ("Wealth Tax") Act (1935) Public Utilities Holding Company Act (1935)
For the Needy	Federal Emergency Relief Act (1933) Civilian Conservation Corps (1933) Civil Works Administration (1933) National Public Housing Act (1937) Emergency Relief Appropriation Act (1935)		
For Protection against Future Depressions			Federal Deposit Insurance Corporation (1933) Securities Exchange Act (1934) Social Security Act (1935)

✓ **REVIEW**

What did the New Deal accomplish, and what did it fail to accomplish? Was it conservative or radical? Why?

History in Global Context >> The Depression shook both the political and material pillars of democratic culture, more turbulently around the world than at home. By 1939, on the eve of World War II, the Soviet Union, Germany, and Italy were firmly under the control of dictators bent on expanding both their powers and their territory. The number of European democracies shrank from 27 to 10. A variety of dictators and military juntas, little different from the new despots of Europe, ruled Latin America. China suffered not only from invasion by Japan but from the corrupt one-party dictatorship of Chiang Kai-shek.

The New Deal attempted to combat the Depression through the methods of parliamentary democracy, but New Dealers recognized that the federal government could not do everything. "It bought us time to think," concluded Eleanor Roosevelt in 1939. Even as she spoke, a measure of doubt crept into her voice: "Is it going to be worthwhile?" With war looming, only future generations could tell.

CHAPTER SUMMARY

The Great Depression of the 1930s was the longest in the history of the nation. It forced virtually all Americans to live leaner lives and it spawned Franklin Roosevelt's New Deal.

- The Great Depression acted as a great leveler that reduced differences in income and status and left many Americans with an "invisible scar" of shame, self-doubt, and lost confidence.
  - ► Unemployment and suffering were especially acute among agricultural migrants, African Americans, Latinos, and Native Americans.
  - ► Rates of marriage and birth declined in all social classes, and many women found themselves working additional hours inside and outside the home to supplement family incomes.
  - ► Popular culture rallied to reinforce basic tenets of American life: middle-class morality, family, capitalism, and democracy.
- President Herbert Hoover represented a transition from the old, do-nothing policies of the past to the interventionist policies of the future. In the end his program of

voluntary cooperation and limited government activism failed, and in 1932 he lost the presidency to Franklin Roosevelt.

- Roosevelt's New Deal attacked the Great Depression along three broad fronts: recovery for the economy, relief for those in need, and reforms to ward off future depressions.
- The New Deal failed to achieve full recovery but did result in lasting changes:
  - ▶ The creation of economic stabilizers such as federal insurance for bank deposits, unemployment assistance, and greater control over money and banking that were designed to compensate for swings in the economy.
  - ▶ The establishment of a limited welfare state to provide minimum standards of well-being for all Americans.
  - ▶ The revitalization of the Democratic Party and the formation of a powerful new political coalition of labor, urban ethnics, women, African Americans, and the South.
  - ▶ The modernization of the presidency.

Digging Deeper

The best overall examination of the period encompassing the Great Depression and the World War II is David M. Kennedy's *Freedom from Fear: The American People in Depression and War, 1929-1945* (1999). For a comparative look at responses to the Great Depression, see John A. Garraty, *The Great Depression* (1987); and Wolfgang Schivelbusch, *Three New Deals: Reflections on Roosevelt's America, Mussolini's Italy, and Hitler's Germany, 1933-1939* (2006). Caroline Bird, *The Invisible Scar* (1966), remains one of the most sensitive treatment of the human impact of the Great Depression; but it should not be read without Studs Terkel, *Hard Times: An Oral History of the Great Depression* (1970); and Robert McElvaine, *The Great Depression: America, 1929-1941* (1984), both especially good on Depression culture and values. Glen Jeansonne's *Herbert Hoover: A Life* (2016) revises our understanding of the president as a progressive and "the most versatile American since Benjamin Franklin."

William Leuchtenburg's *Franklin D. Roosevelt and the New Deal, 1932-1940* (1963) remains the best single-volume study of the New Deal and falls within the liberal tradition of New Deal scholarship that is admiringly critical of Roosevelt's use of power. Robert Dallek's *Franklin D. Roosevelt: A Political Life* (2017) is a balanced and learned biography of the public side of Roosevelt. Stephen Lawson's *A Commonwealth of Hope: The New Deal Response to Crisis* (2006) argues that the New Deal was less a makeshift reaction to the Great Depression and more a part of a longer tradition of planning and reform. Amity Shlaes, *The Forgotten Man: A New History of the Great Depression* (2007), provides a conservative critique of the New Deal that argues that its policies actually prolonged the Great Depression. Ira Katznelson, *Fear Itself: The New Deal and the Origins of Our Time* (2013), stresses the importance of fear in shaping the New Deal's broker state. Neil Maher's *Nature's New Deal: The Civilian Conservation Corps and the Roots of the American Environmental Movement* (2009) explores the impact of the CCC on the environment and the environmental movement, while Sarah Phillips's *This Land, This Nation: Conservation, Rural America, and the New Deal* (2007) takes a broader look at New Deal environmental policies with a narrower focus on rural America. Jill Watt's *The Black Cabinet: The Untold Story of African Americans and Politics During the Age of Roosevelt* (2020) examines some of the early leaders of the civil rights movement who had Roosevelt's ear. For the global impact of the New Deal, see Kiran Klaus Patel, *The New Deal: A Global History* (2016).

Eleanor Roosevelt is analyzed in rich detail and from a frankly feminist viewpoint in Blanche Wiesen Cook, *Eleanor Roosevelt*, 3 vols. (1992-2016). For a biography of the second most powerful female New Dealer, see Kirsten Downey's *The Woman behind the New Deal: The Life and Legacy of Frances Perkins—Social Security, Unemployment Insurance, and the Minimum Wage* (2009). Susan Ware, *Beyond Suffrage: Women and the New Deal* (1981), locates a women's political network within the New Deal. Lauren Rebecca Sklaroff's *Black Culture and the New Deal: The Quest for Civil Rights in the Roosevelt Era* (2009) looks at the New Deal's support for writers, artists, and intellectuals. The culture and politics of workingmen and workingwomen during the Great Depression are the subject of Lisabeth Cohen, *Making a New Deal: Industrial Workers in Chicago, 1919-1939* (1990). In Jill Lepore's *The Secret History of Wonder Woman* (2015), the most popular superheroine of all time becomes part of the women's movement. Food, increasingly a focus of historical scholarship, is the subject of Jane Ziegelman and Andrew Coe's *A Square Meal: A Culinary History of the Great Depression* (2016).

26 The United States's Rise to Globalism

1927–1945

Americans reacted to the destruction of the Japanese attack on Pearl Harbor with shock and near panic. Franklin Roosevelt stirred that frightened nation when he called December 7 "a day that will live in infamy." The declaration of war on Japan and, soon after, its axis allies Germany and Italy, truly united Americans in a crusade that lasted almost four bloody years.

Mary Evans/Media Drum Images/age fotostock

>> An American Story
PEARL HARBOR

John Garcia, a native Hawaiian and a worker at the Pearl Harbor Navy Yard in Honolulu, planned a lazy day for December 7, 1941. By the time his grandmother woke him that morning at eight, he had already missed the worst of the attack. "The Japanese are bombing Pearl Harbor," he recalled her yelling at him. John responded with disbelief. "I said, 'They're just practicing.'" "No," his grandmother replied. It was real. He catapulted his huge frame from the bed, ran to

the front porch, hopped on his motorcycle, and sped to the harbor.

"It was a mess," Garcia remembered. The USS *Shaw* was in flames. The battleship *Pennsylvania* had a bomb nesting one deck above the powder and ammunition and was about to blow. When ordered to put out its fires, he told the navy officer, "There ain't no way I'm gonna go down there." Instead, he spent the rest of the day pulling bodies from the water. Surveying the wreckage the next morning, he noted that the battleship *Arizona* "was a total washout." So was the *West Virginia*. The *Oklahoma* had "turned turtle, totally upside down." It took two weeks to get all the fires out.

The war spreading around the world had, until December 7, spared the United States. After the Pearl Harbor attack, panic spread up and down the West Coast. Crowds in Los Angeles turned trigger-happy, shooting out street lights. A police officer heard "sirens going off, aircraft guns firing." "Here we are in the middle of the night," he said, "there was no enemy in sight, but somebody thought they saw the enemy." In January 1942 worried officials moved the Rose Bowl from Pasadena, California, to Durham, North Carolina. Though overheated, their fears were not entirely imaginary. Japanese submarines shelled Santa Barbara, California, and Fort Stearns in Oregon. Hot-air balloons carrying fire bombs caused several deaths.

Although the Japanese never mounted a serious threat to the mainland, in a world with long-range bombers and submarines, no place seemed safe. This was global war, the first of its kind. Arrayed against the Axis powers of Germany, Italy, and Japan were the Allies: Great Britain, the Soviet Union, the United States, China, and the Free French. Their armies fought from the Arctic to the southwestern Pacific, in the great cities of Europe and Asia and the small villages of North Africa and Indochina, in malarial jungles and scorching deserts, on six continents and across four oceans. Perhaps as many as 100 million people took up arms; some 40 to 50 million lost their lives.

Tragedy on such a scale taught that generation of Americans that they could no longer isolate themselves from any part of the world, no matter how remote. Manchuria, Ethiopia, and Poland had once seemed far away, yet the road to war had led from those distant places to the United States. Retreat into isolation had not cured the worldwide depression or preserved the peace. As it waged a global war, the United States began to assume far wider responsibility for managing the world's geopolitical and economic systems. <<

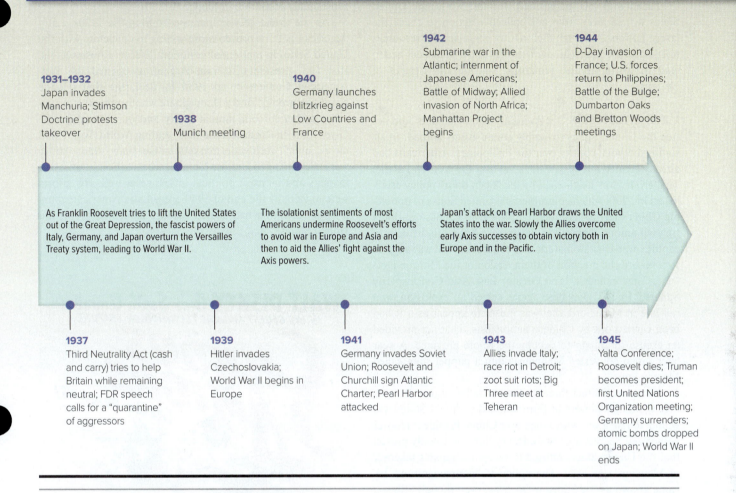

1931–1932
Japan invades Manchuria; Stimson Doctrine protests takeover

1938
Munich meeting

1940
Germany launches blitzkrieg against Low Countries and France

1942
Submarine war in the Atlantic; internment of Japanese Americans; Battle of Midway; Allied invasion of North Africa; Manhattan Project begins

1944
D-Day invasion of France; U.S. forces return to Philippines; Battle of the Bulge; Dumbarton Oaks and Bretton Woods meetings

As Franklin Roosevelt tries to lift the United States out of the Great Depression, the fascist powers of Italy, Germany, and Japan overturn the Versailles Treaty system, leading to World War II.

The isolationist sentiments of most Americans undermine Roosevelt's efforts to avoid war in Europe and Asia and then to aid the Allies' fight against the Axis powers.

Japan's attack on Pearl Harbor draws the United States into the war. Slowly the Allies overcome early Axis successes to obtain victory both in Europe and in the Pacific.

1937
Third Neutrality Act (cash and carry) tries to help Britain while remaining neutral; FDR speech calls for a "quarantine" of aggressors

1939
Hitler invades Czechoslovakia; World War II begins in Europe

1941
Germany invades Soviet Union; Roosevelt and Churchill sign Atlantic Charter; Pearl Harbor attacked

1943
Allies invade Italy; race riot in Detroit; zoot suit riots; Big Three meet at Teheran

1945
Yalta Conference; Roosevelt dies; Truman becomes president; first United Nations Organization meeting; Germany surrenders; atomic bombs dropped on Japan; World War II ends

THE UNITED STATES IN A TROUBLED WORLD

In the aftermath of World War I, many of the victorious as well as the defeated nations resented the peace terms adopted at Versailles. Their efforts to overturn the Versailles system sowed the seeds for World War II. Over the next two decades Germany, the Soviet Union, Italy, Poland, and Japan all sought to achieve on their own what Allied leaders had denied them during the negotiations. War debt payments imposed on Germany at Versailles shackled its economy. The German struggle to recover during the Great Depression imposed a burden on all of Europe. In central and eastern Europe, rivalry among fascists, communists, and other political factions led to frequent violence and instability.

Fascists exploited this instability to undermine democratic governments. Their movement had its roots in Italy, where nationalists under Benito Mussolini gained power in the 1920s. Il Duce, as he was known—"The Leader"— proclaimed that the nation was an organic community in which individuals must sacrifice their wants to the needs of the state. War, fascists believed, kept the nation strong and served the collective interest. Adolf Hitler and his Nazis (the National Socialist German Workers' Party) went further when they assumed control of Germany in 1933. They put in place a totalitarian government, embraced racism (especially anti-Semitism) and homophobia, and pursued a policy of territorial expansion to obtain *Lebensraum* (living space). Japanese fascists erected a militarist state whose leaders were bent on armed conquest and gaining access to raw materials. As political movements of the right, extreme conservatives— whether fascist, national socialist, or militarist—in all three nations preached notions of racial purity. They violently opposed communism with its abolition of private property and its ideal of a classless, collectivist society. They attacked communist and labor parties at home, and abroad they sought to destroy the Soviet Union's worker-state.

Faced with this increasingly unstable world, the United States turned away from any collective action to check the fascist powers. Although their nation possessed the resources to at least ease international tensions, Americans declined to lead in world affairs, remaining outside the League of Nations.

Pacific Interests >> Avoiding "entanglements" did not free the United States to simply ignore events abroad. In assuming colonial control over the Philippines, Americans had already created a rivalry with Japan over the western Pacific. That rivalry was heightened by the "open door" policy established in 1900, which committed the United States to upholding China's territorial integrity. With rival Chinese warlords fighting among themselves, Japan seized the opportunity to capture overseas raw materials and markets. That was a major step toward the creation of their version of the Monroe Doctrine. They called it "The Greater East Asia Co-Prosperity Sphere." In 1931 Japanese agents staged an explosion on a rail line in Manchuria that was meant to appear as if it had been carried out by Chinese nationalists. That act provided an excuse for Japan to occupy the whole province. A year later Japan converted Manchuria into a puppet state called Manchukuo.

Here was a direct threat to the Versailles system. But neither the major powers in Europe nor the United States was willing to risk a war with Japan over China. President Hoover authorized Secretary of State Henry Stimson to only protest that the United States refused to recognize Japan's takeover of Manchuria as legal. The policy of "nonrecognition" became known as the Stimson Doctrine, even though Stimson himself doubted its worth. He was right to be skeptical. Three weeks later Japan's imperial navy shelled the port city of Shanghai, as Japan used force to expand its position in China.

Becoming a Good Neighbor >> Growing tensions in Asia and Europe gave the United States an incentive to improve relations with nations closer to home. By the late 1920s, the United States had intervened militarily in Latin America so often that heavy-handed "Yanqui diplomacy" became notorious. Slowly, however, American administrations began to practice more restraint. In 1927, when Mexico confiscated American-owned properties, President Coolidge sent an ambassador, rather than the marines, to settle the dispute. In 1933, when critics compared the American position in Nicaragua to Japan's in Manchuria, Secretary Stimson ordered U.S. troops to withdraw. In such gestures lay the roots of a "Good Neighbor" policy.

Franklin Roosevelt embraced the good neighbor idea. At the seventh Pan-American Conference in 1933, his administration accepted a resolution denying any country "the right to intervene in the internal or external affairs of another." The following year he negotiated a treaty with Cuba that renounced the American right to intervene set forth under the Platt Amendment of 1902. Henceforth the United States would replace direct military presence with indirect (but still substantial) economic influence.

As the threat of war increased during the 1930s, Latin American nations proved more willing to cooperate with the United States in matters of common defense. Roosevelt—the first U.S. president to visit Argentina—opened the Pan-American Conference in 1936 by declaring that outside aggressors would "find a Hemisphere wholly prepared to consult together for our mutual safety and our mutual good." Given that the peace settlement ending World War I had closed many worldwide markets to Germany, Adolf Hitler was campaigning to increase German access to South American markets and increase political influence as well. His efforts were in vain: by the end of 1940 every Latin American country but Argentina had signed defense agreements with the United States.

˄ As war broke out in Europe, Roosevelt's Good Neighbor policy became even more important in cementing alliances in South America. To that end the State Department commissioned a good-will tour that sent movie studio head Walt Disney to several Latin American nations, some of whom had friendly relations with Nazi Germany. The end result was a documentary of the trip, *Saludos Amigos*, interspersed with animated films in which the popular Donald Duck created mayhem with a new Latin animated character, Joe Carioca, "the Brazilian Jitterbird."
Everett Collection, Inc/Alamy Stock Photo

The Quest for Neutrality >> During the 1920s Benito Mussolini appealed to Italian nationalism and fears of communism to gain power in Italy. Spinning his dreams of a new Roman empire, Mussolini embodied the rising force of fascism. His *Fasci di Combattimento,* or fascists, used terrorism and murder to create an "all-embracing" single-party state outside which "no human or spiritual values can exist, let alone be desirable." Italian fascists rejected the liberal belief in political parties in favor of a glorified nation-state dominated by the middle class, small-business owners, and small farmers.

On March 5, 1933, one day after the inauguration of Franklin Roosevelt, the German legislature granted Adolf Hitler dictatorial powers in Germany. Riding a wave of anti-communism, fanatical patriotism, and anti-Semitism, Hitler's Nazi Party trumpeted its own fascist ideals. It pledged to unite all Germans in a Greater Third Reich that would seek *Lebensraum,* or living space to the east. A week earlier, when the League of Nations had condemned Japan for its attacks on China, the Japanese simply withdrew from the League to pursue their ambition for the Greater East Asia Co-Prosperity Sphere. The rise of fascism and militarism during the 1930s brought the world to war.

As much as Roosevelt wanted the United States to resist aggression against democracies, he found Americans reluctant to follow. "It's a terrible thing to look over your shoulder when you are trying to lead—and to find no one there," he commented during the mid-1930s. For every step the president took toward internationalism, the Great Depression forced him home again. Programs to revive the economy gained broad support; efforts to resolve crises abroad provoked opposition. The move to noninvolvement in world affairs gained in 1935 after Senator Gerald P. Nye of North Dakota held hearings on the role of bankers and munitions makers in World War I. These "**merchants of death**," as Nye's committee described them, had made enormous profits during World War I. The committee report implied, but could not prove, that business interests had steered the United States into war to save their investments. "When Americans went into the fray," declared Senator Nye, "they little thought that they were there and fighting to save the skins of American bankers who had bet too boldly on the outcome of the war and had two billions of dollars of loans to the Allies in jeopardy."

merchants of death term popularized in the 1930s to describe American bankers and arms makers whose support for the Allied cause, some historians charged, drew the United States into World War I.

Sharing Nye's fear of being dragged into foreign conflicts, many in Congress supported a proposal to prohibit the sale of arms to all belligerents. Internationalists argued that an embargo should apply only to aggressor nations. Otherwise, aggressors could strike when they were better armed than their victims. The president, internationalists suggested, should have the freedom to use an embargo selectively. Isolationists, however, had more votes. The Neutrality Act of 1935 required an impartial embargo of arms to all belligerents. The president had authority only to declare that a state of war existed, no matter who attacked first.

Neutrality failed its first test, when in October 1935 Mussolini ordered Italian forces into the North African country of Ethiopia. Against tanks and planes, Ethiopian troops fought back with spears and flintlock rifles. Roosevelt immediately invoked neutrality in hopes of depriving Italy of war goods. Unfortunately for Roosevelt, the aggressor, Italy, needed not arms but oil, steel, and copper—materials not included under the Neutrality Act. When Secretary of State Cordell Hull called for a "moral embargo" on such goods, depression-starved American businesses shipped them anyway. With no effective opposition from the League of Nations or the United States, Mussolini quickly completed his conquest. Congress tried to improve neutrality with a second Neutrality Act banning loans or credits to belligerents.

American noninvolvement also provided opportunities for Nazi dictator Adolf Hitler to push military actions. In March 1936, two weeks after Congress passed the second Neutrality Act, German troops thrust into the demilitarized area west of the Rhine River. Faced with this flagrant violation of the Treaty of Versailles, Britain and France did nothing, while the League of Nations sputtered out a worthless condemnation. Roosevelt remained aloof. The Soviet Union's lonely call for collective action fell on deaf ears, just as Hitler shrewdly expected.

Then came an attack on Spain's fledgling democracy. In July 1936 Generalissimo Francisco Franco, emboldened by Hitler's success, led a rebellion against the newly elected Spanish Popular Front government. Hitler and Mussolini sent supplies, weapons, and troops to Franco's Fascists, while the Soviet Union and Mexico aided the left-leaning government. With Americans sharply divided over whom to support, Roosevelt refused to become involved. Lacking vital support, the Spanish Republic fell to Franco in 1939.

Congress sought a way to allow American trade to continue (and thus to promote economic recovery at home) without drawing the nation into war. Under new "cash-and-carry" provisions in the Neutrality Act of 1937 belligerents could buy supplies other than munitions. But they would have to pay beforehand and carry the supplies on their own ships. If war spread, these terms favored the British, whose navy could better ensure that supplies reached Great Britain.

The policy of cash-and-carry crippled China's defense when Japanese forces pushed into its southern areas in 1937. In order to give China continued access to American goods, Roosevelt refused to invoke the Neutrality Act, which would have cut off trade with both nations. But Japan had by far the greater volume of trade with the United States. Since the president lacked the freedom to impose a selective embargo, he could only condemn Japan's aggression.

Inching toward War >> In 1937 the three aggressor nations, Germany, Japan, and Italy, signed the Anti-Comintern Pact. On its face, the pact pledged them to ally against the

↑ A company of Nazi youths parades past the Führer, Adolf Hitler (in the balcony doorway). Hitler's shrewd use of patriotic symbols, mass rallies, and marches exploited the new possibilities of mass politics.
Alan Band/Photoshot/Getty Images

became synonymous with betrayal, weakness, and surrender.

Hitler's Invasion

Hitler's Invasion >> By 1939 Hitler made little secret that he intended to recapture territory Germany had lost to Poland after World War I. What then would the Soviet Union do? If Soviet leader Joseph Stalin joined the Western powers, Hitler might be blocked. But Stalin, who coveted eastern Poland, suspected that the West hoped to turn Hitler against the Soviet Union. On August 24, 1939, Russia and Germany shocked the world when they announced a nonaggression pact. Its secret protocols freed Hitler to invade Poland without fear of Soviet opposition. In turn, Stalin could extend his western borders by bringing eastern Poland, the Baltic states (Latvia, Estonia, and Lithuania), and parts of Romania and Finland into the Soviet sphere.

On the hot Saturday of September 1, 1939, German tanks and troops surged into Poland. "It's come at last," Roosevelt sighed. "God help us all." Within days France and Britain declared war on Germany. Stalin quickly moved into eastern Poland. German and Russian tanks took just three weeks to crush the outdated Polish army and divide the country. As Hitler consolidated his hold on eastern Europe, Stalin invaded Finland.

Once spring arrived in 1940, Hitler moved to protect his sea lanes by capturing Denmark and Norway. Soon after, German Panzer (armored) divisions supported by airpower knifed through Belgium and Holland in a *blitzkrieg*—a "lightning war." The Low Countries fell in 23 days, giving the Germans a route into France. By May, a third of a million British and

Soviet Union. But the agreement created a Rome-Berlin-Tokyo axis that provoked growing fear of wider war. Roosevelt groped for some way to contain the Axis powers, delivering in October his first foreign policy speech in 14 months. Seeming to favor collective action, he called for an international "quarantine" of aggressor nations. Although most newspapers applauded his remarks, the American public remained skeptical, and Roosevelt remained cautious about matching words with deeds. When Japanese planes sank the American gunboat *Panay* on China's Yangtze River only two months later, he meekly accepted an apology for the unprovoked attack.

In Europe, the Nazi menace continued to grow as German troops marched into Austria in 1938 to forge a union or *anschluss*—in yet another violation of the Versailles treaty. Hitler then insisted that the 3.5 million ethnic Germans in the Sudetenland of Czechoslovakia be brought into the Reich. With Germany threatening to invade Czechoslovakia, the leaders of France and Britain flew to Munich in September 1938, where they struck a deal to appease Hitler. Czechoslovakia would give up the Sudetenland in return for German pledges to seek no more territory in Europe. On his return to Great Britain, British prime minister Neville Chamberlain told cheering crowds that the Munich Pact would bring "peace in our time." Six months later, in open contempt for the European democracies, Hitler took over the remainder of Czechoslovakia. **Appeasement**

appeasement policy of making concessions to an aggressor nation, as long as its demands appear reasonable, in order to avoid war.

↑ The conquest of Czechoslovakia, along with the nonaggression pact with Stalin, freed Hitler to attack Poland. The Polish military's largely antiquated equipment proved no match for the Nazi's mechanized Blitzkrieg.
World History Archive/Alamy Stock Photo

French troops had been driven back onto the Atlantic beaches of Dunkirk. Only a strenuous rescue effort, staged by the Royal Navy and a flotilla of yachts and fishing boats, managed to ferry them across the channel to Britain and safety. With the British and French routed, German forces marched to Paris.

On June 22, less than six weeks after the German invasion, France surrendered. Hitler insisted on signing the truce in the very railway car in which Germany had signed the armistice in 1918. William Shirer, an American war correspondent standing 50 yards away, watched the dictator through binoculars: "He swiftly snaps his hands on his hips, arches his shoulders, plants his feet wide apart. It is a magnificent gesture of defiance, of burning contempt for this place and all that it has stood for in the twenty-two years since it witnessed the humbling of the German Empire."

Retreat from Isolationism >> With France defeated, only Great Britain stood between Hitler and the United States. If the Nazis destroyed the British fleet, what would stop the Atlantic Ocean from becoming a gateway to the Americas? Suddenly, **isolationism** seemed dangerous. Roosevelt thus abandoned impartiality in favor of outright aid to the Allies. In May 1940 he requested funds to motorize the U.S. Army (it had only 350 tanks) and build 50,000 airplanes a year (fewer than 3,000 existed, most outmoded). Over isolationist protests, Congress adopted a bill for the first peacetime draft in history.

isolationism belief that the United States should avoid foreign entanglements, alliances, and involvement in foreign wars.

That summer thousands of German fighter planes and heavy bombers struck targets in Great Britain. In the Battle of Britain, Hitler sought to soften up the country for a German invasion. Radio reporters relayed graphic descriptions of London in flames and Royal Air Force pilots putting up a heroic defense. Such tales convinced a majority of Americans that the United States should help Britain fight the war, though few favored military involvement.

In the fall of 1940 Roosevelt easily won a third term, defeating his Republican opponent, Wendell Willkie. In doing so, the president promised voters that rather than fight, the United States would become "the great arsenal of democracy." The beleaguered British, however, could no longer pay for arms under the strict provisions of cash-and-carry. So Roosevelt proposed a scheme to "lease, lend, or otherwise dispose of" arms and supplies to countries whose defense was vital to the United States. That meant sending supplies to Britain on the dubious premise that they would be returned when the war ended. Roosevelt likened "lend-lease" to lending a garden hose to a neighbor whose house is on fire. Isolationist senator Robert Taft thought a comparison to chewing gum more apt. After a neighbor has used it, "you don't want it back." Still, in March 1941 Congress easily passed the Lend-Lease Act.

Step by step, Roosevelt led the United States to the verge of war with the Nazis. Then in June 1941, Hitler, as audacious as ever, broke his pact with the Russians and launched a surprise invasion. The Allies expected a swift collapse, but when Russian troops mounted a heroic resistance, Roosevelt extended lend-lease to the Soviet Union.

That August Roosevelt secretly met with the new British prime minister, Winston Churchill, on warships off the coast of Newfoundland. Almost every day since Britain and Germany had gone to war, the two leaders had exchanged phone calls, letters, or cables. Now Roosevelt and Churchill drew up the Atlantic Charter, a statement of principles that the two nations held in common. The charter condemned "Nazi tyranny." Roosevelt also proposed, and Churchill acknowledged, what he called the "Four Freedoms": freedom of speech and expression, freedom of worship, freedom from want, and freedom from fear. In that spirit, the Atlantic Charter became an unofficial statement of war aims. Yet despite Roosevelt's increasing involvement, 8 of 10 Americans still opposed entering the war. Few in the United States suspected that an attack by Japan, not Germany, would bring a unified America into the battle.

>> During World War II, President Franklin Roosevelt and British prime minister Winston Churchill developed the closest relationship ever between an American president and the head of another government. These distant cousins shared a sense of the continuities of Anglo-American culture and of the global strategy for pursuing the war to a successful end.
Universal Images Group/Getty Images

Disaster in the Pacific >> Preoccupied by the fear of German victory in Europe, Roosevelt sought to avoid a showdown with Japan. The navy, the president told his cabinet, had "not got enough ships to go round, and every little episode in the Pacific means fewer ships in the Atlantic." But precisely because American and European attention lay elsewhere, Japan was emboldened to expand militarily into Southeast Asia. By the summer of 1941 Japanese forces controlled the Chinese coast and all major cities. When its army marched into French Indochina (present-day Vietnam) in July, Japan stood ready to conquer all of the Southeast Asian peninsula and the Dutch East Indies. Control of East Indian oil would free Japan from its dependence on the United States.

That aggression forced Roosevelt to act. He embargoed trade, froze Japanese assets in American banks, and barred shipments of vital scrap iron and petroleum. Japanese leaders indicated a willingness to negotiate with the United States, but diplomats from both sides were only going through the motions. Japan demanded that its conquests be recognized; the United States insisted that Japan withdraw from China and renounce the Tripartite Pact with Germany and Italy. As negotiations sputtered on, the Japanese secretly prepared to attack American positions in Guam, the Philippines, and Hawai'i.

In late November American intelligence located, and then lost, a Japanese fleet as it left Japan. Observing strict radio silence, the six carriers and their escorts steamed across the North Pacific. On Sunday morning, December 7, 1941, the first wave of Japanese planes roared down on the American ships lying at anchor in Pearl Harbor. For more than an hour the Japanese pounded the ships and nearby airfields. "We were flabbergasted by the devastation," a sailor wrote. Altogether 19 ships were sunk or battered. Practically all the 200 American aircraft were damaged or destroyed. Only the aircraft carriers, sent to reinforce Midway and Wake Island, escaped the worst naval defeat in American history.

In Washington, Secretary of War Henry Stimson could not believe the news relayed to his office. "My God! This can't be true, this must mean the Philippines." Later that day the Japanese did attack the Philippines, along with Guam, Midway, and British forces in Hong Kong and the Malay Peninsula. On December 8, Franklin Roosevelt told a stunned nation that "yesterday, December 7, 1941" was "a date which will live in infamy." America, the "reluctant belligerent," joined the battle at last. Three days later Hitler declared war on the "half Judaized and the other half Negrified" people of the United States; Italy quickly followed suit.

✓ **REVIEW**

Identify at least three major events that pushed the United States to intervene in World War II.

A GLOBAL WAR

British prime minister Winston Churchill greeted the news of Pearl Harbor with shock but also with relief. Great Britain would no longer stand alone in Europe and the Pacific. "We have won the war," he thought, and that night he slept "the sleep of the saved and thankful."

As Churchill recognized, only with the Americans fully committed could the Allies win the war. Now they had access to the enormous material and human resources of the United States. Beyond that, the Allies needed to secure an alliance between the Anglo-American democracies and the Soviet Communist dictatorship that could win both the war and the peace to follow.

Strategies for War >> Within two weeks, Churchill was in Washington, meeting with Roosevelt to coordinate production schedules for ships, planes, and armaments. The numbers they announced were so large that some critics openly laughed—at first. A year later, combined British, Canadian, and American production boards not only met but exceeded the schedules.

Roosevelt and Churchill also planned grand strategy. Outraged by the attack on Pearl Harbor, many Americans thought Japan should be the war's primary target. But the two leaders agreed that Germany posed the greater threat. The Pacific war, they decided, would be fought as a holding action, while the Allies concentrated on Europe. In a global war, arms and resources had to be allocated carefully, for the Allies faced daunting threats on many fronts.

Gloomy Prospects >> At summer's end in 1942, the Allies faced grim prospects. The Nazis stood outside the Soviet Union's three major cities: Leningrad, Moscow, and Stalingrad. In North Africa, General Erwin Rommel, Germany's famed "Desert Fox," swept into Egypt with his Afrika Korps within striking distance of the Suez Canal—a lifeline to the resources of the British Empire. German U-boats (submarines) in the North Atlantic threatened to sever the ocean link between the United States and Britain. So deadly were these U-boat "wolfpacks" that merchant sailors developed a grim strategy about sleeping. Those on freighters carrying iron ore slept above decks, since the heavily laden ships could sink in less than a minute. On oil tankers, however, sailors closed their doors, undressed, and slept soundly. If a torpedo hit, no one would survive anyway.

In the Far East, the Japanese navy destroyed most of the Allied fleet in the western Pacific during the Battle of Java Sea. General Douglas MacArthur, commander of American forces in the Philippines, escaped to Australia in April 1942. In what appeared to be an empty pledge, he vowed, "I shall return." The ill-equipped American and Philippine troops left on Bataan and Corregidor put up a heroic but doomed struggle. By summer no significant Allied forces stood between the Japanese and India or Australia.

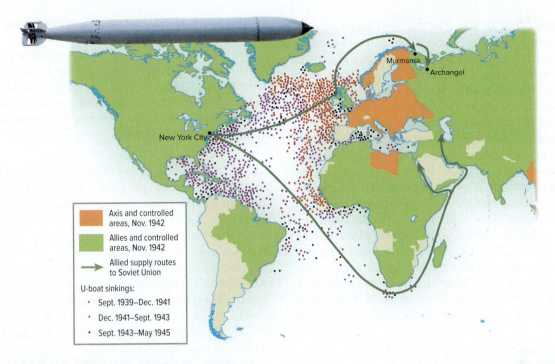

MAP 26.1: THE U-BOAT WAR

In the world's first truly global war, the need to transport troops and supplies became paramount. But as German U-boats took a heavy toll on Allied shipping, it became difficult to deliver American supplies to Europe. Avoiding the North Atlantic route forced an arduous 12,000-mile journey around Africa through Suez and to the Persian Gulf and then across Iran by land. The elimination of German submarines greatly eased the shipping problem and, as much as any single battle, ensured victory. *Why did so many U-boat sinkings occur off the north coast of South America?*
(photo): Panya_/Getty Images

Endless victories disguised fatal weaknesses within the Axis alliance. Japan and Germany never coordinated strategies. Vast armies in both China and Russia drained each other of troops and supplies. Brutal occupation policies made enemies of conquered populations, which forced Axis armies to use valuable forces to limit sabotage and move supplies. The Nazis were especially harsh. They launched a major campaign to exterminate Europe's Jews, Slavs, and Gypsies. Resistance movements grew as the victims of Axis aggression fought back.

A Grand Alliance >> The early defeats also obscured Allied strengths. Chief among these were the human resources of the Soviet Union and the productive capacity of the United States. Safe from the fighting, American farms and factories could produce enough food and munitions to supply two separate wars at once. By the end of the war American industry had turned out vast quantities of airplanes, ships, artillery pieces, tanks, and self-propelled guns, as well as 47 million tons of ammunition.

The Allies benefited, too, from exceptional leadership. The "Big Three"—Joseph Stalin, Winston Churchill, and Franklin Roosevelt—maintained a unity of purpose that

eluded Axis leaders. All three understood the global nature of the war. To a remarkable degree they set aside their many differences to pursue a common goal: the defeat of Nazi Germany. At the war's height 50 countries were among the Allies, who referred to themselves as the United Nations.

To be sure, each nation had its own needs. Russian forces faced 3.5 million Axis troops along a 1,600-mile front in eastern Europe. To ease the pressure on those troops, Stalin repeatedly called upon the Allies to open a second front in western Europe. So urgent were his demands that one Allied diplomat remarked that Stalin's foreign minister knew only four words in English: *yes, no,* and *second front.* But Churchill and Roosevelt felt compelled to turn down Stalin. After an initial surge of anger, Stalin accepted Churchill's rationale for a substitute action. British and American forces would invade North Africa, not Europe, at the end of 1942. Code-named Operation Torch, the North African campaign would bring British and American troops into direct combat with the Germans and stood an excellent chance of succeeding. Here was an example of how personal contact among the Big Three ensured Allied cooperation. The alliance sometimes bent but never broke.

The Naval War in the Pacific >> Despite the decision to defeat Germany first, the Allies' earliest successes came in the Pacific. At the Battle of Coral Sea in May 1942, planes from American aircraft carriers stopped a large Japanese invading force headed for Port Moresby in New Guinea. For the first time in history, two fleets fought without seeing each other. The age of naval aviation had arrived.

To extend Japan's defenses after an American raid on Tokyo, the Japanese military ordered the capture of Midway, a small island west of Hawai'i. The Americans, having decoded secret messages, knew the Japanese were coming. On June 3, American planes surprised the Japanese main fleet as it bore down on Midway. They sank four enemy carriers, a cruiser, and three destroyers. The Battle of Midway broke Japanese naval supremacy in the Pacific and stalled Japan's offensive. In August 1942 American forces went on the offensive, in the Solomon Islands east of New Guinea. With the landing of American marines on the island of Guadalcanal, the Allies started on the bloody road to Japan and victory.

Turning Points in Europe and Africa >> By the fall of 1942 Allied fortunes in the European war improved. In Egypt, at El Alamein, British forces under General Bernard Montgomery broke through Rommel's lines. Weeks later, the Allies launched Operation Torch, the invasion of North Africa. Under the command of General Dwight D. Eisenhower, Allied forces fought eastward through Morocco and Algeria. They were halted in February 1943 at the Kasserine Pass in Tunisia, but General George S. Patton regrouped them. An impressive string of victories followed. By May 1943 Rommel had fled from North Africa, leaving behind 300,000 German troops.

Success in North Africa provided a stirring complement to the dogged Russian stand at Stalingrad against a vast German army. Despite losses in the millions, Stalin's forces went on the offensive, moving south and west through the Ukraine toward Poland and Romania. Stalingrad destroyed the Germans' offensive might.

Those Who Fought >> "The first time I ever heard a New England accent," recalled a midwesterner, "was at Fort Benning. The southerner was an exotic creature to me. The people from the farms. The New York street smarts." Mobilizing for war brought together Americans from all regions, classes, and ethnic backgrounds. More than any other social institution, the army acted as a melting pot. It also offered educational opportunities and job skills. "I could be a technical sergeant only I haven't had enough school," reported one Navajo soldier in a letter home to New Mexico. "Make my little brother go to school even if you have to lasso him."

In waging the world's first global war the U.S. armed forces swept millions of Americans into new worlds and experiences. In 1941 the army had 1.6 million soldiers in uniform. By 1945 it had more than 7 million; the navy, 3.9 million; the army air corps, 2.3 million; and the marines, 600,000. At basic training recruits were subjected to forms of regimentation—the army haircut, foul-mouthed drill sergeants, and barracks life—they had seldom experienced in other areas of America's democratic culture.

In this war, as in most, the foot soldiers (called infantry) bore the brunt of the fighting and dying. They suffered 90 percent of the battlefield casualties. In all, almost 400,000 Americans died in combat and more than 600,000 were wounded. But service in the military did not mean constant fighting. Most battles were reasonably short, followed by long periods of waiting and preparation. The army used almost 2 million soldiers just to move supplies. Yet even during lulls in battle, the soldiers' biggest enemy, disease, stalked them: malaria, dysentery, typhus, and even plague. Weather could also make life miserable. The temperature sometimes rose to over 110 degrees Fahrenheit in the Pacific, while in winter troops in Europe struggled through cold and snow.

<< The violence of amphibious warfare, which required the landing of troops from ships to shores, was evident on the beaches of Tarawa in 1943.
National Archives and Records Administration (NWDNS-80-G-57405)

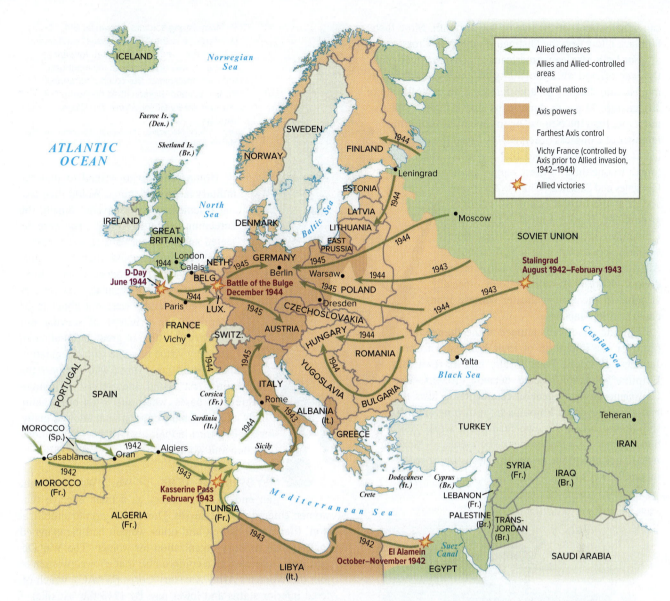

MAP 26.2: WORLD WAR II IN EUROPE AND NORTH AFRICA

Until 1944 Soviet forces carried the brunt of the war in Europe, engaging the Axis armies across a huge front. After winning North Africa the Allies turned north to knock Italy out of the war. The final key to defeating Germany was the Anglo-American invasion of western Europe (D-Day) at Normandy (see Map 26.3).

Why did the first Anglo-American ground campaigns occur in North Africa?

Minorities at War >> Minorities enlisted in unusually large numbers especially since the services offered training and opportunities unavailable in civilian life. Still, prejudice in the ranks remained high. The army was strictly segregated and generally assigned Black soldiers to noncombatant roles. The navy accepted them only as cooks and servants. At first, the air corps and the marines would not take Black recruits at all. The American Red Cross even kept "Black" and "white" blood plasma separated, as if there were a difference. (Ironically, a

Black physician, Charles Drew, had invented the process allowing plasma to be stored.)

Despite such prejudice, more than a million Black men and women served. As the war progressed, leaders of the Black community pressured the military to ease segregation and allow Black soldiers a more active role. The army did form some Black combat units, usually led by white officers, as well as the Tuskegee airmen, a Black air corps unit. By mid-1942 Black officers began to graduate from integrated officer candidate schools at the rate of 200 a month. More than 80 Black pilots won the Distinguished Flying Cross.

For both Mexican Americans and Asian Americans the war offered an opportunity to enter the American mainstream. Putting on a uniform was an essential act of citizenship. Mexican Americans had a higher enlistment rate than the population in general. A California member of Congress observed, "as I read the casualty list from my state, I find that anywhere from one-fourth to one-third of these names are names such as Gonzales and Sanchez." Chinese Americans served at the highest rate of all minority groups. As Harold Liu of New York's Chinatown recalled, "for the first time Chinese were accepted as being friends. . . . All of a sudden we became part of an American dream." Korean Americans were especially valuable in the Pacific theater because many could translate Japanese.

Filipino Americans jumped at the chance to fight for the liberation of their homeland from Japanese invaders. Their loyalty had its rewards. Filipinos who volunteered became citizens. The California attorney general reinterpreted laws that had once prevented Filipinos from owning land. Now they could buy their own farms and work jobs that had opened in war factories. The status of Mexican Americans and other Asian Americans improved in similar ways.

^ In the face of Japanese occupation of the Philippines, many Filipinos actively supported the American war effort. Valentine Untalan survived capture by the Japanese and went on to serve in the American army's elite Philippine Scouts. Like a growing number of Filipinos, he moved to the United States after the war ended.
©James West Davidson

<< Many young soldiers, known as GIs (a reference to the "General Issue" equipment soldiers received), at first looked forward to combat. "I was going to gain my manhood," recalled one soldier. But combat hardened troops. Donald Dickson titled his portrait of one war-weary GI *Too Many, Too Close, Too Long.*
Leatherneck Magazine, The National Museum of the Marine Corps

Homosexuals who wished to join the military faced a dilemma: Would their sexual orientation be discovered during the screening process? And if they were rejected and word got back to their parents or communities, would they be stigmatized? Many took that chance. Charles Rowland from Arizona recalled that he and other gay friends "were not about to be deprived the privilege of serving our country in a time of great national emergency by virtue of some stupid regulation about being gay." Those who did pass the screening test found themselves in gender-segregated bases, where life in an overwhelmingly male or female environment allowed many, for the first time in their lives, to meet like-minded gay men and women.

Women at War >> World War II brought an end to the military as a male enclave that women entered only as nurses. During the prewar mobilization, Eleanor Roosevelt and other women had campaigned for a regular military organization for women. The War Department came up with a compromise that allowed women to join the Women's Army Auxiliary Corps (WAAC), which offered inferior status and lower pay. By 1943 the "Auxiliary" had dropped out of the title: WAACs became WACs, with full status, equal ranks, and equal pay. (The navy had a similar force called the WAVEs.)

Women had reason to look on their wartime military service with a mixture of pride and resentment. Thousands served close to the battlefields, working as technicians, mechanics, radio operators, postal clerks, and secretaries. Although filling a vital need, these were largely traditional female jobs that implied a separate and inferior status. Until 1944 women were prevented by law from serving in war zones, even as noncombatants. There were women pilots, but they were restricted to shuttling planes behind the lines. At many posts, WAVEs and WACs lived behind barbed wire and could move about only in groups under armed escort.

 REVIEW

What strategy did the Big Three adopt to fight the war, and when did it begin to succeed?

^ African Americans enlisted in huge numbers during World War II. This WAC was among the first Black women to arrive in Europe.
National Archives and Records Administration (531333)

WAR PRODUCTION

After the attack on Pearl Harbor, Thomas Chinn sold his publishing business and devoted all his time to war work. Like many Chinese Americans, it was the first time he had a job outside of Chinatown. He served as a supervisor in the Army Quartermaster Market Center, which was responsible for supplying the armed forces with fresh food harvested from across California. Chinn found himself coordinating cold-storage warehouses across the entire state.

Food distribution was only one of many areas that demanded attention from the government. After Pearl Harbor, steel, aluminum, and electric power were all in short supply, creating bottlenecks in production lines. Roosevelt recognized the need for more-direct government management of the economy.

The president used a mix of compulsory and voluntary programs to guarantee an ever-increasing supply of food, munitions, and equipment. Although slow to get under way, eventually the United States worked a miracle of production that proved every bit as important to victory as any battle fought overseas. So successful was war production that civilians suffered inconvenience rather than serious deprivation.

Mobilizing for War >> Who should have priority for materials in short supply? To answer that question and relieve bottlenecks, in 1943 the president made Supreme Court justice James F. Byrnes the dictator the economy needed. His authority as director of the new Office of War Mobilization (OWM) was so great and his access to Roosevelt so direct that he became known as the "assistant president." By

assuming control over vital materials such as steel, aluminum, and copper, OWM was able to allocate them more systematically. Americans learned to do without new cars and Sunday drives. Soon, the bottlenecks disappeared.

Equally crucial, industries large and small converted their factories to turning out war matériel. The "Big Three" automakers—Ford, General Motors, and Chrysler—generated some 20 percent of all war goods, as auto factories were retooled to make tanks and planes. But small businesses also played a vital role. A manufacturer of model trains, for example, made bomb fuses.

War production also created new industrial centers, especially in the West. When production peaked in 1944, the aircraft industry had 2.1 million workers producing almost 100,000 planes. Most of the new plants were located around Los Angeles, San Diego, and Seattle. The demand for workers opened opportunities for many Asian workers who had been limited to jobs within their own ethnic communities. By 1943, 15 percent of all shipyard workers around San Francisco Bay were Chinese.

The government relied on large firms such as Ford and General Motors because they had experience with large-scale production. War contracts helped large corporations increase their dominance over the economy. Workers in companies with more than 10,000 employees amounted to just 13 percent of the workforce in 1939; by 1944 they constituted more than 30 percent. In agriculture a similar move toward bigness occurred. The number of people working on farms dropped by a fifth, yet productivity increased 30 percent, as small farms were consolidated into larger ones that relied on more machinery and artificial fertilizers to increase yields.

Productivity increased for a less tangible reason: pride in work done for a common cause. Civilians volunteered for civil defense, hospitals, and countless scrap drives. Children became "Uncle Sam's Scrappers" and "Tin-Can Colonels" as they scoured vacant lots for valuable trash. Backyard "victory" gardens added 8 million tons of food to the harvest in 1943; carpooling conserved millions of tires. As citizens put off buying new consumer goods, they helped limit inflation. Morale ran high because people believed that their contributions, big or small, helped defeat the Axis.

Science Goes to War >> New technologies transformed the way the Americans fought this global war. At the Battles of the Coral Sea and Midway, the navy used radar gunnery and airplanes to spot and sink enemy ships. Applied mathematics and game theory helped the navy find and destroy the U-boats that preyed on Allied shipping. Improved fighter planes and long-range bombers allowed Allied pilots to take the war to the Axis homelands. As a result, the distinction between civilians and soldiers blurred as the "front line" lost its meaning.

To fight inflation, the Office of Price Administration (OPA) imposed rationing on products in short supply. Consumers received coupons to trade for goods such as meat, shoes, and gasoline. The program was one of the most unpopular of the war.
©James West Davidson

Applied science was not simply about destruction. Production mattered as well. With so many farmers off at war, increased agricultural productivity became vital. In the 1930s plant geneticists had learned to cross-pollinate corn to create new varieties. These hybrids greatly increased yields per acre. Plastics offered an alternative to natural materials such as glass, rubber, wood, steel, and copper in short supply because of the war effort; for example, commercial production of polyvinyl chloride (PVC) began modestly in 1933. Given its stability and flexibility, PVC was ideal for use in construction, plumbing, packaging, and flooring. By 1941, 120 million pounds of PVC were being manufactured annually.

Some scientific advances increased health and life expectancy. Antibiotics had their first widespread application during the war. Infectious diseases such as tuberculosis, syphilis, and pneumonia—once the scourge of armies—could now be contained. Pesticides such as DDT controlled insects that spread malaria, typhus, and other deadly and debilitating diseases. With the use of these chemicals, the health of the nation improved. Life expectancy increased during the 1940s by an average of three years overall and by five years for African Americans. Infant mortality fell by a third overall.

The atomic bomb, DDT, PVC, and hybrid seeds came to represent for Americans humankind's ability to control nature. But those discoveries also posed dangers to the environment. Atomic bombs spewed radiation clouds into the atmosphere. DDT controlled insect pests but killed beneficial insects and proved harmful to wildlife. PVC production gave off carcinogens dangerous to humans. Many such substances existed nowhere in nature, and, once discarded, took ages to degrade. The widespread use of hybrid seeds created through artificial pollination greatly reduced genetic variety. Scientists anticipated some of these dangers, but at the time they had a war to win.

War Work and Prosperity

War Work and Prosperity >> Not only did war production end the Depression; it revived prosperity. Unemployment, which stood at almost 7 million in 1940, virtually disappeared by 1944. Jeff Davies, president of Hoboes of America, reported in 1942 that 2 million of his members were "off the road." Employers, eager to overcome the labor shortage, recruited workers whom they once shunned. People with hearing impairments found jobs in deafening factories; those with dwarfism became aircraft inspectors because they could crawl inside wings and other cramped spaces. By the summer of 1943, nearly 3 million children aged 12 to 17 joined the workforce. When the war ended, average income had jumped to nearly twice what it had been in 1939.

Organized Labor

Organized Labor >> Tensions between business and labor that marked the New Deal era continued into the war.

Scientists began to explore some of the basic forces of nature. Generals and admirals understood all too well that the fortunes of battle could turn on the weather. With the navy's support, the Massachusetts Institute of Technology created a professional program in meteorology. There, scientists applied the principles of physics to better understand climate patterns. Meteorology and other fields of geophysics provided the military with information on the winds, ocean currents, tides, and weather in far-flung theaters of the war. These efforts laid the foundation for future understanding of climate science.

No scientific quest did more to alter the relationship between humans and the natural world than the effort to build an atomic bomb. In 1938 German scientists discovered the process of nuclear **fission**, during which an isotope of uranium-235 is split and releases enormous energy. Leading physicists, many of them refugees from European fascism, understood that a fast fission reaction might be used to build a bomb. In 1939 Albert Einstein, Enrico Fermi, and Leo Szilard warned President Roosevelt that the Germans might be well on the way to creating such a weapon, the use of which could determine the outcome of the war.

fission splitting of a nucleus of an atom into at least two other nuclei, accompanied by the release of energy. The splitting of the nucleus of the uranium isotope U-235 or its artificial cousin, plutonium, powered the atomic bomb.

Once alerted, Roosevelt authorized an enormous research and development effort, code-named the Manhattan Project. More than 100,000 scientists, engineers, technicians, and support staff from Canada, Great Britain, and the United States worked at 39 installations to build an atomic bomb. Yet, even as they spent over $2 billion in their quest, scientists feared the Germans might succeed before they did.

In 1941 alone, more than 2 million workers walked off their jobs to protest low wages and harsh working conditions. To end labor strife Roosevelt established the War Labor Board (WLB) in 1942. Like the similar agency Woodrow Wilson had created during World War I, the new WLB had authority to impose arbitration in any labor dispute.

Despite the WLB, dissatisfied railroad workers in 1943 tied up rail lines in a wildcat strike. To break the impasse, the government seized the railroads and then granted wage increases. That same year the pugnacious John L. Lewis allowed his United Mine Workers to go on strike. "The coal miners of America are hungry," he charged. "They are ill-fed and undernourished." Roosevelt seized the mines and ran them for a time; he even considered arresting union leaders and drafting striking miners. But as Secretary of the Interior Harold Ickes noted, a "jailed miner produces no more coal than a striking miner." In the end the government negotiated a settlement that gave miners substantial new benefits.

Most Americans were less willing to forgive Lewis and his miners. A huge coal shortage along the East Coast had left homes dark and cold. "John L. Lewis—Damn your coal black soul," wrote the military newspaper *Stars and Stripes*. In reaction, Congress easily passed the Smith-Connolly Act of 1943. It gave the president more authority to seize vital war plants shut by strikes and required union leaders to observe a 30-day "cooling-off" period before striking.

Despite these incidents most workers remained dedicated to the war effort. Stoppages actually accounted for only about one-tenth of 1 percent of total work time during the war. When workers did strike, it was usually in defiance of their union leadership, and they left their jobs for just a few days. By war's end, membership in labor unions had grown dramatically.

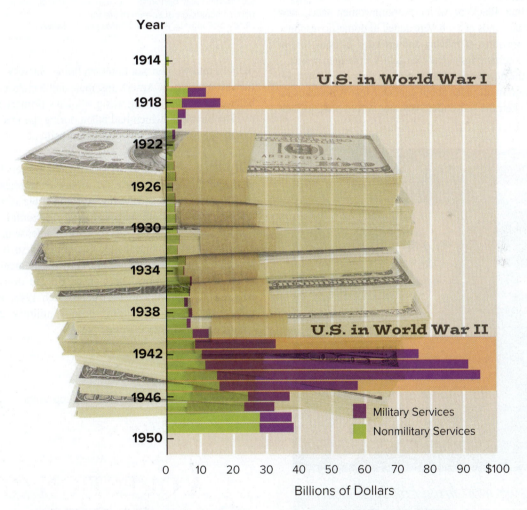

IMPACT OF WORLD WAR II ON GOVERNMENT SPENDING

As the chart shows, the war spurred government spending more than the New Deal, even on nonmilitary sectors. Note that after both world wars, nonmilitary spending was higher than in the prewar years.
(background photo) Comstock Images/Alamy Stock Photo

Women Workers >> With as many as 12 million men in uniform, women (especially married women) became the nation's largest untapped source of labor. During the high unemployment years of the Depression, both government and business had discouraged women from competing with men for jobs. Now, magazines and government bulletins began trumpeting "the vast resource of woman-power." Having accounted for a quarter of all workers in 1940, women amounted to more than a third by 1945. These women were not mostly young and single, as female workers of the past had been. A majority were either married or between 55 and 64 years old.

With husbands off at war, millions of women enjoyed the relative freedom of work and the additional income it provided. Black women in particular realized dramatic gains in the quality of jobs available. Once concentrated in low-paying domestic and farm jobs with erratic hours and tedious tasks, some 300,000 opted for factories that offered higher pay and more-regular hours. Whether Black or white, workingwomen faced new stresses. The demands of a job were added to domestic responsibilities. The pressures of moving and crowded housing tore at families and communities already fearful for their men at war.

Despite the new work roles for women, the war did not create a revolution in attitudes about gender. Most Americans assumed that when the war ended, veterans would pick up their

⌃ Viola Sievers was one of many women during the war who took jobs traditionally performed by men. Here she cleans a locomotive using a scalding hot stream of steam.
Library of Congress, Prints and Photographs Division

old jobs and women would return home. Surveys showed that the vast majority of Americans, male and female, continued to believe that child rearing was a woman's primary responsibility. The birthrate, which had fallen during the Depression, began to rise by 1943 as prosperity returned.

Mobility >> War industries attracted workers from places near and far. Vine Deloria Jr., a Native American, recalled that "the war dispersed the reservation people as nothing ever had. Every day, it seemed, we could be bidding farewell to families as they headed west to work in defense plants on the coast." African Americans left the South in such large numbers that cotton growers began to buy mechanical harvesters to replace their labor. The Census Bureau discovered that between Pearl Harbor in 1941 and March 1945, at least 15.3 million people (not counting those in military service) had changed their county of residence.

> ✓ **REVIEW**
> How did advances in technology support the Allied war effort?

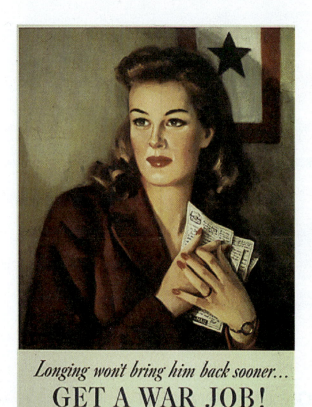
Longing won't bring him back sooner...
GET A WAR JOB!
SEE YOUR U. S. EMPLOYMENT SERVICE
WAR MANPOWER COMMISSION

⌃ Propaganda poster promoting wartime employment as the way to speed a husband's return from the war.
National Archives and Records Administration

A QUESTION OF RIGHTS

President Roosevelt was determined to avoid the patriotic excesses he had witnessed during World War I: mobs menacing immigrants, appeals to spy on neighbors, harassment of pacifists. Even so, the tensions over race, ethnic background, and class differences could not be ignored. In a society in which immigration laws discriminated against Asians by race, the war with Japan made life difficult for loyal Asian Americans of all backgrounds. Black and Hispanic workers still faced discrimination in finding good jobs, much as they had in peacetime.

Italians and Asian Americans >> As the war began,
about 600,000 Italian aliens and 5 million Italian Americans lived in the United States. Most lived in Italian neighborhoods centered on churches, fraternal organizations, and clubs. Some had been proud of Mussolini and supported fascism. "Mussolini was a hero," recalled one Italian American, "a superhero. He made us feel special." Those attitudes changed abruptly after Pearl Harbor. During the war Italian Americans unquestioningly pledged their loyalty to the United States.

At first the government treated Italians without citizenship (along with noncitizen Japanese and Germans) as "aliens of enemy nationality." They could not travel without permission; enter strategic areas; or possess shortwave radios, guns, or maps. By 1942 few Americans believed that German or Italian Americans posed any kind of danger. Eager to keep the support of Italian voters in the 1942 congressional elections, Roosevelt chose Columbus Day 1942 to lift restrictions on Italian aliens.

Not surprisingly, the 127,000 Japanese living in the United States, whether aliens or citizens, faced the most

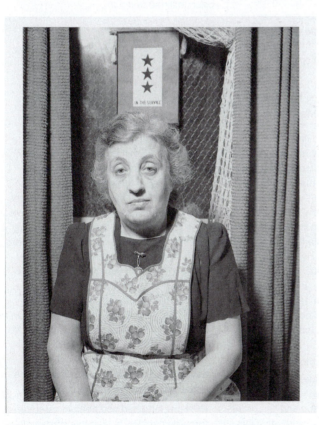

^ Rose Carrendeno, Italian American mother of six children. The three stars indicate that her three sons were in the armed forces.
Library of Congress, Prints and Photographs Division

severe discrimination. Ironically, prejudice against them was lowest in Hawai'i, where the war with Japan had begun. Newspapers there expressed confidence in the loyalty of Japanese Americans, whose labor was crucial to Hawai'i's economy.

On the mainland, Japanese Americans remained segregated from the mainstream of American life. State laws and local custom often threw up barriers to opportunity. In the western states, where they were concentrated around urban areas, most Japanese Americans could not vote, own land, or live in "decent" neighborhoods.

Approximately 47,000 Japanese aliens, known as **Issei**, were ineligible for citizenship under American law. Only their children (**Nisei**) could become citizens. Despite such restrictions, the Japanese showed great resourcefulness in turning marginal land into productive farms that supplied fruits and vegetables to growing cities.

> **Issei** native-born Japanese living in the United States; their U.S.-born children were called Nisei.
>
> **Nisei** U.S.-born children of native-born Japanese (Issei).

West Coast politicians pressed the Roosevelt administration to remove the Japanese from their communities. It did not seem to matter that about 80,000 Nisei were American citizens and that not one was ever convicted of espionage. "A Jap's a Jap," commented General John DeWitt, commander of West Coast defenses. "It makes no difference whether he is an American citizen or not." In response, in February 1942 the War Department drew up Executive Order 9066, which allowed the exclusion of any person from designated military areas. Under DeWitt's authority, the order was applied only on the West Coast against Japanese Americans. By late February Roosevelt had agreed that both Issei and Nisei would be evacuated. But where would they go?

The army shipped the entire Japanese community to temporary "assembly centers." Most Nisei were forced to sell their property at far below market value. Furthermore, many army sites did not offer basic sanitation, comfort, or privacy. "We lived in a horse stable," remembered one young girl. Eventually, most Japanese were interned in 10 camps in remote areas of seven western states. No claim of humane intent could change the reality: these were concentration camps. Internees were held in wire-enclosed compounds by armed guards. Tar-papered barracks housed families or

>> Racism against Japanese Americans was especially powerful in California.
Library of Congress, Prints and Photographs Division

"WHO DO YOU WANT TO WIN THIS WAR?"— JUSTIFYING INTERNMENT

In June 1943, Lieutenant General John L. DeWitt submitted a report on the evacuation of Japanese Americans from the West Coast, justifying his actions (Document 1). Mary Suzuki Ichino grew up in Los Angeles, California, and was interned at Camp Manzanar, about 230 miles northeast of there. Document 2 is a transcript of an interview with her, made decades later.

DOCUMENT 1
Sabotage on a Mass Scale

The Department of Justice had agreed to authorize its special field agents of the Federal Bureau of Investigation to undertake spot raids without warrant to determine the possession of arms, cameras and other contraband by Japanese. . . . In the Monterey area in California a Federal Bureau of Investigation spot raid made about February 12, 1942, found more than 60,000 rounds of ammunition and many rifles, shotguns and maps of all kinds. . . .

The combination of spot raids revealing hidden caches of contraband, the attacks on coastwise shipping, the interception of illicit radio transmissions, the nightly observation of visual signal lamps from constantly changing locations, and the success of the enemy offensive in the Pacific, had so aroused the public along the West Coast against the Japanese that it was ready to take matters into its own hands. . . .

Because of the ties of race, the intense feeling of filial piety and the strong bonds of common tradition, culture and customs, this population presented a tightly-knit racial group. It included in excess of 115,000 persons deployed along the Pacific Coast. Whether by design or accident, virtually always their communities were adjacent to very vital shore installations, war plants, etc. . . .

Throughout the Santa Maria Valley in [Santa Barbara] County, including the cities of Santa Maria and Guadalupe, every utility, air field, bridge, telephone and power line or other facility of importance was flanked by Japanese. They even surrounded the oil fields in this area. Only a few miles south, however, in the Santa Ynez Valley, lay an area equally as productive agriculturally as the Santa Maria Valley and with lands equally available for purchase and lease, but without any strategic installations whatever. There were no Japanese in the Santa Ynez Valley. . . . It was certainly evidence that the Japanese population of the Pacific Coast was, as a whole, ideally situated with reference to points of strategic importance, to carry into execution a tremendous program of sabotage on a mass scale should any considerable number of them have been inclined to do so.

Lieutenant General John L. DeWitt, *Final Report Japanese Evacuation from the West Coast 1942* (Washington, DC: Government Printing Office, 1943), chap. 2.

DOCUMENT 2
Interview with Mary Ichino

RP [Richard Potashin]: Tell us about what your attitude, where your attitude was [about being sent to an internment camp]. . . . Did you form your own ideas about the injustice of this, the unconstitutionality of it? Was that something you were thinking about?

MI [Mary Ichino]: I think I was a little bit naïve that way. I didn't, I think, understand that depth of the, you know, the situation. . . . I told you about that letter I wrote to General DeWitt. It took me until I got in camp for me to realize "What was I doing in this place?" And I go, "Why didn't that hit me before this as a question?"

RP: So your attitude changed—

MI: My attitude changed because—

RP: —when you got into camp?

MI: —I thought, it's sort of like an adventure, you know, for a teenager, when you think about it. You're moving, you're going, you know. But when I started seeing that my dad is losing his business, we're losing all our property, he lost his new car that he worked so darn hard for—what for? We're not from Japan. You know? Then when finally we went to camp is when I realized the injustice of the whole thing. And you're always taught in civics in high school that we're all equal under the law, and I said, "But how can you be equal when you haven't had a hearing as to whether you're guilty or not guilty?" And that's when I wrote that letter to General DeWitt.

RP: There was another friend that you—

MI: Yeah, Marie Hisamune. She was my classmate at Sacred Heart. And we decided to put our—well, she and I, in order to keep busy, decided to write—first we started writing a murder mystery. And we came to a point where we couldn't figure out how to end the darn thing. And then, so then the next thing was, "You know what? We ought to write to General DeWitt.". . . And so Maria and I put our heads together and we wrote, and we said, "We haven't gotten our constitutional hearing before we're declared guilty to be put into this place. Why is it? How is it? And how could it be?" And then we wanted an explanation. And then we're getting a little bit smarter, you know, at that age. "Okay, we better send it to General DeWitt." "Oh," somebody says, "They'll throw it out." "No they won't. We're going to make it registered directly to him." And so he must have gotten it because we never got the letter back, anything. No answer. . . .

RP: How long had you been in camp before you decided to take this course of action?

MI: Not quite six months, I bet. It dawned on us real quick.

RP: You just looked around and—

MI: Says, "Oh my God, can't get out of camp, you can't do this, you can't do that. The food is lousy. The physical facility's lousy. What did I do to deserve this?" You know.

RP: Right.

MI: And then it turned out to be, at that age we were realizing that it was hysteria. We figured that out.

RP: Did you have any second thoughts about writing that letter after you'd sent it? You know, like, Are they going to, you know, are we going to be—

MI: No.

RP: —on a blacklist or anything or—

MI: Nope.

RP: You felt—

MI: Fearless. . . . We're only sixteen. What are they going to do with us? You know? I mean, 'cause, yeah. Mmhmm. I'd been told more than once, "Oh, you're probably on the blacklist." I said, "So?" In a way, it's sort of a compliment, you know?

RP: Right. Yeah, it took a lot of courage to do that.

MI: It's either your courage, or you're so darned innocent. If you're worried about what's going to happen or what will happen to you, you're not going to do a thing. If you think you're right and you need an explanation, it's as simple as that. That was it. So there was no *gaman* [Zen Buddhist term meaning "endurance out of patience or dignity"] there. Tell it like it is.

16. Item # Acc-196 [letter to Mary Ichino]: Mary Suzuki Ichino [MI], MANZ 1216A, interviewed by Richard Potashin [RP] Disc 1, Part 2 (DVD), 22:41–27:53.

THINKING CRITICALLY

What contraband items does DeWitt cite to indicate Japanese disloyalty? Do they substantiate his case? Does anything suggest that Dewitt is overreacting to the Japanese threat in California? What elements does Mary Ichino cite that throw doubt on DeWitt's arguments? What gave Ichino the courage to write directly to General DeWitt? Why might she be proud to be on a blacklist?

---

small groups in single rooms. Each room had a few cots, some blankets, and a single lightbulb. That was home.

Some Japanese Americans protested loudly when government officials asked Nisei citizens if they would be willing to serve in the armed forces. "What do they take us for? Saps?" asked one camp prisoner. "First, they . . . run me out of town, and now they want me to volunteer for a suicide squad so I could get killed for this damn democracy." Yet thousands of Nisei did enlist, and many distinguished themselves in combat.

Concentration camps in America did not mirror the horror of Nazi death camps, but they were built on racism and fear. Worse, they violated the traditions of civil rights and liberties for which Americans believed they were fighting. African Americans, for example, called for "Double V": victory over racism at home and abroad.

Minorities and War Work >> Minority leaders saw the irony of fighting a war for freedom in a country in which civil rights were still limited. "A jim crow army cannot fight for a free world," the NAACP declared. Labor leader A. Philip Randolph, long an advocate of greater Black militancy, launched a campaign to gain entrance to jobs in defense industries and government agencies, unions, and the armed forces, all of them segregated. "The Administration leaders in Washington will never give the Negro justice," Randolph argued, "until they see masses—ten, twenty, fifty thousand Negroes on the White House lawn." In 1941 he began to organize a march on Washington.

President Roosevelt could have issued executive orders to integrate the government, as Randolph demanded. But it took the threat of the march to make him act. He issued Executive Order 8802 in June, which forbade discrimination by race in hiring either government or defense industry workers. To carry out the policy, Order 8802 established the Fair Employment Practices Committee (FEPC). In a society still deeply divided by racial prejudice, the new agency had only limited success in breaking down barriers against African Americans and Hispanics.

The FEPC did open industrial jobs in California's shipyards and aircraft factories, which had previously refused to hire Hispanics. Thousands migrated from Texas, where job discrimination was most severe, to California, where war work created new opportunities. Labor shortages led the

∧ Manzanar, in Owens Valley, California, was the site of 1 of 10 "relocation centers" set up to hold interned Japanese Americans. Here the first group of arrivals carry their few belongings into camp, in March 1942. Prisoners enlivened the drab surroundings with Japanese and American traditions, holding Boy Scout parades, sumo wrestling matches, and pickup games of baseball.
Eliot Elisofon/The LIFE Picture Collection/Getty Images

southwestern states to join with the Mexican government under the bracero program to recruit Mexican labor. In Texas, in contrast, antagonism to braceros ran so deep that the Mexican government tried to prevent workers from going there. Not until late 1943 did the FEPC investigate the situation.

Black Americans faced similar frustrations. More than half of all defense jobs were closed to minorities. For example, with 100,000 skilled and high-paying jobs in the aircraft industry, Blacks held about 200 janitorial positions. Unions segregated Black workers or excluded them entirely. One person wrote to the president with a telling complaint: "Hitler has not done anything to the colored people—it's people right here in the United States who are keeping us out of work and keeping us down."

Eventually the combination of labor shortages, pressure from Black leaders, and initiatives from government agencies opened the door to more skilled jobs and higher pay. Beginning in 1943, the United States Employment Service rejected requests with racial stipulations. By 1944 Blacks, who accounted for almost 10 percent of the population, held 8 percent of the jobs.

Urban Unrest >> At the beginning of the war three-quarters of the nation's 12 million Black Americans lived in the South. Hispanic Americans, whose population exceeded a million, were concentrated in a belt along the U.S.-Mexican border. When jobs for minorities opened in war centers, African Americans and Hispanic Americans became increasingly urban.

To ease crowding and reduce racial tensions, the government funded new housing. In Detroit federal authorities picked a site for minority housing along the edge of a Polish neighborhood. One project, named in honor of the Black abolitionist Sojourner Truth, included 200 units for Black families. When the first of them tried to move in, local officials had to send the National Guard to protect the newcomers from menacing Ku Klux Klan members. Riots broke out in the hot summer of 1943, as white mobs beat up African Americans riding public trolleys or patronizing movie theaters, and Black protesters looted white stores. Six thousand soldiers from nearby bases finally imposed a troubled calm, but not before the riot had claimed the lives of 24 Blacks and 9 whites.

In Southern California, Anglo hostility toward Latinos focused on *pachucos*, or "zoot suiters." These were young Hispanic men who had adopted the stylish fashions of Harlem hipsters: greased hair swept back into a ducktail; broad-shouldered, long-waisted suit coats; baggy pants pegged at the ankles. In June 1943 sailors from the local navy base invaded Hispanic neighborhoods in search of "zooters" who had allegedly attacked servicemen. The self-appointed vigilantes grabbed innocent victims, tore their clothes, cut their hair, and beat them. When Hispanics retaliated, the police arrested them, ignoring the actions of the sailors. Irresponsible

᠈ A "zoot suiter" gets escorted by the police.
Bettmann/Getty Images

newspaper coverage made matters worse. Underlying Hispanic anger were the grim realities of poor housing, unemployment, and white racism, which added up to a level of poverty that wartime prosperity eased but in no way resolved.

Minority leaders acted on the legal as well as the economic front. The Congress of Racial Equality (**CORE**), a civil rights group inspired by the Indian leader Mohandas K. Gandhi, used sit-ins and other nonviolent tactics to desegregate some restaurants and movie theaters. In 1944 the Supreme Court outlawed the "all-white primary," a device used by southerners to exclude Blacks from voting in primary elections within the Democratic Party. In *Smith* v. *Allwright* the Court ruled that since political parties were integral parts of public elections, they could not deny minorities the right to vote in primaries. Such new attitudes opened the door to future civil rights gains.

> **CORE** Congress of Racial Equality, an organization founded in 1942 that believed African Americans should use nonviolent civil disobedience to challenge segregation.

The New Deal in Retreat >> After Pearl Harbor, Roosevelt told reporters that "Dr. New Deal" had retired in favor of "Dr. Win-the-War." Political debates, however, could not be eliminated, even during a global conflict. The growing anti–New Deal coalition of Republicans and rural Democrats saw in the war an opportunity to attack programs they had long resented. They quickly ended the Civilian Conservation Corps and the National Youth Administration, reduced the powers of the Farm Security Administration, and blocked moves to extend Social Security and unemployment benefits.

By the spring of 1944 no one knew whether Franklin Roosevelt would seek an unprecedented fourth term. Pallid skin, sagging shoulders, and shaking hands seemed open signs that his health was failing. In July, a week before the Democratic convention, Roosevelt announced his decision: "All that is within me cries out to go back to my home on the Hudson River. . . . But as a good soldier . . . I will accept and serve." Conservative Democrats, however, replaced FDR's liberal vice president, Henry Wallace, with Harry S. Truman of Missouri, a loyal Democrat. The Republicans chose the moderate governor of New York, Thomas E. Dewey, to run against Roosevelt, but Dewey never had much of a chance. Still, Roosevelt's margin of victory was smaller than any since 1916. Like its aging leader, the New Deal coalition was showing signs of strain.

REVIEW

In what ways did discrimination against minorities continue after the war started?

WINNING THE WAR AND THE PEACE

In a war that stretched across the globe, the Allies had to coordinate their strategies on a grand scale. Which war theaters would receive equipment in short supply? Who would administer conquered territories? Inevitably, the questions of fighting a war turned into discussions of the peace that would follow. What would happen to occupied territories? How would the Axis powers be treated? As Allied armies struggled mile by mile to defeat the Axis, Allied diplomacy concentrated just as much on winning the peace.

The Fall of the Third Reich >> After pushing the Germans out of North Africa in May 1943, Allied strategists agreed to Churchill's plan to drive Italy from the war. Late in July, two weeks after a quarter of a million British and American troops had landed on Sicily, Mussolini fled to German-held northern Italy. Although Italy surrendered early in September, Germany continued to pour in reinforcements. It took the Allies almost a year of bloody fighting to reach Rome, and at the end of the campaign they had yet to break German lines. Along the eastern front, Soviet armies steadily pushed the Germans out of Russia and back toward Berlin.

General Dwight D. Eisenhower, fresh from battle in North Africa and the Mediterranean, took command of Allied preparations for Operation Overlord, the long-awaited opening of a second front in western Europe. By June 1944 all eyes focused on the coast of France, because Hitler, of course, knew the Allies would attack across the English Channel. Allied planners did their best to focus his attention on Calais, the French port city closest to the British Isles. On the morning of June 6, 1944, the invasion began—not at Calais but on the less fortified beaches of Normandy. Almost 3 million troops, 11,000 aircraft, and more than 2,000 vessels took part in D-Day.

Luck and Eisenhower's meticulous planning favored the Allied cause. Convinced that Calais was the Allied target, Hitler delayed sending in two reserve divisions. His indecision allowed the Allied forces to secure a foothold. Still, the Allied advance from Normandy took almost two months, not several weeks as hoped. Once Allied tanks broke through German lines, their progress was spectacular. In August Paris was liberated, and by mid-September the Allies had driven the Germans from France and Belgium. Hitler's desperate counterthrust in the Ardennes Forest in December 1944 succeeded momentarily, pushing back the Allies along a 50-mile bulge. But the "Battle of the Bulge" cost the Germans their last reserves. After General George Patton's forces rescued trapped American units, little stood between the Allies and Berlin.

Two Roads to Tokyo >> In the bleak days of 1942 General Douglas MacArthur—flamboyant with his dark sunglasses and corncob pipe—emerged as America's great military hero. MacArthur believed that the future of America lay in the Far East. The Pacific theater (and his forces, not those in Europe, he argued) should have top priority. In March 1943 the Combined Chiefs of Staff agreed to a compromise plan. MacArthur's forces would advance along the northern coast of New Guinea toward the Philippines and Tokyo. Naval forces, directed by Admiral Chester Nimitz, would use amphibious warfare to pursue a second line of attack, along the island chains of the central Pacific. American submarines played the vital role of cutting Japan's supply lines.

By July 1944 the navy's leapfrogging campaign reached the Mariana Islands, east of the Philippines. From there newly developed B-29 bombers could reach the Japanese home islands. As a result, Nimitz proposed bypassing the Philippines in favor of a direct attack on Formosa (present-day Taiwan). MacArthur insisted on fulfilling a promise he had made "to eighteen million Christian Filipinos that the Americans would return." President Roosevelt himself came to Hawai'i to resolve the impasse, giving MacArthur the green light. Backed by more than 100 ships of the Pacific Fleet, the general splashed ashore on the island of Leyte in October 1944.

↑ During an attack as complicated as the one on D-Day 1944, communication was immensely important for successful coordination of millions of troops and thousands of landing vessels. Here, a navy signaller uses a semaphore light to blink out Morse code to a battleship offshore. Another uses a telescope to pick up the replies from the ship.
Navy Art Collection, Naval History and Heritage Command

The decision to invade the Philippines led to savage fighting until the war ended. As retreating Japanese armies left Manila, they tortured and slaughtered tens of thousands of Filipino civilians. The United States suffered 62,000 casualties redeeming MacArthur's pledge, but a spectacular U.S. Navy victory at the Battle of Leyte Gulf spelled the end of the Japanese Imperial Navy as a fighting force. MacArthur and Nimitz prepared to tighten the noose around Japan's home islands.

MAP 26.3: D-DAY, 1944

The final key to defeating the Nazis was the invasion of western Europe at Normandy. D-Day for the invasion was June 6, 1944, and the massive undertaking would not have been possible had the Allies been unable to use Great Britain as a base to gather their forces. Stalin supported D-Day with a spring offensive in eastern Europe.
Why might Hitler have assumed Calais was the Allies' likely target?

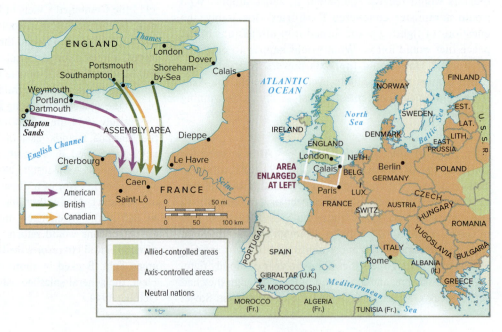

>> MAPPING THE PAST <<

THE PACIFIC CAMPAIGNS OF WORLD WAR II

The extraordinary distances of the Pacific spurred the United States to devise a two-front strategy to defeat Japan. MacArthur's army forces used Australia as a base of operations, aiming for the Philippines and the southeast coast of China. The navy, under the command of Admiral Nimitz, set out to destroy the Japanese fleet and to conduct an "island-hopping" campaign: a series of landings on island chains in the Central Pacific.

MAP READING

1. Where does Admiral Nimitz start his "island-hopping" campaign? Trace its course to the Mariana Islands.
2. Where does General MacArthur's campaign lead, moving out of Australia? What major island group does he attempt to recover?
3. Locate Manchuria. Which nation attacks Japanese positions there?
4. Locate Midway Island. How does its geographic position make it important?

MAP INTERPRETATION

1. What does MacArthur mean when he says his strategy was to "hit 'em where they ain't"?
2. Why did the success of the naval campaign in the central Pacific make it unnecessary to invade the Philippines?
3. Why might the Soviet Union's attack in Manchuria in August 1945 have affected Japan's decision to surrender?

Big Three Diplomacy

>> Agreement over the post-war peace proved even knottier than planning strategies for war. Churchill believed that only a stable European balance of power, not an international agency, could preserve peace. In his view the Soviet Union was the greatest threat to that balance of power. Premier Joseph Stalin left no doubt that an expansive notion of Russian security defined his war aims. For future protection, Stalin expected to annex the Baltic states, once Russian provinces, along with bits of Finland and Romania and about half of prewar Poland. In eastern Europe and other border areas such as Iran, Korea, and Turkey, he wanted "friendly" neighbors. It soon became apparent that *friendly* meant regimes dependent on Moscow.

Early on, Roosevelt had promoted his own version of an international balance of power, which he called the "Four Policemen." Under its framework the Soviet Union, Great Britain, the United States, and China would guarantee peace through military cooperation. But by 1944 Roosevelt was seeking an alternative to this scheme and to Churchill's wish to return to a balance of power that hemmed in the Russians. He preferred to bring the Soviet Union into a peacekeeping system based on an international organization similar to the League of Nations. But this time, all the great powers would participate, including the United States. Whether Churchill and Stalin—or the American people as a whole—would accept the idea was not yet clear.

The Road to Yalta

>> The outlines of a postwar settlement emerged during several summit conferences among the Allied leaders. In November 1943, with Italy's surrender in hand and the war against Germany going well, Churchill and Roosevelt agreed to make a hazardous trip to Teheran, Iran. There, the Big Three leaders met together for the first time. ("Seems very confident," Roosevelt said of Stalin, "very sure of himself, moves slowly—altogether quite impressive.") The president tried to charm the Soviet premier, teasing Churchill for Stalin's benefit, keeping it up "until Stalin was laughing with me, and it was then that I called him 'Uncle Joe.'"

Teheran proved to be the high point of cooperation among the Big Three. It was there that FDR and Churchill finally committed to the D-Day invasion Stalin had so long sought, although Churchill's promise was halfhearted at best. The British hoped to delay D-Day as long as possible in order to minimize British casualties. Stalin, for his part, promised to launch a spring offensive to pin down German troops on the eastern front. He also pledged to declare war against Japan once Germany was beaten.

But thorny disagreements remained. That was clear in February 1945, when the Big Three met at the Russian resort city of Yalta, on the Black Sea. By then Russian, British, and American troops were closing in on Germany. Roosevelt arrived tired, ashen. At 62, limited by his paralysis, he was visibly aged. He came to Yalta mindful that although Germany was all but beaten, Japan still held out in the Pacific. Under no circumstances did he want Stalin to withdraw his promises to enter the fight against Japan and to join a postwar international organization. Churchill remained ever mistrustful of Soviet intentions. The Russians appeared only too eager to fill the power vacuum that a defeated Japan and Germany would leave.

The Allies remained most at odds about Germany's postwar future. Stalin was determined that the Germans would never invade Russia again. Many Americans shared his desire to have Germany punished and its war-making capacity eliminated. At the Teheran Conference, Roosevelt and Stalin had proposed that the Third Reich be split into five powerless parts. Churchill, however, was much less eager to bring low the nation that was the most natural barrier to Russian expansion. The era after World War I, he believed, demonstrated that a healthy European economy required an industrialized Germany.

The Big Three made no firm decisions. For the time being, they agreed to divide Germany into separate occupation zones (France would receive a zone carved from British and American territory). These four powers would jointly occupy the German capital, Berlin, while an Allied Control Council supervised the national government.

<< Joseph Stalin, Franklin Roosevelt, and Winston Churchill, Teheran, 1943.
Library of Congress, Prints and Photographs Division

When the Big Three turned their attention to the Far East, Stalin held a trump card. Fierce Japanese resistance on the islands of Okinawa and Iwo Jima had convinced Roosevelt that only a bloody invasion would force Japan's surrender. He thus secured a pledge from Stalin to declare war within three months of Germany's defeat. The price was high. Stalin wanted to reclaim territories that Russia had lost in the Russo-Japanese War of 1904–1906, as well as control over the Chinese Eastern and South Manchurian railroads.

The agreements reached at Yalta depended on Stalin's willingness to cooperate. In public Roosevelt put the best face on matters. He argued that the new world organization (which Stalin agreed to support) would "provide the greatest opportunity in all history" to secure a lasting peace. "We shall take responsibility for world collaboration," he told Congress, "or we shall have to bear the responsibility for another world conflict." Privately the president was less optimistic. "When the chips were down," he confessed, he doubted "Stalin would be able to carry out and deliver what he had agreed to."

 REVIEW

Over what issues did Stalin, Churchill, and Roosevelt disagree as they planned for peace?

The Fallen Leader >> The Yalta Conference marked one of the last and most controversial chapters of Franklin Roosevelt's presidency. Critics charged that the concessions to Stalin were far too great: Poland and eastern Europe betrayed, China sold out, and the United Nations crippled at birth. Yet Roosevelt gave to Stalin mostly what the Russians had liberated with their blood and could have taken anyway. Four out of five Nazi soldiers killed in action died on the eastern front. Even Churchill, an outspoken critic of Soviet ambitions, concluded that although "our hopeful assumptions were soon to be falsified . . . they were the only ones possible at the time."

What peace Roosevelt might have achieved can never be known. He returned from Yalta visibly ill. On April 12, 1945, while sitting for his portrait at his vacation home in Warm Springs, Georgia, he complained of a "terrific headache," then

suddenly fell unconscious. Two hours later, Roosevelt was dead. Not since the assassination of Lincoln had the nation so grieved. Under Roosevelt's leadership, government had become a protector, the president a father and friend, and the United States the leader in the struggle against Axis tyranny. Eleanor Roosevelt recalled how many Americans later told her that "they missed the way the President used to talk to them. . . . There was a real dialogue between Franklin and the people."

"Who the hell is Harry Truman?" the chief of staff had asked when Truman was nominated for the vice presidency in 1944. As vice president, Truman had learned almost nothing about the president's postwar plans. Sensing his own inadequacies, he adopted a tough pose and made his mind up quickly. People welcomed the new president's decisiveness as a relief from Roosevelt's evasive style. Too often, though, Truman acted before the issues were clear. But he at least knew victory in Europe was at hand as Allied troops swept into Germany from the east and west.

The Holocaust >> The horror of war in no way prepared the invading armies for their liberation of the Nazi concentration camps. **Anti-Semitism**, or prejudice against Jews and Judaism, had a long and ugly history in the Christian Western world. It was particularly strong in central and eastern Europe. As Allied

anti-Semitism hatred, prejudice, oppression, or discrimination against Jews or Judaism.

>> In April 1945, at the concentration camp in Buchenwald, Germany, Senator Alben Barkley of Kentucky views a grisly example of the horrors of the Nazis' "final solution." As vice president under Harry Truman, Barkley urged the administration to support an independent homeland in Israel for Jews.
National Archives & Records Administration

troops discovered, Hitler had authorized the systematic extermination of all European Jews as well as Gypsies, homosexuals, and others considered deviant. The SS, Hitler's security force, had constructed six extermination centers in Poland. By rail from all over Europe, the SS shipped Jews to die in the gas chambers.

No issue of World War II more starkly raised questions of human good and evil than what came to be known as the Holocaust. Tragically, the United States could have done more to save at least some of the 6 million Jews killed. Until the autumn of 1941 the Nazis permitted Jews to leave Europe, but few countries would accept them—including the United States. Americans haunted by unemployment feared that a tide of new immigrants would make competition for jobs even worse. After 1938 the restrictive provisions of the 1924 Immigration Act were made even tighter.

American Jews wanted to help, especially after 1942, when they learned of the death camps. But they worried that highly visible protests might only aggravate American anti-Semitism. They were also split over support for Zionists working to establish a Jewish homeland in Palestine. Roosevelt and his advisers ultimately decided that the best way to save Jews was to win the war quickly. That strategy still does not explain why the Allies did not do more: They could have bombed the rail lines to the camps, sent commando forces, or tried to destroy the death factories.

A Lasting Peace >> Late in the summer of 1944 the Allies met at Dumbarton Oaks, a Washington estate, to lay out the structure for the proposed United Nations Organization (UNO, later known simply as the UN). An 11-member Security Council would oversee a General Assembly composed of delegates from all member nations. By the end of the first organizational meeting, held in San Francisco in April 1945, it had become clear that the United Nations would favor the Western powers in most postwar disputes.

While the United Nations was organizing itself in San Francisco, the Axis powers were collapsing in Europe. After Mussolini attempted to escape to Germany, anti-Fascist mobs in Italy captured and slaughtered him like a pig. Adolf Hitler committed suicide in his Berlin bunker on April 30. Two weeks later General Eisenhower accepted the German surrender.

In one final summit meeting, held in July 1945 at Potsdam (just outside Berlin), President Truman met Churchill and Stalin for the first time. (Before the conference ended, British voters replaced the Tory Churchill with Labor Party leader, Clement Attlee.) The three countries agreed that Germany should be occupied and demilitarized. Stalin insisted that Russia receive a minimum of $10 billion in reparations, regardless of how much it might hurt postwar Germany or the European economy. A complicated compromise allowed Britain and the United States to restrict reparations from their zones. But in large part Stalin had his way. For the foreseeable future, Germany would remain divided into occupation zones without a central government of its own.

Atom Diplomacy >> The issue most likely to shape postwar relations never even reached the bargaining table in Potsdam. On July 16, 1945, Manhattan Project scientists detonated their first atomic device. Upon receiving the news in Germany, Truman seemed a changed man—firmer, more confident. He "told the Russians just where they got on and off and generally bossed the whole meeting," observed Churchill. Several questions loomed: Should the United States now use the bomb? Should it warn Japan before dropping it? And perhaps equally vital, should Truman inform Stalin of the new weapon?

Over the spring and early summer of 1945 administration officials discussed the use of atomic weapons. A few scientists had recommended not using the bomb, or at least attempting to convince Japan to surrender by offering a demonstration of the new weapon's power. A high-level committee of administrators, scientists, and political and military leaders dismissed that idea. Rather than tell Stalin directly about the bomb, Truman mentioned obliquely that the United States possessed a weapon of "awesome destructiveness." Stalin showed no surprise, most likely because spies had already informed him about the bomb. Privately, Truman and Churchill decided to drop the first bomb with only a veiled threat of "inevitable and complete" destruction if Japan did not surrender unconditionally. Unaware of the warning's full meaning, officials in Tokyo, worrying about the future of the emperor, made no formal reply.

Some historians have charged that Secretary of State James Byrnes, a staunch anti-Communist, believed that a combat demonstration of the bomb would shock Stalin into behaving less aggressively in postwar negotiations. Most evidence, however, indicates that Truman decided to drop the

⌃ On August 6, 1945, the bomber *Enola Gay* dropped an atomic bomb on Hiroshima, Japan, as recorded in this photograph taken by an observation plane. Approximately 100,000 people died from the initial bomb blast, with tens of thousands more dying from radiation poisoning.
World History Archive/Alamy Stock Photo

Make a Case

Should the United States have sought an alternative to dropping the atomic bombs on Japan without a clear warning?

bomb in order to end the war quickly. The victory in the Pacific promised to be bloody. Military leaders estimated that an invasion of Japan would produce heavy Allied casualties.

Before leaving Potsdam, Truman gave the final order for B-29s to drop two atomic bombs on Japan. On August 6 the first leveled four square miles of the city of Hiroshima. Three days later a second exploded over the port of Nagasaki. About 140,000 people died instantly in the fiery blasts. A German priest came upon soldiers who had looked up as the bomb exploded. Their eyeballs had melted from their sockets. Tens of thousands more who lived through the horror began to sicken and die from radiation poisoning.

The two explosions left the Japanese stunned. Breaking all precedents, the emperor intervened and declared openly for peace. On September 3 a somber Japanese delegation boarded the battleship *Missouri* in Tokyo Bay to sign the document of surrender. World War II had ended.

THEN&NOW

When World War II, ended the nuclear genie was out of the bottle. Still only the United States possessed an atom bomb, though Great Britain and the Soviet Union had already launched nuclear projects of their own. The arms race that followed confronted humanity with the threat to all life on earth. That threat only deepened over time as France, Israel, China, India, and Pakistan each joined the atomic club. Only after Ronald Reagan, George H. W. Bush, and Mikhail Gorbachev agreed to broad disarmament agreements and the Soviet Union collapsed in 1991 did the world seem to step back from the nuclear brink. That relief was short-lived as Iran and North Korea, two disruptive states, sought to create their own atomic weapons. The prospect of nuclear-armed terrorist groups poses yet another nightmare scenario.

History in Global Context >> "World War II changed everything," observed an admiral long after the war. The defeatism of the Depression gave way to the exhilaration of victory. Before the war Americans seldom exerted leadership in international affairs. Afterward, the world looked to the United States to rebuild the economies of Europe and Asia and to maintain peace. Not only had World War II

shown the global interdependence of economic and political systems, it had also increased that interdependence. Out of the war developed a truly international economy. At home the economy became more centralized and the role of the government larger.

Still, a number of fears loomed. Would the inevitable cut-backs in military spending bring on another depression? Would devastation in Europe and Asia produce conditions the Soviet Union could exploit for its own advantage? Did the Soviets have ambitions to undo the new global peace, much as fascism and economic instability had undermined the Versailles treaty? And then there was the shadow of the atomic bomb, looming over the victorious as well as the defeated. The United States might control the bomb for the present, but what if the weapon fell into unfriendly hands? After World War II launched the atomic age, no nation, not even the United States, was safe anymore.

CHAPTER SUMMARY

World War II deepened the global interdependence of nations and left the United States as the greatest economic and military power in the world.

- As fascism spread in Europe and as militarism spread in Asia, Franklin Roosevelt struggled to help America's allies by overcoming domestic political isolation and the fervor for neutrality.
- Despite German aggression against Poland in 1939, France and the Low Countries in 1940, and the Soviet Union in 1941, the United States did not enter the war until the Japanese surprise attack on Pearl Harbor in December 1941.
- The alliance forged among British prime minister Winston Churchill, Soviet premier Joseph Stalin, and President Franklin Roosevelt did not swerve from its decision to subdue Germany first, even though early defeats and America's lack of preparation slowed the war effort until 1943.
- At home America's factories produced enough goods to supply the domestic economy and America's allies.
- Demands for labor created opportunities for women and minorities.
- War hysteria aggravated old prejudices and led to the internment of Japanese Americans.
- New Deal reform ended as "Dr. Win-the-War" replaced "Dr. New Deal."
- Although the successful landings in France on D-Day and the island-hopping campaign in the Pacific made it clear that the Allies would win the war, issues over Poland, Germany, and postwar boundaries raised doubts about the peace.
- The war ended with the atomic bombings of Hiroshima and Nagasaki, but not soon enough to limit the horrors of the Holocaust.

Digging Deeper

A comprehensive treatment of the war years is David Kennedy, *The American People in World War II: Freedom from Fear: Part II* (2003). Painful and compelling is Adam Hochschild, *Spain in our Hearts: Americans in the Spanish Civil War, 1936-1939* (2016). Equally gripping is Max Hastings, *Inferno: The World at War, 1939-1945* (2011). Richard Lingeman, *Don't You Know There's a War On: The Homefront, 1941-1945* (updated ed., 2003), is a classic study. Possibly the best way to understand the Holocaust is through Timothy Snyder, *Bloodlands: Europe between Hitler and Stalin* (2012). Emily Yellin, *Our Mothers' War: American Women at Home and at the Front during World War II* (2005), explores the many roles women played. Tetsuden Kashima, *Judgment without Trial: Japanese American Imprisonment during World War II* (2003), reveals that planning for internment of the Japanese began well before the war.

The decision to drop two atomic bombs on Japan remains a topic of vigorous debate. For the racial dimension of the decision, see John Dower, *War without Mercy: Race and Power in the Pacific War* (1986). Richard Rhodes, *The Making of the Atomic Bomb* (1987), re-creates the history of the Manhattan Project. Gar Alperowitz, *The Decision to Use the Atomic Bomb* (1995), extends an interpretation he first advanced in *Atomic Diplomacy* (1965): that the Soviet Union was the planners' real target. Martin Sherwin, *A World Destroyed* (rev. ed., 1985); and J. Samuel Walker, *Prompt and Utter Destruction: Truman and the Use of the Atomic Bomb against Japan* (1997), view the decision more as a way to end the war quickly. David Holloway, *Stalin and the Bomb: The Soviet Union and Atomic Energy 1939-1956* (1994), uses Russian sources. For a broader view of the end of the Pacific War, see Robert Frank, *Downfall: The End of the Japanese Imperial Empire* (2001).

27 The United States and the Cold War

1945–1954

The *Queen Elizabeth* docked in New York Harbor on July 20, 1945, with as many of its 14,576 troops as possible crowding the decks or hanging out of portholes in anticipation of the return to home, families, and peacetime.

Anthony Camerano/AP Photo

>> An American Story
GLAD TO BE HOME?

Five months after World War II ended, troopships steamed into New York harbor. Timuel Black was packing his duffel belowdecks when he heard some of the white soldiers shout, "There she is! The Statue of Liberty!"

Black felt a little bitter about the war. He'd been drafted in Chicago in 1943, just after race riots ripped the city. His father, a strong supporter of civil rights, was angry. "What the hell are you goin' to fight in Europe for? The fight is here." He wanted his son to go with him to demonstrate in Detroit, except the roads were blocked and the buses and trains screened to prevent African Americans from coming in to "make trouble."

Instead, Black went off to fight the Nazis, serving in a segregated army. He'd gone ashore during the D-Day invasion and marched through one of the German concentration camps. "The

first thing you get is the stench," he recalled. "Everybody knows that's human stench. You begin to see what's happened to these creatures. And you get—I got more passionately angry than I guess I'd ever been." He thought: if it could happen to Jews in Germany, it could happen to Black folk in America. So when the white soldiers called to come up and see the Statue of Liberty, Black's reaction was, "Hell, I'm not goin' up there. Damn that." But he went up after all. "All of a sudden, I found myself with tears, cryin' and saying the same thing [the white soldiers] were saying. Glad to be home, proud of my country, as irregular as it is. Determined that it could be better."

On the other side of the country, nurse Betty Basye was working at a California hospital that treated soldiers shipped back from the Pacific: "Blind young men. Eyes gone, legs gone. Parts of the face. Burns—you'd land with a fire bomb and be up in flames." She tried to keep up their spirits, joking and talking about times to come. Basye liked to take Bill, one of her favorites, for walks downtown. Half of Bill's face was gone, and civilians would stare. It happened to other patients, too. "Nicely dressed women, absolutely staring, just standing there staring." Some people wrote the local paper, wondering why disfigured vets couldn't be kept on their own grounds and off the streets. Such callousness made Basye indignant. But once the war ended, she had to think about her future. "I got busy after the war," she recalled, "getting married and having my four children. That's what you were supposed to do. And getting your house in suburbia."

Yet as Betty Basye and Timuel Black both discovered, the return to "normal" life was filled with uncertainties. The first truly global war had left large parts of Europe and Asia in ruins. The task of rebuilding was enormous and it soon became clear the United States would have a central role in shaping whatever world order emerged. Isolation seemed neither practical nor desirable in an era in which Americans had global responsibilities to keep the peace, while the Soviet Union and communism seemed to pose new threats.

To blunt those threats the United States converted not so much to peace as to a "cold war" against its former Soviet ally. This undeclared war came to affect almost every aspect of American life. Abroad, it justified a far wider military and economic role for the United States—not just in Europe but also in the Middle East and along the Pacific Rim, from Korea to Indochina. At home, it sent politicians searching for Communist spies and "subversives" everywhere from the State Department to labor unions, college campuses, and the movie studios of Hollywood.

Trying to deter war in times of peace dramatically increased the role of the military-industrial-university complex that had formed during World War II. A people who had once resisted government intrusion into individual lives now accepted a large defense establishment. They voted, too, to maintain New Deal programs that ensured an active federal role in managing the economy. <<

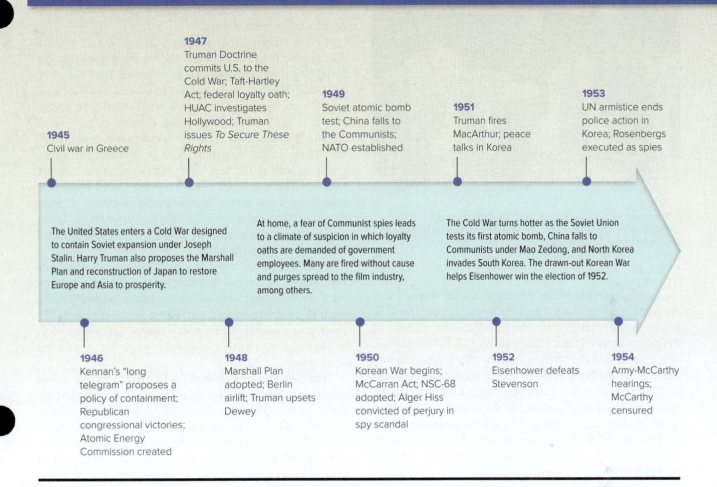

1945
Civil war in Greece

1947
Truman Doctrine commits U.S. to the Cold War; Taft-Hartley Act; federal loyalty oath; HUAC investigates Hollywood; Truman issues *To Secure These Rights*

1949
Soviet atomic bomb test; China falls to the Communists; NATO established

1951
Truman fires MacArthur; peace talks in Korea

1953
UN armistice ends police action in Korea; Rosenbergs executed as spies

The United States enters a Cold War designed to contain Soviet expansion under Joseph Stalin. Harry Truman also proposes the Marshall Plan and reconstruction of Japan to restore Europe and Asia to prosperity.

At home, a fear of Communist spies leads to a climate of suspicion in which loyalty oaths are demanded of government employees. Many are fired without cause and purges spread to the film industry, among others.

The Cold War turns hotter as the Soviet Union tests its first atomic bomb, China falls to Communists under Mao Zedong, and North Korea invades South Korea. The drawn-out Korean War helps Eisenhower win the election of 1952.

1946
Kennan's "long telegram" proposes a policy of containment; Republican congressional victories; Atomic Energy Commission created

1948
Marshall Plan adopted; Berlin airlift; Truman upsets Dewey

1950
Korean War begins; McCarran Act; NSC-68 adopted; Alger Hiss convicted of perjury in spy scandal

1952
Eisenhower defeats Stevenson

1954
Army-McCarthy hearings; McCarthy censured

THE ONSET OF THE COLD WAR

As the world struggled to rebuild after World War II, power that had once been centered in Europe shifted to nations on its periphery. In place of Germany, France, and Great Britain, the United States and the Soviet Union emerged as the world's two reigning superpowers—and as mortal enemies. This rivalry was not altogether an equal one. At war's end the United States had a booming economy, a massive military establishment, and the atomic bomb. In contrast, much of the Soviet Union lay in ruins.

But the defeat of Germany and Japan left no power in Europe or Asia to block the still formidable Soviet army. Many Americans feared that desperate, war-weary peoples would find the appeal of communism irresistible. If Stalin intended to extend the Soviet Union's dominion, only the United States had the economic and military might to block

him. Events in the critical years of 1945 and 1946 persuaded most Americans that Stalin did have such a plan. The Truman administration concluded that "the U.S.S.R. has engaged the United States in a struggle for power, or 'cold war,' in which our national security is at stake and from which we cannot withdraw short of national suicide." What had happened that led Western leaders to such a dire view of their former Soviet allies? How did that wide breach threaten the postwar peace?

American Suspicions >> Long before events deepened American suspicions of the Soviets, conflicting ideologies separated the two nations. The October Revolution of 1917 had shocked most Americans who viewed Lenin's Bolshevik revolutionaries with fear, suspicion, and loathing. As the Bolsheviks grasped power, they often resorted to terrorism to achieve their ends. As Marxists they rejected both religion and the notion of private property, two institutions that defined the American way of life. Furthermore, Soviet propagandists made no secret that they intended to export revolution throughout the world, including to the United States.

^ Clement Atlee (who replaced Churchill), Truman, and Stalin met at Potsdam in July 1945. Their smiles masked disagreements over the shape of the postwar world.
Everett Collection Inc/Alamy Stock Photo

Events leading to World War II had caused Western leaders to be wary of the dangers of "appeasement." In 1938 British prime minister Neville Chamberlain's attempt at Munich to satisfy Hitler's demands on Czechoslovakia had only emboldened the Nazis to expand further. After the war, Secretary of the Navy James Forrestal applied the "lessons" of Munich to the new Europe. Appeasing Russian demands, he believed, would only seem like an attempt "to buy their understanding and sympathy. We tried that once with Hitler. . . . There are no returns on appeasement." Many of Truman's advisers believed the Soviet dictator was as much bent on conquest as Hitler had been.

Communist Expansion >> During the war Stalin made numerous demands to control territory along Soviet borders. And when peace came, he continued to push for control over the Dardanelles, the narrow strait linking Soviet ports on the Black Sea with the Mediterranean Sea. Soviet forces occupying northern Iran also supported rebels seeking a separate state. In Greece local Communists fought to overturn the monarchy.

Asia, too, seemed a target for Communist ambitions. Russian occupation forces in Manchuria turned over captured Japanese arms to Chinese Communist rebels led by Mao Zedong. Russian troops controlled the northern half of Korea. In Vietnam leftist nationalists fought against the return of colonial rule.

Despite Russian actions, many historians have argued that American policy makers consistently exaggerated Stalin's ambitions. At war's end, farms and industry in the Soviet Union lay in ruins. When Stalin looked outward, he saw American occupation forces in Europe and Asia ringing the Soviet Union, their military might backed by a newly developed atomic arsenal. American corporations owned or were gaining control of vast oil fields in the Middle East. Along

with the French and the British, the United States was a strong presence in Southeast Asia. Given that situation, one could interpret Stalin's actions after the war as being defensive. Stalin wanted to counter what he saw as a threatening American-European alliance.

Recent evidence from once-secret Soviet records suggests that, despite the ravages of war, Stalin recognized that the Soviet Union had emerged as a world power. With Germany and Japan defeated, Soviet borders to the east and west were secure from invasion. Only to the south, along the border with Iran, did Stalin see a problem. Further, he recognized that the people of Britain and the United States had tired of war. Their leaders were not about to threaten the Soviet Union, at least in the near term. Equally significant, Soviet spies had informed Stalin in 1946 that the United States possessed only a few atomic bombs. In the short-term, the nuclear threat was more symbolic than real. As a realist, Stalin saw an opportunity to advance Soviet interests so long as his actions did not provoke a war.

Postwar tensions came to a head in the first months of 1946. Stalin announced in February that the Soviet Union would strive to preserve its national security. In a world dominated by capitalism, he warned, future wars were inevitable. The Russian people had to ensure against "any eventuality" by undertaking a new five-year plan for economic development.

Some Americans dismissed the Five Year Plan as a means to rally popular support for renewed sacrifices to rebuild the Soviet Union. Others feared it was a blueprint for military expansion. *Time* magazine, an early voice for a "get tough" policy, called Stalin's speech "the most warlike pronouncement uttered by any top-rank statesman since V-J day." "I'm tired of babying the Soviets," remarked President Truman, who seldom backed away from a fight. Truman's advisers spelled out the political advantages of a tough line. "The worse matters get," they told him, "the more there is a sense of crisis. In times of crisis, the American citizen tends to back up his president." In March, Winston Churchill, now a private citizen, warned that the Soviets had dropped an "Iron Curtain" across Europe between their satellite nations and the free world. Poland, East Germany, Romania, and Bulgaria lay behind it. Iran, Greece, Turkey, and much of Europe seemed at risk.

A Policy of Containment >> As policy makers groped for a way to deal with these developments, the State Department received an extraordinary diplomatic cable in February 1946. It was exceptionally long (8,000 words) and dire in its warning of a Soviet threat. Its author was George Kennan, chargé d'affaires in Moscow and a student of Soviet conduct. His "long telegram" argued that Russian leaders, including Stalin, were so paranoid that no country could reach any useful agreements with them. When this "instinctive Russian sense of insecurity" combined with Marxist conviction that capitalism was evil, the result was a natural tendency toward Soviet expansion, Kennan argued. Soviet

COMMUNIST CONTAGION

TIME Maps by R.M.Chapin Jr.

Quarantined
Infected
Exposed

<< As American fears of Soviet intentions increased, journalists often described communism as a disease, an inhuman force, or a savage predator. In April 1946, anti-Communist *Time* magazine portrayed the spread of "infection" throughout Europe and Asia as the "Red Menace."
AP Photo

power "moves inexorably . . . like a toy automobile wound up and headed in a given direction, stopping only when it meets some unanswerable force."

Kennan recommended a policy that came to be known as "containment." The United States must apply "unalterable counterforce at every point where [the Soviets] show signs of encroaching upon the interests of a peaceful and stable world." Kennan's analysis provided leaders in Washington with a clear rationale for opposing Soviet ambitions. He recommended firm counterpressure that combined diplomatic, economic, and military measures to block Russian aggression. Truman and his advisers embraced containment, but stressed military, over economic and diplomatic, measures.

The Truman Doctrine >> A major crisis came in early 1947, as Europe reeled under severe winter storms and a depressed postwar economy, Great Britain announced that it was no longer able to support the governments of Greece and Turkey. Without British aid, the Greek and Turkish governments seemed vulnerable to a Communist takeover. Truman decided that the United States should shore up their power to resist. He asked Congress to provide $400 million in military and economic aid. To gain support, he spoke to Congress in March, determined to "scare hell out of the country." The world was now divided into two hostile camps, he warned. To preserve the American way of life, the United States must step forward and help "free people" threatened by "totalitarian regimes." This rationale for aid to Greece and Turkey soon became known as the Truman Doctrine.

The Truman Doctrine marked a new level of American commitment to a Cold War. Just what responsibility the Soviets had for unrest in Greece and Turkey remained unclear. But Truman linked communism with insurgencies across the globe. Americans now faced an open-ended struggle, in which the president gained expanded powers to act wherever unrest threatened. Occasionally Congress would regret yielding the executive branch so much power, but by 1947 anticommunism dominated American policy, both foreign and domestic.

The Marshall Plan >> The Truman Doctrine did nothing to aid Western Europe. There, governments were

bankrupt, factories were closed, city streets stood dark, and people faced starvation. American diplomats warned that without aid to revive the European economy, Communists would seize power in Germany, Italy, and France. If Western Europe fell, the Cold War could be lost.

In June 1947 Secretary of State George C. Marshall presented a plan for ensuring European recovery. He invited all European nations, East and West, to request assistance from the United States to rebuild their economies. Unlike Truman, Marshall did not emphasize the Communist menace. Still, his massive aid plan aimed to eliminate conditions that produced the discontent that Communists often exploited. Then, too, humanitarian aid had practical benefits. As Europe recovered, so would its capacity to buy American goods. Marshall did not rule out Soviet participation in the massive aid program. But he gambled—correctly—that fears of American economic domination would lead the Soviets and their allies to reject his offer. At first **neo-isolationists** in Congress argued that the United States could not afford such generosity. But when Stalin further solidified control of the nations behind the Iron Curtain, Congress approved the Marshall Plan, as it became known, in 1948. The blame for dividing Europe fell on the Soviet Union, not the United States. The Marshall Plan provided Western Europe the boost its economies needed.

> **neo-isolationist** an individual who after World War II believed the United States should avoid foreign entanglements.

NATO >> American efforts to stabilize Europe led Stalin to shore up Soviet control over Eastern Europe. In 1947 he moved against the moderate government in Hungary. Soviet

Make a Case

Which nation deserves more blame for the Cold War—the United States or the Soviet Union? And why?

forces replaced the relatively free government with a Communist regime dependent on Moscow. Then in February 1948 Soviet-backed Communists toppled the elected government of Czechoslovakia. News came that the popular Czech foreign minister, Jan Masaryk, had fallen to his death from a small bathroom window. Suicide was the official explanation, but many suspected murder.

The spring of 1948 brought another clash between the Soviets and their wartime allies, this time over Germany. There, the United States, Great Britain, and France decided to transform their occupation zones into an independent West German state. The Western-controlled sectors of Berlin, however, lay over 100 miles to the east, well within the Soviet zone. On June 24 the Soviets suddenly blockaded land access to Berlin. Truman did not hesitate: "We are going to stay, period." But he did reject General Lucius Clay's proposal to have his forces shoot their way through the blockade. Instead, the United States began a massive airlift of supplies that lasted almost a year. In May 1949 Stalin lifted the blockade, conceding that he could not prevent the creation of West Germany.

Stalin's aggressive actions accelerated the American effort to use military means to contain Soviet ambitions. By 1949 the United States and Canada had joined with Britain, France, Belgium, the Netherlands, and Luxembourg to establish the North Atlantic Treaty Organization (NATO) as a mutual defense pact. In his Farewell Address of 1793, George Washington had warned against entangling alliances. Now, for the first time, the United States entered into a peacetime alliance with European nations.

Democrats and Republicans alike praised Truman's firm handling of the Berlin crisis. They were equally enthusiastic about another presidential action. Minutes after Jewish residents of Palestine announced their independence in May 1948, Truman recognized the new state of Israel. He had previously supported the immigration of Jews into Palestine, despite the opposition of oil-rich Arab states and his own State Department. The president sympathized with Jewish aspirations for a homeland. He also faced a tough campaign in 1948 in which Jewish votes would be critical. As British prime minister Clement Attlee observed: "There's no Arab vote in America, but there's a heavy Jewish vote and the Americans are always having elections."

The Atomic Shield versus the Iron Curtain >> The Berlin crisis forced Truman to consider the possibility of war. If it came, would atomic weapons be used? That dilemma raised two other difficult questions. Should the decision to use atomic weapons rest in civilian or military hands? And was it possible to find a way to ease the nuclear threat by creating an international system to control atomic power?

Truman opposed total military control of nuclear weapons. He declared he was not going to

have "some dashing lieutenant colonel decide when would be the proper time to drop one." In 1946 Congress seemed to choose civilian control when it passed the McMahon Act. This bill established the Atomic Energy Commission (AEC) with control of all fissionable materials for both peacetime and military applications. The AEC was a civilian, not a military, agency, but the military maintained a heavy influence.

Proposals for the international control of atomic energy fell victim to Cold War fears. Originally a government committee proposed that the mining and use of the world's atomic raw materials be supervised by the United Nations. The committee argued that in the long run the United States would be more secure under a system of international control than by relying on its temporary nuclear monopoly. But Truman chose Bernard Baruch, a staunch Cold Warrior, to draw up the recommendations to the United Nations in June 1946. Baruch's proposals ensured that the United States would dominate any international atomic agency. The Soviets countered with a plan calling for destruction of all nuclear bombs and a ban on their use. Baruch had no intention of bargaining. It was either his plan or nothing, he announced. And so it was nothing. The Truman administration never seriously considered the possibility of giving up the American nuclear monopoly.

Ironically, because so much secrecy surrounded the bomb, many military planners knew little about it. Even Truman had no idea in 1946 how many bombs the United States possessed. (For the two years after Hiroshima, it was never more than a dozen.) Military planners, however, soon found themselves relying on the concept of nuclear **deterrence**. The Soviet army had at its command over 260 divisions. The United States, in contrast, had reduced its forces by 1947 to little more than a single division. As the Cold War heated up, American military planners believed they could deter any Soviet attack by threatening a devastating atomic counterattack.

ʌ The huge new XB-36 alongside the Boeing B-29 Superfortress: the plane that carried atomic bombs to Hiroshima and Nagasaki.
U.S. Air Force photo

COLD WAR EUROPE

During the first decade of the cold war, the United States fought a hot war in Korea and became involved in Vietnam. Yet the majority of Americans agreed that it was most important to contain the Soviet threat to Western Europe. To that end, the United States adopted the Truman Doctrine and Marshall Plan and created the North Atlantic Treaty Organization (NATO). The Soviets, in response, formed the Warsaw bloc and sent assistance to Egypt and Syria while pressuring Turkey and Iran.

MAP READING

1. Which four nations occupied zones in Berlin?
2. What important Western European countries had not joined NATO by 1956?
3. What feature shown in the insert reveals why the British, French, and Americans preserved their zones in Berlin during the 1948 crisis?

MAP INTERPRETATION

1. Why would Berlin's location make it a focus of East-West tensions? On the inset map, why are there airplane symbols in three of the zones but not the fourth?
2. Of the seven Western European nations that did not belong to NATO in 1956, which do you think made their choice for political reasons and which because of geography?
3. Why would the Dardanelles and Bosporus Straits be so important to both the Warsaw bloc and NATO countries?
4. Why might the Soviet Union put pressure on Iran, Turkey, and Greece, known as the "Northern Tier"?

Duck and Cover

Sound track and music: ". . . and Bert the Turtle was very alert. When danger threatened him, he never got hurt. He knew just what to do . . ."

What tone is set by using "Bert the Turtle:" and a monkey for teaching students the tactic of "Duck and Cover" in an atomic attack?

Go to YouTube and search for "Duck and Cover." Play the film. How do the sound track, animation, music, and script contribute to the impression the film gives to an atomic bomb?

Narrator: "Now, [laughs] you and I don't have shells to crawl into like Bert the Turtle so, we have to cover up in our own way. First you duck . . ."

". . . and then you cover! And very tightly, you cover the back of your neck . . ." How do you react to the idea that "ducking and covering" would protect these children in case of a nuclear attack?

After the Soviet Union exploded an atomic bomb in 1949 American civil defense planners confronted a delicate task. They needed to warn citizens to prepare for a possible nuclear attack against the United States. But to avoid panic and hysteria, they had to reassure Americans they could survive if one occurred. The civil defense film *Duck and Cover* (1951) conveyed to students the message that government had plans in place to protect them. Did the

message get across? And perhaps just as interesting to consider, did the officials making the film believe what they were teaching? If not, why teach the techniques? In the end, *Time* magazine concluded that while Americans feared the bomb, they accepted "the idea they must live with it."

Stills from *Duck and Cover,* Federal Civil Defense Administration

THINKING CRITICALLY

In what ways does the use of cartoon images and humor make the message more or less credible? Can you describe a more effective way to get across the message that to survive, people needed to react immediately in a nuclear crisis? Or is there no effective defense against nuclear weapons?

By 1949, then, the Cold War framed all aspects of American foreign policy. The Joint Chiefs of Staff had committed themselves to a policy of nuclear deterrence. Western Europe was on its way to economic recovery, thanks to the Marshall Plan. Soviet pressures on Greece and Turkey had abated. Many Americans had hopes that the United States might soon defeat communism.

Yet these successes brought little comfort. The Soviet Union was not simply a major power seeking to protect its interests and expand where opportunity permitted. Many Americans believed the Soviets were determined to overthrow the United States from either without or within. This was a war being fought not only across the globe but right in the United States by unseen agents using subversive means. In this way, the Cold War came to shape the lives of Americans at home as much as it did American policy abroad.

 REVIEW

What were Soviet and American strategies after World War II, and what were the hot spots where these strategies clashed?

POSTWAR PROSPERITY

At war's end many business leaders feared that a sudden drop in government spending would bring back the conditions of the 1930s. Instead, despite a rocky year or two of inflation and shortages, Americans entered into the longest period of prosperity in the nation's history, lasting until the 1970s. Even the fear of communism could not deflect Americans from the ideal of a consumer society in which government cooperated with private enterprise and management accepted a partnership with labor leaders.

Two forces drove the postwar economic boom. One was unbridled consumer and business spending that followed 16 years of depression and war. High war wages had piled up in savings accounts and war bonds. Eager consumers set off to find the new cars, appliances, and foods unavailable during the war. Despite the end of government wartime spending, the gross national product fell less than 1 percent and employment actually increased. Consumers had taken up the slack.

Government spending at the local, state, and federal levels provided another boost to prosperity. The three major growth industries in the decades after World War II were health care, education, and government programs. Each of these was spurred by public spending. Equally important, the federal government poured billions of dollars into the military-industrial sector. The defense budget, which fell to $9 billion in 1947, reached $50 billion by the time Truman left office. Over the longer term these factors promoting economic growth became clearer.

Hidden Costs of a Consuming Nation >> In this new consumer economy synthetic goods played a central role, promising a cheaper and more convenient lifestyle. Phosphate detergents got clothes whiter than did traditional laundry soaps. Chemical fertilizers produced greater yields in fields once treated with animal manure. The chemical giant DuPont caught the spirit of the American fascination with new wonders and promised "Better Things for Better Living . . . through Chemistry."

But the ideal of a full-employment society based on mass consumption contained flaws. The new consumer goods depended on cheap and plentiful fossil fuels, since hydrocarbons from petroleum formed the basis for many fertilizers and plastics. Much of the world's future oil resources lay in politically unstable regions such as the Middle East or in ecologically vulnerable areas such as the Gulf of Mexico. Some scientists saw nuclear power as an alternative energy source that would fuel consumer needs. But in 1946 an atomic test on Bikini Atoll in the South Pacific revealed that dangerous levels of radiation persisted long after an atomic blast. Atomic energy would not be the miracle source of cheap, safe power.

In 1948 the industrial town of Donora, Pennsylvania, provided a warning about the dangers of environmental abuse. Donora, located near Pittsburgh, was home to metal smelters and steel mills. During a five-day period, an inversion layer over the town trapped the toxic brew of sulfur dioxide, carbon monoxide, and metal dust spewing from the smelters. Some 20 people died and half the town's 7,000 residents were hospitalized. Industry leaders worried that an outraged public would insist on new government controls. It preferred to view the atmosphere into which it dumped its pollution as "a useful natural resource" to be used "for the dispersion of wastes within its capacity to do so without harm to the surroundings."

A few critics argued that such ideas ignored a fundamental principle of ecology: that substances entering the food chain accumulated in all living things. Aldo Leopold, a pioneering ecologist, proposed in a *Sand County Almanac* (1949) what he called a "land ethic." He observed, "we abuse the land because we see it as a commodity belonging to us" instead of "a community to which we belong," to be used with love and respect. Americans in the postwar years were not ready to heed Leopold's warning.

As the economy made the bumpy transition from war to peace, short-term worries trumped long-term concerns.

Postwar Adjustments >> With millions of veterans looking for peacetime jobs, workers on the home front, especially women and minorities, found themselves out of jobs. War employment had given many women their first taste of economic independence. As peace came, almost 75 percent of the workingwomen in one survey indicated that they hoped to continue their jobs. But when the troops returned home traditional cultural attitudes pushed women out of the workforce. Male social scientists stressed that it was important for

<< For five days in October 1948, an inversion layer in the atmosphere trapped a deadly mix of pollutants over Donora, Pennsylvania. In addition to 20 people, some 800 animals died from the effects of the toxic air.
Bettmann/Getty Images

women to accept "more than the wife's usual responsibility for her marriage" and offer "lavish—and undemanding—affection" to returning GIs.

At the end of the war, minorities found themselves the losers when an old labor practice was implemented: "last hired, first fired." At the height of the war, over 200,000 African Americans and Hispanics were employed in shipbuilding. By 1946 that number had dwindled to fewer than 10,000. The influx of Mexican laborers under the bracero program was temporarily halted. In the South, where the large majority of Black Americans lived, few jobs were available.

At the same time, many Hispanic veterans who had fought for their country during the war resented returning to a deeply segregated society. Such GIs "have acquired a new courage, have become more vocal in protesting the restrictions and inequalities with which they are confronted," noted one white Texan. When a funeral director in Three Rivers, Texas, refused to open a segregated cemetery for the burial of Felix Longoria, a Mexican American soldier killed in battle, his supporters organized. Led by Dr. Hector Garcia, a former army medical officer, the American GI Forum was founded in 1948 to campaign for civil rights. Longoria was finally buried in Arlington National Cemetery after the GI Forum convinced Congressman Lyndon Baines Johnson to intervene.

Black veterans had a similar impact. Angered by violence and frustrated by the slow pace of desegregation, they breathed new energy into civil rights organizations like the NAACP and

^ The Liga Pro Defensa Escolar, or Pro Schools Defense League, pushed to abolish segregated schooling, which affected Latinos as well as African Americans. No doubt deliberately, the league's emblem was written in English.
Benson Latin American Collection, University of Texas

the Congress of Racial Equality. Voting rights was one of the issues they pushed. Registration drives in the South had the greatest success in urban centers like Atlanta. Other Black leaders pressed for improved education. In rural Virginia, for example, a young Howard University lawyer, Spottswood

Robinson, litigated cases for the NAACP to force improvement in all-Black schools, which were always separate, but seldom equal. Robinson and the NAACP won equal pay for Black and white teachers in one school district.

In rural areas, however, segregationists used economic intimidation, violence, and even murder to preserve the Jim Crow system. White citizens in Georgia lynched several Black veterans who tried to vote. Such instances disturbed President Truman, who saw civil rights as a key ingredient in his reform agenda. The president was especially disturbed when he learned that police in South Carolina had gouged out the eyes of a recently discharged Black veteran. Truman in December 1946 appointed a Committee on Civil Rights that a year later published *To Secure These Rights*.

In its report the committee exposed a racial caste system that denied African Americans employment opportunities, equal education, voting rights, and decent housing. But every time Truman appealed to Congress to carry out the committee's recommendations, southern senators threatened to filibuster. Their obstruction forced the president to resort to executive authority to achieve even modest results. In his most direct attack on segregation, he issued an **executive order** in July 1948 banning discrimination in the armed forces. Segregationists predicted disaster, but experience soon demonstrated that integrated units fought well and experienced minimal racial tension.

executive order declaration issued by the president or by a governor possessing the force of law.

The New Deal at Bay >>

In September 1945 Truman pushed to extend the New Deal into the postwar era. He called for legislation to guarantee full employment, subsidized public housing, national health insurance, and a peacetime version of the Fair Employment Practices Commission to fight job discrimination. But inflation, temporary shortages of consumer goods, and a wave of strikes by autoworkers, coal miners, and railroad workers hobbled the recovery. They also undermined Truman's ability to pass such liberal legislation. For two years prices rose as much as 15 percent annually. Consumers blamed the White House for not doing more to ease their burden.

Conservative Republicans and southern Democrats moved to block the president's attempts to revive the New Deal. All the president achieved was a watered-down full-employment bill, which created the Council of Economic Advisers. The bill did establish one key principle: the government rather than the private sector was responsible for maintaining full employment. As the congressional elections of 1946 neared, Republicans stressed the production shortages and labor unrest. "To err is Truman," proclaimed the campaign buttons—or, more simply, "Had enough?" Many voters had. Not since 1928 had the Democrats fared so poorly. The Republicans gained control of both houses of Congress.

Leading the rightward swing was Senator Robert A. Taft of Ohio, son of former president William Howard Taft. Bob Taft not only wanted to halt the spread of the New Deal—he wanted to dismantle it. "We have to get over the corrupting idea we can legislate prosperity, legislate equality, legislate opportunity," he said in dismissing the liberal agenda. Taft especially wished to limit the power of the unions. In 1947 he pushed the Taft-Hartley Act through Congress over Truman's veto. In the event of a strike the bill allowed the president to order workers back on the job during a 90-day "cooling-off" period while collective bargaining continued. It also permitted states to adopt "right-to-work" laws, which banned the closed shop by eliminating union membership as a prerequisite for many jobs. Union leaders hated the new law but learned to live with it, though it did hurt union efforts to organize, especially in the South.

Despite the conservative backlash, most Americans continued to support the New Deal's major accomplishments: Social Security, minimum wages, and a more active role for government in reducing unemployment. The administration maintained its commitment to setting a minimum wage, raising it in 1950 from 45 to 75 cents an hour. Social Security coverage was broadened to include an additional 10 million workers. Furthermore, a growing list of welfare programs benefited not only the poor but also veterans, middle-income families, older people, and students.

The most striking of these was the GI Bill of 1944, which created unparalleled opportunity for returning veterans. Those with more than two years of service received all tuition and fees plus living expenses for three years of college education. By 1948 the government was paying the college costs of almost half of all male students as over 2 million veterans went to college on the GI Bill. The increase in college graduates encouraged a shift from blue- to white-collar work. Veterans also received low-interest loans to start businesses or to buy farms and homes. The GI Bill accelerated trends that would transform American society into a prosperous, better-educated, heavily middle-class, suburban nation.

The Election of 1948 >>

With his domestic program blocked, Truman faced almost certain defeat in the election of 1948. The New Deal coalition that Franklin Roosevelt had put together now fractured. From the left Henry Wallace challenged Truman. Wallace had served as secretary of agriculture and vice president under Roosevelt, and then as secretary of commerce under Truman. He wanted to pursue New Deal reforms even more than Truman and voiced sympathy for the Soviet Union. Disaffected liberals bolted the Democratic Party to support Wallace on a third-party Progressive ticket.

Within the southern wing of the party, arch-segregationists resisted Truman's proposals for either a voting rights bill or an antilynching law. When the liberal wing of the party adopted a civil rights plank at the Democratic convention, delegates from several Deep South states stalked out to create the States' Rights or "Dixiecrat" Party. They chose J. Strom Thurmond, the segregationist governor of South Carolina, as their candidate.

Divisions among Democrats convinced Republicans they would win easily. To control the political center they rejected the conservative Taft in favor of the moderate former New York governor and 1944 nominee Thomas Dewey. Dewey's reserved manner inspired little enthusiasm. "You have to know Dewey well to really dislike him," quipped one critic. Still, it seemed Dewey would walk away with the race.

Truman fought back with a stinging attack against the "reactionaries" in Congress: that "bunch of old mossbacks . . . gluttons of privilege . . . all set to do a hatchet job on the New Deal." From the rear of his campaign train, he made almost 400 speeches in eight weeks. At each stop, he hammered away at the "do-nothing" 80th Congress, which, he told farmers, "had stuck a pitchfork" in their backs. On Election Day, oddsmakers still favored Dewey by as much as 20 to 1. Hours before the polls closed the anti–New Deal *Chicago Tribune* happily headlined "Dewey Defeats Truman." But the experts were wrong. Not only did Truman win by over 2 million popular votes, but Democrats also gained majorities in the House and the Senate.

The Fair Deal >> As he began his new term, Harry Truman declared that all Americans were entitled to a "Fair Deal" from their government. He called for such New Deal programs as national health insurance and regional TVA-style

projects. Echoing an old Populist goal, Truman strove to keep his working coalition together by forging stronger links between farmers and labor. But the conservative coalition of southern Democrats and Republicans in Congress still blocked any significant initiatives. On the domestic front Truman remained largely the conservator of Franklin Roosevelt's legacy.

REVIEW

How did the federal government promote postwar prosperity?

THE COLD WAR AT HOME

Bob Raymondi was no stranger to racketeering or gangland killings. In fact, as a mobster serving a prison term in the late 1940s, he was so feared that he dominated the inmates at Dannemora Prison. Raymondi also befriended a group of Communists who had been jailed for advocating the overthrow of the government. He enjoyed talking with people who had some education. When Raymondi's sister learned about his new friends, she was frantic. "My God, Bob," she told him, "you'll get into trouble."

Was something amiss? Many Americans seemed to believe that Communists were more dangerous than hardened criminals. Out of a national population of 150 million, the Communist Party had a membership of just 43,000 in 1950. (Many of those were undercover FBI agents.) But worry about Communists Americans did. Conservatives still thought of the New Deal as "creeping socialism," only an arm's length short of communism. Leftists, they believed, controlled labor unions, Hollywood, and groups sympathetic to the New Deal. As Stalin extended Soviet control in Eastern Europe and Asia, American domestic fears grew.

The Shocks of 1949 >> The year 1949 proved a pivotal year in the Cold War abroad. American scientists reported in August that rains monitored in the Pacific contained traces of hot nuclear waste. Only one conclusion seemed possible: the Soviet Union possessed its own atomic bomb. Senator Arthur Vandenberg, a Republican with wide experience in international affairs, summed up the reaction of many Americans to the end of the American nuclear monopoly: "This is now a different world." Truman accelerated the nuclear arms race by increasing research into a newer, more powerful hydrogen bomb.

Candidate (Party)	Electoral Vote (%)	Popular Vote (%)
Harry S. Truman (Democratic)	303 (57)	24,105,812 (50)
Thomas E. Dewey (Republican)	189 (36)	21,970,065 (46)
Strom Thurmond (States' Rights)	3 (7)	1,169,021 (2)
Henry A. Wallace (Progressive)		1,157,172 (2)
Other candidates (Communist, Prohibition, Socialist Labor, Liberty)	–	272,713 –

MAP 27.1: ELECTION OF 1948

THE SATURDAY EVENING POST SERIAL THAT JOLTED MILLIONS!

WARNER BROS. BRING IT TO THE SCREEN!

I WAS A COMMUNIST FOR THE F.B.I.
FRANK LOVEJOY

∧ The role of government informer took center stage in this movie derived from articles in *The Saturday Evening Post*. "I had to sell out my own girl—so would you!" went the film's tagline. "I was under the toughest orders a guy could get! I stood by and watched my brother slugged. . . . I started a riot that ran red with terror. . . . I learned every dirty rule in their book—and had to use them—because I was a communist—but I WAS A COMMUNIST FOR THE FBI."
Warner Bros./Photofest, Inc.

December brought more bad news. The Nationalist government of Chiang Kai-shek fled mainland China to the offshore island of Formosa (present-day Taiwan). In January 1950 Communist troops under Mao Zedong swarmed into Beijing, China's capital city. Chiang's defeat came as no surprise to the State Department. Officials there had long regarded Chiang and his Nationalists as hopelessly corrupt and ineffective. Despite major American efforts to save his regime

∧ The fall of China to the forces of Mao Zedong was one of the chilling Cold War shocks of 1949.
Bettmann/Getty Images

and stabilize China, poverty and civil unrest had spread. In 1947 full-scale civil war had broken out. By February 1949 almost half of Chiang's demoralized troops had defected to the Communists. The December defeat was hardly unexpected.

Republicans, who had formerly supported the president's foreign policy, now turned on him. For some time, a group of wealthy conservatives and Republican senators had resented the administration's preoccupation with Europe. Time Life publisher Henry Luce used his magazines to campaign for a greater concern for Asian affairs and especially more aid to defeat Mao Zedong. When Chiang at last collapsed, his American backers, called the China Lobby, charged the Democrats with letting the Communists win.

In 1948 former Communist Whittaker Chambers testified to HUAC that Alger Hiss, an adviser to Roosevelt at the Yalta Conference, had passed secrets to the Soviet Union during the 1930s. Though the evidence in the case was inconclusive, the jury convicted Hiss not for espionage but for lying about his association with Chambers. And in February 1950 Cold War anxieties intensified with news from Britain that a high-ranking physicist, Klaus Fuchs, had spied for the Russians while working on the Manhattan Project. Here was clear evidence of conspiracy.

The Loyalty Crusade >> As fears of subversion and espionage mounted, President Truman sought to deflect Republican accusations that he was "soft" on communism. Only days after proposing the Truman Doctrine in March 1947, the president signed an executive order establishing a Federal Employee Loyalty Program to guard against any disloyalty by "Reds, phonies, and 'parlor pinks.'" The order required government supervisors to testify to a system of federal loyalty review boards about the loyalties of their workers. The FBI was to follow up any "derogatory information" that came to light.

The system quickly got out of hand. Those accused had no right to confront their accusers. And a few years' experience showed that it was difficult to actually prove disloyalty on the part of employees. Truman began allowing the boards to fire those who were "potentially" disloyal or "bad security risks," such as alcoholics, homosexuals, and debtors. Suspected employees, in other words, were assumed guilty until proven innocent. After some 5 million investigations, the program identified a few hundred employees who, though not Communists, had at one time been associated with suspect groups. Rather than calm public fears, the loyalty program made the growing Red Scare seem more credible.

HUAC and Hollywood >> Hollywood, with its wealth, glamour, and highly visible Jewish and foreign celebrities, had long aroused suspicions among traditional Americans. In 1947 the House Committee on Un-American Activities (HCUA or HUAC) began to investigate Communist influences in the film industry. "Large numbers of moving pictures that come out of Hollywood carry the communist line," charged committee member John Rankin of Mississippi.

HUAC called a parade of Hollywood figures to sit in the glare of its public hearings. Some witnesses, such as actors John Wayne and Ronald Reagan, were "friendly" because they answered committee questions or supplied names of suspected leftists. Others refused to inform on their colleagues or to answer questions about earlier ties to the Communist Party. Eventually 10 uncooperative witnesses, known as the "Hollywood Ten," refused on First Amendment grounds to say whether they were or ever had been Communists. They served prison terms for contempt of Congress.

For all its probing, HUAC never offered convincing evidence that the film industry was in any way subversive. Yet the investigation did have a chilling effect on Hollywood. The studios adopted a blacklist that prevented admitted or accused Communists from working. Since no judicial proceedings were involved, victims of false charges, rumors, or spiteful accusations found it nearly impossible to clear their names.

Suspicion of aliens and immigrants as subversives led finally to the passage, over Truman's veto, of the McCarran Act (1950). The act required all Communists to register with the attorney general, forbade the entry of anyone who had belonged to a totalitarian organization, and allowed the Justice Department to detain suspect aliens indefinitely during deportation hearings. That same year, a Senate committee began an inquiry designed to root out homosexuals holding government jobs. Even one "sex pervert in a Government agency tends to have a corrosive influence upon his fellow employees," warned the committee.

The Ambitions of Senator McCarthy >> By 1950 anticommunism had created a climate of fear, as irrational hysteria overwhelmed legitimate concerns. Senator Joseph R. McCarthy, a relatively unknown Republican senator from Wisconsin, saw in that fear an opportunity to improve his political fortunes. Before an audience in Wheeling, West Virginia, in February 1950 he waved a sheaf of papers and announced that he had a list of 205—or perhaps 81, 57, or "a lot" of—Communists in the State Department. (No one, including the senator, could remember the number, which he continually changed.) In the following months McCarthy leveled a string of charges. He had penetrated the "iron curtain" of the State Department to discover "card-carrying Communists," the "top Russian espionage agent" in the United States, "egg-sucking phony liberals," and "Communists and queers" who wrote "perfumed notes."

In a sense, McCarthyism was the bitter fruit Truman and the Democrats reaped from their own attempts to exploit the anti-Communist mood. McCarthy, better than Truman, tapped the fears and hatreds of traditional conservatives, Catholic leaders, and neo-isolationists who distrusted things foreign, liberal, or intellectual. They saw McCarthy and his fellow witch-hunters as the protectors of a vague but deeply felt spirit of Americanism.

By the time Truman stepped down as president, 32 states had laws requiring teachers to take loyalty oaths. Government loyalty boards were asking employees what newspapers they subscribed to or phonograph records they collected. A library in Indiana banned *Robin Hood* because the idea of stealing from the rich to give to the poor seemed too leftish. As one historian commented, "Opening the valve of anti-Communist hysteria was a good deal simpler than closing it."

✓ REVIEW

How did Truman's actions contribute to the Red Scare at home and the rise of McCarthyism?

FROM COLD WAR TO HOT WAR AND BACK

As the Cold War heated up during 1949, the Truman administration searched for a more assertive foreign policy. The new approach was developed by the National Security Council (NSC), an agency created by Congress in 1947 as part of a plan to make the executive branch more effectively during Cold War crises. Rather than "contain" the Soviets, as George Kennan had suggested, the NSC wanted the United States to "strive for victory." In April 1950 the council sent Truman a document, NSC-68, which became the framework for American policy over the next 20 years.

NSC-68 called for a dramatic increase in defense spending, from $13 billion to $50 billion a year, to be paid for with a large tax increase. Most of the funds would go to rebuild conventional forces, but the NSC supported development of the hydrogen bomb to offset the new Soviet nuclear capacity. Efforts to carry out NSC-68 at first aroused widespread opposition. George Kennan argued that the Soviets had no immediate plans for domination outside the Communist bloc. Fiscal conservatives, both Democrat and Republican, resisted any proposal for higher taxes. All such reservations were swept away on June 25, 1950. "Korea came along and saved us," Secretary of State Dean Acheson later remarked.

Police Action >> In 1950 Korea was about the last place Americans imagined themselves fighting a war. Since World War II the country had been divided along the 38th parallel: the north was controlled by the Communist government of Kim Il Sung; the south, by the dictatorship of Syngman Rhee. Preoccupied with China and the rebuilding of Japan, the Truman administration's interest in Korea had dwindled steadily after the war. When Secretary of State Acheson discussed American policy in Asia for the National Press Club in January 1950, he did not even mention Korea.

On Saturday, June 24, Harry Truman was enjoying a leisurely break from politics at the family home in Independence, Missouri. In Korea it was already Sunday morning June 25 when Acheson called the president. North Korean troops had

˄ General Douglas MacArthur launched a risky amphibious attack at Inchon harbor. Because the harbor was shallow, only a narrow window existed at high-tide for landing craft to reach shore without running aground and facing enemy fire.
Navy Art Collection, Naval History and Heritage Command

crossed the 38th parallel, Acheson reported, possibly to fulfill Kim Il Sung's proclaimed intention to "liberate" South Korea. Soon Acheson confirmed that a full-scale invasion was in progress. A third world war, this one atomic, seemed agonizingly possible. Acheson recommended enough force to deter North Korean aggression, but not enough to provoke a larger war with the Soviet Union or China.

Truman did not hesitate. American troops would fight the North Koreans, though the United States would not declare war. The conflict in Korea would be a "police action" supervised by the United Nations and commanded by General Douglas MacArthur. For his part, Stalin secretly gave the Korean dictator the "green light." He told Kim that he did not oppose the attack, but that neither Russian troops nor Russian prestige would be involved.

Americans widely applauded Truman's forceful response. Congress adopted the recommendations of NSC-68. But by the time the UN authorized the police action, on June 27, North Korean forces had already pinned down the South Korean army and its American advisers within an area at the southern tip of Korea around Pusan. In a daring counterstroke, on June 15 General MacArthur launched an amphibious attack behind North Korean lines at Inchon, near the western end of the 38th parallel. Fighting eastward, MacArthur's troops trapped large numbers of the invaders.

The Chinese Intervene >> MacArthur's smashing
victory led Truman to a fateful decision. With the South liberated, he gave MacArthur permission to cross the 38th parallel, drive the Communists from the North, and reunite Korea under Syngman Rhee. Such a victory would help Truman silence Senator Joe McCarthy and boost Democrats in the 1950 congressional elections. By Thanksgiving, American troops had roundly defeated northern forces and were advancing toward the frozen Yalu River, the boundary between

Korea and China. MacArthur, made bold by success, dismissed Chinese warnings and promised that the troops would be home by Christmas.

But on November 26, 400,000 Chinese troops poured across the Yalu, smashing through lightly defended UN lines. At Chosan they trapped 20,000 American and South Korean troops, inflicting one of the worst military defeats in American history. Within three weeks they had driven UN forces back behind the 38th parallel.

Truman versus MacArthur >> Military stalemate
in Korea brought into the open a simmering feud between General MacArthur and Truman. The general, in defiance of Truman, publicized his plans for victory. He argued that UN forces should bomb Chinese and Russian supply bases across the Korean border, blockade China's coast, and unleash Chiang Kai-shek on mainland China. On March 23, 1951, he issued a personal ultimatum to Chinese military commanders demanding total surrender. To his Republican congressional supporters he sent a letter declaring, "We must win. There is no substitute for victory."

Truman saw MacArthur's strategy as risking another world war. Equally alarming, the general's insubordination threatened the tradition that the military remain under clear civilian control. When Truman made plans to discipline MacArthur, General Omar Bradley reported that MacArthur was threatening to resign before Truman could act. "The son of a bitch isn't going to resign on me," Truman retorted. "I want him fired!" Military leaders agreed that MacArthur had to go. On April 11 a stunned nation learned that the celebrated military commander had been relieved of his duties. When MacArthur returned to the States, cheering crowds welcomed him with a ticker-tape parade. Congress gave him the unprecedented opportunity to address a joint session before a national television audience.

The Global Implications of the Cold War >>
While MacArthur crusaded publicly, Truman acted behind the scenes. This was not simply a personal feud. The outcome would determine the future direction of American foreign policy. The Cold War crisis forced American leaders to think globally. Where in the world did the nation's interests lie? What region was most critical to the future? MacArthur believed that the Pacific basin would "determine the course of history in the next ten thousand years." The United States should make an all-out effort, not just to contain the Communist onslaught in Korea, but to play a major role throughout Asia. Many conservative Republicans and groups like the China Lobby shared MacArthur's view. As Senator Robert Taft put it, the United States should pursue "the same policy in the Far East as in Europe."

Truman and his advisers continued to see Western Europe as the key to the world's economic and military future. Political scientist Hans Morgenthau argued that "he who controls Europe is well on his way toward controlling the

MAP 27.2: THE KOREAN WAR

MacArthur's landing at Inchon in September 1950 helped UN forces take the offensive. The drive to the Yalu River provoked Communist China to intervene.

How did Korea's geographic location increase the risk of escalating the scale of the war?

→	North Korean forces, June 1950
┄►	Farthest advance of North Koreans, Sept. 1950
→	U.S. and UN forces, Sept. 1950
┄►	Farthest advance of U.S., Nov. 1950
→	Chinese forces, Nov. 1950–Jan. 1951
┄►	Farthest advance of Chinese, Jan. 1951

whole world." Secretary of State Acheson agreed with the Eurocentrists. Korea was to Acheson but a small link in a global "collective security system." The wider war in Asia that MacArthur favored would make the United States vulnerable elsewhere. Or, as General Bradley told Congress, a war in Asia would lead to "the wrong war, at the wrong place, at the wrong time, and with the wrong enemy." In this debate the Eurocentrists prevailed. Congressional leaders agreed that the war in Korea should remain limited and that American resources should go to rebuilding Europe's defenses.

Still, the war took its toll on Truman's political fortunes as it dragged on and peace talks went nowhere. By March 1952 Truman's popularity had sunk so low that he lost the New Hampshire presidential primary. With that defeat he announced he would not run for reelection in 1952.

The Election of 1952 >> The Republican formula for victory in 1952 played on the Truman administration's weaknesses, the stalemate over Korea in particular. In addition,

several of Truman's advisers were exposed for accepting gifts in return for political favors. The GOP summed up its campaign strategy in the formula K1C2: Korea, corruption, and communism. The Democrats could boast about the economy, which remained remarkably healthy. Wage and price controls put in place by the administration prevented the sharp inflation that was expected to follow increased wartime spending.

Republican Party regulars and the conservative wing committed themselves to Robert Taft. But party leaders nominated the popular military hero Dwight "Ike" Eisenhower. To console disappointed Taft delegates, the convention chose the staunch anti-Communist senator Richard Nixon as Eisenhower's running mate. The Democrats drafted Illinois governor Adlai E. Stevenson, an eloquent speaker but a little-known candidate who lacked the common touch.

The election outcome was never much in doubt. Eisenhower addressed voter unease over Korea by promising that if elected, he would seek an end to the war. In the end, Ike's broad smile and confident manner won him over 55 percent of the vote. "The great problem of America today," he had said during the campaign, "is to take that straight road down the middle."

Once in office Eisenhower renewed negotiations with North Korea but warned that unless the talks made speedy progress, the United States might retaliate "under circumstances of our choosing." The carrot-and-stick approach worked. On July 27, 1953, the Communists and the United Nations forces signed an armistice ending a "police action" in which nearly 34,000 Americans had died. Korea remained divided, almost exactly as it had been in 1950. Communism had been "contained," but at a high price.

The Fall of McCarthy >> It was less clear whether anticommunism could be contained. When Eisenhower called himself a "modern" Republican, he distinguished himself from what he called the more "hidebound" members of the GOP. Senator McCarthy's reckless antics, which at first had been directed at Democrats, began to hit Republican targets as well.

By the summer of 1953 the senator was on a rampage. He dispatched two young staff members, Roy Cohn and David Schine, to investigate the State Department's overseas information agency and the Voice of America radio stations. While there, they insisted on purging government libraries of "subversive" volumes. Some librarians, fearing for their careers, burned a number of books.

The administration's own behavior contributed to the hysteria on which McCarthy thrived. Eisenhower launched another federal loyalty campaign, which he claimed resulted in 3,000 firings and 5,000 resignations of government employees. Furthermore, a well-publicized spy trial led to the conviction of Ethel and Julius Rosenberg, a couple accused of passing atomic secrets to the Soviets. Although the evidence against Ethel was weak, the judge sentenced both Rosenbergs

to death in the electric chair, an unusually harsh punishment even in cases of espionage. When asked to commute the death sentence to life imprisonment, Eisenhower refused, and the Rosenbergs were executed in June 1953.

In such a climate—where Democrats remained silent for fear of being called leftists and Eisenhower cautiously refused to "get in the gutter with that guy"—McCarthy lost all sense of proportion. When the army denied his staff aide David Schine a special assignment, McCarthy launched an investigation into communism in the army. Under the glare of television lights, the public had an opportunity to see McCarthy badger witnesses and make a mockery of Senate procedures. Soon after, his popularity began to slide and the anti-Communist hysteria ebbed as well. The Senate finally moved to censure him. He died three years later, destroyed by alcohol.

THEN&NOW

Joe McCarthy epitomized those public figures who play on popular fears of others to advance their own ambitions. The Salem Witch Trials, lynchings to enforce segregation, arrests of Socialists during World War I, the internment of Japanese citizens during World War II, and the persecution of homosexuals are all instances in American history in which irrational fears led to acts of violence and/or threats to the rule of law. Historians generally find these outbreaks the exception rather than the norm in the nation's past. Yet, recent efforts to stigmatize immigrants, members of the LGBTQ community, and religious minorities again tear at the fabric of

<< At the Army-McCarthy hearings Senator McCarthy continued to claim that the United States faced a serious internal threat from Communists. Army lawyer Joseph Welch barely disguised his impatience with the senator's exaggerations.
Everett Collection Inc/Alamy Stock Photo

our nation. Abraham Lincoln reminded us that in a democratic society "a house divided against itself cannot stand." Political leaders eventually knitted together a divided nation after the Civil War and calmed the Cold War fears of the 1950s. Who will heal the divisions of the 21st century?

Eisenhower Republicanism >> With the Democrats out of the White House for the first time since the Depression and with McCarthyites in retreat, Eisenhower did indeed seem to be leading the nation on a course "right down the middle." Still, it is worth noting how much that sense of "middle" had changed, both domestically and in the international arena.

The Great Depression and World War II made most Americans realize that the nation's economy was closely linked to the international order. The crash in 1929, with its worldwide effects, made that clear. The New Deal demonstrated that Americans were willing to give the federal government power to manage American society in major new ways. And the war led the government to intervene in the economy even more directly.

It became clear that the "middle road" did not mean a return to the laissez-faire economics of the 1920s. Nor would most Americans support the isolationist policies of the 1930s. "Modern" Republicans accepted social welfare programs such as Social Security and recognized that the federal government had a responsibility to lower unemployment, control inflation, and manage the economy in a variety of ways.

The shift from war to peace demonstrated that it was no longer possible to make global war without making a global peace. Under the new balance of power in the postwar world, the United States and the Soviet Union stood alone as "superpowers," with the potential capability to annihilate each other and the rest of the world. After the United States used its resources to rebuild the economies of Western Europe and Japan, a new global economy emerged. And the two superpowers tacitly acknowledged each other's spheres of influence: Eastern Europe and China for the Soviet Union; East Asia, Western Europe, and Latin America for the United States and its NATO allies. Much of the world, however, remained unaligned or outside the cold war boundaries. South Asia, the Middle East, Africa, India, and even Cuba, in America's backyard, would soon become arenas for the continuing cold war rivalry

REVIEW

On what major issues did President Truman and General MacArthur disagree?

CHAPTER SUMMARY

The Cold War between the Soviet Union and the United States affected every aspect of American domestic and foreign policy.

- Americans had long been suspicious of Soviet communism, but Stalin's aggressive posture toward Eastern Europe and the Persian Gulf region after World War II raised new fears among American policy makers.
- In response the Truman administration applied a policy of containment through the Truman Doctrine, the Marshall Plan, and NSC-68.
- The domestic transition from war to peace was slowed because of inflation, labor unrest, and shortages of goods and housing, but consumer and government spending marked the beginning of a 30-year economic expansion.
- Domestic fear of Communist subversion led the Truman administration to devise a government loyalty program and inspired the witch hunts of Senator Joseph McCarthy.
- The Soviet detonation of an atomic bomb and the fall of China to the Communists, followed by the Korean War, undermined the popularity of Harry Truman and the Democrats, opening the way for Dwight Eisenhower's victory in the 1952 presidential election.

Digging Deeper

A good overview of the Cold War is Fredrik Logevall and Campbell Craig, *America's Cold War* (2009). For the science and politics of the H-bomb, see Gregg Herken, *Brotherhood of the Bomb: The Tangled Lives and Loyalties of Robert Oppenheimer, Ernest Lawrence, and Edward Teller* (2003); and Kai Bird and Martin Sherwin, *American Prometheus: The Triumph and Tragedy of J. Robert Oppenheimer* (2006). Melvin P. Leffler and Odd Arne Westad, eds., *The Cold War*, Vol. 1 (2011), covers almost every phase of the early Cold War. Stephen Whitfield, *The Culture of the Cold War* (1991), illuminates the rise of the Red Scare.

Brian Burnes, *Harry S. Truman: His Life and Times* (2003), is a lively account of a president who became more popular with the passage of time. Elizabeth Edwards Spalding, *The First Cold Warrior: Harry Truman, Containment and the Remaking of Liberal Internationalism* (2006), measures Truman as an architect of the postwar world order. The best account of the man who gave his name to the Red Scare is David Oshinsky, *A Conspiracy So Immense: The World of Joe McCarthy* (2005). Two historians have shown how Cold War politics and the civil rights movement intersected: Thomas Borstelmann, *The Cold War and the Color Line: American Race Relations in the Global Arena* (2003); and Mary Dudziak, *Cold War Civil Rights: Race and the Image of American Democracy* (2002).

Just as the United States raced the Soviet Union in a quest for atomic weapons, so the Big Three automakers of the 1950s (GM, Ford, and Chrysler) sought to outdo one another in producing sleek, jet-age-styled cars. This suburban family shows off its 1959 Mercury Monterey.

Archive Photo/Getty Images

>> **An American Story**

DYNAMIC OBSOLESCENCE (THE WONDERFUL WORLD OF HARLEY EARL)

General Motors epitomized the corporate culture of the 1950s. In an age of conformity, GM executives sought to blend in rather than to stand out. They chose their suits in drab colors— dark blue, dark gray, or light gray—to increase their anonymity. Not head car designer Harley Earl. Earl brought a touch of Hollywood into the world of corporate bureaucrats. He had a closet filled with colorful suits. His staff would marvel as he headed off to a board meeting dressed in white linen with a dark blue shirt and blue suede shoes.

Mr. Earl—no one who worked for him ever called him Harley—could afford to be a maverick. He created the cars that brought customers into GM showrooms across the country. Before he came to Detroit, engineering sold cars. Advertising stressed mechanical virtues—the steady ride, reliable brakes, or, perhaps, power steering. Earl made style the distinctive feature. Unlike the boxy look other designers favored, an Earl car was low and sleek, suggesting motion even when the car stood still. No feature stood out more distinctively than the fins he first put on the 1948 Cadillac. By the mid-1950s jet planes inspired Earl to design ever-more-outrageous fins, complemented by huge, shiny chrome grilles and ornaments. These features served no functional purpose. Some critics dismissed Earl's designs as jukeboxes on wheels.

Earl and GM did not care. Design sold cars. "It gave [customers] an extra receipt for their money in the form of visible prestige marking for an expensive car," Earl said. The "Big Three" auto manufacturers—General Motors, Ford, and Chrysler—raced one another to redesign their annual models, the more outrageous the better. Earl once joked, "I'd put smokestacks right in the middle of the sons of bitches if I thought I could sell more cars." The goal was not a better car but what Earl called "dynamic obsolescence," or simply change for change's sake. "The 1957 Ford was great," its

The monstrous tail fins of the 1959 Cadillac.
Transtock/SuperStock

designer remarked, "but right away we had to bury it and start another." Even though the mechanics of cars changed little from year to year, dynamic obsolescence persuaded Americans in the 1950s to buy new cars in record numbers.

Fins, roadside motels, "gaseterias," drive-in burger huts, interstate highways, shopping centers, and, of course, suburbs—all these were part of a culture of mobility in the 1950s. Americans continued their exodus from rural areas to cities and from cities to the suburbs. African Americans left the South, heading for industrial centers in the Northeast, in the Midwest, and on the West Coast. Mexican Americans concentrated in southwestern cities, Puerto Ricans came largely to New York, while Cubans arrived after a 1959 revolution. And for Americans in the Snow Belt, the climate of the West and South (at least when civilized by air conditioning) made the Sun Belt attractive.

Mobility was social, as well as physical. The American middle class grew, as the economy expanded.

Labor unions negotiated wage and benefits packages that moved blue-collar workers into middle-income brackets. In an era of prosperity and peace, some commentators began to speak of a **consensus**—a general agreement

consensus point of view generally shared by a group, institution, or even a culture.

in American culture, based on values of the broad middle class. In a positive light, consensus reflected the agreement among most Americans about fundamental democratic values. Most citizens embraced the material benefits of prosperity as evidence of the virtue of "the American way." And they opposed the spread of communism abroad.

But consensus had its dark side. Critics worried that too strong a consensus bred a mindless conformity. Were Americans becoming too homogenized? Was there a depressing sameness in the material goods they owned, in the places they lived, and in the values they held? The parents of the baby boomers born into this era seldom agonized over such issues. In the White House, President Eisenhower radiated a comforting sense that the affairs of the nation and the world were in capable hands. That left teenagers free to worry about what really mattered: a first date, a first kiss, a first job, a first choice for college, and whether or not to "go all the way" in the back seat of one of Harley Earl's fin-swept Buicks. <<

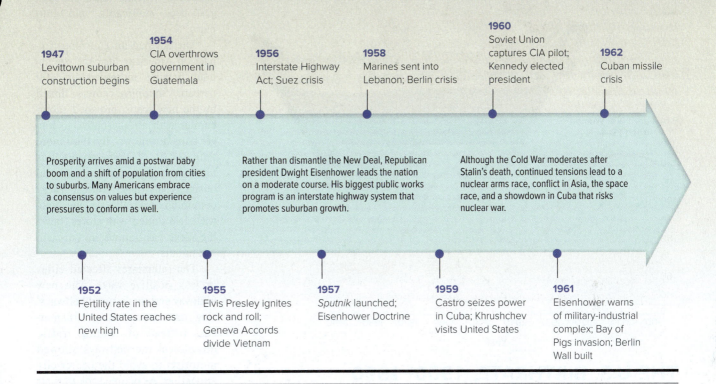

1947
Levittown suburban construction begins

1954
CIA overthrows government in Guatemala

1956
Interstate Highway Act; Suez crisis

1958
Marines sent into Lebanon; Berlin crisis

1960
Soviet Union captures CIA pilot; Kennedy elected president

1962
Cuban missile crisis

Prosperity arrives amid a postwar baby boom and a shift of population from cities to suburbs. Many Americans embrace a consensus on values but experience pressures to conform as well.

Rather than dismantle the New Deal, Republican president Dwight Eisenhower leads the nation on a moderate course. His biggest public works program is an interstate highway system that promotes suburban growth.

Although the Cold War moderates after Stalin's death, continued tensions lead to a nuclear arms race, conflict in Asia, the space race, and a showdown in Cuba that risks nuclear war.

1952
Fertility rate in the United States reaches new high

1955
Elvis Presley ignites rock and roll; Geneva Accords divide Vietnam

1957
Sputnik launched; Eisenhower Doctrine

1959
Castro seizes power in Cuba; Khrushchev visits United States

1961
Eisenhower warns of military-industrial complex; Bay of Pigs invasion; Berlin Wall built

THE RISE OF SUBURBS

The return of prosperity brought a baby boom and a need for new housing. Suburban growth accelerated sharply at the end of World War II. During the 1950s suburbs grew 40 times faster than cities, so that by 1960 half of the American people lived in them. But as suburbs flourished, the cities declined as the middle class moved out. Many urban businesses and industries joined the exodus as well.

A Boom in Babies and in Housing >> The Great
Depression caused many couples to delay beginning a family. Postwar prosperity thus stimulated a "baby boom" so that by 1952 the birthrate passed 25 per 1,000, one of the highest rates in the world. New brides were younger, which translated into increased fertility. And Americans chose to have larger families, with numbers of three-children families tripling and those with four or more quadrupling. "Just imagine how much these extra people, these new markets, will absorb," one journalist predicted.

This extraordinary population bulge was not limited to the United States. In several other developed countries fertility rates also soared—Australia, New Zealand, Britain, and West Germany prime among them in the early 1960s. Yet, following this postwar spurt, the long-term trend in American fertility rates continued downward, as it did in other developed countries.

The boom in marriages and births created a need for housing. At war's end, 5 million families lived in cramped apartments or even dark basements. With the help of the GI Bill and rising incomes, owning a house rather than renting became a reality for over half of American families. And the suburbs offered the kind of residence most Americans idealized: a detached single-family house with a lawn.

In the postwar era inexpensive suburban housing became synonymous with the name of real estate developer William Levitt. Levitt learned how to use mass-production techniques in construction while building houses for war workers. In 1947 he began construction of a 17,000-house community in the Long Island suburb of Hempstead. Buoyed by its success, Levitt later built developments in Bucks County, Pennsylvania, and Willingboro, New Jersey.

The typical early Levitt house was a "Cape Codder." It featured a living room, a kitchen, a bath, and two bedrooms on the ground floor and an expansion attic, all for $7,990. None of the houses had custom details, insulation, or any features that complicated construction. "The reason we have it so good in this country," Levitt said, "is that we can

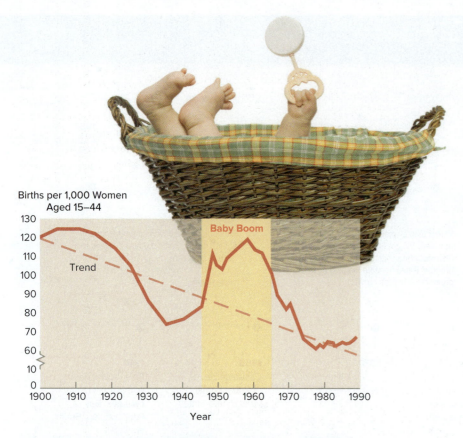

Births per 1,000 Women
Aged 15–44

Baby Boom

Trend

THE U.S. BIRTHRATE, 1900–1990

The Depression years marked the sharpest decline as financially strapped couples deferred child rearing. Younger marriages and postwar prosperity triggered the baby boom, but in general, affluence encourages lower birthrates.
(background photo) James Steidl/Kyle Gruba/jgroup/istock

produce lots of things at low prices through mass production." Uniformity in house style extended to behavior as well. Levitt discouraged owners from changing colors or adding distinctive features to the house or yard. Buyers promised to cut the grass each week of the summer and not to hang out wash on weekends.

Suburbs and Cities Transformed >> Single-family houses with lawns required plenty of open land, unlike the row houses built side by side in urban developments. That meant Levitt and other mass builders chose vacant areas outside major urban centers. With the new houses farther from factories, offices, and jobs, the automobile became indispensable.

Population shifts to suburbs choked old country roads with traffic. To ease congestion the Eisenhower administration proposed a 20-year plan to build a massive interstate highway system. Eisenhower played on Cold War fears to rally support for the plan, arguing that the new system would help cities evacuate in case of nuclear attack. In 1956 Congress passed the National Interstate and Defense Highways Act, setting in motion the largest public-works project in

history. The federal government picked up 90 percent of the cost through a Highway Trust Fund, financed by special taxes on cars, gas, tires, lubricants, and auto parts.

The act had an enormous impact on American life. Average annual driving increased by 400 percent. Shopping centers, linked by the new roads, provided suburbanites with an alternative to longer trips downtown. By 1960 more than 3,840 of them covered as much land as the nation's central business districts. Almost every community had at least one highway strip dotted with stores, bowling alleys, gas stations, and drive-in restaurants.

The interstates affected cities in less positive ways. The new highway system featured beltways, ring roads around major urban areas. Instead of leading traffic downtown, the beltways allowed motorists to avoid the center city altogether. As people took to their cars, intercity rail service and mass transit declined. Seventy-five percent of all government transportation dollars went to subsidize travel by car and truck; only 1 percent was earmarked for urban mass transit. At the same time that middle-class homeowners were moving to the suburbs, many low-paying, unskilled jobs disappeared from the cities. This forced the urban poor into reverse commuting from city to suburb. All these trends made cities less attractive places to live or do business in. With falling property values, city governments lacked the tax base to finance public services. A vicious cycle ensued that proved most damaging to the urban poor, who had few means of escape.

Much of the white population that moved to the suburbs was replaced by African Americans and Latinos. They were part of larger migrations of millions of Black and Latino families leaving rural areas to search for work in urban centers. Most African Americans headed for the Northeast and upper Midwest. While central cities lost 3.6 million white residents, they gained 4.5 million African Americans. Indeed, by 1960 half of all Black Americans were living in central cities.

Earlier waves of European immigrants had been absorbed by the expanding urban economy. During the 1950s, however, the flight of jobs and middle-class taxpayers to the suburbs made it difficult for African Americans and Latinos

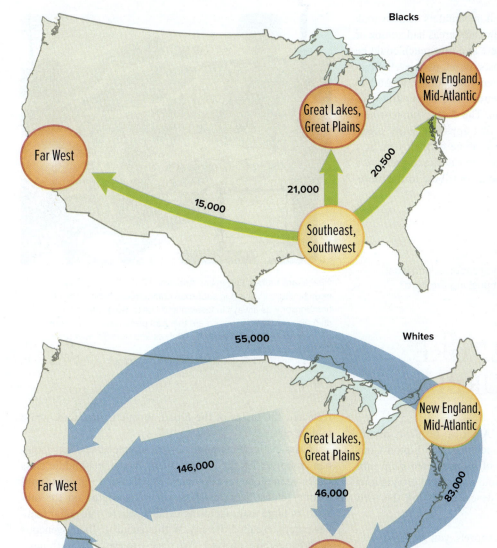

Blacks

Whites

MAP 28.1: AVERAGE ANNUAL REGIONAL MIGRATION, 1947–1960

African Americans moved in significant numbers to urban centers in the Northeast, the Midwest, and the Far West. Whites were drawn to the increasingly diversified economy of the South as well as to the new industries, stimulated by the war, in the Far West. By the 1970s, the trend had become known as the "Sun Belt" phenomenon.
Source: Russell Sage Foundation

to follow the same path. In the cities fewer jobs awaited them, while declining school systems made it harder for newcomers to acculturate. In the hardest-hit urban areas, unemployment rose to over 40 percent.

The suburbs remained beyond the reach of most minorities. Those who could afford a home there faced "red-lining."

In areas outlined in red on maps, real estate agents refused to show houses to minorities; bankers refused them mortgages. And many communities adopted either restrictive covenants or zoning regulations that kept out "undesirable" home buyers. One African American, William Myers, finally managed to buy a house from a white family in Levittown, Pennsylvania, in 1957, but the developers did not sell directly to African Americans until 1960.

Environmental Blues >>

With the spread of suburbs came other growing pains. In late summer of 1956 residents of Portuguese Bend, California, learned a painful lesson about building in unstable areas. Houses along Palos Verde Drive South began to move—slowly at first. By October, 156 houses, along with their lawns, gardens, and swimming pools, had "gently slumped downhill as though they were so much custard pudding." Over time the effluent from septic systems, along with lawn watering, had slicked the underlying layers of shale tilting toward the nearby Pacific Ocean. With no friction to hold the soil and shale in place, gravity took over. Suburbs in Washington, D.C., Cincinnati, and Pittsburgh suffered similar landslide disasters. Other misfortunes occurred where developers built in wetlands and on floodplains.

The disappearance of open space confronted many suburbanites with yet another threat to their dreams. "No more sweep of green," lamented suburban critic William Whyte. "Across the hills are splattered scores of random subdivisions, each laid out with the same dreary curves. Gone are the streams, brooks, woods, and forests that the subdivisions signs talked about." Gone, too, were habitats for birds, small mammals, fish, and amphibians.

During the suburban boom, homebuilders seldom took the environment into account. Few rural areas had zoning or building codes that restricted where and how much could be built. To lower land purchase costs, developers leveled hillsides, filled wetlands, and ignored flood dangers. And to lower construction costs, they cleared mature trees and vegetation and scrimped on insulation. The cost to homeowners and the environment was not at first apparent. Early suburbanites were focused on finding a home of their own at a price they could afford. Years later their desire to preserve a shred of the suburban dream would contribute to the movement to protect the environment.

 REVIEW

What factors pushed the growth of suburbs, and what were the environmental costs of pushing too hard?

THE CULTURE OF SUBURBIA

In suburban tracts across 1950s America, residents discovered the California Dip, the brainchild of the Lipton Company. Wanting to increase sales of its powdered soup mix, Lipton suggested mixing it with sour cream and serving it up with chips. One commentator described eating this new invention:

> Using potato chips as little shovels, you gathered up the deliciously salty but drip-prone liquid and popped it, potato chip and all, into your mouth as quickly and gracefully as possible. There was anxiety in all this—particularly the fear that a great glop of the stuff would land on your tie or the rug—but also immense satisfaction.

Lipton had come up with an ingenious way to Americanize an ethnic food. Sour cream had been a mainstay in such dishes as blintzes (thin Jewish pancakes) and borscht (an Eastern European beet soup). With an all-American name like "California Dip," sour cream's ethnic associations were left behind. The ingredient went mainstream—into the consensus.

The evolving culture of the suburbs encouraged newcomers to shuck off their ethnic associations. In many city neighborhoods, immigrant parents or grandparents lived on the same block or even in the same apartment with their children. In the suburbs, single-family dwellers often left their relatives and in-laws behind, making ethnic lifestyles less pronounced. Also significant, the restrictive immigration policies of the 1920s had reduced the number of newly arrived foreign-born Americans. Thus, suburban culture

⌃ Backyard barbecuing in Los Angeles, 1950. A fairly homogeneous culture evolved in suburban communities, where the classic hamburger was always in fashion and Lipton Soup's fancy new chip dip, made with sour cream that had previously been more often used in ethnic dishes like blintzes and borscht, was now christened "California Dip."
J. R. Eyerman/The LIFE Picture Collection/Getty Images

reflected the tastes of the broad, mostly assimilated, white middle classes.

Class distinctions were more pronounced between suburban communities than within them. The upper-middle class clustered in older developments, which often revolved around country clubs. Working-class suburbs sprouted on the outskirts of large manufacturing centers, where blue-collar families eagerly escaped the city. Within suburbs a homogeneous suburban culture evolved. "We see eye to eye on most things," commented one Levittown resident, "about raising kids, doing things together with your husband . . . we have practically the same identical background."

American Civil Religion >> If suburban residents retained less of their ethnic heritages, most held on to their religious beliefs. Religion continued to be a distinctive and segregating factor during the 1950s. Catholics, Protestants, and Jews generally married within their own faith, and in the suburbs they kept their social distance as well.

Communities that showed no obvious class distinctions were sometimes deeply divided along religious lines. Many Catholics attended parochial rather than public schools, formed their own clubs, and socialized less with their Protestant neighbors. Protestant and Catholic members of the same country club usually did not play golf or tennis in the same foursomes. As for Jews, one historian remarked that whereas a gulf divided many Catholics and Protestants, Jews and Gentiles "seem to have lived on the opposite sides of a religious Grand Canyon."

Although religious affiliation divided the nation along social and residential lines, most Americans agreed that religious commitment was an essential part of their lives. "Our government makes no sense unless it is founded on a deeply religious faith," President Eisenhower declared, "and I don't care what it is." In short, any religion was better than none. Historians have referred to this generalized adherence to faith as American civil religion. Each Friday afternoon the host of TV's *Howdy Doody Show*, Buffalo Bob Smith, urged his young viewers to worship "at the church or synagogue of your choice."

Americans took that advice to heart as church membership rose to over 50 percent for the first time in the twentieth century. The Census Bureau reported that 96 percent of the people polled in 1957 cited a specific affiliation when asked, "What is your religion?" Many leaders saw religion as a weapon in the Cold War. After all, Communists were avowed atheists. Prominent clergy pointed out that the Pledge of Allegiance was so secular that any young Soviet child could recite it. So in 1954 Congress added to the pledge's "one nation indivisible" the phrase "under God."

Patriotic and anti-Communist themes were strong in the preaching of clergy who pioneered the use of television. Billy Graham, a Baptist revival preacher, first attracted national attention at a tent meeting in Los Angeles in 1949. Graham achieved wider impact than nineteenth-century revivalists like Dwight Moody by televising his meetings. Though no revivalist, the Roman Catholic bishop Fulton J. Sheen made the transition from radio to television ministry. In his weekly program he extolled traditional values and attacked communism. Both Graham and Sheen preached an ecumenical faith that religion should unite Americans rather than divide them.

"Homemaking" Women in the Workaday World >> The growth of a suburban culture revealed a contradiction in the lives of middle-class women. Never before were their traditional roles as housewives and mothers so central to American society. Yet never before had more women joined the workforce outside the home.

For housewives the single-family suburban home required more labor to keep clean. At the same time, the baby boom left suburban mothers with more children to tend and less help from relatives, who less often lived nearby. Increased dependence on automobiles made many a suburban housewife the chauffeur for her family. By the 1950s housewives also had do to "errands," as milk carriers, bakeries, and grocers stopped making deliveries.

Yet between 1940 and 1960 the percentage of wives working outside the home doubled, from 15 to 30 percent. While some women took jobs to help make ends meet, more than financial necessity was involved. Middle-class married women went to work as often as lower-class wives, and women with college degrees were the most likely to get a job. Two-income families were able to spend far more on extras: gifts, education, recreation, and household appliances. In addition, women found status and self-fulfillment in their jobs, as well as a chance for increased social contacts.

More women were going to college, too, but increased education did not translate into economic equality. The median wage for women was less than half that for men—a greater gap than in any other developed country. The percentage of women holding professional jobs actually dropped between 1950 and 1960.

<< Once a utilitarian space for food preparation, kitchens became centers of style and even fantasy in the suburban era. They also became larger and brighter. Note that the stainless steel appliances echo the futuristic look of the era's cars. GraphicaArtis/Getty Images

The Flickering Gray Screen >> The new medium of television provided an ideal way to entertain families at home as well as to sell them consumer goods. Television was invented in the 1920s, but the new technology spread widely only after World War II. In 1949 Americans owned only 1 million televisions; by 1960 more Americans had televisions than had bathrooms, some 46 million. Attendance began dropping at movie theaters and sports arenas. As downtown theaters closed, popular suburban drive-ins allowed whole families to enjoy movies from the comfort of their cars. But even that novelty failed to draw viewers away from their televisions in large numbers.

In 1948 politics moved into the television age, as the networks covered both the Democratic and Republican National Conventions. Two years later, they televised hearings on organized crime chaired by Senator Estes Kefauver. Some 30 million viewers watched senators grill mobster Frank Costello about his criminal organization and its ties to city governments. Millions more watched Senator Joseph McCarthy's ill-fated attack on the army in 1954. With such a large audience, television clearly had the potential to shape the nation's politics. But the networks did not want controversy to drive away advertisers. Nor did they see news as a popular topic. By the mid-1950s hostile reaction to coverage of McCarthy led them to downgrade public affairs programs. They relied instead on telefilm dramas, quiz shows, sports, and situation comedies.

THEN&NOW

Many Americans look back at the 1950s as "Happy Days," in the spirit of the popular television sitcom. Prosperity in that era introduced what economists have called "the Great Compression." By that they meant that the gap between rich and poor narrowed further than any other time in the twentieth century. A robust economy with high employment and rising wages drew millions into an expanding middle class. Access to home ownership, college education, health care, and leisure time all increased. Trends today have reversed that pattern. Salaries for corporate executives have soared as blue-collar wages remain flat. The middle class, so important to the optimism of Happy Days, has shrunk as union membership declined and high-wage jobs moved overseas. Deep tax cuts during the presidencies of Ronald Reagan, George W. Bush, and Donald Trump favored the very rich. The top 1 percent now control more wealth than at any time since the 1890s Today sharp divisions over inequality and moral values have shattered any sense of consensus as Americans focus on their differences rather than on what binds them together.

REVIEW

How did religion, the role of women, and television each help define suburban culture?

THE POLITICS OF CALM

As the leader presiding over these changes in American society, President Dwight David Eisenhower projected an aura of paternal calm. Pursuing "modern Republicanism," the new president sought consensus, not confrontation. He rejected conservative calls for a repeal of the New Deal and a return to laissez-faire capitalism. Eisenhower declared that he was "conservative when it comes to money and liberal when it comes to human beings."

The Eisenhower Presidency >> Eisenhower had been raised in a large Kansas farm family. His parents, though poor, offered him a warm, caring home steeped in religious faith. In an era of organizational men, Eisenhower succeeded by mastering the military's bureaucratic politics. In the placid years between the two World Wars, the skills "Ike" demonstrated at golf, poker, and bridge often proved as valuable as his military expertise. Yet these genial ways could not hide his ambition or his ability to judge character shrewdly. It took a gifted organizer to coordinate the D-Day invasion and to hold together the egocentric Allied generals who pushed east to Berlin.

As president, Eisenhower supported key New Deal programs. He even agreed to increases in Social Security, unemployment insurance, and the minimum wage. He accepted a small public housing program and a modest federally supported medical insurance plan for those in need. But as a conservative, Eisenhower remained uncomfortable with big government. He rejected more far-reaching liberal proposals on housing and universal health care through the Social Security system.

FDR and Truman had favored activist government: when the economy faltered, they used deficit spending and tax cuts to stimulate it. Eisenhower preferred to reduce federal spending and the government's role in the economy. When a recession struck in 1953–1954, the administration was concerned more with balancing the budget and holding inflation in line than with reducing unemployment through public spending.

But Eisenhower didn't oppose spending in other areas. When major projects like the Highway Act called for federal

^ Eisenhower was a popular president, and crowds turned out to wave him on at his Inauguration Day parade. Being 1953, the Cadillac in which he rides sports only stubby fins compared with the giant appendages of the 1959 model shown at the opening of this chapter.
Rolls Press/Popperfoto/Getty Images

leadership, he supported them. And in 1954 he signed the St. Lawrence Seaway Act, which joined the United States and Canada in an ambitious engineering project to open the Great Lakes to ocean shipping. Like the highway program, the seaway struck Eisenhower as fiscally acceptable because the funding came from user tolls and taxes rather than from general revenues. Few Seaway supporters considered the environmental threats to the Great Lakes.

Despite several recessions and his own uncertain health, Eisenhower remained popular. Voters gladly reelected him in 1956. But poor economic performance did take its toll. In the wake of the 1954 recession, congressional Democrats gained a 29-member majority in the House and a 1-vote edge in the Senate. Never again would Eisenhower work with a Republican majority. In 1958, when recession again dragged down the economy, the midterm elections gave Democrats an even more commanding advantage. Modern Republicanism did not put down deep roots beyond Eisenhower's White House.

The Conglomerate World >> Corporate America
welcomed the administration's pro-business approach as well as the era's general prosperity. Wages for the average worker rose over 35 percent between 1950 and 1960. Business and labor leaders negotiated generous wage and benefits packages that minimized the strikes of earlier eras. At the same time, corporate executives remained mindful of the economic distress of the 1930s. They devised new ways to minimize the danger that economic downturns posed to their companies.

One expansion strategy took the form of diversification. In the 1930s industrial giant General Electric had concentrated largely in one area: equipment for generating electric power and light. When the Depression struck, GE found its markets shrinking. The company responded by entering markets for appliances, X-ray machines, and elevators—all products developed or enhanced by the company's research labs. In the postwar era, General Electric diversified even further, into nuclear power, jet engines, financial services, and television. Diversification was most practical for large industrial firms, whose size allowed them to support extensive research and development.

Conglomeration enabled some small companies to become giants. Unlike earlier horizontal and vertical combinations, **conglomerate** mergers could join companies with seemingly unrelated products. Over a 20-year period International Telephone and Telegraph branched out from its basic communications business into banking, hotels and motels, car rental, home building, and insurance. Corporations also became multinational by expanding their overseas operations or buying out potential foreign competitors. Large integrated oil companies such as Mobil and Standard Oil of New Jersey developed huge oil fields in the Middle East and markets around the free world.

conglomerate corporation whose various branches or subsidiaries are either directly or indirectly spread among a variety of industries, usually unrelated to one another.

Corporations that manufactured consumer goods increased their advertising to reach potential customers. Madison Avenue in New York became the code name for firms that designed ad campaigns. They often influenced what manufacturers produced. "The only institution which we have for instilling new needs, for training people to act as consumers, for altering men's values, and thus for hastening their adjustment to potential abundance is advertising," historian David Potter concluded. Economist John Kenneth Galbraith agreed that advertising "create[d] desires—to bring into being wants that previously did not exist."

The great "cola war" dramatized Potter's point. Coke had long dominated the market for cola soft drinks. It appealed to tradition in order to maintain its advantage. Pepsi countered by suggesting not that it tasted better, but that its customers were more youthful, fashionable, and popular:

> Be sociable, look smart
> Keep up-to-date with Pepsi
> Drink light refreshing Pepsi
> Stay young and fair and debonair
> Be sociable, have a Pepsi!

Pepsi's decision to target young people and women transformed its corporate fortunes. Coke continued to position itself as the cola leader, with universal appeal that stood the test of time. While Pepsi's sales increased, so did Coke's, as the cola wars expanded the market for soft drinks.

One aid to managing these modern corporate giants was the advent of electronic data processing. In the early 1950s computers were virtually unknown in private industry. But banks and insurance companies saw the new mainframe computers of International Business Machines (IBM) as an answer to their need to manage huge quantities of records and statistical data. Manufacturers, especially in the petroleum, chemical, automotive, and electronics industries, began to use computers to monitor their production lines, quality control, and inventory.

 REVIEW

In what ways did President Eisenhower show his pragmatic approach to governing?

CRACKS IN THE CONSENSUS

In the 1950s many corporations advertised a cultural consensus just as much as the products they sold. They praised prosperity as a reflection of an American way of life. What was good for the country was good for General Motors, GM's president assured the nation. Not all Americans were persuaded of the virtues of consensus and business leadership. Intellectuals and artists found in corporate culture a stifling conformity that crushed individual creativity. On the fringes of society, the Beats scorned traditional behavior and values. Closer to the mainstream, a new generation of musicians created rock and roll, which became the sound of youthful rebellion.

Critics of Mass Culture >> In Levittown, New Jersey, a woman who had invited her neighbors to a cocktail party eagerly awaited them dressed in newly fashionable Capri pants—a tight-fitting calf-length style. One early-arriving couple glimpsed the woman through a window. What on earth was the hostess wearing? Pajamas? Who in their right mind would entertain in pajamas? The couple sneaked home, afraid they had made a mistake about the day of the party. They telephoned another neighbor, who anxiously called yet others on the guest list. The neighbors finally mustered enough courage to attend the party. But when the hostess later learned of their misunderstanding, she decided Levittown was not ready for cutting-edge fashion.

Was the United States creating a vast suburban wasteland, whose residents worried more about Capri pants than their obligations as citizens? Many highbrow intellectuals derided the homogenized lifestyle created by mass consumption, conformity, and **mass media**. Critics such as Dwight

mass media forms of communication designed to reach a vast audience, generally a nation-state or larger, without personal contact between the senders and receivers.

^ Capri pants, 1950s. Were such fashions too radical for the conformist suburbs?
Bettmann/Getty Images

Macdonald sarcastically attacked the culture of the suburban middle classes, including the popularity of Reader's Digest Condensed Books and uplifting film spectacles such as *The Ten Commandments.* "Midcult," as Macdonald called it, was his shorthand for uninspired middlebrow culture.

Other critics charged that the skyscrapers and factories of giant conglomerates housed an impersonal world. In large, increasingly automated workplaces, skilled workers seemed little more than caretakers of machines. Large corporations required middle-level executives to submerge their personal goals to fit into the work routines of large bureaucracies. David Riesman, a sociologist, condemned stifling conformity in *The Lonely Crowd* (1950). In the nineteenth-century United States, Riesman argued, Americans had been "inner directed." It was their own consciences that formed their values and drove them to seek success. In contrast, modern workers had developed a personality shaped not so much by inner convictions as by the opinions of their peers. The new "other-directed" society of suburbia preferred security to success. "Go along to get along" was its motto.

William Whyte carried Riesman's critique from the workplace to the suburb in *The Organization Man* (1956). Here he found rootless families, shifted from town to town by the demands of corporations. (IBM, went one standard joke, stood for "I've Been Moved.") The typical "organization man" was sociable but not terribly ambitious. He sought primarily to "keep up with the Joneses" and the number of consumer goods they owned. He lived in a suburban "split-level trap," as one critic put it, one among millions of "haggard" men, "tense and anxious" women, and "the gimme kids."

No doubt such portraits were overdrawn and overly alarmist. Many suburbanites put up with the constraints of conformity because they preferred the convenience of mass-produced goods. But the critics were on to something. Behind the impersonal facade of bureaucratic organizations and suburban tract houses, millions of Americans experienced a growing sense of discontent.

Juvenile Delinquency, Rock and Roll, and Rebellion >>

Young Americans were among suburbia's sharpest critics. Dance crazes, outlandish clothing, slang, rebelliousness, and sexual precociousness—all these behaviors challenged middle-class respectability. More than a few educators warned that the United States had spawned a generation of rebellious "juvenile delinquents." Psychologist Fredric Wertham told a group of doctors, "You cannot understand present-day juvenile delinquency if you do not take into account the pathogenic and pathoplastic [infectious] influence of comic books." Others laid the blame on films and the lyrics of popular music.

The center of the new teen culture was the high school. Whether in consolidated rural school districts, new suburban schools, or city systems, the large, comprehensive high schools of the 1950s aimed to prepare students for the corporate world. That pressure often led middle-class students into rebellious behaviors that mimicked the style of the lower classes. They wore jeans and T-shirts, challenged authority, and defiantly smoked cigarettes, much like the motorcycle gang leader portrayed by Marlon Brando in the film *The Wild One* (1954).

In many ways the debate over juvenile delinquency was an argument about social class and, to a lesser degree, race. When adults complained that "delinquent" teenagers dressed poorly, lacked ambition, were irresponsible and sexually promiscuous, these were the same arguments traditionally used to denigrate other outsiders—immigrants, the poor, and African Americans. Nowhere were these racial and class undertones more evident than in the hue and cry that greeted the arrival of rock and roll.

Before 1954 popular music had been divided into three major categories: pop, country and western, and rhythm and blues. A handful of major record companies with almost exclusively white singers dominated the pop charts. On one fringe of the popular field was country and western, often split into cowboy musicians such as Roy Rogers and Gene Autry and the hillbilly and blue-grass styles associated with Nashville. The music industry generally treated rhythm and blues as "race music," whose performers and audiences were largely Black. Each of these musical traditions, it is worth noting, grew out of regional cultures. As the West and the South merged into the national culture, these musical

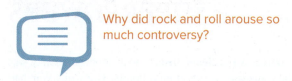

Make a Case

Why did rock and roll arouse so much controversy?

subcultures were gradually integrated into the national mainstream.

By the mid-1950s the distinctiveness of the three styles began to blur. Singers on the white pop charts recorded a few songs from country and from rhythm and blues. The popularity of crossovers such as "Sh-boom," "Tutti-Frutti," and "Earth Angel" indicated that a major shift in taste and market was under way. Lyrics still reflected the pop field's preoccupation with young love, marriage, and happiness, but the music now vibrated with the rawer, earthier style of rhythm and blues. Country and western singer Bill Haley brought the new blend to the fore in 1954 with "Shake, Rattle, and Roll," the first rock song to reach the top-10 on the pop charts.

And then—calamity! Millions of middle-class roofs nearly blew off with the appearance in 1955 of the rhythmic and raucous Elvis Presley. By background Elvis was a country boy whose musical style combined elements of gospel, country, and blues. But it was his hip-swinging, pelvis-plunging performances that electrified teenage audiences. To conservative adults, Presley's long hair, sideburns, and tight jeans seemed menacingly delinquent, an expression of hostile rebellion. What they often resented but rarely admitted was that Elvis looked lower class, sounded Black, and really could sing.

Beyond the frenetic rhythms of rock and roll, and even further beyond the pale of suburban culture, a subculture flourished known as the beat generation. In rundown urban neighborhoods and college towns this motley collection of artists, intellectuals, musicians, and middle-class students dropped out of mainstream society. In dress and behavior the Beats self-consciously rejected what they viewed as the excessive spiritual bankruptcy of U.S. middle-class culture. They were nonconformists in a conformist world. Cool urban "hipsters"—especially Black jazz musicians such as John Coltrane and Sonny Rollins—were their models. They read poetry, listened to jazz, explored Asian philosophy, and experimented openly with drugs, mystical religions, and sex. Their behavior outraged the "square world" they rejected, but aroused widespread curiosity.

REVIEW

Why did social critics worry about conformity in the 1950s?

NATIONALISM IN AN AGE OF SUPERPOWERS

One source of the Beats' dismay with modern society was the dark shadow of the atomic bomb. The Cold War had triggered an arms race in which human survival seemed endangered. Along the Iron Curtain of Eastern Europe and across the battle lines of northern Asia, the Soviet-American rivalry had settled into an uneasy stalemate. But World War II had also disrupted Europe's colonies, where nationalists in the Middle East, Africa, and South Asia fought to gain independence. Which power, the Soviet Union or United States, would draw the emerging nations into its orbit? Across the globe the Eisenhower administration sought ways to prevent the Soviet Union from capturing national independence movements. To do so, it sometimes used the threat of nuclear war to block Communist expansion in Europe or Asia.

To the Brink? >> Eisenhower, no stranger to world politics, shared the conduct of foreign policy with his secretary of state, John Foster Dulles. Coming from a family of missionaries and diplomats, Dulles had within him a touch of both. He viewed the Soviet-American struggle in almost religious terms, as a fight between good and evil. Eisenhower was less hostile toward the Soviets. In the end, the two men's differing temperaments led to a policy that seesawed from confrontation to conciliation.

The Republican Party divided over issues of national security. As a centrist, Eisenhower sought to compromise between those who favored an aggressive policy to defeat communism and those who worried that big defense meant big government. Dulles wanted the United States to aid in liberating the "captive peoples" of Eastern Europe and other Communist nations. However, Eisenhower was equally determined to cut back military spending and troop levels in order to keep the budget balanced. The president was sometimes irked at the "fantastic programs" the Pentagon kept proposing. "If we demand too much in taxes in order to build planes and ships," he argued, "we will tend to dry up the accumulations of capital that are necessary to provide jobs for the million or more new workers that we must absorb each year."

Rather than rely on costly conventional forces, Eisenhower and Dulles used the threat of massive nuclear retaliation to intimidate the Soviets into behaving less aggressively. Dulles insisted that Americans not shrink from the threat of nuclear war: "If you are scared to go to the brink, you are lost." And as Secretary of Treasury George Humphrey put it, a nuclear strategy was cost-effective—"a bigger bang for the buck." Henceforth American foreign policy would have a "new look," though behind the more militant rhetoric lay an ongoing commitment to containment.

Brinkmanship in Asia >> Putting **brinkmanship** into action proved challenging. When Dulles announced U.S. intentions to "unleash" Chiang Kai-shek to attack mainland China from his outpost on Taiwan (formerly Formosa), China threatened to invade

> **brinkmanship** policy of using the threat of nuclear war in order to persuade an opponent to back down.

Taiwan. In response, Eisenhower ordered the Seventh Fleet into the area to protect rather than unleash Chiang. If the Communists attacked, Dulles warned bluntly, "we'll have to use atomic weapons."

Nuclear weapons also figured in the American response to a crisis in Indochina. There, Vietnamese forces led by Ho Chi Minh were fighting the French, who had reestablished their colonial rule at the end of World War II. Between 1950 and 1954, the United States bankrolled the French war in Indochina, providing more than $1 billion in military aid. Eisenhower worried that if Vietnam fell to a Communist revolutionary such as Ho, other nations of Southeast Asia would follow. "You have a row of dominoes set up," the president warned; "you knock over the first one, [y]ou could have the beginning of a disintegration that would have the most profound influences."

Worn down by a war they seemed unable to win, the French tried to force a final showdown with Ho Chi Minh's army at Dien Bien Phu in 1954. Finding themselves besieged and near defeat, the French pleaded for more U.S. aid. Admiral Arthur Radford, head of the Joint Chiefs of Staff, proposed a massive American air raid, perhaps even using tactical nuclear weapons. But again Eisenhower pulled back. The idea of American involvement in another Asian war aroused opposition from both allies and domestic political leaders.

In May 1954 the garrison at Dien Bien Phu collapsed under the siege. At an international peace conference in Geneva, Switzerland, the French negotiated the terms of their withdrawal. Ho Chi Minh agreed to pull his forces north of the 17th parallel, temporarily dividing the nation into North and South Vietnam. Because of Ho's broad popularity, he seemed assured an easy victory in elections scheduled within the next two years. Dulles, however, viewed any Communist victory as unacceptable, even if the election was democratic. He convinced Eisenhower to support a South Vietnamese government under Ngo Dinh Diem. Unlike most South Vietnamese, Diem was a Catholic, not a Buddhist. Dulles insisted that Diem was not bound by the Geneva Accords to hold any election—a position the autocratic Diem eagerly supported. To help keep him in power, the United States sent a military mission to train South Vietnam's army. The commitment was small, but a decade later it would return to haunt Americans.

The Superpowers >> Korea, Taiwan, Indochina—to Dulles and Eisenhower, the crises in Asia and elsewhere could all be traced back to the Soviet dictatorship. But in March 1953 Soviet dictator Joseph Stalin died. Power soon fell to Nikita Khrushchev, a party stalwart with a formidable intellect and peasant origins in the rural Ukraine. In some

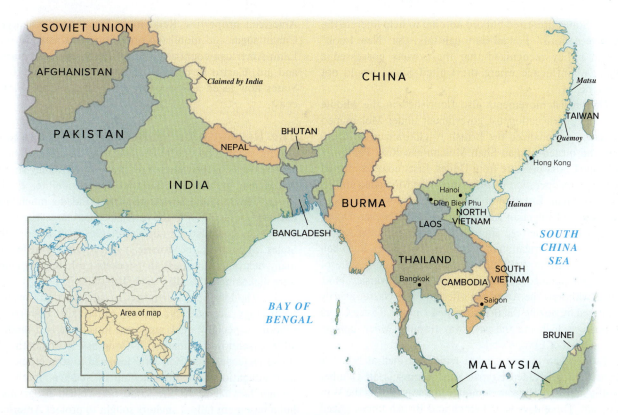

MAP 28.2: ASIAN TROUBLE SPOTS

After the Geneva Accords divided Indochina into North and South Vietnam, Secretary of State Dulles organized the Southeast Asia Treaty Organization (SEATO) to resist Communist aggression in Southeast Asia. In addition to the conflict in Vietnam, tensions were fueled by the mutual hostility between mainland Communist China and Chiang Kai-shek's Taiwan, as well as the issue of the offshore islands Quemoy and Matsu.
What geographic factors caused the United States to make Thailand a key ally?

ways Khrushchev resembled another farm-belt politician, Harry Truman. Both were unsophisticated yet shrewd, earthy in their sense of humor, energetic, short-tempered, and largely inexperienced in international affairs. Khrushchev kept U.S. diplomats off balance. At times genial and conciliatory, he would suddenly become demanding and boastful.

Khrushchev moderated some of the excesses of the Stalin years. At home, he gradually shifted the Soviet economy toward production of consumer goods. Internationally, he called for an easing of tensions and reduced forces in Europe, hoping to weaken Western European dependence on the United States. In Washington the administration was unsure of how to respond to the new overtures. Conservatives generally opposed any compromise with Communists, even though Khrushchev repudiated Stalin's excesses. It was Winston

^ Nikita Khrushchev was by turns boisterous and somber, threatening and conciliatory—a style that both captivated and alarmed Americans.
Bettmann/Getty Images

Churchill who suggested that the Russians might be serious about negotiating. In 1955 the Americans, British, French, and Soviets met in a conference at Geneva, Switzerland. Although little came of the summit other than a cordial "spirit of Geneva," the meeting hinted that a cooling in the arms race was possible.

Nationalism Unleashed >> The spirit of Geneva did not long survive new nationalist upheavals. Khrushchev's moderation encouraged nationalists in Soviet-controlled Eastern Europe to push for greater independence. Riots erupted in Poland, while in Hungary students took to the streets demanding that a coalition government replace Stalin's puppet regime. At first, Moscow accepted the new Hungarian government and began to remove Soviet tanks. But when Hungary announced it was withdrawing from the Warsaw Pact, the tanks rolled back into Budapest to crush the uprising in October 1956. The

United States protested but did nothing to help liberate the "captive nations." For all its tough talk, the "New Look" foreign policy recognized that the Soviets possessed a sphere of influence where the United States would not intervene.

Nationalist movements also flourished in the Middle East. In Iran, a nationalist government under Mohammed Mossadeq nationalized the British Anglo-Iranian Oil Company and ousted Iranian Shah Mohammad Reza Pahlavi, a firm ally. Under pressure from Dulles, Eisenhower approved a covert CIA operation in 1953 to remove Mossadeq and restore the Shah. Eisenhower and Dulles also worried about the actions of Egyptian leader Gamal Abdel Nasser. Dulles had promised American aid to help Nasser build the Aswan Dam, a massive irrigation project on the Nile River. But when Nasser formed an Arab alliance against the young state of Israel and pursued economic ties with the Warsaw bloc, Dulles withdrew the American offer. In 1956 Nasser angrily countered by seizing the British-owned Universal Suez Canal Company, which ran the waterway through which tankers carried most of Europe's oil.

Events then moved quickly. Israel, alarmed at Nasser's Arab alliance, invaded Egypt's Sinai peninsula on October 29–the same day Hungary announced it was leaving the Warsaw Pact. Three days later French and British forces seized the canal in an attempt to restore their own interests and prestige. Angered that the allies had acted without consulting the United States, Eisenhower joined the Soviet Union in supporting a United Nations resolution condemning the attacks and demanding an immediate cease-fire. By December American pressures forced Britain and France to remove their forces. Few events placed as much strain on the Western alliance as the Suez crisis. At the same time, Nasser had demonstrated the potential force of nationalism in less developed countries. The Middle East, with its rich oil reserves and the threat of Arab-Israeli conflict, would remain a major source of superpower tensions.

Nationalist forces were also active in Latin America, where only 2 percent of the people controlled 75 percent of the land. Repressive dictatorships exercised power, and foreign interests—especially American ones—dominated Latin American economies. In 1954 Eisenhower authorized the CIA to send a band of Latin American mercenaries into Guatemala to overthrow a nationalist government there. Similar economic tensions beset Cuba, where the United States owned 80 percent of the country's utilities and operated a major naval base at Guantánamo Bay. A determined revolutionary nationalist, Fidel Castro, gained the support of impoverished peasants in Cuba's mountains and, in January 1959, drove the deeply corrupt and pro-American dictator from power.

At first many Americans applauded the revolution, welcoming Castro when he visited the United States. But Eisenhower was distinctly cool to the cigar-smoking Cuban, who had filled key government positions with Communists, launched a sweeping agricultural reform, and confiscated American properties. Retaliating, Eisenhower embargoed Cuban sugar and mobilized opposition to Castro in other Latin American countries. Cut off from American markets and aid, Castro turned to the Soviet Union. The United States now faced a Soviet threat 90 miles off the Florida coast.

The Response to *Sputnik* >> Castro's turn to the Soviets seemed all the more dangerous because of Soviet achievements in their missile program. In 1957 they stunned Americans by orbiting the first space satellite, dubbed *Sputnik*. By 1959 the Soviets had crash-landed a much larger payload on the moon. If the Russians could target the moon, surely they could launch nuclear missiles against the United States. In contrast, the American space program suffered so many delays and mishaps that rockets exploding on launch were nicknamed "flopniks" and "kaputniks."

How had the Soviets managed to catch up with American technology so quickly? Some Americans blamed the schools, especially weak programs in science and math. In 1958 Eisenhower joined with Congress to enact the National Defense Education Act, designed to strengthen graduate education and the teaching of science, math, and foreign languages. At the same time, crash programs to build basement fallout shelters sought to protect Americans in case of a nuclear attack. Democrats charged that the administration had allowed the United States to face an unacceptable "missile gap."

∧ Even before the launch of *Sputnik* in 1957, Americans had begun devising fallout shelters for protection from the effects of a nuclear attack. *What messages about nuclear war does this photo send?*
Dmitri Kessel/The LIFE Picture Collection/Getty Images

THE KITCHEN DEBATE

On July 24, 1959, Vice President Richard Nixon and Soviet Premier Nikita Khrushchev met at an exhibition in Moscow, showcasing American technology and culture. For Nixon the consumer goods on display offered proof of the superiority of the American free-enterprise system. Khrushchev argued forcefully, though defensively, that the Soviet Union could provide equally well for its housewives. While the event appeared to be spontaneous, Nixon had been looking for an opportunity to stand up to the pugnacious Russian leader. In this primary newspaper account, the perspectives are within a single document.

DOCUMENT 1
Khrushchev-Nixon Debate

Nixon: "There are some instances where you may be ahead of us, for example in the development of the thrust of your rockets for the investigation of outer space, there may be some instances in which we are ahead of you—in color television, for instance."

Khrushchev: "No, we are up with you on this, too. We have bested you in one technique and also in the other."

Nixon: "You see, you never concede anything."

Khrushchev: "I do not give up."

Nixon: "Wait till you see the picture. Let's have far more communication and exchange in this very area that we speak of. We should hear you more on our televisions. You should hear us more on yours."

Khrushchev: "That's a good idea. Let's do it like this. You appear before our people. We will appear before your people. People will see and appreciate this."

Nixon: "There is not a day in the United States when we cannot read what you say. When Kozlov was speaking in California about peace, you were talking here in somewhat different terms. This was reported extensively in the American press. Never make a statement here if you don't want it to be read in the United States. I can promise you every word you say will be translated into English."

Khrushchev: "I doubt it. I want you to give your word that this speech of mine will be heard by the American people."

Nixon: [shaking hands on it] "By the same token, everything I say will be translated and heard all over the Soviet Union?"

Khrushchev: "That's agreed."

Nixon: "You must not be afraid of ideas."

Khrushchev: "We are telling you not to be afraid of ideas. We have no reason to be afraid. We have already broken free from such a situation."

Nixon: "Well, then, let's have more exchange of them. We are all agreed on that. All right? All right?". . .

Khrushchev: [after Nixon called attention to a built-in panel-controlled washing machine] "We have such things."

Nixon: "This is the newest model. This is the kind which is built in thousands of units for direct installation in the houses." [He added that Americans were interested in making life easier for their women.]

Mr. Khrushchev [remarked that in the Soviet Union, they did not have] "the capitalist attitude toward women."

Nixon: "I think that this attitude toward women is universal. What we want to do is make easier the life of our housewives." [He explained that the house could be built for $14,000 and that most veterans had bought houses for between $10,000 and $15,000.] . . .

"Let me give you an example you can appreciate. Our steelworkers, as you know, are on strike. But any steelworker could buy this house. They earn $3 an hour. This house costs about $100 a month to buy on a contract running 25 to 30 years."

Khrushchev: "We have steelworkers and we have peasants who also can afford to spend $14,000 for a house." [He said American houses were built to last only 20 years, so builders could sell new houses at the end of that period.] "We build firmly. We build for our children and grandchildren."

Mr. Nixon [said he thought American houses would last more than 20 years, but even so, after 20 years many Americans want a new home or a new kitchen, the old one being obsolete then. The American system is designed to take advantage of new inventions and new techniques, he said.]

Khrushchev: "This theory does not hold water." [He said some things never got out of date—furniture and furnishings, perhaps, but not houses. He said he did not think houses. He said he did not think that what Americans had written about their houses was all strictly accurate.]

Nixon: [pointing to television screen] "We can see here what is happening in other parts of the home."

Khrushchev: "This is probably always out of order."

Nixon: "*Da* [yes]."

Khrushchev: "Don't you have a machine that puts food into the mouth and pushes it down? Many things you've shown us are interesting but they are not needed in life. They have no useful purpose. They are merely gadgets. We have a saying, if you have bedbugs you have to catch one and pour boiling water into the ear."

Nixon: "We have another saying. This is that the way to kill a fly is to make it drink whisky. But we have a better use for whisky. [Aside] I like to have this battle of wits with the Chairman. He knows his business."

"The Kitchen Debate." Richard Nixon and Nikita Khrushchev, July 24, 1959, Moscow, U.S.S.R.

THINKING CRITICALLY

How does Khrushchev counter Nixon's explanation of "planned obsolescence"? What is Khrushchev's attitude about high-tech American consumer goods? Why was Nixon so insistent that his ideas be broadcast in the Soviet Union? In what way could women be offended by the two leaders' comments?

Thaws and Freezes >> During each crisis, the superpowers found it difficult to interpret one another's motives. The Russians exploited nationalist revolutions where they could—less successfully in Egypt, more so in Cuba. "We will bury you," Khrushchev admonished Americans, though it was unclear whether he meant through peaceful competition or military confrontation. Berlin remained a strategic issue for both powers. In November 1958, when Khrushchev demanded that the Western powers withdraw all troops from West Berlin, Eisenhower viewed this demand as a real threat. If Berlin became a "free city," as Khrushchev insisted, the Allies would have to deal with East Germany, a government they did not recognize. Fortunately, when Eisenhower rejected the ultimatum, Khrushchev backed down.

Rather than adopt a more belligerent course, Eisenhower determined to use the last 18 months of his presidency to improve Soviet-American relations. The shift in policy was made easier because Eisenhower knew from American spying (but could not admit publicly) that the "missile gap" was not real. Since the U.S. missile program was actually more advanced than the Soviets', the president refused to heed the calls for a crash defense program. Instead, he took a conciliatory approach by inviting Khrushchev to visit the United States in September 1959. Though the meetings produced no significant results, they eased tensions.

In May, Eisenhower's plans for a return visit to the Soviet Union were abruptly canceled. Only weeks earlier the Russians had shot down a high-altitude U-2 American spy plane over Soviet territory. At first Eisenhower claimed the plane had strayed off course during weather research, but Khrushchev sprang his trap: the CIA pilot, Gary Powers, had been captured alive. The president then admitted that he had personally authorized the U-2 overflights for reasons of national security.

That episode ended Eisenhower's hopes that his personal diplomacy might create a true thaw in the Cold War. A less mature president might have led the United States into more severe conflict or even war. But Eisenhower was not readily impressed by the promises of new weapons systems. He left office with a warning that too much military spending would lead to "an unwarranted influence, whether sought or unsought" by the **military-industrial complex** at the expense of democratic institutions.

military-industrial complex combination of the U.S. armed forces, arms manufacturers, and associated political and commercial interests, which grew rapidly during the Cold War era.

> ✓ **REVIEW**
>
> How did President Eisenhower's "New Look" foreign policy affect American actions in Asia, the Middle East, and Latin America?

THE COLD WAR ON THE NEW FRONTIER

The 1960 election promised to bring the winds of change to Washington. The opponents—Vice President Richard Nixon and Senator John F. Kennedy of Massachusetts—were the first major presidential candidates born in the twentieth century. At age 43 John Fitzgerald Kennedy would be the youngest person ever elected to the office. Nixon was just four years older. The nation needed to find "new frontiers," Kennedy proclaimed. His rhetoric was noble, but he did not reveal if he would seek accommodation or confrontation in the Cold War or significant reforms at home.

The Election of 1960 >> The biggest issue of the campaign was social as much as political. Jack Kennedy was a Roman Catholic out of Irish Boston, and no Catholic had ever been elected president. Conservative Protestants, many concentrated in the heavily Democratic South, were convinced that a Catholic president would never be "free to exercise his own judgment" if the pope ordered otherwise. Kennedy confronted the issue head-on, addressing an association of hostile ministers in Houston. "I believe in an America where the separation of church and state is absolute," he said, "where no Catholic prelate would tell the President (should he be Catholic) how to act, and no Protestant minister would tell his parishioners how to vote." House Speaker Sam Rayburn, an old Texas pol, was astonished by Kennedy's bravura performance. "My God! . . . He's eating them blood raw."

Vice President Nixon ran on his political experience and reputation as a staunch anti-Communist. His campaign faltered in October as unemployment rose. Nixon was also hurt by a series of televised debates with Kennedy—the first broadcast nationally. Nixon was overtired, and his Lazy Shave makeup failed to hide his five-o'clock shadow. Radio broadcast favored Nixon, a skilled debater, but television gave an edge to the photogenic Kennedy. The election had the largest turnout in 50 years: 64 percent of all voters. Out of 68.3 million ballots cast, Kennedy won by a margin of just 118,000. The whisker-thin victory was made possible by strong Catholic support in key states. "Hyphenated" Americans—Hispanic, Jewish, Irish, Italian, Polish, and German—voted Democratic in record numbers, while much of the Black vote that had gone to Eisenhower in 1956 returned to the Democratic fold.

The Hard-Nosed Idealists of Camelot >> John Kennedy and his cosmopolitan wife Jackie brought a new sense of glamour to Washington. Many observers compared the Kennedy White House to Camelot, King Arthur's magical court. A popular musical of 1960 pictured Camelot as a land where skies were fair, men brave, women pretty, and the days full of noble causes. With similar vigor, Kennedy surrounded

Candidate (Party)	Electoral Vote (%)	Popular Vote (%)
John F. Kennedy (Democratic)	303 (56)	34,226,731 (49.7)
Richard M. Nixon (Republican)	219 (41)	34,108,157 (49.6)
Robert Byrd (Independent)	15 (3)	501,643 (0.7)

MAP 28.3: ELECTION OF 1960

himself with bright, energetic advisers. Touch football games on the White House lawn displayed a rough-and-tumble playfulness, akin to Arthur's jousting tournaments of old.

In truth, Kennedy was not a liberal by temperament. Handsome and intelligent, he possessed an ironic, self-deprecating humor. Yet in Congress, he had led an undistinguished career, supported Senator Joe McCarthy, and earned a reputation as a playboy. He associated with a faction of Cold War Democrats who wanted to overcome the Republican advantage on national security issues. To woo liberals, Kennedy surrounded himself with a distinguished group of intellectuals and academics.

Robert Strange McNamara typified the pragmatic, liberal, but anti-Communist bent of the new Kennedy team. Steely and brilliant, McNamara was one of the postwar breed of young executives known as the "whiz kids." As a Harvard Business School professor and later as president of Ford Motors, he specialized in using new quantitative tools to streamline business. As the new secretary of defense, McNamara intended to find more flexible and efficient ways of spending defense dollars.

Kennedy liked men like this—witty, bright, intellectual—because they seemed comfortable with power and not afraid to use it. If Khrushchev spoke of waging guerrilla "wars of liberation," Americans could play that game, too. The president's leisure reading reflected a similar adventurous taste:

the popular James Bond spy novels. Agent 007, with his license to kill, was sophisticated, a cool womanizer (as Kennedy continued to be), and ready to use the latest technology to deal with Communist villains. Ironically, Bond demonstrated that there could be plenty of glamour in being "hard-nosed" and pragmatic. That illicit pleasure was the underside, perhaps, of Camelot's promise.

The (Somewhat) New Frontier at Home

>> Kennedy and his advisers had no broad vision for domestic reform. In making policy Kennedy found himself hemmed in by a Democratic Congress dominated by conservatives. As a result the president's legislative achievements were modest. He passed a bill providing some financial aid to depressed industrial and rural areas. But on key issues, including civil rights, aid to education, and national health insurance, Kennedy made no headway.

He wavered, too, on how to manage the economy. The president's liberal advisers favored increased government spending to reduce unemployment, even if that meant a budget deficit. Even so, Kennedy believed that prosperity for big business spelled growth for the whole nation. Thus the president asked Congress to ease antitrust restrictions and grant investment credits and tax breaks—actions that pleased corporate interests. But he was convinced that the government needed to limit the power of both large corporations and unions to set prices and wages. The alternative was an inflationary spiral in which wage increases would spark price increases followed by even higher wage demands.

To prevent such a spiral, the Council of Economic Advisers proposed that steel manufacturers agree to hold down prices if labor unions agreed to limit an increase in their wages. When the large steel corporations broke an informal bargain by sharply raising prices, Kennedy angrily called for investigations into price fixing and shifted Pentagon purchases to smaller steel companies that had not raised prices. The intense pressure caused the big companies to drop the price increases but soured relations between the president and the business community.

Kennedy's Cold War

>> During the 1952 election Republicans had exploited the stalemate in Korea, the fall of China, and the fear of domestic communism. The Democrats, they charged, could not protect the nation's security. Kennedy was determined not to be seen as soft on communism. The Cold War contest, he argued, had shifted from the traditional struggle over Europe to the developing nations in Asia, Africa, and Latin America. The United States should be armed with a more flexible range of military and economic options.

^ JFK stands at the center of this Kennedy family portrait. His father, Joe, and mother, Rose, sit to his right; brother Teddy is sitting on the left in front of his brother-in-law, actor Peter Lawford, while brother Bobby, his attorney general, is behind his left shoulder. *What image do you think the picture projects?*
Paul Schutzer/The LIFE Picture Collection/Getty Images

The Alliance for Progress, announced in the spring of 1961, reflected the Kennedy approach. Kennedy promised to provide $20 billion in foreign aid to Latin America over 10 years—about four times the aid given under Eisenhower. In return Latin American nations would agree to reform unfair tax policies and begin agricultural land reforms. If successful, the alliance would discourage future Castro-style revolutions. With similar fanfare, the administration set up the Peace Corps. This program sent idealistic young men and women to less developed countries to provide technical, educational, and public health services. Under the alliance, most Peace Corps volunteers were assigned to Latin America. A few also spied covertly for the CIA.

To back the new economic policies with military muscle, the Pentagon created jungle warfare schools in North Carolina and in the Canal Zone. The programs were designed to train Latin American police and paramilitary groups as well as American special forces like the Green Berets. If the Soviets or their allies entered wars of liberation, U.S. commandos could fight back.

Kennedy believed, too, that the Soviets had made space the final frontier of the Cold War. Only a few months after the president's inauguration, a Russian cosmonaut orbited the world for the first time. In response, Kennedy initiated a program for a crewed space mission to land on the moon by the end of the decade. In February 1962 John Glenn circled the Earth three times in a "fireball of a ride." Before long, the American space program left the Russians far behind.

Cold War Frustrations >> Kennedy had little success in countering "wars of liberation." The Eisenhower administration had authorized the CIA to overthrow Fidel Castro's Communist regime in Cuba, 90 miles south of Florida. Eager to establish his own Cold War credentials, Kennedy approved an attack by a 1,400-member army of Cuban exiles in April 1961. The invasion turned into a disaster. The poorly equipped rebel forces landed at the swampy Bay of Pigs, and no discontented rebels flocked to their support. Within two days Castro's army had rounded them up. Taking responsibility for the fiasco, Kennedy felt bitterly humiliated.

Kennedy's advisers took a similar covert approach in South Vietnam. There, the American-backed prime minister Ngo Dinh Diem grew ever more unpopular. South Vietnamese Communists, known as the National Liberation Front (NLF), waged a guerrilla war against Diem with support from North

THE WORLD OF THE SUPERPOWERS

By the 1960s the Soviet Union and the United States were engaged in an arms race that presented the world with the threat of nuclear destruction. The two powers adopted a policy popularly known as MAD— mutually assured destruction. Each side maintained enough nuclear weapons to discourage the other from launching an attack without fear of receiving a counterattack equal in kind. Movie director Stanley Kubrick captured this situation in his 1964 film *Dr. Strangelove or: How I Learned to Stop Worrying and Love the Bomb.* The movie ends when an American B-52 bomber drops a nuclear weapon that triggers the Soviet's world-ending "Doomsday Machine."

MAP READING

1. Where are most military bases located?
2. Which European countries and which major South Asian country have no bases?
3. Where have a great many of the cold war conflicts been concentrated?
4. Where is the farthest north U.S. base?

MAP INTERPRETATION

1. What advantages does this polar projection—viewing the globe from above the North Pole—provide in understanding the cold war conflict?
2. If the Soviet Union and Communist China were allies, what explains the large number of Soviet bases along the borders of China?
3. The United States created a "triad" (land-based missiles, submarine-based missiles, and strategic bombers) to guarantee surviving a Russian first strike. How does the "triad" strategy affect the distribution of U.S. bases shown on the map?
4. In what ways does the map suggest strategic and tactical advantages each side possesses?

>> The discovery of Soviet offensive missile sites in Cuba, revealed by low-level American reconnaissance fights, led to the first nuclear showdown of the Cold War. For several tense days in October 1962, President Kennedy met with his National Security Council to debate the proper course of action.
Popperfoto/Getty Images

him as weak and inexperienced. By August, events in Berlin confirmed his fears. To keep East Germans from fleeing, the Soviets built a wall to seal West Berlin off from the rest of the eastern zone. Despite American protests, the wall stayed up.

Tensions with the Soviet Union also led the administration to rethink the American approach to nuclear warfare. Under the Dulles doctrine of massive retaliation, almost any incident threatened to trigger a full-scale nuclear war. Kennedy and McNamara sought to establish a "flexible response doctrine" that would limit the level of a first nuclear strike and thus leave room for negotiation.

But what if the Soviets launched a first-strike attack to knock out American missiles? A "flexible response" policy required that enough American weapons survive a surprise attack in order to retaliate. McNamara thus developed a "triad" of nuclear forces: strategic nuclear bombers, long-range missile sites underground, and submarine-launched missiles. One arm of the triad was sure to survive any attack with the capability to launch a counterstrike. The concept of **mutually assured destruction (MAD)** was thus designed to deter a Soviet threat. But the new approach also resulted in a 15 percent increase in the 1961 military budget, compared with only 2 percent increases during the last two years of Eisenhower's term.

> **mutually assured destruction (MAD)** national defense strategy in which a nuclear attack by one side would inevitably trigger an equal response leading to the destruction of both the attacker and the defender.

Vietnam. Buddhists and other groups backed the rebellion, since the Catholic Diem ruthlessly persecuted them. In May 1961, a month after the Bay of Pigs invasion, Kennedy secretly ordered 500 Green Berets and military advisers to Vietnam to prop up Diem. By 1963 the number of "military advisers" had risen to more than 16,000.

As the situation degenerated, Diem's corruption and police-state tactics made it unlikely he could defeat the Vietcong. Thus the Kennedy administration tacitly encouraged the military to stage a coup. The plotters captured Diem and, to Washington's surprise, shot him in November 1963. Despite Kennedy's policy of pragmatic idealism, the United States found itself mired in a Vietnamese civil war, which it had no clear strategy for winning.

Confronting Khrushchev >> Vietnam and Cuba
were just two less developed countries in which the Kennedy administration sought to battle Communist forces. The conflict between the two superpowers soon overshadowed developments in Asia, Africa, and Latin America.

In June 1961 a summit held in Vienna gave the president his first chance to take the measure of Nikita Khrushchev. For two long days, Khrushchev was brash and belligerent. East and West Germany must be reunited, he demanded. The problem of Berlin, where dissatisfied East Germans were fleeing to the city's free western zone, must be settled within six months. Kennedy left Vienna worried that the Soviet leader perceived

The Missiles of October >> The peril of nuclear
confrontation became dramatically clear in the Cuban missile crisis of October 1962. President Kennedy had warned repeatedly that the United States would treat any attempt to place offensive weapons in Cuba as an unacceptable threat. Khrushchev pledged that the Soviet Union had no such intention. Yet, in May 1962 he ordered the building of secret nuclear missile sites in Cuba. Throughout the summer, the buildup went largely undetected by Americans. But by October 14, overflights of Cuba by U-2 spy planes confirmed the presence of offensive missile sites. Kennedy was outraged.

For a week American security advisers secretly debated a course of action. The Joint Chiefs of Staff urged air strikes against the missile sites, and at first Kennedy agreed. "We're certainly going to . . . take out these . . . missiles," he said. But other advisers pointed out that the U-2 flights had not photographed all of Cuba. What if there were more concealed bases with missiles ready to fire? The Soviets could then launch an atomic attack on the United States despite the air strikes. Kennedy finally chose the more restrained option of a naval blockade to intercept "all offensive military equipment under shipment to Cuba."

The blockade allowed time to negotiate. On October 22 word of the confrontation began to leak out. "CAPITAL CRISIS AIR HINTS AT DEVELOPMENTS ON CUBA, KENNEDY TV TALK IS LIKELY," headlined the *New York Times*. In Moscow, Soviet leaders were convinced that an American invasion of Cuba was likely. "The thing is we were not going to unleash war," a nervous Khrushchev complained, "we just wanted to intimidate them, to deter the anti-Cuban forces." American people were stunned that evening when the president's television address revealed the Cuban threat.

Over the next few days, tensions mounted as a Soviet submarine approached the line of American ships. On October 25 the navy stopped an oil tanker. Several Soviet ships reversed course. In Cuba, Soviet general Issa Pliyev assumed the worst—that in addition to the blockade, a U.S. invasion of Cuba was being secretly prepared. The attack was expected "in the night between October 26 and October 27 or at dawn on October 27," he said, in a coded message to Moscow. Equally ominously, he added, "We have taken measures to disperse 'techniki' [the nuclear warheads] in the zone of operations." In other words, Pliyev was making his nuclear missiles operational.

On the morning of October 27 alarmed Soviet technicians detected a U-2 spy plane over Cuba. Was this the beginning of the expected attack? General Pliyev had issued strict instructions not to use force without his go-ahead, but when the air defense command looked to consult him, he could not be found, and the U-2 was about to leave Cuban airspace at any moment. Soviet officers went ahead and shot it down, killing its pilot.

Meanwhile, Kennedy was seeking urgently to resolve the crisis through diplomatic channels. Worried that events might spiral out of control, the president put off a decision on the U-2 incident until the following morning.

He decided to accept a secret offer from Khrushchev to remove Soviet missiles, in return for an American pledge not to invade Cuba. Kennedy also gave private assurances that U.S. missiles stationed in Turkey and pointed at the Soviet Union would be removed within half a year. In Moscow, Khrushchev agreed reluctantly to the deal, telling his advisers somberly that there were times to advance and times to retreat, and this time "we found ourselves face to face with the danger of war and of nuclear catastrophe, with the possible result of destroying the human race." The face-off ended on terms that saved both sides from overt humiliation.

The nuclear showdown prompted Kennedy to seek ways to control the nuclear arms race. "We all inhabit this small planet," he warned in June 1963. "We all breathe the same air. We all cherish our children's future. And we are all mortal." The administration negotiated a nuclear test ban with the Soviets, prohibiting all above-ground nuclear tests. At the same time, Kennedy's prestige soared for "standing up" to the Soviets. Khrushchev soon fell from power.

↑ The Women Strike for Peace organization demonstrated during the Cuban missile crisis. The strikers stressed their concern as mothers to justify their actions.
Bettmann/Getty Images

 REVIEW

How did crises in Berlin and Cuba push President Kennedy to change Cold War policies?

The Cuban missile crisis was the closest the world had come to "destroying the human race," in Khrushchev's words. Such a close call sobered the superpowers. It did not, however, end the Cold War. Ahead lay long, bloody regional wars—for the United States, in Vietnam; for the Soviet Union, in Afghanistan; and elsewhere, between Israel and its Arab neighbors. Conservatives would continue to press for victory in the Cold War, but never again would the two superpowers come so close to an atomic war. The nuclear anxieties of the 1950s—so much a part of the suburban era—gave way to different, equally urgent concerns in the 1960s.

CHAPTER SUMMARY

At midcentury, during an era of peace and prosperity, the United States began to build a new social and political agenda.

- Automobiles and the culture of the highways helped bind Americans to one another in a "consensus" about what it meant to be an American.
- New highways made possible rapid suburban growth.
- Suburbs proved popular with the growing blue- and white-collar middle classes.

- Consensus in the suburbs blurred class distinctions and promoted the notion of "civil religion."
- Suburban life nurtured the ideal of the woman who found fulfillment as a homemaker and a mother, even though more women began to work outside the home.
- President Eisenhower resisted the demands of conservatives to dismantle the New Deal and of liberals to extend it, in favor of moderate, or "middle-of-the-road," Republicanism.
- Cracks in the consensus appeared among discontented intellectuals and among teenagers who, through Elvis Presley and new teen idols, discovered the power of rock and roll.
- Efforts to more vigorously contain the USSR and Communist China through a policy of "brinkmanship" proved difficult to apply because of growing nationalism of less developed countries.
- Eisenhower held back from using tactical nuclear weapons during crises in Vietnam and Taiwan.
- Successful CIA operations in Iran and Guatemala encouraged U.S. policy makers to use covert operations more frequently.
- Postcolonial nationalism contributed to crises in Hungary, Egypt, and Cuba, where President Kennedy was embarrassed by the failure of an invasion attempt to overthrow Fidel Castro.
- Relations between the two superpowers thawed gradually but not without recurring confrontations between the United States and the Soviet Union.
- Under Eisenhower, the Soviet success with *Sputnik* increased fears that the United States was vulnerable to missile attacks, while the U-2 spy plane incident worsened relations.
- John F. Kennedy proved willing to use covert operations as well as diplomatic and economic initiatives like the Peace Corps and the Alliance for Progress.
- The construction of Soviet missile bases 90 miles from American shores triggered the Cuban missile crisis of 1962, the closest the United States and the Soviet Union ever came to nuclear war.

Digging Deeper

David Halberstam profiles suburban United States engagingly in *The Fifties* (1994); using suburban Orange County, California, as her focus, Lisa McGirr looks at grassroots conservatism in *Suburban Warriors: The Origins of the New American Right* (2001). For an environmental perspective, see Adam Rome, *The Bulldozer in the Countryside: Suburban Sprawl and the Rise of American Environmentalism* (2001); and Robert Bruegmann, *Sprawl: A Compact History* (2005). On cars and suburbia see Tom McCarthy, *Auto Mania: Cars, Consumers, and the Environment* (2007). Karal Ann Marling, *As Seen on TV: The Visual Culture of Everyday Life in the 1950s* (1998), dissects the popular aesthetics of the era. For popular culture, see Glenn Altschuler, *All Shook Up: How Rock and Roll Changed America* (2003). As a corrective to the view of women in the 1950s popularized by Betty Friedan, *The Feminine Mystique* (1963), see the provocative essays in Joanne Meyerowitz, ed., *Not June Cleaver: Women and Gender in Postwar America* (1994).

Fred Greenstein, *The Hidden Hand Presidency: Eisenhower as Leader* (rev. ed., 1994), contradicts the view of Ike as a bumbling president. Historians have also refurbished Kennedy's reputation. See, for example, Graham Allison, *The Essence of Decision: Explaining the Cuban Missile Crisis* (2nd ed., 1999); and Warren Bass, *Support Any Friend: Kennedy, the Middle East, and the Making of the U.S.-Israel Alliance* (2003). Two fine books on Kennedy and Vietnam are Fredrik Logevall, *Embers of War: The Fall of an Empire and the Making of America's Vietnam* (2014), as well as his earlier *Choosing War: The Lost Chance for Peace and the Escalation of War in Vietnam* (2003).

29 Civil Rights and Uncivil Liberties

1947–1969

On August 28, 1963, more than 250,000 demonstrators joined the great civil rights march on Washington, D.C., where Martin Luther King gave his "I Have a Dream" speech.

Paul Schutzer/The LIFE Picture Collection/Getty Images

>> **An American Story**

TWO ROADS TO INTEGRATION

Six-year-old Ruby knew her lessons: Look straight ahead—not to one side or the other—and especially not at them. Keep walking. Above all, do not look back once you pass, because that would encourage them. Even though Ruby learned these things, she still struggled to keep her eyes straight. The first day of school, her parents came, along with federal marshals to keep order. And all around hundreds of angry white people were yelling things like, "You little nigger, we'll get you and kill you." A sense of safety came when she was within the building's quiet halls and alone with her teacher. She was the only person in class: none of the white students

had come. As the days went by during that autumn of 1960, the marshals stopped walking with her but the hecklers still waited. And once in a while Ruby couldn't help looking back, trying to see if she recognized the face of one particular woman.

Ruby's parents were not social activists. They signed up their daughter for the white school in this New Orleans neighborhood because "we thought it was for all the colored to do, and we never thought Ruby would be alone." Her father's white employer fired him; letters and phone calls threatened the family. Through it all Ruby seemed to take things in stride, though her parents worried that she was not eating well. Often she left her school lunch untouched or refused anything other than packaged food such as potato chips. It was only after a time that her parents traced the problem to the hecklers. "They tells me I'm going to die, and that it'll be soon. And that one lady tells me every morning I'm getting poisoned soon, when she can fix it." Ruby was convinced that the woman owned the variety store nearby and would carry out her threat by poisoning the family's food.

Over the course of a year white students gradually returned to class and life settled into a new routine. By the time Ruby was 10 she had developed a remarkably clear perception of herself. "Maybe because of all the trouble going to school in the beginning I learned more about my people," she told Robert Coles, a psychologist studying children and the effects of segregation. "Maybe I would have anyway; because when you get older you see yourself and the white kids; and you find out the difference. You try to forget it, and say there is none; and if there is you won't say what it be. Then you say it's my own people, and so I can be proud of them instead of ashamed."

The new ways were not easy for white southerners either—even those who saw the need for change. A teacher from segregated Atlanta, recalled for Robert Coles a summer 10 years earlier, when she went to New York City to take courses in education. Finding Black students in her dormitory was something she'd never experienced. One day as she stepped from her shower, so did a Black student from the nearby stall. "When I saw her I didn't know what to do," the woman recalled. "I felt sick all over, and frightened. What I remember—I'll never forget it—is that horrible feeling of being caught in a terrible trap, and not knowing what to do about it." So she ducked back into the shower until the other woman left.

Weeks passed before she felt comfortable eating with Black students. Back in Atlanta she told no one about her experiences. "At that time people would have thought one of two things: I was crazy (for being so upset and ashamed) or a fool who in a summer had become a dangerous 'race mixer.'" She continued to love the South and to defend its traditions of dignity, neighborliness, and honor, but she saw the need for change. And so in 1961 she volunteered to teach one of the first integrated high school classes in Atlanta. "I've never felt so useful," she concluded after two years; "not just to the children but to our whole society. American as well as Southern. Those children, all of them, have given me more than I've given them."

For Americans in all walks of life, the changes that swept the United States in the 1960s were wrenching. From the schoolrooms and lunch counters of the South to the college campuses of the North, from eastern slums to western migrant labor camps, American society was in ferment.

On the face of it, such agitation seemed a dramatic reversal of the placid 1950s. Turbulence and controversy had overturned stability and consensus. Yet the events of the 1960s grew naturally out of the social conditions that preceded them. The civil rights movement was brought about not by a group of farsighted leaders in government but by ordinary people who sought change, often despite the reluctance or even fierce opposition of those in power. After World War II, grassroots organizations such as the NAACP for Blacks and the American GI Forum for Latinos acted with a new determination. Both peoples sought to achieve the equality of opportunity promised by the American creed. <<

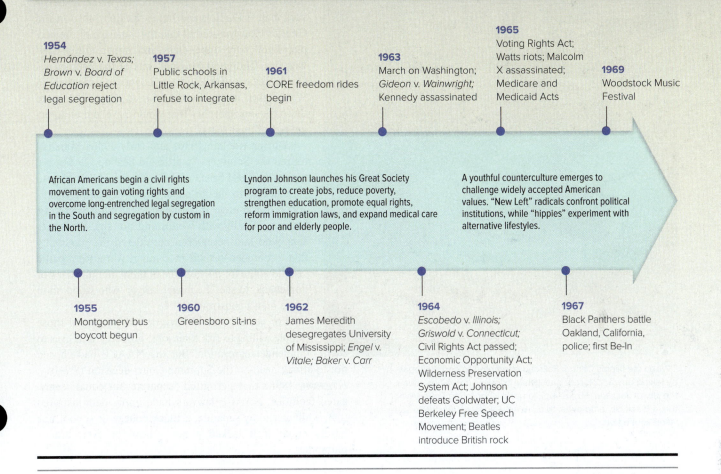

1954
Hernández v. *Texas;*
Brown v. *Board of*
Education reject
legal segregation

1957
Public schools in
Little Rock, Arkansas,
refuse to integrate

1961
CORE freedom rides
begin

1963
March on Washington;
Gideon v. *Wainwright;*
Kennedy assassinated

1965
Voting Rights Act;
Watts riots; Malcolm
X assassinated;
Medicare and
Medicaid Acts

1969
Woodstock Music
Festival

African Americans begin a civil rights movement to gain voting rights and overcome long-entrenched legal segregation in the South and segregation by custom in the North.

Lyndon Johnson launches his Great Society program to create jobs, reduce poverty, strengthen education, promote equal rights, reform immigration laws, and expand medical care for poor and elderly people.

A youthful counterculture emerges to challenge widely accepted American values. "New Left" radicals confront political institutions, while "hippies" experiment with alternative lifestyles.

1955
Montgomery bus
boycott begun

1960
Greensboro sit-ins

1962
James Meredith
desegregates University
of Mississippi; *Engel* v.
Vitale; Baker v. *Carr*

1964
Escobedo v. *Illinois;*
Griswold v. *Connecticut;*
Civil Rights Act passed;
Economic Opportunity Act;
Wilderness Preservation
System Act; Johnson
defeats Goldwater; UC
Berkeley Free Speech
Movement; Beatles
introduce British rock

1967
Black Panthers battle
Oakland, California,
police; first Be-In

THE CIVIL RIGHTS MOVEMENT

The struggle of African Americans for equality during the postwar era is filled with ironies. By the time barriers to legal segregation in the South began to fall, millions of Black families had departed for regions where they faced less easily challenged de facto discrimination. The South they left behind was in the early stages of an economic boom. The cities to which many migrated had entered a period of decline. Yet, as if to close a circle, the rise of large Black voting blocs in major cities gave African Americans more power to force the nation to dismantle the worst legal and institutional barriers to racial equality.

The Changing South and African Americans >>

Before World War II, 80 percent of African Americans lived in the South. Most raised cotton as sharecroppers and tenant farmers. The war created job opportunities in industrial cities. As millions went off to fight and others to do war work, cotton growers faced a labor shortage. They thus had an incentive to mechanize cotton picking. In 1950 only 5 percent of the crop was picked mechanically; by 1960 at least half was. Tenant farmers, sharecroppers, and hired labor of both races continued to leave the countryside for the city.

The national level of wages also profoundly affected southern labor. When federal minimum-wage laws forced lumber and textile mills to raise their pay scales, the mills no longer expanded. In addition, steel and other industries with strong national unions and manufacturers with plants around the country set wages by national standards. This brought southern wages closer to the national average by the 1960s. As the southern economy grew, what had for many years been a distinct regional economy integrated into the national economy.

As wages rose and unskilled work disappeared, job opportunities for Black southerners declined. New high-wage jobs were reserved for white southerners, since outside industries arriving in the South made no effort to change local

↑ When the Illinois Central Railroad attempted to end segregation by taking down "colored" and "white" signs in its waiting rooms, the city of Jackson, Mississippi, jumped in, ordering Robert Wheaton, a Black city employee, to paint new signs, as two white supervisors looked on.
AP Photo

the school and the school was turning out sharp, dedicated lawyers. Not only was Marshall sharp; he had the common touch as well. "Before he came along," one observer noted, "the principal black leaders— such men as Du Bois and James Weldon Johnson and Charles Houston—didn't talk the language of the people. They were upper-class and upper-middle-class Negroes. Thurgood Marshall was of the people. . . . Out in Texas or Oklahoma or down the street here in Washington at the Baptist church, he would make these rousing speeches that would have 'em all jumping out of their seats."

During the late 1930s and early 1940s Marshall toured the South (in "a little old beat-up '29 Ford"), typing out legal briefs in the backseat while trying to get teachers to sue for equal pay or defending Blacks accused of murder in a Klan-infested Florida county. He was friendly with whites and not shy. Black citizens who had never even considered the possibility that a member of their race might win a legal battle "would come for miles, some of them on mule-back or horseback, to see 'the nigger lawyer' who stood up in white men's courtrooms."

For years NAACP lawyers had supported those people willing to risk their jobs, property, and lives to challenge segregation. But the NAACP had chosen not to attack head-on the Supreme Court decision (*Plessy* v. *Ferguson*, 1896) that permitted "separate but equal" segregated facilities. NAACP lawyers had simply demonstrated that, while certainly separate, a Black college or school was hardly equal if it lacked a law school or even indoor plumbing.

patterns of discrimination. As per capita income rose and industrialization brought in new jobs, Black laborers poured out of the region in search of work. They arrived in cities that showed little willingness to hire unskilled Black labor or integrate urban neighborhoods.

The NAACP and Civil Rights >> In the

postwar era the National Association for the Advancement of Colored People (NAACP) led the legal fight against racial segregation. Its hard-hitting campaign reflected the increased national political influence of African Americans as they migrated out of the South. No longer could northern politicians readily ignore the demands that Black leaders made for greater equality. At first, however, the NAACP focused its campaign on the courts.

Thurgood Marshall was the NAACP's leading attorney. Marshall had attended law school in the 1930s at Howard University in Washington, D.C. There, the law school's dean, Charles Houston, was in the midst of revamping

The *Brown* Decision >> In 1950 the NAACP changed
tactics: it would now try to convince the Supreme Court to overturn the separate-but-equal doctrine itself. Oliver Brown of Topeka, Kansas, was one of the people who provided a way.

Brown was bothered that his daughter Linda had to walk past an all-white school on her way to catch the bus to her segregated Black school and brought suit against the Topeka Board of Education. A three-judge federal panel rejected Brown's suit on the grounds that the schools in Topeka met the legal standards for equality. The NAACP appealed the case to the Supreme Court and, in 1954, won a striking decision. *Brown v. Board of Education of Topeka* overturned the lower court ruling and rejected the doctrine of separate but equal.

Marshall and his colleagues succeeded in part because of a change in the Court itself. The year before, President Eisenhower

<< Thurgood Marshall.
Library of Congress, Prints and Photographs Division
[LC-DIG-ppmsc-01271]

had appointed Earl Warren, a liberal Republican from California, as chief justice. Warren, a forceful advocate, managed to persuade even his reluctant judicial colleagues that segregation as defined in *Plessy* rested on an insupportable theory of racial supremacy. The Court ruled unanimously that separate facilities were inherently unequal. To keep Black children segregated solely on the basis of race, it ruled, "generates a feeling of inferiority as to their status in the community that may affect their hearts and minds in a way unlikely ever to be undone."

At the time of the *Brown* decision, 21 states and the District of Columbia operated segregated school systems. All had to decide, in some way, how to comply with the new ruling. The Court allowed some leeway, handing down a second ruling in 1955 that required states to carry out desegregation "with all deliberate speed." Some border states reluctantly decided to comply, but in the Deep South, many pledged diehard defiance. In 1956, a "Southern Manifesto" was issued by 19 U.S. senators and 81 representatives: They intended to use "all lawful means" to maintain legalized segregation.

Latino Civil Rights >> Mexican Americans also considered school desegregation key to their civil rights campaign. In the years after World War II, only 1 percent of children of Mexican descent graduated from Texas high schools. Two Latino organizations, the American GI Forum and the League of United Latin American Citizens (LULAC; see Chapter 25), supported legal challenges to the segregated school system in Texas.

In 1947 the superintendent in the town of Bastrop, Texas, refused a request to enroll first-grader Minerva Delgado in a nearby all-white school. Civil rights activist Gus Garcia, a legal adviser to both LULAC and the GI Forum, helped bring a case on Minerva's behalf against the school district. But before *Delgado et al.* v. *Bastrop et al.* could even be tried, a Texas judge ordered an end to segregated schools beyond the first grade (the exception was based on the assumption that the youngest Mexican American children needed special classes to learn English). *Delgado* served notice that Mexicans would no longer accept second-class citizenship. It also served as a precedent in *Brown* v. *Board of Education* in 1954.

Two weeks before the Supreme Court made that landmark civil rights ruling, it also decided a case of great importance to Latinos. Unlike African Americans, Latinos did not face a Jim Crow system of laws imposing segregation. Throughout the Southwest the states recognized just two races: Black and white. That left Mexican Americans in legal limbo. Though legally grouped with whites, by long-standing social custom they were barred from many public places, could not serve on juries, and faced widespread job

discrimination. To remedy the situation, Mexican Americans had to establish themselves in the courts as a distinct class of people. Only then could they seek legal remedies.

An opportunity to make that point arose in the case of Pete Hernández, who had been convicted of murder by an all-white jury in Jackson County, Texas. As Gus Garcia and other Mexican American attorneys realized, no Mexican American had served on a Jackson jury in the previous 25 years. Taking a leaf from the tactics of Thurgood Marshall, they appealed the Hernández case before the Supreme Court, hoping to extend to Mexicans the benefits of the Fourteenth Amendment's equal protection clause.

The key to the Hernández case was ingenious but direct. Lawyers for Texas argued that because Mexicans were white, a jury without Mexicans was still a jury of peers. Yet the courthouse in which Hernández was convicted had two men's rooms. One said simply "MEN." The other had a crude, hand-lettered sign that read "COLORED MEN" and below that, in Spanish, "HOMBRES AQUÍ" ["MEN HERE"]. As one of Garcia's colleagues recalled: "In the jury pool, Mexicans may have been white, but when it came to nature's functions they were not." Such examples of discrimination persuaded the Supreme Court, in *Hernández* v. *Texas*, to throw out the state's argument. "The Fourteenth Amendment is not directed solely against discrimination due to a 'two-class theory,' that is, based on differences between 'white' and Negro," ruled Chief Justice Earl Warren. Warren's reasoning made it possible for Latinos to seek redress as a group rather than as individuals.

⌃ Attorney Gus Garcia was one of the key leaders of the American GI Forum, founded by Mexican American veterans to pursue their civil rights. He and his colleagues successfully appealed the conviction of Pete Hernández before the Supreme Court in 1954.
©Zuma Press, Inc,a27

A New Civil Rights Strategy >> Neither the *Brown* nor the *Hernández* decision ended segregation, but they helped usher in a new era of southern race relations. In December 1955 Rosa Parks, a 43-year-old Black civil rights activist, was riding the bus home in Montgomery, Alabama. When the driver ordered her to give up her seat for a white man, as Alabama Jim Crow laws required, she refused. Police took her to jail and eventually fined her $14.

Determined to overturn the law, a number of women from the NAACP, led by Jo Ann Robinson, met secretly at midnight to draft a letter of protest:

> Another Negro woman has been arrested and thrown into jail because she refused to get up out of her seat on the bus and give it to a white person. . . . Until we do something to stop these arrests, they will continue. The next time it may be you, or you or you. This woman's case will come up Monday. We are, therefore, asking every Negro to stay off the buses on Monday in protest of the arrest and trial.

Thousands of copies of the letter were distributed, and the Monday **boycott** was such a success it was extended indefinitely.

boycott tactic used by protestors, workers, and consumers to pressure business organizations through a mass refusal to purchase their products or otherwise do business with them.

Many in the white community, in an effort to halt the unprecedented Black challenge, resorted to various forms of legal and physical intimidation. No local insurance agent would insure cars used to carpool Black workers. A bomb exploded in the house of the Reverend Martin Luther King Jr., the key boycott leader. Still the boycotters held out until November 13, 1956, when the Supreme Court ruled that bus segregation was illegal.

The triumph was especially sweet for Martin Luther King Jr., whose leadership in Montgomery brought him national fame. Before becoming a minister at the Dexter Street Baptist Church, King had had little personal contact with the worst forms of white racism. He had grown up in the relatively affluent middle-class Black community of Atlanta, Georgia, the son of one of the city's most prominent Black ministers. He attended Morehouse College, an academically respected Black school in Atlanta, and Crozer Theological Seminary in Philadelphia before entering the doctoral program in theology at Boston University. As a graduate student, King embraced the pacifism and nonviolence of the Indian leader Mohandas Gandhi and the activism of Christian reformers of the Progressive Era.

As boycott leader, King sought to rally support without triggering violence. Since local officials were all too eager for any excuse to use force, King's nonviolent approach proved an effective strategy. Preaching his nonviolent message, King rejected the cross-burnings, kidnappings, and legally sanctioned murder practiced by extremists such as the Ku Klux Klan. A combination of Christian love and republican ideals would guide his followers when they protested with courage,

Governor Faubus of Arkansas called out the National Guard to prevent African American students from integrating Little Rock's Central High School. Once President Eisenhower federalized the Guard, soldiers stayed at the school to protect the nine students who dared to cross the color line.
John Bryson/The LIFE Picture Collection/Getty Images

dignity, and restraint. In that way history would view the civil rights activists as those with "the moral courage" to fight for their rights and, in that way, earned the respect of future generations.

Indeed, the African Americans of Montgomery did set an example of moral courage that attracted national attention and rewrote the pages of American race relations. King and his colleagues were developing the tactics needed to launch a more aggressive phase of the civil rights movement.

Little Rock and the White Backlash >> The following year, the civil rights spotlight moved to Little Rock,

Arkansas. There, reluctant white officials had adopted a plan to integrate the schools with a most deliberate lack of speed. Nine Black students were scheduled to enroll in September 1957 at the all-white Central High School. The school board urged them to stay home. Governor Orval Faubus, generally a moderate on race relations, called out the Arkansas National Guard on the excuse of maintaining order. President Eisenhower, who had refused to endorse the *Brown* decision, tacitly supported Faubus in his defiance of court-ordered integration by remarking that "you cannot change people's hearts merely by laws."

Still, the Justice Department could not let Faubus defy the federal courts, and it won an injunction against the governor. When the nine Blacks returned to school on September 23, a mob of a thousand abusive protesters greeted them. So great was national attention to the crisis that Eisenhower felt compelled to send in a thousand federal troops and take control of the National Guard. For one year the Guard preserved order until Faubus, in a last-ditch maneuver, closed all the schools. Only in 1959, under the pressure of another federal court ruling, did the Little Rock schools reopen and resume the plan for gradual integration.

King and other civil rights leaders recognized that the skirmishes of Montgomery and Little Rock were a beginning, not the end. Cultural attitudes and customs were not about to give way overnight. Black leaders were unable to achieve momentum on a national scale until 1960. Then, a series of spontaneous demonstrations by young people changed everything.

> ✅ **REVIEW**
>
> In what way did the Brown and Hernández cases promote the cause of civil rights?

A MOVEMENT BECOMES A CRUSADE

On January 31, 1960, Joseph McNeill got off the bus in Greensboro, North Carolina, a first-year student on the way back to college. When he looked for something to eat at the lunch counter, the server gave the familiar reply. "We don't serve Negroes here."

It was a refrain repeated countless times and in countless places. Yet for some reason this refusal particularly offended McNeill. He and his roommates had read a pamphlet describing the 1955 bus boycott in Montgomery, Alabama. They decided it was time to make their own protest against segregation. Proceeding the next day to the "whites only" lunch counter at a local store, they sat politely waiting for service. Rather than comply, the manager closed the counter. Word of the action spread. A day later—Tuesday—the four students were joined

by 27 more. Wednesday, the number jumped to 63, Thursday, to over 300. That weekend, 1,600 students rallied to plan further action. Within two weeks, the courage of the Greensboro students had inspired 15 **sit-ins** across the South. By year's end, 70,000 people had demonstrated; thousands had gone to jail.

> **sit-in** form of direct action in which protesters nonviolently occupy and refuse to leave an area.

The campaign for Black civil rights gained momentum not so much by the power of national movements as through a host of individual decisions by local groups and citizens. When New Orleans schools were desegregated in 1960, young Ruby's parents had not intended to make a social statement. But once involved, they refused to back down. The students at Greensboro had not been approached by the NAACP but acted on their own initiative.

Riding to Freedom >> Even as individual acts inspired protests, organizations channeled discontents and aspirations. Martin Luther King's Southern Christian Leadership Conference (SCLC) continued to advocate nonviolent protest as a direct challenge to the status quo. A second organization, the Congress of Racial Equality (CORE), was equally dedicated to nonviolent confrontations as a way to challenge segregation. A new group, the Student Nonviolent Coordinating Committee (SNCC, pronounced "Snick"), grew out of the Greensboro sit-in. SNCC represented the more militant, younger generation of activists, impatient with the slow pace of reform.

In May 1961 CORE director James Farmer led a group of Black and white "freedom riders" on a bus trip from Washington to New Orleans. They intended to focus national attention on the lack of integrated facilities throughout the South. Violent mobs attacking freedom riders and their buses raised the kind of attention they feared. In South Carolina, thugs beat divinity student John Lewis as he tried to enter an all-white waiting room. Mobs in Anniston and Birmingham, Alabama, assaulted the freedom riders as police ignored the violence. One of the buses was burned.

Sensitive to the power of conservative southern Democrats, President Kennedy tried to avoid sending federal forces to protect the demonstrators. But mounting violence dashed his hopes. From a phone booth outside the bus terminal, John Doar, a Justice Department official in Montgomery, relayed the situation to Attorney General Robert Kennedy:

> Now the passengers are coming off. They're standing on a corner of the platform. Oh, there are fists; punching! A bunch of men led by a guy with a bleeding face are beating them. There are no cops. It's terrible! It's terrible! There's not a cop in sight. People are yelling. "There those niggers are! Get 'em; get 'em!" It's awful.

Appalled, Robert Kennedy ordered in 400 federal marshals, who barely managed to hold off the crowd. King, addressing a meeting in town, phoned the attorney general to say that

^ In May 1961 a mob in Montgomery, Alabama, surrounded the Negro First Baptist Church where Martin Luther King Jr. was leading an all-night vigil. King put in a call to Attorney General Robert Kennedy, who sent 400 federal marshals to keep order.
Bettmann/Getty Images

the segregated University of Mississippi to admit James Meredith, a Black applicant. When Governor Ross Barnett personally blocked Meredith's registration in September 1962, Kennedy ordered several hundred federal marshals to escort Meredith into a university dormitory. A mob confronted the marshals, shot out streetlights, and threw rocks and bottles. The president finally sent in federal troops, but not before 2 people were killed and 375 wounded. Reacting to the violence in Mississippi, the House of Representatives debated a number of civil rights measures.

In 1963, from a prison cell in Birmingham, Alabama, Martin Luther King Jr. produced one of the most eloquent documents of the civil rights movement, his "Letter from Birmingham Jail." Addressed to local ministers who had called for an end to confrontation, the letter defended the use of civil disobedience. The choice, King warned, was not between obeying the law and nonviolently breaking it to bring about change. It was between his way and streets "flowing with blood," as frustrated Black citizens turned toward more militant ideologies.

their church had been surrounded by a mob that was throwing rocks and carrying firebombs. "I said that we were doing the best that we could," Kennedy later recalled, "and that he'd be as dead as Kelsey's nuts if it hadn't been for the marshals and the efforts that we made."

Both Kennedys understood that civil rights was the most divisive issue the administration faced. The president needed the votes of African Americans and liberals to win reelection. Yet an active federal role threatened to drive white southerners from the Democratic Party. Thus Kennedy hedged on his promise to introduce civil rights legislation. He assured Black leaders that executive orders would eliminate discrimination in the government and in businesses filling government contracts. He appointed several Blacks to high positions and five, including Thurgood Marshall, to the federal courts. But the freedom riders, by their bold actions, forced the Kennedys to do more.

Civil Rights at High Tide >> In the fall of 1961 Robert Kennedy persuaded the Student Nonviolent Coordinating Committee to shift its energies to voter registration, which he assumed would stir up less violence. Voting booths, Kennedy noted, were not like schools, where people would protest, "We don't want our little blond daughter going to school with a Negro."

Despite the Kennedys' desire to ease tensions, they continued to worsen. A federal court ordered

^ In Birmingham, Alabama, firefighters used high-pressure hoses to disperse civil rights demonstrators. The force of the hoses was powerful enough to tear bark off trees. Photographs like this one aroused widespread sympathy for the civil rights movement.
Bettmann/Getty Images

Make a Case

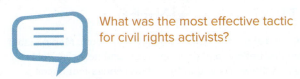

What was the most effective tactic for civil rights activists?

Once freed, King led new demonstrations. Television cameras were on hand that May as Birmingham police chief "Bull" Connor, a man with a short fuse, unleashed vicious dogs, club-wielding police, and fire hoses powerful enough to peel the bark off trees against peaceful marchers. When bombs went off in African American neighborhoods, Black mobs retaliated by burning a number of white-owned Birmingham businesses. In the following 10 weeks more than 750 protests and marches erupted in 186 cities and towns, both North and South. King's warning of streets "flowing with blood" no longer seemed far-fetched.

Kennedy sensed that he now had to deliver on his promise to promote civil rights. "If [an American with dark skin] cannot enjoy the full and free life all of us want," he asked Americans, "then who among us would be content to have the color of his skin changed and stand in his place? Who among us would then be content with counsels of patience and delay?" The president supported a strong bill to end segregation and protect Black voters.

When King announced a massive march on Washington for August 1963, Kennedy objected that it would undermine support for his bill. "I have never engaged in any direct action movement which did not seem ill-timed," King replied. Faced with the inevitable, Kennedy convinced the organizers to use the event to promote the administration's bill, to the disgust of militant CORE and SNCC factions seeking a stronger response.

Kennedy received support from the nation's leading preacher, the Reverend Billy Graham. Though born and raised in segregated North Carolina, Graham had preached widely in Africa and had invited many African leaders to come to the United States. Graham was embarrassed to learn about the discrimination they faced when they stopped at hotels and restaurants. He feared their exposure to segregation would aid Soviet efforts to gain a foothold in Africa.

On August 28, 250,000 people gathered at the Lincoln Memorial in support of civil rights and racial harmony. The day belonged to King. In the powerful tones of a southern preacher, he reminded the crowd that the Declaration of Independence was a promise that applied to all people, Black and white. He spoke passionately of his dream that one day all people regardless of race, ethnicity, or religion could live together in spirit of freedom and mutual respect.

The Fire Next Time >> As civil
rights politics fractured the Democratic Party, the president scheduled a trip to Texas to

^ Malcolm X.
AP Photo

recoup some southern support. On November 22, 1963, the people of Dallas lined the streets to view his motorcade. Suddenly a sniper's rifle fired several times and Kennedy slumped into his wife's arms, fatally wounded. His assassin, Lee Harvey Oswald, was caught several hours later. Emotionally unstable, he had spent several years in the Soviet Union. Oswald never fully explained his actions, because only two days after his arrest—in full view of television cameras—a disgruntled nightclub operator named Jack Ruby gunned him down.

In the face of such violence, many Americans came to doubt that gradual reform or nonviolence could hold the nation together. Younger Black leaders observed that civil rights received the greatest national coverage when white, not Black, demonstrators were killed. They wondered, too, how Lyndon Johnson, who became president following Kennedy's death, would approach the civil rights programs.

Johnson, a consummate politician, knew he must act forcefully. He was convinced that if he failed on civil rights, "I'd be dead before I could ever begin." On his first day in office, Johnson promised one civil rights leader after another that he would pass Kennedy's bill. His skillful management of reluctant senators pushed the Civil Rights Act of 1964 through Congress. Embodying the provisions of the Kennedy bill, it barred discrimination in public accommodations like lunch counters, bus stations, and hotels. It also prohibited employers from discriminating by race, color, religion, sex, or national origin.

The Civil Rights Act, however, did not strike down literacy tests and other laws used to prevent Black citizens from voting. With King and other Black leaders keeping up the pressure, Johnson persuaded Congress to pass a strong Voting Rights Act in August 1965. The act outlawed literacy tests and permitted federal officials to monitor elections in many southern districts. Johnson called the act "one of the most monumental laws in the entire history of American freedom." Within a five-year period Black voter registration in the South jumped from 35 to 65 percent.

Black Power >> Despite
their breadth, the new civil rights laws did not address the **de facto segregation** found outside the South. This was segregation not codified in laws

> **de facto segregation** spatial and social separation of populations brought about by social behavior rather than by laws or legal mechanisms.

but practiced through unwritten custom. In large areas of the United States, African Americans were denied mortgages, kept out of decent schools, barred from clubs, and eligible for only menial jobs. Nor did the Voting Rights Act deal with the sources of urban Black poverty. The median income for urban Black residents was about half of what white residents earned.

In such an atmosphere, militants sharply questioned the goal of integration. Since the 1930s the Nation of Islam religious sect, dedicated to complete separation from white society, had attracted as many as 100,000 members,

>> MAPPING THE PAST <<

CIVIL RIGHTS—PATTERNS OF PROTEST AND UNREST

The earliest civil rights protests such as those in Montgomery, Alabama, in 1955, took place largely in the South. Martin Luther King Jr. proclaimed a doctrine of "nonviolence" would prevail. Over time, frustrations and passions rose, and new civil rights activists pressed for a more aggressive approach. Violence erupted both in the South and in the urban centers that became home to African Americans leaving the region in search of more opportunities and better lives.

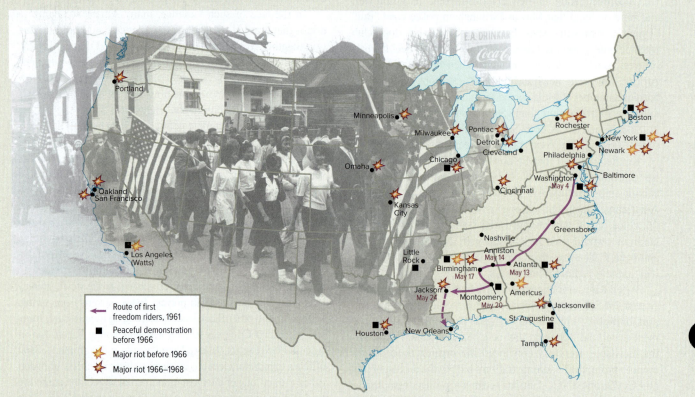

(background photo): Library of Congress, Prints and Photographs Division [LC-DIG-ppsca-08102]

MAP READING

1. Where did the first freedom riders depart? What was their final destination? What on the map suggests they did not reach it?
2. Where were the most peaceful protests held?
3. Which cities had major riots both before and after 1966?
4. Did more riots occur before or after the passage of the Civil Rights Act in 1964 and the Voting Rights Act in 1965?

MAP INTERPRETATION

1. What characteristics did the cities that experienced major riots outside the South have in common?
2. What explains the large number of racially charged events in Georgia, Alabama, and Mississippi?
3. Type "list of riots" in your browser and go to the article of that name in Wikipedia. Look at the riots listed for the 1960s and choose one from a southern city and one from a northern or western city. Compare the two accounts for similarities and differences. Is there mention of any riots from earlier in the city's history?

mostly young men. During the early 1960s the sect drew wider attention through the efforts of Malcolm X. Provocative, shrewd, and charismatic, Malcolm had learned the language of the downtrodden from his own past as a hustler, gambler, and prison inmate. His militancy after converting to Islam alarmed whites, though by 1965 he was in fact becoming more moderate. He accepted integration but emphasized

Black community action. After breaking with the Black Muslims, Malcolm was assassinated by rivals.

By 1965 even CORE and SNCC chose not to work with white liberals for nonviolent change. If Black Americans were to liberate themselves fully, militants argued, they could not merely accept rights "given" to them by whites: they had to claim them. Some members began carrying guns to defend themselves. In 1966 Stokely Carmichael of SNCC gave the militants a slogan—"Black Power"—and the defiant symbol of a gloved fist raised in the air.

In its moderate form, the Black Power movement encouraged African Americans to discover their cultural roots, their African heritage, and a new sense of identity. African clothes and natural hairstyles became popular. On college campuses Black students pressed universities to hire Black faculty, create Black studies programs, and provide segregated residential space.

For some Black militants, however, violence became a revolutionary tool. The Black Panther Party of Oakland, California, called on the Black community to arm. Leader Huey Newton and his followers openly brandished shotguns and rifles as they patrolled the streets protecting Blacks from police harassment. After being wounded in a gun battle with police, Newton went to jail. Eldridge Cleaver assumed his place as leader of the party. Even at the height of their power, the Panthers never counted more than 2,000 members nationwide.

Violence in the Streets >> No ideology organized the violent outbreaks that erupted in the ghettos. Often, a seemingly minor incident such as an arrest or an argument on the streets would trigger rioting. A mob would gather, and police cars and white-owned stores would be firebombed or looted. Riots broke out in Harlem and Rochester, New York, in 1964; the Watts area of Los Angeles in 1965; Chicago in 1966; and Newark and Detroit in 1967. It took nearly 5,000 troops to end the bloodiest rioting in Detroit, where 40 died, 2,000 were injured, and 5,000 were left homeless.

To most white Americans the violence was unfathomable and inexcusable. Martin Luther King, still preaching nonviolence, found the destruction saddening, but understood the anger behind it. Touring Watts only days after the riots, he was approached by a band of young Blacks. "We won," they told him proudly. "How can you say you won," King countered, "when thirty-four Negroes are dead, your community is destroyed, and whites are using the riot as an excuse for inaction?" The youngsters were unmoved. "We won because we made them pay attention to us."

For Lyndon Johnson, ghetto violence and Black militance stymied his efforts to achieve racial progress. The Civil Rights and Voting Rights Acts were essential parts of the "Great Society" he hoped to build. In that regard he had achieved a legislative record virtually unequaled by any other president in the nation's history. What Kennedy had promised, Johnson delivered. But the anger exploding in the nation's cities exposed serious flaws in the theory and practice of liberal reform.

✓ **REVIEW**

How did SCLC and SNCC differ in their tactics for promoting civil rights?

LYNDON JOHNSON AND THE GREAT SOCIETY

Like the state he hailed from, Lyndon Baines Johnson seemed bigger than life. His gifts were great, and his flaws glaring. Insecurity was his Achilles' heel and the engine that drove him. As president, Johnson aimed to be "the greatest of them all, the whole bunch of them." He was occasionally driven to ask why so few people genuinely liked him; one courageous diplomat answered, "Because, Mr. President, you are not a very likable man."

Johnson was born in the Hill Country outside Austin, Texas, where the dry, rough terrain grudgingly yielded up a living. He arrived in Washington in 1932 as an ardent New Dealer who loved politics. As majority leader of the Senate after 1954, Johnson was regarded as a moderate conservative who knew what strings to pull to get the job done. On an important bill, he latched on to the undecided votes until they succumbed to the famous "Johnson treatment," a combination of arguments, threats, rewards, and patriotic appeals. (Once, before meeting with Johnson, President Eisenhower pleaded with his attorney general, William Rogers, to run interference: "Bill, if Lyndon tries to get around my desk, block him off. I can't stand it when he grabs me by the lapel.")

Despite his compulsion to control every person and situation, Johnson was best at hammering out compromises. To those who served him well, he could be loyal and generous. And as president, he cared sincerely about society's underdogs. His support for civil rights, aid to the poor, education, and the welfare of the older people arose out of genuine conviction. In that sense he stood squarely in the liberal political tradition that flowered during the 1960s.

Like the New Dealers of the 1930s and the progressives before them, liberals were pragmatic reformers who wished to refine rather than overturn capitalism. Like Franklin Roosevelt and John F. Kennedy, Johnson believed that the government could and should actively manage the economy in order to soften the boom-and-bust swings of capitalism. Like progressives from the turn of the century, Johnson looked to improve society by applying the intelligence of "experts." With the nation still in shock over the Kennedy assassination, Johnson possessed the horse-trading skills—and the leverage with the southern wing of the Democratic Party—to accomplish far more of the liberal dream than Kennedy ever could.

The Origins of the Great Society >> In his first months, Johnson acted as the conservator of the Kennedy legacy. "Let us continue," he told a grief-stricken nation. Liberals who had dismissed Johnson as an unprincipled power broker came to respect the energy he showed in quickly steering Kennedy's Civil Rights Act and tax-cut legislation through Congress.

Kennedy had come to believe that prosperity alone would not ease the plight of the poor in the United States. In 1962 Michael Harrington's book *The Other America* brought attention to the persistence of poverty despite the nation's affluence. Harrington focused attention on the hills of Appalachia, which stretched from western Pennsylvania south to Alabama. In some Appalachian counties a quarter of the population survived on a diet of flour and dried-milk paste supplied by federal surplus food programs. Under Kennedy, Congress had passed a new food stamp program as well as laws designed to revive the economies of poor areas. Robert Kennedy also headed a presidential committee to fight juvenile delinquency in urban slums by involving the poor in **community action** programs.

community action programs designed to identify and organize local leaders to take steps to alleviate poverty and crime in their neighborhoods.

It fell to Lyndon Johnson to fight Kennedy's "War on Poverty." By August 1964 this master politician had driven through Congress the most sweeping social welfare bill since the New Deal. The Economic Opportunity Act addressed almost every major cause of poverty. It included training programs such as the Job Corps, which brought poor and unemployed recruits to rural or urban camps to learn new job skills. It granted loans to rural families and urban small businesses as well as aid to migrant workers. The price tag for these programs was high—almost $1 billion to fund the new Office of Economic Opportunity (OEO). Unfortunately the speed Johnson demanded in implementing the programs led in more than one instance to confusion, conflict, and waste.

The Election of 1964 >> Johnson's political stock remained high in 1964 as he announced his ambition to forge a "Great Society," in which poverty and racial injustice no longer existed. The chance to fulfill his dreams seemed within reach, for the Republicans nominated Senator Barry Goldwater of Arizona as their presidential candidate. Though ruggedly handsome and refreshingly candid, Goldwater believed that government should not dispense welfare, subsidize farmers, or aid public education. He was so determined to combat the spread of communism that he favored a nuclear showdown, if necessary, to achieve victory. Few Americans subscribed to such extreme views.

The election produced the landslide Johnson craved. Carrying every state except Arizona and four in the Deep South, he received 61 percent of the vote. Democrats gained better than two-to-one majorities in the Senate and House. The president moved rapidly to exploit the momentum.

The Great Society >> In January 1965 Johnson announced a legislative vision that would extend welfare programs on a scale beyond even Franklin Roosevelt's New Deal. By the end of 1965 some 50 bills had passed, many of them major pieces of legislation.

As a former teacher Johnson believed better schools would compensate the poor for their disadvantages at home. Under the Elementary and Secondary School Act, students

⌃ Lyndon Johnson's powers of persuasion were legendary. He applied the "Johnson treatment" (as here, in 1957, to Senator Theodore Green) whenever he wanted people to see things his way. Few could say no, as he freely violated their personal space and reminded them who dominated the situation.
George Tames/The New York Times/Redux Pictures

in low-income school districts were to receive educational equipment, money for books, and enrichment programs like Project Head Start for nursery-school-age children. However, as schools scrambled to spend federal money, they sometimes paid more for middle-class educational professionals' salaries than on resources for disadvantaged students.

Johnson also pushed through the Medicare Act to provide older people with health insurance to cover their hospital costs. Studies had shown that this demographic used hospitals three times more than other Americans did and generally had incomes only half as large. Since Medicare made no provision for the poor who were not elderly, Congress also passed a program called Medicaid. Participating states would receive matching grants from the federal government to pay the medical expenses of those on welfare or those too poor to afford medical care.

The Great Society also reformed immigration policy in ways that brought it up to date with modern population trends. The National Origins Act of 1924 reflected the deeply Eurocentric orientation of American society. It guaranteed that almost all the annual admissions quota of 154,000 were northern Europeans. Asians were barred almost entirely.

The Immigration Act of 1965 abolished the national origins system. Besides increasing annual admissions from the Eastern Hemisphere to 170,000, it gave marked preference to reuniting families of those immigrants already in the United States—so much so that some observers nicknamed it the "brothers and sisters act." Asians and Eastern Europeans were among its prime beneficiaries. Such liberal provisions were offset, however, by prejudice toward Latin Americans. Many in Congress feared a massive influx of poverty-stricken workers from south of the border. Hence the new act capped arrivals from the Western Hemisphere at 120,000 annually.

Johnson did not forget the environment in his efforts to outdo the New Deal. By the mid-1960s many Americans had become increasingly concerned about symptoms of environmental damage such as smog generated by factories and automobiles; lakes and rivers polluted by detergents, pesticides, and industrial wastes; and the disappearance of wildlife. One popular insecticide, DDT, became the focus of such concerns.

For years public health and agriculture officials had viewed DDT as a kind of magic bullet that could wipe out disease-spreading insects and pests that attacked crops. Assuming the pesticide was harmless, farmers and health officials sprayed it on farmland, forests, golf courses, beaches, and even people. Marine biologist and nature writer Rachel Carson warned against such indiscriminate use. "The contamination of man's total environment with such substances of incredible harm," she wrote in her 1962 book *Silent Spring*, could "alter the very material of heredity upon which the shape of the future

depends." More fundamentally, Carson challenged the popular belief that humans could improve on nature through science and technology. "The 'control of nature,'" she wrote, "is a phrase conceived in arrogance, born of the Neanderthal age of biology and philosophy when it was supposed that nature exists for the convenience of man." Echoing Aldo Leopold, she advocated a biocentric approach in which humans sought harmony with the natural world. Her critics dismissed her as romantic or even hysterical. One linked her to "the organic gardeners, the anti-fluoride leaguers, the worshippers of 'natural foods' . . . and other pseudo-scientists and faddists."

But the outcry sparked by *Silent Spring* could not be suppressed. The Kennedy administration formed a committee to study the problem and it largely vindicated Carson. "The elimination of the use of persistent toxic pesticides should be the goal," the investigators concluded. More important, Carson taught Americans to think ecologically. She showed the interconnection of living things and how toxic chemicals moved through the food chain, affecting beneficial and harmful insects alike, along with birds, animals, and humans.

Carson's alarm helped inspire a broad movement to protect the environment, and Congress, prodded by Lyndon Johnson, took note. In 1964 and 1965 it established pollution standards for interstate waterways and provided funds for sewage treatment and water purification. New laws tightened standards on air pollution. In addition Congress passed the National Wilderness Preservation System Act to set aside 9.1 million acres of wilderness as "forever wild."

The Great Society produced more legislation and more reforms than the New Deal. It also carried a higher price tag than anyone predicted. Economic statistics suggested that

⌃ This truck sprayed DDT on the beach, and beachgoers, at Jones Beach in Long Island in 1945. Convinced that pesticides such as DDT posed no threat, public health and agriculture officials sprayed it with such reckless abandon that Rachel Carson felt compelled to advocate curbs on pesticide abuse.
Keystone-France/Gamma-Keystone/Getty Images

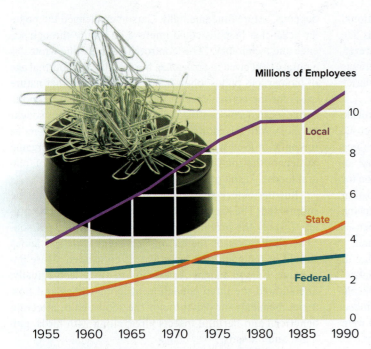

GROWTH OF GOVERNMENT, 1955–1990

Government has been a major growth industry since World War II. Most people think of "big government" as federal government. But even during the Great Society, far more people worked in state and local government. (background photo) DRB Images, LLC/iStock.com

general prosperity, boosted by the tax cut, did more to fight poverty than all the OEO programs. Conservatives and radicals alike objected that the liberal welfare state was intruding into too many areas of people's lives.

For all that, the Great Society was the high-water mark of a trend toward activist government that had grown steadily since the Progressive Era and the Great Depression. While Americans continued to pay lip service to the notion that government should remain small and interfere little in citizens' lives, programs such as Medicare or Medicaid remained widely popular. Few Americans disputed the right of the government to regulate industrial pollution or to control the excesses of large corporations or powerful labor unions. In this sense, the tradition of liberalism prevailed.

The Reforms of the Warren Court >> Although Lyndon Johnson and Congress led the liberal crusade in the 1960s, the Supreme Court played an important role. Under Chief Justice Earl Warren, the Court handed down landmark decisions in broad areas of civil liberties and civil rights.

As of 1960, the rights of citizens accused of a crime but not yet convicted were often unclear. Those too poor to afford lawyers could be forced to go to trial without representation. Often they were not informed of their constitutional rights when arrested. In a series of decisions, the Court ruled that the

Fourteenth Amendment provided broad guarantees of **due process** under the law. *Gideon* v. *Wainwright* (1963), an appeal launched by a Florida prisoner, made it clear that all citizens were entitled to legal counsel in any case involving a possible jail sentence. In *Escobedo* v. *Illinois* (1964) and *Miranda* v. *Arizona* (1966), the Court declared that individuals detained for a crime must be informed of the charges against them, of their right to remain silent, and of their right to have an attorney present during questioning. Though these decisions applied to all citizens, they were primarily intended to benefit the poor, who were most likely to be in trouble with the law and least likely to understand their rights.

> **due process** constitutional concept, embodied in the Fifth and Fourteenth Amendments, that no person shall be deprived of life, liberty, or property without legal safeguards such as being present at a hearing, having an opportunity to be heard in court, having the opportunity to confront hostile witnesses, and being able to present evidence.

Other decisions promoted a more liberal social climate. In *Griswold* v. *Connecticut* (1964) the Warren Court overturned a nineteenth-century law banning the sale of contraceptives or giving medical advice about their use. The Court also greatly narrowed the legal definition of obscenity and ruled that a book had to be "utterly without redeeming social value" to permit censorship. And the Court strengthened the constitutional separation of church and state by ruling in *Engel* v. *Vitale* (1962) that prayers could not be read in public schools.

Banning school prayer may have been one of the Court's most controversial decisions; *Baker* v. *Carr* (1962) was one of its most far-reaching. Most states had not redrawn their legislative districts to reflect the growth of urban and suburban population since the nineteenth century. The less populated (and most often conservative) rural areas elected the most legislators. In *Baker* v. *Carr* the Court ruled that the states must redraw legislative lines to follow as closely as possible the principle of "one person, one vote."

 REVIEW

What were three major legislative achievements of Johnson's Great Society?

YOUTH MOVEMENTS

In 1964 some 800 students from UC Berkeley, Oberlin, and other colleges met in western Ohio to be trained for the voter registration campaign in the South. Middle-class students who had grown up in quiet white suburbs learned sobering lessons from protest-hardened SNCC coordinators. When beaten by police, the SNCC staff advised, assume the fetal position—hands protecting the neck, elbows covering the

Edie Black from Smith College was one of hundreds of middle-class students who volunteered during Freedom Summer of 1964. Many students returned to their campuses in the fall radicalized, ready to convince others to join them in finding alternatives to "the system."
BH, File/AP Photo

temples, in order to minimize injuries from nightsticks. A few days later, grim news arrived. Three volunteers who had left for Mississippi two days earlier and already been arrested by local police were now reported "missing." Six weeks later, their mangled, bullet-riddled bodies were found, bulldozed into the earthworks of a freshly finished dam.

By the mid-1960s conservatives, civil rights organizations, and the poor were not the only groups questioning liberal solutions. Dissatisfied members of the middle class—and especially the young—had joined them. The students who returned to campus from the voter registration campaign that summer of 1964 were the shock troops of a much larger movement.

Activists on the New Left and Right >> More
than a few students had become disillusioned with the slow pace of reform. Tom Hayden, from a working-class family in a suburb of Detroit, went to the University of Michigan, then traveled to UC Berkeley, and soon joined civil rights workers in Mississippi. Along with other radical students, Hayden helped form Students for a Democratic Society (SDS). Members of SDS gave up on change through electoral politics. Direct action was needed if the faceless, bureaucratic society of the "organization man" were to be made truly democratic. SDS advocated a "participatory democracy" that made full use of sit-ins, protest marches, and confrontation.

These discontents surfaced dramatically in the Free Speech Movement at the University of California's Berkeley campus. To those in the SDS, Berkeley was a bureaucratic monster, enrolling more than 30,000 students who filed into large impersonal halls to endure lectures from remote professors. After the university banned political recruiting and fund-raising along a

narrow strip of sidewalk in the fall of 1964, university police tried to remove a recruiter for CORE. Thousands of angry student protesters surrounded their police car for 32 hours.

To Mario Savio, a graduate student in philosophy and veteran of the Mississippi Freedom Summer, the issue was clear: "In our free-speech fight, we have come up against what may emerge as the greatest problem of our nation—depersonalized, unresponsive bureaucracy." When the university's president, Clark Kerr, threatened to expel Savio, 6,000 students engaged in organized civil disobedience. They took control of the administration building, stopped classes, and convinced many faculty members to join them. Kerr backed down, placing no limits on free speech on campus except those that applied to society at large. Berkeley was not the only university where students felt aggrieved. The rebellious spirit spread to Michigan, Yale, and Columbia, and then to other campuses across the nation.

Political activism on college campuses was not limited to students on the left. The clean-cut members of Young Americans for Freedom (YAF) criticized students in the Free Speech Movement as beatniks, liberals, and Communists. To YAF Eisenhower's "middle-of-the-road Republicanism" and Kennedy's liberalism were both forms of "statism." Growth of government, these young conservatives believed, threatened individual liberty and freedom. Their hero, Barry Goldwater, embodied the **libertarian** values and anticommunism they cherished. Undaunted by Goldwater's defeat in 1964, YAF was the seedbed of a new generation of conservatives who gained control of the Republican Party in the 1970s.

> **libertarian** advocate of a minimalist approach to governing, in which the freedom of private individuals to do as they please ranks paramount.

THEN&NOW

At the heart of the upheavals of the 1960s era were wars over political and cultural values. By the 1970s conservatives were winning the political wars as they gained ever greater influence over Congress, the Supreme Court, and the White House. Liberals, however, continued to redefine American lifestyles. Consider, for example, how people dress. In 1960, most middle-class men wore suits and hats for work, travel, worship services, and even sporting events. Women donned dresses and white gloves when in public, even to go shopping. Now ask yourself where today you see a man in a three-piece suit or wearing something other than a baseball cap? When outside an operating room or on a cold winter's day do you see women wearing gloves? Americans now choose to wear more informal and

^ Members of Young Americans for Freedom protest at the offices of IBM in St. Louis, for trading with Communist nations in Eastern Europe. Though less prominent than student activists on the left, members of YAF proved to be the seedbed of a generation of conservatives who would gain influence in the 1970s and 1980s.. Bettmann/Getty Images

comfortable clothes. This shift in fashion is political as well as cultural, since it signifies a more democratic presentation of self in public spaces.

Vatican II and American Catholics >> Catholics played a prominent role in the creation of YAF. Many Catholics and conservatives condemned the secular trends of modern life as a threat to their traditional faith. But other American Catholics sought a greater engagement with the currents of change. They were pleased when, in October 1962, Pope John XXIII summoned church leaders to a reformist ecumenical council, popularly known as Vatican II.

Pope John instructed the council to weigh issues facing the world in the 1960s, including poverty, nuclear war, atheism, and birth control. He wished, as well, to bring the church hierarchy into closer touch with lay members and the modern world in which they lived. Although Pope John died before the council finished, his successor, Pope Paul VI, supported changes that would transform the church. Gone were "fish Fridays" and Saturday confessions. Priests would now face the congregation, not the altar, and deliver the service in English, not Latin. In addition, Vatican II encouraged Catholics to reach out to other Christians in a spirit of **ecumenism**.

> **ecumenism** movement encouraging unity among religions, especially among Christian denominations and between Christians and Jews.

The reforms initiated by John XXIII inspired many Catholics to activism both inside and outside the church. Fathers

Daniel and Philip Berrigan were among a number of priests and nuns who joined anti-poverty and antiwar movements. Some female Catholics sought a greater role for women in religious life. As one historian concluded, "Catholics live in a different world since the Council."

The Rise of the Counterculture >>
Spiritual matters also aroused less-religious rebels who found their culture too materialistic and shallow. These alienated students began to grope toward spiritual, nonmaterial goals. "Turn on to the scene, tune in to what is happening, and drop out of high school, college, grad school, junior executive," advised Timothy Leary, a Harvard psychology professor. Those who heeded Leary's call to spiritual renewal rejected politics for experimentation with music, sex, and drugs. Observers labeled their movement a "counterculture."

The counterculture of the 1960s had much in common with earlier religious revival and utopian movements. It admired the quirky individualism of Henry David Thoreau. Like Thoreau, it turned to Asian philosophies such as Zen Buddhism. Like Brook Farm and other nineteenth-century utopian communities, the new "hippie" communes sought perfection along the fringes of society. Communards "learned how to scrounge materials, tear down abandoned buildings, use the unusable," as one member of the "Drop City" commune put it. Sexual freedom became a means to liberate members of the counterculture from the repressive inhibitions that distorted the lives of their "uptight" parents. Drugs appeared to offer access to a higher state of consciousness or pleasure. Timothy Leary began experimenting with hallucinogenic mushrooms in Mexico and soon moved on to LSD. The drug "blew his mind," he announced, and he became so enthusiastic in making converts that Harvard blew him straight out of its hallowed doors. By 1966 Leary was lecturing across the land on the joys of drug use.

Where Leary's approach to LSD was cool and contemplative, novelist Ken Kesey (*One Flew over the Cuckoo's Nest*) embraced it with antic frenzy. His ragtag company of druggies and freaks formed the "Merry Pranksters" at Kesey's home outside San Francisco. In *The Electric Kool-Aid Acid Test*, Tom Wolfe chronicled their travels as the Pranksters headed east on a **psychedelic** school bus in search of Leary. Their example inspired others to drop out.

> **psychedelic** characterized by or generating shifts in perception and altered states of awareness, often hallucinatory, and usually brought on by drugs such as LSD, mescaline, or psilocybin.

The Rock Revolution >> In the 1950s rock and roll defined a teen culture preoccupied with young love, cars, and

STUDENT VOICES FOR A NEW UNITED STATES

In 1960 students created three organizations committed to ideals of political and moral regeneration for the United States. The organizations were the Student Nonviolent Coordinating Committee (SNCC; see the section "Riding to Freedom"), Young Americans for Freedom (YAF), and the Students for a Democratic Society (SDS). Each organization addressed the issue of justice but in different ways.

DOCUMENT 1
SNCC Statement of Purpose

We affirm the philosophical or religious ideal of nonviolence as the foundation of our purpose, the presupposition of our belief, and the manner of our action. Nonviolence as it grows from the Judaic-Christian tradition seeks a social order of justice permeated by love. Integration of human endeavor represents the crucial first step towards such a society.

Through nonviolence, courage displaces fear, love transcends hate. Acceptance dissipates prejudice; hope ends despair. Peace dominates war, faith reconciles doubt. Mutual regards cancel enmity. Justice for all over-throws injustice. The redemptive community supersedes systems of gross immorality.

Love is the central motif of nonviolence. Love is the force by which God binds man to Himself and man to man. Such love goes to the extreme; it remains loving and forgiving even in the midst of hostility. It matches the capacity of evil to inflict suffering with an even more enduring capacity to absorb evil, all the while persisting in love.

By appealing to conscience and standing on the moral nature of human existence, nonviolence nurtures the atmosphere in which reconciliation and justice become actual possibilities.

Adopted at Raleigh, North Carolina, April, 1960.

Lewis, John, and D'Orso, Michael, *Walking with the Wind: A Memoir of the Movement*, New York: NY Simon & Schuster, 1998, p. 189.

DOCUMENT 2
YAF Sharon Statement

In this time of moral and political crises, it is the responsibility of the youth of America to affirm certain eternal truths.

We, as young conservatives, believe:

That foremost among the transcendent values is the individual's use of his God-given free will, whence derives his right to be free from the restrictions of arbitrary force:

That liberty is indivisible, and that political freedom cannot long exist without economic freedom:

That the purpose of government is to protect those freedoms through the preservation of internal order, the provision of national defense, and the administration of justice:

That when government ventures beyond these rightful functions, it accumulates power, which tends to diminish order and liberty. . . .

That we will be free only so long as the national sovereignty of the United States is secure; that history shows periods of freedom are rare, and can exist only when free citizens concertedly defend their rights against all enemies:

That the forces of international Communism are, at present, the greatest single threat to these liberties:

That the United States should stress victory over, rather than coexistence with, this menace; and

That American foreign policy must be judged by this criterion: does it serve the just interests of the United States?

Adopted in conference at Sharon, Connecticut, September 11, 1960.

Young Americans for Freedom.

DOCUMENT 3
SDS Port Huron Statement

INTRODUCTION: AGENDA FOR A GENERATION We are people of this generation, bred in at least modest comfort, housed now in universities, looking uncomfortably to the world we inherit. . . . Many of us began maturing in complacency.

As we grew, however, our comfort was penetrated by events too troubling to dismiss. First, the permeating and victimizing fact of human degradation, symbolized by the Southern struggle against racial bigotry, compelled most of us from silence to activism. Second, the enclosing fact of the Cold War, symbolized by the presence of the Bomb, brought awareness that we ourselves, and our friends, and millions of abstract "others" we knew more directly because of our common peril, might die at any time. We might deliberately ignore, or avoid, or fail to feel all other human problems, but not these two, for these were too immediate and crushing in their impact too challenging in the demand that we as individuals take the responsibility for encounter and resolution. . . .

Some would have us believe that Americans feel contentment amidst prosperity—but might it not be better called a glaze above deeply felt anxieties about their role in the new world? And if these anxieties produce a developed indifference to human affairs, do they not as well produce a yearning to believe there is an alternative to the present, that something can be done to change circumstances in the school, the workplaces, the bureaucracies, the government? It is to this latter yearning, at once the spark and engine of change, that we direct our present appeal. The search for truly democratic alternatives to the present, and a commitment to social experimentation with them, is a worthy and fulfilling human enterprise, one which moves us and, we hope, others today. On such a basis do we offer this document of our convictions and analysis: as an effort in understanding and changing the conditions of humanity in the late twentieth century, an effort rooted in the ancient, still unfulfilled conception of man attaining determining influence over his circumstances of life.

Adopted at Port Huron, Michigan, June 15, 1962.

Hayden, Tom, *The Port Huron Statement: The Visionary Cell of the 1960s, Revolution.* New York: NY, Thunder's Mouth Press, 2005, pp. 45–48.

the pressures of the adult world. One exception was the Kingston Trio, which in 1958 popularized folk music and historical ballads, especially among college audiences. As the interest in folk music grew, the lyrics increasingly focused on social or political issues. Bob Dylan joined other folk singers in the civil rights march on Washington in 1963, singing "We Shall Overcome" and "Blowin' in the Wind." Their music reflected the activist side of the counterculture as they sought to provoke their audiences to social activism. Dylan, who had played his protest songs on an acoustic guitar, shocked fans in 1965 by donning a black leather jacket and shifting to a "folk rock" style featuring an electric guitar. His new songs seemed to suggest that the old United States was almost beyond redemption.

In 1964 a new sound, imported from Great Britain, exploded on the American scene. The Beatles, four musicians from Liverpool, attracted frenzied teen audiences everywhere they played. Along with other British groups, such as the Rolling Stones, the Beatles reconnected American audiences with the rhythm-and-blues roots of rock and roll. And, like Dylan, their style influenced pop culture almost as much as their music. After a spiritual pilgrimage to India, they returned to produce *Sergeant Pepper's Lonely Hearts Club Band,*

possibly the most influential album of the decade. It blended sound effects with music, alluded to trips taken with "Lucy in the Sky with Diamonds" (LSD), and welcomed listeners into a turned-on world. Out in San Francisco, bands such as the Grateful Dead pioneered "acid rock" with long pieces aimed at echoing drug-induced states of mind.

The debt of white rock musicians to rhythm and blues led to increased integration in the music world. Before the 1960s Black rhythm-and-blues bands played primarily to Black audiences in segregated clubs or over Black radio stations. Black artists such as Little Richard, Chuck Berry, and Ray Charles wrote many hit songs made popular by white performers. Black social and political consciousness gave rise to "soul" music. "Soul brothers" and "soul sisters," for the first time heard their music played on major radio stations. One Black disc jockey described soul as "the last to be hired, first to be fired, brown all year round, sit-in-the-back-of-the-bus-feeling." Soul was the quality that expressed Black pride and separatism. Out of Detroit came the Motown sound, which combined elements of gospel, blues, and big-band jazz.

The West Coast Scene >> The vibrant counterculture also signaled the increasing importance of the West Coast in American popular culture. In the 1950s the shift of television production from the stages of New York to the film lots of Hollywood helped establish Los Angeles as a communications center. San Francisco became notorious as a center of the beat movement. By 1963 the "surfing sound" of West Coast rock groups such as the Beach Boys and Jan and Dean had made Southern California's preoccupation with surfing and cars into a national fad.

Before 1967 Americans were only vaguely aware of another West Coast phenomenon, the "hippies." But in January a loose coalition of drug freaks, Zen cultists, and political activists banded together to hold the first well-publicized "Be-In." The Beat poet Allen Ginsberg was on hand to offer spiritual guidance. The Grateful Dead and Jefferson Airplane, acid rock groups based in San Francisco, provided entertainment. An unknown organization called the Diggers somehow managed to supply free food and drink, while the notorious Hell's Angels motorcycle gang policed the occasion.

In the summer of 1969 all the positive forces of the counterculture converged on Bethel, New York, in the Catskill Mountains resort area, to celebrate the promises of peace,

⋏ The Beatles had a major impact on men's style as well as on popular music. This 1963 photo shows their "mod" look popular first in Britain. Later they adopted a hippie look.
Bettmann/Getty Images

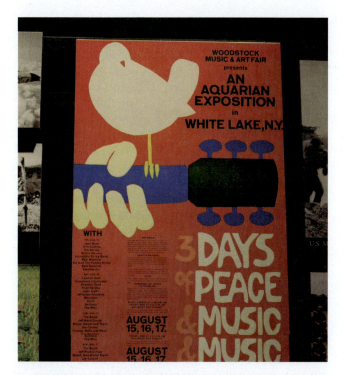

In the summer of 1969, over 400,000 people converged on the Woodstock Music Festival in Bethel, New York. A society rent by violence defied their determination to spread the spirit of brotherhood and sisterhood, peace, and love.
B Christopher/Alamy Stock Photo

love, and freedom. The Woodstock Music Festival attracted over 400,000 people to the largest rock concert ever organized. For one long weekend the audience and performers formed an ephemeral community based on sex, drugs, and rock and roll. Yet even then, the counterculture was dying. Violence intruded on the laid-back urban communities that hippies had formed. Organized crime and drug pushers muscled in on the lucrative trade in LSD, amphetamines, and marijuana. Bad drugs and addiction took their toll. Free sex often became an excuse for exploitation, loveless gratification, and even rape.

What failure could not doom was finished off by success. Much that once seemed outrageous in the hippie world was soon absorbed into the mainstream marketplace. Rock groups became big business enterprises commanding huge fees. Yogurt, granola, and herbal teas appeared on supermarket shelves. Ironically, much of the world that hippies forged was embraced and tamed by the society hippies had rejected.

 REVIEW

How did the following elements influence the counterculture: drugs, music, religion?

History in Global Context >> The civil rights movement and counterculture changed the United States in fundamental ways. Although de facto segregation and racism remained entwined in American life, segregation as a legal system had been overturned. No longer was it enshrined by the decisions of the highest court in the land, as it had been in *Plessy* v. *Ferguson*. And the rise of Black power—in both its moderate and radical forms—reflected a political and cultural current that was international as well as national. In Africa the drive for civil rights revolved around the effort to overthrow the imperial powers of Europe. In colony after colony, African nationalists fought for their independence, with Ghana leading the way in 1957. Too often the new governments devolved into dictatorships; while in South Africa the white regime maintained a system of *apartheid* that strictly segregated the races and smothered Black political and economic progress. But colonial empires continued to fall across the globe.

The United States granted independence to its principal Asian colony, the Philippines, in 1946. Yet Americans, too, found themselves ensnared by the conflicts of colonialism. More than any other factor, a growing war in France's former colony, Vietnam, destroyed the promise of Lyndon Johnson's Great Society and distracted from the campaign for civil rights. After 1965 the nation divided sharply as the American military role in Southeast Asia grew. Radicals on the left looked to rid the United States of a capitalist system that promoted race and class conflict at home and imperialism and military adventurism abroad. Conservatives who supported the war called for a return to more traditional values, such as law and order. Both the left and the right attacked the liberal center. Their combined opposition undermined the consensus Lyndon Johnson hoped to build.

CHAPTER SUMMARY

Largely excluded from the prosperity of the 1950s, African Americans and Latinos undertook a series of grassroots efforts to gain the legal and social freedoms denied them by racism and, in the South, an entrenched system of segregation.

- Early postwar campaigns focused on legal challenges to the system, winning victories in the Supreme Court decisions of *Brown* v. *Board of Education* and *Hernández* v. *Texas*.
- Later in the 1950s Martin Luther King Jr. and other civil rights activists used new techniques of protest, such as the boycott, to desegregate the bus system in Montgomery, Alabama.
- Continued resistance by white southerners sparked a school integration dispute in Little Rock, Arkansas.
- Beginning in 1960 widespread grassroots efforts from Black churches, students, and political groups accelerated the drive for an end to segregation.
- Violence against sit-ins, freedom rides, voter registration drives, and other forms of nonviolent protest made the nation sympathetic to the civil rights cause.
- In the wake of the assassination of President Kennedy, Lyndon Johnson persuaded Congress to adopt the Civil Rights Act of 1964 and the Voting Rights Act of 1965.

- The Supreme Court under Chief Justice Earl Warren expanded civil liberties through its *Gideon, Escobedo*, and *Miranda* decisions, and also eased censorship, banned school prayer, and expanded voting rights.
- Lyndon Johnson delivered on the liberal promise of his Great Society through his 1964 tax cut, aid to education, Medicare and Medicaid, wilderness preservation, and urban redevelopment and through the many programs of his War on Poverty.
- Johnson's liberal reforms did not satisfy student radicals, minority dissidents, and the counterculture whose members sought to transform the United States into a more just and less materialistic society.

Digging Deeper

Steven Lawson, Charles Payne, and James Patterson provide an excellent overview in *Debating the Civil Rights Movement, 1945–1968* (2006). Also useful is Robert Weisbrot, *Freedom Bound: A History of America's Civil Rights Movement* (1990). Though exhaustive in detail (nearly 3,000 pages in all), Taylor Branch's three-volume biography of Martin Luther King Jr. is superb: *Parting the Waters: America in the King Years, 1954–63* (1988); *Pillar of Fire: America in the King Years, 1963–65* (1998); and *At Canaan's Edge: America in the King Years, 1965–68* (2006). The prominent role of women, sometimes slighted, receives its due in Bettye Collier-Thomas and V. P. Franklin, eds., *Sisters in the Struggle: African-American Women in the Civil Rights–Black Power Movements* (2001). Latino civil rights movements are covered in Henry A. J. Ramos, *American G.I. Forum* (1998); and F. Arturo Rosales, *Chicano! The History of the Mexican-American Civil Rights Movement* (1997).

Todd Gitlin, *The Sixties* (1987), set the early tone for books that are part history and part memoir. Maurice Isserman and Michael Kazan, *America Divided: The Civil War of the 1960s* (2011), is politically engaged and scholarly. On the spiritual side of the era see Mark Oppenheimer, *Knocking on Heaven's Door: American Religion in the Age of Counterculture* (2003), Mark H. Lytle, *The Gentle Subversive: Rachel Carson, Silent Spring and the Rise of the Environmental Movement* (2007), provides a brief biographical approach. For a narrative overview, also consult Lytle, *America's Uncivil Wars: The Sixties Era from Elvis to the Fall of Richard Nixon* (2006). Robert Dallek, *An Unfinished Life: John F. Kennedy, 1917–1963* (2004), draws a portrait that balances Kennedy's virtues and vices. A good political biography of Lyndon Johnson is Randall Woods, *LBJ: Architect of Ambition* (2006), and more recently *Prisoners of Hope: Lyndon Johnson, the Great Society and the Limits of Liberalism* (2015).

30 The Vietnam Era
1963–1975

In Vietnam, helicopters gave infantry unusual mobility, critical in a war with no real front line, because troops could be quickly carried from one battle to another. Tim Page, who snapped this photo, described the chaos of such warfare: "On the ground it's always confusion, dust, smoke, unfamiliar territory wet or dry. Everyone seems to mill around in mad ant-like patterns waiting for the seething to calm down; maybe it will, maybe it won't, and when it's hot, it's very hot."

Tim Page/Getty Images

>> **An American Story**

WHO IS THE ENEMY?

From afar, Vietnam looked like an emerald paradise. Thomas Bird, an infantry soldier sent there in 1965, recalled his first impression: "A beautiful white beach with thick jungle background. The only thing missing was naked women running down the beach, waving and shouting 'Hello, hello, hello.' " Upon landing, Bird and his buddies were each issued a "Nine-Rule" card outlining proper behavior toward the Vietnamese. "Treat the women with respect, we are guests in this country and here to help these people."

But whom were they helping and whom were they fighting? When American troops searched out the enemy, whom they called Vietcong (VC), the VC generally disappeared into the jungle or blended in among the villagers. John Muir, a Marine, walked into a typical hamlet with a Korean lieutenant. To Muir the place looked peaceful, but the Korean had been in Vietnam awhile. "We have a little old lady and a little old man and two very small children," he pointed out. "According to them, the rest of the family has been spirited away . . . either been drafted into one army or the other. So there's only four of them, and they have a pot of rice that's big enough to feed fifty people. And rice, once it's cooked, will not keep. They gotta be feeding the VC." Muir watched in disbelief as the lieutenant set the house on fire. The roof "started cooking off ammunition, because all through the thatch they had ammunition stored."

GIs soon learned to walk down jungle trails with a cautious shuffle, looking for a wire or a piece of vine that seemed too straight. "We took more casualties from booby traps than we did from actual combat," recalled David Ross, a medic. "It was very frustrating because how do you fight back against a booby trap? You're just walking along and all of a sudden your buddy doesn't have a leg. Or you don't have a leg." Yet somehow the villagers would walk the same paths and never get hurt. Who was the enemy and who the friend?

The same question was being asked back home, on the campus of Kent State University on May 4,

1970. By then the escalated phase of the Vietnam War had dragged on for more than five years, driving President Lyndon Johnson from office and embroiling his successor, Richard Nixon, in controversy. When Nixon expanded the war beyond Vietnam into Cambodia, protest erupted at Kent State, just east of Akron, Ohio. Opposition to the war had become so intense in this normally apolitical community that 300 students had torn the Constitution from a history text and, in a formal ceremony, buried it. "President Nixon has murdered it," they charged. That evening demonstrators spilled into the nearby town, smashed shop windows, and returned to campus to burn down an old army ROTC building. Governor James Rhodes ordered in 750 of the National Guard. Student dissidents were the "worst type of people we harbor in America," he announced. "We are going to eradicate the problem."

When demonstrators assembled for a rally on the college commons, the guard ordered them to disperse. Whether they had the authority to do so was debatable. The protesters stood their ground. Then the members of the guard advanced, wearing full battle gear and armed with M-1 rifles, whose high-velocity bullets had a horizontal range of almost two miles. Some students scattered; a few picked up rocks and threw them. The guard members suddenly fired into the crowd, many of whom were students passing back and forth from classes. Incredulous, a young woman knelt over Jeffrey Miller; he was dead. By the time calm was restored,

three other students had been killed and nine more wounded, some caught innocently in the guard's indiscriminate fire.

News of the killings swept the nation. At Jackson State, a Black college in Mississippi, antiwar protesters seized a women's dormitory. On May 14 state police surrounding the building opened fire without provocation, killing two more students and wounding a dozen. In both incidents the demonstrators had been unarmed. The events at Kent State and Jackson State turned sporadic protests against the American invasion of Cambodia into a nationwide student strike. Many students believed the ideals of the United States had been betrayed by those forces of law and order sworn to protect them.

Who was the friend and who the enemy? Time and again the war in Vietnam led Americans to ask that question. Not since the Civil War had the nation been so deeply divided. As the war dragged on, debate moved off college campuses and into the homes of middle Americans, where sons went off to fight and the war came home each night on the evening news. As no other war had, Vietnam seemed to stand the nation on its head. When American soldiers shot at Vietnamese "hostiles," who could not always be separated from "friendlies," or when National Guard members fired on their neighbors across a college green, who were the enemies and who were the friends? Division over Vietnam added to forces that would destroy the consensus that unified the nation in the 1950s. <<

1954
French defeated at Dien Bien Phu; Geneva Accords

1965
Rolling Thunder begins bombing of North Vietnam; Ralph Nader's *Unsafe at Any Speed*

1968
U.S. Vietnam troop levels peak at 536,000; Tet offensive; Johnson withdraws from presidential race; Martin Luther King Jr. and Robert Kennedy assassinated; George Wallace candidacy; Nixon wins election

1971
Nixon adopts wage and price controls; Pentagon Papers published

1973
Vietnam peace treaty; *Roe v. Wade;* AIM supporters occupy Wounded Knee

1975
Thieu government falls in South Vietnam

Lyndon Johnson sharply increases the U.S. role in Vietnam against Communist forces. Protest at home grows as the war drags on with little progress.

Richard Nixon wins the presidency promising to end the war. He travels to China and to the Soviet Union to ease Cold War rivalries and to reduce nuclear arms.

A new sense of identity leads Latinos, Native Americans, feminists, and gay men and women to press for equal rights. In addition, activists seek greater protection for consumers and the environment.

A scandal arising out of a politically motivated burglary forces Nixon to resign before the Vietnam War ends.

1964
Johnson uses Gulf of Tonkin incident to escalate U.S. involvement in Vietnam

1966
César Chávez campaign; Betty Friedan founds National Organization for Women

1970
First Earth Day; U.S. troops invade Cambodia; NOW organizes Strike for Equality; Clean Air and Water Acts; repeal of Tonkin Gulf Resolution

1972
Nixon policy of détente to ease Cold War tensions; Watergate burglary

1974
House adopts articles of impeachment; Nixon resigns; Gerald Ford becomes president; Ford pardons Nixon

THE ROAD TO VIETNAM

For several thousand years Vietnam had struggled periodically to fight off foreign invasions. Buddhist culture had penetrated eastward from India. Indochina repeatedly faced invasion and rule by the Chinese from the north. After 1856 the French entered as a colonial power, bringing with them a strong Catholic tradition.

Ho Chi Minh hoped to throw off French influence as well as Chinese. Since the end of World War I, he had worked to create an independent Vietnam. After World War II he organized a guerrilla war against the French, which finally

⌃ Nguyen Ai Quoc, who became Ho Chi Minh, once worked at London's posh Carlton Hotel in the pastry kitchen of the renowned chef Escoffier. He was soon swept up in socialist and nationalist politics, appearing at the Versailles Peace Conference (*left*) to plead for an independent Vietnam. Ho spent a lifetime in anticolonialist and revolutionary activity and became a revered leader of his people (*right*). He died in 1969, six years before his dream of a united Vietnam became a reality.
(left): AFP/Getty Images; (right): Bettmann/Getty Images

led to their defeat at Dien Bien Phu in 1954 (Chapter 28, "Brinkmanship in Asia" section). At the Geneva peace conference, Ho agreed to withdraw his forces north of the 17th parallel in return for a promise to hold free elections in both the North and the South. The Eisenhower administration, having supported the French struggle against Ho, helped install Ngo Dinh Diem in South Vietnam. It then supported Diem's decision not to hold elections, which Ho's followers seemed sure to win. Frustrated South Vietnamese Communists—the National Liberation Front—renewed their guerrilla war. "I think the Americans greatly underestimate the determination of the Vietnamese people," Ho remarked in 1962, as President Kennedy was committing more American advisers to South Vietnam.

THE WAR IN VIETNAM

For the United States, one strategic problem was to locate and destroy the supply routes known as the Ho Chi Minh Trail. Rugged mountains and triple canopy jungles hid much of the trail from aerial observation and attack.

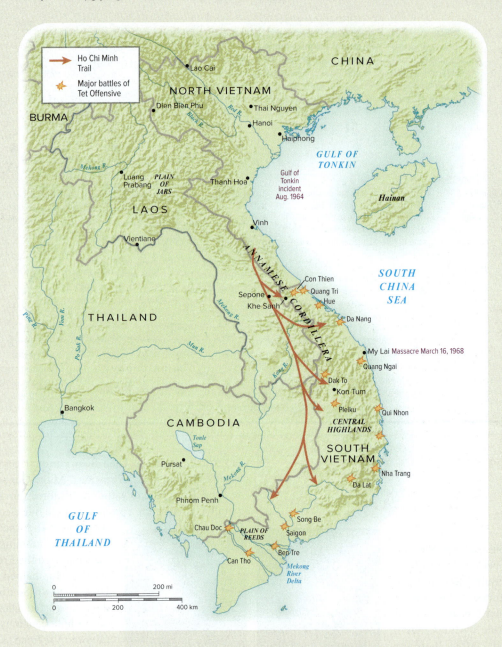

MAP READING

1. Locate the Gulf of Tonkin. What larger body of water is it a part of?
2. How many countries does the Ho Chi Minh Trail pass through?
3. What is the dominant terrain feature in South Vietnam?
4. How many major battles of Tet are noted on the map? Are they concentrated in any particular region of South Vietnam?

MAP INTERPRETATION

1. Why would the Gulf of Tonkin location suggest that the United States might have provoked the North Vietnamese attack on USS Turner Joy?
2. What geographic factors help explain why Richard Nixon secretly extended the war into Laos and Cambodia?
3. Despite heavy bombing, why were the Soviet Union and China able to send supplies into North Vietnam?

Lyndon Johnson's War

>> For Kennedy, Vietnam had been just one of many anti-Communist skirmishes his activist advisers wanted to fight. As attention focused increasingly on Vietnam, he came to discount President Eisenhower's "domino theory," which insisted that if Diem's pro-Western government fell to the Communists, the other nations of Southeast Asia would collapse one after the other. Still, he saw a Communist victory as unacceptable. But what to do? Even 16,000 American "advisers" had been unable to help the unpopular Diem, who was executed by a military coup in November 1963, which had the tacit support of the United States. When Kennedy was assassinated a few weeks later, Lyndon Johnson inherited the problem of Vietnam.

Johnson's political instincts told him to keep the Vietnam War at arm's length. He felt like a catfish, he remarked, who had "just grabbed a big juicy worm with a right sharp hook in the middle of it." Johnson's heart was in his Great Society programs. Yet the fear of "losing" Vietnam to Communists led him to escalate American involvement.

Until August 1964 American advisers focused mainly on training and supporting the South Vietnamese army. Its reluctance to fight the Vietcong, however, sometimes drew the "advisers" into combat. North Vietnam, for its part, had been infiltrating men and supplies along the Ho Chi Minh Trail, a network of jungle routes threading through Laos and Cambodia into the highlands of South Vietnam. With the Vietcong controlling some 40 percent of the South, Johnson decided to relieve the pressure on the South by engaging North Vietnam itself.

American ships patrolling the Gulf of Tonkin began to provide cover for secret South Vietnamese raids against the North. On August 2, three North Vietnamese patrol boats exchanged fire with the American destroyer *Maddox*. Two nights later, in inky blackness and a heavy thunderstorm, a second incident occurred. But a follow-up investigation could not be sure whether enemy ships had even been near the scene. President Johnson was not pleased. "For all I know our navy might have been shooting at whales out there," he remarked privately.

Whatever his doubts, the president publicized both incidents as "open aggression on the high sea" and ordered retaliatory air raids on North Vietnam. He did not disclose that the navy and South Vietnamese forces had been conducting secret military operations at the time. When Johnson then asked for the authority to take "all necessary measures" to "repel any armed attack" on American forces and to "prevent future aggression," Congress overwhelmingly passed what became known as the Tonkin Gulf Resolution.

Senator Ernest Gruening of Alaska, one of only two lawmakers to vote no, objected that the resolution gave the president "a blank check" to declare war, a power the Constitution reserved to Congress. Johnson insisted that he had limited aims. But with his victory in the 1964 election the president felt free to exploit the powers the resolution gave him.

Rolling Thunder

>> In January 1965 Johnson received a disturbing memorandum from National Security Advisor McGeorge Bundy and Secretary of Defense Robert McNamara.

"Both of us are now pretty well convinced that our present policy can lead only to disastrous defeat," they said. The United States should either increase its attacks—*escalate* was the term coined in 1965—or simply withdraw. In theory, **escalation** would increase military pressure to the point at which further resistance would cost more than the enemy was willing to pay. By taking gradual steps the United States would demonstrate its resolve to win while leaving the door open to negotiations.

> **escalation** process of steady intensification, rather than a sudden or marked increase, applied to the increasing American military presence in Vietnam.

The theory that had made so much sense in the White House did not work well in practice. Each stage of American escalation only hardened the resolve of the Vietcong and North Vietnamese. When a Vietcong mortar attack in February killed seven marines stationed at Pleiku air base, Johnson ordered U.S. planes to begin bombing North Vietnam.

Restricted air strikes did not satisfy more hawkish leaders. Retired Air Force chief of staff Curtis LeMay complained, "We are swatting flies when we should be going after the whole manure pile." In March Johnson ordered Operation Rolling Thunder, a systematic bombing campaign aimed at bolstering confidence in South Vietnam and cutting the flow of supplies from the North. Rolling Thunder achieved none of its goals. American pilots could seldom spot the Ho Chi Minh Trail under its dense jungle canopy. Equally discouraging, South Vietnamese leaders quarreled among themselves and jockeyed for power instead of uniting against the Vietcong.

Once the Americans established bases from which to launch the new air strikes, these too became targets for guerrilla attacks. General William Westmoreland, the chief of American military operations in Vietnam, requested combat troops to defend the bases. Johnson's decision to send 3,500 marines proved to be a crucial first step toward Americanizing the war. Another 40,000 soldiers arrived in May and 50,000 more by July.

The shadow of the Korean War hung over the decision to increase the role of the United States. McNamara ordered that the escalation be carried out in a "low-keyed manner to avoid undue concern and excitement in the Congress and in domestic public opinion." He worried also about how China and Russia might react. Restricting American operations below the 17th parallel reduced the danger of Chinese forces joining the war as they did in Korea. By 1966 almost 185,000 American troops had landed—and the call for more continued. In 1968, at the height of the war, 536,000 American troops were being supported with helicopters, jet aircraft, and other advanced military technologies. This was "escalation" with a vengeance.

 REVIEW

Why did Lyndon Johnson choose to escalate the war in Vietnam, and how did he do it?

SOCIAL CONSEQUENCES OF THE WAR

The impact of the war fell hardest on the baby-boom generation. As these young people came of age, draft calls for the armed services were rising. At the same time, the civil rights movement and the growing counterculture were encouraging students to question the goals of the establishment in the United States. Whether they fought in Vietnam or protested at home, supported the government or demonstrated against it, eventually these baby boomers—as well as Americans of all ages—were forced to take a stand on Vietnam.

The Soldiers' War >> Most Americans who fought in Vietnam were drafted. Under the Selective Service System, as it was called, many young people in the middle and upper classes could avoid being drafted: they could be deferred as students or by working in "critical" occupations, such as teachers and engineers. As the war escalated, the draft switched to a lottery system under which luck more than social class determined who went to Vietnam. That did not prevent the more privileged from gaming the system. They were better able to produce a doctor's affidavit certifying a weak knee, bone spurs, or bad eyes—all grounds for flunking the physical. Of the 1,200 men in Harvard's class of 1970, only 56 served in the military, and only 2 of them in Vietnam.

The poorest and least educated were also likely to escape service, because the Armed Forces Qualification Test and the physical often screened them out. Thus the sons of blue-collar Americans were most likely to accept Uncle Sam's letter of induction. Once in uniform, Hispanic and Black Americans, who typically had fewer skills. were more often assigned to combat duty. The draft made Vietnam a relatively young man's war. The average age of soldiers serving in Vietnam was 19, compared to 26 for World War II.

Most American infantry came to Vietnam ready and willing to fight. Over time physical and psychological hardships took their toll. An American search-and-destroy mission would fight its way into a Communist-controlled hamlet, clear and burn it, and move on—only to be ordered back days or weeks later because the enemy had moved in again. Since success could not be measured in territory gained, the measure became the "body count": the number of Vietcong killed. Unable to tell who was friendly and who was hostile, GIs sometimes took out their frustrations on innocent civilians. Officers counted those victims as Vietcong in order to inflate the numbers that suggested their tactics were working.

Most Americans assumed that superior military technology guaranteed success. But technology alone could not tell friend from foe. Since the Vietcong routinely mixed with the civilian population, the chances for deadly error increased. Bombs of napalm (jellied gasoline) and white phosphorus rained liquid fire from the skies, coating everything from village huts to the flesh of fleeing humans. Since the enemy hid in the jungle, the Americans made war on its vegetation. American planes spread more than 100 million pounds of defoliants that destroyed more than one-third of South Vietnam's timberlands—an area approximately the size of the state of Connecticut. The long-term health and ecological effects were severe, while the military benefits were minimal.

By 1967 war costs reached more than $2 billion a month. The United States dropped more bombs on South Vietnam over the course of the war than dropped during all of World War II. After one air attack on a Communist-held provincial capital, American troops walked into the smoldering ruins. "We had to destroy the town in order to save it," an officer explained. As the human and material costs of the war increased, that logic disturbed many observers. What sense was there in a war that saved people by burning their homes? Out of a population of around 14 million in South Vietnam, over 2 million became refugees.

^ The Vietcong often fought in small groups, using the dense vegetation to cover their movements. These suspects faced an arduous interrogation as U.S. soldiers tried to learn more about the location of Vietcong units.
Tim Page/Getty Images

The War at Home

The War at Home >> As the war dragged on, it provoked anguished debate among Americans, especially on college campuses. Faculty members held "teach-ins" to explain the issues to concerned students. Scholars familiar with Southeast Asia questioned every major assumption the president used to justify escalation. The United States and South Vietnam had brought on the war, they charged, by violating the Geneva Accords of 1954. Moreover, the Vietcong were an indigenous rebel force with legitimate grievances against Saigon's corrupt government. The war was a civil war among the Vietnamese, not an effort by Soviet or Chinese Communists to conquer Southeast Asia, as Eisenhower, Kennedy, and Johnson claimed.

Few Americans knew how cynical the rationale for war might be. One policy maker ranked the well-being of Vietnam and its people as just 10 percent of the reason to fight. Another 20 percent he assigned to keeping China from controlling South Vietnam. The major reason by far, 70 percent, was not to win the war, but to avoid a national humiliation. That made Vietnam and its people mere pawns in the American crusade to contain communism.

hawks and doves nicknames for the two opposing positions in American policy during the war in Vietnam. Hawks supported the escalation of the war and a "peace with honor." Doves argued that the United States had wrongly intervened in a civil war and should withdraw its troops.

By 1966 national leaders were divided into opposing camps of **"hawks" and "doves."** The hawks privately accepted the 70 percent rationale for fighting the war. Most Americans supported this view. The doves were nonetheless a prominent minority. African Americans as a group were far less likely than white Americans to support the war. Some resented the diversion of resources from the cities to the war effort. Many Black Americans' heightened sense of racial consciousness led them to identify with the Vietnamese people. Martin Luther King, SNCC, and CORE all opposed the war. Heavyweight boxing champion Muhammad Ali, a Black Muslim, refused on religious grounds to serve in the army, even though the decision cost him his title.

By 1967 college students and faculty were turning out in crowds to express their outrage, asking "Hey, hey, LBJ, how many kids have you killed today?" Over 300,000 people demonstrated in April 1967 in New York City. Some protesters even burned their draft cards in defiance of federal law. In the fall more protests erupted as antiwar radicals stormed a draft induction center in Oakland, California. The next day 55,000 protesters ringed the Pentagon in Washington, D.C. Mass arrests followed.

As protests flared, key moderates became increasingly convinced the United States could not win the war. Defense Secretary McNamara became the most dramatic defector. For years the statistically minded secretary had struggled to quantify the success of the war effort. By 1967 McNamara had become skeptical. If Americans were killing 300,000 Vietnamese, enemy forces should be shrinking. Instead, intelligence estimates indicated that North Vietnamese

ˆ Before and after. The devastating impact of American bombing and use of defoliants such as Agent Orange on the Vietnamese countryside. Some critics likened chemical defoliation to the use of poison gases.
(top): CPA Media Pte Ltd/Alamy Stock Photo; (bottom): Archive Image/Alamy Stock Photo

infiltration had risen from 35,000 a year in 1965 to 150,000 in 1967.

McNamara came to have deep moral qualms about continuing the war indefinitely. "The picture of the world's greatest superpower killing or seriously injuring 1,000 noncombatants a week, while trying to pound a tiny, backward nation into submission on an issue whose merits are hotly disputed, is not a pretty one," he advised. When Johnson, who did not want to be remembered as the first American leader who lost a war, continued to side with the hawks, McNamara resigned.

As the war's cost soared to more than $50 billion a year, it fueled rising inflation at home. Medicare, education, housing, and other Great Society programs raised the domestic budget sharply too. Through it all Johnson refused to raise taxes, even though wages and prices rose rapidly. From 1965 to 1970 inflation jumped from about 2 percent to around 4 percent. The economy was headed for trouble.

REVIEW

What factors complicated conducting the war in Vietnam and managing the war at home?

THE UNRAVELING

Almost all the forces dividing the United States seemed to converge in 1968. Until January of that year, most Americans had reason to believe General Westmoreland's assessment of the war. There was, he suggested, "light at the end of the tunnel." Johnson and his advisers, whatever their private doubts, painted an optimistic picture. With such hope radiating from Washington, few Americans were prepared for the massive attacks on the night of January 30, 1968.

Tet Offensive >> As the South Vietnamese began their celebration of Tet, the Vietnamese lunar New Year, Vietcong guerrillas assaulted major targets including Saigon's airport, the South Vietnamese presidential palace, and Hue, the ancient Vietnamese imperial capital. Most unnerving to Americans, 19 Vietcong commandos blasted a hole in the American Embassy compound in Saigon and stormed in. They fought in the courtyard until all 19 lay dead. One reporter, stunned by the carnage, compared the courtyard to a butcher shop.

Tet ranks as one of the great American intelligence failures, on par with the failure to anticipate Japan's attack on Pearl Harbor or Al Qaeda's terrorist attacks on September 11, 2001. For nearly half a year the North Vietnamese had lured American troops away from Vietnam's cities into pitched battles at remote outposts. As American forces dispersed, the Vietcong infiltrated major population centers. A few audacious VC, disguised as South Vietnamese soldiers, even hitched rides on American jeeps and trucks. Though surprised by the Tet offensive, American and South Vietnamese troops repulsed most of the assaults. General Westmoreland announced that the Vietcong's "well-laid plans went afoul."

In a narrow military sense, Westmoreland was right. The enemy had been driven back, sustaining perhaps 40,000 deaths. Only 1,100 American and 2,300 South Vietnamese soldiers had been killed. But Americans at home received quite another message. Tet created a "credibility gap" between the administration's optimistic reports and the war's harsh reality. The president had repeatedly claimed that the Vietcong were on their last legs. Yet, as Ho Chi Minh had coolly informed the French after World War II: "You can kill ten of my men for every one I kill of yours . . . even at those odds, you will lose and I will win." Respected CBS news anchor Walter Cronkite drew a gloomy lesson from Tet for his national audience: "To say that we are mired in stalemate seems the only realistic, yet unsatisfactory, conclusion." With Chronkite's defection, Lyndon Johnson sensed he had lost the war of public opinion.

That sense of looming defeat spread in Washington. When Johnson's new secretary of defense, Clark Clifford, joined the cabinet, he was persuaded the war could be won. But as Clifford reviewed the American position in Vietnam, his own doubts grew. He could get no satisfactory answers when he questioned the Joint Chiefs of Staff, who had requested an additional 206,000 troops. "How long would it take to succeed in Vietnam?" he recalled asking them:

> They didn't know. How many more troops would it take? They couldn't say. Were two hundred thousand the answer? They weren't sure. Might they need more? Yes, they might need more. Could the enemy build up [their own troop strength] in exchange? Probably. So what was the plan to win the war? Well, the only plan was that attrition would wear out the Communists, and they would have had enough. Was there any indication that we've reached that point? No, there wasn't.

Clifford decided to build a case for deescalation and formed a panel of "wise men," respected veterans of the Cold War establishment, to help formulate appropriate policy. The war could not be won, they concluded, and Johnson should seek a negotiated settlement.

Meanwhile, the antiwar forces found a political champion in Senator Eugene McCarthy from Minnesota. McCarthy was something of a maverick who wrote poetry in his spare time. He announced that no matter how long the odds, he intended to challenge Lyndon Johnson in the 1968 Democratic primaries. Idealistic college students got haircuts and shaves in order to look "clean for Gene" as they campaigned for McCarthy in New Hampshire. Johnson won the primary, but his margin was so slim (300 votes) that it amounted to a stunning defeat. To the anger of McCarthy supporters, Robert Kennedy, John Kennedy's younger brother, announced his own antiwar candidacy.

"I've got to get me a peace proposal," the president told Clifford. White House speechwriters crafted an announcement that bombing raids against North Vietnam would be halted, at least partially, in hopes that peace talks could begin. They were still working on an ending when Johnson told them, "Don't worry; I may have a little ending of my own." On March 31 he announced: "I have concluded that I should not permit the presidency to become involved in the partisan divisions that are developing in this political year. . . . Accordingly I shall not seek, and I will not accept, the nomination of my party for another term as your president."

The announcement shocked nearly everyone. The Vietnam War had pulled down one of the savviest, most effective politicians of the era. North Vietnam responded to the speech by sending delegates to a peace conference in Paris, where negotiations quickly faltered. The two sides could not even agree on the shape of the table. And American attention became focused on the chaotic situation at home, where the divisions over Vietnam exacerbated the turbulence, discontent, and violence of the 1960s.

LEVELS OF U.S. TROOPS IN VIETNAM (AT YEAR END)

This graph suggests one reason why protest against the war increased after 1964, peaked by 1968, and largely ended after 1972.
(background photo) Andriusha/iStock

NUMBER OF TROOPS (THOUSANDS)

KENNEDY   JOHNSON   NIXON

Year

The Shocks of 1968 >> On April 4 Martin Luther King Jr., by then an outspoken opponent of the war, traveled to Memphis to support striking sanitation workers. He was relaxing on the balcony of his motel when James Earl Ray, an escaped convict, fatally shot him with a sniper's rifle. The violent reaction to King's murder overshadowed his campaign for nonviolence. Riots broke out in ghetto areas of the nation's capital; by the end of the week, disturbances rocked 125 more neighborhoods across the country. Then, on the evening of June 5, a disgruntled Palestinian nationalist, Sirhan Sirhan, assassinated Robert Kennedy. Running in opposition to the war, Kennedy had just won a crucial primary victory in California.

King and Kennedy, each in his own way, exemplified the liberal tradition which reached its high-water mark in the 1960s. King had retained his faith in a Christian theology of nonviolence and had sought reform for the poor of all races without resorting to the language of the fist and the gun.

Robert Kennedy had come to reject the war his brother had supported, and seemed to genuinely sympathize with minorities and the poor. At the same time, he was popular among traditional white ethnics and blue-collar workers. King's and Kennedy's deaths persuaded many Americans that violence was the new normal.

Though a lame duck, Lyndon Johnson was able to ensure that his loyal vice president, Hubert Humphrey, would be nominated to succeed him. Humphrey had begun his career as a progressive and a strong supporter of civil rights. But as vice president, he was intimately associated with the war and the old-style liberal reforms that could never satisfy the activist, antiwar wing of the party. The Republicans nominated Richard Nixon, a traditional anti-Communist now reborn as the "new," moderate Nixon. As much as radicals disliked Johnson, they truly despised Nixon, "new" or old.

Chicago, where the Democrats met for their 1968 national convention, was the fiefdom of Mayor Richard Daley, the ultimate old-style political boss. Daley was determined that the protestors who poured into Chicago would not disrupt "his" Democratic National Convention. Radical elements were equally determined that they would. For a week the police skirmished with demonstrators: police clubs, riot gear, and tear gas met the demonstrators' eggs, rocks, and balloons filled with paint and urine. When Daley refused to allow a peaceful march past the convention site, protesters marched anyway and the police, with the mayor's blessing, turned on the crowd in what a federal commission later labeled a police riot. In one pitched battle, many officers took off their badges and waded into the crowd, nightsticks swinging, chanting "Kill, kill, kill." Reporters, medics, and other innocent bystanders were injured; at 3 a.m. police invaded candidate Eugene McCarthy's hotel headquarters and pulled some of his assistants from their beds.

With feelings running so high, President Johnson did not dare appear at his own party's national convention. Theodore White, a veteran journalist covering the assemblage, scribbled

^ Despite the liberal achievements of the Great Society, antiwar protestors vilified Lyndon Johnson.
Rolls Press/Popperfoto/Getty Images

his verdict in a notebook as police chased hippies down Michigan Avenue. "The Democrats are finished," he wrote.

Revolutionary Clashes Worldwide >> The

clashes in Chicago took place against the backdrop of a global surge in radical, often violent, student upheavals. In 1966 Chinese students were in the vanguard of Mao Zedong's Red Guards, formed to enforce a Cultural Revolution that sought to purge China of all bourgeois cultural influences. Although that revolution persecuted millions among the educated classes and left the country in economic shambles, Mao became a hero to radicals outside China. Radicals also lionized other revolutionaries who took up arms: Fidel Castro and Che Guevara in Cuba and Ho Chi Minh in Vietnam.

Radical targets varied. In Italy students denounced the official Marxism of the Soviet Union and the Italian Communist Party. French students at the Sorbonne in Paris rebelled against the university's efforts to discipline political activists. Students in Czechoslovakia launched a full-scale rebellion, known as Prague Spring, in 1968 against the Soviet domination of their nation—until Soviet tanks crushed the uprising. Though the agenda varied from country to country, virtually all student revolutionaries condemned the American war in Vietnam.

Whose Silent Majority? >> Radicals were not

the only Americans alienated from the political system in 1968. Governor George Wallace of Alabama sensed the frustration among the "average man on the street, this man in the textile mill, this man in the steel mill, this barber, this beautician, the policeman on the beat." As a presidential candidate, Wallace sought the support of blue-collar workers and the lower middle classes.

Wallace had first come to national attention in 1963, when he barred integration of the University of Alabama. Briefly, he pursued the Democratic presidential nomination in 1964. For the race in 1968 he

formed his own American Independent Party. Wallace's enemies were the "liberals, intellectuals, and long hairs [who] have run this country for too long." Wallace did not simply appeal to law and order, militarism, and white backlash. With roots in southern populism, he called for federal job-training programs, stronger unemployment benefits, national health insurance, a higher minimum wage, and a further extension of union rights. Many Robert Kennedy voters shifted to Wallace. A quarter of all union members backed him.

Richard Nixon, too, sought the votes of disgruntled Democratic voters, especially in the once solidly Democratic South. Populists of old had condemned Republicans as servants of the monied elite. Nixon had modest roots. He came from a middle-class family and at Duke Law School was so pinched for funds that he lived in an abandoned toolshed. His dogged hard work earned him the somewhat dubious nickname of "iron pants." And Nixon well understood the disdain ordinary laborers felt for "kids with beards from the suburbs" who seemed always to be insisting, protesting, *demanding*.

Nixon believed himself a representative of the "**silent majority**," as he later described it, not a vocal minority.

Nixon set two goals for his campaign: to distance himself from President Johnson on Vietnam and to turn Wallace's

silent majority phrase coined by President Richard Nixon in a 1969 speech, referring to the large number of Americans who supported his policies but did not express their views publicly.

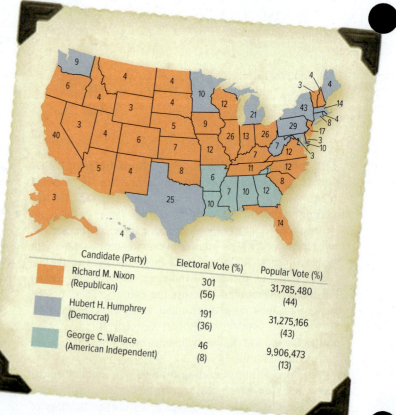

Candidate (Party)	Electoral Vote (%)	Popular Vote (%)
Richard M. Nixon (Republican)	301 (56)	31,785,480 (44)
Hubert H. Humphrey (Democrat)	191 (36)	31,275,166 (43)
George C. Wallace (American Independent)	46 (8)	9,906,473 (13)

MAP 30.1: ELECTION OF 1968

"average Americans" into a Republican majority. The Vietnam issue was delicate. As he told one aide, "I've come to the conclusion that there's no way to win the war. But we can't say that, of course. In fact, we have to seem to say the opposite." During the campaign he hinted that he had a secret plan to end the war but steadfastly refused to disclose it. He pledged only to find an honorable solution. As for Wallace's followers, Nixon promised to promote "law and order" while cracking down on "pot," pornography, protest, and permissiveness.

Hubert Humphrey had the more daunting task of surmounting the ruins of the Chicago convention. All through September antiwar protesters dogged his campaign with "Dump the Hump" posters. Although Humphrey picked up steam late in the campaign (partly by cautiously criticizing Johnson's war policies), the last-minute surge was not enough. Nixon captured 43.4 percent of the popular vote to 42.7 percent for Humphrey and 13.5 percent for Wallace. The outcome left the nation deeply divided.

REVIEW

What events in 1968 made that year a turning point in the war in Vietnam and in politics at home?

THE NIXON ERA

Americans had elected a Sphinx to the presidency. The public Nixon appeared to be a traditional small-town conservative who cherished individual initiative, chamber-of-commerce capitalism, Fourth of July patriotism, and middle-class propriety. The private Nixon was a troubled man. His language among intimates was caustic and profane, and he waxed bitter toward those he saw as enemies. That list included Jews, liberals, the media, African Americans, and other minorities. The public Nixon seemed to search out challenges—"crises" to face and conquer; the private Nixon avoided intimacy with almost everyone.

Vietnamization—and Cambodia >> A settlement of the Vietnam "crisis" became one of Nixon's first priorities. He found a congenial ally in National Security Advisor Henry Kissinger. Kissinger, an intensely ambitious Harvard academic, shared with the new president a global vision of foreign affairs. Like Nixon, Kissinger had a tendency to pursue his ends secretly, circumventing the traditional channels of government such as the State Department.

Both men wanted to end the war, but insisted on "peace with honor." That meant leaving a pro-American South Vietnamese government behind. The strategy Nixon adopted was "Vietnamization," a gradual withdrawal of American troops as a way to advance peace talks in Paris. The burden of fighting would shift to the South Vietnamese army. Critics likened

this strategy to little more than "changing the color of the corpses." All the same, as the media shifted their focus to the peace talks, the public had the impression the war was winding down.

At the same time, Nixon hoped to drive the North Vietnamese into negotiating peace on American terms. Quite consciously, he traded on his reputation as a Cold Warrior who would stop at nothing. As he explained to his chief of staff, Robert Haldeman:

> I call it the Madman Theory, Bob. I want the North Vietnamese to believe that I've reached the point where I might do anything to stop the war. We'll just slip the word to them that, "for God's sake, you know Nixon is obsessed about Communists. We can't restrain him when he's angry—and he has his hand on the nuclear button"—and Ho Chi Minh himself will be in Paris in two days begging for peace.

In the spring of 1969 the president launched a series of bombing attacks against North Vietnamese supply depots inside neighboring Cambodia. Johnson had refused to widen the war in this manner, fearing domestic reaction. Nixon simply kept the raids secret.

The North Vietnamese refused to cave in, nor did Ho Chi Minh's death in 1969 enhance peace prospects. Ho's successors rejected any offer that did not end with complete American withdrawal and an abandonment of the South Vietnamese military government. Once again Nixon turned up the heat. Over the opposition of his secretaries of defense and state, he ordered American troops into Cambodia to wipe out North Vietnamese bases there. On April 30, 1970, he announced the "incursion" of American troops, proclaiming that he would not allow "the world's most powerful nation" to act "like a pitiful helpless giant."

The wave of protests that followed included the fatal clashes between authorities and students at Kent State and Jackson State as well as another march on Washington by 100,000 protesters. Congress was upset enough to repeal the Tonkin Gulf Resolution, a symbolic rejection of Nixon's invasion. After two months American troops left Cambodia, having achieved little.

Fighting a No-Win War >> For a time Vietnamization seemed to be working. As more American troops went home, the South Vietnamese forces improved modestly. But for American GIs still in the country, morale became a serious problem. Why were the "grunts" in the field still being asked to put their lives on the line, when it was becoming clear there would be no victory? The anger surfaced increasingly in incidents known as "fragging," in which GIs threatened officers with fragmentation grenades when they pursued the war too aggressively.

Nor could the army isolate itself from the trends dividing American society. Just as young Americans "turned on" to marijuana and hallucinogens, so soldiers in Vietnam used drugs. Black GIs shared with their brothers at home a desire for Black power. One white medic noticed that when Muhammad Ali refused to be drafted, African Americans in his unit began "to question why they were fighting the Honky's war against other Third World people."

The Move toward Détente >> Despite Nixon's insistence on "peace with honor," Vietnam was not a war he had chosen to fight. And both Kissinger and Nixon recognized that by 1968 the United States no longer had the resources to pursue a policy of containment around the globe. The Soviet Union remained their prime concern. Ever since Khrushchev had backed down at the Cuban missile crisis in 1962, the Soviets had steadily expanded their nuclear arsenal. The Vietnam War also diverted valuable military and economic resources from easing instability in the Middle East and from aiding other less developed countries.

Under what the White House labeled the "Nixon Doctrine," the United States planned to shift some of the military burden for containment to other allies: Japan in the Pacific, the shah of Iran in the Middle East, Zaire in central Africa, and the apartheid government in South Africa. One concrete outcome was massive arms sales to Iran that included resources useful in developing a nuclear capacity. At the same time, Nixon and Kissinger looked for new ways to contain Soviet power not simply through nuclear deterrence but also through negotiations to ease tensions. This policy was named, from the French, **détente**.

détente relaxation of strained relations between nations, especially among the United States, the Soviet Union, and China in the 1970s and late 1980s.

Kissinger and Nixon sought to use these negotiations to link separate Cold War issues. The arms race burdened the Soviet economy; why not offer American concessions on nuclear missiles? In return, the Soviets would be asked to pressure North Vietnam to negotiate an end to the war. Nixon also decided to reach out to Mao Zedong, the Communist Chinese dictator. In some ways, the Soviets viewed China as more of a threat than the United States. Nixon calculated that the Soviets would cooperate in order to discourage the Americans from allying with China. Playing this "China card" was a real break from Nixon's conservative past. Republicans had long supported the Nationalist Chinese in Taiwan and viewed the Soviet Union and China as part of a Communist monolith.

To activate this new strategy, Kissinger slipped off to China on a secret mission and then reappeared to that announce the president would travel to China. During that visit in early 1972, Nixon pledged to normalize relations between the United States and China, a move the public applauded. Later that year, Nixon traveled to the Soviet Union to join Premier Leonid Brezhnev in signing the first Strategic Arms Limitation Treaty (SALT I). Under the agreement, both sides pledged to limit the number of intercontinental ballistic missiles (ICBMs) they would deploy, and agreed not to develop a new system of antiballistic missiles (ABMs).

Most Americans, except the staunchest conservatives, were pleased at the prospect of lowering Cold War tensions. But it was not clear that the diplomatic maneuvering with Moscow and Beijing would help the United States in Vietnam.

An End to Vietnam >> Nixon's maneuvering in Moscow and Beijing did not cause Hanoi to accept American terms for peace in Vietnam. The North Vietnamese continued to reject any agreement that left the South Vietnamese government in power. Unwilling to return American troops to Vietnam, in May 1972 Nixon instead ordered the mining and blockade of North Vietnam's major port, Haiphong, along with a sustained bombing campaign. In December he launched an even greater wave of aerial attacks, with American planes dropping more bombs in 12 days than they had during the entire campaign from 1969 to 1971.

South Vietnamese leaders at first refused to sign the settlement for they were rightly convinced that General Thieu's regime would not last once the United States departed. But in January 1973, Kissinger returned to Paris to negotiate a final treaty. Three months later the last American units were home.

The nightmare of Vietnam did not end with the Paris accords. North Vietnamese forces continued their battle against the southern government. In January 1975, with

<< Richard Nixon's trip to China included this visit to the Great Wall. Precisely because he had been so staunch an anti-Communist, Nixon appreciated the enormous departure his trip marked in Sino-American relations.
Pictures From History/Newscom

Members of Nixon's "silent majority" resented antiwar and minority group protestors. This man, who lost his son in Vietnam, attacks "America's noisy scum."
Bill Ray/The LIFE Picture Collection/Getty Images

Defeat in Vietnam marked the end of triumphant liberalism and offered a stark reminder of the limits of American power. No longer did most Americans believe that the world could be remade in their image. Nor did they see the Communist bloc as a monolith ruled from Moscow. Nixon's trip to Beijing made clear that China was an independent actor on the world stage, one Americans would soon see as a rival to their own efforts to dominate the world stage.

THEN&NOW

Americans now generally agree that the Vietnam War was a tragic mistake. After decades of bloodshed and the waste of vast American resources, the North Vietnamese united the country under Communist rule—the very result Ho Chi Minh sought after World War II. "No more Vietnams" became a fundamental principle of the nation's foreign policy. But did Americans truly learn that lesson? In the 1980s Ronald Reagan involved the United States in Guatemala's internal unrest and sent troops to Lebanon and Grenada. George H. W. Bush formed a broad coalition of nations to drive Saddam Hussein's Iraqi forces out of Kuwait. His son George W. Bush committed troops to endless wars in Iraq and Afghanistan that cost thousands of lives and trillions of dollars. Now Russia, Iran, and North Korea threaten their neighbors. Does Vietnam offer guidance in how the United States should respond to threats these states pose?

 REVIEW

How did Richard Nixon both escalate the war in Vietnam and wind it down?

Hanoi's forces closing in on Saigon, Nixon's successor, Gerald Ford, implored Congress to grant $1 billion in emergency aid, but the nation's political will was exhausted. "My God, we're all tired of it, we're sick to death of it," exclaimed one citizen in Oregon. "55,000 dead and $100 billion spent and for what?" In April 1975 Saigon fell, amid scenes of desperate Americans and South Vietnamese fighting to squeeze onto evacuation helicopters. North Vietnam had outlasted the Americans.

"The enemy must fight his battles far from his home base for a long time," a Vietnamese strategist once wrote. "We must further weaken him by drawing him into protracted campaigns. Once his initial dash is broken, it will be easier to destroy him." The enemy in question here was not the Americans, nor the French, but the Mongol invaders of 1284 CE. The strategy of resistance and attrition that kept the Chinese at bay for centuries also defeated the United States. The cost to save Southeast Asia from communism was incalculable. Much of the land lay devastated, and some 6.5 million South Vietnamese had become refugees, along with 3 million Laotians and Cambodians. In excess of 3 million Vietnamese soldiers and civilians died during the war.

THE NEW IDENTITY POLITICS

While Vietnam weakened the liberal consensus on the need to contain communism, minority activism challenged liberal assumptions on integration. The liberal tradition had long embraced a belief in the common humanity of all people. Lyndon Johnson expressed the notion pungently, updating Shakespeare's Shylock with a Texas twang: "They cry the same tears, they feel hungry the same, they bleed the same." Differences among individuals, liberals argued, came not from race or gender but from cultural circumstances and historical experiences. Out of such beliefs, civil rights advocates had committed themselves to an integrated United States.

pluralist idea that identity cannot be reduced to a single shared essence. The philosophy contrasts with the belief, in American politics, that citizens should assimilate into a uniform cultural identity of shared values.

The politics of the late 1960s substituted a **pluralist** model for the unified model sought by integrationists. Traditionally, Latino civil rights groups such as LULAC and World War II veterans in the American GI Forum had looked to assimilate into American society. Now minorities began to forge identities in opposition to the prevailing culture. By 1970 Black nationalists had abandoned integration for the politics of Black pride. To these activists the qualities that distinguished Black Americans should be valued and maintained—their music, clothing, hairstyles, and religion. In similar ways radical feminists, Latinos, Native Americans, and gays and lesbians demanded that the nation respect and accept their essential differences.

To some degree the Supreme Court had already granted that point in both the *Brown* and *Hernández* decisions of 1954 (Chapter 29, "Latino Civil Rights"). In each case the Court declared that Latinos and African

affirmative action practice of actively seeking to increase the number of racial and ethnic minorities, women, persons in a protected age category, persons with disabilities, and veterans with disabilities in a workplace or school.

Americans had suffered not simply as individuals but as groups. To correct past injustices, identity politics called for positive steps—what the Johnson administration called **affirmative action**—to repair the damage done by past injustices.

Latino Activism >> The distinct identities of minorities became more visible owing to new waves of immigration in the 1950s and 1960s from Puerto Rico, Mexico, and Cuba. Historical and cultural ethnic differences among the three major Latino groups made it difficult to develop a common political agenda. Still, some activists did seek greater Latino unity.

After World War II a weak island economy and the lure of prosperity on the mainland brought more than a million Puerto Ricans to New York City. As citizens of the United States, they could move freely to the mainland and back home again. That dual consciousness discouraged many from establishing deep roots stateside. Equally important, the newcomers discovered that, whatever their status at home, on the mainland they were subject to racial discrimination and often segregated into urban slums. Light-skinned migrants escaped those conditions by blending into the middle class as "Latin Americans." The Puerto Rican community thereby lost some of the leadership it needed to assert its political rights.

Make a Case

Is affirmative action an effective way to address past inequalities based on race, ethnicity, gender, or other minority status? Why or why not?

Still, during the 1960s the urban barrios gained greater political consciousness as groups such as *Aspira* adopted the strategies of civil rights activists and organizations such as the Black and Puerto Rican Caucus created links with other minority groups. The Cubans who arrived in the United States after Fidel Castro came to power in 1959—some 350,000 over the course of the decade—forged fewer ties with other Latinos. Most settled around Miami. An unusually large number came from Cuba's professional, business, and government class and were racially white and politically conservative.

Mexican Americans constituted the largest segment of the Latino population. Until the 1940s most were farmers and farm laborers in Texas, New Mexico, and California.

˄ Living conditions were harsh for Mexican American agricultural workers. César Chávez mobilized these workers into the United Farm Workers union. Here he meets with Dolores Huerta, his vice president in the UFW, in January 1968. Note the three iconic symbols displayed in the office. Why are they there?
Arthur Schatz/The LIFE Picture Collection/Getty Images

A Farmworkers' Boycott Poster

Si se puede is translated here as "It can be done." Can you think of a different translation that a more recent political campaign used to recruit Latino voters?

United Farm Workers' Eagle. Use Google to discover why the eagle was chosen as an emblem for the farmworkers and how it was designed.

Why is lettuce called a "stoop crop"?

What elements of the group suggest the UFW considers itself not only a union movement but also a community organization?

Artwork can often serve as a lens that reveals the values of political movements. César Chávez and the United Farm Workers (UFW) used this poster to arouse public support for a 1968 national boycott on California lettuce and grapes. Boycotts have often been seen as ineffective or even un-American, because they involve collective action. For the UFW three potential benefits offset the risks. First, lettuce and grapes were highly perishable, so any delay in harvesting them could cause growers large losses. Second, the boycott gave American consumers distant from farm fields an effective way to support UFW efforts to organize California's farmworkers. Finally, the campaign promoted a new sense of pride and solidarity among Latinos.

THINKING CRITICALLY

Why might a national boycott be a risky strategy? What sense does this poster give you of the labor that farmworkers perform? What are the links between this poster and the "new identity politics" described in the text?

©Estelle Carol/CWLU Herstory Project

During the 1950s the process of mechanization pushed them off farms into cities—by 1969 some 85 percent of Mexicans lived in urban areas. With urbanization came a slow improvement in the quality of jobs held. A body of skilled workers, middle-class professionals, and entrepreneurs emerged.

Meanwhile Mexican agricultural workers continued to face harsh working conditions and meager wages. Attempts to unionize faltered partly because workers migrated from job to job and strikebreakers were easily imported. In 1963 a soft-spoken but determined farmworker, César Chávez, recruited fellow organizers Gil Padilla and Dolores Huerta to make another attempt. Their efforts over the next several years led to the formation of the United Farm Workers labor union.

Chávez, like Martin Luther King, proclaimed an ethic of nonviolence. Also like King, he was guided by a deep religious faith, in his case Roman Catholicism. During a strike of Mexican and Filipino grape workers in the summer of 1966, Chávez led a 250-mile march on Sacramento, California.

("Dr. King had been very successful" with such marches, he noted.) Seeking additional leverage, the union used consumers as an economic weapon by organizing a boycott of grapes in supermarkets across the nation. Combined with a 24-day hunger strike by Chávez—a technique borrowed from Mohandas Gandhi—the boycott forced growers to negotiate contracts with the UFW beginning in 1970.

Just as King's nonviolent approach was challenged by more radical activists, a new generation of Mexican Americans took up a more aggressive brand of identity politics. Many began calling themselves Chicanos. Like Blacks, Chicanos saw themselves as a people whose heritage had been rejected, their labor exploited, and their opportunity for advancement denied. In Denver, Colorado, Rodolfo "Corky" Gonzales laid out a blueprint for a separatist Chicano society, with public housing set aside for Chicanos and the development of economically independent barrios. "We are Bronze People with a Bronze Culture," declared Gonzales. "We are a Nation. We are a union of free pueblos. We are Aztlán."

The new activism came from both college and high school students. Like others of the baby-boom generation, Mexican Americans attended college in increasing numbers. In addition, Lyndon Johnson's Educational Opportunity Programs, part of the War on Poverty, brought higher education to thousands more Latinos. By 1968 some 50 Mexican American student organizations had sprung up on college campuses. Two years later La Raza Unida (The United Race) launched a third-party movement to gain power in communities in which Chicanos were a majority. The more militant "Brown Berets" adopted the paramilitary tactics and radical rhetoric of the Black Panthers.

The Choices of Native Americans >>

The civil rights movement affected Native Americans too, but in unexpected ways. Radicalization came not from indigenous people on reservations, but from those living in cities. FDR's New Deal had tried to strengthen the reservation system and tribal cultures, rather than assimilating Native Americans into mainstream American life. But during the Eisenhower administration the Bureau of Indian Affairs changed course once again, working to replace the reservation system with a policy of "termination." To encourage the tribes to leave, the BIA cut federal services and began to sell off tribal lands. Liberal reformers of 1960s did not strongly object to this policy. They had come to see reservations as rural ghettos, rather than oases of Native American culture. Although most full-blooded tribal members objected to the policy of termination, others who had already assimilated into white society supported the move away from rural life. In 1940, barely 30,000 Native Americans lived in cities. By the 1970s, more than 300,000 did.

The activism of the 1960s inspired native leaders to shape their own political agenda. In 1968 urban activists in Minneapolis created AIM, the American Indian Movement. A year later like-minded Native Americans living around the San Francisco Bay Area formed Indians of All Tribes. More militant members of the organization seized the abandoned federal prison on Alcatraz Island in San Francisco Bay in protest of the Bureau of Indian Affairs's failure to address the problems of urban native peoples. The Alcatraz action inspired calls for a national pan–Native American rights movement.

In 1973 AIM organizers Russell Means and Dennis Banks led a dramatic takeover of a trading post at Wounded Knee, on a Sioux reservation in South Dakota. Ever since white cavalry gunned down over 100 Sioux there in 1890 (Chapter 18, "Killing with Kindness"), Wounded Knee symbolized for Native Americans the betrayal of white promises and the bankruptcy of reservation policy. Wounded Knee now demonstrated how difficult it was to achieve unity when tribes were determined to go their own ways. Not all native people supported the militant takeover of Wounded Knee,

In 1890 the U.S. cavalry killed 146 Sioux at Wounded Knee, South Dakota. In 1973 members of the American Indian Movement seized the hamlet of Wounded Knee, making it once again a symbol of conflict.
Bettmann/Getty Images

and federal officers soon forced its occupiers to leave. The movement splintered further as more than 100 different organizations were formed during the 1970s to pursue reform at the local, state, and federal levels.

Asian Americans >>

By striking down the old quota system, the 1965 Immigration Reform Act led to a sharp increase in the numbers of immigrants from Asia. Asians, who in 1960 made up less than 1 percent of the American population (about 1 million people), made up 2 percent (about 5 million) by 1985. This new wave included many middle-class professionals, a lower percentage of Japanese, and far more newcomers from Southeast and South Asia. These new immigrants benefited from earlier civil rights reforms that had swept away the legal barriers to full citizenship that had once stigmatized Asians.

Many Americans saw these new immigrants as "model minorities." They possessed skills in high demand, worked hard, were often Christian, and seldom protested. The 1970 census showed Japanese and Chinese Americans with median incomes well above the median for white Americans. Such statistics, however, hid fault lines within communities. Although many assimilated into the American mainstream, agricultural laborers and sweatshop workers remained trapped in poverty. And no matter how much Anglos praised their industry, Asian Americans still wore what one sociologist defined as a "racial uniform." They were nonwhites in a white society.

Few Americans were aware of Asian involvement in identity politics. That was in part because the large majority of Asian Americans lived in just three states—Hawai'i, California, and New York. Further, Asian Americans were less likely to join the era's vocal protests. Nonetheless some Asian students did join with African Americans, Chicanos, and Native Americans to advocate a "third world revolution" against the white establishment and to demand a curriculum that recognized their histories and cultures.

Gay Rights >>

In 1972 Black Panther Huey Newton observed that homosexuals "might be the most oppressed people" in American society. Certainly Newton was qualified to recognize oppression when he saw it. But by then a growing number of homosexuals had embraced liberation movements that placed them among minorities demanding equal rights.

Even during the "conformist" 1950s, gay men founded the Mattachine Society (1951) to fight bias attacks against homosexuals and to press for wider public acceptance. Lesbians formed a similar organization, the Daughters of Bilitis, in 1955. Beginning in the mid-1960s, more radical gay and lesbian groups began organizing to raise individual consciousness and to establish a gay culture in which they felt free. One group called for "acceptance as full equals . . . basic rights and equality as citizens; our human dignity; . . . [our] right to love whom we wish."

The movement's defining moment came on Friday, June 27, 1969, when New York police raided the Stonewall Inn, a Greenwich Village bar. Such raids were common enough: The police regularly harassed gays and lesbians by raiding the places where they gathered. This time the patrons fought back, first with taunts and jeers, then with paving stones and parking meters. Increasingly, gay activists called on homosexuals to "come out of the closet" and publicly affirm their sexuality. In 1974 gays achieved a major symbolic victory when the American Psychiatric Association removed homosexuality from its list of mental disorders.

Feminism >>

Organized struggle for women's rights and equality in the United States began before the Civil War. Sustained political efforts had won women the vote in 1920. But the women's movement of the 1960s and 1970s began to push for equality in broader, deeper ways.

Writer Betty Friedan was one of the earliest to voice dissatisfaction with the cultural attitudes that flourished after World War II. Even though more women were entering the job market, the media routinely glorified housewives and homemakers while discouraging those who aspired to independent careers. In *The Feminine Mystique* (1963), Friedan identified the "problem that has no name," a dispiriting emptiness in the midst of affluent lives. "Our culture does not permit women to accept or gratify their basic need to grow and fulfill their potentialities as human beings."

The Feminine Mystique gave new life to the women's rights movement. The Commission on the Status of Women appointed by President Kennedy proposed the 1963 Equal Pay Act and helped add gender to the forms of discrimination outlawed by the 1964 Civil Rights Act. Women also assumed an important role in both the civil rights and antiwar

movements. They accounted for half the students who went south for the "Freedom Summers" in 1964 and 1965. But even women who joined the protests of the 1960s often found themselves ignored in policy debates and limited to providing menial services such as cooking and laundry. Casey Hayden, a veteran of SDS and SNCC, told her male comrades that the "assumptions of male superiority are as widespread . . . and every much as crippling to the woman as the assumptions of white superiority are to the Negro."

By 1966 activist women were unwilling to remain silent. Friedan joined a group of 24 women and two men who formed the National Organization for Women (NOW). By arguing that "sexism" was much like racism, they persuaded President Johnson in 1967 to include women along with African Americans, Hispanics, and other minorities as a group covered by federal affirmative action programs.

Broader social trends created a receptive climate for the feminist appeal. After 1957 the birthrate began a rapid decline; improved methods of contraception, such as the birth control pill, permitted smaller families. By 1970 an unprecedented 40 percent of all women were employed outside the home. Education also spurred the shift from home to the job market, as higher educational levels allowed women to enter an economy oriented increasingly toward white-collar service industries.

Equal Rights and Abortion >>

As its influence grew, the feminist movement translated women's grievances into a political agenda. In 1967 NOW proclaimed a "bill of rights" that called for paid maternity leave for working mothers, federally supported day care facilities, child care tax deductions, and equal education and job training. But feminists divided on two other issues: the passage of an "equal rights amendment" to the Constitution and a repeal of state anti-abortion laws.

At first, support seemed strong for an equal rights amendment that forbade all discrimination on the basis of gender. In 1972 both the House and the Senate passed the Equal Rights Amendment (ERA) virtually without opposition. Within a year, 28 of the necessary 38 states had approved the ERA. It seemed only a matter of time before 10 more state legislatures would complete its ratification. Many in the women's movement also applauded the Supreme Court's decision, in *Roe* v. *Wade* (1973), to strike down 46 state laws restricting a woman's access to abortion. In his opinion for the majority, Justice Harry Blackmun observed that a woman in the nineteenth century had "enjoyed a substantially broader right to terminate a pregnancy than she does in most states today." As legal abortion in the first three months of pregnancy became more readily available, the rate of maternal deaths from illegal operations, especially among minorities, declined.

But the early success of the Equal Rights Amendment and the feminist triumph in *Roe* v. *Wade* masked underlying divisions among women's groups. *Roe* v. *Wade* triggered a sharp backlash from many Catholics, Protestant evangelicals, and socially conservative women. Their opposition inspired a

↥ Despite her genteel manner, Phyllis Schlafly was a fierce supporter of conservative causes. She joined the far-right John Birch Society and organized opposition to abortion rights, feminism, and entente with the Soviet Union.
Everett Collection Inc/Alamy Stock Photo

crusade for a "right to life" amendment to the Constitution. A similar conservative reaction breathed new life into the "STOP ERA" crusade of Phyllis Schlafly, an Illinois political organizer. Although a professional workingwoman herself, Schlafly believed that women should embrace their traditional role as homemakers subordinate to their husbands. "Every change [that the ERA] requires will deprive women of a right, benefit, or exemption that they now enjoy," she argued. By 1979 supporters of ERA were forced to admit that they would not succeed in convincing the necessary three-fourths of the state legislatures to ratify the amendment.

 REVIEW

In what ways were the movements for the rights of Latinos, Native Americans, Asian Americans, gays, and women similar and in what ways different?

VALUE POLITICS: THE CONSUMER AND ENVIRONMENTAL MOVEMENTS

Some of those seeking to change the United States were reformers who defined themselves by their ideas and values rather than by personal identity. Where many participants in identity politics viewed themselves as outsiders, consumer advocates and environmentalists generally came from the social mainstream. Still, they shared with the counterculture a worry that excessive materialism wasted resources and generated pollution, and that too many corporations exploited the public through misleading advertising and shoddy, even dangerous, products.

Technology and Unbridled Growth >> As early as 1962, marine biologist Rachel Carson had warned in *Silent Spring* against the widespread use of chemical pesticides, especially DDT. Pesticides were only one aspect of what environmentalists considered misguided technology. A report issued in 1965 indicated that every river near an urban area in the United States was polluted, save one (the St. Croix near St. Paul, Minnesota). Certainly, no one could doubt the pollution in the industrially fouled Cuyahoga River running through Cleveland, Ohio, which burst into flames in 1969. Smog, radioactive fallout, lethal pesticides, and polluted rivers were the by-products of a society that valued technology and unbridled economic growth over a healthy environment.

To consumer advocates, rising fatality rates on American highways signaled another kind of corporate failure. Besides contributing to smog and other forms of pollution, many automobiles were inherently dangerous to their occupants. That was a conclusion announced by an intense young lawyer, Ralph Nader, in his 1965 exposé *Unsafe at Any Speed*. Nader's particular target was the rear-engine Chevrolet Corvair. General Motors knew the Corvair had design flaws and internal studies confirmed crash data showing that it tended to flip over even during mild turns. Though the company fixed the problem, it also hired private investigators to try to discredit Nader.

The company picked the wrong target. Nader was the son of immigrant Lebanese parents who supported his success at Princeton and Harvard Law School. He lived simply and had no vices. And when he discovered GM's campaign against him, he successfully sued. GM's embarrassed president publicly apologized, but by then Nader had become a counterculture hero. In 1966 Congress passed the National Traffic and Motor Vehicle Safety Act and the Highway Safety Act. For the first time, the government required seat belts and set safety standards for cars, tires, and roads.

With the money from his lawsuit, Nader founded a consumer advocacy organization in 1969, the Center for the Study of Responsive Law. His staff of low-paid but eager lawyers, student interns, and volunteers investigated a wide range of consumer and environmental issues. "Nader's Raiders," as his staff was called, shared their leader's view that it was time for corporations "to stop stealing, stop deceiving, stop corrupting politicians with money, stop monopolizing, stop poisoning the earth, air and water, stop selling dangerous products, stop exposing workers to cruel hazards." In the tradition of progressive reform, Nader counted on interventionist government and informed citizen-consumers to regulate corporate behavior.

Many environmentalists, too, had links to the Progressive Era, believing that government action could police corporate irresponsibility. Others emphasized the need to preserve scenic and natural wonders for the benefit of future generations.

^ "Some river! Chocolate brown, oily, bubbling with subsurface gases, it oozes rather than flows." So *Time* magazine described the Cuyahoga River when it caught fire in 1969. Newspaper photographers arrived too late to record that fire, but *Time* was able to run a photo of the blazing Cuyahoga anyway—because the river had also caught fire in 1868, 1883, 1887, 1912, 1936, 1941, 1948, and—most disastrously— in 1952, as shown here. The wide publicity surrounding polluted rivers helped spark the first Earth Day in 1970.
Bettmann/Getty Images

What made modern environmentalism distinct was a growing focus on the field of ecology. Since the early twentieth century, this biological science had demonstrated that life processes throughout nature were interdependent. Small changes could have large unintended consequences. New groups such as the Environmental Defense Fund (EDF) and Friends of the Earth used legal challenges and civil disobedience to advocate for nature. Inspired by Rachel Carson's *Silent Spring*, the EDF filed lawsuits in Michigan and Wisconsin to have DDT declared a toxin subject to state regulation.

Barry Commoner, a politically active biologist, argued in his book *The Closing Circle* (1971) that modern society courted disaster by trying to "improve on nature." American farmers, for example, greatly increased their crop yields by switching from animal manures to artificial fertilizers. But the change consumed large quantities of energy, raised costs, often left soils sterile, and polluted nearby water. By the 1970s chemical discharges had virtually killed Lake Erie. Technology might prove profitable in the short run, Commoner argued, but in the long run modern methods were bankrupting the environment.

Political Action >> While he was no friend of liberal reform, President Nixon sensed that these value movements had broad popular appeal. His administration supported the passage of the National Environmental Policy Act of 1969, which required environmental impact statements for all major public projects. And in 1970 Nixon established the Environmental Protection Agency (EPA), whose first major act

banned most domestic uses of DDT. The president also signed a bill establishing an Occupational Safety and Health Administration (OSHA) to enforce health and safety standards in the workplace, and signed the Clean Water and Clean Air Acts into law.

On April 22, 1970, millions of Americans demonstrated their commitment to a healthy environment by celebrating the first Earth Day. For a few hours, pedestrians strolled city streets closed to motor vehicles, schoolchildren planted trees and picked up litter, and college students demonstrated. The enthusiasm reflected the movement's dual appeal: it was both practical in seeking to improve the quality of air, water, and earth and spiritual in celebrating the unity of living things. Senator Gaylord Nelson of Wisconsin, who helped bring about Earth Day, also appreciated the occasion's more radical implications: "The Establishment sees this as a great big antilitter campaign. Wait until they find out what it really means . . . to clean up our earth."

The Legacy of Identity and Value Politics >>
Earth Day did not signal a consensus on an environmental ethic. President Nixon, for one, was unwilling to impose regulations that stifled growth, especially when facing a troubled economy. Radical activists "aren't really one damn bit interested in safety or clean air," he commented to one industry group. "What they are interested in is destroying the system." He said that if he faced "a flat choice between jobs and smoke," nature would be the loser.

After *Apollo 11* reached the moon in 1969, President Richard Nixon told the astronauts "this is the greatest week in the history of the world since the Creation." Reverend Billy Graham took exception to this rhetorical flourish. What about Christ's birth, his death, and his resurrection, he asked the president. "Tell Billy," Nixon instructed his chief of staff, "RN referred to a week, not a day." NASA Johnson Space Center (NASA-JSC)

Most labor leaders also opposed affirmative action. Their older workers had been hit hard by rising inflation and the dwindling number of high-wage union jobs in the auto and steel industries. Union negotiators worried more about providing security and benefits to workers with seniority rather than about younger workers and their concerns with job safety, working conditions, and opportunities for racial/ ethnic minorities and women. When Jock Yablonski, a union district leader, led an insurgent movement to oust the corrupt leadership of the United Mine Workers, the union president, Tony Boyle, hired professionals to murder Yablonski and his wife and daughter.

Despite the backlash against reform, the upheavals of the 1960s had clearly opened doors to jobs, careers, and avenues of success previously closed to all but white males. Inevitably, however, a pluralistic approach to equality tended to fragment rather than unify the nation. The road to equality— whether in the workplace, schools, or even the bedroom— remained a fault line dividing the nation.

✓ REVIEW

What were the philosophies behind the consumer and environmental movements, and how well did they succeed in the political arena?

PRAGMATIC CONSERVATISM

Nixon's political instincts were cynical, but shrewd. Rather than fight the tides of reform, he rode those that were popular, basking, for example, in the triumphant *Apollo 11* moon landing in 1969. At the same time, he resisted those that offended Republicans and traditional Democrats, such as affirmative action. Both the 1968 and 1972 presidential elections revealed a shift in political power toward the southern and western rims of the United States, where traditional values flourished and whites, in the wake of the civil rights revolution, were deserting the Democrats in droves. These were the voters Nixon courted, in what he sometimes referred to as his "southern strategy" to replace the old New Deal coalition with a new Republican majority. By the early 1970s his silent majority worried more about job security than clean air and water. As one bumper sticker declared: "Out of work? Hungry? Eat an environmentalist."

Nixon sought to channel a similar backlash against identity politics. Conservatives opposed many of the era's reforms, including the Equal Rights Amendment, the integration of private clubs, and the use of racial and gender quotas for jobs and college admissions. Merit, not race or gender, should determine an individual's opportunities, they argued. Ethnic identity organizations such as the Italian American Civil Rights League spoke out against affirmative action for minorities.

In August 1969, 4,000 angry white union workers marched on city hall in Pittsburgh, Pennsylvania. There, a confrontation with police turned violent, leaving 50 protesters injured and 200 under arrest. A month later the scene repeated itself in Chicago, where hundreds of construction workers "slugged it out with 400 policemen." In both cases the issue was the "Philadelphia Plan" for affirmative action. Under it, the Nixon administration adopted the rule set forth under Lyndon Johnson in 1967 that government funding would be provided only if contractors' bids had "the result of producing minority group representations in all trades and in all phases of the construction project." The building trades unions wanted to know why they had been singled out when so many other industries did not meet those goals. Ethnicity played a role as well. "Why should these guys be given special consideration, just because they happen to be Black?" one angry white worker asked.

By 1969 affirmative action had become a political hot potato and Richard Nixon knew it. Over the course of his first term the president charted a pragmatic course, preserving and even expanding popular entitlements such as Social Security, seeking a middle ground on civil rights and affirmative action, and following the liberal tides in areas such as environmental protection.

Nixon's New Federalism >> Nixon envisioned his New Federalism as a conservative counter to liberal programs run by the federal government. Passed in 1972, a revenue sharing act distributed $30 billion over five years in federal block grants to state and local governments. Instead of the funds being earmarked for specific purposes, localities could decide which problems needed attention and how best to attack them. A similar approach influenced aid to individuals. In the past, liberal programs from the New Deal to the Great Society often provided specific services to individuals: job retraining programs, Head Start programs for preschoolers, food supplement programs for nursing mothers. Republicans argued that such a "service strategy" too often assumed that federal bureaucrats best understood what the poor needed. Nixon favored an "income strategy," which gave recipients money to spend as they saw fit. Such grants were meant to encourage initiative, increase personal freedom, and reduce government bureaucracy. Even if Nixon was determined to reverse the liberalism of the 1960s, critics were wrong to dismiss him as a knee-jerk conservative.

Stagflation >> Ironically, an economy weakened by the inflationary impact of Vietnam and Great Society programs forced Nixon to adopt liberal remedies. By 1970 the nation had entered its first recession in a decade. Traditionally a recession brought a decrease in demand for goods and a rise in unemployment as workers were laid off. Manufacturers then cut prices to encourage demand for their goods and cut wages to preserve profit margins. But in the recession of 1970, while unemployment rose as economists expected, wages and prices also rose in an inflationary spiral—a condition described as "stagflation."

Unfriendly Democrats labeled the phenomenon "Nixonomics," although in truth Lyndon Johnson had brought on inflation by refusing to raise taxes In addition, wages continued to rise partly because powerful unions had negotiated automatic cost-of-living increases into their contracts. Similarly, where a few large corporations dominated an industry, like steel and oil, prices and wages ignored market forces and continued to rise as demand and employment fell. Nixon's decision to extend Social Security to millions more added to inflationary pressures.

Social Policies and the Court >> Affirmative action, school prayer, contraception, criminal rights, obscenity, and school busing were all issues on which Supreme Court decisions offended the silent majority. Under Earl Warren, the liberal Court placed rights and liberties ahead of traditional values and law enforcement. The justices recognized, for example, that 15 years after its Brown v. Board of Education decision, most school districts remained segregated. Busing, one remedy they approved, provoked wide opposition. In white neighborhoods, parents opposed having their children bused to more distant, formerly all-Black schools to achieve racial balance. Although Black parents for their part worried about how their children might be treated in hostile white neighborhoods, by and large they supported busing as a means to better education.

Under Nixon, federal policy on desegregation took a 180-degree turn. In 1969 the Justice Department supported lawyers for Mississippi who asked the Supreme Court to delay an integration plan. The Court not only rejected that proposal but two years later ruled, in Swann v. Charlotte-Mecklenburg Board of Education (1971), that busing and redrawing school district lines were acceptable ways to achieve integration. The president looked to change the liberal direction of the court by filling vacancies with more conservative justices. When Warren retired in 1969 Nixon appointed Warren Burger, a centrist jurist who respected precedents. When another vacancy occurred in 1969, Nixon tried twice to appoint conservative southern judges with reputations for opposing civil rights and labor unions. Congress rejected both nominees. In the end, the president nominated Minnesotan Harry Blackmun, a moderate judge of unimpeachable integrity. Following Nixon's two conservative appointments, the Court no longer led the fight for minority rights, but neither did it reverse the achievements of the Warren Court.

Triumph and Revenge >> As the election of 1972 approached, Nixon's majority seemed to be falling into place, especially after the Democrats nominated Senator George McGovern of South Dakota. McGovern's nomination gave Nixon the split between "us" and "them" he sought. The Democratic platform embraced all the activist causes that the silent majority resented. It called for immediate withdrawal from Vietnam, abolition of the draft, amnesty for war resisters, and a guaranteed minimum income for the poor.

By November the only question that remained to be settled was the size of Nixon's majority. An unsolved burglary at the Watergate complex in Washington, D.C., while vaguely linked to the White House, had not touched the president, who received almost 61 percent of the popular vote.

Yet the overwhelming victory did not relieve the urge to settle scores. In his political battles, Nixon exhibited a tendency to see issues in terms of "us against them." With his consent (and with Lyndon Johnson's before him), the FBI and intelligence agencies conducted a covert, often illegal war against antiwar groups and political opponents. "We have not used the power in the first four years, as you know," he remarked to his chief of staff, H. R. Haldeman, during the campaign. "We haven't used the Bureau [FBI] and we haven't used the Justice Department, but things are going to change now." The administration began compiling an "enemies list"— everyone from television news correspondents to student activists—to be targeted for audits by the Internal Revenue Service or other forms of harassment.

In truth, Nixon had already begun to abuse his presidential powers. In June 1971 the New York Times published a secret, often highly critical military study of the Vietnam War, soon dubbed the "Pentagon Papers." Even though the papers focused on Johnson's escalation of the war, Nixon was angry that "Top Secret" information had become public. Mistrusting

J. Edgar Hoover and the FBI, the president authorized the creation of "the plumbers," a secret group he authorized to take illegal actions against his enemies. That included a burglary of the office of a psychiatrist who was treating Daniel Ellsberg, the disillusioned official who had leaked the Pentagon Papers.

Nixon also took his battle to Congress. When Democrats passed a number of programs the president opposed, he simply refused to spend the appropriated money. By 1973 Nixon had used this policy of "impoundment" to cut some $15 billion out of more than 100 federal programs. The courts eventually ruled that impoundment was illegal.

Break-In >> Nixon's fall from power began with what seemed a minor event. In June 1972 police arrested burglars at the Democratic National Committee headquarters, located in Washington's plush Watergate apartment complex. The five burglars did seem an unusual lot. They wore business suits and carried bugging devices, tear-gas guns, and more than $2,000 in crisp new 100-dollar bills. One had worked for the CIA. Another was carrying an address book whose phone numbers included that of a Howard Hunt at the "W. House." Nixon's press secretary dismissed the break-in as "a third-rate burglary attempt," and Nixon himself announced that a thorough investigation had concluded "no one on the White House staff . . . was involved in this very bizarre incident. What really hurts in matters of this sort is not the fact that they occur," the president continued. "What really hurts is if you try to cover up."

In January 1973 the burglars went on trial along with former White House aides E. Howard Hunt Jr. and G. Gordon Liddy. Judge John Sirica was not satisfied with the defendants' guilty plea. He wanted to know who had directed the burglars and why "these 100-dollar bills were floating around like coupons." Facing a stiff jail sentence, one of the Watergate burglars admitted that the defendants had been bribed to plead guilty and that they had perjured themselves to protect higher officials.

To the Oval Office >> Over the summer of 1973 televised Senate hearings grilled a string of officials. Each witness linked the burglary and its cover-up to higher officials in the White House. Then John Dean, Nixon's former legal counsel, gave his testimony. Young, with a Boy Scout's face, Dean declared in a quiet monotone that the president had personally been involved in the cover-up. The shocking testimony remained Dean's word against the president's until Senate committee staff discovered, almost by chance, that since 1970 Nixon had been secretly recording all conversations and phone calls in the Oval Office. The reliability of Dean's testimony was no longer central, for the tapes could tell all.

^ Under the leadership of the folksy but razor-sharp Senator Sam Ervin of North Carolina, the Senate committee investigating the Watergate scandal attracted a large television audience. John Dean (*above*), the former White House legal counsel, provided the most damning evidence linking President Nixon to the cover-up—until the existence of secretly recorded White House tapes became known.
ASSOCIATED PRESS/AP images

Obtaining that evidence proved no easy task. In an effort to restore confidence in the White House, Nixon agreed to the appointment of a special prosecutor, Harvard law professor Archibald Cox, to investigate the new Watergate disclosures. When Cox subpoenaed the tapes, the president refused to turn them over, citing executive privilege and matters of national security. The courts, however, overruled this position.

As that battle raged and the astonished public wondered if matters could possibly get worse, they did. Evidence unrelated to Watergate revealed that Vice President Spiro Agnew had systematically solicited bribes, both as governor of Maryland and while serving in Washington, D.C. He resigned the vice presidency in October. Under provisions of the Twenty-Fifth Amendment, Nixon appointed Representative Gerald R. Ford of Michigan to replace Agnew.

Meanwhile, when Special Prosecutor Cox demanded the tapes, the president offered to submit written summaries instead. Cox rejected the offer and on Saturday night, October 20, Nixon fired Cox. Reaction to this "Saturday Night Massacre" was overwhelming: 150,000 telegrams poured into Washington, and by the following Tuesday, 84 House members had sponsored 16 different bills of impeachment. The beleaguered president agreed to hand over the tapes and appointed Texas lawyer Leon Jaworski as a new special prosecutor. By April 1974 Jaworski's investigations led him to request additional tapes. Again the president refused, although he grudgingly supplied some 1,200 pages of typed transcripts of the tapes.

Even the transcripts damaged the president's case. Littered with cynicism and profanity, they revealed Nixon talking with John Dean about how to "take care of the jackasses who are in jail." When Dean estimated it might take a million dollars to buy their silence, Nixon replied, "We could get that. . . . You could get a million dollars. And you could get it in cash. I know where it could be gotten."

Even those devastating revelations did not produce the "smoking gun" demanded by the president's defenders. When Special Prosecutor Jaworski petitioned the Supreme Court to order release of additional tapes, the Court in *United States* v. *Nixon* ruled unanimously in Jaworski's favor.

Resignation >> The end came quickly. The House Judiciary Committee adopted three articles of impeachment, charging that Nixon had obstructed justice, abused his constitutional authority in improperly using federal agencies to harass citizens, and hindered the committee's investigation.

The tapes produced the smoking gun. Conversations with White House chief of staff Bob Haldeman on June 23, 1972, only a few days after the break-in, showed that Nixon knew the burglars were tied to the White House staff and knew that his attorney general had acted to limit an FBI investigation. Not willing to be the first president convicted in a Senate impeachment trial, Nixon resigned on August 8, 1974. The following day Gerald Ford became president. "The Constitution works," Ford told a relieved nation. "Our long national nightmare is over."

Ford tried to put Watergate behind the nation by quickly issuing Richard Nixon a full pardon for any crimes he might have committed. The pardon succeeded only in deepening the nation's cynicism, because Nixon would never face prosecution nor assume responsibility for his crimes. Watergate was just one of the many events and issues of the 1960s era that divided Americans over the decades to follow.

Had the system worked? In one sense, yes. For the first time, a president had been forced to leave office and numerous members of his administration served prison terms for crimes related to the break-in and cover-up. Yet the corrupt campaign practices that financed Watergate continue to plague the political system. The system works, as the Founders understood, only when citizens and public servants respect the limits of government power.

✓ **REVIEW**

In what ways was Richard Nixon a conservative, and why did he adopt some liberal policies?

CHAPTER SUMMARY

Though presidents from Truman to Nixon sent American forces to Indochina, Vietnam came to be known as Lyndon Johnson's war. The political divisions it caused ended both his presidency and the consensus on liberal reform.

- To force the North Vietnamese to negotiate, Johnson escalated the American war effort, pouring in troops and bombing North Vietnam heavily.
- As the nation divided into prowar hawks and antiwar doves, the Vietcong's Tet offensive shocked Americans. In the face of opposition Johnson abandoned his reelection campaign.
- After the assassinations of Martin Luther King and Robert Kennedy, Hubert Humphrey became the Democrats' presidential nominee. But riots at the Chicago convention so damaged Humphrey's candidacy that Richard Nixon won the election, promising a "peace with honor" in Vietnam.
- A wide range of minorities—Latinos, Native Americans, Asian Americans, gays and lesbians, and feminists—adopted identity politics as a way to claim their full civil rights.
  - Mexican American migrant workers led by César Chávez established a farmworkers' union, the UFW, while a rising generation of Latino students adopted more militant techniques for establishing a Chicano identity.
  - Though often divided by tribal differences, Native Americans called attention to the discrimination faced by native people in urban settings as well as on reservations.
  - Feminists campaigned for civil and political equality as well as to change deep-seated cultural attitudes of a "patriarchal" society.
- In addition to reform movements based on identity, the value politics of environmentalists and consumer advocates extended the spirit of reform.

⌃ Nixon's farewell; his daughter Tricia looks on.
National Archives and Records Administration (194597)

- White House involvement in the Watergate break-in and the president's subsequent cover-up led to the first resignation of an American president.
- President Gerald Ford inherited an office weakened by scandal, an economy in recession, and a Congress determined to rein in an "imperial presidency."

Digging Deeper

Melvyn Leffler and Odd Arne Westad, eds., *The Cold War: Crises and Detente,* vol. II (2011), contains essays that cover topics discussed in this chapter. See also Frank Costigliola, "US Foreign Policy from Kennedy to Johnson"; Frederik Logevall, "The Indochina Wars and the Cold War, 1945–1975"; Robert Schulzinger, "Detente in the Nixon-Ford Years"; and Francis J. Garvin, "Nuclear Proliferation and Non-proliferation during the Cold War." John Farrell, *Richard Nixon: A Life* (2017), shows that Nixon did scuttle the peace talks in 1968. For the soldiers' experience, look at the classic by Michael Herr, *Dispatches* (1977). Two important and comprehensive one-volume histories are Christian Appy, *American Reckoning: The Vietnam War and Our National Identity* (2015); and Max Hastings, *Vietnam: An American Tragedy, 1945–1975* (2018).

Keith Olsen, *Watergate: The Presidential Scandal That Shook America* (2003), is a lively brief account of Nixon's fall; while Stanley Kutler, *The Wars of Watergate: The Last Crisis of Richard Nixon* (1992), provides more detail. A historically rich way to understand the scandal is Thomas Mallon, *Watergate: A Novel* (2013). J. Brooks Flippen, *Nixon and the Environment* (2000), explores his legacy as "the greenist" president. Richard Reeves, *President Nixon: Alone in the White House* (2002), offers a nonpartisan look. A dissenter from the camp of Kissinger admirers is Jussi Hanhimaki, *The Flawed Architect: Henry Kissinger and American Foreign Policy* (2004).

Bruce Shulman, *The Seventies: The Great Shift in American Culture, Society, and Politics* (2002), argues that the 1970s were more significant than the 1960s. Gender politics are widely explored in Gail Collins, *When Everything Change: The Amazing Journey of American Women from 1960 to the Present* (2009). An excellent history of the environmental movement is Robert Gottlieb, *Forcing the Spring: The Transformation of the American Environmental Movement* (2005).

31 The Conservative Challenge

1976–1992

On June 12, 1987, speaking in West Berlin, Germany, President Ronald Reagan invited Soviet Premier Mikhail Gorbachev to "tear down" the Berlin Wall, a vestige of Cold War conflict.

Piero Oliosi/Polaris/Newscom

>> An American Story

BORN AGAIN

When 1976 presidential candidate Jimmy Carter declared himself a "born-again Christian," many Americans were puzzled. Carter's outspoken religious faith drew attention to the world of evangelical preachers. Many of these preachers traced their roots back to the Fundamentalist movement that flourished during the 1920s (see Chapter 25). More recently, however, their

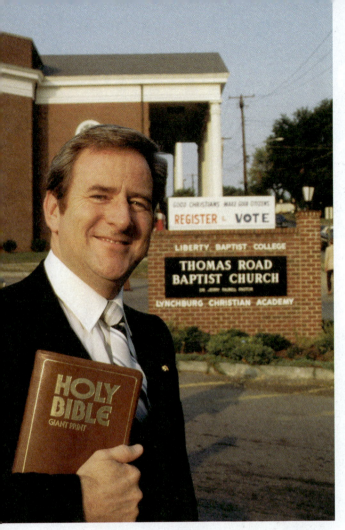

^ The Reverend Jerry Falwell in 1980, outside his Thomas Road Baptist Church in Lynchburg, Virginia. By the time Ronald Reagan was making a run for the presidency, Falwell had left behind his aversion to involvement in politics, as the sign behind him makes clear: "Good Christians Make Good Voters."

Wally McNamee/Corbis/Getty Images

role in mainstream American life had been muted, partly because many chose to separate themselves from an increasingly secular society.

For years, the Reverend Jerry Falwell followed this path of separation. Though his father had been a Prohibition bootlegger and his father's father an avowed atheist, Falwell absorbed the beliefs of his devout mother and attended Baptist Bible College in Missouri. Returning home in 1956 to Lynchburg, Virginia, he founded the Thomas Road

Baptist Church, as well as the *Old-Time Gospel Hour,* a radio and television program. Falwell steered clear of preaching politics. "Servicing the church and letting government take care of itself had been my lifelong policy," he recalled later.

His attitude shifted in response to the tumult of the 1960s and 1970s. Falwell and other conservative Christians never reconciled themselves to the 1962 Supreme Court decision in *Engel* v. *Vitale,* which banned prayer in public schools, or to the political protests and countercultural lifestyles of the era. And the *Roe* v. *Wade* decision, which made abortion legal in 1973, seemed to many on the Christian right to authorize the murder of the unborn. Falwell began to talk politics, right in church. And he told his fellow pastors they should do the same.

Traveling to Florida, he helped spearhead a fight against the Equal Rights Amendment for women. "Here's what you do," he told Florida pastors. "You tell everybody in your congregation to bring two stamped envelopes to church on Sunday. You show them a couple of sample letters. And don't assume they know who their state representative is.

Show them a map of their district. Make them write those letters in church. It's all perfectly legal as long as you don't use the building for special meetings. Do it right during the service."

Falwell also fought a ruling by the Internal Revenue Service denying tax exemptions to segregated Christian schools. He himself had created the all-white Lynchburg Christian Academy—not to segregate, he insisted, but to protect his students from the evils of "secular humanism." Where evangelicals saw God, the Bible, the family, and the church as the moral foundation of a Christian society, humanists believed that people were capable of moral and ethical behavior without God or religion. Falwell championed homeschooling and Christian academies. "I hope to see the day when, as in the early days of our country," he said, "we won't have any public schools. The churches will take them over again and Christians will be running them."

Though Jimmy Carter was born-again, in the end he was far too sympathetic to feminist aspirations and too accepting of racial and sexual diversity for Falwell's taste. In 1979 the crusading pastor joined with other evangelicals to form the Moral Majority, an organization that campaigned openly for Ronald Reagan in the 1980 election. Ironically, Reagan was far more secular than Carter in his personal beliefs. But his values were more in tune with Falwell's. That election marked a turning point, as evangelicals joined other conservatives to challenge the liberal direction of American politics and culture. <<

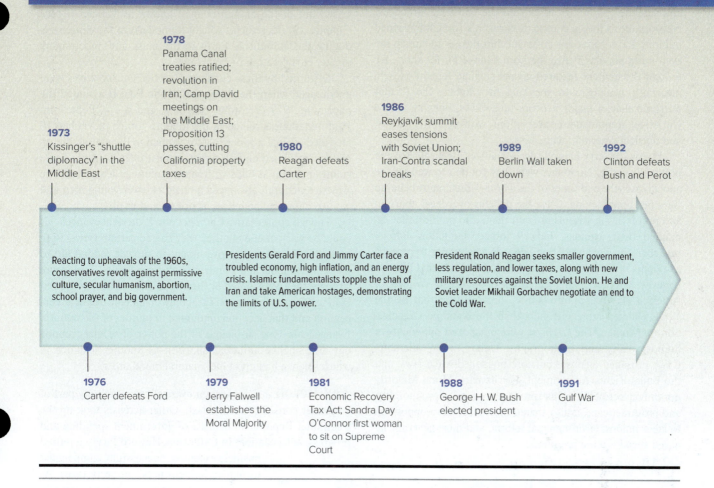

1973
Kissinger's "shuttle diplomacy" in the Middle East

1978
Panama Canal treaties ratified; revolution in Iran; Camp David meetings on the Middle East; Proposition 13 passes, cutting California property taxes

1980
Reagan defeats Carter

1986
Reykjavík summit eases tensions with Soviet Union; Iran-Contra scandal breaks

1989
Berlin Wall taken down

1992
Clinton defeats Bush and Perot

Reacting to upheavals of the 1960s, conservatives revolt against permissive culture, secular humanism, abortion, school prayer, and big government.

Presidents Gerald Ford and Jimmy Carter face a troubled economy, high inflation, and an energy crisis. Islamic fundamentalists topple the shah of Iran and take American hostages, demonstrating the limits of U.S. power.

President Ronald Reagan seeks smaller government, less regulation, and lower taxes, along with new military resources against the Soviet Union. He and Soviet leader Mikhail Gorbachev negotiate an end to the Cold War.

1976
Carter defeats Ford

1979
Jerry Falwell establishes the Moral Majority

1981
Economic Recovery Tax Act; Sandra Day O'Connor first woman to sit on Supreme Court

1988
George H. W. Bush elected president

1991
Gulf War

THE CONSERVATIVE REBELLION

Jerry Falwell and his Moral Majority were only one strand of an evangelical world that had been changing over the past two decades. During those years mainline Protestant churches struggled over how their religious beliefs should engage with civil rights, the war in Vietnam, issues of sex and gender, and more liberated lifestyles. As some congregations moved to embrace liberal definitions of faith, many found themselves yearning for a traditional religious experience. They moved in large numbers from long-established denominations such as Presbyterian and Congregational denominations to evangelical churches. By the mid-1980s some 36 percent of Americans described themselves as "born again." Similar trends occurred among Catholics and Jews, many of whom also resisted the liberalization of their faith.

Moving Religion into Politics >> Among evangelicals the Southern Baptists and Assemblies of God attracted large national memberships. But their real focus was local, centered in church communities. Such congregations insisted that salvation came through a spiritual rebirth (being "born again") after a person had acknowledged sinfulness and embraced Christ's atonement. Evangelical tradition encouraged the faithful to make converts, often by sponsoring mass revivals under the direction of charismatic preachers, similar to earlier "Great Awakenings." And most evangelicals anticipated the rapture, when Christ would return to transport true believers into his Father's kingdom. These shared beliefs, when combined with a commitment to piety, put evangelicals squarely at odds with modern society. They demanded a strict personal morality, often insisted on the central role of the father in the family, and in some churches forbade such "worldly evils" as dancing, cosmetics, movies, gambling, and premarital sex.

Though evangelicals condemned much of modern culture, many preachers advocated a "prosperity theology" that encouraged economic success. They also used modern media to spread the word. Pat Robertson, a magnetic Southern Baptist preacher based in Virginia, like Jerry Falwell, used cable and satellite technology to expand the Christian Broadcast Network into a media empire. Robertson's 700 Club reached millions and inspired his colleague Jim Bakker to launch the even more popular Praise the Lord Club—PTL for short. Although the content featured gospel singing, fervent preaching, faith healing, and speaking in tongues, the format mirrored that of major network talk shows, opening with a Christian monologue, conversations with celebrity guests, and musical entertainment.

Following Jerry Falwell's lead, many evangelicals became politically active. No longer were they content to wait for the apocalypse—the end times of the world—which many believed were fast approaching. Once the debates over legal abortion and prayer in the schools brought them into politics, they expanded their agendas. Falwell joined his fellow Baptist preacher Tim LaHaye of San Diego in a campaign to repeal a gay rights ordinance in Miami, Florida. LaHaye and his wife Beverly, a writer, had formed the Concerned Women of America (CWA), a "pro-family" organization that by the 1980s claimed more members than the National Organization for Women. The LaHayes were outspoken opponents of homosexuality and pornography. Under their leadership, CWA crusaded against abortion, no-fault divorce laws, and the Equal Rights Amendment. For its part, Moral Majority not only described itself as "pro-life, pro-family, pro-morality, and pro-American," it also shared the conservative opposition to labor unions, environmental reform, and most government-based social welfare programs.

The Catholic Conscience >> American Catholics

faced their own decisions about the lines between religion and politics. In the 1960s a social activist movement had arisen out of the church council known as Vatican II (see Chapter 29). Its reforms sought to modernize the church, reducing the amount of Latin in the mass and encouraging greater participation by laypeople.

Disturbed by these currents, Catholic conservatives were encouraged when the charismatic John Paul II assumed the papacy in 1979. Vigorous, outgoing, and warm, Pope John Paul nonetheless reined in the modern trends of Vatican II. He ruled against a wider role for women in the church hierarchy and stiffened church policy against birth control. These rulings put him at odds with many American Catholics. The American church also faced a crisis as fewer young men and women chose celibate lives as priests and nuns.

Though conservative Catholics and Protestant evangelicals could be wary of one another, they shared certain views. Both groups lobbied for the government to provide federal aid to parochial schools and Fundamentalist academies. Even more strongly, they were united by their opposition to abortion. John Paul reaffirmed the church's teaching that all life began at conception and that abortion amounted to murder of the unborn. Evangelicals, long suspicious of the power of secular technology and science, attacked abortion as another instance in which science had upset life's natural moral order.

Tax Revolt >> Protestant evangelicals were only part of

a broader conservative backlash. Other activists took up the traditional Republican distrust of government spending and progressive legislation. In California, Howard Jarvis, a retired business executive, successfully campaigned to reduce homeowners' property taxes. At stake was not merely lower taxes but the equity of the system. Small homeowners often paid taxes at much higher rates than large property owners and businesses. Although Jarvis was extremely conservative, he framed his antigovernment agenda in Populist terms. His supporters, he claimed, were the small individuals: teachers, blue-collar workers, and "a great number of Negroes." His group, the United Organizations of Taxpayers, received no money from oil companies, bankers, land speculators, or insurance companies.

By the late 1970s California was ripe for the Jarvis rebellion. Inflation imposed a

<< During the late 1970s and the 1980s, conservatives increasingly spoke out against abortion and in favor of the right to life for an unborn fetus. Adopting the tactics of protest and civil disobedience once common to radicals in the 1960s, they clash here with pro-choice demonstrators outside Faneuil Hall in Boston. Bettmann/Getty Images

crushing burden on middle- and lower-class homeowners. At the same time their taxes rose steadily. An old radical and union organizer described state politicians and bureaucrats as "those leeches who must have more and more taxes." Mounting anger helped the United Organization of Taxpayers collect 1.25 million signatures to place Proposition 13 on the California ballot in 1978. The measure cut property taxes 57 percent and made it difficult for the state and local legislatures to raise them in the future. Opponents warned that the loss of revenue would force school closings, job losses, and reduced police and fire protection, but the measure passed with widespread support.

The tax rebellion spread across the nation. Over the next four years 12 states passed similar resolutions, while many legislatures cut public spending and taxes, hoping to avoid the voters' wrath. Even liberal Massachusetts capped local property taxes and set strict limits on future increases.

The Media as Battleground >> Both evangelicals and political conservatives believed that the mass media corrupted family values. Their permissive, even positive, portrayal of premarital sex, drug use, profanity, homosexuality, nudity, and violence offended their moral sensibilities. The conservative determination to censor media content clashed with a liberal commitment to free speech and toleration for diversity.

Hollywood movies had long pushed the boundaries of acceptable content, but by the 1970s television also introduced controversial and politicized programming. In 1971 producer Norman Lear introduced *All in the Family,* whose main character, Archie Bunker, embodied the blue-collar backlash against liberal and permissive values. The ultimate male chauvinist, Archie treated his wife Edith like a servant, clashed with his modestly rebellious daughter, Gloria, and heaped verbal abuse on his leftist Polish American son-in-law. All things liberal or cosmopolitan—"Hebes," "Spics," and "Commie crapola"— became targets for Archie's coarse insults. Despite its popularity the show was attacked from both the left and the right. Many conservatives who shared Archie's values found the language offensive, while some minority leaders charged that the show legitimized the prejudices it attacked.

Saturday Night Fever >> As *All in the Family* defined the class anger of blue-collar Americans, the hugely popular disco movie *Saturday Night Fever* revealed their alienation. The film explores the Brooklyn world of Tony Manero, played by John Travolta, who holds a dead-end job as a hardware store clerk during the day but at night transforms himself into a white-suited disco king. While his loser friends walk down Brooklyn's mean streets, Tony struts. When asked by his boss to think about his future, Tony snarls back that he couldn't care less what the future brings. His boss, recognizing the lost prospects of blue-collar Americans, suggests that Tony will only get what he deserves.

The glitter of disco offers Tony a world in which he can be somebody. In the end, however, he rejects his suffocating

∧ John Travolta, the blue-collar Brooklyn boy with aspirations, dressed to the nines and "Stayin' Alive" to the beat of the Bee Gees. Michael Ochs Archives/Getty Images

family, loser friends, and blue-collar roots for a future across the Brooklyn Bridge in Manhattan, where his girlfriend is bent on a professional career. He embraces the notion that those with talent and dreams can escape the past and reinvent themselves. In the end, *Saturday Night Fever,* the most popular movie of the 1970s, looked to have its cake and eat it. On the one hand, it glamorized the youthful blue-collar culture whose vulgar language, violence, explicit sexuality, and drug use so offended conservative critics of the media. At the same time, the escapist ending offered audiences fantasy rather than a practical guide to success.

Perhaps inevitably, the wars for the soul of prime-time entertainment spilled into the political arena. Fearful that the Moral Majority's political pressure would lead television producers to censor themselves, the creator of Archie Bunker, Norman Lear, formed People for the American Way. The organization self-consciously opposed the agenda set by LaHaye and Falwell. People for the American Way campaigned for diversity and tolerance. In turn, conservatives, particularly the religious right, advanced their pro-life and pro-family agenda.

 REVIEW

Why did evangelical Christians become more politically active in the 1970s, and what tactics did they use?

THE PRESIDENCY IN TRANSITION: GERALD FORD AND JIMMY CARTER

Restraining the Imperial Presidency >> The cross-currents in American culture shook the political system as well. In the wake of Watergate and the Vietnam War, Congress was determined to place limits on the presidency which, under Nixon, had seemed to grow too imperial. The War Powers Resolution, passed in 1973 before Gerald Ford took office, required the president to consult Congress before committing troops to the battlefield, report within two days of taking action, and withdraw troops after 60 days unless Congress voted to retain them.

Meanwhile, congressional hearings revealed that the CIA had routinely violated its charter forbidding it to spy on Americans at home. Abroad, the agency had attempted to assassinate foreign leaders in Cuba, the Congo, South Vietnam, and the Dominican Republic. The FBI had also used illegal means to infiltrate and disrupt domestic dissidents. FBI director J. Edgar Hoover had authorized an (unsuccessful) operation to drive Martin Luther King Jr. to commit suicide. Determined to rein in the executive branch, the Senate established committees to oversee intelligence operations.

Energy and the Middle East >> Hemmed in by a newly assertive Congress, President Gerald Ford relied on Henry Kissinger, who served as both National Security Advisor and secretary of state. After Nixon's fall, Kissinger became the darling of the media. He was a realist whose manipulation of power offended idealists on both the political left and right. Quoting the German writer Goethe, Kissinger explained, "If I had to choose between justice and disorder, on the one hand, and injustice and order, on the other, I would always choose the latter." During the final years of the Nixon administration, Kissinger had (with the president's blessing) used the CIA to engineer the overthrow in Chile of the democratically elected socialist leader, Salvador Allende Gossens. Allende was killed and a brutal military regime assumed power. Kissinger argued that the United States had the right to limit democratic disorder in Latin America in order to guard against the evils of communism.

Under President Ford, Kissinger faced an energy crisis brought to a head by events in the Middle East. The United States and its allies had long depended on Middle Eastern oil and, so long as the pipelines flowed, low oil prices discouraged conservation or the use of alternative energy. Prime among the nation's foreign suppliers were the 13 nations of the Organization of the Petroleum Exporting Countries (OPEC)—and chief among those were seven Arab states and Iran.

The vulnerability of that supply became clear in the autumn of 1973, when on Yom Kippur, the holiest day of the Jewish year, troops from Egypt and Syria launched a surprise attack on Israel. The seven Arab members of OPEC, who supported Egypt and Syria, imposed a boycott on oil exports to countries seen as friendly to the Israelis. Lasting six months, the boycott staggered the economies of Western nations and Japan. The price of crude oil had been rising in any case, from under $2 a barrel in 1972 to over $12 by 1976. As the price of petroleum soared, so did the cost of carbon-based plastics used in a huge range of consumer goods from phonograph records to raincoats to tires. Inflation reached an annual rate of 14 percent. Meanwhile, with gasoline scarce, motorists found themselves waiting in line for hours at the pump, in hopes of purchasing a few gallons.

The oil crisis pushed many cities toward financial disaster. In October 1975 New York City announced it was near bankruptcy and petitioned the Ford administration for relief. When the president refused, the *New York Daily News* headline blared, "Ford to City: Drop Dead." The administration eventually extended a loan, but the political damage had been done.

To ease the crisis, Kissinger mediated the conflict between Israel and the Arab states. In negotiating, he flew back and forth so often between Jerusalem in Israel and Cairo in Egypt that observers nicknamed his efforts "shuttle diplomacy." Eventually the Israelis agreed to withdraw from the west bank of the Suez Canal and to disengage from Syrian troops along the Golan Heights, which overlooked Israel (see Mapping the Past). As an uncertain peace returned, OPEC lifted its boycott. The following year Congress addressed the energy crisis by ordering electric utilities to switch from expensive oil to more abundant and cheaper (though more polluting) coal. The new legislation also ordered the auto industry to improve the efficiency of its cars.

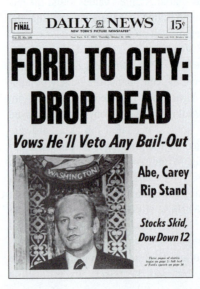

<< As the energy crisis contributed to New York City's near-bankruptcy, Gerald Ford at first opposed federal assistance. New Yorkers were not amused. New York Daily News/Getty Images

OIL AND CONFLICT IN THE MIDDLE EAST, 1948–1988

After World War II the Middle East became a vital geopolitical region beset by big-power rivalry and complicated by local, tribal, ethnic, and religious divisions. Much of the world's oil reserves lie along the Persian Gulf. Proximity to the former Soviet Union and vital trade routes such as the Suez Canal have defined the region's geographic importance. Revolutions in Iran and Afghanistan, intermittent warfare between Arabs and Jews, the unresolved questions of Israel's borders and a Palestinian homeland, the disintegration of Lebanon, and a long war between Iran and Iraq were among the conflicts that unsettled the region.

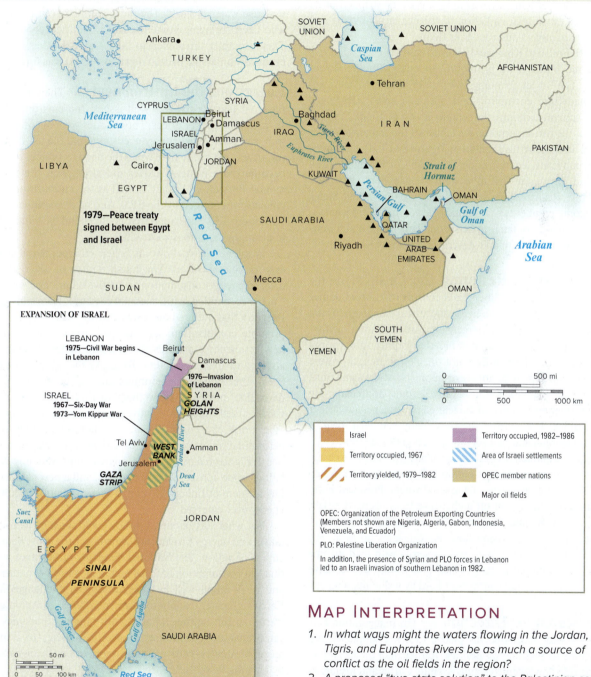

1979—Peace treaty signed between Egypt and Israel

EXPANSION OF ISRAEL

LEBANON
1975—Civil War begins in Lebanon

1976—Invasion of Lebanon

ISRAEL
1967—Six-Day War
1973—Yom Kippur War

Legend:
- Israel
- Territory occupied, 1967
- Territory yielded, 1979–1982
- Territory occupied, 1982–1986
- Area of Israeli settlements
- OPEC member nations
- ▲ Major oil fields

OPEC: Organization of the Petroleum Exporting Countries (Members not shown are Nigeria, Algeria, Gabon, Indonesia, Venezuela, and Ecuador)

PLO: Palestine Liberation Organization

In addition, the presence of Syrian and PLO forces in Lebanon led to an Israeli invasion of southern Lebanon in 1982.

MAP INTERPRETATION

1. In what ways might the waters flowing in the Jordan, Tigris, and Euphrates Rivers be as much a source of conflict as the oil fields in the region?
2. A proposed "two-state solution" to the Palestinian conflict calls for an independent State of Palestine, including the West Bank, alongside the State of Israel. What does the map insert tell you about the difficulties of executing such a solution?
3. What makes the Suez Canal and the Strait of Hormuz so strategically important?
4. Why would Iraq's invasion of Kuwait in 1990 pose a threat to Saudi Arabia?

MAP READING

1. Locate the Sinai Peninsula. What is its relationship to the Suez Canal?
2. Which countries border Israel?
3. Which countries do the Tigris and Euphrates Rivers cross?
4. Which countries on the map have the most oil fields?

Limits across the Globe >> In addition to the energy crisis and rampant inflation, the United States faced mounting competition from Europe and the expanding economies of the Pacific Rim (Japan, South Korea, Taiwan, Hong Kong, Singapore, the Philippines, and, eventually, Vietnam). Lower wages there convinced many American manufacturers to move high-wage jobs overseas. The AFL-CIO complained that as skilled union jobs disappeared, what remained would be "a nation of hamburger stands, a country stripped of its industrial capacity . . . a nation of citizens busily buying and selling hamburgers and root beer floats."

Both Ford and Kissinger looked to ease the United States's economic burdens by promoting détente with the Soviet Union. The Soviet economy, even more than the American, stagnated from corruption and mismanagement. During a pair of summit meetings, the second held at Helsinki, Finland, in 1975, the two superpowers established the framework for a second Strategic Arms Limitation Treaty (SALT II). Conservative Republicans, led by presidential contender Ronald Reagan, opposed the treaties as unnecessary concessions. Kissinger and Ford, Reagan claimed, were allowing the United States "to become number two in military power in a world where it is dangerous—if not fatal—to be second best." That claim exaggerated Soviet strength and American weakness.

Jimmy Carter: Restoring the Faith >> In the escalating war between liberal and conservative forces, James Earl "Jimmy" Carter launched a successful campaign for the presidency. He succeeded largely because he fell into neither camp. Carter represented a new breed of southern governors—they came from the Sun Belt, not the Cotton Belt; they were economic progressives, not segregationists. At the same time, Carter had credentials conservatives could appreciate. He was a former navy man and nuclear engineer, a peanut farmer and business leader from the thoroughly southern town of Plains, Georgia, and had served as Georgia's governor.

Carter exploited his outsider's status by promising to bring honesty and openness to a nation still smarting from Watergate. "I will not lie to you," he assured voters. President Ford, for his part, had to fight off a challenge from his party's right wing, led by Ronald Reagan, a former California governor, movie actor, and television host. Reagan grew up as a New Deal Democrat, but deeply held concerns with high income taxes and communism had turned him toward conservative causes. In the election Carter beat Ford by a slim margin.

The Search for Direction >> On Inauguration Day Jimmy Carter redeemed his pledge to bring simplicity and directness to Washington politics. Rather than the usual limousine ride down Pennsylvania Avenue, Carter and his family walked. The imperial presidency, he made clear, was a thing of the past. Congress remained determined to rein in the executive branch. To succeed in governing, Carter and his brash Georgia outsiders would have to prove they could swim among the political sharks.

Carter possessed disciplined work habits, a mastery of detail, and a wealth of plans to address the energy crisis, economic stagnation, the financial woes of major cities, and a host of foreign policy issues. What he and his advisers lacked was a clear set of priorities. Veteran politicians warned not to try too much too soon, but Carter admitted, "it's almost impossible for me to delay something that I see needs to be done." Almost immediately the president called for the elimination of 19 financially wasteful and environmentally destructive water projects. The move stunned even Democrats, who liked "bringing home the bacon" to their communities. They promptly threatened to bury Carter's other legislative proposals unless he backed down, which he was forced to do.

Energy and the Environment >> The water project fiasco at least raised two vital issues: the environment and skyrocketing energy prices. Those issues were in constant tension, since satisfying energy needs required the use of natural resources, just at the time when the need to protect them had become more evident. Carter did strengthen the Environmental Protection Agency as well as the clean air and water regulations enforced by the EPA. And he championed legislation to create a Superfund that could spend $1 billion a year to clean up hazardous waste sites.

Problems arose, however, when environmental and energy policies clashed. The harsh winter of 1977–1978 increased energy consumption and drove oil prices even higher. Carter responded with a comprehensive National Energy Program that outlined measures environmentalists favored to promote conservation, such as "gas guzzler" taxes on cars, new efficiency standards for building materials and appliances, and solar tax credits. To please the oil and gas industries, the president recommended a complex plan to deregulate prices to allow them to find their "true value." Carter urged Congress to move quickly, calling his energy bill "the moral equivalent of war." He had not counted on the determination of special interests to block virtually every proposal. Eighteen months later Congress approved only deregulation, some conservation tax credits, and a new cabinet-level Department of Energy. No comprehensive national policy on energy ever emerged.

But what sort of energy policy made sense? Environmentalists and energy producers clashed over the most beneficial course of action. The National Academy of Sciences warned that the consumption of fossil fuels—oil, gasoline, natural gas, and coal—might well be causing long-term changes in the Earth's climate, leading to a potentially catastrophic global warming. But neither scientists nor energy companies were yet prepared to recommend specific policies to limit the greenhouse gases—carbon dioxide prime among them—produced by burning fossil fuels.

Some utility companies argued for nuclear power plants, since fission energy emitted no carbon dioxide. That was an option few environmentalists accepted. No solution yet existed to dispose of the radioactive wastes that nuclear plants produced. The dangers of nuclear power became obvious in

^ In 1979 the four cooling towers at Three Mile Island nuclear reactor had to be shut down, due to a leak of radioactive steam.
Bettmann/Getty Images

March 1979, when a plume of radioactive steam unexpectedly spewed from an overheated reactor at Three Mile Island in Pennsylvania. Local authorities evacuated some 100,000 panicked residents from nearby communities. After the incident, prospects for nuclear power dimmed. While existing nuclear plants continued to operate, no new ones would be built for decades to come.

The Sagging Economy >> Throughout the 1970s wages stagnated, unemployment rose, and so did inflation, spurred by rising energy costs, falling industrial productivity, and foreign competition. President Carter at first proposed stimulating the economy with a series of popular tax rebates. And he pleased progressive politicians by finding new funding for federal programs such as food stamps, Social Security, Medicare, and Medicaid.

But the president's fiscal conservatism undermined these attempts to cushion the blow of hard times. Confronted by the large deficit from the Nixon and Ford years, Carter canceled his proposed tax rebates. "Government cannot solve our problems," he insisted, nor "eliminate poverty, or provide a bountiful economy, or reduce inflation, or save our cities, or cure illiteracy or provide energy." That sentiment, spoken by a Democrat, indicated how successful conservatives had been in promoting their ideas.

Foreign Policy: Principled or Pragmatic? >> In foreign policy, Jimmy Carter again gravitated between conservative and liberal impulses, between being practical and being idealistic. Like Nixon and Kissinger, Carter recognized that the United States no longer had either the strength or the resources to impose its will across the globe. But unlike his conservative critics, Carter believed Soviet power was

declining. Too often, the knee-jerk fear of Soviet power led Americans to build wasteful weapons systems and support brutal and corrupt dictators simply because they professed to be anti-Communist.

Carter insisted that the United States do more to promote human rights. He spoke publicly on behalf of political prisoners and reduced foreign aid to some dictatorships (though strategic allies such as the Philippines under the autocratic Ferdinand Marcos were largely spared). Argentinian Nobel Peace Prize winner Adolfo Pérez Esquivel claimed he owed his life to Carter's policies. Hundreds of other journalists and dissidents, who routinely faced imprisonment, torture, and even murder, benefited as well.

Carter also eased decades of distrust toward Yankee imperialism by negotiating a treaty to turn over to Panama control of the Canal Zone, the 10-mile-wide strip that the United States administered under a perpetual lease. For many conservatives, Carter's initiative offered further evidence of declining American power. Presidential hopeful Ronald Reagan condemned the proposed treaty as "appeasement," while Senator S. I. Hayakawa of California quipped: "It's ours; we stole it fair and square." Despite such criticisms the Senate ratified the final agreement in 1978.

For conservatives, however, the real test lay in relations with the Soviets. The president's first impulse was to continue the policy of détente scorned by the right wing. The Soviet Union's economy had long been saddled by inefficient industries and obligations to poor client states such as Cuba, Vietnam, and East Germany. When Carter announced he would extend diplomatic recognition to Communist China—playing "the China card" as Kissinger and Nixon once had—Soviet premier Leonid Brezhnev became even more willing to negotiate. In 1979 Carter and Brezhnev agreed on SALT II, finalizing talks on strategic arms limitation set in motion by President Ford. Although neither side agreed to scrap its major weapon systems, conservatives still attacked the treaty as a sell-out and blocked its approval in the Senate.

The Middle East: Hope and Hostages >> Throughout the Cold War, instability in the oil-rich Middle East continually threatened to set off a larger conflict. Dictators in Iran, Egypt, Syria, and Iraq vied with autocratic monarchies in Saudi Arabia, Kuwait, Jordan, and the Arab emirates. Tensions simmered between rival Islamic religious sects, the Sunnis and Shi'ites, while at the same time Arab nations were united in their hostility toward Israel.

American policy for the region pulled in two directions. On the one hand, the United States wanted to ensure the free flow of Middle Eastern oil to the industrial world; on the other, it was committed to the survival of Israel. The energy crises of the 1970s heightened the tensions within these goals, as did Israel's decision to refuse Palestinian demands for a homeland in the West Bank. The diplomatic impasse eased somewhat when Egyptian president Anwar Sadat

It was at Camp David, in private talks sponsored by President Jimmy Carter (*center*), that Egyptian president Anwar Sadat (*left*) and Israeli prime minister Menachem Begin (*right*) hammered out a "Framework for Peace in the Middle East" as a first step toward ending decades of war and mistrust. David Rubinger/Getty Images

traveled to Israel to meet Israeli prime minister Menachem Begin. Sensing an opportunity to promote peace, Carter invited the two leaders to Camp David in September 1978.

For 13 days the two antagonists argued, while Carter kept them at the table. Each feared a backlash at home if he gave the other side too much. Finally, they struck a limited compromise: Sadat would recognize Israel; Israel would return the Sinai Peninsula to Egypt. On the question of a Palestinian state in the West Bank and Gaza, Begin would not yield. Even so, the discussions had been historic. Begin and Sadat shared the Nobel Peace Prize for their courageous diplomacy, but it could just as well have gone to Carter, who brokered the peace.

Amid the Middle East's ongoing turmoil, the shah of Iran had long seemed a stabilizing force. But in the autumn of 1978, Shi'ite fundamentalists rebelled against his rule. Long dismayed by the increasing Westernization of their society, they found the presence of tens of thousands of non-Muslim American military advisers particularly offensive. When the regime collapsed in February 1979, the religious leader Ayatollah Ruhollah Khomeini established an Islamic republic. Later that year, the United States admitted the ailing shah to an American hospital for medical treatment. In reaction, several hundred Iranian students stormed the U.S. Embassy in Teheran and took 53 Americans hostage. That action violated every convention of Western diplomacy, and yet the United States was helpless to respond.

A President Held Hostage >> While American officials debated how to respond to Islamic fundamentalists in Iran, the Soviet Union faced a similar uprising along its own southern borders. In Afghanistan, Islamic rebels had overthrown a government that had long been friendly to the Soviets, leading Premier Brezhnev to send troops into Afghanistan to restore the old government. President Carter condemned the Soviet invasion, but there was little the United States could do to stop it. As a symbolic gesture, Carter announced that the United States would boycott the 1980 Olympics in Moscow.

Once again, the problem of energy dependence interacted with the region's political instability to create a political crisis. Nightly newscasts aired the spectacle of "America Held Hostage" in Iran. And the turbulence in the Middle East set off another round of OPEC oil price increases. Soaring energy costs soon drove up inflation and pushed some interest rates to above 20 percent.

With polls giving Carter a negative rating of 77 percent, the president revived the Cold War rhetoric of the 1950s and accelerated the development of new classes of nuclear weapons. But whereas the CIA in 1953 had successfully overthrown an Iranian government, an airborne mission launched in April 1980 to rescue the hostages ended in disaster. Eight marines died when two helicopters and a plane collided in Iran's central desert in the midst of a blinding sandstorm. The United States, as even the president admitted, was mired in "a crisis of confidence."

The administration's mistakes had no doubt contributed to it. Yet the obstacles to projecting American power internationally were not simply a result of Carter's mismanagement. Vietnam had demonstrated the clear limits of what U.S. forces could accomplish in distant lands, while the long lines for expensive gas rose from an energy crisis decades in the making. The problems in the Middle East had proved intractable over many centuries. Finally, Carter could not be blamed for the reluctance of Americans to sacrifice personal comforts for the general good. American culture had long defined wealth as having more, not wanting less. In 1980 the discouraged electorate discovered in Ronald Reagan a political leader who shared that faith.

 REVIEW

How did Jimmy Carter's presidency demonstrate that he could be both liberal and conservative in his approach to governing?

PRIME TIME WITH RONALD REAGAN

The recession of the 1970s and the accompanying runaway inflation brought about a major political realignment, only the third since the Civil War. Republicans undermined the Democrats' New Deal coalition and established a conservative majority that would shape American politics for at least four decades. In the 1980 presidential campaign, Ronald Reagan asked Americans, "Are you better off now than you were four years ago?" Many thought not, and Reagan swept the election with an unexpectedly large majority. The fight against inflation and high taxes would be the cornerstone of his administration. No longer would federal economic policy make full employment its priority.

The Great Communicator >> Reagan's message was clear: "It is time to reawaken the industrial giant, to get government back within its means, and to lighten the punitive tax burden." To both liberals and conservatives this signaled the onset of what came to be called "the Reagan revolution." Liberals feared—and conservatives hoped—that the revolution meant a harder line against the Communists and an assault on a wide range of social programs and regulations at home. What both groups ignored at first were the moderating forces at work. As governor of California, Reagan had showed a willingness to accommodate, at times increasing both spending and taxes. The liberal *Washington Post* commented that the new president was not someone who allowed rigid ideas to block flexible policies. Equally important, noted the *Post,* almost anyone who met him thought he was "a nice guy, a happy secure person who likes himself and most other people."

In other ways Reagan contradicted expectations. With his jaunty wave and jutting jaw, he projected an aura of physical vitality and movie-star good looks. Yet at 69 he was the oldest person to become president, and no president since Calvin Coolidge slept as soundly or as often. Such serenity demonstrated his refusal to become bogged down in the details of his job. Outsiders applauded his "hands-off," style after four years under detail-oriented Jimmy Carter. Reagan set his administration's direction, while leaving the rest to his advisers. Sometimes that left him in the dark about major programs. Donald Regan, his first treasury secretary, once noted: "The Presidential mind was not cluttered with facts."

The effectiveness of Reagan's message was no accident. The president had honed his public speaking skills as an actor, as a spokesperson for General Electric, and as a politician. His communications staff planned everything from the president's words to a speech's location and the camera angles and lighting. The elaborate preparation complemented Reagan's discipline as a performer. The president understood how to use a battlefield, a classroom, or the flag to communicate a hopeful message.

Luck seemed to be on Reagan's side as well. Problems that handcuffed Carter eased on Reagan's watch. The day he took office Iran announced it would release the American hostages after 444 days of captivity. Three aging Russian leaders, beginning with Leonid Brezhnev in 1982, died suddenly, thereby greatly reducing the influence of the Soviet Union. And when a disturbed assassin shot Reagan in the chest two months after his inauguration, the wounds proved non–life-threatening. Even Reagan's critics admired his courage in the face of death.

The Reagan Agenda >> Reagan viewed the economic downturn as an opportunity to push for his revolution in government. That agenda called for massive tax cuts, deregulation of the economy, and a reduction in spending for social programs. Only the military would be spared the budget cutters' ax, because the president planned a forceful foreign policy to contain Soviet power.

MAP 31.1: ELECTION OF 1980

Candidate (Party)	Electoral Vote (%)	Popular Vote (%)
Ronald Reagan (Republican)	489 (91)	43,904,153 (51)
Jimmy Carter (Democratic)	49 (9)	35,483,883 (41)
John B. Anderson (Independent)	—	5,719,437 (7)
Minor parties	—	1,395,558 (1)

supply-side economics theory that emphasizes tax cuts and business incentives to encourage economic growth rather than deficit spending to promote demand.

A commitment to **supply-side economic** theory became the cornerstone of the Reagan revolution. Supply-side advocates argued that high taxes and government regulation stifled business. The key to revival lay in a large tax cut—a politically popular proposal, though economically controversial. Supply-side economist Arthur Laffer calculated that lower tax rates would stimulate the economy so greatly, tax revenues would actually grow and the deficit shrink. Conservative economists also suggested that broad cuts in social programs would further reduce deficits.

After little more than half a year in office, Congress handed the president most of the cuts he requested. Taxpayers in the highest brackets were far and away the biggest winners. The Economic Recovery Tax Act (ERTA) lowered income tax rates over the next three years by 25 percent, capital gains from the sale of stock by 40 percent, and investment income rates by 28 percent. At the same time, Reagan signed the Omnibus Budget Reconciliation Act, which slashed some $35 billion spent on government programs. The *Wall Street Journal* hailed the two measures as a "spectacular tax victory," and news commentators suggested that Reagan had ended 50 years of liberal government.

Liberal government relied on the support of big labor. Here, too, Reagan struck a decisive blow. In 1981 members of PATCO, the air traffic controllers union, struck against what they claimed were dangerous and debilitating working conditions. PATCO workers were, however, both highly paid and public employees. Reagan declared their strike illegal and, without addressing the issues they raised, summarily fired them. Large corporations seized on the antiunion climate to wrest significant concessions on wages and work rules.

Reagan likewise sought to decrease government involvement in protecting the environment. Many conservatives dismissed warnings about global warming and calls to adopt renewable energy sources as a strategy to regulate business. Under Reagan the National Climate Program Office, created during the Carter years, became "an outpost in enemy territory." Anne Gorsuch, the new head of the Environmental Protection Agency, cut her budget so drastically, the agency almost ceased to function. Under her leadership, the EPA filed no new enforcement cases against hazardous waste sites, even though it knew of some 18,000 that qualified for cleanup under the Superfund law passed during Carter's final year in office.

The Occupational Safety and Health Administration also faced severe cutbacks that ended its efforts to set health and safety standards and regulate toxic work environments. Workers were at particular risk in plants that produced polyvinyl chloride (PVC) and related plastics used in a wide array of consumer products. Members of the Oil, Chemical, and Atomic Workers union (OCAW) had documented chemical wastes that the German firm BASF dumped into the Mississippi River at its Louisiana plant. There, they constantly smelled "this chlorine all day, twenty-four hours a day, depending on what job you're working at." When OCAW called a strike to gain improved wages and safer working conditions, the company locked out the workers for five years. OSHA, under Reagan, began to ignore such cases.

Reagan's secretary of the interior, James G. Watt, fought environmentalists and federal regulations. An evangelical Christian and a self-proclaimed **sagebrush rebel**, Watt wanted to force the Department of the Interior to open the public grazing lands, forests, and wilderness to private development. His abrasive style (he once denied the Beach Boys a permit to perform on the Washington Mall because he considered their music immoral) offended so many people that he resigned in 1983. Scandal forced EPA director Gorsuch to resign the same year, but the campaign to reduce or eliminate environmental regulation continued.

sagebrush rebels group of western cattle ranchers, loggers, miners, developers, and others who argued that federal ownership of huge tracts of land and natural resources violated the principle of states' rights.

A Halfway Revolution >> Soon after the tax cuts went into effect, evidence emerged that supply-side policies did not produced the tax revenues Laffer predicted. Continued recession, rising interest rates, and a mounting federal deficit compounded the problem. So Reagan reversed course and accepted the Tax Equity and Fiscal Responsibility Act of 1982, a measure including $98 billion in tax increases disguised as "revenue enhancements." A year later Social Security reform led to further tax increases. In both cases Reagan allowed pragmatism to trump ideology.

After reversing course on tax cuts, the economy began a strong upturn that extended through both of the president's terms in office. Labor productivity improved,

⌃ Striking air traffic controllers protest their firing.
Yvonne Hemsy/Getty Images

inflation subsided to 4.3 percent, unemployment fell, and the stock markets rose sharply. Falling energy costs played a major role as crude oil, having sold for as much as $30 per barrel, fell to as low as $10 a barrel.

The benefits of an improved economy were distributed unevenly across economic classes and regions. For the wealthiest Americans the 1980s were the best of times. The top 1 percent commanded a greater share of wealth (37 percent) than at any time since 1929. Their earnings per year were 25 times greater than those of the 40 percent of Americans at the bottom of the economic ladder. Good times meant new jobs—more than 14.5 million. Three million of these were concentrated in unskilled, minimum-wage areas such as hotels, fast-food restaurants, and retail stores. High-paying jobs in financial services, real estate, insurance, and law went largely (70 percent) to white males. Only 2 percent went to African Americans.

The 1980s also saw an acceleration of the trend toward **outsourcing**, or relocating, high-wage industrial jobs to low-wage areas such as Mexico and Asia. Given its commitment to free markets and free trade, the Reagan administration resisted pressure to develop a plan to keep jobs at home. Thus, even as the economy grew and inflation dropped below 2 percent, unemployment persisted at over 6 percent, and poverty levels ranged from 11 to 15 percent. Cuts in programs such as food stamps, Medicaid, and school lunches increased the burden on the poor.

> **outsourcing** the contracting of goods or services from outside a company or organization in order to maintain flexibility in the size of the organization's workforce.

Winners and Losers in the Labor Market >>

Several characteristics distinguished workers in the new technology industries from those in older industrial sectors. In general, workers in the new technologies were much younger and better educated. The media began referring to young, upwardly mobile, urban professionals as yuppies—part of the younger generation that rejected the anti-materialistic values of their hippie forebears. To Gen-Xers, those born after 1963 (the end of the baby boom), computers and other electronic devices seemed second nature. Data processing and information technologies streamlined the workplace so that the time it took to develop and bring new products to market fell sharply, along with the cost. Increased productivity also reduced the demand for low-skill workers. By contrast, demand for workers with education and technical skills rose (as did wages) and thereby increased the income gap between those at the top and bottom of the labor market.

In an economy in which brains displaced brawn, educated women were among the big winners. Not only did they find more jobs in high-tech areas and computerized offices, but they also greatly increased their presence in law, medicine, business, and other professional schools. Still, many women continued to work lower-paying jobs in health care, education, social services, and government. The net result was that well-educated women gained far more economic independence and a more substantial political voice, while women with fewer skills and less education saw their earnings eroded. Single mothers with children, many who worked in low-wage jobs, were the nation's most impoverished group.

Job displacement in the 1980s had a devastating impact on African American men and organized labor. Beginning in

Percentage of Group Living in Poverty

(chart, 1970–1993)
- Single Mothers with Children
- Children under 18
- Persons Aged 65 and Over

Percentage of Group Living in Poverty

(chart, 1970–1993)
- Black
- Hispanic
- White

Year

POVERTY IN THE UNITED STATES, 1970–1993

⌃ Social Security and other income supplements to older Americans reduced their rate of poverty. For all other traditionally impoverished groups the prosperity of the Reagan-Bush years (1981–1989) left them slightly worse off than in 1980. The charts also indicate that during the years 1970–1993, poverty was most severe for single mothers and their children and for people of color.

(top right) David Buffington/Photodisc/Getty Images; (top left) Stock Shop/iStock; (center left) James Pauls/eyecrave LLC/Vetta/iStockphoto; (bottom left) Plush Studios/Blend Images LLC

↑ Introduced in 1977, the Apple II transformed the market for personal computers. Customers welcomed it as the first "computer appliance" that was "a completed system that is purchased off the retail shelf, taken home, plugged in and used."
INTERFOTO/Alamy Stock Photo

the 1970s, Black males lost much of the gains they had made over the previous three decades. The decline in the unionized manufacturing industries such as steel and autos struck hardest in the older industrial cities where Blacks had gained a foothold in the economy. Often lacking the education required in the technology sector, Black men had difficulty finding new jobs and many simply dropped out of the labor market. Sociologists began to describe an underclass of Black Americans, trapped in poverty, while middle-class Blacks escaped devastated urban neighborhoods.

As manufacturing declined, so did membership in unions. Labor organized 27 percent of all workers in 1953, 20 percent in 1980, and 16 percent in 1990. Only the increase in the number of unionized government workers helped offset the shrinkage in the industrial sector. Deregulation made matters worse. With increased competition in the airlines, trucking, and telecommunications industries (all areas where membership had been strong), unions were forced to make concessions on wages and benefits. A two-tier system emerged in which younger workers received lower pay and hence had less incentive to join unions. A shrinking membership reduced labor's political clout, weakened the Democratic Party, and spurred the conservative revolution.

 REVIEW

What were the major goals of the Reagan revolution?

STANDING TALL IN A CHAOTIC WORLD

Ronald Reagan's view of international affairs was primal. "The Soviet Union underlies all the unrest in the world," he stated in his 1980 campaign. Thus he made the defeat of the Communist menace a central mission of his administration. To that end he believed Americans must put Vietnam behind them and once again stand tall in the world. Although he was pleased to see the Soviet threat dissolving by the end of his years in office, the president also discovered that firmness and military force alone were not sufficient to calm regional crises across the world.

The Military Buildup >> Reagan described the Soviet Union as the "evil empire." His plan to defeat that enemy centered on a massive buildup of the American military. Whereas Richard Nixon had thought the United States needed enough force to fight one and one-half wars at any time, Reagan pushed for enough to fight three and one-half around the globe. That required expenditures of over $1.6 trillion over his first five years (Carter had planned for $1.2 trillion). The combination of massive defense spending and tax cuts created huge deficits.

The massive military buildup expanded the size of the government that conservatives were so eager to reduce. Cost overruns and wasteful spending were yet another problem. Exposés of $600 toilet seats and $7,000 coffeepots symbolized spending run amok. Worse yet were the multibillion-dollar weapons systems that were unneeded. Air Force planners, for example, persuaded Congress to fund the B-2 bomber, a plane costing $2 billion each and designed to penetrate Soviet air defenses. Only later did investigators determine that those Soviet air defenses did not exist. In general, advocates of the defense buildup exaggerated Soviet capabilities in order to pressure Congress to appropriate money.

Controversy arose, too, when Reagan's tough-talking defense planners spoke out about winning any nuclear exchange with the Soviet Union. In *Fate of the Earth* author Jonathan Schell warned that no one would win a nuclear war, in which radiation and debris in the atmosphere would create conditions potentially fatal to life on Earth. Such warnings revived the antinuclear movement across East Asia, Europe, and the United States. Bishops of the American Catholic Church felt moved to announce their opposition to nuclear war.

Disaster in the Middle East >> The Middle East continued to be a flashpoint of U.S.-Soviet tensions. In 1982 Israel invaded neighboring Lebanon to destroy missiles supplied by Syria, a Soviet client state. The Israelis also used the invasion to strike a decisive blow against forces of the Palestine Liberation Organization (PLO) that were camped in Lebanon. As the Israeli offensive bogged down, international outrage over the killing of Palestinians in Israeli-controlled camps forced the Israelis to withdraw.

Reagan decided to send American troops to Beirut, Lebanon's capital, to protect the Palestinians and keep the peace between warring Christian and Muslim factions. Unfamiliar with the terrain or the politics, the Americans were drawn into supporting Christian militias. Muslim radicals responded by bombing the American Embassy and then, in October 1983, a U.S. marine barracks. Some 239 troops died. Confronting a chorus of criticism, including some from his own Defense Department, Reagan withdrew American troops from Lebanon.

The president also groped for a response to terrorist attacks and hostage-taking by Islamic fundamentalists. In speeches, the president was forceful and uncompromising: "Let terrorists beware: . . . our policy will be one of swift and effective retribution." But against whom should the United States seek retribution? Intelligence agencies had only sketchy profiles of the many terrorist factions and their political allies. In 1986 the president launched an attack against Libya, which sponsored terrorism. But so, too, did Syria and Iran, against whom the administration did nothing.

Frustrations in Central America >> At first, Reagan had more success closer to home. On the pretext of protecting American medical students studying on the Caribbean island of Grenada, American troops crushed a band of pro-Cuban rebels and evacuated the students, who were hardly at risk. As the rebel uprising had posed no significant security threat, the incursion was largely symbolic.

More challenging was a campaign to overthrow the left-wing Sandinista government in Nicaragua. The president justified arming the anti-Sandinista "Contras" as aid to "freedom fighters" who battled in the spirit of America's Founders. True, the Contras included a few democrats and disillusioned

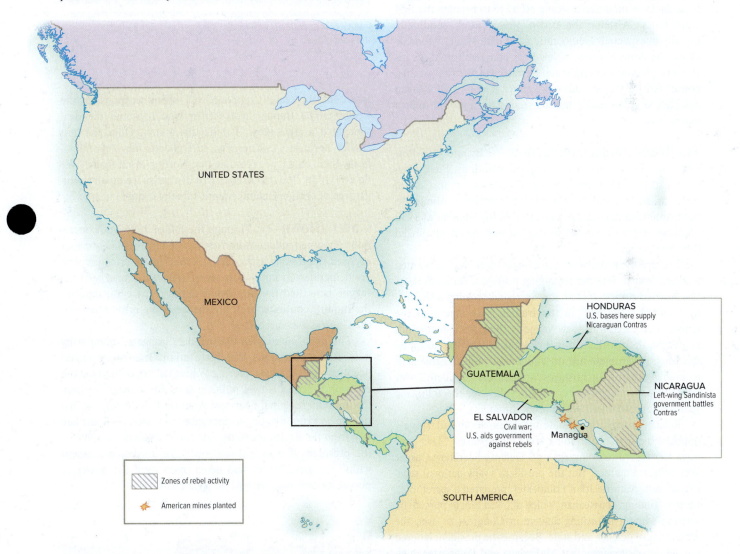

MAP 31.2: NICARAGUA AND ITS NEIGHBORS IN THE 1980S

The strong anti-Communist tilt of the Reagan administration led it to actively intervene in Central America, particularly with aid toward the overthrow of the left-leaning Sandinista government in Nicaragua. But Congress reacted to the mining of Nicaraguan harbors by forbidding any American aid to the Contra forces.
What part did El Salvador and Honduras play in Reagan's anti-Communist strategy?

Sandinistas, but most had served in the brutal and corrupt dictatorship of Anastasio Somoza, which the Sandinistas overthrew in 1979.

Reagan had no desire to broker a settlement between the opposing forces. Instead, he authorized the CIA to help the Contras mine Nicaragua's harbors, in hopes of destabilizing the Sandinistas. When the mines damaged foreign ships—a violation of international law—Congress adopted the Boland Amendment, which explicitly forbade the CIA or "any other agency or entity involved in intelligence activities" to spend money to support the Contras "directly or indirectly." Bowing to criticism, Reagan reluctantly signed the measure, though he remained determined to overthrow the Sandinistas.

Conflict with Congress coincided with the 1984 presidential race. Though Reagan's reelection was expected, the campaign did bring two surprises. In the Democratic primaries Jesse Jackson mounted a strong effort to to become the first major-party African American presidential candidate. Equally unexpected, Democratic candidate Walter Mondale chose Geraldine Ferraro, a New York congresswoman, as his vice presidential running mate. Ferraro was the first woman nominated for vice president by either major party. Reagan defeated Mondale easily, but his second term proved to be a bumpy ride.

The Iran-Contra Connection >> By mid-1985 Reagan policy makers faced two major frustrations. First, Congress had forbidden any support of the Contras in Central America, and second, Iranian-backed terrorists continued to hold American hostages in Lebanon. In the summer of 1985 a course of events was set in motion that eventually linked these two issues.

The president made it increasingly clear that he wanted to find a way to free the remaining hostages. National Security Advisor Robert McFarlane suggested opening a channel to "moderate factions" in the Iranian government. If the United States sold Iran a few weapons, the grateful moderates might use their influence in Lebanon to free the hostages. But Iran's government had no "moderates" and an agreement to exchange arms for hostages violated the president's vow never to pay ransom to terrorists. Still, over the following year, Iran received four secret arms shipments.

Reagan's secretaries of state and defense both had strongly opposed the notion of trading arms for hostages. "This is almost too absurd to comment on," Defense Secretary Caspar Weinberger remarked. But the president's new national security advisor, Admiral John Poindexter, prepared a secret intelligence "finding" for Reagan, which allowed him to pursue the mission without informing anyone in Congress or even the secretaries of defense and state. Because the president ignored the details of foreign policy, McFarlane and Poindexter in effect had assumed the power to act on their own.

The man most often pulling the strings for them was Lieutenant Colonel Oliver "Ollie" North, a Vietnam veteran with a flair for the dramatic. Impatient with bureaucratic procedures, North hit on the idea that the profits made selling arms to

^ Lieutenant Colonel Oliver North successfully took the offensive in his testimony before the congressional committee investigating the Iran-Contra scandals. Here North delivers a pro-Contra lecture to the committee.
Lana Harris/AP Images

Iran could be secretly siphoned off to buy weapons for the Contras. The Iranian arms dealer who brokered the deal thought it a great idea. "I think this is now, Ollie, the best chance, because . . . we never get such good money out of this," he laughed, on a tape recording that North himself made. "We do everything. We do hostages free of charge; we do all terrorists free of charge; Central America free of charge."

Cover Blown >> Through the fall of 1986 both operations remained hidden from view until a Lebanese newspaper exposed the Iranian arms deal. Astonished American reporters demanded to know how secret arms sales to a terrorist regime benefited the president's antiterrorist campaign. As the inquiry continued, the link between the arms sales and the Contras was discovered.

The press nicknamed the scandal "Irangate," comparing it to Richard Nixon's Watergate affair. Irangate revealed deeply troubling issues. During Watergate, Nixon had led the cover-up to save his own political skin. But during the Iran-Contra congressional hearings, Admiral Poindexter testified that he had kept Reagan in ignorance "so that I could insulate him from the decision and provide some future deniability for the president if it ever leaked out." An unelected segment within the government had taken upon itself the power to pursue its own policies beyond legal channels.

Make a Case

Why was Irangate as much a threat to democratic institutions as was Watergate?

From Cold War to Glasnost >> Because few members of Congress wanted to impeach a genial president, the hearings came to a sputtering end. Reagan's popularity returned, in part because of substantial improvement in Soviet-American relations. By the 1980s the Soviet Union had become far weaker. The Soviet economy stagnated; the Communist Party was mired in corruption. The war in Afghanistan had become a Soviet Vietnam. By accelerating the arms race, Reagan placed additional pressure on the Soviet Union.

In 1985 a fresh spirit entered the Kremlin. Unlike the aged leaders who preceded him, the youthful Mikhail Gorbachev saw the need for reform. Gorbachev's fundamental restructuring, or *perestroika,* set about improving relations with the United States. He reduced military commitments and adopted a policy of openness (*glasnost*) about problems in the Soviet Union. In October the two leaders held their second summit in Reykjavík, Iceland. Gorbachev dangled the possibility of abolishing all nuclear weapons. Reagan was receptive to the idea, but in the end did not accept so radical a proposal. Even so, a summit in Moscow two years later

⌃ In October 1986 President Reagan and General Secretary Mikhail Gorbachev met for arms talks at Reykjavík, Iceland. At their second summit meeting Gorbachev proposed that the two superpowers agree to "the liquidation of nuclear weapons." Reagan liked that ambitious goal (considerably more than his skeptical advisers), but he was unable to agree because he wanted to continue development of an antiballistic missile system.
David Hume Kennerly/Getty Images

eliminated an entire class of nuclear missiles with ranges of 600 to 3,400 miles. Both sides agreed to allow on-site inspections of missile bases and the facilities where missiles would be destroyed. A disastrous meltdown at a nuclear power station at Chernobyl in the USSR in 1986 made Gorbachev all the more eager to denuclearize the Cold War.

As the election of 1988 approached, the president could claim credit for improved relations with the Soviet Union. Loyalty to Ronald Reagan made Vice President George H. W. Bush the Republican heir apparent. The Democratic challenger, Governor Michael Dukakis of Massachusetts, never mounted a strong challenge, allowing Bush to win by a comfortable margin.

 REVIEW

How did Reagan's foreign policy try to overcome the legacy of Vietnam?

AN END TO THE COLD WAR

President George Herbert Walker Bush was born to both privilege and politics. The son of a Connecticut senator, he attended an exclusive boarding school and Yale University. His background made him part of the East Coast establishment often scorned by Populist Republicans. Yet once the oil business lured Bush to Texas, he became a Goldwater Republican and ran unsuccessfully for the Senate in 1964. Foreign policy interested him far more than domestic politics. In the end, inattention to domestic issues proved his undoing as the economy slid into recession.

A Post-Cold War Foreign Policy >> To the astonishment of most Western observers, Mikhail Gorbachev's reform policies led not only to the collapse of the Soviet Empire but also to the breakup of the Soviet Union itself. In December 1988 Gorbachev spoke in the United Nations of a "new world order." To that end, he began liquidating the Soviet Cold War legacy, with Russian troops leaving Afghanistan and then Eastern Europe.

Throughout 1989 Eastern Europeans began to test their newfound freedom. In Poland, Hungary, Bulgaria, Czechoslovakia, and, most violently, Romania, Communist dictators fell from power. Nothing more inspired the world than the stream of celebrating East Germans pouring through the Berlin Wall in November 1989. Within a year, the wall, a symbol of Communist oppression, had been torn down and Germany reunified. Although Gorbachev struggled to keep together the 15 republics that made up the Union of Soviet Socialist Republics, the forces of nationalism and reform pulled it apart. The Baltic republics—Lithuania, Latvia, and Estonia—declared

The Berlin Wall

This platform was erected in 1969 when President Richard Nixon visited the Berlin Wall.

In what way do these paintings suggest a difference between the public cultures of East and West Berlin?

Which side of the wall is East and which is West? How can you tell?

No place in the world reflected Cold War tensions more than the city of Berlin. And East Germany's erection of a wall there in August 1961—launched in great secrecy in the dead of night—struck many Americans as an escalation of the Cold War. Suddenly, the outpouring of educated and skilled East Germans escaping to West Germany ceased. For some 28 years the Wall stood as a stark symbol of a divided Germany, and historians can use the Wall to help track the ups and downs of the long conflict between East and West: attempted escapes, the addition of barbed wire and guard posts, espionage novels such as *The Spy Who Came in from the Cold,* the scaffolding periodically erected so that American presidents could project their messages to captive citizens.

By 1987 tensions had begun to ease. President Ronald Reagan, while in the city commemorating Berlin's 750th anniversary, challenged Soviet Premier Mikhail Gorbachev to "tear down this wall." Two years later the Wall came down.

(top) National Archives and Records Administration (NLNP-WHPO-MOF-0388(13A)); (bottom) Owen Franken/Getty Images

THINKING CRITICALLY

What geographic difficulties prompted East Germany to build the Wall? (See Mapping the Past: Cold War Europe.) What symbolic meanings does a wall suggest? Why did so many East Germans want to move to the West? Can you think of ways in which building a wall might have been a good thing?

---

their independence in 1991. Then, in December, the Slavic republics of Ukraine, Belarus, and Russia formed a new Commonwealth of Independent States. By the end of December eight more of the former Soviet republics had joined the loose federation. Boris Yeltsin, the charismatic president of Russia, became the Commonwealth's dominant figure. With no Soviet Union left to preside over, Gorbachev resigned as president.

Although President Bush supported Gorbachev's reforms, he did so with caution. Even if he had wished to aid Eastern Europe and the new Commonwealth states, soaring deficits at home limited his options. The administration seemed to accept the status quo in Communist China, too. When in June 1989 China's aging leadership crushed students rallying for democratic reform in Beijing's Tiananmen Square, Bush offered only muted protests.

The fall of the Soviet Union signaled the end of a Cold War that, over the span of half a century, had threatened a nuclear end to human history. At a series of summits with Russian leaders, the United States and its former rival agreed to sharp

MAP 31.3: WAR WITH IRAQ: OPERATION DESERT STORM

When Saddam Hussein invaded oil-rich Kuwait on August 2, 1990, the United States formed a coalition to defeat the Iraqis. (Although Turkey was not a formal member, it allowed its airfields to be used. Israel remained uninvolved to avoid antagonizing Arab coalition members.) The coalition launched Operation Desert Storm in January 1991; land forces invaded on February 24, routing Iraqi troops, who left Kuwait in ruin and its oil fields aflame.
What geographic reason would Iraq have for wanting to invade Kuwait?

reductions in their stockpiles of nuclear weapons. The Strategic Arms Reduction Treaty (or START, concluded in July 1991) far surpassed the limits negotiated in earlier SALT talks. By June 1992 Bush and Yeltsin had agreed to even sharper cuts.

The Gulf War >> With the United States now the world's sole superpower, many wondered what the "new world order" would be like. If anything, regional crises loomed larger. Instability in the Middle East continued to pose the greatest foreign policy challenges. From 1980 to 1988, Iran and Iraq had battered each other in a debilitating war. During those years the Reagan administration assisted Iraq with weapons and intelligence, until at last it won a narrow victory over Iran's fundamentalists. But Iraq's ruthless dictator, Saddam Hussein, had run up enormous debts. To ease his financial crisis, Hussein cast a covetous eye on his neighbor, the small oil-rich sheikdom of Kuwait. In August 1990, 120,000 Iraqi troops invaded and occupied Kuwait, catching the Bush administration off guard. Would Hussein stop there?

"We committed a boner with regard to Iraq and our close friendship with Iraq," Reagan admitted. Embarrassed about having supported the pro-Iraqi policy, Bush likened the Iraqi leader to Hitler and coordinated a United Nations–backed economic boycott. Increasing the pressure further, he deployed half a million American troops in Saudi Arabia and the Persian Gulf to liberate Kuwait. By November Bush had won a resolution from the UN Security Council permitting the use of military force if Hussein did not withdraw.

On January 17, 1991, planes from France, Italy, Britain, Saudi Arabia, and the United States began bombing Baghdad and Iraqi bases. Operation Desert Storm had begun. After weeks of merciless pounding from the air, ground operations shattered Hussein's vaunted Republican Guards in less than 100 hours. In an act of spite, Hussein resorted to ecoterrorism. His forces set Kuwait's oil fields ablaze and dumped huge quantities of crude oil into the Persian Gulf ecosystem. It did him no good: by the end of February Kuwait was liberated, and nothing stood between Allied forces and Iraq's capital, Baghdad. Bush was unwilling to advance that far—and most other nations in the coalition agreed. If Hussein were toppled, who would prevent Iran from stepping into the power vacuum?

Domestic Doldrums >> Victory in the Gulf War boosted the president's popularity so high that aides brushed aside the need for any bold domestic program. "Frankly, this president doesn't need another single piece of legislation, unless it's absolutely right," asserted his cocky chief of staff. "In fact, if Congress wants to come together, adjourn, and leave, it's all right with us." That attitude suggested a lack of direction that proved fatal to Bush's reelection hopes.

At first Bush envisioned a domestic program that would soften the harsher edges of the Reagan revolution. He promised to create a "kinder, gentler" nation. Yet pressures from conservative Republicans kept the new president from straying too far in the direction of reform. When delegates from 178 nations met at an "Earth Summit" in Rio de Janeiro in 1992, the president opposed efforts to draft stricter rules to lessen the threat of global warming. Bush did sign into law the sweeping Clean Air Act, passed by Congress in 1990. But soon after, Vice President Dan Quayle established a Council on Competitiveness to rewrite regulations that corporations found burdensome.

The president did call for reform of the educational system, whose quality had declined through the 1980s. But while he convened a well-publicized Education Summit in 1989, the delegates issued only a modest set of goals, and only after the president was urged to do so by his co-chair at the summit, Governor Bill Clinton of Arkansas.

THEN&NOW

As early as 1958 researcher Dave Keeling measured an increase in atmospheric carbon dioxide, a key greenhouse gas linked to global warming. Keeling later produced one of the world's most famous graphs that charted atmospheric carbon levels in what looked like a hockey stick. A few years later, his boss showed the graph to a class of Harvard students that included Al Gore. That graph, by emphasizing the growing threat of global warming, changed the trajectory of Gore's life. Atmospheric carbon dioxide stood just over 300 parts per million when Keeling first measured it. By the time George H. W. Bush scuttled an ambitious climate agreement at Rio de Janeiro in 1991, it had increased more than 20 percent to around 360 ppm. In 2019, it reached over 410 ppm—the highest in 800,000 years. As Al Gore warned in his documentary *An Inconvenient Truth* (2006), we understand that carbon dioxide does more than raise global temperatures. It leads to melting ice sheets, rising ocean levels, increasing acidification of seawater that threatens marine life, and creating ever more catastrophic natural disasters including desertification, floods, forest fires, hurricanes, and tornadoes.

The Conservative Court >> Although Presidents Reagan and Bush both spoke out against abortion, affirmative action, the banning of prayer in public schools, and other conservative social issues, neither made action a legislative

priority. Even so, both presidents shaped social policy through their appointments to the Supreme Court. Reagan placed three members on the bench, including in 1981 Sandra Day O'Connor, the first woman to sit on the high court. Bush nominated two justices. As more liberal members of the Court retired (including William Brennan and Thurgood Marshall), the decisions handed down became distinctly more conservative. The appointment of Antonin Scalia in 1986 gave the Court its most outspoken conservative.

In 1991 the Senate hotly debated President Bush's nomination of Clarence Thomas, an outspoken Black conservative and former member of the Reagan administration. The confirmation hearings became even more contentious when Anita Hill, a woman who had worked for Thomas, testified that he had sexually harassed her. Women's groups blasted the all-male Judiciary Committee for keeping Hill's allegations private until reporters uncovered the story. Thomas and his defenders accused his opponents of using a disgruntled woman to help conduct a latter-day lynching. In the end the Senate narrowly voted to confirm, and Thomas joined Scalia as one of the Court's most conservative members.

Evidence of the Court's changing stance came most clearly in its attitude toward affirmative action—those laws that gave preferred treatment to minority groups with the intent of remedying past discrimination. State and federal courts and legislatures had used techniques such as busing and the setting of quotas—minimum proportional shares of minorities or women as part of an institution's makeup—to move toward equality. As early as 1978, however, the Court began to set limits on affirmative action. In *Bakke* v. *Regents of the University of California* (1978), the majority ruled that college admissions staffs could not set fixed quotas, although they could still use race as a guiding factor in trying to create a more diverse student body. Increasingly, the Court made it easier for white citizens to challenge affirmative action programs. At the same time, it set higher standards for those who wished to put forward a claim of discrimination. "An amorphous claim that there has been past discrimination in a particular industry cannot justify the use of an unyielding racial quota," wrote Justice O'Connor in 1989.

Disillusionment and Anger >> Ronald Reagan had given a sunny face to conservatism. He had assured voters that if taxes were cut, the economy would revive and deficits would fall. He promised that if "big government" could be scaled back, there would be a new "morning in America." Yet a decade of hands-off conservative leadership left the deficit ballooning and state and local governments larger than ever, with fewer resources to address the nation's needs. A growing number of Americans felt that the institutions of government had come off track. Indeed, Reagan's and Bush's attacks on big government fueled such cynicism.

A series of longer-term crises contributed to this sense of disillusionment. One of the most threatening centered on the nation's savings and loan institutions. By the end of the decade, they were failing at the highest rate since the Great Depression.

Reagan's advisers, as well as members of Congress, ignored the warnings that fraud and mismanagement had increased sharply. Only during the Bush administration did it become clear that the cost of rebuilding the savings banks and paying off huge debts might run into hundreds of billions of dollars.

The late 1980s also brought a public health crisis. Americans were spending a higher percentage of their resources on medical care than were citizens in other nations, yet they were no healthier. As medical costs soared, more than 30 million Americans had no health insurance. The crisis was worsened by a fatal disorder that physicians began diagnosing in the early 1980s: acquired immunodeficiency syndrome, or AIDS. With no cure available, the disease threatened to take on epidemic proportions not only in the United States but also around the globe. Yet because the illness at first struck hardest at the male homosexual community and intravenous drug users, many groups in American society were reluctant to address the problem.

Bank failures, skyrocketing health costs, anger over poverty and discrimination—none of these problems by itself had the power to derail the conservative revolution. Still, the various crises demonstrated how pivotal government had become in providing social services and limiting the abuses of powerful private interests in a highly industrialized society.

The Election of 1992

>> In the end, George Bush's inability to rein in soaring government deficits proved most damaging to his reelection prospects. "Read my lips! No new taxes," he pledged to campaign audiences in 1988. But the president and Congress remained at loggerheads over how to reach the holy grail of so many conservatives: a balanced budget. In 1985 Congress had passed the Gramm-Rudman Act, establishing a set of steadily increasing limits on federal spending. By 1990 the law's automatic spending limits were threatening popular programs such as Medicare. To preserve them, Bush agreed to a package of new taxes along with budget cuts. Conservatives felt betrayed, and in the end, the deficit grew larger all the same.

As the election of 1992 approached, unemployment stood at more than 8 percent, penetrating to areas of the economy not affected by most recessions. Statistics showed that wages for middle-class families had not increased since the early 1970s and had actually declined during Bush's presidency. Many Reagan Democrats seemed ready to return to the party of Franklin Roosevelt, who had mobilized an activist government in a time of economic crisis.

The Democrats nominated Governor Bill Clinton of Arkansas and his running-mate Al Gore to challenge Bush in the presidential election. Clinton arose out of the ranks of the baby boomers born after World War II. Like many of his generation he had opposed the war in Vietnam and experimented with marijuana (but "did not inhale," he assured a skeptical reporter). In the campaign he accused Bush of failing to combat the recession. "It's the economy, stupid!" read the sign tacked up at his election headquarters. Clinton painted himself as a new kind of Democrat: centrist, independent of liberal interest groups, and willing to work with business.

At the voting booth, middle-of-the-road voters turned to Clinton and, in smaller numbers, to third-party challenger H. Ross Perot. Clinton captured 43 percent of the popular vote (to Bush's 38 and Perot's 19) in the largest turnout—55 percent—in 20 years. The election of four women to the Senate, including the first African American woman, Carol Moseley Braun, indicated that gender had become an electoral factor.

The 1992 election left the fate of the conservative revolution unresolved. In foreign affairs, Reagan and Bush presided over the end of the cold war. Despite a growing isolationist sentiment among Democrats and Republicans, both presidents had shown a willingness to assert American power—in Libya, Lebanon, Nicaragua, and the Persian Gulf.

Domestically, the economy had grown and inflation had subsided. Yet prosperity benefited mostly those at the upper end of the income tax scale. Poor and average Americans saw their financial situation stagnate or grow worse. Reagan and Bush had both supported a conservative social agenda that sought to restrict abortion rights, return prayer to the schools, and end

<< As the AIDS epidemic spread in the 1980s, quilts such as these expressed sorrow for lost friends and loved ones. The quilts also served to raise public awareness of the need for a more effective policy to help people living with AIDS and fight the disease.
Kristoffer Tripplaar/Alamy Stock Photo

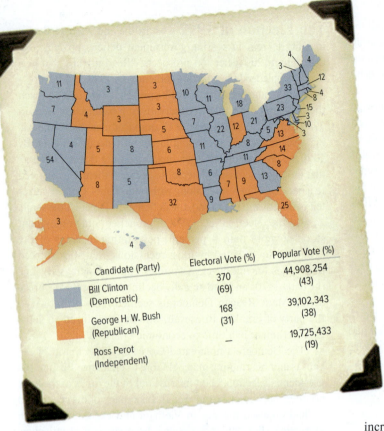

MAP 31.4: ELECTION OF 1992

Candidate (Party)	Electoral Vote (%)	Popular Vote (%)
Bill Clinton (Democratic)	370 (69)	44,908,254 (43)
George H. W. Bush (Republican)	168 (31)	39,102,343 (38)
Ross Perot (Independent)	–	19,725,433 (19)

affirmative action, but neither had done much to advance those goals. Both presidents weakened the capacity of the federal government to implement social programs. No longer did Americans expect Washington to solve all the issues of the day.

How, then, would the nation meet the needs of the increasing number of poor, minority, older, and immigrant Americans? And what role would the United States play in the post–Cold War era, as the lone superpower in the world? Those were questions for president-elect Bill Clinton as he sought to lead the United States into the post–Cold War world.

 REVIEW

What steps did Reagan, Gorbachev, and Bush take to stop the arms race and end the Cold War?

CHAPTER SUMMARY

During the years of the Carter, Reagan, and Bush administrations, the nation's political and social agenda was increasingly determined by a conservative movement, including newly politicized evangelical Christians, that sought to restore traditional religious and family values, patriotism, and a more limited role for government.

- An energy crisis brought on by Arab-Israeli conflict and an oil boycott by the OPEC nations worsened an already ailing American economy.
- Secretary of State Henry Kissinger used shuttle diplomacy to bring an uneasy peace to the Middle East. He and President Ford sought to ease diplomatic tensions by pursuing détente with the Soviet Union.
- Jimmy Carter, unable to end the recession at home, pursued success abroad with a human rights policy and the negotiation of the Camp David Accords between Israel and Egypt—only to have the Soviet invasion of Afghanistan and the Iranian hostage crisis undermine his foreign policy.
- Ronald Reagan led the conservative tide with a program to limit the power of labor unions, reduce government regulation, lower taxes, and sharply increase spending on the military.
- Despite a revived economy, Reaganomics had two undesirable outcomes: huge government budget deficits and a growing gap in income between the rich and the poor.
- Conservative appointments to the federal judiciary and the Supreme Court led to decisions increasing limits on government intervention in the areas of civil rights, affirmative action, abortion rights, and the separation of church and state.
- Reagan's efforts to "stand tall" in foreign policy led to the Iran-Contra scandal, which revealed a broad pattern of illegal arms shipments to right-wing rebels in Nicaragua and the trading of arms to Iran in an unsuccessful attempt to win the release of hostages in Lebanon—actions for which the president was sharply criticized but not impeached.
- Both Reagan and George Bush welcomed reforms set in motion by Mikhail Gorbachev that led by 1991 to the breakup of the Soviet Union, reductions in nuclear arms, and an end to the Cold War.
- In the post–Cold War era, regional conflicts proved more troublesome as Iraq's invasion of Kuwait led Bush to form a UN coalition that routed the forces of Saddam Hussein in Operation Desert Storm.
- For George Bush a continuing recession, high budget deficits, and high unemployment undermined his bid for reelection.

Digging Deeper

Bruce Shulman, *The Seventies* (2002), follows the transition from the 1960s to the Reagan era. Judith Stein, *Pivotal Decade: How the United States Traded Factories for Finance in the Seventies* (2010), explores economic trends. An intriguing look at cultural trends is Philip Jenkins, *Decade of Nightmares: The End of the Sixties and the Making of Eighties*

America (2006). An even-handed treatment of Jimmy Carter is Robert A. Strong, *Working in the World: Jimmy Carter and the Making of American Foreign Policy* (2000). Two books that look favorably on Ronald Reagan and the politics of the right are John Ehrman, *The Eighties: America in the Age of Reagan* (2006); and Gil Troy, *Morning in America: How Ronald Reagan Invented the 1980s* (2005). Considering the transformation into the digital world is Fred Turner, *From Counterculture to Cyberculture: Stewart Brand, the Whole Earth Network, and the Rise of Digital Utopianism* (2006).

A rich source for understanding the divisions in American politics is Danial T. Rogers, *The Age of Fracture* (2012). Steven Miller, *The Age of Evangelicalism: America's Born Again Years* (2013), explores the evangelicals' return to politics.

Randall Balmer, *Mine Eyes Have Seen the Glory: A Journey into the Evangelical Subculture in America* (2006), offers the perspectives of someone raised in the evangelical tradition. The issue of income inequality is well explained in Jefferson Cowie, *Stayin' Alive: The 1970s and the Last Days of the Working Class* (2010). Racial currents of the era are powerfully conveyed in Nicholas Lemann, *The Promised Land* (1995). The reasonably friendly treatment of George H. W. Bush by Ryan Barilleaux and Mark Rozell, *Power and Prudence: The Presidency of George H. W. Bush* (2004), can moderate the often insightful Kevin Phillips, *American Dynasty: Aristocracy, Fortune, and the Politics of Deceit* (2004). On military operations in the first Gulf War see Rick Lowry, *The Gulf War Chronicles: A Military History of the First War with Iraq* (2008).

32 The United States in a Global Community

1989–Present

Farmworkers harvest lettuce, a backbreaking "stoop crop," in California's Imperial Valley. Between 1990 and 2020 more than 30 million legal immigrants arrived in the United States, underlining the global nature of the American community and economy.

Jenny E. Ross/Getty Images

>> An American Story

OF GROCERY CHAINS AND MIGRATION CHAINS

Juan Chanax was born in San Cristóbal, a small village in the Guatemalan highlands. In that region, some 2,000 years earlier, his Maya ancestors had created one of the world's great civilizations. During the twentieth century, San Cristóbal had escaped the political upheavals that disrupted much of

Guatemala. All the same, Chanax struggled to earn enough at a nearby American textile factory to support his young family. His relatives discouraged him from seeking a job in the United States: "All you will eat there will come out of cans and the only job they will give you is sweeping trash." Still, in 1978 he decided that the only way he could help his sick son and improve himself was to go north. After a difficult journey, Chanax reached Houston, Texas, with a letter introducing him to several Guatemalans. Through them he learned of a job at a Randall's supermarket.

In the late 1970s, high oil prices brought a boom to Houston. As the city prospered, Randall's expanded. That expansion meant plenty of low-wage jobs for people like Chanax, even though he had almost no education and had entered the United States illegally. Randall's did not want just any low-wage workers. The chain specialized in high-priced goods in fancy suburban stores. Its upscale customers received valet parking, hassle-free shopping, and service from uniformed employees. Shortly before Chanax began work, one of Randall's managers had quarreled with several African American employees. The argument had escalated, until one employee finally threw a mop at the manager and quit.

The incident gave Chanax an opportunity. Unlike the worker who stormed out, he was willing to do any job without complaint—and the pay was more than twice what he received in Guatemala. Within several weeks he began to wire money home to his family. And when the manager said Randall's would soon need more workers, Chanax arranged for relatives to come north. Over time Randall's appointed him to hire Guatemalans exclusively.

Within five years the grocery chain employed more than a thousand Maya from San Cristóbal. A single person had created what scholars call a migration chain. Through Chanax, the supermarket found a minimum-wage workforce who would perform willingly—in the company's words—as "cheerful servants." The Maya, in turn, found opportunities unavailable in Guatemala. Chanax and other early immigrants became department managers and supervising assistants. Many of their wives worked as maids and servants in the homes of Houston's upper-income communities.

Juan Chanax and his fellow Guatemalans embody the classic tale of immigrants realizing the American Dream. In suburban Houston they formed their own community in an area that came to be known as Las Americas. There, Central American immigrants established churches and social clubs amid some 90 apartment complexes. The growth of Las Americas in the late twentieth century echoed the growth of other immigrant communities at the century's opening.

Immigration patterns had changed in important ways. Although cities remained the destination of most immigrants, many newcomers of the 1980s and 1990s settled in suburban areas, particularly in the West and Southwest. Industrial factories had provided the lion's share of work in the 1890s, but a century later the service industries—grocery stores, fast-food chains, janitorial positions—absorbed many more of the new arrivals. Even the faces had changed, as European immigration dwindled while that from Mexico and Central America as well as the Philippines, China, Korea, Southeast Asia, and the Indian subcontinent increased. Russians, Arabs, Africans, and Eastern Europeans also joined the ranks of newcomers.

The global nature of immigration was only one aspect of an American society more tightly linked to the world community. With the end of the Cold War, diplomacy shifted toward managing regional conflicts. The international economy forged close links. A financial collapse in Thailand or a bank default in France could easily spread to other countries in a matter of weeks or even days. Finally, the dawn of the twenty-first century witnessed a communication revolution as the Internet tied together correspondents, consumers, manufacturers, and information systems. The movement of people, financial capital, and data around the globe forced a nation of nations to adapt. And not least, the threat of terrorism was evidence of the dark side of that globalism. <<

Juan Chanax.
©Robert Suro/Alicia Patterson Foundation

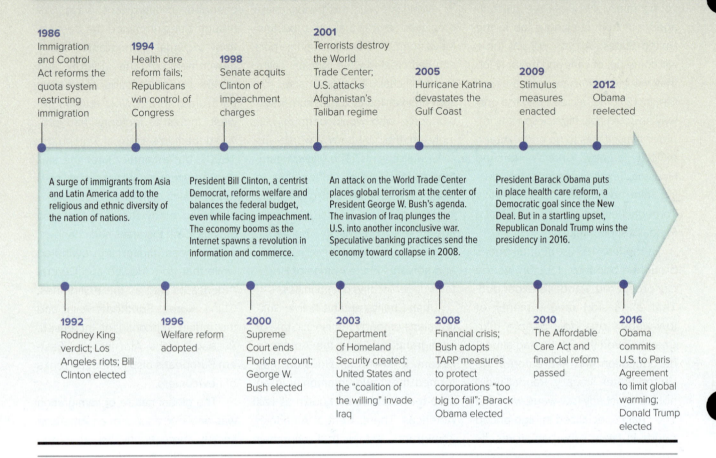

1986
Immigration and Control Act reforms the quota system restricting immigration

1994
Health care reform fails; Republicans win control of Congress

1998
Senate acquits Clinton of impeachment charges

2001
Terrorists destroy the World Trade Center; U.S. attacks Afghanistan's Taliban regime

2005
Hurricane Katrina devastates the Gulf Coast

2009
Stimulus measures enacted

2012
Obama reelected

A surge of immigrants from Asia and Latin America add to the religious and ethnic diversity of the nation of nations.

President Bill Clinton, a centrist Democrat, reforms welfare and balances the federal budget, even while facing impeachment. The economy booms as the Internet spawns a revolution in information and commerce.

An attack on the World Trade Center places global terrorism at the center of President George W. Bush's agenda. The invasion of Iraq plunges the U.S. into another inconclusive war. Speculative banking practices send the economy toward collapse in 2008.

President Barack Obama puts in place health care reform, a Democratic goal since the New Deal. But in a startling upset, Republican Donald Trump wins the presidency in 2016.

1992
Rodney King verdict; Los Angeles riots; Bill Clinton elected

1996
Welfare reform adopted

2000
Supreme Court ends Florida recount; George W. Bush elected

2003
Department of Homeland Security created; United States and the "coalition of the willing" invade Iraq

2008
Financial crisis; Bush adopts TARP measures to protect corporations "too big to fail"; Barack Obama elected

2010
The Affordable Care Act and financial reform passed

2016
Obama commits U.S. to Paris Agreement to limit global warming; Donald Trump elected

THE NEW IMMIGRATION

The Immigration Act of 1965 (see Chapter 29) altered the face of American life—perhaps more than any other legislation from Lyndon Johnson's Great Society. Those who passed the act assumed that the newcomers would continue to be Europeans. Yet reform of the old quota system opened the way for a new wave of immigrants unequaled since the beginning of the century.

More than 30 million immigrants arrived legally in the United States between 1990 and 2020, and millions more illegally. The greatest numbers came from Asia (People's Republic of China, the Philippines, and India) and Latin America (Mexico, Cuba, Central America, and Colombia). Immigrants settled largely in seven states: California, New York, Florida, Texas, Pennsylvania, New Jersey, and Illinois. The influx raised the nation's foreign-born population to about 12 percent—a significant percentage, though lower than

the high-water mark of 20 percent in 1900. The numbers were especially concentrated among the young. As of 2015 a quarter of the residents of the United States under 18 were immigrants or immigrants' children. When the nation prospered in the 1990s, Americans welcomed these newcomers as a vital source of labor. But when the economy went into recession in 2008, immigration again became a divisive political issue.

The New Look of the United States—Asian Americans >> In 1970, 96 percent of Asian Americans were Japanese, Chinese, or Filipino. By the year 2000, those same three groups made up only about half of that group, as Asian Indians, Koreans, and Vietnamese joined the incoming stream. The newcomers also varied dramatically in economic background.

The higher end included many Chinese students who, beginning in the 1960s, sought out the United States for a college education, then found a job and stayed, eventually bringing in their families. Asian Indians were even more acculturated upon arrival because about two-thirds entered the United States with college degrees in hand. Indian engineers

PROJECTED POPULATION SHIFTS, 1980–2050

The millions of immigrants who arrived between 1990 and 2015 accounted for 32 percent of the increase in the total U.S. population. Census figures project an increasing racial and ethnic diversity. White population is projected to drop from 80 percent in 1980 to about 53 percent in 2050, with the nation's Latino population rising most sharply.
(background photo) Ryan McVay/Getty Images

played a vital role in the computer and software industries. Korean and Filipino professionals also took skilled jobs, particularly in medical fields.

Many highly educated Asian immigrants found it difficult to land jobs in their professions. To American observers, Korean shopkeepers seemed examples of success, when in fact such owners often enough had been professionals before emigrating. One Filipino surgeon, unable to open his own medical practice, found himself working as a restaurant meat cutter, for employers who had no idea of his training. "They thought I was very good at separating meat from the bone," he commented ironically.

The New Look of the United States— Latinos >> Like Asian Americans, Latino newcomers in the United States came from dozens of immigrant streams.

Although the groups shared a language, they usually settled in distinct urban and suburban barrios across the United States. Such enclaves provided support to newcomers and an economic foothold for newly established businesses. Money tended to circulate within a community and support it. For example, the workers and owners of an ethnic grocery might spend their wages at neighboring stores, whose profits fueled other immigrant businesses.

Washington Heights, at the northern tip of New York City, became such an enclave, as nearly a quarter of a million Dominicans settled there in the 1970s and 1980s. Shopkeepers' stereos boomed songs featuring trumpets and congas, while peddlers pushed heavily loaded shopping carts through busy streets, crying "¡A peso! ¡A peso!" ("For a dollar!"). In addition, Dominican social clubs planned dances and hosted political discussions. Similarly, in Miami and elsewhere in South Florida, Cuban Americans created their own enclaves. A large professional class and strong community leadership brought prosperity and political influence.

Along the West Coast, Los Angeles was the magnet for many Latino (and Asian) immigrants. Mexicans had long flocked to East Los Angeles, which was convenient to jobs in factories, warehouses, and railroad yards across the river. Many Mexican Americans now owned businesses and homes in East LA. By the 1990s, the neighborhood of MacArthur Park became the focal point for the newest immigrants from Mexico and Central America. Because Mexico and the United States share a long common border where peoples and cultures mingle, many Mexicans have entered the United States illegally. That illegal flow increased during the 1980s, and now included Central Americans. By 1985 the number of illegal immigrants in the United States was estimated at anywhere from 2 to 12 million.

Congress tried to stem the tide with the Immigration and Control Act of 1986. Tightened border security was coupled with a requirement that American employers certify their workers as legal residents. At the same time, illegal immigrants who had arrived before 1986 were allowed to become legal residents. In the end, however, the law failed to create the clean slate Congress had hoped for. Worried about a labor shortage, California's fruit and vegetable growers gained exceptions to the rules.

Religious Diversity >> The new immigration also reshaped religious faiths in the United States. During the 1950s, most Americans' sense of religious diversity encompassed

Sikhs—seen marching here in the New York City annual Sikh Day Parade in 2003—trace their origins to India's Punjab region.
JENNIFER SZYMASZEK/Associated Press/AP Images

the mainline Protestant churches, Roman Catholicism, and Judaism. But immigrants brought with them not only their own brands of Christianity and Judaism but also Buddhist, Hindu, and Islamic beliefs. By 2009 there were perhaps 2 to 3 million Muslims in the United States. Many had emigrated from Arab states, but adherents from South Asia made up an even greater number. Buddhists and Hindus numbered about a million adherents each.

Mainline Protestants and Catholics changed as well. The Presbyterian Church (U.S.A.) grew from about 20 Korean-speaking congregations in 1970 to over 350 by the turn of the century. In New York City, Episcopalian services were held in 14 different languages. And Catholic churches increasingly found themselves celebrating mass in both English and Spanish. Such arrangements took place not only in urban congregations, but increasingly even in rural areas, like Columbus Junction, Iowa, whose Catholic church was energized by Mexican Americans working in a nearby meat-processing plant.

Whatever their religion or point of origin, the new immigrants found it easier to maintain links with their home country in an increasingly interdependent world. In the 1980s Pacoima, a small suburban barrio near Burbank, California, boasted 13 different currency exchanges to handle the funds that immigrants wired home to relatives. By 1992 the amount of money sent worldwide was so great that it was surpassed in volume only by the currency flows of the global oil trade.

 REVIEW

What were the major sources of immigration during the 1980s and 1990s, and how did the composition of those immigrants change from earlier decades?

THE CLINTON PRESIDENCY

In 1993, William Jefferson Clinton became the first baby boomer to occupy the White House. His wife, Hillary Rodham Clinton, would be the most politically involved presidential wife since Eleanor Roosevelt. Like so many couples of their generation, the Clintons were a two-career family. Bill chose politics as his career, becoming governor in his home state of Arkansas, while Hillary mixed private legal practice with public service. Their marriage had not been easy. Revelations of Clinton's sexual affairs almost ruined his presidential campaign.

Clinton chose to be an activist president. He pledged to revive the economy and rein in the federal deficit, which had grown enormously during the Bush-Reagan years. Beyond that, he called for systematic reform of the welfare and health care systems as well as measures to reduce the increasing violence that had turned many urban neighborhoods into war zones. An activist executive could achieve much, he believed, with "a disciplined, aggressive agenda."

The new president's desire for major initiatives ran up against the election results of 1992. Clinton had received just 43 percent of the popular vote, while the Republicans had narrowed the Democratic majorities in Congress. Furthermore, the president's high energy levels did not always seem to be directed solely at his political agenda. One observer shrewdly noted that there were two Bill Clintons—the idealistic young man from Hope, Arkansas (his hometown), and the boy from Hot Springs (his mother's home). The latter was a resort town associated with the seamier side of Arkansas night life. With increasing frequency, the character flaws of the boy from Hot Springs undermined the leadership exercised by the idealistic politician from Hope.

The New World Disorder >> Clinton's plan to concentrate on domestic rather than foreign policy ran into the realities of regional disorders. By using American power in a limited way, Clinton gained considerable public support.

In sub-Saharan Africa, brutal civil wars broke out in both Somalia and Rwanda. As president-elect, Clinton had supported President Bush's decision in December 1992 to send troops to aid famine-relief efforts in Somalia. But attempts to install a stable government proved difficult. Tragically, the United States as well as European nations failed to intervene in Rwanda before more than a million Hutu people were massacred.

Europe's most difficult trouble spot proved to be Yugoslavia, a nation divided by ethnic rivalries within a number of provinces, including Serbia, Croatia, Kosovo, and Bosnia. After Bosnia became independent in 1992 both Serbs and Croats, but especially the Serbs, resorted to what was euphemistically referred to as "ethnic cleansing"—the massacre of rival populations—to secure control. The United States at first viewed the civil war in Yugoslavia as Europe's problem. But as the civilian death toll mounted to a quarter of a million, the conflict became difficult to ignore.

Many members of Congress feared the prospect of American troops bogged down in a civil war, as had happened in Vietnam. Over Republican objections, Clinton committed the United States to support NATO bombing of Serb forces and then brokered peace talks held in Dayton, Ohio. The Dayton Accords created separate Croatian, Bosnian, and Serbian nations. Some 60,000 NATO troops, including 20,000 Americans, moved into Bosnia to enforce the peace. Clinton had intervened successfully without the loss of American lives.

Clinton also worked to mediate conflict in the Middle East. Sporadic protests and rioting by Palestinians in the Israeli-occupied territories of Gaza and the West Bank gave way in the 1990s to negotiations. At a ceremony hosted by the president in 1993, Palestinian leader Yasir Arafat and Israeli prime minister Itzak Rabin signed a peace agreement permitting self-rule for Palestinians in the Gaza Strip and in Jericho on the West Bank. Still, a full settlement remained elusive. Whether in the Middle East, Eastern Europe, Africa, or the Caribbean, regional crises demonstrated how difficult it was to maintain a new global "world order."

Recovery without Reform at Home >> Throughout Clinton's presidency the nation experienced a powerful economic expansion, which sustained his popularity despite a sex scandal and attacks by conservatives. But the increasing prosperity did not provide Clinton the momentum to enact his ambitious plan for health care reform.

Reversing the deficits of the Reagan and Bush years was the president's first domestic goal. He also proposed investments to stimulate the economy and repair the nation's decaying public infrastructure. In August 1993 a compromise budget bill passed by only a single vote in the Senate, with Republicans blocking the stimulus portion of the program. Still, deficit reduction was a significant achievement. And victory in the budget battle provided Clinton the necessary leverage to pass the North American Free Trade Agreement (NAFTA). With the promise of greater trade and more jobs, the pact linked the U.S. economy more closely with those of Canada and Mexico.

Gun control became more contentious as the National Rifle Association and its congressional allies fought against any restrictions. The president overcame NRA resistance to pass the 1993 Brady Bill, which required a five-day waiting period on gun purchases. In 1994 Congress adopted a 10-year ban on assault weapons and some large-capacity magazines.

But health care reform topped the legislative agenda for both Clintons. Hillary Clinton led a task force to design a

>> President Clinton's most ambitious reform aimed to overhaul the nation's health care system to provide all Americans with basic health care. Medical interest groups lobbied successfully to defeat the proposal.
Jeffrey Markowitz/Sygma/Getty Images

plan to provide insurance for all Americans, including the 37 million who in 1994 remained uninsured. It was not to be. A host of interest groups rallied to defeat the proposal, especially small businesses that worried that they would bear the brunt of the system's financing. The failure of health care reform heightened the perception of an ill-organized administration and a Congress content with the status quo. The 1994 midterm elections confirmed the public's anger over political gridlock, as Republicans captured majorities in both the House and the Senate.

The Conservative Revolution Reborn >> When the new Congress assembled, the combative Speaker of the House, Newt Gingrich of Georgia, proclaimed himself a "genuine revolutionary." Gingrich used the first hundred days of the new session to vote on 10 proposals from his campaign document "The Contract with America." The contract proposed a balanced-budget amendment, tax cuts, and term limits for all members of Congress. To promote family values, an anticrime package included a broader death penalty and welfare restrictions aimed at reducing teen pregnancy. Although the term-limits proposal did not survive, the House passed the other 9 proposals. "When you look back five years from now," boasted a Republican leader, "you're going to say 'they came, they saw, they conquered.'"

But the Senate was in a less revolutionary mood, and the public worried about what Gingrich and his rebels proposed. To balance the federal budget and still cut taxes, they planned to reduce Medicare expenditures while allowing premiums to double. They also sought to roll back environmental protections for endangered species, pollution controls set up by the Clean Water Act, and restrictions on mining, ranching, and logging on public lands.

When Clinton threatened to veto the Republican budget, Republicans forced a confrontation by shutting down the federal government for 27 days. Older adults on Social Security, visitors to national parks, and soldiers on active duty all felt the consequences and Congress retreated.

In the end, the president made some of the Republican agenda his own. He adopted a balanced budget and signed into law a sweeping reform of welfare. The bill ended guaranteed federal aid to poor children and turned over programs to the states. Food stamp spending was cut, and under welfare-to-work requirements, most adults receiving payments had to find a job within two years. With a robust economy in full swing, voters readily supported Bill Clinton's reelection bid in 1996. The president became the first Democrat since Franklin Roosevelt to win a second term in the White House.

Women's Issues >> As First Lady, Hillary Clinton used her influence to promote opportunity for women and to draw attention to feminist issues. Bill Clinton shared many of his wife's concerns, and appointed Ruth Bader Ginsburg to the Supreme Court as well as four women to cabinet posts, including Madeleine Albright as the first female secretary of state. Women continued to assume higher profiles in such formerly male-dominated professions as law, medicine, veterinary medicine, and business, though they still lagged in the so-called STEM areas of science, technology, engineering, and math.

Both Clintons supported a woman's right to make her own decisions on reproduction, an issue that remained hotly contested. Because antiabortion conservatives had been unable to secure the repeal of *Roe* v. *Wade*, they sought to limit its application as much as possible.

Scandal >> Almost every two-term president has faced some crisis in his second term. Watergate brought down Richard Nixon, and the Iran-Contra controversy tarnished Reagan. Bill Clinton's scandal was in some ways more puzzling. At once smaller and more personal, it nonetheless threatened him with the ultimate constitutional sanction: **impeachment**, conviction, and removal from office.

> **impeachment** the constitutional process whereby members of the House of Representatives bring charges against a government official for "Treason, Bribery, or other high Crimes and Misdemeanors." If impeached, the individual is tried before the Senate, where a vote of two-thirds is needed to convict. Conviction results in removal from office.

ʌ "I am a genuine revolutionary," House Speaker Newt Gingrich proclaimed. Illustrator Anita Kunz associated Gingrich and his followers with Mussolini and overzealous Black Shirts.
Illustration by Anita Kunz for the New Yorker Magazine. Anita Kunz Limited. Reproduced by permission of the artist

Conservative Republicans who disliked Clinton referred to him derisively as "Slick Willie." During his first term they pressured Attorney General Janet Reno to appoint Kenneth Starr as a special prosecutor to investigate the president's involvement in an old Arkansas real estate venture known as Whitewater. Years of digging and millions of dollars later, neither Starr nor two Senate committees had produced any evidence of wrongdoing. Then in January 1998 Starr hit what looked like a political jackpot. A former Bush administration appointee had secretly taped her conversations with White House intern Monica Lewinsky who revealed that she and the president had had an affair in the White House.

Without revealing the tapes existed, Starr deposed the president and Lewinsky about their relationship. Both swore under oath that they had not had "sexual relations." Then news leaked about the tapes. Political pundits generally agreed that the president would have to resign or face impeachment—if not for his indiscretion with Lewinsky, then for lying under oath.

To the astonishment of the news media, polling indicated that impeachment had little public support. Although most Americans disapproved of Clinton's behavior, they seemed to distinguish between public and private actions. The Republican majority in the House pressed their attack anyway, voting three articles of impeachment for lying to the grand jury, encouraging perjury, and orchestrating a cover-up. In January 1999 the matter went to the Senate for trial. Unlike with the Watergate scandals, in which a bipartisan consensus had determined that impeachment was necessary, the accusers and defenders of Bill Clinton divided along party lines. The Senate voted to acquit, with 5 Republicans joining all 45 Senate Democrats in the decision.

The impeachment controversy left the president weakened, but hardly powerless. Throughout the political tempest the nation's economy grew strongly. By 1999 the rate of unemployment had dropped to 4.1 percent, the lowest in nearly 30 years. As the economy expanded, federal tax receipts grew with it. By 1998 Bill Clinton faced a situation that would have seemed improbable at the beginning of his term—a budget surplus.

✔ **REVIEW**

What were President Clinton's greatest successes and failures in foreign and domestic policy?

The Election of 2000 >> Al Gore, Bill Clinton's vice president, received the Democratic presidential nomination in 2000. Both Gore and his Republican opponent, George W. Bush (the son of former president George H. W. Bush), ran cautious, centrist campaigns. Pollsters predicted a race "too close to call," but none were prepared for the razor-thin

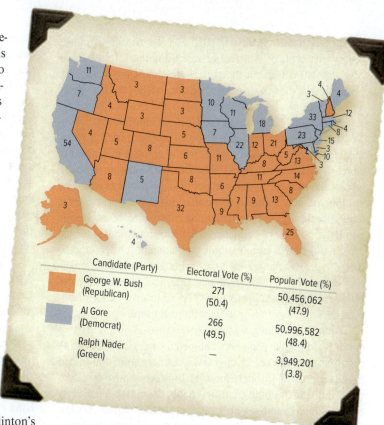

Candidate (Party)	Electoral Vote (%)	Popular Vote (%)
George W. Bush (Republican)	271 (50.4)	50,456,062 (47.9)
Al Gore (Democrat)	266 (49.5)	50,996,582 (48.4)
Ralph Nader (Green)	—	3,949,201 (3.8)

MAP 32.1: ELECTION OF 2000

margin. The outcome came down to Florida, where, two days after the election, Bush led by just 300 votes. Nationwide, Gore held a lead of 500,000 in the popular vote, but without Florida's 25 electoral votes neither candidate could claim a majority in the Electoral College. In *Bush* v. *Gore*, the Supreme Court's conservative majority, all Republican appointees, ruled 5–4 to end the recount of contested Florida ballots. The unelected Court, rather than the American voter, made George W. Bush the president of the United States.

THE UNITED STATES IN A NETWORKED WORLD

In 1988 economist Lawrence Summers was in Chicago working on the Michael Dukakis presidential campaign. When the staff assigned him a car with a telephone, Summers was so impressed, he called his wife to tell her. A decade later as a member of the Clinton administration, he visited a village in Africa's Ivory Coast that could be reached only by dugout canoe. As Summers stepped into the canoe for his return trip, an aide handed him a cell phone: "Washington has a question for you."

The Internet Revolution >> By the dawn of the twenty-first century, Americans were using the Internet to access a global communications network almost anywhere they went. Most of the scientists who had created the Internet shared a democratic vision of the web as open and free to all, without restrictions and with access to any form of information.

Such openness was the bane of authoritarian governments. They struggled to control public opinion in a world in which information flowed freely. But the web's unregulated format raised legal, moral, and political questions as well. The millions of sites included those that dispensed pornography, hate speech, and even instructions on how to build atomic bombs. A number of politicians and civic groups called for the censorship of the more extreme web content. Others argued that the greater danger lay in allowing large telecommunication companies to dominate the Internet. These advocates called for legislation protecting "Net neutrality." That meant providers could not favor those who paid more.

Equally intriguing was the emergence of a new virtual culture. Computer engineers competed to devise effective algorithms to power search engines, a business soon dominated by Google. And through Internet browsers and other software, individuals could chat, find a job, download music, buy and sell merchandise, or locate potential mates. Within 10 years, political blogs offered instant responses to the issues of the day. Grassroots organizations formed mass social and political movements using e-mail and networking sites such as Facebook, Twitter, and Snapchat. Virtual communities came into being in cyberspace. No longer did people have to turn to major media outlets to stay in touch with the news.

The revolution in microchip technologies contributed substantially to the economic expansion of the 1990s. Whereas in 1965 businesses had committed just 3 percent of their spending to high technology, they were committing 45 percent in 1996. That increase contributed to a significant rise in labor productivity, a critical factor in economic growth. Online merchandiser Amazon.com and others began to challenge such giant brick-and-mortar retailers as Sears and Walmart. By 1998 e-commerce was generating nearly half a million jobs.

American Workers in a Two-Tiered Economy >> The benefits of prosperity were not evenly distributed. Economists described the United States after the 1980s as a two-tiered labor market in which most increases in earning went to people with the highest wages. Despite prosperity, the median income of American families was barely higher in 2018 than in 1973. Indeed, the earnings of the average white male worker actually fell. Only because so many women entered the job market did the family standard of living remain the same. In the early 1970s some 37 percent of women over 16 worked outside the home; in 2010 about 58 percent did.

Education was a critical factor in determining winners in the high-tech, global economy. In the early years of the Internet, families with college-educated parents were three times more likely to have home access than those in which parents' education ended with high school. Because average education levels were relatively lower among African Americans and Latinos (and relatively higher among Asian Americans), the computer divide took on a racial cast. The implications went beyond mere access to the web and its wealth of information and commerce. The high-wage sector of the computer economy required educated workers, and the demand for them drove up their salaries. Most semiskilled and unskilled workers saw little growth in earnings despite full employment. "The most important economic division is not between races, or genders, or economic sectors," one economist argued, "but between the college-educated and the non-college-educated."

The Persistence of a Racial Divide >> In the 1990s the highest-paid celebrity in the world was an African American basketball star—Michael Jordan. Oprah Winfrey, also an African American and media mogul, was among the wealthiest women in the United States. Although the situation of African Americans had improved vastly since the 1950s, race still mattered, as the case of Rodney King showed.

In 1991 Los Angeles police officers, all white, arrested King for speeding and drunken driving. As King lay on the ground, four officers proceeded to beat him with nightsticks more than 50 times. When Blacks complained about such police brutality, public officials often ignored them. But this time a man in a nearby apartment videotaped the beating, which the news media broadcast to the entire nation. Yet the following year, an all-white suburban jury acquitted the officers, concluding that King had been threatening and that the officers had acted within their authority.

The verdict enraged the African American community in Los Angeles, where widespread riots erupted for three days. It was the worst civil disturbance in the city's history. By the time order was restored, nearly 2,000 people had been injured, 40 people had died, more than 4,500 fires burned, and $500 million of property had been looted, damaged, or destroyed.

The 1992 riots were multiracial in character, exposing divisions in Los Angeles's multicultural communities. Rioters, both Black and Latino, damaged more than 2,000 small groceries, liquor stores, and other businesses run by Korean American immigrants. African Americans also attacked Latinos; and after the first day, Latinos joined in the disturbances. But there was a revealing pattern. In the more established Latino communities of East Los Angeles, where families had more to lose, residents remained quiet or worked actively to maintain the peace. In contrast, fires and looting destroyed many businesses in the MacArthur Park area, where the newest Latino immigrants lived.

African Americans in a Full-Employment Economy >> The prosperity of the late 1990s did benefit African Americans in increasing numbers. Homeownership

^ The Los Angeles riots of 1992 revealed divisions in the city's multicultural communities of African Americans, Latinos, and Asian Americans, as well as between those communities and the predominantly white police force.
Don Emmert/AFP/Getty Images

Global Pressures in a Multicultural United States

>> Clearly the transformations wrought by the new global economy affected not just the immigrant enclaves but American culture as a whole. Salsa rhythms became part of the pop-culture mainstream, and Latino foods competed with Indian curries, Japanese sushi, and Thai takeout.

During the 1990s immigration restriction again became a goal of citizens worried that the United States would lose its national identity if it became too diverse. Lawrence Auster published *The Path to National Suicide* (1990), in which he complained of the "browning of America." In California, opponents of immigration supported Proposition 187, a ballot initiative that denied health, education, and welfare benefits to illegal immigrants. Despite the opposition of most major religious, ethnic, and educational organizations, the measure passed with 59 percent of the vote. In the end, the proposition did not go into effect because a federal judge ruled unconstitutional the provision denying education to children of illegal immigrants.

Although the tides of immigration diminished somewhat over the next decades, the issue of illegal immigration and how to deal with it remains contentious. Even the idea of a "nation" takes on new meaning in a global economy in which jobs, people, and goods move wherever markets for them exist. As international migrations bring new people to the shores of the United States, the American political system will continue to evolve ways of encompassing a diversity that now reflects the entire world.

 REVIEW

How did the Internet and multiculturalism reflect a new global order?

TERRORISM IN A GLOBAL AGE

reached 46 percent, and employment increased significantly as well. Some African Americans became leaders of corporate America. Others started their own businesses. Within the nation's inner cities, crime and poverty decreased, especially rates of murder and violence. Fewer Blacks lived below the poverty level and fewer were on welfare than in the 1980s.

Opposition to affirmative action continued to concern civil rights leaders. In 1996 California voters passed a ballot initiative, Proposition 209, that eliminated racial and gender preferences in hiring and college admissions. The proposition's leading advocate, a conservative Black business executive, argued that racial preferences patronized Black and other minority students by suggesting they could not compete on an equal basis. Proposition 209 had a striking effect: enrollments of Latinos and Blacks at the elite California universities dropped sharply. Similar laws banning racial preference in admissions resulted in enrollment declines at leading state universities in Texas, Washington, and Michigan.

The Supreme Court addressed the issue in 2003, when it ruled on the University of Michigan's affirmative action admissions program, in *Gratz* v. *Bollinger*. Michigan's point system, the Court argued, was unconstitutional, because it gave minorities preference in undergraduate admissions. At the same time, the Court did not remove race as a consideration in the admissions process. In so doing the justices allowed the nation's public universities as well as other institutions to consider race in less overt ways. Affirmative action had been reduced in scope, but not abolished.

On September 11, 2001, Francis Ledesma was sitting in his office on the sixty-fourth floor of the South Tower of the World Trade Center, when a friend suggested they go for coffee. In the cafeteria he heard and felt a muffled thump: a boiler exploding, he thought. But then he saw bricks and glass falling by the window. When he started to head back to his office for a nine o'clock meeting, his friend insisted they leave immediately. Out on the street Francis saw the smoke and gaping hole where American Airlines Flight 11 had hit the North Tower. At that moment a huge fireball erupted as United Airlines Flight 175 hit their own South Tower. "We kept looking back," Francis recalled as they escaped the area, "and then all of a sudden our building, Tower 2, collapsed. I really thought that it was a mirage."

That was only the beginning of the horror. Shortly after takeoff from Dulles Airport, American Airlines Flight 77 veered from its path and crashed into the Pentagon. Several passengers on United Airlines Flight 93 from Newark to San Francisco heard the news over their cell phones before hijackers seized their plane. Rather than allow another attack, passengers stormed the cockpit. Moments later the plane crashed into a wooded area of western Pennsylvania.

Not since Pearl Harbor had the United States experienced such a devastating strike on its homeland. Most directly the tragedy claimed approximately 3,000 lives. More than 20,000 residents living in Lower Manhattan had to evacuate their homes. The attack had economic consequences as well. Before September 11 the booming economy of the 1990s was already showing signs of strain, as overextended technology companies cut back or went out of business. The World Trade Center attack pushed the nation into a recession.

The attacks were not the work of enemy nations but of an Arab terrorist group known as al-Qaeda, led by a shadowy figure, Saudi national Osama bin Laden. After the World Trade Center attack, the United States focused less on the danger from other nations and more on terrorism, initiated by local and regional groups, such as Hamas and Hezbollah, and international actors like al-Qaeda.

A Conservative Agenda at Home >> Bush's inaugural address promised a moderate course but his influential

White House adviser Karl Rove persuaded him to rule as a conservative. Vice President Richard Cheney pushed a similar approach favoring massive tax cuts, fewer social programs, and less government regulation, especially of the energy industry. When Cheney brought the industry's leaders together in the summer of 2001 to discuss policy, he included no one from the environmental community.

Tax cuts formed the cornerstone of the Bush agenda. Many conservatives wanted lower taxes in order to limit the government's ability to initiate new policies—a strategy referred to as "starving the beast." With a recession looming, Bush defended his proposals as a means to boost the economy and create jobs. Congress supported the proposed cuts, passing the first in 2001 and another the following year. The cuts did little to create jobs and earners in high-income brackets received most of the benefits. Very quickly the federal budget surpluses of the late 1990s turned into massive deficits.

Unilateralism in Foreign Affairs >> Even before the events of September 11, the president rejected multilateralism—the policy of working together with international allies—that had guided American presidents, including his father, since World War II. Bush was determined that the United States would play a global role largely on its own terms. In particular, conservatives bitterly distrusted the United Nations as rife with corruption and an impediment to forceful action.

Bush's unilateral approach became clear when he rejected the 1997 Kyoto Protocol on global warming to which 178 nations had subscribed. "We have no interest in implementing that treaty," announced Christie Whitman, head of the Environmental Protection Agency. She argued that compliance would add an unfair burden on American energy producers. Environmentalists around the globe protested the decision. With only 4 percent of the world's population, the United States produced about 25 percent of the Earth's greenhouse gas emissions.

The tragedy of September 11 reoriented American foreign policy priorities. At home the president was careful to distinguish between the majority of "peace-loving" Muslims and "evildoers" such as Osama bin Laden. But he made it clear that the enemy was "a radical network of terrorists" and that governments around the world had a simple choice: "Either you are with us or you are with the terrorists."

In a struggle with so many shadowy opponents, it was not easy to agree on which radical groups most threatened American security. The network spread across dozens of nations, and in most cases was not a

⌃ The Cold War of the 1950s had imagined a Manhattan like this after a nuclear attack: debris everywhere, buildings in ruin, the city shrouded in smoke and fumes. On September 11, 2001, disaster on such a scale came not from confrontation with another superpower but through the actions of international terrorists.
Doug Kanter/AFP/Getty Images

network at all. Even the states hospitable to al-Qaeda proved hard to single out. Afghanistan was an obvious target. It was the seat of the Taliban, extreme Islamic fundamentalists, and a haven for bin Laden. Yet 15 of the 19 hijackers in the World Trade Center attacks hailed from Saudi Arabia, long an ally of the United States.

The Roots of Terror

>> Before September 11 Americans had paid little attention to terrorist movements. Indeed, only a few American radicals had resorted to terrorism. In 1995 Timothy McVeigh, a right-wing terrorist, detonated a bomb that killed 161 people in the federal building in Oklahoma City. Yet that event was shocking precisely because, in the United States, it was relatively rare. More common were mass-shootings in which the perpetrators were usually white males who acted alone.

Most terrorists resort to violence not because they are strong, but because they are weak. By attacking civilians and creating widespread fear, they hope to undermine the legitimacy of governments and force their enemies to recognize their grievances. In both Northern Ireland and Israel, two centers of terrorist activities, the ruling governments possessed far more power than the insurgents.

While booming populations and high unemployment in the Middle East fostered terrorist movements, ironically it was the Cold War—and, indirectly, the United States—that provided terrorists with training and weapons. After the Soviet Union invaded Afghanistan in 1980, the CIA, with help from Pakistan, Saudi Arabia, and the United Kingdom, encouraged Muslims from all over the world to join the Afghan rebels. One of the militants who journeyed to Afghanistan was Osama bin Laden, a devout Muslim and son of a Saudi business leader. During the 1980s bin Laden founded al-Qaeda to forge a broad-based alliance of Arab rebels. When Iraq invaded Kuwait in 1990, bin Laden was outraged that infidel troops from the United States used Saudi bases to invade Iraq. It was not the kind of holy war he had imagined. From his hidden camps in Afghanistan he began directing a terror network to strike back.

Bin Laden's organization differed from previous terrorist movements in that it had no national home—unlike the Irish Republican Army, which struggled to unify Ireland, or Palestinians, who wanted an independent state of their own. Al-Qaeda's primary motivation was religious rather than nationalist.

The group's anti-American campaign began with a bombing at the World Trade Center in 1993. Further attacks occurred in places far from the United States. Twice the Clinton administration retaliated against al-Qaeda with missile attacks; once it narrowly missed killing bin Laden himself in one of his Afghan camps.

The War on Terror: First Phase

>> In response to September 11, George Bush made the fateful decision: to launch a military offensive against terrorism, rather than treat bin Laden and al-Qaeda as criminals. That often meant using massive firepower that inflicted civilian casualties. The military phase began in early October 2001, after the Taliban rulers of Afghanistan rejected American demands to deliver bin Laden "dead or alive." The United States launched air attacks followed by an invasion, which quickly toppled the Taliban, and then established a coalition government in Kabul to help rebuild the nation.

The war on terrorism posed daunting challenges. The United States was an open society, where citizens expected to travel freely and valued their privacy. But widespread fears led the administration to propose the USA Patriot Act. Congress passed it so quickly, some members did not even read the bill before voting for it. The act broadly expanded government powers to use electronic surveillance, monitor bank transactions (to fight money laundering), and investigate suspected terrorists. To administer the Patriot Act, Bush created the cabinet-level Department of Homeland Security that included such diverse agencies as the Transportation Security Administration (TSA), the Immigration and Customs Enforcement Service (ICE) and the Federal Emergency Management Agency (FEMA).

The War in Iraq

>> The president's focus shifted from Osama bin Laden to Iraq's brutal dictator, Saddam Hussein. Indeed, many in the Bush administration had long wished to overthrow Hussein, even before the September 11 attacks. These "neoconservatives" argued that regime change in Iraq would promote democracy in the Middle East and protect Israel.

Bush and his administration built a case for war against Iraq. "If we know Saddam Hussein has dangerous weapons today—and we do—," he proclaimed, "does it make any sense for the world to wait . . . for the final proof, the smoking gun that could come in the form of a mushroom cloud?" The president had already laid the groundwork for a policy of not waiting, by asserting that the United States would be "ready for preemptive action when necessary to defend our liberty and to defend our lives." This **doctrine of preemption**—announcing that the United States might attack before it was itself attacked—was a major departure from the Cold War policy of containment. "A preventive war, to my mind, is an impossibility," President Eisenhower had declared in 1954. In fact, much of the evidence for Iraq possessing weapons of mass destruction (WMDs) was based on what administration officials, including the president, knew was faulty intelligence.

> **doctrine of preemption** attacking in anticipation of imminent attack or invasion by another nation or in hopes of gaining a strategic advantage when war seems unavoidable.

UN weapons inspectors had found no evidence of WMDs or even programs to build them. Thus, the Security Council refused to support an American resolution giving the United States the authority to lead a UN-sponsored invasion. Only the United Kingdom, Spain, and Italy, among the major powers, were willing to join the United States. On March 19, 2003, without a UN mandate, a "coalition of the willing" consisting of 30 nations attacked Iraq in "Operation Iraqi Freedom." (The actual troops, however, were virtually all

THE WAR ON TERRORISM: AFGHANISTAN AND IRAQ

In the wake of the attacks of September 11, 2001, President Bush declared a global war on terrorism. The first American attacks targeted the Taliban rulers of Afghanistan, who sheltered al Qaeda forces. The following year Bush extended the war into Iraq. Ethnic and religious divisions influenced allegiances in both wars. In Afghanistan, al Qaeda forces were concentrated in the mountainous region along the border with Pakistan. In Iraq the most severe resistance to American occupation occurred from around Baghdad to Fallujah in the west and Tikrit to the north.

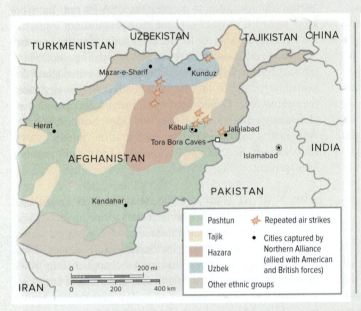

MAP READING

1. What are the three major population groups in Iraq?
2. Which major adversary of the United States borders both Afghanistan and Iraq?
3. What geographic feature does Iraq have that Afghanistan lacks?
4. From which country did the "coalition of the willing" invade Iraq?

MAP INTERPRETATION

1. In what major ways do Iraq and Afghanistan face divisions within their nations?
2. What difference makes Iran more of a threat to Iraq than to Afghanistan?
3. If ethnic and religious differences influenced allegiances in these wars, what does the pattern of airstrikes in Afghanistan suggest about the difficulty of the war?
4. What does the map show that might explain why resistance to American occupation in Iraq was strongest toward Fallujah and Tikrit?

American and British.) The invasion was accomplished with amazing speed and precision. Within days U.S. forces were halfway to Baghdad. On May 1 Bush announced an end to major combat operations. Coalition casualties (135 dead and 1,511 wounded) were remarkably low.

A Messy Aftermath >> The decision to invade Iraq, without adequate plans to govern it, has proven to be perhaps the most misjudged war an American president has ever launched (and the most expensive: over $2 trillion would be spent). Yet at the time, a large majority of Americans, including many Democrats, supported the invasion. Opponents pointed out that no solid evidence linked the secular Saddam Hussein

with the religious al-Qaeda. If the United States toppled Saddam, who would rule? And who would block Iranian fundamentalists from exporting terrorism or even invading Iran's neighbors?

Ethnic and religious factions divided Iraq—Shia Muslims in the southeast, **Sunni** Muslims around Baghdad, and Kurds in the north. Without Saddam's tyranny to hold the country together, the burden of

Shia and Sunni two major branches of Islam. After the death of the Prophet Muhammad, most believers accepted the tradition of having their leader chosen by community consensus (the Sunni branch), but a minority supported the claim of Ali, the Prophet's cousin. Over the years theological differences have separated Shia and Sunni Muslims as well.

Make a Case

Is torture justified against potential enemies, when the United States is under threat from terrorists? Why or why not?

peacekeeping fell to the American military. In the years to come, over 4,400 American troops died in Operation Iraqi Freedom, to say nothing of approximately half a million Iraqi deaths.

The intangible costs of the war were also high. In the spring of 2004 Americans were stunned to learn that Iraqi prisoners of war being held in the Abu Ghraib prison near Baghdad had been abused and tortured by American soldiers guarding them. The Bush administration blamed a handful of "bad apples" in the military. In fact the administration had excused such abuses in a Justice Department memo that argued that cruel, inhuman, or degrading acts did not qualify as torture.

The Second Term >> Despite the chaos in Iraq, in 2004 President Bush narrowly defeated his Democratic opponent, Senator John Kerry of Massachusetts. Conservatives saw an opportunity to achieve long-sought goals.

The president exerted the most significant impact on conservative values by appointing two justices to the Supreme Court, John Roberts and Samuel Alito. In 2007 the Court issued a number of decisions demonstrating that it had moved to the right. By a 5–4 majority, it weakened campaign finance laws that set limits on how much individuals or parties could contribute, limited free speech on the part of students in schools, and protected religious groups offering social programs financed by public funds. Roberts and Alito joined the majority in the controversial 2010 decision in *Citizens United* v. *FEC* (Federal Elections Commission). The decision granted to corporations the First Amendment's protection of free speech. In so ruling the Court removed many limits on campaign donations and allowed Political Action Committees (PACs) to keep their donor lists secret.

Disasters Domestic and Foreign >> Controversy over the Iraq War proved to be no more than a mild headwind to Bush's political popularity—compared to the gale from Hurricane Katrina. That storm slammed the Gulf Coast in September 2005, crippling New Orleans's levees and inundating the city. Most well-to-do citizens escaped before the storm, but no one had made adequate provision to evacuate those who were elderly, disabled, or poor, most of whom were African American. For days desperate survivors hung to rooftops. Well over a thousand died, while tens of thousands huddled in the damaged Superdome sports arena.

The president and his administration at first failed to respond decisively. The Federal Emergency Management Agency suffered from incompetent leadership as well as staff and budget cuts. Gulf Coast residents waited helplessly and

^ A plea from New Orleans residents threatened by Hurricane Katrina. DAVID J. PHILLIP/ASSOCIATED PRESS/AP Images

with growing anger for federal relief to arrive. Katrina reminded Americans that there are some problems that only an effective government can address.

Halfway across the globe in Iraq, sectarian violence between Shia and Sunni Muslims threatened to erupt into a full-scale civil war. As critics charged that the administration lacked a coherent exit strategy for the war, Bush changed course. In 2007, he ordered more troops to Iraq—a surge—rather than a withdrawal. The surge temporarily reduced violence, but political stability remained elusive, while the Taliban in Afghanistan posed a growing threat.

Suddenly the impregnable Republican stranglehold on Washington seemed to slip. Voters voiced their displeasure in the 2006 congressional elections. Democrats took control of both the House and the Senate.

Collapse >> As President Bush's popularity plummeted, the Democrats prospects for 2008 improved. And then the economy went into free fall. Over the previous decade, banks, investment firms, and hedge funds had poured trillions of dollars into unregulated mortgage-backed securities. Lenders routinely granted loans to prospective homeowners who possessed virtually no assets and little capacity to make monthly payments. One fruit picker in California received a $750,000 mortgage, though he earned just $14,000 a year. Financial markets bundled such subprime mortgages with other forms of debt, creating financial instruments that were so complicated, few bankers recognized their underlying risks. As the housing market contracted, many of these securities proved worse than worthless. The global financial system verged on bankruptcy.

The Bush administration, which normally championed the free market, hastily extended massive government loans to save the banking system. The Troubled Asset Relief Program (TARP) allowed the Treasury Department to purchase or insure up to $700 billion of mortgages and securities ("toxic assets" with no evident value) in order to stabilize financial markets. Later the administration modified the program to invest money directly into troubled banks. Critics complained that while desperate homeowners faced foreclosure, the government bailed out those who had created the problem in the first place.

The 2008 presidential election played out against this global financial crisis. For the Democrats, Hillary Clinton was the odds-on favorite, with high name recognition and long experience in government. However, Barack Obama, a junior senator from Illinois, possessed the advantages of relative youth—he was 47 when he ran—and an ability to inspire audiences. Even more striking, Obama was an African American, born in Hawai'i to a white mother and a Kenyan father. He overcame Clinton in a strongly contested primary season and then, with his running mate, Senator Joe Biden of Delaware, defeated the Republican nominee, Senator John McCain of Arizona, and his vice presidential running mate, Governor Sarah Palin of Alaska.

Forty-five years after Martin Luther King Jr. shared his dreams of freedom on the Washington Mall, the United States had elected the first African American as its president.

REVIEW

What issues made the Republicans vulnerable in the 2008 election?

A DIVIDED NATION

Barack Obama inherited an economy in free fall. Millions had lost jobs. many others faced eviction from their homes, and major corporate icons such as General Motors and Chrysler faced bankruptcy. Climate change continued to pose a global threat, as did ongoing wars in Iraq and Afghanistan.

Obama moved quickly in February 2009 to propose measures designed to stimulate the collapsing economy: tax cuts, expanded unemployment benefits and social welfare provisions, as well as spending on education, health care, and infrastructure. The stimulus package carried a $787 billion price tag. Republicans dismissed it as ineffective federal spending that added to the national debt; none would vote for it in the House and only three in the Senate. Liberals warned that more than a trillion dollars in spending might be needed to fully revive the economy.

First-Term Reforms >> Partisanship similarly complicated Obama's pledge to reform the nation's health care system. Americans paid far more for medical care than any other nation, but were no healthier. Over 40 million people had no health insurance, and rising unemployment threatened millions more with loss of coverage. Many Republicans supported the idea of reform—Mitt Romney had established a comprehensive plan similar to Obama's when he was governor of Massachusetts. But congressional Republicans opposed any deal with Obama. After a year of bitter negotiation, the Democrats passed the Affordable Care Act (ACA) in March 2010, with only one Republican member of Congress voting yes. The ACA's provisions extended Medicaid to some 16 million poor people, guaranteed coverage for children, and prevented insurers from denying coverage because of preexisting conditions. By 2017 it had extended care to over 20 million who had been uninsured.

With the president's support, Congress also passed the Dodd-Frank Act, which many observers considered "the toughest financial reform" since the aftermath of the Great Depression. Among other provisions, the law tightened bank requirements and established a consumer protection agency to reduce credit card abuses. Major banks faced periodic "stress tests" to ensure they could survive another financial meltdown.

The milestones in health care and financial reform did not translate into electoral success for either the president or the Democrats. Republicans were determined to make Obama a one-term president. They obstructed even compromise measures they privately supported. (Senate Republicans threatened to filibuster the Democratic majority 256 times between 2007 and 2010, compared with 130 filibuster threats from the Democrats during the Republican-controlled Congress between 2003 and 2007.) In foreign affairs, the president ended the American combat role in Iraq. Soon after a terrorist group called ISIS threatened to destabilize not only Iraq but also Syria and Afghanistan. Thus, Obama poured an additional 30,000 troops into Afghanistan to fight Taliban insurgents, with little to show for the effort.

⌃ In June 2015, White House photographer Pete Souza caught this quick succession of photos as an aide stepped in to tell President Obama that the Supreme Court had upheld a key portion of the Affordable Care Act, known informally as Obamacare.
White House/Zuma Press/Newscom

As the midterm elections of 2010 approached, disgruntled conservatives and independents formed a loosely coordinated alliance dubbed the Tea Party. Like the original demonstrators in Boston in 1773, the modern-day Tea Party protested high taxes. Its followers wanted less government in their lives, not more, although many also opposed any reduction in Social Security and Medicare benefits. The election gave Republicans a decisive majority in the House and significant gains in the Senate.

Although the economy recovered only slowly, the president gained a major victory in the war on terrorism. In the spring of 2011, the CIA tracked bin Laden to a house in Pakistan and Obama dispatched Navy SEALs on a daring nighttime mission.

The SEALs found and killed the al-Qaeda leader, escaping with his body as well as a cache of valuable intelligence.

Domestic issues framed the election of 2012. Republican Mitt Romney, the first Mormon to be nominated for president, promised to bring business skills to the presidency. But in selecting Romney, the GOP failed to address the changing profile of American voters. Latino and Asian Americans overwhelmingly favored Obama, since Romney had spoken out against immigration reform. Women voters, especially younger single women, rejected conservatives' antiabortion stance and their opposition to contraception coverage as part of health care reform. The president was reelected by a comfortable margin.

MAP 32.2: ENVIRONMENTAL STRESSES ON THE GULF OF MEXICO

After an oil rig explosion in 2010, millions of gallons of crude oil erupted into the Gulf of Mexico. In addition, the gulf had already been plagued by a hypoxic zone, where the lack of oxygen killed all marine life. The zone expanded over decades as fertilizers from farm fields washed into the Mississippi River system and flush into the gulf along with chemical discharge, storm runoff, and sewage. *Which problems receive the most attention, the short- or the long-term ones?*
U.S. Coast Guard photo

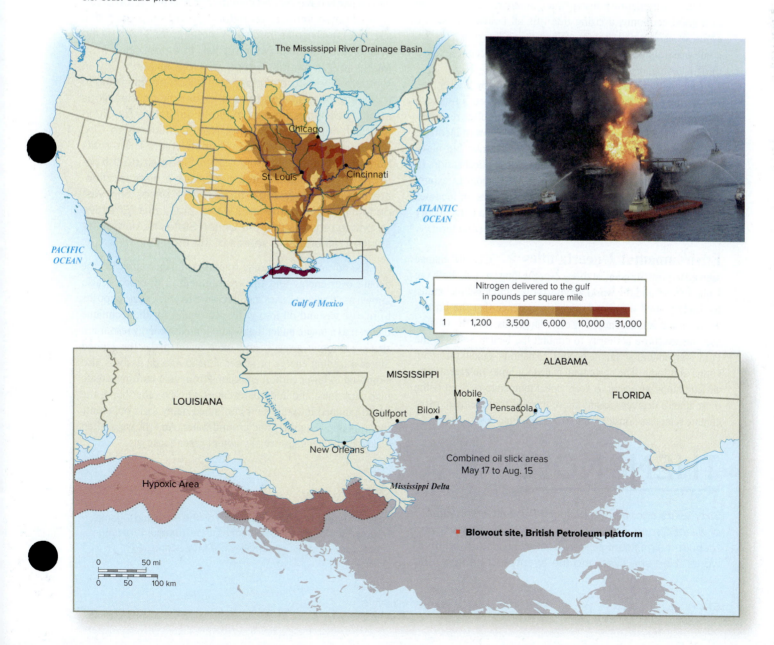

Short, Medium, Long

>> Every president must make choices. Short-term crises such as the financial collapse of 2008 demanded immediate attention. Health care and financial reforms could be called medium-term issues, and their success remained to be measured as they went into effect. But long-term problems began crowding the president's second term. They centered on economic inequality and global warming.

On the surface, the economy seemed on an upswing. Corporate profits and the stock market rebounded, while the number of home foreclosures and evictions declined. The job market continued its slow improvement. Yet the gap between the richest and poorest Americans continued to widen. By 2012 the CEOs of the 350 largest corporations earned over $14 million a year on average, 273 times more than the average worker. The average incomes of the 400 wealthiest families in the United States exceeded $200 million a year.

↑ A midwestern farmer surveys cropland ruined by drought. The year 2015 was the hottest year yet since such records began being recorded in 1880. The next four years were even hotter. The level of greenhouse gases is higher now than anytime in the last 3 million years.
Andrew Lichtenstein/Getty Images

The traditional response to such numbers was to say that in a good economy, a rising tide lifts all boats. But as one group of economists noted, "When a handful of yachts become ocean liners while the rest remain lowly canoes, something is seriously amiss."

Inequality inspired protesters to form Occupy Wall Street, a movement that took over a portion of New York's financial district for two months. They proclaimed themselves representatives of the 99 percent of Americans with the lowest incomes. The movement spread to cities around the country but never set a clear agenda or an effective strategy for political action. In Congress, as the 10-year Bush tax cuts were about to expire, Democrats succeeded in slightly raising the rates on incomes of over $250,000 a year. But the longer-term issue of inequality was never squarely addressed during Obama's second term.

Environmental Uncertainties

>> Climate change seemed to pose the greatest threat over the long term, for both the United States and the world. Conservatives and fossil fuel industry leaders often dismissed scientific evidence that the Earth's warming was human-caused or even dangerous. In 2016, Obama used his executive authority to commit the United States to the Paris Agreement, a climate accord 72 nations signed, including China and India. The agreement called for limits on greenhouse gas emissions sufficient to keep global temperatures from rising more than 2 degrees Celsius above preindustrial averages. Most climate scientists consider that to be a minimal goal.

would likely have placed climate change at the top of her list of human impacts on nature. Scientists predict that sea levels will rise as much as 1 meter (over 3 feet) by the end of the century. Flooding will threaten cities from Miami to Alexandria, Egypt, to Ho Chi Minh City in Vietnam. The future of close to a billion people living in low-lying coastal floodplains depends on decisions about greenhouse gases made in capitals as far flung as Washington, D.C., Beijing, New Delhi, Mexico City, and Brussels, home to the European Union. The threats humankind faces are truly global. So must be the response. The United States generates a disproportionate share of the world's greenhouse gases and vast quantities of airborne and water pollutants. Effective response requires that the United States be part of the solution rather than a source of the problem.

The advance of hydraulic fracturing further unsettled the debate over energy and the environment. The process, also known as "fracking," uses high pressure to crack shale deposits to release gas and oil into wells. Advocates for the technique hailed it as a magic bullet that would increase energy resources, spark economic growth, and once again make the United States a leading energy producer. Cheap natural gas was also supposed to lower carbon emissions from coal burning, create high-wage jobs, and add tax revenues. On the other hand, the liquid pumped into the wells contained many toxic pollutants that threatened aquifers and ground water. And the wells often leaked methane, an especially potent greenhouse gas.

THEN&NOW

Sixty years ago, marine biologist Rachel Carson, author of *Silent Spring*, came to understand how humans had "acquired significant power to alter the nature of [their] world." Had she lived into the twenty-first century, she

 REVIEW

List the major problems dealt with by the Bush and Obama administrations, and rank them as short-, medium-, or long-term crises. How successfully were they addressed?

COLD WAR OVER GLOBAL WARMING

Is the Earth warming, and have human activities been responsible? James Inhofe, the senior Republican senator from Oklahoma, is one of the most vocal spokespersons for those who deny global warming is a threat. More recently, the U.S. government issued a report, the National Climate Assessment, prepared by a panel of 300 scientists. "Climate change," they concluded, "once considered an issue for a distant future, has moved firmly into the present."

DOCUMENT 1
Climate Change: "The Greatest Hoax"

As I said on the Senate floor on July 28, 2003, "much of the debate over global warming is predicated on fear, rather than science." I called the threat of catastrophic global warming the "greatest hoax ever perpetrated on the American people," a statement that, to put it mildly, was not viewed kindly by environmental extremists and their elitist organizations. . . .

For these groups, the issue of catastrophic global warming is not just a favored fundraising tool. In truth, it's more fundamental than that. Put simply, man-induced global warming is an article of religious faith. Therefore contending that its central tenets are flawed is, to them, heresy of the most despicable kind. Furthermore, scientists who challenge its tenets are attacked, sometimes personally, for blindly ignoring the so-called "scientific consensus." But that's not all: because of their skeptical views, they are contemptuously dismissed for being "out of the mainstream." That is, it seems to me, highly ironic; aren't scientists supposed to be non-conforming and question consensus? . . .

I have insisted all along that the climate change debate should be based on fundamental principles of science, not religion. Ultimately, I hope, it will be decided by hard facts and data—and by serious scientists committed to the principles of sound science. Instead of censoring skeptical viewpoints, as my alarmist friends favor, these scientists must be heard, and I will do my part to make sure that they are heard.

Since my detailed climate change speech in 2003, the so-called "skeptics" continue to speak out. What they are saying, and what they are showing, is devastating to the alarmists. They have amassed additional scientific evidence convincingly refuting the alarmists' most cherished assumptions and beliefs. . . .

This evidence has come to light in very interesting times. Just last month [December 2004] the 10th Conference of the Parties (COP-10) to the Framework Convention on Climate Change convened in Buenos Aires to discuss Kyoto's implementation and measures to pursue beyond Kyoto. As some of my colleagues know, Kyoto goes into effect on February 16th. I think the nations that ratified Kyoto and agreed to submit to its mandates are making a very serious mistake.

In addition, last month, popular author Dr. Michael Crichton, who has questioned the wisdom of those who trumpet a "scientific consensus," released a new book called "State of Fear," which is premised on the global warming debate. . . . Dr. Crichton, a medical doctor and scientist, very cleverly weaves a compelling presentation of the scientific facts of climate change—with ample footnotes and documentation throughout—into a gripping plot. From what I can gather, Dr. Crichton's book is designed to bring some sanity to the global warming debate. In the "Author's Message" at the end of the book, he refreshingly states what scientists have suspected for years: "We are also in the midst of a natural warming trend that began about 1850, as we emerged from a 400-year cold spell known as the Little Ice Age." Dr. Crichton states that. "Nobody knows how much of the present warming trends might be a natural phenomenon," and, "Nobody knows how much of the present trend might be manmade." And for those who see impending disaster in the coming century, Dr. Crichton urges calm: "I suspect that people of 2100 will be much richer than we are, consume more energy, have a smaller global population, and enjoy more wilderness than we have today. I don't think we have to worry about them."

Senator James M. Inhofe, "Climate Change Update," January 4, 2005.

DOCUMENT 2
"The Warming Can Only Be Explained by Human Influences"

Evidence for changes in Earth's climate can be found from the top of the atmosphere to the depths of the oceans. . . . The sum total of this evidence tells an unambiguous story: the planet is warming. . . .

In the past, climate change was driven exclusively by natural factors: explosive volcanic eruptions that injected reflective particles into the upper atmosphere, changes in energy from the sun, periodic variations in the Earth's orbit, natural cycles that transfer heat between the ocean and the atmosphere, and slowly changing natural variations in heat-trapping gases in the atmosphere. . . .

Natural factors are still affecting the planet's climate today. The difference is that, since the beginning of the Industrial Revolution, humans have been increasingly affecting global climate, to the point where we are now the primary cause of recent and projected future change.

The majority of the warming at the global scale over the past 50 years can only be explained by the effects of human influences, especially the emissions from burning fossil fuels (coal, oil, and natural gas) and from deforestation. The emissions from human influences affecting climate include heat-trapping gases such as carbon dioxide (CO_2), methane, and nitrous oxide, and particles such as black carbon (soot), which has a warming influence, and sulfates, which have an overall cooling influence. . . .

Carbon dioxide has been building up in the atmosphere since the beginning of the industrial era in the mid-1700s, primarily due to burning coal, oil, and gas, and secondarily due to clearing of forests. Atmospheric levels have increased by about 40% relative to pre-industrial levels. Methane levels in the atmosphere have increased due to human activities including agriculture (with livestock producing methane in their digestive tracts and rice farming producing it via bacteria that live in the flooded fields); mining coal, extraction and transport of natural gas, and other fossil fuel-related activities; and waste disposal including sewage and decomposing garbage in landfills. Since pre-industrial times, methane levels have increased by 250%.

"Our Changing Climate," from *The National Climate Assessment*, issued by the U.S. Global Change Research Program.

THINKING CRITICALLY

How does Inhofe's lack of training in science affect your reaction to his views on global warming? Does Michael Crichton's training as a doctor validate the claims Inhofe makes about him? Which human activities are primary contributors to global warming, according to the National Climate Assessment? How would you compare the tone of the two excerpts and how would that affect your assessment of them?

TRUMP

At a 2011 Washington event Barack Obama roasted TV reality star and real estate mogul Donald Trump. Trump had joined the rank of "birthers," conspiracy theorists who questioned whether Obama had a legitimate U.S. birth certificate and hence was qualified to be president. Obama produced his official birth certificate and suggested the occasion freed "the Donald" to focus on issues that really mattered: whether the government had faked the moon-landing, what really happened at Roswell, New Mexico (UFO and alien sitings), and where were rappers "Biggy" and "Tupac."

Trump's fixation on the birther issue revealed themes that would define his presidency. Chief among them was his obsession with undoing every success Obama had achieved, including repealing Obamacare. Trump also attracted people who believed the greatest threat to the country in the twenty-first century lay in immigration, legal and illegal. Among them were nativists and white supremacists. Though he denied it, racial stereotyping and thinly veiled racialized rhetoric would inform his approach to both foreign and domestic policy.

The Greatest Upset since Truman versus Dewey >> In the run-up to the 2016 election, both major parties found themselves divided. Hillary Rodham Clinton, the leading Democratic candidate, faced a challenge from the left by Senator Bernie Sanders of Vermont, a self-proclaimed democratic-socialist. Sanders appealed to voters who resented inequality and the influence exercised over politics by the super rich. Clinton won the nomination, though she was tarnished by the millions of dollars she had earned giving speeches to major banks and corporations. Many voters, even Democrats, simply did not like her. Clinton's long career in public life gave critics an opportunity to cherrypick her record to find damaging information.

Eighteen candidates competed for the Republican nomination—including business conservatives, evangelicals, and libertarians. Among them, most observers at first dismissed the prospects of reality TV celebrity and real estate mogul Donald Trump. Trump had never held political office nor did he possess any deep experience in world affairs. He touted his business successes as proof that he possessed the executive experience necessary to master the presidency. Yet his past included at least four bankruptcies, fraud charges against Trump University, and dozens of lawsuits for nonpayment of debts. Voters struggling to make a living and feeling ignored by traditional politicians flocked to his rallies. After all, Trump was a Washington outsider, who opposed illegal immigration and undocumented immigrants. And he delighted attendees at rousing campaign rallies with his politically incorrect attacks on Democratic rivals, minorities, and immigrants.

In some ways, Trump followed conservative Republican principles. He vowed to end Obamacare, without specifying

⌃ Having criticized Obama for playing too much golf, Trump spent virtually every weekend on one of his own courses. The expense to taxpayers exceeded $100 million.
WENN Rights Ltd/Alamy Stock Photo

how he would replace it. He promised massive tax cuts, privatization of government services, and protection of gun rights. In other ways, however, Trump rejected traditional Republican positions, arguing against free trade policies, promising to reduce American involvement abroad, and displaying a pronounced affection for Russia's strongman, Vladimir Putin. His insistent call for immigration restriction led him to vow to build a "really great wall" to secure the southern U.S. border and force Mexico to pay for it.

Style more than substance set Trump apart. His lavish living suggested power and success. From his experience in reality TV, he knew how to attract the publicity, good or bad, which shaped his campaign. The media slavishly reported the tweets he sent out at all hours often without fact-checking his claims. Many of the controversies he sparked would have torpedoed a traditional campaign: he was caught bragging about groping women and tarred Mexican immigrants as "rapists." With tongue in cheek, his campaign later said, he invited Russia to hack the Clinton campaign even after U.S. intelligence had warned that the Russians had already leaked Democratic e-mails.

When the results were in, Clinton won the popular vote by a margin of nearly 3 million. But the Electoral College went for Trump, making 2016 one of only five presidential elections in which the losing candidate won the popular vote. Class and race played a role. Eighty-five percent of Trump voters were white; at a time when police shootings of unarmed Black men had inspired protesters to launch a "Black Lives Matter" campaign, African Americans joined Latinos in support of Clinton, but not as much as they did Barack Obama. Better educated voters favored Clinton. In some key states, such as Michigan and Wisconsin, traditionally Democratic workers who feared globalization rejected Clinton and chose Trump, as did those in fossil fuel–producing states. Trump also carried evangelicals and socially conservative rural and suburban areas, especially in the South. Control of both the Senate and the House gave the Republicans the opportunity to fill three crucial Supreme Court seats and control all three branches of government.

Making America Great?

>> During his campaign rallies, Donald Trump often sported a red baseball cap with his signature slogan: "Make America Great Again." That meant putting "America First" abroad and appealing to nationalism and xenophobia at home.

Trump as President   Donald Trump viewed the world in the transactional terms with which he ran his businesses. Each interaction between two people or two nations produced a winner and loser. Compromise was not an option, since Trump insisted on always being the winner. He regarded himself as the smartest person around, a brilliant billionaire many times over, and a huge celebrity. His record seemed to belie those claims. The Trump organization was actually a tightly held family company run by a small group that included his sons, Eric and Donald Jr., and his daughter Ivanka. Loyalty to the boss counted for more than any business acumen.

Ethnic and Racial Nationalism   Trump described himself as "the least racist" person he knew. The history of the Trump organization and his behavior as president caused many to question that claim. In the late 1980s Trump explained why he never wanted an African American accountant, "Black guys counting my money! I hate it. . . . I think that the guy is lazy. And it's probably not his fault, because laziness is a trait in blacks."

From the moment he launched his campaign, Trump railed against immigrants and people of color. He condemned undocumented immigrants and singled out a new wave of those escaping civil war, poverty, and religious persecution in the Middle East and Latin America. "They're bringing drugs," he said of Mexicans. "They're bringing crime. They're rapists. And some, I assume, are good people."

Judges routinely rejected his executive orders concerning immigration, including those that divided families by placing the children of detained immigrants in detention centers. Trump also blocked a path to citizenship for a group known as "Dreamers," children of immigrants who had entered the country illegally and were now integrated into American life. Reformers wanted them to have a path to citizenship. Trump and his supporters wanted them deported.

Trump and the Alt Right   Trump's nationalism was both racial and religious. He issued several orders restricting immigrants from Muslim countries, even those friendly to the United States. As president, he called African nations "sh**hole countries" and suggested that African Americans and Hispanics were "living in hell . . . you're living in poverty; . . . your schools are no good; you have no jobs."

Trump's closest advisers nurtured those prejudices. Several were closely associated with white supremacists who called themselves the "alt-right." The decision of some southern cities to remove statues of former heroes of the Confederacy provoked alt-right groups to protest. White supremacists flocked to the city of Charlottesville, Virginia, after the city decided to move a statue of Robert E. Lee. One of them drove his car into a crowd of counterprotestors, killing a woman. Others marched Klan- and Nazi-style with torches chanting, "Jews will not replace us" and other racist slogans. The president refused to condemn their actions, insisting instead "There were very fine people on both sides."

Tragedy sometimes followed the president's pandering to white supremacists. In a Pittsburgh synagogue, a Walmart in El Paso, Texas, and, the same night, on a crowded street in Dayton Ohio, white terrorists murdered people because of their skin color and religion. In August 2019 mass-murders claimed over 50 lives with hundreds wounded. After each shooting, Trump pledged to toughen background checks on gun purchases—until the NRA objected.

Repeal, Replace, and Deceive   Trump's election seemed to ensure the repeal of the Affordable Care Act. Yet, Republicans could never agree on how to fulfill Trump's promise to replace Obamacare "with insurance for everyone" that was "a lot less expensive."

The Republicans did pass the Tax Cuts and Jobs Act of 2017, fulfilling a major Trump campaign promise. The need for such cuts was dubious, since the economy was strong, unemployment low, and the stock market robust. While most taxpayers received a few hundred dollars, cuts in capital gains rates, estates taxes, and business savings conferred benefits of some $1.5 trillion on the wealthiest 1 percent and corporations. Most companies spent their savings on stock buybacks and executive benefits rather than capital investment, research and development, and job creation. By 2020 the federal deficit exceeded $1 trillion a year, leaving annual interest costs close to $400 billion. Under Trump, the Republicans ceased to be the party of fiscal conservatism.

Russians and Election Meddling   Throughout his presidency, a cloud hung over Trump. National security agencies uncovered evidence that during the 2016 election Russian meddling helped Trump win. His links to Russia were undeniable. As a real estate developer, he received funding from Russian investors, though his refusal to reveal his taxes obscured the extent and exact nature of their involvement. He continued during the campaign to seek a hotel deal in Moscow. Evidence later emerged that members of Trump's campaign and Trump himself knew of illegal Russian moves to promote his election. Some half dozen Trump campaign staff members, including his son Donald Jr., son-in-law Jared Kushner, and campaign manager Paul Manafort, held secret meetings with Russian operatives promising to find "dirt" on the Clinton campaign.

Flynn, Comey, and Mueller   Less than a month after taking office, Trump reluctantly dismissed his National Security Advisor, former army terrorism expert Michael Flynn. Flynn not only lied about his secret contacts with the Russians, but also failed to disclose money he received for lobbying on behalf of Russia and Turkey. To limit the investigation, Trump asked FBI Director James Comey to pledge his loyalty. When Comey refused, Trump fired him, triggering suspicions that he was obstructing justice.

With so many questions about the president's actions, the Justice Department appointed former FBI director Robert Mueller as a special counsel. Mueller had the power to investigate Russian election meddling and the possible collusion between the Trump campaign and the Russians. Over the next year, as Mueller's team worked in total secrecy, Trump issued hundreds of tweets insisting there was "no collusion" and condemning his attorney general, Jeff Sessions, for recusing himself from the investigation. Those opposing Trump hoped Mueller's final report would lead either to impeachment or criminal indictments.

Those expectations were largely disappointed, though the investigations led to numerous indictments and conviction of several Trump advisers. When Mueller filed his report in March 2019, Trump's new attorney general, William Barr, issued a summary in which he insisted that the Mueller Report showed there had been "no collusion." That was far from the truth, as Mueller angrily informed him. Barr also released a redacted (sensitive information removed) version that concealed key evidence.

Mueller in fact had dismissed "collusion" only because the term had no legal basis. His investigators did conclude that Russian interference was "sweeping and systematic," that numerous campaign members were linked to Russian operatives and lied about it, and that Russian interference "deserves the attention of every American."

The World Stage   Early in his presidency Barack Obama won a Nobel Peace Prize; Trump was determined to do the same. To that end, he reached out to North Korea's young autocrat, Kim Jong-un. Kim had systematically starved his people while he poured scarce funds into developing missiles and nuclear weapons. He and Trump at first traded insults. Kim called him a "mentally deranged dotard," while Trump demeaned Kim as little "Rocket Man." Their decision to meet face-to-face in Singapore in June 2018 came as a surprise. But what Trump demanded, full denuclearization, Kim was not prepared to give. They failed to reach an agreement and a follow-up meeting in Hanoi in February 2019 ended abruptly with no resolution. Kim went back to testing missiles.

The courtship of Kim revealed a curious feature of Trump's approach to world

⌃ President Donald Trump fired FBI director James Comey (left) and in the ensuing controversy Robert Mueller, former head of the FBI (right), was appointed to head a special commission investigating Russian meddling in the 2016 presidential election.
Kevin Dietsch/UPI/Newscom

affairs. Toward autocrats and dictators in Russia, the Philippines, Turkey, Hungary, and Saudi Arabia he was almost deferential. For example, after evidence emerged that Saudi Crown Prince Mohammed bin Salman had ordered the murder of *Washington Post* journalist Jamal Khashoggi, Trump refused to condemn the prince. The only democratic leader toward whom he showed such deference was Israel's Benjamin Netanyahu who, like Trump, was under investigation for corruption. As a show of support, in December 2018 Trump ignored the opposition of almost all U.S. allies and announced he would move the American embassy from Tel Aviv to Jerusalem. The move outraged Palestinians who favored a "two-state" solution to their conflict with Israel.

The "America First" approach to international relations became a hallmark of the Trump presidency. Trump pulled the United States out of the Paris Agreement on global warming, ended negotiations for a Trans-Pacific trade deal, and forced a renegotiation of NAFTA. He also picked fights with such long-time allies as Canada, Germany, and other members of NATO. He then entered into a trade war with China whose commercial restrictions and theft of intellectual property had long troubled American political and business leaders. Assuring the public that "trade wars are easy to win," Trump slapped heavy tariffs on Chinese imports. When China retaliated, the ensuing uncertainty threw financial markets into turmoil, while American influence in the world steadily eroded.

Impeachment >>
Shortly after Trump claimed exoneration from the Mueller Report, a whistleblower revealed that Trump had pressured the newly elected president of the Ukraine to announce an investigation into the activities of former vice president Joe Biden and his son Hunter. Biden had emerged as Trump's most likely opponent in the 2020 election; his son had ties to a corrupt oil company. As a stick, Trump ordered a hold on U.S. military aid vital to the Ukrainians' war with Russian invaders in its eastern provinces.

Had the president exceeded his authority? Was it an impeachable offense for him to use U.S. aid to promote his own election? Democrats in the House decided that it was. Trump had abused his powers for personal gain. The House sent three articles of impeachment to the Senate for trial, where the outcome was never in doubt. In lock-step loyalty to the president, Republicans refused to call any witnesses who might shed light on his actions. In a nakedly partisan contest all Democratic senators voted to convict, while all the Republicans, except for Mitt Romney of Utah, voted to acquit.

Pandemic >>
Impeachment was a mere bump in the road compared to the crisis that followed. Ten years earlier, as the Obama administration struggled to revive the economy, Homeland Security Advisor John Brennan warned that an H1N1 virus, called "Swine Flu," was spreading in Mexico, while cases had popped up in California and Texas. Virologists identified this H1N1 virus as one that had caused the 1918 pandemic (See "The Influenza Pandemic of 1918–1919" in Chapter 23).

That pandemic afflicted one-third of the world's population and killed between 17 and 50 million people.

In 2009 no pandemic broke out. Swine flu did infect some 60 million Americans, but claimed only 12,469 lives. Because children were vulnerable, Congress appropriated money needed to buy protective equipment (PPE) and fund research that produced a vaccine. Then in 2014 Ebola, a deadly filiovirus, appeared in West Africa. An American doctor who volunteered to fight the outbreak tested positive for Ebola after he returned to New York. Far less infectious than H1N1, Ebola was also far deadlier. This case provoked outrage from New York business executive and TV celebrity Donald Trump. In October 2014, he tweeted, "I am starting to think that there is something seriously wrong with President Obama's mental health. Why won't he stop the flights [from Africa]. Psycho!" Trump's outburst proved misguided, as Ebola never spread to the United States.

In 2019 it was Trump who faced a viral scourge. On December 31, Chinese authorities confirmed rumors that they were treating dozens of cases of a mysterious infection from the city of Wuhan. The World Health Organization (WHO) later named this coronavirus COVID-19. It was similar to those that caused the SARS outbreak in 2002 and MERS in 2012 (see "Recent Pandemics"). The Chinese initially denied any evidence of human-to-human transmission, yet by January 20, 2020 the disease had spread through Asia and claimed its first fatality. Ten days later WHO declared a public health emergency.

The Trump administration at first adopted few precautions but did restrict travel from China to the United States. The president tweeted two weeks later, "The Coronavirus is very much under control in the USA." Then he added, "Stock Market starting to look very good to me!" That optimism proved premature as major outbreaks erupted in South Korea, Iran, Italy, and Spain. Cases also appeared in the United States, which recorded its first death on February 29. The Dow Jones Industrial stock index had peaked above 29,000 in mid-February and plummeted below 19,000 within a month.

Only then did the United States begin to adopt more aggressive measures. Much of the initiative came from governors in Washington State, California, New York, Maryland, Louisiana, and New Jersey, where infection hotspots had erupted. Public health officials, led by epidemiologist Anthony Fauci, called for social distancing measures, contact tracing, and quarantining in place. Schools and colleges closed across the nation, major sports organizations canceled their seasons, and travel for business and tourism virtually ceased. Unemployment soared to levels not seen since the Great Depression 90 years earlier.

Perhaps, only the crises of the Civil War and Great Depression have tested the nation and its leaders so severely. On one hand, governors' and mayors' offices, hospital workers, first responders, supermarket employees, and those who have put their lives on hold have emerged as heroes. At the same time, partisan politics hampered the efforts to find the

RECENT PANDEMICS

	Type	Transmission	First Reported Case	Source	Deaths	Threat Level
1918 Pandemic	H1N1	Respiratory mist	Ft. Riley, Kansas Spring 1918	Birds to human	Worldwide, 17–50 million; United States, 500,000 to 850,000	One-third of world infected (500 million people 2-3% mortality rate); Unites States: 0.48–0.81 fatality rate. Disease affected mostly young, pregnant women and those under age 65. Outbreak came in four waves, with the second in Fall 1918 the most severe.
SARS (Severe Acute Respiratory Syndrome)	CoV-1 coronavirus	Respiratory mist infecting mucous membranes	Yunnan China, November 2002	Animal to human	Worldwide, 774; United States, 0 (4 Americans contacted it overseas and died)	55% fatality rate especially in those over 65
Swine Flu	H1N1	Respiratory mist, not from eating pork	Central Mexico, Fall 2008		Worldwide, estimated 150,00–575,000; United States, 12,500	Low mortality rate but most dangerous to children and young people
Ebola	Filovirus with virions	Direct contact with fluids of infected animals or people	South Sudan and Democratic Republic Congo near Ebola River, 1976	Fruit bats	1,590 from 1976–2013, mostly in West Africa	Low transmission rate but 50% death rate from infection
MERS (Middle East Respiratory Syndrome)	Coronavirus	Not known	Saudi Arabia, 2012	Animals (camels and bats) to humans	871, mostly Saudi Arabia and South Korea	34.3% fatality rate
COVID-19 (Coronavirus)	Coronavirus	Respiratory mist human to human; some surface contact	Wuhan China, December 2019	Most likely animal to human.	(As of Jan 27. 2021) Worldwide, over 2 million; United States, 425,000	Highest in Western Europe and North America; most affected are those over 65 and with preexisting conditions

equipment, vaccine, and treatments needed to fight the virus. Despite warnings from his health advisers of greater outbreaks, Trump pressed to reopen the economy. "Easter is a special day for me. And I see it in that sort of timeline I'm thinking about. And I say wouldn't it be great to have all the churches full?" Despite warnings from public health experts, the president refused to wear a mask, while most Republican governors opened their states' economies without imposing mask ordinances and social distancing. Medical providers faced a shortage of tests to identify those with COVID-19, while they searched for a preventive vaccine and treatments for those afflicted. Seven months after the first reported COVID-19 death, the epidemic claimed more than 200,000 American lives.

Public health experts warned that even as cases declined in the warm summer months, an upsurge would strike when cold weather returned. The president continued to ignore their advice and dismiss the virus as a hoax. He refused to wear a mask and urged his supporters to ignore this and other basic health measures. Many Republican governors opened their states' economies without imposing mask ordinances and social distancing. Rural areas once spared the worst of the epidemic, such as the Dakotas and mountain states, became hot spots in the fall.

2020 Election >> Donald Trump reopened his reelection campaign office the day after his inauguration in January 2017. All the same he faced an uphill battle as the 2020 election approached. Over his first term, his approval ratings never reached 50 percent. The Democrats faced a glut of choices as more than 20 candidates vied for the nomination. They included an independent socialist, Bernie Sanders; the first openly gay man, Pete Buttigieg; the first mixed-race female, Senator Kamala Harris; billionaire Michael Bloomberg; and Barack Obama's former vice president, Joseph Biden. A surge of support from African American voters in South Carolina turned the hotly contested Democratic primary into a runaway for Biden.

Trump hinged his hopes for victory on a booming economy and the loyal support of his largely blue-collar and rural base. Suburban women, offended by accusations of sexual misconduct and his insulting male chauvinism, generally favored Biden. One highlight of the campaign came from a group called the "Lincoln Project." These were disillusioned Republican conservatives who considered Trump corrupt, autocratic, and fundamentally incompetent. They ran a sophisticated ad campaign designed to infuriate Trump and give Republican voters a reason to vote Democratic.

Trump largely campaigned in red states before crowds chanting "Four More Years" and "Lock Them Up," as he insulted his Democratic opponents. His bullying style appealed to his base but offended more moderate voters. That became clear during the first campaign debate when he ranted, raved, blustered, and interrupted both Biden and the debate moderator. After Trump contracted COVID-19, the second debate became virtual. To avoid a repetition of the first fiasco, debate planners gave the moderator power to turn off a candidate's microphone as his opponent answered a question. Trump refused to participate under the new rules. During the final debate, Trump insisted Americans had to learn to live with the virus to which Biden responded that, under Trump, Americans were "learning to die from" the virus.

Disregard for scientific advice on containing the epidemic proved Trump's undoing. It did not help Trump that the *New York Times* made public some of his tax returns. For years, even with an income in the hundreds of millions of dollars, he had paid no taxes and twice paid just $750. Voting split along class and gender lines, as better-educated and more affluent voters blamed Trump for his ineffective response to the COVID-19 crisis. Suburban areas, once Republican strongholds, turned the traditionally red states Georgia and Arizona to blue. Victory in Pennsylvania, Michigan, and Wisconsin, states that Trump carried in 2016, gave Biden the electoral college majority he needed.

Rather than concede defeat, an outraged Trump launched an unprecedented legal campaign to overturn the election results. He amassed over $200 million in donations, much of which was available for his personal expenses. Judges, some of whom he appointed, dismissed his lawsuits as without merit, since his lawyers provided no evidence of voting irregularities. Dedicated state election officials, many of them Republicans, certified that the 2020 election had fairly made Joseph Biden the 46th president of the United States. Yet, many congressional Republicans continued to support Trump's lie that the Democrats stole the election. On January 6, 2021, an angry pro-Trump mob led by white supremacists chanting "Stop the Steal," stormed the Capitol building. The ensuing riot left five people dead and forced senators and congresspersons to seek shelter. Even Republican Senate Majority Leader Mitch McConnell blamed Trump and his allies for promoting a terrorist insurrection.

On January 20, as Joseph Biden was sworn in as the nation's 46th president, Trump left Washington in disgrace: the only president in history who refused to attend his successor's inauguration as well as the first and only one who faced two impeachments. To Biden fell the monumental challenge of bringing order out of the chaos Trump left in his wake. In his inaugural speech he pledged to unite a divided nation and revive trust in government as it faced a sea of troubles. They included the COVID-19 epidemic, racial tensions, inequality, loss of faith in government, and the sense around the world that the United States had lost its way.

CHAPTER SUMMARY

Over the past two decades the United States has become increasingly involved in economic, financial, and demographic relationships that have increased both the nation's diversity and global interdependence.

- The Immigration Act of 1965 opened the United States to new waves of immigration hailing from South and Southeast Asia as well as more traditional flows from China, Japan, and the Philippines.
- Both legal and illegal immigrants from Mexico, Cuba, and Central America contributed to the growing Latino population, settling in urban and suburban barrios.
- During the Clinton and Bush presidencies, Islamic radicalism and terrorism as well as regional conflicts in the Middle East, Eastern Europe, Africa, and the Caribbean replaced Cold War rivalry as the central challenge of foreign policy.
- A divided and (after the elections of 1994) hostile Congress limited President Clinton's legislative program aimed at health care, education, and welfare reform. The campaign of Republicans to impeach President Clinton ended when the Senate failed to convict the president.
- The growth of the Internet, the World Wide Web, social networks, and e-commerce was part of a revolution in communications and information management made possible by advances in microchip and computer technology.
- President George W. Bush advanced a conservative agenda in domestic affairs, revolving around lower taxes, education reform, and faith-based initiatives in social policy. In foreign policy he pursued a unilateralist approach that led him to reject the Kyoto Protocol on global warming.
- The attacks of September 11 gave new stature to the president, as he declared war on al-Qaeda and global terrorism. He launched a successful attack on Afghanistan's Taliban regime in 2001, before invading Iraq, in a preemptive war.
- Hurricane Katrina, the protracted wars in Afghanistan and Iraq, and the collapse of the housing and financial markets undermined public confidence in the Bush administration.
- Voter dissatisfaction allowed Democrats to gain control of the House and Senate in 2006 and send Barack Obama to the White House in 2008.
- A weak economy, ongoing wars in Iraq and Afghanistan, and political factionalism in Congress limited President Obama's ability to deliver on his promise to bring "change" to Washington.
- Over a unified Republican opposition, Obama legislated a stimulus package and reform of the nation's health care system and financial markets, but his opponents stymied his plans for environmental and economic reforms.
- Donald Trump won an upset victory in 2016 that put Republicans in control of all three branches of the federal government.

- Trump's opposition to immigration and support for white nationalism promoted deep divisions and occasional violence.
- Investigation by special counsel Robert Mueller confirmed suspicions of Trump's involvement with Russians to win the election of 2016.
- Voter dissatisfaction with Trump's handling of the COVID-19 crisis and his autocratic, combative leadership style led to his loss to Joseph Biden in the 2020 presidential election.

Digging Deeper

Accounts of the most recent past often reflect the partisan spirit of those engaged in ongoing controversies. Michael I. Days, *Obama's Legacy: What He Accomplished as President* (2016), offers a thorough, if partisan, look at the politics of eight years. Sidney Blumenthal, *The Clinton Wars* (2003), is an insider's unabashed defense of the Clintons. Peter Baker, *Days of Fire: Bush and Cheney in the White House* (2013), follows Cheney's declining influence in the second term. Joseph Stiglitz, *The Roaring Nineties: A New History of the World's Most Prosperous Decade* (2004), offers a liberal perspective on economic inequalities. To appreciate the Mueller Report see the U.S. Department of Justice, Special Counsel Robert S. Mueller III, *Report on the Investigation into Russian Interference in the 2016 Presidential Election* (2019), Volume I and II, though this is a redacted version, not the full report. For insight into the chaos and dangers of Trump's approach to government see Michael Lewis, *The Fifth Risk* (2018). Steven Levitsky and Daniel Ziblatt, *How Democracies Die* (2018), use the lessons of history to show how Trump and his Republican enablers are undermining democratic institutions.

Jacob S. Hacker and Paul Pierson, *Winner-Take-All Politics: How Washington Made the Rich Richer—and Turned Its Back on the Middle Class* (2010), trace the influence of financial markets on politics. Jeff Madrick, *Age of Greed: The Triumph of Finance and the Decline of America, 1970 to the Present* (2011), tells how the pursuit of private wealth has come to dominate economics. In a powerful memoir, J. D. Vance, *Hillbilly Elegy* (2016), explores the culture and worldview of "Blue Dog Democrats" who now vote Republican. Lawrence Wright, *The Looming Tower: Al-Qaeda and the Road to 9/11* (2006), makes the case that Osama bin Laden purposely drew George Bush into a trap. Ron Suskind, *The One Percent Doctrine* (2006), uses CIA sources to follow the road to war in Iraq. Beth Bailey and Richard Immerman, *Understanding the U.S. Wars in Iraq and Afghanistan* (2015), explores the political and diplomatic sides; while Andrew Bacevich, *America's War for the Greater Middle East: A Military History* (2016), covers 30 years of U.S. fighting in the region. Spencer Weart, *The Discovery of Global Warming* (2008), is a fascinating look at the science of climate change.

Appendix

- **The Declaration of Independence**

- **The Constitution of the United States of America**

Royalty-Free/CORBIS
Background paper: sbayram/Getty Images

The Declaration of Independence

The Unanimous Declaration of the Thirteen United States of America

When, in the course of human events, it becomes necessary for one people to dissolve the political bands which have connected them with another, and to assume, among the powers of the earth, the separate and equal station to which the laws of nature and of nature's God entitle them, a decent respect to the opinions of mankind requires that they should declare the causes which impel them to the separation.

We hold these truths to be self-evident, that all men are created equal; that they are endowed by their Creator with certain unalienable rights; that among these, are life, liberty, and the pursuit of happiness. That, to secure these rights, governments are instituted among men, deriving their just powers from the consent of the governed; that, whenever any form of government becomes destructive of these ends, it is the right of the people to alter or to abolish it, and to institute a new government, laying its foundation on such principles, and organizing its powers in such form, as to them shall seem most likely to effect their safety and happiness. Prudence, indeed, will dictate that governments long established, should not be changed for light and transient causes; and, accordingly, all experience hath shown, that mankind are more disposed to suffer, while evils are sufferable, than to right themselves by abolishing the forms to which they are accustomed. But, when a long train of abuses and usurpations, pursuing invariably the same object, evinces a design to reduce them under absolute despotism, it is their right, it is their duty, to throw off such government and to provide new guards for their future security. Such has been the patient sufferance of these colonies, and such is now the necessity which constrains them to alter their former systems of government. The history of the present King of Great Britain is a history of repeated injuries and usurpations, all having, in direct object, the establishment of an absolute tyranny over these States. To prove this, let facts be submitted to a candid world:

He has refused his assent to laws the most wholesome and necessary for the public good.

He has forbidden his governors to pass laws of immediate and pressing importance, unless suspended in their operation till his assent should be obtained; and, when so suspended, he has utterly neglected to attend to them.

He has refused to pass other laws for the accommodation of large districts of people, unless those people would relinquish the right of representation in the legislature; a right inestimable to them, and formidable to tyrants only.

He has called together legislative bodies at places unusual, uncomfortable, and distant from the depository of their public records, for the sole purpose of fatiguing them into compliance with his measures.

He has dissolved representative houses repeatedly for opposing, with manly firmness, his invasions on the rights of the people.

He has refused, for a long time after such dissolutions, to cause others to be elected; whereby the legislative powers, incapable of annihilation, have returned to the people at large for their exercise; the state remaining, in the meantime, exposed to all the danger of invasion from without, and convulsions within.

He has endeavored to prevent the population of these States; for that purpose, obstructing the laws for naturalization of foreigners, refusing to pass others to encourage their migration hither, and raising the conditions of new appropriations of lands.

He had obstructed the administration of justice, by refusing his assent to laws for establishing judiciary powers. He has made judges dependent on his will alone, for the tenure of their offices, and the amount and payment of their salaries.

He has erected a multitude of new offices, and sent hither swarms of officers to harass our people, and eat out their substance.

He has kept among us, in time of peace, standing armies, without the consent of our legislatures.

He has affected to render the military independent of, and superior to, the civil power.

He has combined, with others, to subject us to a jurisdiction foreign to our Constitution, and unacknowledged by our laws; giving his assent to their acts of pretended legislation:

For quartering large bodies of armed troops among us:

For protecting them by a mock trial, from punishment, for any murders which they should commit on the inhabitants of these States:

For cutting off our trade with all parts of the world:

For imposing taxes on us without our consent:

For depriving us, in many cases, of the benefit of trial by jury:

For transporting us beyond seas to be tried for pretended offences:

For abolishing the free system of English laws in a neighboring province, establishing therein an arbitrary government, and enlarging its boundaries, so as to render it at once an example and fit instrument for introducing the same absolute rule into these colonies:

For taking away our charters, abolishing our most valuable laws, and altering, fundamentally, the powers of our governments:

For suspending our own legislatures, and declaring themselves invested with power to legislate for us in all cases whatsoever.

He has abdicated government here, by declaring us out of his protection, and waging war against us.

He has plundered our seas, ravaged our coasts, burnt our towns, and destroyed the lives of our people.

He is, at this time, transporting large armies of foreign mercenaries to complete the works of death, desolation, and tyranny, already begun, with circumstances of cruelty and perfidy scarcely paralleled in the most barbarous ages, and totally unworthy the head of a civilized nation.

He has constrained our fellow citizens, taken captive on the high seas, to bear arms against their country, to become the executioners of their friends, and brethren, or to fall themselves by their hands.

He has excited domestic insurrections amongst us, and has endeavored to bring on the inhabitants of our frontiers, the merciless Indian savages, whose known rule of warfare is an undistinguished destruction of all ages, sexes, and conditions.

In every stage of these oppressions, we have petitioned for redress, in the most humble terms; our repeated petitions have been answered only by repeated injury. A prince, whose character is thus marked by every act which may define a tyrant, is unfit to be the ruler of a free people.

Nor have we been wanting in attention to our British brethren. We have warned them, from time to time, of attempts made by their legislature to extend an unwarrantable jurisdiction over us. We have reminded them of the circumstances of our emigration and settlement here. We have appealed to their native justice and magnanimity, and we have conjured them, by the ties of our common kindred, to disavow these usurpations, which would inevitably interrupt our connections and correspondence. They, too, have been deaf to the voice of justice and consanguinity. We must, therefore, acquiesce in the necessity which denounces our separation, and hold them as we hold the rest of mankind, enemies in war, in peace, friends.

We, therefore, the representatives of the United States of America, in general Congress assembled, appealing to the Supreme Judge of the world for the rectitude of our intentions, do, in the name, and by the authority of the good people of these colonies, solemnly publish and declare, that these united colonies are, and of right ought to be, free and independent states: that they are absolved from all allegiance to the British Crown, and that all political connection between them and the state of Great Britain is, and ought to be, totally dissolved; and that, as free and independent states, they have full power to levy war, conclude peace, contract alliances, establish commerce, and to do all other acts and things which independent states may of right do. And, for the support of this declaration, with a firm reliance on the protection of Divine Providence, we mutually pledge to each other our lives, our fortunes, and our sacred honor.

The foregoing Declaration was, by order of Congress, engrossed, and signed by the following members:

JOHN HANCOCK

NEW HAMPSHIRE
Josiah Bartlett
William Whipple
Matthew Thornton

MASSACHUSETTS BAY
Samuel Adams
John Adams
Robert Treat Paine
Elbridge Gerry

RHODE ISLAND
Stephen Hopkins
William Ellery

CONNECTICUT
Roger Sherman
Samuel Huntington
William Williams
Oliver Wolcott

NEW YORK
William Floyd
Philip Livingston
Francis Lewis
Lewis Morris

NEW JERSEY
Richard Stockton
John Witherspoon
Francis Hopkinson
John Hart
Abraham Clark

PENNSYLVANIA
Robert Morris
Benjamin Rush
Benjamin Franklin
John Morton
George Clymer
James Smith

George Taylor
James Wilson
George Ross

DELAWARE
Caesar Rodney
George Read
Thomas M'Kean

MARYLAND
Samuel Chase
William Paca
Thomas Stone
Charles Carroll,
   of Carrollton

VIRGINIA
George Wythe
Richard Henry Lee
Thomas Jefferson

Benjamin Harrison
Thomas Nelson, Jr.
Francis Lightfoot Lee
Carter Braxton

NORTH CAROLINA
William Hooper
Joseph Hewes
John Penn

SOUTH CAROLINA
Edward Rutledge
Thomas Heyward, Jr.
Thomas Lynch, Jr.
Arthur Middleton

GEORGIA
Button Gwinnett
Lyman Hall
George Walton

Resolved, That copies of the Declaration be sent to the several assemblies, conventions, and committees, or counsils of safety, and to the several commanding officers of the continental troops; that it be proclaimed in each of the United States, at the head of the army.

The Constitution of the United States of America[1]

We the People of the United States, in Order to form a more perfect Union, establish Justice, insure domestic Tranquility, provide for the common defence, promote the general Welfare, and secure the Blessings of Liberty to ourselves and our Posterity, do ordain and establish this CONSTITUTION for the United States of America.

ARTICLE I

SECTION 1. All legislative Powers herein granted shall be vested in a Congress of the United States, which shall consist of a Senate and House of Representatives.

SECTION 2. The House of Representatives shall be composed of Members chosen every second Year by the People of the several States, and the Electors in each State shall have the Qualifications requisite for Electors of the most numerous Branch of the State Legislature. No Person shall be a Representative who shall not have attained to the Age of twenty-five Years, and been seven Years a Citizen of the United States, and who shall not, when elected, be an Inhabitant of that State in which he shall be chosen.

[Representatives and direct Taxes[2] shall be apportioned among the several States which may be included within this Union, according to their respective Numbers, which shall be determined by adding to the whole Number of free Persons, including those bound to Service for a Term of Years, and excluding Indians not taxed, three fifths of all other Persons.][3] The actual Enumeration shall be made within three Years after the first Meeting of the Congress of the United States, and within every subsequent Term of ten Years, in such Manner as they shall by Law direct. The Number of Representatives shall not exceed one for every thirty Thousand, but each State shall have at Least one Representative; and until such enumeration shall be made, the State of New Hampshire shall be entitled to chuse three, Massachusetts eight, Rhode-Island and Providence Plantations one, Connecticut five, New York six, New Jersey four, Pennsylvania eight, Delaware one, Maryland six, Virginia ten, North Carolina five, South Carolina five, and Georgia three. When vacancies happen in the Representation from any State, the Executive Authority thereof shall issue Writs of Election to fill such Vacancies. The House of Representatives shall chuse their Speaker and other Officers; and shall have the sole Power of Impeachment.

SECTION 3. The Senate of the United States shall be composed of two Senators from each State, chosen by the Legislature thereof, for six Years; and each Senator shall have one Vote.

Immediately after they shall be assembled in Consequence of the first Election, they shall be divided as equally as may be into three Classes. The Seats of the Senators of the first Class shall be vacated at the Expiration of the second Year, of the second Class at the Expiration of the fourth Year, and of the third Class at the Expiration of the sixth Year, so that one-third may be chosen every second Year; and if Vacancies happen by Resignation, or otherwise, during the Recess of the Legislature of any State, the Executive thereof may make temporary Appointments until the next Meeting of the Legislature, which shall then fill such Vacancies. No Person shall be a Senator who shall not have attained to the Age of thirty Years, and been nine Years a Citizen of the United States, and who shall not, when elected, be an Inhabitant of that State for which he shall be chosen.

The Vice President of the United States shall be President of the Senate, but shall have no vote, unless they be equally divided.

The Senate shall chuse their other Officers, and also a President pro tempore, in the absence of the Vice President, or when he shall exercise the Office of President of the United States.

The Senate shall have the sole Power to try all Impeachments. When sitting for that purpose they shall be on Oath or Affirmation. When the President of the United States is tried, the Chief Justice shall preside: And no person shall be convicted without the Concurrence of two thirds of the Members present.

Judgment in Cases of Impeachment shall not extend further than to removal from Office, and disqualification to hold and enjoy any Office of honor, Trust, or Profit under the United States: but the Party convicted shall nevertheless be liable and subject to Indictment, Trial, Judgment, and Punishment, according to Law.

---

1 This version follows the original Constitution in capitalization and spelling. It is adapted from the text published by the United States Department of the Interior, Office of Education.

2 Altered by the Sixteenth Amendment.

3 Negated by the Fourteenth Amendment.

SECTION 4. The Times, Places and Manner of holding Elections for Senators and Representatives, shall be prescribed in each State by the Legislature thereof; but the Congress may at any time by Law make or alter such Regulations, except as to the Places of Chusing Senators. The Congress shall assemble at least once in every Year, and such Meeting shall be on the first Monday in December, unless they shall by Law appoint a different Day.

SECTION 5. Each House shall be the Judge of the Elections, Returns and Qualifications of its own Members, and a Majority of each shall constitute a Quorum to do Business; but a smaller number may adjourn from day to day, and may be authorized to compel the Attendance of absent Members, in such Manner, and under such Penalties, as each House may provide.

Each House may determine the Rules of its Proceedings, punish its Members for disorderly Behaviour, and, with the Concurrence of two thirds, expel a Member. Each House shall keep a Journal of its Proceedings, and from time to time publish the same, excepting such Parts as may in their Judgment require Secrecy; and the Yeas and Nays of the Members of either House on any question shall, at the Desire of one fifth of those Present, be entered on the Journal.

Neither House, during the Session of Congress, shall, without the Consent of the other, adjourn for more than three days, nor to any other Place than that in which the two Houses shall be sitting.

SECTION 6. The Senators and Representatives shall receive a Compensation for their Services, to be ascertained by Law, and paid out of the Treasury of the United States. They shall in all Cases, except Treason, Felony, and Breach of the Peace, be privileged from Arrest during their Attendance at the Session of their respective Houses, and in going to and returning from the same; and for any Speech or Debate in either House, they shall not be questioned in any other Place. No Senator or Representative shall, during the Time for which he was elected, be appointed to any civil Office under the Authority of the United States, which shall have been created, or the Emoluments whereof shall have been increased, during such time; and no Person holding any Office under the United States shall be a Member of either House during his continuance in Office.

SECTION 7. All Bills for raising Revenue shall originate in the House of Representatives; but the Senate may propose or concur with Amendments as on other bills. Every Bill which shall have passed the House of Representatives and the Senate, shall, before it become a Law, be presented to the President of the United States; If he approve he shall sign it, but if not he shall return it, with his Objections, to that House in which it shall have originated, who shall enter the

Objections at large on their Journal, and proceed to reconsider it. If after such Reconsideration two thirds of that House shall agree to pass the bill, it shall be sent, together with the objections, to the other House, by which it shall likewise be reconsidered, and if approved by two thirds of that House, it shall become a Law. But in all such Cases the Votes of both Houses shall be determined by Yeas and Nays, and the Names of the Persons voting for and against the Bill shall be entered on the Journal of each House respectively. If any Bill shall not be returned by the President within ten Days (Sundays excepted) after it shall have been presented to him, the Same shall be a Law, in like Manner as if he had signed it, unless the Congress by their Adjournment prevent its Return, in which Case it shall not be a Law. Every Order, Resolution, or Vote to which the Concurrence of the Senate and House of Representatives may be necessary (except on a question of Adjournment) shall be presented to the President of the United States; and before the Same shall take Effect, shall be approved by him, or being disapproved by him, shall be repassed by two thirds of the Senate and House of Representatives, according to the Rules and Limitations prescribed in the Case of a Bill.

SECTION 8. The Congress shall have Power To lay and collect Taxes, Duties, Imposts and Excises, to pay the Debts and provide for the common Defence and general Welfare of the United States; but all Duties, Imposts and Excises shall be uniform throughout the United States;

To borrow money on the credit of the United States;

To regulate Commerce with foreign Nations, and among the several States, and with the Indian Tribes;

To establish an uniform rule of Naturalization, and uniform Laws on the subject of Bankruptcies throughout the United States; To coin Money, regulate the Value thereof, and of foreign Coin, and fix the Standard of Weights and Measures;

To provide for the Punishment of counterfeiting the Securities and current Coin of the United States;

To establish Post Offices and post Roads; To promote the Progress of Science and useful Arts, by securing for limited Times to Authors and Inventors the exclusive Right to their respective Writings and Discoveries;

To constitute Tribunals inferior to the Supreme Court;

To define and punish Piracies and Felonies committed on the high Seas, and Offenses against the Law of Nations;

To declare War, grant Letters of Marque and Reprisal, and make Rules concerning Captures on Land and Water;

To raise and support Armies, but no Appropriation of Money to that Use shall be for a longer Term than two Years;

To provide and maintain a Navy;

To make Rules for the Government and Regulation of the land and naval forces;

To provide for calling forth the Militia to execute the Laws of the Union, suppress Insurrections and repel Invasions;

To provide for organizing, arming, and disciplining the Militia, and for government such Part of them as may be employed in the Service of the United States, reserving to the States respectively, the Appointment of the Officers, and the Authority of training the Militia according to the discipline prescribed by Congress;

To exercise exclusive Legislation in all Cases whatsoever, over such District (not exceeding ten Miles square) as may, by Cession of particular States, and the acceptance of Congress, become the Seat of the Government of the United States, and to exercise like Authority over all Places purchased by the Consent of the Legislature of the State in which the Same shall be, for the Erection of Forts, Magazines, Arsenals, Dockyards, and other needful Buildings;—And

To make all Laws which shall be necessary and proper for carrying into Execution the foregoing Powers, and all other Powers vested by this Constitution in the Government of the United States, or in any Department or Officer thereof.

SECTION 9.
The Migration or Importation of such Persons as any of the States now existing shall think proper to admit, shall not be prohibited by the Congress prior to the Year one thousand eight hundred and eight, but a tax or duty may be imposed on such Importation, not exceeding ten dollars for each Person.

The privilege of the Writ of Habeas Corpus shall not be suspended, unless when in Cases of Rebellion or Invasion the public Safety may require it.

No bill of Attainder or ex post facto Law shall be passed.

No capitation, or other direct, Tax shall be laid unless in Proportion to the Census or Enumeration herein before directed to be taken.

No Tax or Duty shall be laid on Articles exported from any State.

No Preference shall be given by any Regulation of Commerce or Revenue to the Ports of one State over those of another: nor shall Vessels bound to, or from, one State, be obliged to enter, clear, or pay Duties in another.

No Money shall be drawn from the Treasury, but in Consequence of Appropriations made by Law; and a regular Statement and Account of the Receipts and Expenditures of all public Money shall be published from time to time.

No Title of Nobility shall be granted by the United States: And no Person holding any Office of Profit or Trust under them, shall, without the Consent of the Congress, accept of any present, Emolument, Office, or Title, of any kind whatever, from any King, Prince, or foreign State.

SECTION 10.
No State shall enter into any Treaty, Alliance, or Confederation; grant Letters of Marque and Reprisal; coin Money; emit Bills of Credit; make any Thing but gold and silver Coin a Tender in Payment of Debts; pass any Bill of Attainder, ex post facto Law, or Law impairing the Obligation of Contracts, or grant any Title of Nobility.

No State shall, without the Consent of the Congress, lay any Imposts or Duties on Imports or Exports, except what may be absolutely necessary for executing its inspection Laws; and the net Produce of all Duties and Imposts, laid by any State on Imports or Exports, shall be for the use of the Treasury of the United States; and all such Laws shall be subject to the Revision and Control of the Congress.

No state shall, without the Consent of Congress, lay any duty of Tonnage, keep Troops, or Ships of War in time of Peace, enter into any Agreement or Compact with another State, or with a foreign Power, or engage in War, unless actually invaded, or in such imminent Danger as will not admit of delay.

ARTICLE II

SECTION 1.
The executive Power shall be vested in a President of the United States of America. He shall hold his Office during the Term of four years, and, together with the Vice President, chosen for the same Term, be elected, as follows:

Each State shall appoint, in such Manner as the Legislature thereof may direct, a Number of Electors, equal to the whole Number of Senators and Representatives to which the State may be entitled in the Congress: but no Senator or Representative, or Person holding an Office of Trust or Profit under the United States, shall be appointed an Elector.

[The Electors shall meet in their respective States, and vote by Ballot for two persons, of whom one at least shall not be an Inhabitant of the same State with themselves. And they shall make a List of all the Persons voted for, and of the Number of Votes for each; which List they shall sign and certify, and transmit sealed to the Seat of the Government of the United States, directed to the President of the Senate. The President of the Senate shall, in the Presence of the Senate and House of Representatives, open all the Certificates, and the Votes shall then be counted. The Person having the greatest Number of Votes shall be the President, if such Number be a Majority of the whole Number of Electors appointed; and if there be more than one who have such Majority, and have an equal Number of Votes, then the House of Representatives shall immediately chuse by Ballot one of them for President; and if no Person have a Majority, then from the five highest on the List the said House shall in like Manner chuse the President. But in chusing the President, the Votes shall be taken by States, the Representation from each State having one Vote; a quorum for this Purpose shall consist of a Member or Members from two-thirds of the States, and a Majority of all the States shall be necessary to a Choice. In every Case, after the Choice of the President, the Person having the greatest Number of Votes of the Electors shall be the Vice President. But if there should remain two or more who have equal votes, the Senate shall chuse from them by Ballot the Vice President.][4]

4 Revised by the Twelfth Amendment.

The Congress may determine the Time of chusing the Electors, and the Day on which they shall give their Votes; which Day shall be the same throughout the United States.

No person except a natural-born Citizen, or a Citizen of the United States, at the time of the Adoption of this Constitution, shall be eligible to the Office of President; neither shall any Person be eligible to that Office who shall not have attained to the Age of thirty-five years, and been fourteen Years a Resident within the United States.

In Case of the Removal of the President from Office, or of his Death, Resignation, or Inability to discharge the Powers and Duties of the said Office, the same shall devolve on the Vice President, and the Congress may by Law provide for the Case of Removal, Death, Resignation, or Inability, both of the President and Vice President, declaring what Officer shall then act as President, and such Officer shall act accordingly, until the disability be removed, or a President shall be elected.

The President shall, at stated Times, receive for his Services a Compensation, which shall neither be increased nor diminished during the Period for which he shall have been elected, and he shall not receive within that Period any other Emolument from the United States, or any of them.

Before he enter on the execution of his Office, he shall take the following Oath or Affirmation:—"I do solemnly swear (or affirm) that I will faithfully execute the Office of President of the United States, and will, to the best of my Ability, preserve, protect, and defend the Constitution of the United States."

SECTION 2. The President shall be Commander in Chief of the Army and Navy of the United States, and of the Militia of the several States, when called into the actual Service of the United States; he may require the Opinion, in writing, of the principal Officer in each of the executive Departments, upon any subject relating to the Duties of their respective Offices, and he shall have Power to Grant Reprieves and Pardons for Offenses against the United States, except in Cases of Impeachment.

He shall have Power, by and with the Advice and Consent of the Senate, to make Treaties, provided two-thirds of the Senators present concur; and he shall nominate, and by and with the Advice and Consent of the Senate, shall appoint Ambassadors, other public Ministers and Consuls, Judges of the supreme Court, and all other Officers of the United States, whose Appointments are not herein otherwise provided for, and which shall be established by Law: but the Congress may by Law vest the Appointment of such inferior Officers, as they think proper, in the President alone, in the Courts of Law, or in the Heads of Departments.

The President shall have Power to fill up all Vacancies that may happen during the Recess of the Senate, by granting Commissions which shall expire at the End of their next Session.

SECTION 3. He shall from time to time give to the Congress Information of the State of the Union, and recommend to their Consideration such Measures as he shall judge necessary and expedient; he may, on extraordinary occasions, convene both Houses, or either of them, and in Case of Disagreement between them, with respect to the Time of Adjournment, he may adjourn them to such Time as he shall think proper; he shall receive Ambassadors and other public Ministers; he shall take care that the Laws be faithfully executed, and shall Commission all the Officers of the United States.

SECTION 4. The President, Vice President and all civil Officers of the United States, shall be removed from Office on Impeachment for, and Conviction of, Treason, Bribery, or other high Crimes and Misdemeanors.

ARTICLE III

SECTION 1. The judicial Power of the United States, shall be vested in one supreme Court, and in such inferior Courts as the Congress may from time to time ordain and establish. The Judges, both of the supreme and inferior Courts, shall hold their Offices during good Behaviour, and shall, at stated Times, receive for their Services, a Compensation, which shall not be diminished during their Continuance in Office.

SECTION 2. The judicial Power shall extend to all Cases, in Law and Equity, arising under this Constitution, the Laws of the United States, and Treaties made, or which shall be made, under their Authority;—to all Cases affecting ambassadors, other public ministers and consuls;—to all cases of admiralty and maritime Jurisdiction;—to Controversies to which the United States shall be a Party;—to Controversies between two or more States;—between a State and Citizens of another State;[5]—between Citizens of different States—between Citizens of the same State claiming Lands under Grants of different States, and between a State, or the Citizens thereof, and foreign States, Citizens, or Subjects. In all Cases affecting Ambassadors, other public Ministers and Consuls, and those in which a State shall be Party, the supreme Court shall have original Jurisdiction. In all the other Cases before mentioned, the supreme Court shall have appellate Jurisdiction, both as to Law and Fact, with such Exceptions, and under such Regulations as the Congress shall make.

The trial of all Crimes, except in Cases of Impeachment, shall be by Jury; and such Trial shall be held in the State where the said Crimes shall have been committed; but when

5 Qualified by the Eleventh Amendment.

not committed within any State, the Trial shall be at such Place or Places as the Congress may by Law have directed.

SECTION 3. Treason against the United States, shall consist only in levying War against them, or in adhering to their Enemies, giving them Aid and Comfort. No Person shall be convicted of Treason unless on the Testimony of two Witnesses to the same overt Act, or on Confession in open Court.

The Congress shall have power to declare the Punishment of Treason, but no Attainder of Treason shall work Corruption of Blood, or Forfeiture except during the Life of the Person attainted.

ARTICLE IV

SECTION 1. Full Faith and Credit shall be given in each State to the public Acts, Records, and judicial Proceedings of every other State. And the Congress may by general Laws prescribe the Manner in which such Acts, Records and Proceedings shall be proved, and the Effect thereof.

SECTION 2. The Citizens of each State shall be entitled to all Privileges and Immunities of Citizens in the several States.

A Person charged in any State with Treason, Felony, or other Crime, who shall flee from Justice, and be found in another State, shall on demand of the executive Authority of the State from which he fled, be delivered up, to be removed to the State having Jurisdiction of the crime. No Person held to Service or Labour in one State, under the Laws thereof, escaping into another, shall, in Consequence of any Law or Regulation therein, be discharged from such Service or Labour, but shall be delivered up on Claim of the Party to whom such Service or Labour may be due.

SECTION 3. New States may be admitted by the Congress into this Union; but no new State shall be formed or erected within the Jurisdiction of any other State; nor any State be formed by the Junction of two or more States, or parts of States, without the Consent of the Legislatures of the States concerned as well as of the Congress. The Congress shall have Power to dispose of and make all needful Rules and Regulations respecting the Territory or other Property belonging to the United States; and nothing in this Constitution shall be so construed as to Prejudice any Claims of the United States, or of any particular State.

SECTION 4. The United States shall guarantee to every State in this Union a Republican Form of Government, and shall protect each of them against Invasion; and on Application of the Legislature, or of the Executive (when the Legislature cannot be convened) against domestic Violence.

ARTICLE V

The Congress, whenever two-thirds of both Houses shall deem it necessary, shall propose Amendments to this Constitution, or, on the Application of the Legislatures of two-thirds of the several States, shall call a Convention for proposing Amendments, which, in either Case, shall be valid to all Intents and Purposes, as part of this Constitution, when ratified by the Legislatures of three-fourths of the several States, or by Conventions in three-fourths thereof, as the one or the other Mode of Ratification may be proposed by the Congress; Provided that no Amendment which may be made prior to the Year One thousand eight hundred and eight shall in any Manner affect the first and fourth Clauses in the Ninth Section of the first Article; and that no State, without its Consent, shall be deprived of its equal Suffrage in the Senate.

ARTICLE VI

All Debts contracted and Engagements entered into, before the Adoption of this Constitution, shall be as valid against the United States under this Constitution, as under the Confederation.

This Constitution, and the Laws of the United States which shall be made in Pursuance thereof; and all Treaties made, or which shall be made, under the Authority of the United States, shall be the supreme Law of the Land; and the Judges in every State shall be bound thereby, any Thing in the Constitution or Laws of any State to the Contrary notwithstanding.

The Senators and Representatives before mentioned, and the Members of the several State Legislatures, and all executive and judicial Officers, both of the United States and of the several States, shall be bound by Oath or Affirmation to support this Constitution; but no religious Tests shall ever be required as a qualification to any Office or public Trust under the United States.

ARTICLE VII

The Ratification of the Conventions of nine States shall be sufficient for the Establishment of this Constitution between the States so ratifying the same.

Done in Convention by the Unanimous Consent of the States present the Seventeenth Day of September in the Year of our Lord one thousand seven hundred and Eighty seven, and of the Independence of the United States of America the Twelfth. In Witness whereof We have hereunto subscribed our Names.[6]

6 These are the full names of the signers, which in some cases are not the signatures on the document.

Articles in Addition to, and Amendment of, the Constitution of the United States of America, Proposed by Congress, and Ratified by the Legislatures of the Several States, Pursuant to the Fifth Article of the Original Constitution[7]

[AMENDMENT I]

Congress shall make no law respecting an establishment of religion, or prohibiting the free exercise thereof; or abridging the freedom of speech, or of the press; or the right of the people peaceably to assemble, and to petition the Government for a redress of grievances.

[AMENDMENT II]

A well regulated Militia, being necessary to the security of a free State, the right of the people to keep and bear Arms shall not be infringed.

[AMENDMENT III]

No Soldier shall, in time of peace, be quartered in any house, without the consent of the Owner, nor in time of war, but in a manner to be prescribed by law.

[AMENDMENT IV]

The right of the people to be secure in their persons, houses, papers, and effects, against unreasonable searches and seizures, shall not be violated, and no Warrants shall issue, but upon probable cause, supported by Oath or affirmation, and particularly describing the place to be searched, and the persons or things to be seized.

[AMENDMENT V]

No person shall be held to answer for a capital or otherwise infamous crime, unless on a presentment or indictment of a Grand Jury, except in cases arising in the land or naval forces, or in the Militia, when in actual service in time of War or public danger; nor shall any person be subject for the same offence to be twice put in jeopardy of life or limb; nor shall be compelled in any criminal case to be a witness against himself, nor be deprived of life, liberty, or property, without due process of law; nor shall private property be taken for public use, without just compensation.

[AMENDMENT VI]

In all criminal prosecutions, the accused shall enjoy the right to a speedy and public trial, by an impartial jury of the State and district wherein the crime shall have been committed, which district shall have been previously ascertained by law, and to be informed of the nature and cause of the accusation; to be confronted with the witnesses against him; to have compulsory process for obtaining witnesses in his favour, and to have the Assistance of Counsel for his defence.

7 This heading appears only in the joint resolution submitting the first ten amendments, known as the Bill of Rights.

[AMENDMENT VII]

In suits at common law, where the value in controversy shall exceed twenty dollars, the right of trial by jury shall be preserved, and no fact tried by a jury, shall be otherwise reexamined in any Court of the United States, than according to the rules of the common law.

[AMENDMENT VIII]

Excessive bail shall not be required, nor excessive fines imposed, nor cruel and unusual punishments inflicted.

[AMENDMENT IX]

The enumeration of the Constitution, of certain rights, shall not be construed to deny or disparage others retained by the people.

[AMENDMENT X]

The powers not delegated to the United States by the Constitution, nor prohibited by it to the States, are reserved to the States respectively, or to the people. [Amendments I-X, in force 1791.]

[AMENDMENT XI][8]

The Judicial power of the United States shall not be construed to extend to any suit in law or equity, commenced or prosecuted against one of the United States by Citizens of another State, or by Citizens or Subjects of any Foreign State.

[AMENDMENT XII][9]

The Electors shall meet in their respective States and vote by ballot for President and Vice-President, one of whom, at least, shall not be an inhabitant of the same State with themselves; they shall name in their ballots the person voted for as President, and in distinct ballots the person voted for as Vice-President, and they shall make distinct lists of all persons voted for as President, and of all persons voted for as Vice-President,

and of the number of votes for each, which lists they shall sign and certify, and transmit sealed to the seat of the government of the United States, directed to the President of the Senate;— The President of the Senate shall, in the presence of the Senate and House of Representatives, open all the certificates and the votes shall then be counted;—The person having the greatest number of votes for President, shall be the President, if such number be a majority of the whole number of Electors appointed; and if no person have such majority, then from the persons having the highest numbers not exceeding three on the list of those voted for as President, the House of Representatives shall choose immediately, by ballot, the President. But in choosing the President, the votes shall be taken by states, the representation from each state having one vote; a quorum for this purpose shall consist of a member or members from two-thirds of the states, and a majority of all the states shall be necessary to a choice. And if the House of Representatives shall not choose a President whenever the right of choice shall devolve upon them, before the fourth day of March next following, then the Vice-President shall act as President, as in the case of the death or other constitutional disability of the President.—The person having the greatest number of votes as Vice-President, shall be the Vice-President, if such number be a majority of the whole number of Electors appointed, and if no person have a majority, then from the two highest numbers on the list, the Senate shall choose the Vice-President; a quorum for the purpose shall consist of two-thirds of the whole number of Senators, and a majority of the whole number shall be necessary to a choice. But no person constitutionally ineligible to the office of President shall be eligible to that of Vice-President of the United States.

[AMENDMENT XIII][10]

SECTION 1. Neither slavery nor involuntary servitude, except as a punishment for crime whereof the party shall have been duly convicted, shall exist within the United States, or any place subject to their jurisdiction.

SECTION 2. Congress shall have power to enforce this article by appropriate legislation.

[AMENDMENT XIV][11]

SECTION 1. All persons born or naturalized in the United States, and subject to the jurisdiction thereof, are citizens of the United States and of the State wherein they reside. No State shall abridge the privileges or immunities of citizens of

8 Adopted in 1798.
9 Adopted in 1804.

10 Adopted in 1865.
11 Adopted in 1868.

the United States; nor shall any State deprive any person of life, liberty, or property, without due process of law; nor deny to any person within its jurisdiction the equal protection of the laws.

SECTION 2. Representatives shall be apportioned among the several States according to their respective numbers, counting the whole number of persons in each State, excluding Indians not taxed. But when the right to vote at any election for the choice of electors for President and Vice-President of the United States, Representatives in Congress, the Executive and Judicial officers of a State, or the members of the Legislature thereof, is denied to any of the male inhabitants of such State, being twentyone years of age, and citizens of the United States, or in any way abridged, except for participation in rebellion, or other crime, the basis of representation therein shall be reduced in the proportion which the number of such male citizens shall bear to the whole number of male citizens twenty-one years of age in such State.

SECTION 3. No person shall be a Senator or Representative in Congress, or elector of President and Vice-President, or hold any office, civil or military, under the United States, or under any State, who, having previously taken an oath, as a member of Congress, or as an officer of the United States, or as a member of any State legislature, or as an executive or judicial officer of any State, to support the Constitution of the United States, shall have engaged in insurrection or rebellion against the same, or given aid or comfort to the enemies thereof. But Congress may by a vote of two-thirds of each House, remove such disability.

SECTION 4. The validity of the public debt of the United States, authorized by law, including debts incurred for payment of pensions and bounties for services in suppressing insurrection or rebellion, shall not be questioned. But neither the United States nor any State shall assume or pay any debts or obligation incurred in aid of insurrection or rebellion against the United States, or any claim for the loss or emancipation of any slave; but all such debts, obligations, and claims shall be held illegal and void.

SECTION 5. The Congress shall have the power to enforce, by appropriate legislation, the provisions of this article.

[AMENDMENT XV][12]

SECTION 1. The right of citizens of the United States to vote shall not be denied or abridged by the United States or by any State on account of race, color, or previous condition of servitude.

12 Adopted in 1870.

SECTION 2. The Congress shall have power to enforce this article by appropriate legislation.

[AMENDMENT XVI][13]

The Congress shall have power to lay and collect taxes on incomes, from whatever source derived, without apportionment among the several States, and without regard to any census or enumeration.

[AMENDMENT XVII][14]

The Senate of the United States shall be composed of two Senators from each State, elected by the people thereof, for six years; and each Senator shall have one vote. The electors in each State shall have the qualifications requisite for electors of the most numerous branch of the State legislatures.

When vacancies happen in the representation of any State in the Senate, the executive authority of such State shall issue writs of election to fill such vacancies: Provided, That the legislature of any State may empower the executive thereof to make temporary appointments until the people fill the vacancies by election as the legislature may direct. This amendment shall not be so construed as to affect the election or term of any Senator chosen before it becomes valid as part of the Constitution.

[AMENDMENT XVIII][15]

SECTION 1. After one year from the ratification of this article the manufacture, sale, or transportation of intoxicating liquors within, the importation thereof into, or the exportation thereof from the United States and all territory subject to the jurisdiction thereof for beverage purposes is hereby prohibited.

SECTION 2. The Congress and the several States shall have concurrent power to enforce this article by appropriate legislation.

SECTION 3. This article shall be inoperative unless it shall have been ratified as an amendment to the

13 Adopted in 1913.
14 Adopted in 1913.
15 Adopted in 1918.

Constitution by the legislatures of the several States, as provided in the Constitution, within seven years from the date of the submission hereof to the States by the Congress.

[AMENDMENT XIX][16]

The right of citizens of the United States to vote shall not be denied or abridged by the United States or by any State on account of sex.

Congress shall have power to enforce this article by appropriate legislation.

[AMENDMENT XX][17]

SECTION 1. The terms of the President and Vice-President shall end at noon on the 20th day of January, and the terms of Senators and Representatives at noon on the 3d day of January, of the years in which such terms would have ended if this article had not been ratified; and the terms of their successors shall then begin.

SECTION 2. The Congress shall assemble at least once in every year, and such meeting shall begin at noon on the 3d day of January, unless they shall by law appoint a different day.

SECTION 3. If, at the time fixed for the beginning of the term of the President, the President elect shall have died, the Vice-President elect shall become President. If a President shall not have been chosen before the time fixed for the beginning of his term or if the President elect shall have failed to qualify, then the Vice-President elect shall act as President until a President shall have qualified; and the Congress may by law provide for the case wherein neither a President elect nor a Vice-President elect shall have qualified, declaring who shall then act as President, or the manner in which one who is to act shall be selected, and such person shall act accordingly until a President or Vice-President shall have qualified.

SECTION 4. The Congress may by law provide for the case of the death of any of the persons from whom the House of Representatives may choose a President whenever the right of choice shall have devolved upon them, and for the case of the death of any of the persons from whom the Senate may choose a Vice-President whenever the right of choice shall have devolved upon them.

16 Adopted in 1920.

17 Adopted in 1933.

SECTION 5. Sections 1 and 2 shall take effect on the 15th day of October following the ratification of this article.

SECTION 6. This article shall be inoperative unless it shall have been ratified as an amendment to the Constitution by the legislatures of three-fourths of the several States within seven years from the date of its submission.

[AMENDMENT XXI][18]

SECTION 1. The eighteenth article of amendment to the Constitution of the United States is hereby repealed.

SECTION 2. The transportation or importation into any State, Territory, or possession of the United States for delivery or use therein of intoxicating liquors, in violation of the laws thereof, is hereby prohibited.

SECTION 3. This article shall be inoperative unless it shall have been ratified as an amendment to the Constitution by conventions in the several States, as provided in the Constitution, within seven years from the date of the submission hereof to the States by the Congress.

[AMENDMENT XXII][19]

No person shall be elected to the office of the President more than twice, and no person who has held the office of President, or acted as President, for more than two years of a term to which some other person was elected President shall be elected to the office of the President more than once.

But this Article shall not apply to any person holding the office of President when this Article was proposed by the Congress, and shall not prevent any person who may be holding the office of President, or acting as President, during the term within which this Article becomes operative from holding the office of President or acting as President during the remainder of such term.

This article shall be inoperative unless it shall have been ratified as an amendment to the Constitution by the legislatures of three-fourths of the several states within seven years from the date of its submission to the states by the Congress.

18 Adopted in 1933.

19 Adopted in 1951.

[AMENDMENT XXIII][20]

SECTION 1. The District constituting the seat of Government of the United States shall appoint in such manner as the Congress may direct:

A number of electors of President and Vice-President equal to the whole number of Senators and Representatives in Congress to which the District would be entitled if it were a State, but in no event more than the least populous State; they shall be in addition to those appointed by the States, but they shall be considered, for the purpose of the election of President and Vice-President, to be electors appointed by a State; and they shall meet in the District and perform such duties as provided by the twelfth article of amendment.

SECTION 2. The Congress shall have power to enforce this article by appropriate legislation.

[AMENDMENT XXIV][21]

SECTION 1. The right of citizens of the United States to vote in any primary or other election for President or Vice-President, for electors for President or Vice-President, or for Senator or Representative in Congress, shall not be denied or abridged by the United States or any state by reason of failure to pay any poll tax or other tax.

SECTION 2. The Congress shall have the power to enforce this article by appropriate legislation.

[AMENDMENT XXV][22]

SECTION 1. In case of the removal of the President from office or of his death or resignation, the Vice-President shall become President.

SECTION 2. Whenever there is a vacancy in the office of the Vice President, the President shall nominate a Vice President who shall take office upon confirmation by a majority vote of both Houses of Congress.

SECTION 3. Whenever the President transmits to the President Pro Tempore of the Senate and the Speaker of the House of Representatives his written declaration that he is unable to discharge the powers and duties of his office, and

until he transmits to them a written declaration to the contrary, such powers and duties shall be discharged by the Vice-President as Acting President.

SECTION 4. Whenever the Vice-President and a majority of either the principal officers of the executive departments or of such other body as Congress may by law provide, transmit to the President Pro Tempore of the Senate and the Speaker of the House of Representatives their written declaration that the President is unable to discharge the powers and duties of his office, the Vice President shall immediately assume the powers and duties of the office as Acting President.

Thereafter, when the President transmits to the President Pro Tempore of the Senate and the Speaker of the House of Representatives his written declaration that no inability exists, he shall resume the powers and duties of his office unless the Vice President and a majority of either the principal officers of the executive departments or of such other body as Congress may by law provide, transmit within four days to the President Pro Tempore of the Senate and the Speaker of the House of Representatives their written declaration that the President is unable to discharge the powers and duties of his office. Thereupon Congress shall decide the issue, assembling within forty-eight hours for that purpose if not in session. If the Congress, within twenty-one days after receipt of the latter written declaration, or, if Congress is not in session, within twenty-one days after Congress is required to assemble, determines by two-thirds vote of both Houses that the President is unable to discharge the powers and duties of his office, the Vice President shall continue to discharge the same as Acting President; otherwise, the President shall resume the powers and duties of his office.

[AMENDMENT XXVI][23]

SECTION 1. The right of citizens of the United States, who are eighteen years of age or older, to vote shall not be denied or abridged by the United States or by any State on account of age.

SECTION 1. The Congress shall have power to enforce this article by appropriate legislation.

[AMENDMENT XXVII][24]

No law, varying the compensation for the services of the Senators and Representatives, shall take effect, until an election of Representatives shall have intervened.

Index

Note: Page numbers in *italics* indicate illustrations and their captions; numbers followed by *m* indicate maps

A

AAA (Agricultural Adjustment Administration), 508
ABMs (antiballistic missiles), 620
Abortion, 395, 432, 625–626, 634, 636, *636*
Abu Ghraib prison, 669
ACA (Affordable Care Act), 670, 675
Acheson, Dean, 562
"Acid rock," 606
Activism, 389, 406, 408, 414, 503
  civil disobedience, *636*
  environmental, 626–627, *627*
  labor, 378, 379
  Latino activism, *622,* 622–624
Adams, Charles Francis, Jr., 412
Addams, Jane, *389, 391, 429,* 431, 433, 436, 438, 447
Additives in fuel oils, 474
Advertisements, 355
  railroad and steamship, 355
Advertising, 476–477, 575
  lithographed posters, 394
Affirmative action, 622, 625, 628, 629, 652, 654, 665
Affordable Care Act (ACA), 670, 675
Afghanistan, 587, 639*m*
  Soviet invasion of, 642
  U.S. attack on, 667, 668*m*
AFL (American Federation of Labor), 377–378, 460, 482, 514
AFL-CIO, 640
Africa, 416, 418*m,* 586, 597, 607.
    See also specific countries
  North Africa, 528, 531*m*
African Americans, 398, 401, 405, 410, 415, 416, 540, 597, 665, 669, *669,* 675. *See also* Segregation
  Black power movement, 599
  churches, 342. *See also* Churches
  civil rights of. *See* Civil rights movement
  disenfranchisement. *See* Disenfranchisement
  dream of economic independence, 318–319
  education of
    Black colleges, 398
    busing for desegregation, 629
    literacy, 415
  employment of, 327, 343, 591
  Exodusters, 337, 344
  free Blacks. *See* Freedmen

full-employment economy and, 664–665
impact of Great Depression on, 498, *498*
migration to cities, 364, 365, 461, 483*m,* 570, 571*m*
of Montgomery, 594
music, 392, 401, 478–479
during Reconstruction, 327–330
  Black codes, 322
  land issue, 325
  property ownership, 318–319
of 1920s, 480–481
South and, 591–592
in sports, 401
in suburban era, 570
suburban nation, 559
suffrage, 322
Trump on, 675
in Vietnam War, 615
violence against
  by Ku Klux Klan, 483, *484*
  lynchings. *See* Lynchings
World War II, 591
Afrika Korps, 528
Agent Orange, 615, *615*
Agnew, Spiro T., 630
Agribusiness, 514, 533
Agricultural Adjustment Act of 1933, 507
Agricultural Adjustment Act of 1938, 508
Agricultural Adjustment Administration (AAA), 508
Agriculture, 441, 507–508, *514.*
    See also specific crops; specific plants and animals
  commercial, 498
    cotton. *See* Cotton
    tobacco. *See* Tobacco
  domesticated animals, 347
    disease and, 347
  plant cultivation. *See also specific crops*
    cotton. *See* Cotton
    Dust Bowl, 497
    hybrid seeds, 534
  in South, 338, 341, 3440
  village-centered, 344
Aguinaldo, Emilio, 422, 423
AIDS epidemic, 653, *653*
AIDS quilts, *653*
AIM (American Indian Movement), 624, *624*

Aircraft, 665–666
  B-2 bomber, 646
  helicopters, *609*
  U-2 spy plane, 582, 586
Aircraft carriers, 528, 530
Aircraft industry (WWII), 533
Air moisture, 346
Air pollution, 601
Alabama, 340, *341*
Alaska, acquisition of, *405*
Alaska "Seward's Folly," 420
Albuquerque
  rail lines, 351
Albuquerque, New Mexico, 351
Alcatraz Island, 624
Alger, Horatio, *375*
Algonquin, sinking of, 457
Ali, Muhammad (Cassius Clay), 615, 620
Alienation, 479
Alien Land Law of 1887, 356
All-American Canal, 511
Allen, Frederick Lewis, 472, 477, 491
Allen, Gracie, 495
Allende Gossens, Salvador, 638
Alliance Exchanges, 410
Alliance for Progress, 584
Alliance movement, 410
Allied Control Council, 544
Allies (World War I), 455*m*
All in the Family (TV series), 637
al Qaeda, 666, 667, 668*m,* 671
Altgeld, Gov. John, 404
"Alt right," 675
Amalgamated Association of Iron and Steel Workers, 379
Amateur Hour, 495
Amazon.com, 664
"America First" slogan, 675
American Birth Control League, 477
American Catholic Church, 646
American Catholics, 604
American civil religion, 572–573
American Expeditionary Force, 461
American Federation of Labor (AFL), *361,* 377–378, 460, 482, 514
American GI Forum for Latinos, 590, 593, 622
American Independent Party, 618
American Indian Movement (AIM), 624, *624*
Americanization, 431, 459
American Liberty League, 509
American Plan, 476
American Psychiatric Association, 625
American Railway Union (ARU), 379

C

Cadillac, 568, *568*
Caldwell,. Charles, 330
Caldwell, Erskine, 516
California, 344, *348*, 352, 353, *354*
  commercial farming, 498
    Hetch Hetchy valley, 443
  progressive reform in, 429–430
California Dip, 572
Camelot, 582–583
Campaign buttons, 414, 559
Campaign for Black civil rights, 595
Camp David accords, 642
Camp Manzanar, 538, *539*
Camp meetings, 342, 356
Canada, *348*, 349, *354*, 554, 661
  trade wars with, 677
Canals
  All-American Canal, 511
  Suez Canal, 379, 528, 639*m*
Canal Zone, 450, 450*m*, 584
Cannery and Agricultural Workers
    Industrial Union (CAWIU), 514
Cannon, Joseph, 443
Cape Codder, 569
Capital. *See* Investment capital
Capital deepening, 364
Capitalism
  associationalism, 486
  industrial. *See* Industrial capitalism
  welfare capitalism, 460, 476
Capone, Alfonse ("Scarface"), 483
Captive nations, 580
Cardozo, Justice Benjamin, 507
Caribbean, 324, 451–452, 453, 453*m*
Carlisle Indian School Band, 350
Carmichael, Stokely, 599
Carnegie, Andrew, 368, *369*, 370, 375,
    379, 411, 416, 422
  philanthropy of, 370, 416
  steel mills built by, 369, 372
Carnegie Hall, 480
Carnegie integrates steel, 368–369
Carnegie Steel Company, *361*
Carpentier, George, 479
Carranza, Venustiano, 454
Carrendeno, Rose, *537*
Carson, Rachel, 601, 626, 627
Carter, James Earl ("Jimmy"), 633, 640,
    646, 654
  energy issues, 640–641
  foreign policy, 641, *642*
  sagging economy, 641
Cash-and-carry policy, 525
Cassatt, *399*
Castle Garden, 385
Castro, Fidel, 580, 584, 618
Catholic Church, 356
Catt, Carrie Chapman, 433
Cattle corporations, 354

Cattle drives, 353
Cattle trails, *354*
CAWIU (Cannery and Agricultural
    Workers Industrial Union), 514
CBS News, 616
CCC (Civilian Conservation Corps),
    505, 513
Census Bureau, 573
Center for the Study of Responsive
    Law, 626
Central America, 647–648, 647*m*,
    658, 659
Central and Union Pacific Railroads,
    352–353
Central Intelligence Agency (CIA), 642,
    648, 667
  illegal acts of, 638
Central Pacific Railroad, 353
Central Park (NYC), *383*, 397
Central Powers, 455, 455*m*, 466
A Century of Dishonor (Jackson), 350
Chain stores, 399, 476
Chain stores, 399
Chamberlain, Neville, 526, 552
Chamber of Commerce, 476
Chambers, Whittaker, 561
Chanax, Juan, 656–657, *657*
Charles, Ray, 606
"Charleston," *471*
Charlottesville, Virginia, 675
Château Thierry, battle of, 461, 463*m*
Chatham, Lord. *See* Pitt, William
Chattanooga, 340
Chávez, César, 498, *622*, 623, 631
Chávez, Sen. Dennis, 513
Cheney, Richard, 666
Chevrolet Corvair, safety of, 626
Cheyenne, 344, 346, 348, 353
Cheyenne River Agency, *340*, 349
Chiang Kai-shek, 519, 561, 563, 578
Chicago, Illinois
  Democratic convention of 1968,
    617, *618*
  Hull House, 438
  race riots, 461
  union violence in, 628
  ward bosses, 438
  World's Columbian Exposition, 404,
    411, 425
The Chicago Defender, 461
Chicago Tribune, 560
Chicago Vice Commission, 436
Chicano activists, 623–624
Chief Joseph (of Nez Percé), *348*, 349
Child labor, 377, 507, 534
  abolition of, 433
  Knights of Labor, 377
  legislation of, 433
Children, 533
  child labor. *See* Child labor
  civil defense planners, 556

education of. *See* Education
  school busing for desegregation, 629
Children's Bureau, 433, 440, 444
China, 418*m*, 422, 424, 425, 519, 524,
    578, 583, *620,* 677
  Boxer Rebellion, *405*
  cash-and-carry policy and, 525
  under Communist rule, 552
    diplomatic recognition of, 640
    Tienanmen Square protest, 650
  Cultural Revolution, 618
  fall of, 561
  Japanese occupation of, 524,
    525, 528
  Nationalist government of, 561
  open door policy, 420, 425, 524
  Tienanmen Square protest, 650
China card, 620, 641
China Lobby, 561, 563
Chinese Americans, 532, 533, 658
Chinese Communist, 552
Chinese Exclusion Act of 1882, 390, *390*
Chinese immigrants, 393, 401
  laws banning, 390, *390*
  migration patterns of, 384
Chinese laborers, 390, 392, 393
Chinese Six Companies, 500
Chinese worked on rail lines, 353
Chinn, Thomas, 533
Chin Shee, *384*
Chisholm Trail, 353, 354*m*
Cholera, 384, 387, 402
Christian academies, 634
Christian Broadcast Network, 636
Chrysler, 567, 568
Chrysler Corporation, 533, 670
Churches, 342
  African American, 342
  evangelical, 635
Churchill, Winston, 528, 529, 544, *544,*
    552, 579
  Potsdam Summit, *552*
  Roosevelt and, 527, *527*
  Truman and, 545
CIA. *See* Central Intelligence Agency
Cigarettes, 339
Cigar Makers' Union, 378
Cincinnati, 387
CIO (Congress of Industrial
    Organizations), 515
Circo Azteca, *514*
Circuses, 401, *514*
Cities
  American life, 447
  city charters, 388, 439
  city life, 392–396
  deterioration of, 570
  new urban age, 383–384
  in Trans-Mississippi West, 340
  urban culture, 383, 397
  walking cities, 402